The Leadership Quotient

The Leadership Quotient

✦

12 Dimensions for Measuring and Improving Leadership

Bill Service, Ph.D.
Dave Arnott, Ph.D.

iUniverse, Inc.
New York Lincoln Shanghai

The Leadership Quotient
12 Dimensions for Measuring and Improving Leadership

iUniverse books may be ordered through booksellers or by contacting:

iUniverse
2021 Pine Lake Road, Suite 100
Lincoln, NE 68512
www.iuniverse.com
1-800-Authors (1-800-288-4677)

ISBN-13: 978-0-595-38741-0 (pbk)
ISBN-13: 978-0-595-83123-4 (ebk)
ISBN-10: 0-595-38741-1 (pbk)
ISBN-10: 0-595-83123-0 (ebk)

Printed in the United States of America

Dedication

To our students—who teach us.

Contents

Acknowledgments

My life, learning, and meaning come from the relationships I have formed with so many people I have worked with, enjoyed, taught, and loved. To all of those I say thank you.

In addition to my family, I especially want to thank Dave Arnott, a cherished friend who has taught me much, and Ed Gerloff, who inspired me to become a student-focused learner, not simply a professor.

Jan, my beloved wife and friend, keeps me grounded in the importance of life and what we do with it.

Bill Service
rwservic@samford.edu
Birmingham, Alabama
February 1, 2006

In the last days of writing this book, I was honored to be visiting the Dallas office of the famous motivational speaker, Zig Ziglar. I started to leave when Zig called me back. "Let me show you my pictures," he beamed. In the entry hall of his office are pictures of more than 20 people whom he acknowledges made him a success. It is essentially his "people whose shoulders I stand upon" wall of recognition. Zig is right. We all stand on the shoulders of others. Here are some that I stand on:

Harold Arnott is the best leader I have ever known. He's also a good father.

If Bill Service had not taken the time and consideration to coach me through my research comprehensive exams, I would not have the academic career I have been privileged to enjoy. I am so pleased he invited me to write this book with him. My hope for you, the reader, is that you are as blessed with your career as I am with mine: I get to do what I want with people I like. I like Bill Service.

Bob Briner was the only mentor I ever had, and he modeled the most important aspect of leadership: Do what's right, no matter what the cost.

My fellow Board of Trustees members at Central Christian College are great examples of leading because it benefits others, not you. Davey Naugle taught me how to be a Christian academic. I still need a lot of practice.

Leading the next generation is perhaps the most important thing we do. I led my children, Lindsay and Lance into adulthood, and now they're leading me. I watch with admiration the way my wife, Cynde, leads her children. She is a constant encouragement to me.

The two "Larry's" in my life are responsible for any academic skills I have: Larry Linamen at Colorado Christian University and Larry Rottmeyer at Taylor University.

Dr. Gary Cook, President of Dallas Baptist University, lives out the mission statement of the University as a servant leader. I admire the leadership of Gail Linam as Provost and Charlene Connor as Dean at Dallas Baptist University. I would never try to lead a bunch of people like me.

I have learned a lot about applying leadership in an organization from Kathleen Klaviter at Hanson Building Materials of America, along with David Deviney, Elizabeth Dunn, Rod Hilpirt, Jerry McNeil, Don Powell, and Travis Twomey.

Sandee Smith has elegantly produced everything I've authored, including this book. If it reads well, she gets the credit.

Dave Arnott
davea@dbu.edu
Dallas, Texas
February 1, 2006

1

Introduction

You ain't no more gonna do what you ain't planned than you are gonna get back from where you ain't never been!

A graduate student with an engineering background grew tired of the "soft" side of leadership and demanded of his professor, "Just give me a formula for leadership!" The professor, *LQ*© co-author Bill Service, responded, "There isn't one." "Well, there should be," retorted the engineer. He was right, and now there is a formula: *The Leadership Quotient.*

The *LQ*© formula is research-based, yet it is practical enough to be considered the "pocket guide" for leadership measurement and improvement. Because the *LQ*© is a measurable quotient, it provides a clear guide to help everyone reach their leadership potential.

So What: The *LQ*© Book!

"It is possible to make progress on a seemingly impossible problem if one just ignores the skeptics and gets on with it" (Smolin's book on Quantum Gravity, 2001, p. 6).

As we read many of the books and articles about Colin Powell's leadership, it occurred to us that perhaps none of them provide prescriptions that would yield leadership improvement because the lessons are limited to the specific environment in which Colin Powell was successful. Together, we've reviewed most of those twenty writings, and we're grateful for the authors who have described Powell's great leadership ability. But we're frustrated that the lessons are mostly limited to one specific individual within a unique environment and don't give us principles that we can apply in our complicated, everyday lives.

Powell's 1995 *My American Journey* is a great read, as is Harari's 2002 *The Leadership Secrets of Colin Powell.* While we are awed by Colin Powell's leadership presence, inspired trust, dignity, image, and direct approach, we doubt the value of these and other books of this sort because of their lack of applicability. Frankly, we could not find a single book that brought it all together in a manner that would help all of those seeking leadership development direction, whether the direction be for self or others. Actually, many leadership books provide more negative than positive learning. That's because the reader may be left with the impression that he can lead just as Powell did. Most of us can't, or indeed would not, take those leadership positions even if the opportunity were afforded us. Most of us simply have different designs for our leadership than the Chairman of the Joint Chiefs of Staff or the Secretary of State—those are life-altering commitments.

These types of "my leadership style" books can't tell the rest of us how to lead in a different environment. First, the reader is in a different situation. Second, few of us have the leadership characteristics of Colin Powell, Rudy Giuliani, Bill Clinton, George Bush, or even Attila the Hun or Machiavelli. And again, most of us just don't aspire to these leadership positions and wouldn't take them even if they were offered to us. And yes, we all have different levels of leadership potential. *The Leadership Quotient* acknowledges this difference and offers to everyone a measurable $LQ^©$ that can be tailored to you. That's what the $LQ^©$ is. Here's what it's not.

The $LQ^©$ is not a fleeting fad. In our media-hyped world, we are constantly bombarded with the fad du jour that promises to tell us how to be the leader of all time in just 200 short pages of obnoxious, obvious, and just plain envious "John Q's principles of leadership." John Q is anyone from the leader of the free world to some raving maniac who has been dead for 2,000 years, or even a fictional Mafia or cartoon character. Be leery of those books; they will lead you astray. You are not Attila the Hun, Dilbert, Lewis and Clark, or Tony Soprano! We are here to tell you it just ain't possible to read an easy story about someone else and do as they do and have it make you a better leader. If you memorize a book about mice scurrying around after some cheese, it won't help you be a better leader. Trying to learn to be a leader in a few short pages by following what someone else did in a different environment with way different followers than you will ever have just won't cut it. Yes, the person makes the situation, but to no greater extent than the situation makes the person; yes, the leader determines the path, but to no greater extent than do the followers; yes, the leader picks the followers but to no greater extent than the followers pick the leader; and there are many other "yes-buts" you've got to understand to become a successful leader. A need exists to understand the principles of leaders, followers, and environments and how they interact before you can be a successful leader. We will promise you the fad-of-fads and the secret-of-secrets for leadership success, but to get them you must embark on a journey of study and struggle. You must have a definite bias for action—to learn leadership and ultimately to practice it. Build solid willpower for a lifetime of accomplishment.

You have to know yourself and be able to read others and the situation at hand and adapt and adjust to those unique circumstances. Yes, the methods of old are good, and the fads work, but not well enough; you've simply got to understand the basics and commit to practicing those in a lifelong journey of leadership development and improvement. It's like the fad diets—yes, they work, but at a price ranging from death to a roller coaster ride. To control your health and weight over a lifetime, you eventually have to understand and practice the basics of weight control for the rest of the time you want to control your weight. Precisely the same thing is true for leadership. The fads will help, but the price will be the death of you as a leader or the fading in and out of your leadership influence. We promise you that through the diligent study and application of $LQ^{©}$ principles you will become a better leader capable of a lifetime of successful and sustainable leadership.

There are no magic pills, miracle solutions, or simple secrets. The real key is foundational understanding of leaders, followers, and environments, and how they interact and play out as leadership influence occurs. Therefore, the $LQ^{©}$ is not a simplistic, self-help, motivational book. It's not a fairytale parable about mice, Edg the surfer, or why Tony whacks someone. On the other end of the spectrum, it's not an overly academic analysis of theory. $LQ^{©}$ is a solid set of logical guidelines developed from all the fads, academic research, popular press, and experience, and allows you to measure and improve your leadership through understanding and application. We're glad you've joined us for a look at your leadership capabilities. The journey will help you realize your leadership improvement. Study Figure 1.1 before you start your learning journey.

Figure 1.1: *LQ*© THE LIFESTYLE FOR LEADERSHIP SUCCESS

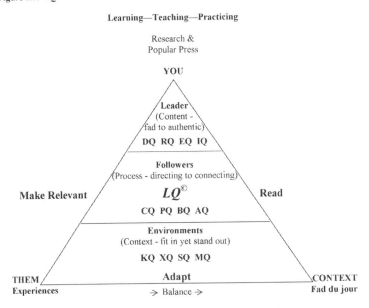

$$LQ^© = f(AQ\text{-Apperance} + BQ\text{-Behavior} + CQ\text{-Communications} + DQ\text{-Desire} +$$
$$EQ\text{-Emotional} + IQ\text{-Intelligence} + KQ\text{-Knowledge} + MQ\text{-Management} +$$
$$PQ\text{-People} + RQ\text{-Reality} + SQ\text{-Situation} + XQ\text{-eXperience a no-fad zone})$$

Categorize your strengths and weaknesses versus the ideal for all 12 Quotients.

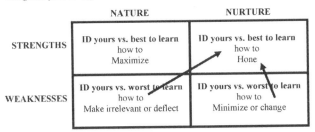

Purpose

Every person has the potential to become a leader (Maxwell, 2000, p. 3), and you are the only person on earth who can use your potential. The *LQ*© allows you to recognize what you have and don't have in your leadership toolbox, and directs your discovery of how to leverage your leadership characteristics. If you want to improve your capabilities as a leader, or help others do so, you've got to learn and practice the fundamentals of leadership regardless of the leadership level you now occupy or the level to which you aspire.

The Leadership Quotient uses scientific research, experience, intuition, and just plain common sense in a logically considered yet emotionally balanced way to measure and then improve your leadership effectiveness. This book is a guide through your Leadership Quotients, helping you become a better leader by showing you how to identify your weaknesses and strengths and then how to use the max-min principle to improve your leadership performance.

One of our favorite slogans is, "Measure it and it will improve." We'll show you how to measure your leadership potential and then how to improve what you have measured. Every organization is trying to develop more leaders who will help their organization deal with a dynamically changing environment. This part of leadership is clear: Measuring and improving your leadership capabilities will increase your value in the marketplace.

Defining Leadership

Let's start by reframing or redefining leadership so we can understand it in a different light. In this age of global enterprise and instant communications, the relationship between leaders and followers acting in varied environments has changed from one of dependence to mutual acceptability. Churchill is an example of moving followers from dependence to mutual acceptance. He asked for blood, sweat, and tears to persevere toward realization of "their finest hour." Likewise, John F. Kennedy urged Americans to "[a]sk not what your country can do for you—ask what you can do for your country." These two examples make it clear that improvement demands some self-reflection, study, and work.

We are defining leadership through 12 quotients that separately and interactively measure leadership for any individual with unique sets of followers operating in differing environments. The 12 quotients include the following:

1. Appearance

2. Behavior

3. Communications

4. Desire

5. Emotions

6. Intelligence

7. Knowledge

8.   Management

9.   People

10. Reality

11. Situation

12. eXperience

These 12 quotients are described in the $LQ^©$ as it guides you through the journey of increasing your personal $LQ^©$ or helping others do so. The $LQ^©$'s comprehensive quotients define leadership in a more universal and applicable way than has been done before.

The cost of inaction is huge. Failure to identify and improve the $LQ^©$ results in the loss of better leaders, and organizations suffer as a result. Improving your $LQ^©$ even a small amount will leverage your leadership capacities and result in acknowledged improvement of the effectiveness and efficiency of your leadership.

People want direction, inspiration, validation, and relationships. "I think it is a great tragedy in life that people live and die and never find a dream around which they can feel resonance, a tragedy in part because a dream is available to people who seek it and a tragedy in part because of the lost and unrealized potential of individuals" (Clawson, 1999, p. 95). In today's turbulent environment, organizations want leaders to guide them to the next level. "During organizational transitions—when things are confusing, stressful, and generally destabilized—employees look for leadership....Your job title is just a label. *Leader* is a reputation...and you personally have to earn it" (Pritchett and Pound, 1991, p. 27).

Leadership is about moving people into an unknown where a leap of faith is required on the part of the followers. As we will remind you many times in this book, in the end, leadership becomes influence—nothing more and nothing less. If there is no influence, there is no leadership.

Everyone has the Potential to be a Leader

Think of several of the world's best singers: Andrea Bocelli, Elvis Presley, Barbra Streisand. The commonality among them? They are good. But can we define good? Not really. So it is with leadership. The definition of good leadership is as nebulous as the definition of good singing. As we continue to study and practice leadership, we learn how little we know, and we're continually faced with the fact that many leadership styles can lead to success or failure. Leadership is hard to define in terms that are replicable and transferable to various situations. That's because leadership is an organic, not a mechanistic, thing: It lives and breathes. Drama provides a good example. A Broadway musical is a success because of the total experience, not just one component. Even masters like Andrew Lloyd Webber have a hard time producing a string of hit shows.

As legendary Dallas Cowboys football coach Tom Landry used to say, "Getting people to do what they don't want to do in order to achieve what they want to achieve is a pretty good description of any kind of leadership because the greatest challenge of every leader is getting the best out of people" (Landry, 1990, p. 279). Landry goes on to say that leadership requires knowledge, innovation, a basic philosophy, shared goals, motivation, ability to handle adversity and criticism, a commitment to excellence, and a plan of action. This seems to sum it all up, but is this all we need to know?

Like many other human behaviors, leadership is a concept that is visible and not thoroughly definable. Yet we all agree it can be used for accomplishment. All leadership requires some level of self-discovery. We use numerous models, frames, modes, metaphors, and filters to make sense of our world. It is not a matter of whether or not we have these views of reality, but whether or not we know and understand those that determine our ability to guide others to accomplishment. We don't describe the world we see; we see the world we describe.

> The fact is that people do not actually go empty-handed but take with them various frameworks.…[T]he choice is not between taking a framework and not taking one, but between taking one that is implicit and unconsidered, and one that is explicit and susceptible to conscious thought and challenge. (Bate and Child, 1987, p. 37)

> Leadership is about *commitment and necessity* directed toward accomplishment:
> [A] common series of management processes seems required.…Most important among these are: sensing needs, amplifying understanding, building awareness, creating credibility, legitimizing viewpoints, generating partial solutions, broadening support, identifying zones of opposition and indifference, changing perceived risks, structuring needed flexibilities, putting forward trial concepts, creating pockets of commitment, eliminating undesired options, crystallizing focus and consensus, managing coalitions, and finally formalizing agreed-upon commitments. (Quinn, 1980, p. 146)

Leadership is an interactive phenomenon where leaders share a vision that results in communication and ultimately empowerment. The science of leadership does not describe reality; it simply tries to represent reality with models and frameworks. In fact, any science is *our* reality, it is not **the** reality. The more we discover about organic systems, which leadership certainly is, the more we see irreducible complexity. All living systems require many matched parts in order to function, and the removal of any one part can cause the system to cease functioning. This relates to our topic, because leadership is a living system that is precariously balanced. *The Leadership Quotient* explains this balance. With all the problems we see in the world, it seems the only thing mankind really has to fear is mankind. "I have more problems with (insert your name) than any other person I've met." Measuring and improving your $LQ^©$ will help you lower the problems you've been having with yourself, your followers, and your situations.

The fact that leadership comes in all shapes and sizes and in varying levels of effectiveness and success is well understood. What is not well understood is what you can do to improve your own leadership success. The $LQ^{©}$ provides a foundation for rectifying this situation. Just begin by thinking as Dennis Hastert, Speaker of the House, said: "I have come to understand the truth behind the saying 'leaders aren't born, they are made'" (in Despain and Converse, 2003, first unnumbered introductory page). We know the $LQ^{©}$ will help make you and others better leaders.

The Initial Case for the $LQ^{©}$

"If a man will begin with certainties, he shall end in doubts; but if he will be content to begin with doubts, he shall end in certainties" (Francis Bacon, 1605, quoted in Boa and Bowman, 2002, p. 7). "If a belief system doesn't claim to correspond to reality, head for the nearest exit!" (Boa and Bowman, 2002, p. 13).

In this constantly evolving and increasingly complex globally diverse world, executives, managers, supervisors, team leaders, and aspiring students of management and leadership must all understand the need to shift their thinking from that of a manager to that of a modern leader. A modern leader must deal not only with many external and internal ambiguities, but also with external and internal people who demand and indeed deserve equal treatment. Foremost among these people are *followers*. The simple models, paradigms, and rules of the past are being replaced by unknowns and complexity coupled with more information than even the most brilliant person can perceive. Modern leaders must see these needs and then realize success through the improvement of their own $LQ^{©}$. Or, as Wayne Gretzky said, "I don't go where the puck is; I go where it is going to be." This is what modern leaders must do through improvement of their $LQ^{©}$.

Everyone can become a more effective leader. The $LQ^{©}$ not only simplifies what a modern leader is but also directs you in your journey to becoming a more successful leader. Attachment 1, at the end of this chapter, gives a picture of the management and leadership dichotomies you need to understand. Understanding will come through the study and application of the $LQ^{©}$.

"Leadership is influence—nothing more, nothing less" (Maxwell, 2000, p. 17). More specifically, leadership is about human influence and impact used to leverage others through courage, priorities, direction, motivation, teamwork, and innovativeness, directed toward improving a situation. Learning to lead better is about the art and the science of leadership. However, it's mostly about the wisdom to discern the differences between art and science in the drive to realize successful leadership. It is about understanding that leadership learning and development is a lifelong process. It is about the years it takes to perfect the things that work for you as a leader. It is about realizing why specific things work for some leaders and not others. It is about presenting leadership effectiveness as a formula that can be measured, and realizing that as influence increases, so does the impact of leadership. It is about accepting that "[l]eadership takes many forms, but understanding leadership as encouraging, supporting and assisting others allows those of us with modest abilities to contribute" (Harris, 2002b, p. i).

Yes, people can have influence and leverage the power of others. It is about the heart and the mind. People change what they do because they see a truth that influences their feelings (Kotter and Cohen, 2002). "The litmus test of all leadership is whether it mobilizes people's commitment to putting their energy into actions designed to improve things. It is individual commitment, but it is above all collective mobilization" (Fullan, 2001, p. 9).

The discipline of leadership is one of the most significant innovations of all time. "We are in the midst of a major managerial paradigm shift that is transforming what it means to be an effective leader" (Clawson, 1999, p. 171). "But leadership isn't a position; it's a process. It's an observable, understandable, learnable set of skills and practices available to everyone, anywhere in the organization" (Hesselbein and Cohen, 1999, p. 37). The *LQ*© clarifies the complexities of interactions of people and processes involved in you becoming a better leader.

From the Documented Past to the *LQ*© Formula

Humans have exhibited leadership for as long as history has been recorded. The Greek and Latin classics, Chinese philosophy, and the Bible have all recorded much about leadership, but leadership as a measurable discipline has only been in existence for the last hundred years or so. Leadership has yet to be reduced to a formula of ideal behaviors, types, traits, or characteristics. The *LQ*© does this through very definite *quotients,* that is, traits, abilities, and behaviors that clearly define successful leadership. The *LQ*© formula will serve anyone well, since a slight improvement in leadership can yield dramatic results in today's environment where so many followers are searching for effective leaders. We need leaders who can help people reach their potential by developing a closer match between the natural and nurtured abilities we all have. We must continually seek new and better ways to meet the void of leadership that exists in the world today, remembering all the while, as Einstein said, "The significant problems we face today cannot be solved at the same level of thinking we were at when we created them" (cited in Oakley and Krug, 1991, p. 13).

Traits, Abilities, and Behaviors

The Leadership Quotient helps you, the leader, realize the traits, abilities, and behaviors that you naturally have and don't have and how to adapt those to followers and environments. Then, it helps you hone those possibilities (maximize strengths) and figure out a way around your shortcomings (minimize weaknesses) so you can improve your success as a leader. This is the application of the max-min principle. Once you realize what is possible, then you can exhibit wisdom through appropriate leadership that matches capabilities with the situation at hand. This is not a simple task and we are not offering a pseudoscientific pill to cure all leadership ills, but you can improve and become a more effective and successful leader. Remember, however, "The more complex society gets, the more sophisticated leadership must become. Complexity means change, but specifically, it means rapidly occurring, unpredictable, nonlinear change" (Fullan, 2001, p. ix). Some will misinterpret this quote and think they need to lead with complexity. Nothing could be further from the truth. The successful leader is a simplifier, not a complexifier. The successful leader is the one who can interpret the difficult and complex, and present it in a simplified and understandable way to followers. Simplifying complexity is the beauty of *The Leadership Quotient*. Your leadership style can be developed and honed as appropriate using the 12 simple measures developed through our extensive research. Though the measures are simple, their development and eventual application are rather complex. That has to be so because leadership is a complex human interaction that can be simplified only so much. We wish we could say otherwise, but it's just not true. Dedicated effort is required; if you desire a quick fix and seek one, you will be wasting your time. Pay me now or pay me later, but pay you will if leadership excellence is your eventual goal.

That's Then; and Now's Now

We have evolved to the point in the free world where all effective and enduring leadership situations include voluntary and reciprocal relationships. An understanding of self, others, and the basic principles of leadership is required as a starting point to building those kinds of enduring relationships. But beyond understanding of self and others, there must be the willingness and desire to: a) identify real issues, not just present complaints; b) admit the state of reality for the leader and the situation; c) define and plan an approach; d) take action; e) measure; f) improve; and, g) go back to "step a" again. You can realize more of what you can be as a leader by following this self-improvement model.

We are in a paradigm shift from the effective leader of the past, where power, position, and fear were paramount, to a new model based on openness, trust, and knowledge. We are also in the midst of change to an interinfovideotechnoreligiosity society where everything "works through sound bites and film clips" (Barber, 1996, p. 17). Management is being replaced with leadership as we begin to work with people who can think and are as educated and informed as their managers. It requires leadership to move people into the unknown and management to keep them in the known. The science side of leadership is simply management, which is reducible to measurable principles and policies, and the leadership side is the art component, which is much more difficult to systematize and measure, though the lines between leadership and management are indeed blurring. An understanding of management and leadership, and the art and science of both, is a precursor to improvement. Attachment 1 provides an overview of the difference between management and leadership. The importance of this difference will be a recurrent theme in *The Leadership Quotient*.

Linking Leaders, Followers, and Environments

The two imperatives of organizational survival today are: 1) understanding why someone would deal with your organization, and 2) knowing how to get people to become and remain innovative. Both of these imperatives require leadership: a higher form of management. Or, as Bennis and Nannus state, "Management controls, arranges, does things right; leadership unleashes energy, sets the vision, does the right thing" (p. 701). For "…leadership plays the prime role for the creation of excellence in an organization" (1985, p. 21, cited in Kanji and Moura e Sa, 2001, p. 701). As we move into the arena of global competition, we must begin to shift managing with a focus on stability and control to leadership with a focus on speed, experimentation, flexibility, change, and innovativeness. "Leadership is the art of accomplishing more than the science of management says is possible" (Colin Powell quoted in Harari, 2002, p. 13).

A lot of leadership studies have focused on power—power that was inherent in a position, was appointed, legitimate, and formal; but now we must move to studying leadership that emerges with influence that is beyond formal authority or power as people work together to accomplish shared purposes. In a rich society, organizations have become more like volunteer organizations where people can easily come and go, working because they want to as much as because they have to.

The authors of *The Leadership Quotient* exemplify this. Neither of us wanted the next step in our careers, so we both dropped out and returned to the university for Ph.D.s that led us to become college professors, seminar leaders, and consultants. We're both making less money than we did before becoming academics, but we've gained more freedom and flexibility of time that makes our lives meaningful. Creating *The Leadership Quotient* is an example of how time flexibility has made our lives richer. We've also visited many foreign countries, and we make hundreds of new acquaintances each year. We work because we *want* to, not because we *have* to.

The Progression of Leadership Studies

The history of leadership study starts with the analysis of great leaders and the traits that differentiated them from less effective leaders. Researchers first looked at physical characteristics and traits. Later, they began to add intangibles like desire, drive, integrity, self-confidence, and intelligence. When this did not work well, traits and situational factors produced such things as managerial grids looking at concern for people versus situational concerns. Studies then moved to contingency models, leader-member relations models, task-structure models, exchange theories, and path-goal and extended path-goal models. These leadership explanations were based on tasks (ambiguity, routine, extrinsic and intrinsic factors), cohesiveness, environments, characteristics of followers and leaders, picking and matching a style (directive, supportive, participative, achievement oriented, charismatic, transactional, and transformational), and finally servant leadership (Maas, 1998). Of late, much attention has been given to the emotional quotient and the adversity quotient (Stoltz, 2000). Also, there has been a proliferation of successful leaders writing books on their personal leadership style. While these are informative to varying degrees, they don't offer universal lessons that can be applied by you (a unique individual) across many situations. The combination of elements needed for success as a leader is complex, and very individualistic and situational. Leadership must be approached with a consideration and realistic understanding of the individuals and situations involved, or it is doomed for failure. Awareness of the leader, the follower, and the environment is the foundation for leadership improvement, and it's the three-point outline for *The Leadership Quotient.*

We often encourage our college students to rephrase their personal stories in a form that can be generalized to other situations so it can be used by their fellow students. This process requires follow-up questions: how, what, so what, how so, explain it as a principle we can all use, etc. This process is necessary to make the many books now being written by *mediagenic* leaders applicable to their readers. In an open and easy way, the *LQ*© provides enduring principles, not what and why "I'm great" stories. We are not belittling the value of other leadership books. However, you need to learn to measure your leadership using the *LQ*©, and then to apply the knowledge of the quotients to your environment to make yourself a better leader.

The three-point outline used to characterize the interactive influences of leadership is represented in Figure 1.2: The Quotients of the Leadership Triangle. This triangle describes the interactive relationship between leaders, followers, and environments. Study it now, for it will help you picture the interactive complexities of realizing leadership as you progress through the *LQ*©.

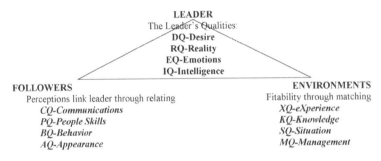

Figure 1.2: **THE QUOTIENTS OF THE LEADERSHIP TRIANGLE**

LEADER
The Leader's Qualities:
DQ-Desire
RQ-Reality
EQ-Emotions
IQ-Intelligence

FOLLOWERS
Perceptions link leader through relating
CQ-Communications
PQ-People Skills
BQ-Behavior
AQ-Appearance

ENVIRONMENTS
Fitability through matching
XQ-eXperience
KQ-Knowledge
SQ-Situation
MQ-Management

- Really understanding the three angles of leadership and the 12 associated Leadership Quotients allows you to understand how to become a more effective leader with lasting impact.

- Leadership success starts with understanding of self, others, and situations, and ends only when you decide you no longer want to be a leader.

- Put in the time and effort and you will see results. You will become a better leader.

Road to the *LQ*©?

Much of the leadership literature has stressed Intelligence Quotient, Emotional Quotient, or a combination of traits that produce leadership success. Yet most of those efforts have found what Peter

Drucker expresses, "There seems to be little correlation between a man's effectiveness and intelligence….Brilliant men are often strikingly ineffectual; they fail to realize that the brilliant insight is not by itself achievement" (cited in Henninger, 2002, p. A16). Likewise, none of the behavioral traits, nor situational, contextual, and contingent approaches fully answer our need to understand leadership as a definable, teachable, and improvable circumstance.

The *LQ*©'s comprehensive view includes research theories, popular press, fads, anecdotes, and suppositions, blended with experience, logic, and observations into definable, measurable, and improvable *quotients*. These *quotients* help organizations and individuals assess leadership strengths and weaknesses so they can be improved.

"Leadership has, for a long time, been a topic that attracts the attention of both academics and practitioners. In spite of the extensive literature on this matter, there is almost a complete absence of models to explain how leadership works" (Kanji and Moura e Sa, 2001, p. 715). The *LQ*© fills this void, and its *quotients* of leadership are useful for selection and development.

Can Personal *LQ*©'s Be Controlled or Modified?

Both. It is important to note that the leadership nature-versus-nurture debate has been settled. It is nature *plus* nurture, and anyone can improve as a leader by correctly identifying those leadership enablers they naturally have and those they don't. Next, the leader begins developing or improving those that they have the potential to mold, while at the same time compensating for those that they cannot develop. As we will document clearly in this book, the leader must move past the dichotomist view of nature and nurture to a realization that all behaviors come from both.

You Are in Control

Among the authors' strongest personal and professional agreements is that the single greatest determinant of personality and subsequent success is an individual's locus of control. People who have a strong internal locus of control know they are in charge of their environment. Leaders who know they are in charge of their environment can develop a higher *LQ*©. Individuals with an external locus of control are not able to change their *LQ*© or much of anything else about themselves or their circumstances (see Arnott's *Corporate Cults*, 2000).

Internal locus of control is important in our professional lives. Though we (authors Dave and Bill) were raised in totally different places at different times in totally different manners, we both know we can accomplish anything we want to in life simply because we have. Dave was given that by his family. Bill was not; he discovered it at about age 30. We have known so many people who do not realize the simple fact that each person is in control of his or her life.

Through completing the *LQ*©, hundreds of people have come to realize how few things are totally outside their control. The *LQ*© discusses many of the things that will help individuals improve their leadership. These things have been categorized into quotients: leaders, followers, and environments.

Nature Versus Nurture

Steven Pinker's book, *The Blank Slate*, is a great foundation for the *LQ*©, saving many hours of research and replication of effort (Thanks, Steven!). Steven's coverage of nature and nurture and their interactive and individual influences on human development is a discourse that stresses the latest scientific evidence and research coupled with the current thinking on the topics. *The Blank Slate*'s common sense conclusion is that human behavior is a combination of nature and nurture: We are born with SOME abilities and traits that contribute to leadership ability.

Pinker continually adds philosophical and psychological aspects to the current thinking in his scientifically oriented treatment of the nature versus nurture topic. We cannot recommend a book more highly for anyone who wants to gain clarity about the complexities of cultural, environmental, personal, evolutional, heritable, and other influences on the development of the human mind and the socialization that allows us to exist in a confusing, distracting, and complex world. Indeed, Pinker's dialogue on the evils that have been done in the name of science and the opponents of discovery who push an agenda and ignore the evidence makes reading *The Blank Slate* worthwhile.

Pinker states directly that the nature versus environment debate has been settled as a combination of both, but that giving exact percentages on the influence of each is meaningless. Nevertheless, Pinker does give some general guidelines, while warning against absolutes and the need to understand where his assessments are coming from. He ultimately succumbs to the felt pressure of his readers and assigns weights that roughly equate to a 50%-50% split for the influence of nature and nurture. He explains in great detail how the influence of genes and the hundreds of traits, viewed in every society ever chronicled, must be understood under probabilistic, not deterministic, illumination. This builds the platform for *The Leadership Quotient*, which enables you, the reader, to analyze your leadership capability based on what you've inherited from nature and what you've gained—and can continue to gain—from nurture. The nature and nurture influences are very interactive in producing the type of leadership a person should strive to exemplify.

Pinker establishes that the behavioral traits that contribute to leadership interact in a way that allows individuals to live successfully within a society (Pinker, 2002, p. 425). His findings give significant credence to the *LQ*© and the idea that leadership can be improved.

When writing the *LQ*©, we had a huge advantage because of Pinker's treatment of nature and nurture. This allowed us to avoid having to reinvent the nature-nurture wheel. *The Blank Slate* is a launching pad for the *LQ*© and many other behavioral studies in and out of the leadership category. If you disagree with us about the natural or nurtured traits of leadership, read Pinker.

From IQ to EQ to the *LQ*©

Pinker's book provides the nature versus nurture framework, and Daniel Goleman's book, *Emotional Intelligence* (*EQ*), builds the conceptual groundwork for the *LQ*©. *EQ* covers extensively what one needs to know about IQ: how it has evolved to mean more and cover more types of intelligence, and how IQ relates to leadership success. Goleman then extends the idea to include emotional intelligence, which can be applied and used for the betterment of leadership and management. Goleman determined that *EQ* can be improved, and spelled out how and why it was necessary to do so. *EQ* has established credibility for the notion of extending traditional measures, such as IQ, to other quotients that lead to life and leadership success. This naturally leads to Leadership Quotients.

The *LQ*© uses *EQ's* support and combines it with *The Blank Slate*'s ideas to jump-start a practical, comprehensive, yet focused explanation of how to improve your leadership effectiveness.

Our Part in the *LQ*©

Admitting to the complexity of the nature versus nurture debate cannot be seen as admitting defeat in the drive to determine what it takes to become a more effective leader. We simply have identified some practicalities that are controllable and impressionable, given the identification of the need and the desire to do so. Understanding what you have as a leader, naturally or otherwise, will only help you in understanding how you can better use what you have, or how you can conceivably obtain new quotient abilities for a better overall advantage.

Even people who claim to understand quantum physics don't totally understand it. Likewise, those who think they understand all of the ramifications of the situation in the Middle East simply do not. Those who say they have figured out violence in America have not, as people who think they know all the differences between men and women do not. And yes, those who know the exact requirements of religion don't; for if they do, they are implying that they are God.

Similarly, anyone who thinks they fully understand *The Leadership Quotient* does not. First, this is because a complete *absolute* formula does not exist. And even if it did, by the time we figured it out exactly it would have changed. As authors, we are not saying we know the complete and absolute formula, but we do know the best *useful* leadership guidance formula that exists. That formula can be used by ordinary people wishing to improve as leaders. The *LQ*© is simply the best current formulation of existing science and logical thought that can be practically adapted for more effective leadership application. Empirical validation of the *LQ*© is not strong, nor is it likely to be, since we kill leadership when we measure it in an experiment. But the logical practicality of the *LQ*© is supported by evidence from many views and examples.

The *LQ*© is a new framework for leadership improvement. Pinker wrote, "For all its limitations, human cognition is an open-ended combinational system, which in principle can increase its mastery over human affairs, just as it has increased its mastery of physical and living worlds" (2002, p. 299). The *LQ*© gets all of us closer to a mastery of leadership.

We want everyone to be able to easily answer the following two questions for every principle demonstrated in the *LQ*©: 1) So what? and 2) What does it mean to me?

Finally, We're Ready for the *LQ*©

In Howard Gardner's pioneering book, *Frames of Mind* (1993), the notion of many types of intelligence was presented. Gardner noted seven basic types of intelligence: verbal, mathematical-logical, spatial, kinesthetic, musical, interpersonal, and intrapersonal. Gardner's work seems to explain why traditional IQ tests are poor at predicting success in many of life's endeavors. Goleman's (1995) work extended Gardner's into the area of emotional intelligence (EQ—how well someone manages his or her own emotions), which is presented as more predictive of managerial and leadership success. The next logical step is to propose that, just as there are many ways to measure intelligence (IQ), there are many ways to measure leadership. Here is the *LQ*© formula and its *quotients* for successful leadership.

Generally:

LQ © = *f*(**Leader Quotients + Follower Quotients + Environmental Quotients**)

Specifically:

LQ © = *f*(AQ + BQ +CQ + DQ + EQ + IQ + KQ + MQ + PQ + RQ + SQ + XQ)

Learning to be an effective leader in any organization or group requires principles that we express as the Leadership Quotients listed above. Even though business schools have the intention of teaching the latest leadership concepts, business school research lags behind practitioner innovations with business schools not properly innovating their teaching (Vroman, 1995), especially in the area of leadership development. Future theories are being practiced in the real world even now as you read this. Academicians need to reinvent teaching for leadership excellence just as they instruct competitive organizations to continuously redefine excellence.

Many teachers and students resist change, much as IBM and GM did in the 1970s and 1980s, not seeming to realize that all institutions, including universities and individuals, must become more market- and customer-driven—in other words, innovative. We must change the model where professors are more comfortable with research than with their real constituents: business people and students. Likewise, most individuals are too satisfied with the status quo, and they must change. From our *constituent's* perspective, excellence in teaching, learning, and improving leadership requires innovation and change via constant improvement. Personal and enterprise application and university education should not be separated; we must seek excellence in everything related to leadership.

The next section introduces the 12 quotients and serves as a preview for the remainder of the *LQ*©.

The 12 Leadership Quotients Introduced

While we present the Quotients as individual elements, we understand that there is a great deal of interaction between them. However, they must be separated for explanation purposes. In the following brief descriptions, the quotients are organized in the three categories shown in Figure 1.2: leader, followers, and environments. From this point forward, we will present the quotients in *LQ*© chapter order versus alphabetical order.

Leader Quotients

These are the traits and characteristics that you must have or develop to become all you can be as a leader. The old notions about some of these traits and characteristics must change!

DQ—Desire Quotient: DQ is effort, drive for results, persistence, hunger, need, tenacity, exhibited commitment and passion, sense of urgency—basically a willingness to do whatever it takes. The desire to build a successful organization is more highly correlated with success than is the desire to be better personally (Collins, 2001). Here we see that desire can compensate for the lack of many natural characteristics, as witnessed time and again in every endeavor man has ever attempted.

The world is full of examples of people most interested in doing the things necessary to become leaders who realize true leadership success. Likewise, as many examples can be found of people most interested in merely becoming leaders who fail as leaders (Hesselbein and Cohen, 1999). The high-jump record for a person with only one leg is 6' 8"! The bar on desire is rising. Nelson Mandela spent 27 years in prison when he could have simply disavowed his principles and gone free. Desire was the quotient that propelled him to become one of the great leaders of our time.

Billy Martin, Jr., has been a guest speaker in Dave's Professional Sports Management class at Dallas Baptist University. When asked about the leadership ability of his father, the legendary Billy Martin of the New York Yankees, Billy hesitated for a long time. Then, haltingly, he said, "I can't explain it very well…but my Dad could just WILL his team to win." That's the Desire Quotient.

RQ—Reality Quotient: RQ is correctly clarifying inclusiveness, consensus, objectives, forward-sightedness, and visions. All of the great ideas in the world are of no value to the leader if he cannot make them "real." The more accurately the leader can interpret the reality for her followers, the more influence she will exercise over the group. Everyone defines a reality, and the better you are at interpreting the reality for and of your followers, the better leader you will be. When the majority defines reality a certain way, the leader has to interpret and react to that reality.

The leader's ego contributes a great deal to his ability to interpret the reality of his followers. An inflated ego makes the leader *unwilling* to deflate his self-image enough to understand where the group's reality exists. Is this possibly the problem witnessed with Ken Lay (his guilty verdict was vacated when he passed away after he was convicted but before he could be sentenced and given the right to appeal) and Richard Scrushy (can you believe Scrushy was acquitted in his first trial)? The opposite, a poor self-image, means the leader is *unable* to understand the followers' view of reality as it relates to you as the leader.

The results of good reality definition often are not clear until history tells us. The leader who thinks she has the ability to perfectly interpret reality—meaning the group's future—should remember what Warren Buffett said: "I have never met a person who could forecast the market. Forecasts may tell you a great deal about the forecaster; they tell you nothing about the future. Technicians and academics study the measurable, rather than the meaningful." Or as Alan Greenspan put it: "History is strewn with visions of such 'new eras' that, in the end, have proven to be a mirage."

Some people have such high self-perception that they bluff themselves into successfully doing virtually anything, as demonstrated in the real-life version of the movie, *Catch Me If You Can.* Yet others like Abraham Lincoln and Winston Churchill have demonstrated the value of understanding reality even when it was filled with bad news.

President George W. Bush attempted to tie Iraqi leadership to the threat of terrorist attacks on the U.S. The use of the phrase, "Axis of Evil," was his attempt to define reality for his followers.

EQ—Emotional Quotient: EQ is self-awareness, social awareness, empathy, exhibited mood, ability to control first impressions of self, and level of validity of assessment of self and others. The ability to read emotions of others and think like others relates to the continuum along the right side of the leadership leverage triangle in Figure 1.2: Fit. This quotient looks at whether the leader's emotions fit with what is demanded by the followers and the environments.

Common sense, practicality, intuition, preconceptions, and basic assumptions are mentioned as a part of EQ, and are also found in the subsequent quotients, KQ and XQ.

The effective EQ leader will create an environment that will help ensure success. As Kenny Rogers sang, "You gotta know when to hold 'em, know when to fold 'em, know when to walk away, know when to run." Goleman, Boyatzis, and McKee (2001) say clearly, "Emotionally intelligent men and women finish first" (p. 44). They go on to say that beyond the emotional maturity of self-awareness and empathy, "The leader's mood and behavior drive the moods and behaviors of everyone else….It requires an executive to determine, through reflective analysis, how his emotional leadership drives the moods and actions of the organization, and then, with equal discipline, to adjust his behavior accordingly" (p. 44). "But taken as a whole, the message sent by neurological, psychological, and organizational research is startling in its clarity. Emotional leadership is the spark that ignites a company's performance, creating a bonfire of success or a landscape of ashes. Moods matter that much" (p. 51). Surely we can all recall how Rudy Giuliani, "Mayor of the World" (a title Giuliani was given as *Time*'s Person of the Year 2001), exemplified EQ in his responses to 9/11.

A day after Billy Boat was declared winner of the 1999 Indy Racing League event at Texas Motor Speedway in Fort Worth, officials admitted they had miscounted the laps and the true winner was Arie Luyendyk. Track General Manager Eddie Gossage is usually calm and controlled. This day, he rushed to the press conference podium. Beating his fist on the lectern, he shouted, "The Race Car

Club of America counts the laps, not Texas Motor Speedway." We're convinced he was not really that upset. It was just a very good example of applying the correct emotion to the situation.

IQ—Intelligence Quotient: IQ is the best known of the quotients and is commonly thought of as "mental capacity." However, intelligence is a highly complex set of wide-ranging knowledge, skills, and abilities that are hard to define and measure. IQ is most often measured with tests that approximate reasoning power. Many feel that IQ tests measure how well someone can adapt to the form of assessment and that is in itself indicative of a person's intelligence. We feel that IQ as we know it simply predicts how well someone can perform in the American educational system, not how successful they will be in life nor as a leader. The "Asian intelligence myth" provides a good example. In American colleges, Asian students perform at a level that indicates their IQs are about 20 points higher. Actually, they are only a couple of points higher.

IQ is certainly a factor in leadership, but by no means is it the only factor or the most important. A high IQ can help an interested person learn more about a situation and the people involved in that situation, thus leading everyone to be more effective or successful. That's because of their IQ. Or it can be that because of IQ someone just coasts along. We've seen both, but more of the latter.

Though IQ is important, it does not take as much intelligence as many think to be a great leader. History has shown that people like Ronald Reagan and John Kennedy were great leaders who certainly were intelligent but by no means mental giants; yet, others have been held back because of their high IQs. We suppose that some are so smart they simply don't see the need to build their other quotients. In our Ph.D. quest (this is where we met in 1990), we saw the smartest person never complete the program. As we all have witnessed, in many endeavors brains are not enough.

Follower Quotients

Though these are still traits and characteristics you must have as a leader, you must begin to think of them in a different light. Shift your thinking to communicating for your followers—being the people person they want and worrying about how they think you behave—and yes, the way you appear as a leader to them. In the past, we have stressed these leadership skills from the leader's perspective: to be successful, shift your thinking to match that of your followers. It requires some new kinds of thinking because these aren't things you do, they are things they get!

CQ—Communications Quotient: CQ includes verbal, written, and body language: tone, dialect, clarity, conviction, command, use of silence, volume, vocabulary, presentation skills, and listening effectiveness. All of these aspects of communication must fit with the leader's followers and environments.

In one of Bill's management jobs with Blue Cross and Blue Shield of Texas, he had two project managers working for him. Roy was a member of Mensa and so smart it hurt. He was polite and tried very hard. However, Bill ultimately had to fire him because he could not communicate effectively. The other manager, Glen, used crude language and was offensive, yet people loved him. Glen got promoted and is today a top executive in an information systems department because he has the right Communications Quotient.

To get people to truly talk, you must know when to be quiet and listen without problem solving, judging, or interrupting (Goldsmith et al., 2003, p. 173). Communication is a commitment to generating and sharing knowledge. The chapter on CQ presents a formula and real world examples of how every leader can improve in this area. Adolf Hitler, Martin Luther King Jr., Winston Churchill, and Ronald Reagan are well-known examples of leaders with good Communications Quotients.

PQ—People Quotient: PQ is the ability to relate *with* people that includes relationships, social skills, use of poise and demeanor, teaming, facilitating others, networking, and reading others. All of these People Quotient concepts must be exercised in a way that produces a fit between the leader, followers, and environments, as shown in Figure 1.2.

In the past, we have seen the need for followers to be dependent on a leader; we are now moving to the only valid relationships being those that are mutually acceptable and benefiting. This includes having the organizational savvy to network within and outside organizations (Kilmann, Kilmann and Associates, 1991). The People Quotient means being able to understand diversity, and managing conflicts and disagreement. It also includes an understanding of rewards, development, coaching, feedback, evaluation, and enrichment used to tap the talents of others and to motivate them.

John was the worst manager we'd ever witnessed, though he was a Rhodes scholar and the nicest guy you'd ever want to meet. He was an imposing 6' 4", 250-pound ex-college football player, who was frightful when he was mad, as he often appeared to be. He had a lousy People Quotient.

Then overnight John became the best manager we'd ever seen. We found out that during the period preceding the abrupt change, John had been obtaining oil leases for his father-in-law, and once he decided he was quitting to pursue that business, he just overnight became a great manager. John's situation changed, so John just changed the way he related to people, not in his management principles. There was not time for him to change management principles, just his view of handling people: his PQ.

Adolf Hitler and Barbara Bush illustrate this quotient in sharply contrasting ways. Ask yourself, "Could I use Hitler's oratory style or Barbara Bush's motherly instinct as guides to my leadership behavior?"

BQ—Behavioral Quotient: BQ contains the exhibited external focus, ethics, values, credibility, direction, flexibility, savvy, social graces, timing, inspiration, and dependability. As shown in Figure

1.2, the relationship between the leader and followers is the key to the Behavioral Quotient: Does the leader behave in a way that appeals to the followers?

The effective behavioral leader performs actions that reflect what he wants to accomplish through his exhibited values, beliefs, assumptions, and mental models. Since this quotient maintains that leadership is behaviorally oriented, it assumes that leader behavior has to be consistent with the leader's real worldview. If a leader wants to behave in certain ways, she can begin by acting in those ways and soon she will become as she desires.

"Each time a man stands up for an ideal, or acts to improve the lot of others, or strikes out against injustice, he sends forth a tiny ripple of hope, and crossing each other from a million different centers of energy and daring, those ripples build a current that can sweep down the mightiest walls of oppression and resistance" (Robert Kennedy, 1966, as cited in MacArthur, 1999, unnumbered introductory page). Exemplars in this area are former Presidents Bill Clinton and Jimmy Carter.

Dave spent one year as Director of Marketing for the Great American Race. It was an across-the-country staged rally race of cars built before 1937, sponsored by Interstate Batteries. As a second-tier event, the TV broadcast had found a respectable home on ESPN. Because of a shortage of programming in 1990, the race had a chance to appear on ABC. Race organizers were talking to both ESPN and ABC, without telling the other network what was going on. In a private meeting about the matter, Interstate Batteries CEO, Norm Miller, observed, "Maybe we should do unto others." A long silence ensued. He was right, but it would mean losing a chance to be on ABC. Norm's advice carried the day because he exhibited an effective Behavioral Quotient.

AQ—Appearance Quotient: AQ starts with the manifestation of the correct level of confidence and then goes on to include voice, appropriate dress, vitality, alertness, mannerisms, physical appearance, posture, and an outward show of poise and demeanor. This is another example of the importance of fit in Figure 1.2. The leader's appearance must fit with the environment in which leadership takes place.

Bill was in London when the Queen Mother died. He was struck by how energetic she appeared in public just months before her death. She just didn't appear that old. Perhaps all of us would appear more energetic if we knew that each time we were in public millions of people would be watching.

We are in a "new McWorld of global sales, [where] the trademark has surpassed the sales item and the image has overtaken the product…" (Barber, 1996, p. 67). Image has surpassed substance, and indeed an ounce of image is worth a pound of performance. "Politicians can do no right; celebrities can do no wrong—homicide included. Nothing is quite what it seems" (Barber, 1996, p. 85).

Men over 6' tall and women over 5' 6" have an advantage in leadership. The fact that appearance is important is something that leaders must understand. Some examples of high Appearance Quotient are George Washington, Napoleon, Mother Teresa, and Princess Di. Former Senator Phil Gramm was arguably a highly qualified presidential candidate; but, by his own admission, appearance kept him from being elected.

Dave, accompanied by his wife, Cynde, was the guest speaker at a Christian college. Dave was very impressed with the college president's intellectual and people skills. After a private lunch in the president's conference room, Cynde offered her analysis: "A president of a conservative Christian college should not have a tan in the winter and be wearing a designer watch." Oops! His appearance did not match the environment.

Environment Quotients

The skills and traits you see in this section are a little tricky. The key here is to learn what and how to fit with the environments within which you must lead before you try to stand out as a leader in those environments. It's a delicate balancing act!

XQ—eXperience Quotient: XQ includes past accomplishments learned and earned, mistakes, seizing the moment, discernment, maturity, insights, and generalizations; and shows how one can learn through reflection. A person with a high XQ can mobilize commitment, can foster consensus, has *good* hunches, can spread revitalization—institutionalize it, can monitor and adjust strategies and plans, and has assumptions that build our mental models on how we view the world. XQ includes intuition, sound judgment, decisiveness, learning and showing by example, understandability, adaptability, and people and organizational savvy.

No decision *is* a decision and quite often the worst decision. Let experience teach you how to be successfully decisive. "Find one or two people who have leadership styles you really admire. Follow them, observe them, listen to them and imitate the things that you like" (Motley, 1995, pages unnumbered).

We often tell students we are certifiably the most ignorant people in the classroom because we can make a longer list of the things we don't know than any of them can. Yes, we realize more of what we don't know than they do. That is XQ and the beginning of the wisdom of experience. Henry Kissinger has been described as one of the world's greatest negotiators, although he has not been used in that capacity for years. Wonder why? Al Gore had great experience but could not take advantage of it, possibly because he was lacking in other quotients?

KQ—Knowledge Quotient: KQ includes the leader's ability to learn, pay attention, recognize, imagine, and keep up to date on workplace technologies. It also includes adaptability, innovativeness, and the ability to evolve.

Indeed, it is possible to redefine or enact an environment that is more suitable for your success. Many of the executives laid off in the late 1990s and the 2000s never learned to use technology, and this caused them problems in their next phase of life. Bill was the V.P. of an information services division of a major organization and an Assembler Language programmer. Thus, it seems strange that he never used e-mail, typed his own letters, nor used a spreadsheet or word processor. When he left the corporate world to pursue his Ph.D., his main learning curve was for typing skills as well as how to use several other PC-based products.

When reading about the D-Day experience of young American troops as they quickly learned under fire or died, we thought of our recent experience with 23 college-age students who went to Europe for the first time and within days were traveling all over the Continent, realizing there was no place or person they could not handle. They gained confidence in the knowledge that knowledge is easily obtained. On the other hand, never forget what Satchel Paige said: "It's not what you don't know that hurts you, it's what you know that just ain't so."

Warren Buffett has used this to great advantage; but in the movie, *Rain Man,* Raymond had a high KQ but could not use it (as we suspect many in real life cannot).

SQ—Situational Quotient: SQ is the ability to interpret environmental cues and develop appropriate strategies for addressing the cues. This quotient includes timing, instinct, political savvy, curiosity, flexibility, ability to simplify complexity, fitability, imagination, and circumstances. This includes the Situational Leadership model developed by Hersey (1985) and Blanchard (all dates), which asserts that an effective manager varies structure and support based on those being managed and the situation at hand. This is the ability to realize when and where is the time to tell, sell, work for consensus, empower, or delegate.

Did Al Sharpton create a situation or meet the need of a situation? Did Rudy Giuliani change after the situational effect of 9/11, or did that terrible crime make his strengths shine? Martin Luther King Jr. was a great leader in part because of a great cause that needed him, and he molded himself to the need.

Dave spent two college summers working in a family bakery in Spirit Lake, Iowa. Since work started at about 2:00 a.m., sometimes the young workers were a little bleary-eyed and didn't perform exactly as they were supposed to. One night, as bakers were quietly going about their duties, the master baker continually checked the bread in the "proof-box." Laymen say bread is "rising"; bakers say it is "proofing," because the heat and humidity "prove" whether the bread contains the right ingredients.

Dudley, the master baker, would lower his glasses to avoid the steam, pull down the lid of the "proof-box," and glance accusingly at the baker running the mixer. After four or five checks, it was obvious something was wrong. Dudley went through the trash and found an empty bag of cake flour. We were baking bread, not cakes. The wrong ingredients, from nature or nurture, will cause leadership to "flop," much like the bread flopped.

MQ—Management Quotient: MQ includes general administrative skills that could be categorized under systems and procedures, planning, organizing, controlling, and staffing. Other subcategories of the Management Quotient include teaming, process, ability to motivate, evaluating and managing personnel, information and knowledge management, efficiency and effectiveness, quality, technological savvy, strategic thinking, and mentoring. MQ also includes understanding how to use financial and quantitative data, and technical and functional expertise as well as industry and organizational understanding. MQ is the knowledge of time-honored principles useful for getting groups to accomplish shared objectives.

Real managers know how to link their employees with the resources they need to be effective. This includes applying technology to solve basic business problems and building a sense of camaraderie. Collins (2001) said professional managers can kill entrepreneurial spirit through bureaucracy and hierarchy while good to great leaders use freedom and responsibility within a framework of discipline and resolve. He also said, "'Stop doing' lists are more important than the 'to do' lists" (Collins, 2001, p. 143).

Jerry was a great young manager. He simply "managed" everything in a sincere and easy manner. Bob was exceptionally bright, but he could not manage his way out of a wet paper sack if he had an ax. Appropriate MQ helps explains the difference between their managerial effectiveness. Herb Kelleher and Jack Welch are legends, but in very different ways. Kelleher's humor and self-degradation and Welch's brains and guts are great examples of effective yet very different Management Quotients.

Usefulness of the 12 Quotients to You

To "raise" your leadership to its highest level, you need to evaluate yourself in each of the 12 quotients and identify clearly those that are under your control versus those that are not. Then you can work to improve those under your control in order to offset negative effects of factors over which you have no control. In each of the 12 areas, as you identify your individual quotients, remember that the quotients can be viewed in the following ways: 1) real—totally objective, 2) perceived—as each individual sees it, or 3) enacted—as it plays out in given circumstances. Your goal is to try to get your perceptions closer to reality in order for you to play out as an effective leader. We will keep going back to these three views in the *LQ*©, but for now the 2X2 matrix shown in Figure 1.3 gives you the idea of what you are to do with each quotient and your self-evaluation.

Figure 1.3: *LQ°* MEASUREMENT AND IMPROVEMENT MATRIX

	NATURE (uncontrollable-born)	NURTURE (controllable-developed)
STRENGTHS (enablers—advantages)	Quadrant 1 — Maximize	Quadrant 2 — Hone
WEAKNESSES (derailers—disadvantages)	Quadrant 3 — Make Irrelevant or Deflect	Quadrant 4 — Minimize or Change

Get accustomed to this 2X2 matrix, because we build one for each of the next 12 quotient chapters. You will use a matrix for each of the 12 quotients to evaluate your own *LQ°* and ultimately plan how you can become a better leader.

Perception

Dave learned an important lesson about perception via his vision. While wearing hard contacts for 30 years, he could see like a hawk. So he was frustrated when his vision got bad and the optometrist couldn't seem to adjust the contacts correctly.

"Why can't you get the vision in my right eye perfect, like it used to be?" Dave asked. (You're probably thinking the problem was age, but you're wrong.)

"It's because you have a cataract in that eye," said the optometrist matter-of-factly.

"I'm only 45 years old. Cataracts are for old people!" Dave exclaimed.

"Well, you've got one," said the optometrist.

Dave visited an ophthalmologist and the cataract was confirmed. The natural lens was growing yellow, limiting his vision. He had cataract surgery and a new, clear lens was implanted in his right eye.

The day after the surgery, the patch was removed. Dave looked out of the right eye only, then the left eye only. Then back to the right, then back to the left.

"Why is it that through my new lens in my right eye everything looks white, while out of the old lens in the left eye everything looks buff-colored?" Dave asked.

"That's because you have a cataract growing in your left eye also," the ophthalmologist calmly replied. "We'll watch it, and you'll probably have surgery on that eye in a few years."

Dave sat blinking rapidly: left eye, right eye, left eye, right eye. To this day he sees things out of his right eye much as you see a clean sheet of white copy paper. He sees everything out of his left eye about the color of newspaper print.

Without having cataract surgery, how would Dave have ever known reality? How do you know how your followers perceive reality? The cataract incident has given Dave two very different views of reality: white from the right eye, and buff from the left. It's a good lesson to keep in mind as you struggle to understand the version of reality your followers are seeing.

The key is to make perceptions as near reality as possible, but with an understanding that perceptions are in fact reality for the perceiver! For example, in your Appearance Quotient, if you felt your negatives were being short and stout and your positive was the way you dressed, then you could be very careful about clothing and work out to obtain a better physique.

A college friend wore a wig throughout college because he was essentially bald, but he was also totally out of shape physically. Others knew about the wig and wondered why he simply didn't junk it and just dress better and get into better physical condition. In another situation, one of the authors was discussing the Southern Baptists and how they are intolerant of women and homosexuals. An *expert* on the Southern Baptist beliefs became incensed and stated that this was simply not the truth. The author could not get the expert to understand that he was wrong according to the vast majority of informed people in America. Yes—264,000,000 Americans are not Southern Baptist! In this example, intolerance must be treated as "the" truth regardless of the "real" truth if one wants to change anything.

In each chapter, we'll provide a self-assessment worksheet for each of the quotients. What Galileo said is a good guide as you complete these self-assessments: "You cannot teach a man anything. You can only help him discover it within himself" (cited in Oakley and Krug, 1991, p. 166). It takes time and effort to become an effective leader. The only limits on your success as a leader are those limits you allow to hold you back. The world has had great leaders who were short and tall, men and women, attractive and just plain ugly, smart and slow. There are few successes without sacrifice. If you are willing to invest in yourself by learning more about your leadership style, then continue reading *The Leadership Quotient*. As the famous general, Stonewall Jackson, said, "Gentlemen, if we are going to be successful, we have got to go to the sound of battle."

Get Moving on Your *LQ*© Journey!

> *Just think, some night the stars will gleam*
> *Upon a cold gray stone and trace a name with silver beam,*
> *And lo, will be your own.*
> *That night is speeding on…(Just Think, by Robert W. Service)*

It's time to get started; if not now, when? The development of any solution should start with kaleidoscope thinking, remembering that most often when something seems impossible with a certain worldview, it is easier to accomplish with another view (Hesselbein et al., 2002). The *LQ*© sheds light on how that new view might come to you, and indeed, why it must be realized. The *LQ*© asks, "What can anyone do to become a more successful, effective leader?"

The quotients presented here measure **Key Success Factors** *of effective leadership—considering fit among leaders, followers, and the environments.* These Qs are the factors of the 1) content (the facts or technical details), primarily about the leader; 2) process (the way things are done), primarily focuses on followers, their needs and perceptions; 3) context (the environments within which the leadership occurs); how relationships of the leader and followers in an environment find the proper balance; the three are linked by 4) intra-interpersonal relationships, components of leadership where success is determined by fitting in yet standing out.

In this dynamic, information-overloaded world, increasingly it is important to have the judgment to recognize change, get feedback, analyze the circumstances, and become more quickly adaptable in leading for finite action under varying degrees of uncertainty. Situations facing leaders today are ambiguous and murky at best, but the Leadership Quotients codify and simplify the factors that can be measured and improved to increase leadership effectiveness.

We've all tried to put a leader on a pedestal, and we might think the leader's presence is so strong that the leader exhibits all 12 of the Leadership Quotients to perfection. But it's not true. No leader has perfected all 12 of the quotients. What you're observing is the leader's ability to make up for shortcomings in the quotients where she has weaknesses. If you will think about your favorite leader, you will realize that he plays on his strong quotients to overcome his weak quotients. You must first discover the presence you can develop and then hone your presence to its highest potential. Address your tangibles as fundamentals before you address your intangibles. Ultimately, your intangibles will drive your success, but only if you develop some solid tangibles. You've got to get in position to succeed before you will succeed.

The higher the level of leadership to which you aspire, the more complete you as a package must become. We have known executives who were not moved up because they ordered beer when everyone else was drinking wine, had a bad comb-over, dressed great except for their belt or their watch's crummy band, and so on. These actions were not in themselves bad, but they did indicate to someone that a person just could not see the appropriate intricacies and refinements necessary for leadership in that environment.

Many will know these things when they see them but won't be able to measure them. The *LQ*© helps you identify these issues and helps those who want to help themselves. Remember: Looking the part may not seem important, but if you don't look the part, you won't get the part.

Understand that it is becoming increasingly difficult to lead in a global information environment. As Arnold Schwarzenegger reportedly said (if he didn't, he should have!), "Nobody ever got muscles by watching me lift weights." Or as Vince Lombardi said, "Luck is a combination of preparation and opportunity."

We know that in leadership research, profiles and cases run ahead of theory and academic ideas. The lab is out there in the world of organizations. No existing theory explains leadership, yet theories are important. Leadership qualities include adaptive capabilities, ability to engage others, ability to share meanings, ability to appeal to people's emotions as well as their logic, and effectiveness in communicating. But all must lead to a zest for knowledge that is exhibited by your ability to embrace and learn from life's transformational experiences (Bennis and Thomas, 2002; and Campbell, 2002). "Beware of leaders who are always sure of themselves" (Fullan, 2001, p. 123).

The research process is a continuous expansion of knowledge that involves the generation, refutation, and repeated attempted application of theories. Anticipation, research, learning, and continual improvement and innovation are used by many successful organizations. But the current press, and the academic and instructive literature are filled with examples of organizations that did not learn the lessons provided by these innovative examples. Remember: It is not who said it, but whether it works, that counts.

The study of leadership started with great-man theories, defining traits and characteristics, then progressed to contingencies, and ultimately to credibility, knowledge, servant leadership, and empowerment. The Leadership Quotient is the most effective formula we've found in our attempts to get a handle on this thing called leadership and put it into terms that can be measured and improved. A tall order, but one that is worthwhile, because even a small improvement in your $LQ^{©}$ will leverage great organizational and individual accomplishment.

Effective leadership requires a balanced fit among the leader, followers, and environments. Existing theories are useful in explaining leadership, but the dimensions of the $LQ^{©}$ are among the most critical because leadership is first and foremost about human influence. Understanding that we all do as we do to take care of what's important to us, to serve our values, is a basic requirement. Yet this requirement fails when we continue to think that others value what we do as leaders.

Figure 1.2 shows the interaction of 1) the leader, 2) the followers, and 3) the environments, which all need to fit. The leader portion is the process, behaviors, and traits of the leader. The follower portion is the content, relations, tasks, trust, influences, perceptions, and processes; and is very individualistic, though there are normally many followers. Lastly, the environment is the context of the organization and the leader-follower interactions. Overall, the Leadership Leverage Triangle (Figure 1.2) is indeed like a three-legged stool that will not stand without all three legs.

Plan for the Book

So Why Worry About This?

People want direction, inspiration, validation, and relationships. Thus all organizations need leadership development. Realize that people need 1) direction with goals, objectives, measurements, and rewards; 2) knowledge—skills, development, training, information, etc., as a foundation for knowledge; 3) resources—a place, tools, materials, money, recognition in the form of "things," etc.; and 4) support—approval, recognition, pats on the back, good and necessary feedback, coaching, managing, encouragement, etc. Yes, to improve as a leader you've got to come up with a plan and stick with it; you can't just wish things will get better. The *LQ*© provides the foundation for your plan.

Leadership is a fusion of work and human relations, a dream around which those inclined can rally. It is the realization of the potential of individuals, influencing and leveraging the power of others. Leadership is considering the heart and the mind, taking care of what's important to us, serving joint values and motivating toward organizational goals. It's measuring desire, effort, and performance; giving rewards; and honoring intellect. Leadership is about limiting and expanding solutions and learning from failures. It's mobilizing people's commitment to putting their energy into actions designed to improve things: individual commitment with collective mobilization. It's pushing for a culture of personal accountability, the hard and the soft side of leadership and management, tangibles and intangibles, and content and the context. It's being technically perfect in the ways we appeal to others as only those with the highest of *LQ*©s can. The *LQ*© directs this quest if you understand that leadership is as much a matter of how to be or become as about how to do or what you are!

Many of the old ways and arguments continue, yet they have failed. The *LQ*© guides those who want to improve their leadership. We can make failure into success only when we learn from failure.

Start by appreciating what makes each individual and organization unique, and focusing on solutions not problems. This doesn't mean you ignore problems; it just means you work toward positive solutions once you have a clear idea of where you need to go. Most often the solutions are within your control and are relatively simple if you try for small, focused solutions versus saving the world. Yesterday's answers may have nothing to do with today's problems; sometimes they caused them (Jackson and McKergow, 2002).

OK, So What's to Follow?

> *"Everything comes to him who hustles while he waits."—Thomas A. Edison*
> *"The world belongs to the energetic."—Ralph Waldo Emerson*
> *(Both cited in Bruun and Getzen, 1996, p. 543.)*

The quotients have been grouped under the major headings in the *LQ*© chapters as follows:

Part 1: *Leader Quotients:* Chapter 2, DQ—desire; Chapter 3, RQ—reality; Chapter 4, EQ—emotional; and Chapter 5, IQ—intelligence: quotients the leader needs.

Part 2: *Follower Quotients:* Chapter 6, CQ—communications; Chapter 7, PQ—people; Chapter 8, BQ—behavioral; and Chapter 9, AQ—appearance: quotients that must be viewed in light of the followers' perspectives.

Part 3: *Environmental Quotients:* Chapter 10, XQ—experience; Chapter 11, KQ—knowledge; Chapter 12, SQ—situation; and Chapter 13, MQ—management: quotients that need to fit the environment where the leader operates.

Part 4: Chapter 14, Putting it all together. This will include enduring principles and some next steps. Remember, as Machiavelli said, "Fortune favors the bold."

It's not the math, stupid! In all things related to human relations, you should prefer intuitively logical over statistically significant. We will discuss as we go how to adjust leadership style to meet the needs of those you serve while fitting your particularities. As you progress through this book, reflect with an understanding of the following: 1) differing leadership styles, 2) the competency level of everyone, 3) assessment of commitment level of everyone, and 4) use of different leadership styles with different people at different times.

You will in the end be able to fill in the relational triangle with the measures of your quotients. You will understand your particular $LQ^{©}$ strengths and weaknesses and how they fit appropriately. You will begin to see how leaders must understand FISO: *Fit In—Stand Out.*

What's the Bottom Line Thus Far?

Remember: Beyond talent lie all the usual words: discipline, love, luck—but most of all, endurance. Leadership, like all of life, is a test, and does not come with exact directions! IQ, EQ, and many other things help, but it can be that, "The problem is that he is so bright that he stops listening as soon as he has understood the point" (Fullan, 2001, p. 124). This could be said of any Q. Don't stop because you've got a few exceptional Qs. Leadership comes in all shapes and sizes and in levels of effectiveness and success. Understand equally as well what you can do to improve your own leadership success regardless of your $LQ^{©}$ scores. The fundamentals provided in the $LQ^{©}$ are the foundation for improving both the effectiveness and efficiency of leadership. Attachment 2 is the instrument you can use for your initial self-evaluation of your own $LQ^{©}$. It might be a good idea to fill it out now and then see if you changed much at the end of the book. Do as you like—many benefit by doing a before-and-after assessment.

The effective and efficient leaders of the future will be learners who are open to new ideas and value change. The new leaders will be trustworthy, respect-worthy, change-worthy. We will value what others can do, and learn how to highlight and build on that. We will be clear on who we are and what we stand for, because without a central pool of guiding principles, the changes ahead of us would overwhelm. Unlike most aristocratic and many bureaucratic leaders, we will be deeply respectful of the value and dignity of individuals in and near our organizations.

The new leaders of tomorrow will be systems thinkers, able and eager to see ever-larger pictures of systems within systems. We will respect individuals, regardless of race or gender or religion, for what they can do and how they do it. We will be designers and initiators, people who are always looking for a better way, always willing to fix things that are not yet broken, but with a specific purpose in mind. The new leaders will be "and/also" thinkers instead of "either/or" thinkers. The new leaders will be coaches and caretakers, teachers and students, workers as well as managers, and role models as well as instructors.

Continually ask yourself: What is my work? What is our work? What do I value? What do we value? Whom do I serve? Whom do we serve? Whom should I serve? Whom should we serve? Where am I going? Where are we going? How do I fit in? How do we fit in? How do I stand out? How do we stand out? Ask for yourself and your organization as appropriate, but always remember: Only you are in control of you!

So—What Really Works? What Do We Really Know?

After spending many years in the practice and study of leadership, we realize we know only one thing for sure about leadership: We have a lot to learn about it. So, where to start? With the simplest of concepts: the definition of what we are studying. Leadership and the principles outlined here are a great foundation.

What Really Counts in Studying Leadership?

In the study of leadership, it's not solving problems that counts but being open to new ideas. We need to try the "Hawthorne Effect" on ourselves because ideas are funny things. They don't work unless we do. Our goal is not to win the debate on how to become better leaders; our goal as leadership improvement facilitators must become how to develop the best questions and answers to help others realize more of their potential. Leading anything is about leverage, and we need to leverage ourselves and our followers. There are no magic formulas, pills, or miracle moments; only diligence, credibility, desire, and a lot of hard work.

In 1999, Bill was doing some work with a law firm in Birmingham, and he was talking with a young lawyer named Penny. She told him she had a degree in Business from Samford University, but she didn't always have great experiences at Samford. In fact, she had to go talk to one of her professors about how he treated her and the only other girl in her class. She meekly told the professor his behavior was really not what Samford University was about as a Christian school. She went on to explain to Bill that the professor was just so confrontational and would not let up on either of the two girls in the class. This professor had even been critical during Penny's visit to complain, just saying, "That's too bad, deal with it."

Bill asked her if that professor was Ed Felton, and she said yes, it was him.

Bill asked, "Do you suppose that his treatment of you helped you in law school?"

She stopped and said, "You know, I guess it did."

That encounter with Ed was in 1989. It took her ten years to realize the value he added to her, and then she needed some help to realize it. Think about this as you're learning about leadership from the

LQ©, but most importantly, as you go about the daily living of your life. As Lamarkus, one of the African-Americans who make up only 2% of the student body at Samford University, said, "I came here because I knew I wouldn't be comfortable here. I only improve when I'm uncomfortable." He has improved and he is successful.

Gifted leadership is where the heart and head—that is, feelings and thoughts—meet. Leaders need enough intellect to handle the tasks, but they also must motivate, guide, inspire, listen, and persuade, which requires EI—emotional intelligence (Goleman, Boyatzis, and McKee, 2002). Remember on your *LQ*© journey: "The trail is the thing, not the end of the trail. Travel too fast and you miss all you are traveling for" (from Louis L'Amour, *Ride the Dark Trail*). Or maybe you'll like this one better: "The goal isn't worth arriving at unless you enjoy the journey" (Norman Lear). Realization of the interactive implications and complexities of leaders and followers within various situations is the first step of your leadership improvement journey. Before you go further, look back at Figure 1.1 and study it a while, and the reading will mean more to you.

On to DQ: The Desire Quotient

We are starting the first quotient chapter with the Desire Quotient. Without DQ, humans just can't accomplish anything of value. Throughout our lives we have witnessed what DQ can do for or against people. Indeed it has allowed innumerable people to overcome every possible hurdle in sports, fighting a fatal illness, making a failed marriage work, writing a book, obtaining Ph.D.s, fighting as kids, fighting in wars, religious survival, learning about leadership, becoming Miss America, becoming Mr. Universe, becoming a multibillionaire, and basically any pursuit of value.

Katye Jackson is a 13-year-old who has fought several bouts with cancer, losing an arm in the fight. *Katye's Story* is an inspiration to all who have met her or read her book. As we are writing this, Katye is working hard on making the track team in the throwing events. Just tell her she can't do it, her mother says, and watch her do it. The DQ chapter will address this linking and foundational quotient in much more detail.

Attachment 1: Dichotomies in Management Versus Leadership

Helps stay in the known	*Versus*	Moves to the unknown
Content	*Versus*	Process and context
Power with vertical integration	*Versus*	Empowerment and Alliances
Drives with authority	*Versus*	Coaches with goodwill
Experts – I – fixes blame	*Versus*	Teams – We – fixes it
Lifetime employment	*Versus*	Dejobbing
Stability	*Versus*	Innovativeness/change
Invention – watches bottom line	*Versus*	Innovation – watches horizon
Caution	*Versus*	Experimentation/speed
In-house	*Versus*	Outsourcing
I win – demands respect	*Versus*	We win – is respected
Control - doing things right	*Versus*	Trust – doing the right things
Autocrat - fear	*Versus*	Coach – enthusiasm
How – not enough time	*Versus*	Why – makes time
Credit or blame	*Versus*	Shared responsibility
Information hub	*Versus*	Gets problems solved
Steady Administrator	*Versus*	Innovative Leader
Maintains and prefers things	*Versus*	Develops and prefers people
Accepts status quo	*Versus*	Challenges
Surrenders to context	*Versus*	Masters context
A good soldier	*Versus*	Own person

Attachment 2: *LQ*© Self-Assessment (evaluate yourself in each area as indicated):

1. **AQ**—Appearance Quotient—appears correctly confident, voice, dress (eye for appropriate fashion), mannerisms, physical appearance, posture, poise, demeanor, etc.

    a. a positive which you control—

    b. a positive over which you have **NO** control—

  c. a negative over which you have **NO** control—

  d. a negative which you control—

2. **BQ**—Behavioral Quotient—exhibited ethics, values, credibility, sense of necessity, courage, direction, motivation, and commitment.

  a. a positive which you control—

  b. a positive over which you have **NO** control—

  c. a negative over which you have **NO** control—

  d. a negative which you control—

3. **CQ**—Communications Quotient—the primary tool of leadership—verbal, written, body language, tone, dialect, appropriateness of words, presentation skills, listening effectiveness, sounds and body language: fitability.

  a. a positive which you control—

  b. a positive over which you have **NO** control—

  c. a negative over which you have **NO** control—

  d. a negative which you control—

4. **DQ**—Desire Quotient—effort, drive for results, persistence, conveying a sense of urgency, investing of self in accomplishment, hunger, need, tenacity, commitment, high-need type person, exhibited commitment and passion, sense of urgency, belief of usefulness and purpose.

  a. a positive which you control—

  b. a positive over which you have **NO** control—

  c. a negative over which you have **NO** control—

  d. a negative which you control—

5. **EQ**—Emotional Quotient—self-awareness and management, social awareness, empathy, exhibited mood, ability to control first impressions of self, and level of validity of assessment of self and others.

  a. a positive which you control—

  b. a positive over which you have **NO** control—

    c.   a negative over which you have **NO** control—

    d.   a negative which you control—

6. **IQ**—Intelligence Quotient—intellect—commonly thought of as "mental capacity."

    a.   a positive which you control—

    b.   a positive over which you have **NO** control—

    c.   a negative over which you have **NO** control—

    d.   a negative which you control—

7. **KQ**—Knowledge Quotient—ability to learn, paying attention, recognizing, growing and changing as "things" change, continuous expansion of base of useful information, and keeping up to date on workplace technologies.

    a.   a positive which you control—

    b.   a positive over which you have **NO** control—

    c.   a negative over which you have **NO** control—

    d.   a negative which you control—

8. **PQ**—People Quotient—ability to relate *with* people; relationships, social skills, listening—reading the reality of others, poise, demeanor, facilitating others, and reading others: fitability.

    a.   a positive which you control—

    b.   a positive over which you have **NO** control—

    c.   a negative over which you have **NO** control—

    d.   a negative which you control—

9. **MQ**—Management Quotient—developing systems, procedures, and structures: SOP, planning, organizing, controlling, executing, efficiency, quality, directing, staffing, mentoring, and coaching, as well as strategic analysis and thinking.

    a.   a positive which you control—

    b.   a positive over which you have **NO** control—

    c.   a negative over which you have **NO** control—

    d.   a negative which you control—

10. **RQ**—Reality Quotient—clarifying inclusiveness, consensus, objectives, and seeing the current state as it really is and as it is becoming.

    a.   a positive which you control—

    b.   a positive over which you have **NO** control—

    c.   a negative over which you have **NO** control—

    d.   a negative which you control—

11. **SQ**—Situational Quotient—ability to read a situation and fit into it, timing, and circumstances.

    a.   a positive which you control—

    b.   a positive over which you have **NO** control—

    c.   a negative over which you have **NO** control—

    d.   a negative which you control—

12. **XQ**—eXperience Quotient—past accomplishments learned and earned, mistakes, firsthand observations, and assumptions that build our mental models on how we view the world.

    a.   a positive which you control—

    b.   a positive over which you have **NO** control—

    c.   a negative over which you have **NO** control—

    d.   a negative which you control—

PART I
Leader Quotients

The human genetic map is done—Wow, that's about 3,000,000,000 pairs of DNA that control human development! Wanna bet there are a few that relate to leadership?

The purpose of the $LQ^©$ is for you to learn how to lead your followers in your environment as shown in the Leadership Quotient Triangle. It should be your goal as a leader to ***fit in*** *(with your followers and environments)* yet ***stand out*** as a leader who makes a difference. The road to personal leadership improvement starts with the Desire Quotient in Chapter 2; continues through the Reality Quotient in Chapter 3 and the Emotional Quotient in Chapter 4; and ends with the Intelligence Quotient in Chapter 5. These chapters help you understand who you are as a leader. The quotients in Part 1 will help you understand the strengths and weaknesses—from both nature and nurture—that make up your leadership style. This section helps you leverage your strengths and avoid your weaknesses.

Don't get "lost in the forest" as we introduce you to many "trees." Keep in mind the very simple framework of the Leadership Quotient Triangle and you won't get lost. As Einstein said even about the equation that will ultimately define the universe, "Tricky (crafty, shrewd) is the Lord God, but malicious He is not" (Aczel, 1999, p. 13). The $LQ^©$ is simple and logical with only three major points: leader, followers, and environments. Don't make it more complex than that until you have mastered the basics.

Goldsmith et al., wrote (2003, p. 96), "Much has been written about leadership. Some of this literature is based on sound theory and research, but much of it is merely opinion, if not hype." The $LQ^©$ is not hype, but is solidly grounded in theory, research, experience, and logic. Leadership must be simple and logical or it has no application. Leadership ideas must make sense to *you* in order for *you* to be successful in using them; therefore, we admonish you to really understand every principle and trait before you accept them and attempt to use them.

The $LQ^©$ approach includes sound research, exemplars, how to's, popular press reports, experience, case reports, case research, emotionally based concepts, fads, fiction and fact, and finally, logic to give you leadership steps you can use again and again. Scientific research often lacks usefulness in the real world of leadership application. You will notice the use of statistics and research in the $LQ^©$, but they are used in ways that provide "rubber meeting the road" applications. Empirically based findings *are* useful, but they can distract and lead to a false sense of applicability. This is because human interactions are so complex that reducing them to a handful of testable propositions or hypotheses simply can't reflect the level of intricacy that exists within the leader-followers-environments interactions. As mentioned earlier, when you dissect something, you tend to kill it. We want to bring leadership alive in you through application, not kill it through studying it in others.

This section includes **Chapter 2, DQ—Desire Quotient; Chapter 3, RQ—Reality Quotient; Chapter 4, EQ—Emotional Quotient; and Chapter 5, IQ—Intelligence Quotient**. These four elements make up the quotients that define who the leader is and how she is seen by her followers in her environment. As you read about DQ, RQ, EQ, and IQ, think about *balance, fit, appropriateness,* and *authenticity*. Trying to be something you are *not* is a sure ticket to leadership failure.

On to DQ

A leader who has the proper Desire Quotient will have the balance, fit, appropriateness, and authenticity mentioned above. Without desire, the leader will have a noxious blend that makes his leadership unbalanced, poorly fitting, inappropriate, or unreal. These fits must be viewed in light of your wisdom to improve and contribute. Picture a favorite personal leader as well as current leaders you admire. We think of President Bush, Tony Blair, Tom Daschle, Jesse Jackson, Michael Jordan, Kofi Annan, Rudy Giuliani, Bill Clinton, Colin Powell, Sir Richard Branson, Jacques Chirac, and Vladimir Putin, all as exemplars of current leaders who exhibit the Desire Quotient—not all are *good* exemplars!

2

DQ, The Desire Quotient

Why Start Here?

We are continually struck with the realization that those who are successful and those who fail fear the same things, but in successful people we see fear being overcome by the sheer force of their desire to accomplish a goal.

The introductory chapter ended with a story about a young girl named Katye Jackson, and we'd like to start the Desire Quotient chapter with something from Katye's book:

> I have learned that I can do almost anything I want to do just using my one arm. I can swim (and win races), I can play miniature golf and I can play tennis. I can still paint and make things and do my homework. I can tie my shoes and cross-stitch. There are still some things I am working on learning how to do, but I know that I will be able to do them. Sometimes you just have to do them in a different way....I'm just a normal ten-year-old girl. (Jackson, 2000, pp. 23 and 29)

Whenever you think you're having a hard time, remember this brave young lady. We'd even suggest that you order a copy of her amazing story because a portion of the proceeds goes to Camp Smile-A-Mile. A leader who exhibits half the desire Katye does will have a great start toward an appropriate DQ. Not only does Katye exhibit great desire, she exhibits much self-discipline. Carlos Santana recently said that the key to success is self-discipline, yet most people don't want to hear that; they just want to just snap their fingers, forgetting about the work and practice success takes (Fong-Torres, 2003).

One of Dave's favorite seminar questions is to ask the attendees to share the worst job they've ever had. In a recent group of 20-somethings, the expected convenience store and fast-food jobs were mentioned. The very last respondent from the back row, Van Tran from Vietnam, said, "In the refugee camp in Thailand, I had to get up at 4:00 a.m. and clean the toilets." A solemn silence fell over the group. Finally, the guy next to her said, "Geez, it makes us all seem like such whiners!" He was right. We are. Let's see if we can find some of Van's desire to make our lives, and the lives of those we lead, better.

In the Desire Quotient introduction, we noted a necessity to admit to the complexity of the nature-versus-nurture debate. We identified some practicalities that are controllable and impressionable, and said that a leader needs to work on those. Understanding what you have as a leader, naturally or otherwise, will only help you in understanding how you can better use what you have or how you can conceivably obtain new quotient abilities. But all of the identification in the world cannot help if you don't truly desire to improve.

Many factors are important in successful leadership, but it is hard to find a more influential one than desire. In fact, we state flatly that a leader's passionate enthusiasm generates an intense magnetism among the followers, which is directed toward accomplishment of that leader's purpose. This is leadership at its most successful level. We have felt that magnetism many times as we encountered successful leaders.

Both of us have adult children. As we look back at the people they dated in their teens, we have often wondered what they saw in those louses! Our kids were dating teens who had little intelligence, stability, looks, or social graces. They certainly weren't fit to date our kids, so what did our kids see in those cretins? Desire. That's it. Sometimes we call it "enthusiasm." Everyone, but especially teenagers, is attracted to the Desire Quotient.

Looking at recent theories of leadership, specifically Contingency Models and Normative Decision Models, we see the need for a fit between the leader and his environment. While these theories certainly make a contribution to the leadership literature, we maintain that regardless of the leader or the situation, desire is a great predictor of leadership success. Leadership that attains organizational goals must be accompanied by a high level of desire. That's what makes a leader a role model. Desire is a "disease" that infects followers. A leader's level of desire to accomplish goals becomes a guiding light for others that captures people, creates an emotional bond, and becomes the glue in the leader-follower relationship. Followers are continually gauging your Desire Quotient. If it is not high enough, you will not be successful. If you don't like your own personal level of desire, change it. Your desire can generate positive emotional energy in others. Remember: The only continually successful leaders in the future will be those capable of adapting their quotients to the demands of their followers in their environment. Those leaders will be able to attain rapid self-innovativeness by adapting their quotients.

Successful leadership must start with the Desire Quotient because this is the quotient that supplies the drive, motivation, and energy for you to get a leadership role. Once you are a leader, your DQ becomes a mediating variable; that is, DQ is the catalyst that allows the leader-follower relationship to succeed beyond individual capabilities, to accomplish what is beyond individual capabilities. Desire strikes at the heart of the purpose of leadership: goal accomplishment. DQ is characterized by intensity; hard-driving, boundless energy; being keen-to-do; hard work; obsession; ambition; and motivation. Your desire to lead others leads to inspiration and appeal power for you. It creates and encourages actions by others as it helps them show and express confidence by their accomplishments. Desire is a big part of conscientiousness, which is a requirement for leadership success. You need to develop a sense of urgency about your desire to accomplish a goal. That's because when desire is strongly expressed, it is catching. DQ creates committed inertia.

A friend of ours had been in marriage counseling for months without much success. Finally, the counselor asked the husband and wife, "Do you *want* to stay married?"

"No," the wife answered emphatically.

The session—and the marriage—was over. How much energy and resources were lost in a futile attempt to make something happen that one of the parties didn't want to happen? Please take this example and think about the people you're leading in the environment you're in. Do you *want* to succeed? While this may seem like an obvious question, psychologists tell us that often the greatest impediment to success is the fear of success.

Humans don't accomplish anything of value without the desire to do so. And the more daunting the task being attempted, the more desire is needed. It is not always fun, but many often grudgingly go into something and build anew their desire because they have become convinced of the awful consequences of inaction. Desire is a part of the most innate of all living organisms—that of survival. When a human has his back against the wall, his innate desire mechanism is triggered. The fight-or-flight mechanism enables that person to do almost anything to achieve continued existence. Indeed, everyone has a tremendous amount of natural desire that is just awaiting the right followers and environment for expression.

Countless stories are told of people who have overcome seemingly insurmountable hurdles by the extreme force of their desire. When leadership desire is properly channeled, it allows the person and her followers to accomplish much more than could have been conceived without the Desire Quotient present. Yes, so many evils have been done because of twisted desires, but at this point in history, surely everyone can see that the goods of desire have outweighed the evils. DQ is one of the quotients where people have an almost infinite potential, and the DQ exhibited is limited only by the intensity one is willing to expend. Anything of value, and a lot of other things of questionable value, has only been accomplished through a leader's Desire Quotient. Everyone has the inherent desire to survive, as we mentioned earlier. Can you raise your desire to accomplish closer to that kind of instinctual level? If you can, you can accomplish almost anything. How much could you do if someone was holding a gun to your head?

Let's look again at the Leadership Quotient Triangle in Figure 2.1. Note in particular the key position of DQ. DQ is the foundation that holds up the leader's traits and actions that produce leadership success. It is no mistake that we show DQ four times. Yes, it's that much more important than the other Leadership Quotients. The Desire Quotient is made up of many components. The next section unpacks some of the more important ones.

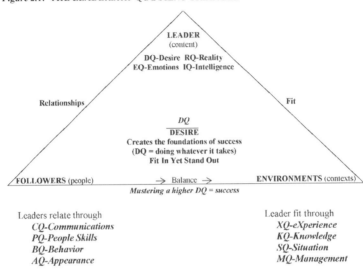

Figure 2.1: THE LEADERSHIP QUOTIENT TRIANGLE

High DQers are intense and hard-driving, have tons of energy, and often seem obsessed with loads of ambition and motivation. They get on our nerves sometimes! But this rubs off on others, encouraging, inspiring, showing, and building confidence and a sense of urgency.

Do you really want to succeed as a leader? We accomplish little of value without desire. DQ properly channeled allows the leader and followers to accomplish the seemingly undoable. Everyone has inherent desire. The purpose of this chapter is to help you channel it to your leadership cause.

The Desire Quotient and its Dimensions

"Leadership does not simply happen. It can be taught, learned, developed....It's about balance" (Giuliani, 2002, pp. xii and xiii).

The personal responsibility of leadership can be observed when looking more closely at DQ where everyone needs to be made to feel they are part of the leadership success story. Without your personal drive, commitment, and ultimate desire, that level of shared responsibility simply will not happen. "You cannot ask those who work for you to do something you're unwilling to do yourself. It is up to you to set a standard of behavior" (Giuliani, 2002, p. 209).

The Desire Quotient can be divided into four distinct dimensions: 1) the personal desire side of you, 2) the desire you can foster in others, 3) the desire it takes to be effective in your given situation, and 4) the desire it takes to be effective in the many areas that are vying for your attention and talent. First, the personal desire side is easy to understand. It's simply what you personally have and can exhibit. Second, the desire you can foster in others is a product of successful leadership. Without it, you can't lead. Third, the desire it takes to be successful in given organizations, industries, or environments can be vastly different. Think about how much Desire it takes to make it in the movies or professional sports, where accomplishments are very public and the competition is fierce, as opposed to what it takes to succeed in some bureaucratic jobs: lots of difference. Lastly, when many problems compete for your attention, desire is important. When unemployment is high it is tougher to gain entrance into an organization, and promotions are difficult to get. More desire is demanded when your industry is fiercely competitive than when it is stable. When things are a mess, more leadership is required, thus more desire.

As an individual desiring to become a better leader, you must think about your personal level of desire and let that be the primary driver that shows for the followers and fits the environment within which you lead. Others should be able to feel your desire!

We see within DQ descriptives such ideas as effort, drive for results, and persistence. But basically we're talking about the willingness to do whatever it takes. Desire alone has compensated for many lacking natural characteristics in every situation and time in all of recorded history. We can logically conclude that if there were a gene that had a tendency toward lack of desire it would have been selected out by evolution long ago. The case could be made that if human fallenness could be cured there would be no need for the Desire Quotient. But the worldview that allows for imperfections in humans demands that the Desire Quotient will always be required of leaders. The billions of bases of human genome, and hundreds of billions of neurons in the trillions of connections in human brains, all work together to guide us to survival and ultimately the ability to have a huge DQ. Admittedly, it seems that much of DQ appears unused. Those who can muster a higher percentage of their DQ are the most successful among us. And they will continue to be. You can be among them, if you can make good use of the $LQ^{©}$ Measurement and Improvement Matrices at the end of this chapter.

Dave was so fascinated and frustrated by the wrong assumptions in Spencer Johnson's book, *Who Moved My Cheese?*, that he wrote a self-published response titled, *Who MADE My Cheese?* He argued that persistence (which we call the Desire Quotient) is the greatest predictor of success, disagreeing with Johnson's claim for "sniffing and scurrying." Dave also argued that production is a better economic indicator than consumption; thus, his book uses the "MADE" verb instead of the "Moved" verb. You can sniff and scurry your entire life, but until you find something you desire, you will not lead successfully.

That we have the ability to select our own futures to a great extent, depending somewhat on our circumstances and genes, has not at this point much empirical verifiability. Yet this choice is logical and intuitive, and ultimately practical, especially as it relates to DQ. Your level of desire will ultimately determine your level of achievement in many areas of life, but none more so than in the area of leadership accomplishment. Recall stories of people doing phenomenal feats when they simply had no choice during times of crisis, or just when others were watching. While it's difficult to put a number on the nature-versus-nurture argument, we're probably without choice (programmed by nature) about 50% or so.

The Desire Quotient can be improved by writing down and repeating a desire. This identification and recording has the effect of solidifying the desire and making it a bigger and better part of the leader. There can be the desire to desire more! In fact, the following quote from a *Business Week* book of the year serves us well at this point.

> I have a very simple thesis: All people have untapped leadership potential, just as all people have untapped athletic potential. There are clear differences due to nature and nurture, that is, genes and development, as to how much untapped potential there may be. But no matter what level of athletic or leadership performance a person currently exhibits, he or she can make quantum improvements. Not everyone can be the CEO of a multibillion-dollar corporation….The important teaching point is: leadership is there in you. (Tichy, 2002, p. 8)

Before we leave the general discussion of DQ, you need to recognize that we diverged from Goleman's more-than-outstanding EQ works (both the 1995 and 2000 versions). We have decided that self-motivation is not EQ as we are defining it here within the $LQ^©$ formula. In *Emotional Intelligence,* Goleman defined motivation as the traits or tendencies of: 1) achievement drive, 2) commitment, and 3) initiative (2000, p. 26). Goleman includes them as components of the Emotional Quotient. We consider them a part of the Desire Quotient. We will discuss EQ in Chapter 5. Our Desire Quotient includes drive, commitment, and initiative.

Goleman is not necessarily wrong, but our logic is clear for the $LQ^©$. We see clear tendencies that are not always emotionally based. Drive, commitment, and initiative are often the products of logic and intellect, with or without the emotional component.

There are no quick fixes to a person's Leadership Quotient weaknesses. There is, however, a lot to be gained by recognition and acceptance of change via the $LQ^©$ Measurement and Improvement Matrices. Once you really understand something about yourself, then you can change it! The only successful leaders in the long term will be rapid self-innovative individuals. Talents and gifts are not enough. The successful leader needs a full understanding of all 12 Leadership Quotients. There is great danger in depending on only one quotient, i.e., charisma, IQ, etc. So is it with DQ. A mite of improvement here will be a mountain of payback later. Guard against an exhibited desire so strong that everyone else will just quit and let the leader do it. Choose and hone your distinctive competency, but don't be stuck in the middle of the Desire Quotient. As *Star Wars'* Yoda said, "Do or don't do; there is no try." Think the unthinkable and do the undoable!! Look for your zone of comfort and then put yourself in uncomfortable positions if you want to grow. It is a most natural thing to desire; perhaps the most natural of all desires is self-preservation. Hardheadedness, pushing yourself, and using all of your capacity to more than your fullest ability are facets of DQ. Leaders make things happen. C. S. Lewis could have been writing about the Leadership Quotient Triangle of Leader, Followers, and Environments when he wrote, "Every single note is right at one time and wrong at another" (1952, p. 11).

Colin Powell's response to his own question, "'Why do you follow somebody around a corner?'…Demonstrate the key attribute and personal traits that are likely to build people's confidence in you" (Harari, 2002, p. 203). This should tell us a lot about desire. Leadership authors Trompenaars and Hampden-Turner (2002, p. 2) support the concept of our *LQ*© Measurement and Improvement Matrices: "We all have weaknesses, but unless the leader recognizes his or hers, the team surrounding the leader will fail to compensate for that weakness."

Look at the *LQ*© Measurement and Improvement Matrix in Figure 2.2. This is your opportunity to make some application of the Desire Quotient. Note we have labeled Quadrants 1, 2, 3, and 4. Refer to this figure as we explain how you can apply the Desire Quotient to your leadership style.

Figure 2.2: DQ MEASUREMENT AND IMPROVEMENT MATRIX

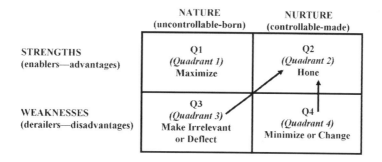

Think about honesty, improvement, and "do you want it enough?" as you review the traits associated with DQ. Perhaps you want it, but without the effort? If so, cut your losses and study something else. Perhaps Hamburger U is for you!

Normal Natural DQ Strengths—Quadrant 1 of the DQ 2X2 Matrix

Survival is the most innate of all things human, and it is deeply rooted in desire. It is needed to make anything work or to accomplish any goal. Making leadership work becomes more a function of desire as the level of leadership increases. A great deal of Desire Quotient is required to be president of the United States or of IBM. To climb mountains in New Mexico you have to have some desire. Both of us have done it.

Natural traits or characteristics in this area are normally associated with personality. Personality has fixed components and components that can be changed though with great difficulty. Recognition that personality disorders are among the least curable of psychological disorders will help you as you study this. Most feel that true personality disorders can seldom be changed. We are not going to judge that but leave it to the reader. What we are doing here is identifying natural strengths that have been reported to us in our testing of the $LQ^{©}$. These strengths are very individualistic. So we suggest that, as you read our examples, you try to make applications to your own Desire Quotient.

Drive for results, persistence, tenacity, conveying a sense of urgency, hunger, and high-need are all traits we have witnessed and most often associated as innate characteristics. Roger Staubach, the famed Dallas Cowboys quarterback, has a high Desire Quotient. The title of his book—*Time Enough to Win* (1980)—exemplifies an attitude and drive that many would call innate. These traits are most often seen as positive, but can be seen as negative when we label them stubbornness or hardheaded-ness. Again, we see that often a strength taken to an extreme becomes a negative—be careful in over-doing most anything. See if you can think of examples where extraordinary persistence worked and where it failed. Then think about the differences in the people or situations involved in the success or failure. Perhaps your personal observations can help you decide on the proper amount of persistence and the factors that make differing levels and types of any high-need endeavor succeed or fail for a leader or a would-be leader. This selection of a comparison other—person or situation—is a good habit to form to assist you in your continuing leadership development.

Other areas associated with desire have been exhibited by some very famous people. As Whitney and Whitney (1996) reported, "Theodore Roosevelt brought a vim, vigor, and vitality to the White House that swept away the cobwebs of the nineteenth century" (p. 205). Or more generically, as Trompenaars and Hampden-Turner (2002) said, "What DOES IT take for a firm to stake its future on a huge, groundbreaking decision? Clearly, it requires a convinced and passionate chief executive officer (CEO) with a daring vision and the stamina to see the project through its tribulations to success" (p. 101). These characteristics again might be weaknesses as well as strengths when they are reported in more negative terms, such as Attention Deficit Disorder, hyperactivity, gambling, and so on.

The first of the natural *born* traits that was reported to us and most often associated with strengths in the DQ area was a **high-need type** person. This is a strength many of us have witnessed, some-times for the good and sometimes for the bad. The key here is, if you have it, don't make it a negative, but use it to the fullest extent. We think of Donald Trump and maybe even Al Gore in this area. Which example fits you and which would you rather follow?

The second most often reported natural positive trait was a **persistent personality**. Again, this could be used in a negative way, though the potential for good is certainly very strong. President George W. Bush has one, as does Michael Moore. But then again so do Osama bin Laden, Saddam Hussein, Oprah Winfrey, and Dr. Phil McGraw. Persistence is a must, but it needs to be tempered for the cause and the followers involved. Most often those who are evil do have this trait; it's just too bad it's used for evil. Can you imagine the good all of the evildoers could have done if their persistence had been to a better cause?

Third, we found **appropriate tenacity** often reported as a natural strength. Though it may not be a born trait, we have witnessed that it forms early in life and changes little as one matures. Tenacity is a great trait to have when properly used and expressed! Rocky Balboa indeed had tenacity. If you follow all the *Rocky* movies, maybe he should have quit before his brains were beaten out, but you can't deny this fictional character has a special tenacity. Again, think of cases where you have seen appropriate tenacity, and compare and contrast that with a case where the tenacity was inappropriate. The differences in the people and situations should point you to personal lessons you can use to learn to be appropriate with your obstinacy.

Last among the natural strengths, we see **selfless passion**. Don't confuse this with selfish passion, for selfish passion is among the most devastating of the desire weaknesses. A passion for others over self is rare, but when we see it, we love the person who exhibits it. There is something so special about a missionary who gives up her life for others. Look at the Lottie Moon story if you want a good exemplar of selfless passion.

As always, when you are completing the DQ Matrix you can round out the list with a personalized trait if you are very careful to select something that fits our DQ mold and not use it to cop out on clearly identifying how you stand on the normally identified traits. At the end of this section you will be able to put a +1 by any traits you feel you have in Q1 of Figure 2.3 (note: this is the next 2X2, not the prior one).

Normal Natural DQ Weaknesses—Quadrant 3 of the DQ 2X2 Matrix

Poor or no exhibited commitment and passion, asking of others instead of giving, exhibiting no real sense of urgency, no belief in usefulness and purpose, poor attention and lack of focus, are some of the most common areas we have seen that have been reported as weaknesses of many less successful leaders. Additionally, the words from Montgomery's 1911 volumes on management still apply today—if you don't have it, your followers won't either: "Enthusiasm…Show faith and real belief in every word you say, and let your manner be as enthusiastic as your words" (v. II, p. 604). This enthusiasm, when it does **not** result in investing yourself in accomplishment, is just bluff. For success, every leader must ultimately "[c]ommit to a proactive role in improving his or her company" (Pritchett,

1995, p. 8). "Motivate your people by rallying them around a shared vision—not your vision, but a collective vision" (Pritchett, 1995, p. 120.)

We have seen very few people exhibit a high Desire Quotient when a goal needs to be accomplished. Often, **no natural enthusiasm** is directed toward overall organizational effectiveness and commitment to the shared purposes. Most often enthusiasm is directed toward *self*-realization, not *group* realization. It truly seems that some simply do not have any natural enthusiasm. Watch young children and you will start to believe that maybe there is a gene for enthusiasm!

Our *LQ*© research indicates that enthusiasm is relatively rare, and this is quite often an inhibitor to effective leadership. We have found many leaders who are enthusiastic about something, but often that something is just not of use to that leader. Bill loves to collect guitars, but doesn't play or use them. Dave loves to plant trees. Both of those are fine as individual satisfiers, but they don't help the authors lead anyone else toward an organizational goal!

Somewhat related to enthusiasm are commitment and passion. These traits are seldom exhibited in the amount necessary to produce an effective Desire Quotient. Everyone has commitment and passion to something. The *LQ*© helps you determine if your passion and commitment are relevant to the followers in the environment in which you work. When that's the case, you have a high Desire Quotient.

We tell students how easy it is to compete and become a leader. We tell them that in a group of ten they are probably only competing with a couple of people at most. We're breaking from our empirical observations when we admit that in a normal group of ten you would find a couple who have the desire of a doorknob. Another two or three want no part of leadership and have no passion for it. Then there are some who simply will not prepare for the task. And finally there will be about three who will not do *whatever it takes* to reach a leadership role; that is, they have **no commitment**. We now see that if we are adding right, you get the job by default simply because everyone else has excluded themselves! Yes, this is a little dramatic and contrived, but it is really not as far from reality as you would expect. For a humorous look at this effect, watch the movie *Being There,* starring Peter Sellers. His character, Chauncey Gardiner (Chauncey is a form of "Chance"), knows only gardening, but others think he is so brilliant because they relate his stories of growth, pruning, patience, and fertilizing to the national economy. He succeeds by…you guessed it…"Being There." Exhibiting commitment and passion sets you up for success. Individuals who have commitment and passion for leadership are actually quite rare. If you have no commitment you have little likelihood of becoming a leader, but if you exhibit some commitment then it is possible to improve this weakness.

Another area many feel is natural and normally a weakness related to desire is **lack of attention and focus**. We are lumping this with commitment because they often go together. People pay attention to those things they commit to and visa versa. We know that some people have attention disorders and this affects their focus, but we have not witnessed this very often. In fact, when we are notified of students with clinically verified attention deficit disorders, we often find those to be among the better students. How did they overcome this? Some with medication, yes; but still, many do not need medication. We wonder why. Their lack of attention and focus are often not as apparent as in many others, yet theirs is certifiably a natural weakness! We think it's because they have analyzed, understood, and recognized their natural weakness. Having done so, they accept it and go on with life. The improvement you will find by completing the *LQ*© Measurement and Improvement Matrices could be invaluable in your leadership success if it results in a plan to improve attention and focus on building your level of commitment.

When completing the *LQ*© instrument, many reported a **misplaced sense of urgency** as a natural weakness. We have a hard time knowing if this is natural or nurtured, but we will go with it as it has been reported most often. A belief of usefulness and purpose as it relates to leadership aspirations and the associated urgency is of course a requirement for leadership, whereas just being urgent about something is not sufficient to help you become a leader. We are urgent about getting tickets to an event we want to attend. In Bill's case it's *The Phantom of the Opera* tickets (he has seen it 25 times). Dave forgot to get tickets to the NASCAR races in Fort Worth, so he took the drastic step of giving his credit card number to a track official with authorization to buy two tickets…without setting a dollar limit! We are urgent about our hobbies and distractions in life, but we were not nearly as urgent about learning what it takes to become a better leader, until we started thinking about writing this book. Urgency to lead may not come naturally to you. That's why we encourage you to discover your current level of urgency, via the *LQ*© Measurement and Improvement Matrices, and then make *urgent* adjustments as necessary.

As with urgency, most of us do not see our potential to be useful as leaders simply because we have not yet identified a purpose in which to get involved. Everyone at some point in their life has a purpose for which they will spend vast amounts of energy, but not that often is it a useful purpose, especially a leadership purpose. We all wish we had more natural urgency and sense of purpose for leadership. Perhaps we all should have more urgency and sense of purpose for leadership *development*.

Lastly, we see **selfish passion**. Everyone is passionate about something, but if it's sex, drugs, or rock and roll, it doesn't move society forward or make the person a very successful leader. To be a sustainably successful leader in modern times, with educated volunteer followers, one's passion must shift from self to a greater cause. Few can do this, and when people identify that a leader is passionate only about his own personal desires, the followers will be turned off.

When you get to Figure 2.3 Q3, think about yourself and rate a -1 for any of the weaknesses you feel you naturally exhibit. First, low or no natural enthusiasm is an area where a lot of people say they are weak. We have seldom seen leadership work without a fair amount of leader enthusiasm. Second, we see commitment—most often accompanied by lack of attention and focus. Many feel they are not very attentive or committed to things for which they don't have affection. We often hear the phrase, "I just don't love that task." And when they are attentive, they simply focus on the wrong things: me versus the group. Third, we see a misplaced sense of urgency. We all exhibit urgency once in awhile, but can it be applied when needed and at a high level? And, lastly, we see as a huge weakness passion that is not properly placed on something other than self. When completing the *LQ*© Measurement and Improvement Matrices, be truthful with yourself. You are the worst person for you to lie to!

Normal Nurtured DQ Strengths—Quadrant 2 of the DQ 2X2 Matrix

We see desire reported as a nurtured trait at the same frequency it is reported as natural. Interestingly, most respondents who reported desire as a natural trait don't have it. Conversely, those who say they have it tell us it is a nurtured trait. This is a common theme we see throughout our studies. When someone has a strength, they think it's developed; and when they don't have it they think it's natural. There are exceptions to this, especially when someone identifies traits their parents or others have convinced them they have, but seldom do we think it's natural when it's a trait we have identified within ourselves.

Within the overall Desire Quotient we see **self-discipline** as the most often touted developed trait. Some seem to have this in some areas but not in others. Often great athletes, just to name one group of many to which this applies, may have self-discipline in their chosen field and not in the personal aspects of their lives. Can you think of a few examples here? What about O.J. Simpson, Lance Armstrong, Mike Tyson, and maybe even Michael Jordan—look into his stint in minor league baseball.

It seems that most of us want to think that we have developed all of the self-discipline that we have, yet we see for those we love that we do not have much trouble attributing their self-discipline to something they inherited. What we've been discussing is called attribution theory.

Attribution theory is complex in many ways but simple in others. According to theories related to attributions, humans need to attribute their actions to something to maintain a balance in their self-worth: not too high or too low. Most people have a good, balanced level of self-worth, not because of what they do and think, but because of what they attribute those feelings and actions to. This balance in some ways seems a little odd at first glance, but it is generally true that people attribute good things to their own actions and nurtured traits. They attribute bad things to the external environment that is beyond their control. Attribution can be summed up by saying that good things happen because of my ability, while bad things happen to me because of my lineage or what others do to me. We tend to take credit for our successes and blame our failures on something else; but regardless, **really believing you are in control is a nurtured strength**. Oh, how important this trait has been for so many who have seen their fortunes go up and down. It seems that some people always feel they can get it back, do it again, because they always think, "It's up to me."

We tend to think the opposite of others. Their success is because of the environment for which they cannot take credit, while their failures are their fault. Their self-discipline would all be under their control from my perspective, but out of their control from their perspective. Jim, a practicing psychologist who suffers from major clinical depression, says that depressed people are actually "more in reality than other more mentally healthy people because if they realized the reality of the temporal nature of themselves they'd all be really depressed!" Can you apply this to your strengths or weaknesses in DQ?

Those who have **passion** feel it is a trait that is the result of nurture. Those who don't have it see it as inheritance. We are reporting passion under nurtured DQ strengths because we have seen it listed here very often. We might need to ask again, "What does it take for an organization to make a groundbreaking decision?" Without a doubt, it takes a leader with a passion that rubs off on the followers. If you want to be successful as a leader, you need to exhibit passion regardless of where it comes from.

"**Commitment to contribution** is commitment to responsible effectiveness. Without it, a man shortchanges himself, deprives his organization, and cheats the people he works with" (Drucker, 1967, p. 58). We find that people with commitment see it as something they chose to do and those without it report it as a natural trait. Where do you stand? You will have a chance to evaluate yourself on the *LQ*© Measurement and Improvement Matrices later in this chapter.

Next, looking at Q2 in Figure 2.3, we come to what positives you have personally made of your own DQ. Most people who are really self-disciplined feel it is a trait they have built, and those with almost no self-discipline feel that's how they were born. You should not give yourself a +1 here unless you have a significant amount of self-discipline. Ask yourself what others would say. Again, you can be a passionate person, and the passion can be of no use in leadership. Can you become passionate about something in order to lead others? Second, we talked earlier about locus of control, and this is what we meant in our introductory chapter. Leaders who really exhibit an understanding of how much control they have exhibit a high internal locus of control. They take the praise and failures as theirs alone without blaming external forces. Third, among the nurtured strengths is the area of passion. Last, we see a committed contributor and realize that a leader has to contribute in the area of desire more than most of the followers if she is to be effective. Add a trait if it definitely fits your DQ. Be truthful when completing this analysis. The results are yours!

Normal Nurtured DQ Weaknesses—Quadrant 4 of the DQ 2X2 Matrix

Few weaknesses are as glaring as the **lack of enthusiasm**. As we have said, most have enthusiasm for something, but here it needs to be an enthusiasm for becoming a better leader or for doing things to become a better leader. If you are not enthusiastic, we suggest you start acting that way. Lack of enthusiasm rubs off, and followers catch this from their leaders. Interestingly, every major innovation occurring within organizations has occurred because of product champions—champions that literally jumped up and down with enthusiasm. So many of our students, young and old, say, "I can get enthusiastic if it's something I'm interested in, like the Final Four NCAA basketball tournament." We say you'll never be successful unless you can learn to become enthusiastic about things that most people aren't enthusiastic about: practice, work, study, etc. All these are necessary to *become* a leader before reaping the *rewards* of being a leader.

This points us directly to the second reported nurtured weakness, which is **favoring rewards or results**. It's as obvious as a person saying, "Yes, I want the pay and recognition, but no, I'm not willing to work for it; but I really am enthusiastic about going to Italy on a 15-day vacation this summer." More often in life we must pay the price before we get the rewards. Many understand this and many don't; that is perhaps why only about 25% of our population has a college education. They can see the rewards that will come, and they pay some price up front for a lifetime of extended earnings and often more rewarding work. This does, however, leave 75% of us that just won't pay the price up front.

The third nurtured DQ weakness we see reported is **the lack of a sense of urgency**. We reported a misplaced sense of urgency as a natural weakness in another section. This nurtured lack of a sense of urgency seems to be of a more universal nature. We all know people who just don't get urgent about anything. They move slowly, think slowly, speak slowly, and so on. And it seems that they all wait on us every single time we are in a hurry at a store or bank—right? Often it may be a medical problem; a drug, intellect, or even weight problem; but for whatever reason, some people just never get urgent about anything. We are not sure which came first—the drugs, the weight, or the no sense of urgency. Regardless, if you lack a sense of urgency in any area of your life, you should realize it will be hard for you to become an effective leader.

The last nurtured weakness is one of the key areas of weakness, and we have labeled it **lack of recognition of strengths and weaknesses of desire**. Perhaps FDR's last written words belong here with nurtured weaknesses: "The only limit to our realization of tomorrow will be our doubts of today. Let us move forward with strong and active faith" (Whitney and Whitney, 1996, p. 277). Perhaps it would be better to just say, "My lack of desire is a weakness; I'm responsible," and go on about your business of becoming a better leader.

Self-discipline directed toward effectiveness is a problem with many people who desire leadership positions. As a leader, you must ask effectiveness of others: "The man who does not first ask, 'What can a man do?' is bound to accept far less than the associate can really contribute" (Drucker, 1967, p. 74). But you must also be effective yourself: "Effectiveness is, after all, not a 'subject,' but a self-discipline" (Drucker, 1967, p. 166). Whether it's you or someone else, "[t]o make the boss effective is therefore usually fairly easy. But it requires focus on his strengths and on what he can do….Effective executives lead from strength in their own work" (Drucker, 1967, p. 95). Admit and clearly know your strengths and weaknesses in the DQ area, and you will be way ahead of most others who are working on being better leaders.

Now, we finish on a negative! In Figure 2.3 Q4, we see those controllable traits that are negative and must be scored a -1 if you have them. Your level of enthusiasm is something you should obtain from asking others, because it is nothing if you think you have it and others can't feel it. Rewards over results is the second trait. Most people seem to want what they can get out of leadership, yet they don't want to put in the effort to become better leaders. Which are you? Third, we see a negative sense of urgency. Yes, you need to be calm, but you've got to have the ability to be urgent when it counts. Last, we see a good assessment of your own strengths and weaknesses in the desire area. Again, we encourage you to verify this with others. Most of us are not that good at admitting strengths and weaknesses as they relate to DQ. Finally, add a trait if you see one we have not clearly identified as constituting your real DQ nurtured weaknesses. Stop for a few minutes and ponder why you have not already addressed these areas and made improvements.

Figure 2.3: YOUR DQ MEASUREMENT AND IMPROVEMENT MATRICES

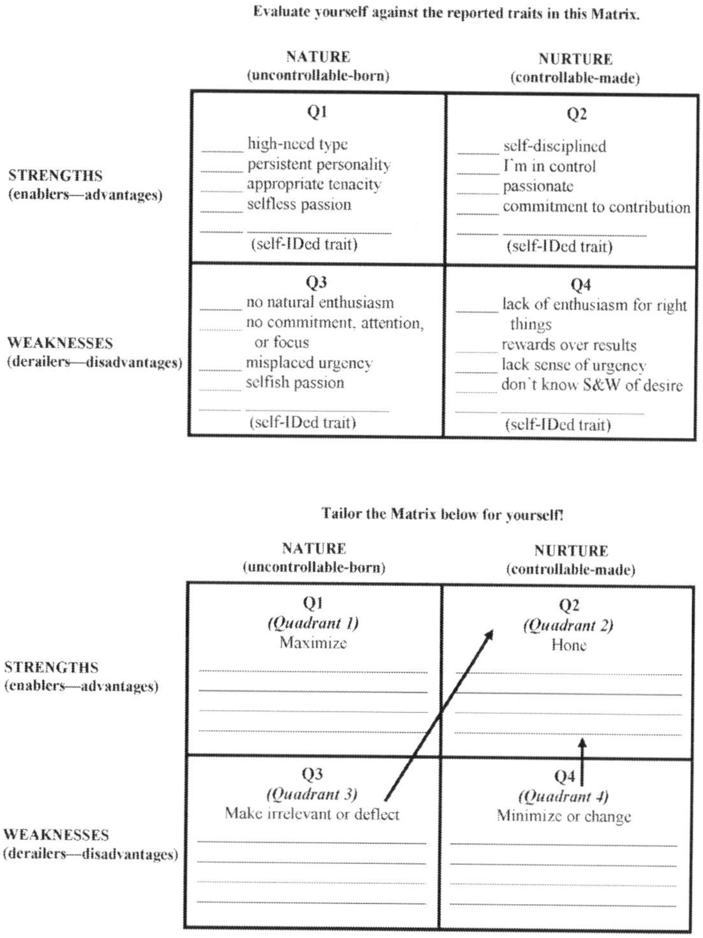

Evaluate yourself against the reported traits in this Matrix.

	NATURE (uncontrollable-born)	NURTURE (controllable-made)
STRENGTHS (enablers—advantages)	**Q1** ___ high-need type ___ persistent personality ___ appropriate tenacity ___ selfless passion ___ (self-IDed trait)	**Q2** ___ self-disciplined ___ I'm in control ___ passionate ___ commitment to contribution ___ (self-IDed trait)
WEAKNESSES (derailers—disadvantages)	**Q3** ___ no natural enthusiasm ___ no commitment, attention, or focus ___ misplaced urgency ___ selfish passion ___ (self-IDed trait)	**Q4** ___ lack of enthusiasm for right things ___ rewards over results ___ lack sense of urgency ___ don't know S&W of desire ___ (self-IDed trait)

Tailor the Matrix below for yourself!

	NATURE (uncontrollable-born)	NURTURE (controllable-made)
STRENGTHS (enablers—advantages)	**Q1** *(Quadrant 1)* Maximize	**Q2** *(Quadrant 2)* Hone
WEAKNESSES (derailers—disadvantages)	**Q3** *(Quadrant 3)* Make irrelevant or deflect	**Q4** *(Quadrant 4)* Minimize or change

Using the DQ Matrix

In summary, evaluate yourself in each of the four quadrants. Give yourself a +1 for each of the strengths and a -1 for each of the weaknesses you have. If you can think of more appropriate strengths or weaknesses you have, list those and again score them +1 to -1; but be careful about just making up some traits. Try to be realistic about a replacement trait; it's preferable to use those we have developed from our research.

The maximum score would be +10 and the minimum would be -10 for DQ. This is the same scoring process you will use for the other 11 quotients. A +10 would say you have all of the good traits we have identified, plus two more you have identified, with no negative items. A perfect overall $LQ^©$ would be +120, where someone has every positive trait and no negative traits. And, sadly, it would be possible for someone to have an $LQ^©$ of -120. We think we've both worked with the latter, though never with the former!

Evaluating Your DQ Personal Profile: Strengths and Weaknesses

Doing Something About Your DQ!

Now you should have identified what you feel is under your control and what you feel is not. Basic skills of identifying, limiting distractions, studying, learning, relearning, and ultimately using new-found skills for DQ development will serve you well, as will practicing improvement in your DQ by expressing outwardly your emotions about doing, getting, or being, versus just saying you have the desire. As cheesy as it sounds, pump yourself up about your own development and it will simply go great. Remember: If you dwell on the negatives, you'll stay where you are.

We have observed two things when people evaluate their strengths and weaknesses in DQ. First, others often disagree with your self-assessment as to what your strengths and weaknesses are. And second, others normally think that a lot more of your negative traits are on the controllable side than you do. In both instances, you must realize that in leadership DQ, it's more important for others to see it than for you to see it. Yes, many people aspiring for leadership growth think they have desire, but others simply don't see it.

So, you've identified your Desire Quotient. What now? First, check your evaluations with some trusted people. You can often do this on the sly, or if you have trusted mentors, use them. Then come up with a realistic plan and strategy to address how you can work to improve those things identified as under your control. This will enable you to offset the negative effects of factors over which you have no control.

In each of the four quadrant areas, you want your perceptions to be as close to reality as possible. For example, manager Charles Hague's natural strength is a fundamental enthusiasm for everything he starts. This can be seen as a negative by many because he has an unusually high DQ. In reality, he has never used his enthusiasm against others, yet some perceive it that way. Yes, a sticky situation exists because only God can correctly interpret reality.

This book is about leading others, not yourself. You can't lead others unless you have a clear understanding of their reality. We will have much more to say about this topic in the Reality Quotient chapter.

In the 2003 Iraqi war, Americans were very convinced that we were liberating a people from untold hardships and cruelty. Yet hundreds of millions around the world felt America had imperialistic designs on the riches of Iraq. How do you change either perception? Press reports are always given by humans with humanistic inabilities to know the Truth.

Don Taylor was a smoker from age 15 until he was over 50. Then one day he quit smoking and started running, and he ran for over two years without missing a day. Early on, he was running three to seven miles a day. Don thinks he has a great amount of self-discipline. His mother feels that the self-discipline is something Don inherited from her father. Don's own father left his family when Don was very young. Is Don's self-discipline because of his work and nurture, or is it just something he inherited? According to Don's mom: all nature. According to Don: all his own nurture. Interestingly, Don's son was a college distance running champion. Maybe there is a gene?

Dave has the same self-discipline. He rode his bike across the U.S., but he's not sure WHY! There is something about a desire to accomplish a goal. When the environment doesn't give him one, he makes up a goal. In 2000, Bill decided to average doing 2,000 sit-ups a day. About October 2000, he decided he might get sick and not finish his goal. So he did 4,000 a day because of his desire to accomplish the goal. He finished the year with 100,000 to spare! In Dave and Bill, is it nature or nurture? Ask them, and ask their moms, and you'll get different answers…as they did!

As We Said in the Introduction, "It's Time to Get Started; If Not Now, When?"

The DQ strengths and weaknesses you've identified here will serve you well as a starting point to improve your overall *LQ*© mainly because desire is the foundation of leadership development. A first step is to work hard to use your natural strengths for their maximum impact. Second, work even harder to improve your nurtured strengths, because you already think those are the result of nurture, so nurture them some more. Third, look at your natural weaknesses and decide some way to make them irrelevant or to mask them since you feel they cannot be changed. In most cases, you'll find a natural or nurtured strength that will enable you to make the identified natural weaknesses mostly non-issues. Lastly, your nurtured weaknesses should not be an issue because you can change them—so just do it!

List your personal **DQ Key Success Factors—factors that can be used** *for your improved effectiveness as a leader* in Figure 2.4. Now it becomes important to have the judgment to recognize needed change, get continuous feedback on progress, and become more quickly adaptable in improving your DQ. **YOU** must get a handle on this thing called leadership and put it into terms about your DQ that can be observed, measured, studied, and learned. This is tough to do, but it's worthwhile. Even a small improvement in your leadership DQ will ultimately be leveraged for organizational and individual accomplishment.

Before we go on to the next chapter, we want to remind you that effective leadership requires a balanced fit among the many environments, behaviors, contexts, processes, contents, and needs. Figure 2.4, The $LQ^{©}$ Triangle, shows the interaction of 1) the leader, 2) the followers, and 3) the environments, which all need to fit. Assess the DQ values you listed in Figure 2.4 and see if your DQ is enough of a foundation to help you proceed to the next level of improving your $LQ^{©}$.

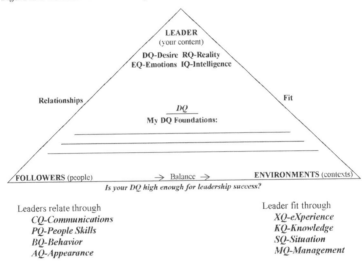

Figure 2.4: YOUR LEADERSHIP QUOTIENT TRIANGLE

Desiring to put energy and enthusiasm, and just old-fashioned work, into becoming a leader is so much more critical than simply desiring to be a leader. This desire requires a life's commitment to identifying, modifying, planning, and improving yourself, using all the principles you can find and logically understand, with all the passion and force you can muster. May the $LQ^{©}$ force be with you!

DQ Conclusions

As we have stressed, leadership is a fusion of work and human relations, a dream around which you can commit and develop a passion. You must realize more of your potential to influence and leverage the power of others. You must use your heart and mind to take care of what's important to you. You must motivate your desire and prove to yourself first with effort and performance that you are learning from realization of strengths and weaknesses. Become committed with personal accountability for leadership improvement!

Our next chapter, The Reality Quotient, demonstrates something that leaders have to exhibit to be able to influence others. As we build toward your complete $LQ^©$ formula, remember: Improvement is very possible and really not that complex. Our formula is relatively simple, for even the most complex equations are being developed as Aczel (1999) said: "When the final equation is constructed, we should be able to use it to solve the wonderful riddle of creation. And perhaps that's why God sent us here in the first place" (p. 220). Do you have as much desire to move your $LQ^©$ equation to more of what it can be, as do those who are set to develop God's Equation? We'd like to see more people who are!

3

RQ, The Reality Quotient

"The reader of these pages in future years should realize how dense and baffling is the veil of the Unknown. Now in the full light of the after-time it is easy to see where we were ignorant or too much alarmed, where we were careless or clumsy" (Churchill, 1949, VII, p. 143).

Remember the ***fit in—stand out*** goal? We will make the **FISO** point many times in *The Leadership Quotient* because it is the key to advancing your leadership potential. The subject of this chapter—the Reality Quotient—is perhaps the most important chapter for understanding how you **stand out** as a leader.

The road to personal leadership improvement will indeed be bumpy and crooked without a healthy self-awareness of your Reality Quotient. Close behind the need for self-awareness is the need to understand the reality of continuous commitment to development and practice, i.e., can your leadership be applied in a real-life situation? The Desire Quotient we discussed in Chapter 2 and the Reality Quotient are about how you can use what you have (and don't have) to lead. But most importantly, they require you to look inside at who you really are and what you really want. It's good to be assured and confident in your quest for leadership improvement, but don't forget, "There is a very fine line between self-confidence and arrogance" (Motley, 1995, pages unnumbered).

Four questions are key to your understanding of your Reality Quotient. Realistically think about the terms *might, can, want,* and *ought* as they relate to the reality of you as a leader. First, think what *might* you practically do. Ask, "Is there a market for me as a leader as I currently am?" Second, address the *can* dimension. Ask, "Can I do it with my current knowledge, skills, and abilities?" Third, address what you really *want*. Ask yourself, "Do I have the desire to be a better leader; do I really want it?" Lastly, examine closely whether you should be a leader or not. Simply ask, "Is leadership something I *ought* to do; is it the right thing for me to do?" Being sensible with the *might, can, want,* and *ought* dimensions of you as a leader is key to your initial, and even continued, development. *Might, can, want,* and *ought* are the foundations for your RQ.

The strategic road that takes you to leadership improvement is much simpler than most people want to believe. It starts with that understanding of *might, can, want,* and *ought.* The *might* part gives you the template for what followers and others need in a leader. When you reach a realistic understanding of what you *might* do in life, sometimes reality dashes dreams. For example, it is a foolish high school senior who relies on her mother's encouragement, "You can be anything you want to be." That's not true. A 4' 11" girl cannot be a professional basketball player. There is not a market for what she might be able to do on a basketball court. Likewise, there is not a market for a lot of things we all love to do. Make sure it is something others want before you seek to do it. That's the *might* part. Many things are doable with super efforts and unusual approaches, but often those things don't produce value for society, so you can't do it for a living. A good RQ makes your limitations clear to you.

The next understanding is close to *might,* but a little different. What you *can* do is most often limited by natural or inherited traits. Physically and mentally you must meet the most basic requirements that are demanded by the specific vocation or avocation. Many people *can* learn to do something well enough to enjoy it or be relatively good at it, but still not perform well enough to make a living at it. Through effort, many people could earn a spot on a junior high school tennis team. Fewer could qualify at the high school level, and even fewer at the collegiate level. The percentage that could succeed at the pro level is miniscule. So it is with leadership, we all *can* do it at some level, but not that many of us will ever succeed at the level of General Electric's legendary Jack Welch or President George W. Bush. The Reality Quotient of being honest about yourself involves true self-esteem. Having false expectations—a poor RQ—is a ticket to disappointment and failure.

We come next to the *want* part. This will remind you of the Desire Quotient to some extent. Also, you will be reminded of the old saying, "Be careful what you ask or pray for—you might get it!" In the 1960s, a television show, *The Twilight Zone,* was on the air. The person appearing on the show would ask for eternal youth, riches beyond compare, a beautiful mate, and so on. The "catch" that accompanied their lifelong wish was a nightmare. Be sure of what you want as a leader and clarify it via a rigorous Reality Quotient. When you do, it's quite likely you will get what you want. Think back to something you have really sought: a special classic car, the next academic degree, a promotion, that girl or guy, that trip of a lifetime. Did you really feel gratified when you got it? Even if the answer is yes, the feeling probably didn't last very long. Perhaps this is because, in reality, you were the same person before you earned this coveted thing as you were after you earned it!

So far in this chapter, we have written about reality *within* you and what you desire to do with your life. In the case of a leader, it must extend beyond your personal understanding of your reality and go to the reality of the situation. Winston Churchill, Ronald Reagan, and Rudy Giuliani all demonstrated some level of reality thinking that was ahead of what others were thinking. Winston Churchill was years ahead of others in his predictions about the dangers of Nazi Germany and Hitler. He was also ahead of the curve when he coined the phrase, "The Iron Curtain." Similarly, Ronald Reagan understood that Communism was an evil empire, and indeed, America had the ability to out-produce it. Rudy Giuliani's leadership in the aftermath of 9/11 was due to his ability to see the terrorist attack as reality and move ahead in repairing the lives of his city and its inhabitants. In the realm of commerce, Jack Welch had the ability to understand what was needed in the future, as did Louis Gerstner of IBM. They had the ability to understand reality and move their followers in that direction. Steven Jobs of Apple saw the reality of widespread computer use before anyone else did. He tapped into that Reality Quotient to give Apple the first-mover advantage in computer hardware. Leaders are good at interpreting reality and making it something followers can buy into. A certain level of RQ is a requirement. Great leaders have exhibited the Stockdale Paradox: They confronted the brutal facts, but believed they would prevail in the end (Collins, 2001).

Look at the following statement made in 1911 and ask if things have really changed: "It can hardly be believed that there are so many manufacturers and businessmen who are blind to the new era of business" (Montgomery, VI, 1911, p. 175). This statement from almost a hundred years ago reminds us that there has always been a shortage of Reality Quotient among leaders. In the following sections, you will learn how to improve your RQ.

On to RQ

"It certainly was odd that it should all work out this way; and once again I had the feeling, for mentioning which I may be pardoned, of being used, however unworthy, in some appointed plan."—Winston Churchill

Reality is more complicated than it at first looks. We feel that people are simply incapable of understanding total reality. Two preconceptions contribute to this: First, the Reality Quotient is indeed complicated; and second, we are biased. The following is just a sampling of the complexities of the cultural subsystems within which we exist:

1. An ecological system, which includes all aspects of the physical environments.

2. A subsistence methods system, which shows how people make a living.

3. The cultural or man-made and psychological systems aspects of interactive life.

4. The social systems that define interactions, roles, and laws.

5. The psychology systems of each person's individuality.

6. The inter-individual side, which is the topic of sociology.

7. The projective aspects, which include myths, fantasies, and religion.

Other more common environmental descriptions would be the ecosystems; demographic classifications; and economic, cultural, political, legal, competitive, family, and organizational cultures. These views overlap somewhat with the seven cultural subsystems above, but all allow for many combinations and permutations of complexity in forming a realistic view of our world. These are just a sampling of the different effects going on in any particular milieu. With so many different viewpoints to choose from, it's amazing that there is any kind of agreed-upon version of reality. But if you want to lead, you must reach an understanding of the Reality Quotient that exists in the particular environment in which you intend to lead.

With varying interpretations of reality, the societal implications and interactions of different Reality Quotients can produce imbalance and inappropriate actions that limit a leader's ability to perform the leadership function. As with DQ, these fits between the leader and the environment must be viewed in light of the leader's ability to understand the RQ of the followers so they can be led. Increasing your leadership Reality Quotient requires two things: 1) more information, and 2) the wisdom to interpret and use the information.

Picture a favorite personal leader as well as current leaders you admire. In recent terms, you might think about President Ronald Reagan's ability to create a worldwide reality that the Soviet Union really would "tear down this wall!" when he challenged Mikhail Gorbachev to do so. Bill Clinton has the Reality Quotient to make followers think he "feels their pain."

There are also examples of leaders who used their Reality Quotient for ill. Dethroned HealthSouth CEO Richard Scrushy was absolutely admired by his young staff of executives because he hired untrained youngsters with the purpose of adjusting their Reality Quotient to his. The reality in Iraq under the brutal foot of Saddam Hussein was that dissidents would be dealt cruel and immediate judgment. Winston Churchill had a good sense of the reality of the Nazi threat, but his predecessor, Neville Chamberlain, did not. We've encouraged you to think about these examples, and your own more personal examples, so you can derive from them the distinctive parts of their Reality Quotients that are applicable to your leadership situation.

Why Is RQ Next?

We are continually amazed that third-party observers have a greater Reality Quotient than those who are intimately involved in the situation. Maybe that's because "when you're up to your belt in alligators, it's hard to remember your objective was to drain the swamp." Leaders often think that wishing a problem would go away makes it go away. While we don't want to undermine the effect of a positive attitude, we also know that the most effective leaders are those who have a high Reality Quotient and thus are able to lead with a realistic goal in mind.

The Leadership Triangle is shown in Figure 3.1 to exhibit the key position of the Reality Quotient. RQ is another foundational quotient that holds up the leader's traits and actions leading to greater leadership success. The RQ abbreviation is shown three times because it is one of the most important traits among the Leadership Quotient. The following section explains the components that make up RQ.

Figure 3.1: THE LEADERSHIP LEVERAGE TRIANGLE

LEADER
(content)
DQ-Desire RQ-Reality
EQ-Emotions IQ-Intelligence

Relationships   Fit

RQ
Reality Quotient
Without it you are wrong for the situation
RQ = Reality over perceptions

FOLLOWERS (people)   → Balance →   ENVIRONMENTS (contexts)
Being close to reality means RQ = success?

Leaders relate through   Leader fit through
  CQ-Communications   *XQ-eXperience*
  PQ-People Skills   *KQ-Knowledge*
  BQ-Behavior   *SQ-Situation*
  AQ-Appearance   *MQ-Management*

RQ is a predictor of success in a given situation with distinctive followers and purposes.
This is the key point of *LQ*©. A fit to reality must occur for success!

The Reality Quotient and its Dimensions

We have read, and believe that it is true, that a schoolboy today knows more than Sir Isaac Newton knew.

Some of the most valuable lessons in life are learned not by seeking answers, but rather by working through difficult situations. We learn the best lessons by the successes and failures that we encounter along life's path. The highest Leadership Quotients are owned by the leaders who are able to learn from every experience. Leaders also help others learn. Learning must not be limited to a subject, person, place, or time. When you recall your greatest lessons in life, you will probably find that the moments when you learned are the ones that stand out. This seems to be how many develop a good

RQ. Those with high RQs have learned lessons, and those with lower RQs didn't quite understand what just happened to them.

A student in an MBA/Law program recently said, "Professor, I don't understand what you mean." The professor ignored his comment. The professor had just said that sometimes you need to accept criticism without responding. About 45 minutes later in the class, the professor said, "Rob, tell me what you like least about me as a professor." Rob replied, "I'm not going to do that." The professor restated the command: "Do it because I told you to." Rob said, "You let us get off the topic too much and don't slam people back into the topic." The professor said, "I see; thank you for your insights." And the professor went on to another subject. Rob whispered to the student next to him, "What the hell was that all about!" He didn't get it. Rob is a 52-year-old who quit his medical practice to get an MBA/Law degree, and one of the things he talks about in every class is the lack of EQ on the part of Law students. Does Rob have an appropriately high EQ? And how about his RQ!

Some of your behaviors are more obvious to others than to you. A valuable lesson is to understand something about yourself or your situation that others already know. There are four dimensions to RQ: 1) your personal self-assessment and orientation, 2) your ability to accurately understand how others perceive you, 3) your ability to read your current situation, and 4) your ability to perceive the direction of larger environments.

Successful people and leaders want to help others in their learning journey. And they start with themselves and understand that, to be successful, any leader must be able to do the following:

- learn from all people and all situations;

- handle the abstract, obscure, and cryptic;

- understand and handle conflicts of human interaction;

- learn to read others: understand what motivates you and others—what they value, and what you value; understand and apply the intricacies and nuances of leadership and organizations;

- understand what's important and what's urgent;

- learn what to pay attention to and focus on;

- adapt or intellectually "wing it" when you have no choice; and

- see the esoteric nature of leading into the unknown, not just managing the known.

Your goal is to understand these complexities and make them meaningful and applicable to you as a leader and to your followers in the leadership environment you happen to be in: that's a big part of your RQ.

Most often it is very clear to others what lessons someone needs to learn and it's unmistakably not in any book. If anyone is incapable of reading and applying what's in most of the modern self-help books or college texts, normally there is little hope they'll advance anyway. So what's needed?

Let's think about personal health as a simple analogy. We want a doctor to help us with a prescription that will provide a no-effort solution. If the doctor were truthful, she would tell us we need a life-style change: "Quit smoking, eat right, get the proper amount of sleep, improve the quality of your life by learning how to deal with stress, balance work and play, cut out excessive alcohol, get the right amount of exercise, watch your weight," and many other general things. Note: A doctor's orders would include things like "proper amount," "right," "quality," "lifestyle," "excessive," and "balance." The same is true of gaining a leadership role in an organization. Some of the prescriptions are hard to define and require judgment and wisdom for effective application. Many times we concentrate on **knowing** things, when what's really important is the ability to **apply** them.

Continue to work on your checklist of new knowledge, skills, abilities, experiences, and credentials, but realize they are not the key to a high Reality Quotient. The key is how you integrate and use those tools to leverage yourself as a leader with your followers in your specific environment. A much less important factor is that you have checked those things off your to-do list. The greatest lessons in life don't normally come from a book or another person. They come from a self-awareness of your Leadership Quotients, and they are there for your taking from this book. Will you take them? However, the route to self-awareness as an effective leader is the acceptance and openness to comprehend reality in your environment.

Low Reality Quotient leaders:

- are just inexperienced.

- know much yet can apply little.

- can't handle the truth.

- think wishing makes it so.

- don't care to learn.

- don't know what they don't know.

- want to blame versus take the blame.

- ask for rather than seek on their own.

- have never been confronted in a meaningful way.

- confuse desire with being ready.

- think they know versus understand they've got much to learn.

- think remembering is learning.

- think facts are all there is to a situation.

- think telling is communication.

- think talking is thinking or listening.

- believe their own hype.

- think policies negate people.

- prefer measurable over meaningful.

- prefer appearance over substance.

- take a TQM function over quality.

- prefer efficiency over effectiveness.

- are politically correct rather than ethically correct.

- prefer legal over right.

- prefer to blame versus change.

- give the responsibility instead of taking the responsibility.

- think obsession is good or bad (it's both).

- think optimism beats pessimism (reality beats either).

- think self-esteem comes from others.

- believe success is a matter of luck.

- think they know leadership—but some just don't get it and never will.

Sometimes you can tell people repeatedly something about the complexities of leadership and they never get it. It's like someone who just can't figure out when and how to apply linear regression. They can run the numbers and read the results, but they don't know what's being done: its use, purpose, when it is the method of choice, what the assumptions are, etc. Another example is the person who has a good understanding about how to play golf, yet he cannot play golf competitively. Likewise, when you are being prepared for expanded leadership roles, you often don't understand what it's all about until you begin to apply the leadership principles. Many leaders say they understand and can quote all the right principles, but they are weak at leadership practice because they have a low Reality Quotient.

It has been said that if you really want to understand something about yourself, change it. Talents and gifts are not enough. The successful leader needs experience and exposure to situations that force them to make choices in an environment full of opportunities and dangers. You'll never be successful unless you learn to become enthusiastic about things most people aren't that interested in. Success will likely pass you by if you are enthusiastic about becoming a success rather than being enthusiastic about the practice of leading people to change their lives for the better. That enthusiasm comes through the self-discovery you are experiencing by developing your Leadership Quotient.

The Reality Quotient is intended to give you a realistic preview of yourself as a leader of the future, not of the past. Recently, a review of over 200 studies relating to self-esteem had some startling results. Healthy self-esteem was shown to be negative when it was praise for the undeserving. Self-esteem must be built on achievement in order for "wonderful outcomes" to occur. "Psychologists should reduce their own self-esteem a bit and humbly resolve that next time they will wait for a more thorough and solid empirical basis before making policy recommendations to the American public" (Begley, 2003, p. B1).

We both feel that the job of a professor is not necessarily to teach someone what they want to learn. As we see it, our job as professors is to help you learn things you need to know. A psychiatrist friend recently asked me, "Do you know when you have a fool for a doctor?" I said no. He said, "When you are your own doctor." If your prescripts are from only your perspective, you will have a weak Reality Quotient that will produce leadership failure.

The only thing we want you to believe about Bill and Dave is that we want to help you become a better leader. We assume that will help you become who you want to be in your vocation, avocation, and—most importantly—your life. Some chapters in this book will help you more than others. Some of the quotients we won't explain correctly for you, and some you will misunderstand. We all make mistakes. But the joint goal of your authors and this book is to help in your development, which must be based on a solid RQ.

Real Lessons and RQ

As we said earlier, the most lasting lessons of the Leadership Quotient are not sought after but are learned the hard way, through experiencing successes and failures. What about you? Bill asked a former student, "What do you want out of this course, Joey?" Joey replied, "I want you to teach me to be a manager." Bill said, "Wow—you're going to be disappointed." A few years later, Joey came by and said, "I now understand what you meant."

The ability to see yourself and the situation the way others see it is what we call the Reality Quotient. Ten years ago, an accountant friend told Dave he really wanted to earn the Certified Public Accountant designation. Instead of taking the traditional preparation course, he went to a hypnotist to get ready for the exam. Needless to say, it didn't work. Ten years later, he still is not a CPA. Ten years later, he still has a very bad Reality Quotient. The reality is that passing the CPA exam requires a lot of study, and being hypnotized makes a very small (if any) contribution to passing the test.

There are many well-known examples of people who should have understood something about the future of their industry but did not because they had a very low Reality Quotient. Lord Kelvin was the president of the British Royal Society in 1895 when he predicted, "Heavier-than-air flying machines are impossible." *BusinessWeek,* August 2, 1968, reported: "With over fifty foreign cars already on sale here, the Japanese auto industry isn't likely to carve out a big slice of the U.S. Market for itself." Then there was Thomas J. Watson, Chairman of IBM, a founder of the computer revolution, who said in 1943, "I think there is a world market for about five computers." Another famous founder of the computer age, Ken Olson, president of DEC, said in 1977, "There is no reason for any individual to have a computer in their home." Finally one of our favorites, though it did not end well, was quoted of General J. B. Sedgwick, whose last words, at the Battle of Spotsylvania in 1864, were, "They couldn't hit an elephant at this dist—" These rather famous people had low RQs. How's yours?

Figure 3.2 will be your guide to the improvement of your Reality Quotient. Quadrants 1, 2, 3, and 4 have been labeled for your ease of analysis. Refer to this figure as we explain what normally is in each of these quadrants.

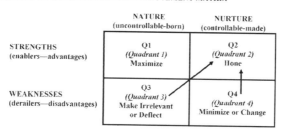

Figure 3.2: RQ MEASUREMENT AND IMPROVEMENT MATRIX

Before you see what others have said about the natural and nurtured components of RQ, think about what you feel are your characteristics related to reality.

Normal Natural RQ Strengths—Quadrant 1 of the RQ 2X2 Matrix

The most commonly cited trait here is, "I'm a born realist." Bud Anderson said of Chuck Yeager: "If he is a little cocky about his abilities, that's okay with me. It's not bragging if you can back it up. And this guy has backed it up with all the spades in the deck" (Yeager and Leerhsen, 1988, p. 203). That's a form of RQ. Or, as Jack Welch said, "The most important quality of leadership is the capacity to see the world as it actually is, not as you would like it to be" (Tracy, 2002). That's a very good definition of RQ.

People who claim to have a natural RQ strength say they are realistic about themselves, others, and their situations. There are three things to be realistic about: First is an **RQ about self**, second is an **RQ about others**, and finally there is an **RQ about the situation**.

The major problem we see with self-realism is that we just don't think too straight when we are contemplating ourselves. When realism relates to others, our pragmatism is clouded by what we wish rather than what is! Lastly, when we are most mired in the muck of the moment it is most difficult to move back, stop, look, and listen to really comprehend the situation as it is developing, not as we wish it were or as it has been in the past. Yes, realism has some difficulties; and some people seem to have a natural way of seeing reality, not their own personal wants. Can't you recall people exemplifying these traits? How's your natural RQ in these areas?

We are not going to attempt to separate realists into differing areas within the three areas we have identified. Perhaps there are those who assess people well in the personal arena and not the organizational arena, or vice versa, but we simply don't feel it is productive to go there. In the area of situational realism, we are talking about the ability to read a current situation and developing situations.

Another natural strength often reported about leaders is **self-esteem**. In an earlier section, we cited a recent finding that said self-esteem is positive only if it is grounded in reality. There are those who will argue that praise is good whether realistic or not. In leadership, we disagree. When the results are in, unfounded self-esteem does not contribute to an effective Leadership Quotient because it lowers the Reality Quotient.

These *reported* natural strengths do have a definite nurture component. However, it seems that by the time you can practice these traits, they are indeed set in your personality to a great extent and really need to be viewed as natural traits. Think of it this way: Are these traits that appeared early in life and could be measured and shown to be relatively stable over periods of time with standardized psychological tests? We would logically conclude that they would be, so we will classify them as natural.

Normal Natural RQ Weaknesses—Quadrant 3 of the RQ 2X2 Matrix

Again, we see identified natural weaknesses that are surely part nurture, but nevertheless many identify them as natural, so we will go with those classifications. The first is an **inflated ego**. This has to be a part of the sense-making that individuals must do in order to live in an imperfect world. Often it does not get in the leader's way, but in some cases it causes a seriously low Leadership Quotient. Clint Eastwood's line in *Magnum Force* provides a good example, "A man has got to know his limitations." When someone didn't, Eastwood's character made the person history. The same thing can happen to a leader who has an inflated ego. They often commit organizational suicide. And when they don't, many follow leaders like former HealthSouth CEO Richard Scrushy, who created such a high profile for himself that he seemed to be trapped into making his own press clippings come true at any cost.

The opposite of inflated ego is a **poor self-image**. A poor self-image often has more of a proximate cause in someone's demise as a leader, while an inflated ego is normally the ultimate cause of demise. We are classifying this as a natural weakness because the evidence from mental health studies indicates that there may be a gene for self-image. "[R]arely does a person speak of only one family member with depression or manic-depression. Most often there are two or more relatives affected, as these illnesses tend to concentrate in families. Familial tendencies suggest a genetic transmission…" (Papolos and Papolos, 1997, p. 56).

The inability to interpret reality from obvious information is another indication of a low Reality Quotient in leaders. The Internet has supplied leaders with more information than they need. So finding information is no longer the challenge. High Reality Quotient leaders have the wisdom to sift for the information they can use to point their followers in the direction they need to go.

Also, high RQs have the strength of character to accept with reality the bad news they receive. How many times have you heard someone say, "I don't want to hear that"? Low RQs choose not to hear many things that point to a new reality that is harmful to them. The last to know that a new innovation is replacing his is the person who created the old way of doing things. Why were airlines slow to follow the low-cost model that was tested and proven successful by Southwest Airlines? Why was IBM so late in realizing the value of computers and then PCs? Why didn't McDonald's open Subway-type shops when they were in the best position to do so? Why did American automobile manufacturers have to wait for Japanese competition before they improved? The examples of low RQ among leaders are legendary. It is alarming how few leaders have the ability to adapt to the future even when identifiable facts predicted it.

Game theory is a discipline that studies how others react in a competitive situation. When a baseball manager sends a left-handed hitter to the plate, the opposing manager reacts by calling for a left-handed pitcher. In poker, competitors often use a bluff to see how their competitors will respond. It works well in baseball and poker—not at all in leadership. A leader who has an unrealistically high self-perception often tries to **bluff** his followers. It's a bad tactic because it indicates a low Reality Quotient. Bluffing is a part of the animal kingdom when appearance and sound are used to scare away rivals. It works for animals, not for leaders. Dave has rabbits as pets. When he does something that is threatening to a rabbit, the rabbit will respond by stomping his hind foot as hard as he can. We suppose that works to ward off some threat in nature, but against the 220-pound Dave, it's not a good bluff. We think leaders who try to bluff their followers are about as ineffective as Dave's rabbits.

Bill was in a taco-eating contest with a 300-pounder. When Bill got up to get his 32nd taco he said loudly, "I think I'm only going to get five this time." Bill *knew* he could eat only one or two more, but it worked. The opponent quit and Bill won the contest. Bluffing is a workable strategy in short-term situations, like a taco-eating contest, but leadership is a long-term venture where bluffing does not work. Bluffing is a definite weakness when it is used to attempt to make others think highly of you because you appear to think highly of yourself. Think about this: "Rationalizations are more important than sex....Have you ever gone a week without a rationalization?" (Pinker, 2002, p. 264).

Normal Nurtured RQ Strengths—Quadrant 2 of the RQ 2X2 Matrix

Inclusiveness is an RQ strength that many feel they have developed. "Include everyone in everything" has become a mantra in the writings of Tom Peters. This is good advice for leaders, because by exhibiting inclusiveness, you share the responsibility for decisions. The high-RQ leader will attempt to let his direct reports convince him to hire someone. It's good to ask for help and advice, but having sought it, plan to use it. It is unwise to ask for advice when you are sure of what you are going to do. In the case where you have already decided, present it so others can be aware, not so they can help decide. This is another form of inclusiveness. Faking inclusiveness on decisions can really backfire and destroy your credibility and change inclusiveness into a decided weakness.

Objectivity is a strength related to RQ that many think they have but few really have. Each of us *thinks* we are objective, but we are simply being objective based on our determination, not on what others think. We can attempt to be objective, but we can't be totally objective because we are not objects, we are individual humans. We think differently because we are made (nature) and socialized (nurture) differently. Our message to leaders is, "Don't try to be totally objective." The leader who attempts to be totally objective will try to lead people in all different directions. That's not leadership. Leadership is taking a group of people in a singular direction. That means you have to shake off objectivity and subjectively state the direction you're going. Understanding your own lack of total objectivity is being as objective as you can be.

"The Iron Lady," Margaret Thatcher, said, "It is probably true that a woman—even a woman who has lived a professional life in a man's world—is more emotionally vulnerable to personal abuse than most men" (Thatcher, 1995, p. 182). Do you think Lady Thatcher worries about admitting her reality? Does she exhibit the RQ trait of objectivity?

Objectivity is another way to say "the correct level of optimism and pessimism." This is indeed a great strength for a leader. Perhaps an exemplar in this area would have to be Franklin Delano Roosevelt, the 32nd president of the United States. His personal circumstances were racked with physical and marital difficulties. He faced the Great Depression and World War II with a campaign song, "Happy Days Are Here Again." Ask yourself: Was Roosevelt, as Seinfeld's Kramer said of the fictional Billy Mumphrey, "a wild-eyed optimist," or was he being a realist?

The vision thing has been overplayed in today's organizational arena in many ways. But being a visionary who can clearly state where her organization is going is a strength for a leader. A leader who can see how the future will look, given likely scenarios, is going to come out ahead. Picture a future state in your mind for yourself and visualize what it will be like. If it's based in realistic projections, you have a high Reality Quotient.

Bill can visualize colors, construction, and ways furniture will look in a redecorated and rearranged room. Dave doesn't have a clue and doesn't care. Conversely, Dave gives dozens of speeches each year on a multitude of topics and never uses a note. What have nature and nurture given you the ability to organize? Can you organize *things*, like Bill, or *words* that motivate people, like Dave? They are similar skills to visualizing your future or your organization's future in an emerging environment. Developing those skills requires practice and patience, but mostly concentrated effort. Leaders must ultimately put their visualizations in a form that their followers can see as a guiding light to reaching the common purposes of the leader. "Visionary" does describe a desirable nurtured leader trait you can develop. **Envisioning** is an RQ trait that can serve you well, and it can be honed and developed. Envisioning is a step beyond visioning. It puts the legs on a vision.

Consensus outside your normal comfort zone is a developed RQ trait that leaders use to increase their effectiveness. It's easy to be able to work with a consensus you have engineered among your followers, but it's much more important to be able to handle consensus when the concept is not invented by you. Your goal as a leader is to put all resources at your disposal toward accomplishing the organization's goals. The only way you can do that is to learn to handle things outside your normal comfort zone. "No one can predict the ultimate effect of the recent dot-com shakeout, or the many other global economic and political forces that set in motion so much change in the early years of the new millennium" (Jick and Peiperl, 2003, p. 283). But high RQ leaders are prepared to handle the various possible outcomes. In most situations, it's not so important *what* you commit to, only that you commit to a course of *action* and proceed. You can adjust when you are doing something, but when you are doing nothing there is nothing to adjust. Riding a Jet Ski is a good example. When the rider turns the handlebars, the jet that propels the watercraft actually turns, "jetting" the boat in another direction. If there is no power to the jet, there is no ability to turn. Many accidents are caused by riders who get in dangerous situations and freeze up. They turn off the power and try to steer. The Jet Ski keeps going straight until the rider gives it some power to "jet" it in another direction. The same is true of leadership. An organization moving is easier to turn than one that has no momentum.

Normal Nurtured RQ Weaknesses—Quadrant 4 of the RQ 2X2 Matrix

One of the more common Reality Quotient weaknesses we see is the constriction that is caused by the models and frames we use to view our world. Some call these our filters, or the "rose-colored glasses" through which we see. Our frames, models, modes, filters, or ways we view the world create the following common traps into which we fall: We anchor things to past events and our preferences. You probably have a favorite solution just looking for a problem. We all have a very strong preference for the status quo. No one gives the status quo the level of scrutiny they give other alternatives. We all believe we make rational and objective decisions, but in reality we have an extreme bias toward perpetuating the status quo. And what's more, the greater the number of choices, the stronger the pull of the status quo.

The first relatively natural weakness is witnessed when we see people who simply **can't reframe their views**. This is largely caused by normal biases that we all have, plus some that are specific to each individual: Do you know your normal biases that prevent you from reframing new issues? Below are the biases we all have. You need to become familiar with these and realize when they are indeed influencing your decision-making too greatly:

- We will follow **sunk cost** to the bitter end. Will you stop putting money in a vending machine when it's already taken much of your change? Warren Buffet simply said, "When you find yourself in a deep hole, stop digging!"

- **Deciding without knowing the "why"** is as normal a thing in businesses as it is at home. "Because I said so!" "Why?" may be as important as "What?"

- We all have a **preference for confirming evidence**. Do you read the same number of articles that disagree with your opinion as those that agree with you, i.e., those that are right? We can listen to the same thing and hear different things, but we often choose to listen to only what we want to hear. This applies to what we read or view, questions we ask, where we go, and many other actions. We look for evidence that confirms our biases.

- **Framing** is the way something is presented or asked, and we frame things for our advantage. The way a problem, opportunity, threat, situation, etc., is presented defines how we look at the problem.

- **Your models**, frames, paradigms, norms, and reference points **define you** and are very predictive of how you will respond. It's far better to approach a decision knowing what your models are than to go in thinking you don't have any!

- We are **poor at forecasting and estimating**. Extremes, recent events, and preferences all get too much attention.

- We all have a tendency to be either **over- or under-confident**. Confidence is formed by our perceptions of experiences.

- Most of us have a **preference for an approach that's on the safe side**. Thus, entrepreneurs number relatively few. An economic model called the Bellman dynamic program says that National Football League teams should "go for it" on fourth down instead of punting in almost every field situation. Why don't they? Because they have a preference for an approach that's on the safe side. They play to avoid losing, not to win.

The lesson is simple: We don't describe the world we see; we see the world we describe. Our lens on the world is not perfect. Dave authored an article in *Leadership Perspectives* explaining that leaders see the world through four different lenses:

1. Strategists look through a telescope at the future.

2. Organizational theorists choose a lens that is the correct shape.

3. Organizational behaviorists choose a contact lens.

4. Human resource leaders look through a microscope at the person-job fit.

Leaders also tell us that **unfounded pessimism** is a nurtured weakness. The Chicken Little Effect is often difficult to see in leaders. It seems counter-intuitive that a leader would be pessimistic, but we have known many who were. Bill's dad said for about 10 years that he would be dead in a couple of weeks. Since he is now deceased, you can say he was right at least once. The strange thing is that he didn't make that prediction for the last couple of months of his life!

Oracle founder Larry Ellison has written a sober account predicting a lasting downturn in technology. The article is based on economic principles, but his view of the data makes one wonder whether it is reality or whether Mr. Ellison is a hardcore pessimist (Mangalindan, 2003). We have seen many students accept defeat early in a semester when they utter, "I'm not good at this subject." It is usually unfounded pessimism that the student has just made a reality. When a leader predicts that her organization won't be able to do something, she dooms her followers to a defeatist attitude. Jimmy Carter was widely criticized for declaring the nation in a "general malaise." He created a self-fulfilling prophecy for the country. When statements of inability are warranted, they are valid; when they're not warranted, they are examples of unfounded pessimism.

At a 2000 Halloween party, Sally asked Mike, a very successful broker, what he thought would happen in the stock markets. Mike said, "I don't think it will come back for three to ten years." Sally replied, "You are such a pessimist. Dick and I retire in a couple of years, and it will be back by then, I'm sure!" Sally could have been correct, but it would have been for the wrong reasons. Her reason for predicting the return of the market was her need for its return. The market does not respond to Sally's need. She was not using logic, so she was exhibiting unfounded optimism. **Unfounded optimism** is a reported weakness that is just as dangerous as unfounded pessimism.

On a similar note, many business people have yet to understand that "globalization and the rise of the Internet are the two most powerful forces affecting business now—and probably will continue to be for at least the next decade" (George, 2003a, p. 31). They are optimistic that the way they want and know how to do business will continue. Thinking does not make it so. The facts make it so!

Lastly, we see leaders whose Reality Quotient is based on seeking consensus in all decision making. It seems they prefer **consensus simply for consensus' sake**! They fail to realize that consensus on the wrong things is more dangerous than dissention. When you are in a meeting and everyone agrees quickly, often you need to say, "Let's adjourn and come back together when we come up with some varied opinions about this issue." Consensus is good only when the ideas behind the decision making are good or when they are on meaningless items. As one young man said to his wife, "I'm in charge of the unimportant things." Well, it would be OK to just do it for consensus' sake on unimportant items. We are concerned when we see leaders who seek consensus on every significant item. Leadership is *not* seeking consensus. As a matter of fact, we rather like the definition of leadership offered by Joel Barker: "Leadership is taking people to a place they would not go without you." In this definition, the leader is taking some action that is not always consensus-oriented.

Figure 3.3: YOUR RQ MEASUREMENT AND IMPROVEMENT MATRICES

Evaluate yourself against the reported traits in this Matrix.

	NATURE (uncontrollable-born)	**NURTURE** (controllable-made)
STRENGTHS (enablers—advantages)	**Q1** ___ self-realist ___ realist about others ___ situation-realist ___ self-esteem ___ (self-IDed trait)	**Q2** ___ inclusive ___ better objectivity ___ envisioning ___ consensus—not yours ___ (self-IDed trait)
WEAKNESSES (derailers—disadvantages)	**Q3** ___ inflated ego ___ poor self-image ___ inability to interpret reality ___ self-image bluff ___ (self-IDed trait)	**Q4** ___ can't reframe views ___ unfounded pessimism ___ unfounded optimism ___ consensus for its sake ___ (self-IDed trait)

Tailor the Matrix below for yourself!

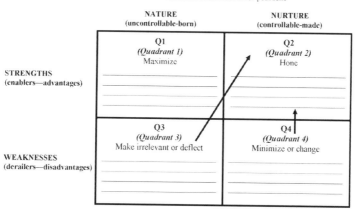

	NATURE (uncontrollable-born)	**NURTURE** (controllable-made)
STRENGTHS (enablers—advantages)	**Q1** *(Quadrant 1)* Maximize	**Q2** *(Quadrant 2)* Hone
WEAKNESSES (derailers—disadvantages)	**Q3** *(Quadrant 3)* Make irrelevant or deflect	**Q4** *(Quadrant 4)* Minimize or change

Using the RQ Matrix

Evaluate yourself in each of the four quadrants, giving yourself a +1 for each of the strengths and a -1 for each of the weaknesses you have. If you can think of more appropriate strengths or weaknesses that are not listed here, include those and score them +1 to -1, but be careful about just making up some traits. Try to be realistic about a replacement trait. It's preferable to use those we have developed from our research.

Evaluating Your RQ Personal Profile: Strengths and Weaknesses

Doing Something About Your RQ!

"Who Moved My Cheese? makes three assumptions: You are dumber than a mouse. You create value by consuming. You should sniff and scurry your way to success" (Arnott, 2002, p. ix). We feel all of you are much smarter than a mouse, create value by producing, and will ultimately produce your way to success by doing exactly what you are doing. In reading and studying how you might improve yourself and your leadership success, you have made the first critical step. Just don't let up! As for organizations, a leader who wants to change an organization must first understand the organization's reality (Goleman, Boyatzis, and McKee, 2002).

The matrix in Figure 3.3 helps you identify what you feel is under your control and what you feel is not. The basic skills of identifying, limiting distractions, studying and learning, then relearning, and using newfound skills for RQ development will ultimately serve you well. Practicing will improve your RQ, because actual repetition builds skills much more effectively than just saying you have a good Reality Quotient. One of the major assumptions of the Leadership Quotient is that we all can become better leaders through the analysis contained in this book and through practice in your leadership environment.

Glance back over the words contained in each quadrant of Figure 3.3. Remember what we wrote in the early parts of this chapter: There seldom is agreement between you and those around you about your strengths and weaknesses in the Reality Quotient. First, others simply don't often agree with your self-assessment as to what your strengths and weaknesses are. Second, others normally think that a lot more of your traits are on the controllable side than you do. Only through an honest and comprehensive self-analysis can you become a more effective leader by increasing your Reality Quotient.

So, you've identified your strengths and weaknesses—some that are under your control and others that aren't. What now? First, validate your analysis with some trusted people. You can often do this on the sly, or if you have trusted mentors, use them. Then come up with a realistic strategy to address how you can work to improve the controllable elements to offset negative factors over which you have no control. Your plan for becoming a better leader must result in actions or they are just empty dreams.

Remember: In each of the four quadrants of the quotient there are three views. First is the real or totally objective view. We simply don't believe humans can have this view, only God can. Second, we see the "perceived as each individual sees it" view. In this area, you need to clearly rectify any discrepancies of how you perceive yourself and how others perceive you. If there is a continual disconnect between what you perceive and what others see, you should change your perception, because the perception of others is more representative of reality. Your goal is to get your perceptions as close to reality as humanly possible, but with a realization that if the majority of those involved perceive something as true, you have to treat it as truth also. Third, and finally, we see that regardless of perceptions, everything will eventually reach a definitive truth where facts show themselves in each leadership circumstance.

This is an important topic that we want to unpack more in depth. The key is to make perceptions as near reality as possible, but with an understanding that perceptions are in fact reality for the perceiver! As we've written earlier, only God can correctly interpret reality. Just never kid yourself, because you're not kidding anyone else. A fact for those wishing to adjust the behavior of others is that the perceptions of the majority are simply facts, true or otherwise. Jack Welch recalled that GE's stock climbed nearly a dollar when Wall Street got the news of his heart problem! This caused him to rethink his importance.

Or, as Walt Disney said, "You can dream, create, design, and build the most wonderful idea in the world, but it requires people to make the dream a reality." You are not in leadership alone. It takes followers. Churchill, in his 1948-1954 volumes on the Second World War, tells us why a leader must be decisive: "To wait till everything was ready was probably to wait till all was too late" (VI, p. 203). Don't wait until it's too late to see the coming tides, or they will sweep you away.

As We Said in the Introduction, "It's Time to Get Started; If Not Now, When?"

Effective leadership requires a balanced fit among the many environments, behaviors, contexts, processes, contents, and needs. Figure 3.4 shows the interaction of 1) the leader, 2) the followers, and 3) the environments, which all need to fit. Put your RQ values in the triangle and see if your RQ forms a foundation to help you proceed to the next level of improving your *LQ©*.

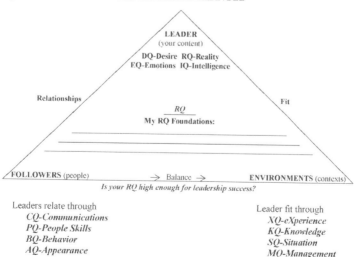

Figure 3.4: YOUR LEADERSHIP LEVERAGE TRIANGLE

LEADER
(your content)
DQ-Desire RQ-Reality
EQ-Emotions IQ-Intelligence

Relationships   Fit

RQ
My RQ Foundations:

FOLLOWERS (people)   → Balance →   ENVIRONMENTS (contexts)
Is your RQ high enough for leadership success?

Leaders relate through
CQ-Communications
PQ-People Skills
BQ-Behavior
AQ-Appearance

Leader fit through
XQ-eXperience
KQ-Knowledge
SQ-Situation
MQ-Management

Living as a leader in reality is not as easy as it sounds, for reality is often tough to take. We don't want to believe certain things about ourselves or about those we love and trust. Likewise, situations are so hard to be realistic about when the heat of the moment is clouding our every thought. Ego, self-esteem, objectivity, inclusiveness, pessimism, and optimism are tough human concepts to get right!

RQ Conclusions

The commercially most successful poet of all time was a namesake of Bill's, Robert W. Service. Service said something we all should consider:

> When I was young I never had the courage to be a coward. We get from a writer what we bring to him, and sometimes we get more than he intended. I have no regret for so much time wasted, for the happiness they gave me made them a success. Once again I had failed to live up to my conception of myself. I was beginning to learn the lesson that success is often failure, and that only by work and achievement can happiness be gained. I should have forced myself to take the hard road and thereby saved my soul. Take the hard road and you'll develop toughness to succeed. (*Ploughman of the Moon*, 1945)

We want to be clear in this chapter that we are talking about reality and your ability to see it developing. We must move beyond phraseology and develop a deeper understanding to lead others into the foggy unknown. You won't be a successful leader by employing short-term tricks. The high $LQ^{©}$ leader pays attention to everything and then learns to focus on the important things. Don't take any predictions as absolutes but understand that all of them have some meaning.

An old TV show was depicting the home and car of the future. In just one case, the show had a robot that changed the TV channel for the viewer. The scriptwriters knew that one day you would not have to get up to change the TV channel, but they never considered you would change it using a handheld remote control! This is how it is with the future: You never quite see it coming in a perfect finished form. High $LQ^{©}$ leaders build their future by first understanding their reality as well as the reality of their organization, their followers, and their environment as much as is possible. The most successful among us will be those who most closely envision the future and their leadership position in that enacted future circumstance.

The ability to effectively receive ideas from *yourself* and others is the essential skill needed to be ultimately successful as a leader. The critical thinking skills, behavioral skills, and decision-making skills all must start with a healthy dose of reality. Reality in part says that there is no real learning without some level of pain or giving up of some level of pleasure. Do a gap analysis of yourself and determine where you are versus where you should be; then develop a speed map of priorities that clarify how you will get there. Don't be one of the many who just continue to work only with their strengths and ignore their weaknesses. Put yourself in uncomfortable positions that force you to confront your weaknesses head on with the danger of failure. That indicates a high Reality Quotient. You might ask, "What happens if I get scared half to death more than once?" First, we like the quip that "51.205% of all statistics are made up on the spot." And second, though statistically it would kill you, in reality it won't! See, statistics don't prove much of anything.

Our next chapter will be "EQ: The Emotional Quotient." Much work has been done on this topic, and we will extend that some and point out how we feel *The Leadership Quotient* version of EQ is different from Goleman's Emotional Quotient. For now, take life and leadership seriously, but remember to live along the way:

> I LAUGH at Life:
> its antics make for me a giddy game,
> where only foolish fellows take themselves with solemn aim.
> I laugh at pomp and vanity, at riches, rank and pride;
> At social inanity, at swagger, swank and side.
> At poets, pastry-cooks and kings, at folk sublime and small,
> Who fuss about a thousand things that matter not at all;
> At those who dream of name and fame, at those who scheme for self…
> But best of all the laughing game—is laughing at myself.
> (Service, 1940, "Laughter," p. 697)

4

EQ, The Emotional Quotient

To avoid criticism, stand still and do nothing; avoid all difficult situations and uncomfortable moments, and then there will be nothing to criticize about you, because you'll be nothing. On the other hand, you can guarantee criticism by taking nobody's advice or taking everyone's advice. The real you is revealed by how you balance these choices. To have a successful Leadership Quotient, it must become second nature for you to know when and how to act and not stand quietly still. Everything you do will be difficult before it is easy.

Thanks to Daniel Goleman's important book, the term, "Emotional Intelligence," is well-known in organizations. Goleman's original book, *Emotional Intelligence* (we call it EQ), was a *New York Times* and *Wall Street Journal* bestseller for good reason. His work extended the definition of what it takes to be successful in organizations. People began to understand that IQ was only one contributor to success and that a much larger factor was an amalgamation of competencies that describes an individual's ability to regulate and use emotions to improve human interactions. Goleman lists the following components of the Emotional Quotient: 1) self-awareness, 2) self-regulation, 3) motivation, 4) empathy, and 5) social skills (see pages 26-27 of Goleman, 1998, for a summary of these competencies). Goleman's EQ makes a great contribution for the leader to understand his own *LQ*$^{©}$.

In another best-selling leadership book, *Good to Great: Why Some Companies Make the Leap...and Others Don't,* Jim Collins wrote: "The good-to-great companies faced just as much adversity as the comparison companies, but responded to that adversity differently....As a result, they emerged from adversity even stronger" (p. 88). "I believe that it is no harder to build something great than to build something good" (2001, p. 205). One of the basic assumptions of the Leadership Quotient is that *companies* don't face adversity, *people* do. It is the response of people in leadership positions that determines the company's success. We feel that the emotional intelligence levels of the dominant coalition of leaders in an organization are key predictors of success. This is borne out with a careful reading of *Good to Great* where Collins discounts charisma and self-centered leadership and points instead to those who are adept at handling their followers' emotions.

"'Emotional intelligence' refers to the capacity for recognizing our own feelings and those of others, for motivating ourselves, and for managing emotions well in ourselves and in our relationships" (Goleman, 1998, p. 317). The $LQ^{©}$ element we refer to as "Emotional Quotient (EQ)" is not being nice or letting it all hang out. It is not related to IQ. It comes from a different part of the brain than rational or logical thoughts. It is the leader's "outer self," which has been called social aptitude and dexterity. It is the ability to regulate outburst and kindness, expressiveness and stoicism, love and hate, and a number of other emotions we will discuss later in this chapter. Emotional intelligence measured by EQ is the sum total of your ability to know and use your emotions and to read and use the emotions of others.

Some would say EQ is a measure of emotional maturity. EQ is about temper, locus of control, teamwork, leadership, anger, love, hate, and a lot of other words that carry much meaning related to our humanness. We have found no quick fixes for EQ, but it is possible to *improve* yours, no matter where you begin. The easiest improvements will be among leaders who are emotionally incompetent. In fact, just studying the EQ concept will improve the EQ of the worst among us. Experience in EQ is often among the most painfully gained lessons, for we often have to be shamed or hurt into understanding the interactions of our emotions with the emotions of others. Despite the potential pain, EQ is worthy of study because EQ is a huge determinant in leadership success.

The competencies that guide a leader in managing relationships with others in differing situations helps bring an awareness to the fit between the leader, the followers, and the environmental situations in which leadership takes place. We've often seen a leader get by without a high IQ, but seldom does a leader succeed without the ability to understand the emotional context that she brings to the leader-follower relationship.

The story of the death of Jesus Christ has been told for 2,000 years in the best-selling book in publishing history. Mel Gibson's movie, *The Passion of The Christ*, is a great example of how relating the same old facts, but in an emotional package, can increase the power of the message. You've been working with people for one, five, ten, or twenty years. You can ignite their emotions, just as Mel Gibson did, by telling the story of your organization with emotional appeal.

The leader who can't understand his own emotions or those of others has little chance of succeeding in a leadership role. A person with a low EQ might be successful as a research scientist, computer programmer, book-level accountant, or even a geeky college professor. But leaders in people-based, competitive environments must understand EQ. There is no substitute for knowing and controlling your emotions and being able to read the emotions of others. Humans are the only species known to have feelings about their emotions, and emotions about their feelings, and so on, into infinity. You can't stop people from thinking, but you sure can start them thinking if you can get them emotionally attached to your organization's mission or vision.

A leader must know his own emotional "blind spots" because they will ultimately determine success at higher levels of leadership. Many leaders survive at lower levels with a poor EQ, but that is not possible at the upper ends of leadership. Of the 12 quotients we write about in this book, we encourage you to get the most feedback about your EQ. In fact, many leaders should seek some form of professional executive-level assessment if they are not totally aware of the weaknesses in their EQ. Some qualities of your EQ will not serve you well at the upper reaches of leadership. EQ traits can be stumbling blocks or steppingstones, depending on your view and enactment of those traits.

Emotions are mostly inherited. Striking similarities among the emotions in the many historical societies have been researched. They all had basically the same fears, loves, hates, humors, and facial expressions. They all participated in the same kind of bargaining and valuing understanding, fear and mourning of death, sneers, loathing, sexual desires and no-no's, fear of taboos, and a search for meaning and understanding of their worlds and themselves. How did this happen if emotional traits are not heritable?

On to EQ

> *"Life could be described as: A sexually transmitted disease in which the mortality rate is 100%....Much too important a thing ever to talk seriously about it" (R.D. Laing and Oscar Wilde in Dillon-Malone, 2000, p. 162).*

As with the other quotients presented in previous chapters, the individual and interactive effects of EQ often get applied in an unbalanced or inappropriate way that does not fit the followers or the environments for which directed EQ is intended. All Leadership Quotients must fit the followers and the environments in which leadership is intended to be expressed. All elements of the Leadership Quotient must be viewed as a means to contribute to the improved leadership of the individual. The understanding of emotions and the wisdom to make application of them are the very essence of EQ. Your intangible qualities related to EQ will drive your success as a leader regardless of any credentials you might have.

Marsha told a story about a job search for the top hospital administrator when she was the Human Resource Director of a large, Florida-based health care organization. The selection committee had mostly agreed to hire Dan, and they were taking him to dinner at the end of the interview. After the dinner, they decided *against* hiring him because he ordered a beer with dinner. While that may seem like a rather small social mistake, the committee felt that since everyone else at the table ordered wine, it was just a touch inappropriate to order beer and Dan's Emotional Quotient should have told him that. Entertaining the very particular stakeholders of the hospital was an important part of the job, and he needed to know precisely what was appropriate and when.

As president, Bill Clinton was great at "feeling your pain." Hillary Rodham Clinton, however, had a public reputation as more coarse and demanding. Martin Luther King Jr. could tune into a crowd's emotions using his preaching style. When she was First Lady, Barbara Bush became "America's Mom," exhibiting a nurturing EQ. Former Federal Reserve Board Chairman Alan Greenspan carefully crafted a public EQ as a tough but thoughtful analyzer of facts and trends. Former U. S. Senator Tom Daschle's soft voice and use of the phrase, "I'm concerned," delivered an EQ that told his audience he was a uniter, not a divider, but he lost in 2004 anyway! While these are well-known public figures, we're confident you can think of people in your own organization who exemplify positive or negative EQs. We are also confident you can predict leadership success or failure based on EQ. It's a great exception when a person of low EQ rises to a position of high leadership. Conversely, it's almost expected when a person of high EQ does so.

Emotional intelligence is buried deep in the developmental scheme of human existence. All animals exhibit some level of emotional intellect, which can be seen when they react quickly to danger, cower to a stronger animal, or use many forms of bluff. In humans, the emotions are more developed and intermingled with our Intelligence Quotient, which allows us to control our emotional response. Danger, anger, bluster, excitement, love, hate, sadness, loss, gain, confidence, sadism, humor, debasement, rationalization, and feelings of all types are emotionally based. In fact, humans are much more a product of emotions than of rational logic. We are emotional beings looking for a way to rationalize the way we feel. Feelings are real, whether they are based in physical pain or emotional stress.

A favorite mother-in-law saying is, "Your headache is all in your head…but my head really hurts!" Ask yourself: "Is there really any difference in those two statements?" Both hurt. An arm that's been cut off hurts and so does losing a loved one. Which would you rather experience? If you don't think emotions count, try this: The next time your boss tells you about a tragedy in his or her life, say, "Let's run a spreadsheet on that. I'll bet you are better off without the burden of your wife, mother, son, daughter, or whomever." That type of poor EQ would soon prove that the boss is also better off without *you* in the organization.

It seems that facts often get in the way of emotions or are used only to justify feelings. Logic is not as commonplace as you might think. Decision-making is so highly based in emotions that it makes us wonder why we even worry with trying to use logic. Witness the number of corporate buyouts that go bad, and the number of change initiatives that don't work as planned. More corporate efforts of those types result in failure than in success. That's not the kind of record you would expect from good rational logic. This is because those human-based activities end up being completed because of emotions versus logic. As leaders, we are very good at rationalizing our poor actions and congratulating ourselves for good actions! Remember the "Bellman equation" that uses dynamic programming to determine that a National Football League team should "go for it" on fourth down in almost every situation? This is a solidly validated principle. Why don't they? Because the coaches are making emotional, not rational, decisions.

In a previous chapter, we discussed locus of control and the fact that so many successful people have an internal locus of control versus an external locus. Having an internal locus of control says you feel that you are in control of yourself and your future. Sure, you realize that there is some level of luck. But for the most part it will always be smart luck, and you will succeed in your endeavors. Even when you experience some really bad luck, you realize the law of averages will catch up and you'll experience some good luck. Also, being emotionally stable and dedicated, you'll learn from tough times and be a better person for the suffering. Or as we've often seen, good luck is the way we define what happens to successful people we don't like, but bad luck is what causes us to fail! In fact, Bernstein (1998), in his remarkable book on risk, asserts that the mastery of risk separates the distant past from the modern times. So, to a great extent, high EQs control their own luck!

One of our heroes of emotional stability is Viktor Frankl. He showed great EQ under the direst of circumstances. Frankl spent years in concentration camps and developed logotherapy as a result of his experiences. He went on to help many people through his personal story and therapy innovations. Frankl also touched millions through his book, *Man's Search for Meaning,* which is often considered one of the most influential books of all time. In his book, Frankl tells of almost dying many times. A couple of his scrapes with death were caused by his inability to control his emotions. Once he told a Nazi guard that he was a doctor, even though he knew the guard might beat him to death. Another time Frankl became indignant when a guard threw a rock at him as if he were not human. He understood the EQ he *should* have exhibited, but he simply had reached the limits of his ability to endure more indignations. Frankl's story says that we can control our emotions most of the time but that often we reach the end of our rope. We all have a point we simply can't go beyond in emotional self-control. Frankl said that "responsibility is the very essence of human existence." Be responsible for your own emotions because followers can see your EQ, and they will choose not to follow a blamer. Fortunately, most of us will never be in a concentration camp to test our EQ limits.

Frankl provides many EQ lessons in his powerful book. One more is helpful to us at this point. He demonstrated with his actions and words throughout his book that he had learned to stop asking, "Why me?" He replaced this lament with "OK, I'm here and it's bad. Now what do I do?" We make *most* choices because of emotions. High EQ leaders are able to understand the emotional part and the logical part of any decision. Their understanding enables them not to dwell on the bad things that may happen, but simply to have the EQ to say, "It happened and I'll deal with it."

The combination of IQ and EQ is what makes us human. It is this emotional side that makes humans vastly superior to any artificial intelligence put together as neural networks that attempt to mimic the human brain. It is this combination of IQ and EQ that enables humans to adapt to the environment in a way that has made human life so good for the species.

In summary, perhaps the real question should not be, "Why is humankind so emotional?" but, "How can some people be at the other end of the spectrum and be so logical and rational?" That indeed might point us to a creative path to improving our emotions to the point that they are useful in leadership. EQ is never static. It is either getting better or worse every day, and in the area of EQ, it is not enough to be able to *handle* your emotions. You have to *control* your EQ or you can become a negative impact on others who have a very low EQ and an equivalently low Leadership Quotient.

Goleman, Boyatzis, and McKee, in *Primal Leadership: Realizing the Power of Emotional Intelligence* (2002), said that gifted leadership is where feelings and thoughts meet; where emotions and logic are both used. They said that, indeed, leaders need a high enough IQ to handle their tasks, but mostly they must be able to motivate, guide, inspire, listen, and persuade. These most-needed skills require emotional intelligence: EQ. They write about the power of negative emotions and how strong positive emotions are for "lubricating mental efficiency." *Primal Leadership* could be summarized by saying that good leaders must be able to control their own emotions and read the emotions of others.

Why Is EQ Next?

> We are repeatedly flabbergasted by people who don't understand that the most valuable lessons in life are not sought but are, rather, gained through difficulty. Those lessons are gained by life's successes and failures. Leaders who limit their learning to a subject, person, place, or time are doomed to failure. Recall your greatest lessons in life, the moments that stand out, because that's when you really lived and learned. We'd bet they were not in a classroom or even from a book but were the times when you had to handle the abstract, obscure, and cryptic in order to settle a conflict of human interactions.

The most basic of emotions—anger—is a good one to consider when you think about EQ. Anger is generally bad, but a person with a great EQ can use even this bad emotion for good purposes. When someone is continually abusing you, at some point anger will take over and you will begin to handle the situation in a way that defends your human rights. All emotions have this good and bad part, but an understanding of the proper *use* of your emotions is the foundation of EQ. Goleman's groundbreaking bestseller, *Emotional Intelligence* (1995), can provide you with more scientific and research findings if you desire. Our goal is not to repeat those findings but to show how EQ can be a key to leadership success. The part that is genetic heritage versus the developed part is important, but only as it pertains to what you feel you have inherited and what you've developed. Bringing together head, heart, values, desires, attention, and effort will help you improve your EQ.

Acting emotionally rather than logically would mean that feelings have overcome reason. But who is to say what reason is? When you realize that the purpose of emotions is to protect us at the most basic levels of danger, maybe the most reasonable thing is to go with emotions versus so-called reason. We are the amalgam of all that we have learned in our life experiences. We have a dilemma of the logical self versus the emotional self. In most recent times, we have been called upon to control the emotional self through logic and reason. That is easier said than done, though it is possible.

Perhaps the favorite emotion is love, yet few can define love. We'd say that love is the case where the strongest of desires—survival—can be overlooked because you care more about another person than you care about yourself. Yes, we all have biological predispositions, but our experiences and feelings can overcome even the strongest of urges. Remember this as you attempt to adjust your EQ.

In most of human history, a hair-trigger temper might have been the thing needed to spur you to quick action and preserve your life. But with modern weapons, temper is a ticket for disaster. Temper may be selected out of humans in a few hundred thousand years, but if you don't want to wait, work on your EQ now. EQ is more than natural traits and more than what you are now, it is how hard you work to control yourself emotionally. It's about balancing logic and reason with emotion and reaction. Humans have been blessed with the ability to use reason and to think long-term, but few of us choose to do it to any great extent. Do you really think we marry, go to college, buy a car, discipline our children, misbehave at work, and so on with more logic than emotion? Watch when small kids get hurt. When they are really hurt, their reaction is most often not as bad as when it's a small injury that's coupled with some indignity. It seems that our emotions can act totally independently of our rational mental self.

Emotions can be good or faulty guides. A good EQ is simply the wisdom to separate the faulty from the appropriate emotion. Most real failures we see in America today are not failures of intellect, but the results of emotional impairment. In fact, Goleman says, "At best, IQ contributes about 20 percent to the factors that determine life success, which leaves 80 percent to other forces…ranging from social class to luck" (1995, p. 34).

It is enormously difficult—in fact, we say humanly impossible—to separate out the effects of nurture from nature. An ongoing study of identical twins separated at birth has produced some interesting results on the subject. A true human clone would effectively separate the two effects as well, but in the meantime, nature and nurture remain closely intermingled.

Through nurturing, we develop social and personal prejudices and biases. As authors, we know that our biases are showing. That's OK, as long as you, the reader, understand when we are expressing an opinion and what it might mean to you. Realize that what we are doing is not like the painter who paints the picture that she wants you to see and feel. We are more like your ophthalmologist. We want to help you toward a unique prescription for your leadership in your situation. It must be customized to you.

Let's look at the Leadership Triangle in Figure 4.1. Note in particular the key position of EQ. EQ is the foundation that holds up the leader's traits and actions that make for leadership success. It is no mistake that we show EQ two times. Yes, it's that much more important than IQ. The next section of this chapter explores the many components that make up EQ.

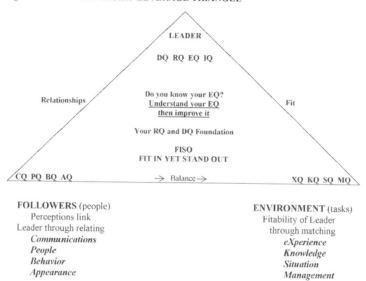

Figure 4.1: THE LEADERSHIP LEVERAGE TRIANGLE

EQ is beyond your own emotions—know and understand how.

Description of the Emotional Quotient and its Dimensions

Human societies have effloresced to levels of extreme complexity because their members have the intelligence and flexibility to play roles of virtually any degree of specification, and to switch them as the occasion demands. Modern man is an actor of many parts who may well be stretched to his limit by the constantly shifting demands of the environment. (Wilson, 2000, p. 554)

In the original version of the Measurement and Improvement Matrices, the quadrants are labeled as follows: Quadrant 1—the natural strengths; Quadrant 2—the nurtured strengths; Quadrant 3—the natural weaknesses; and Quadrant 4—the nurtured weaknesses. You will want to refer to Figure 4.2 as we explain the content of each quadrant. The goals of the matrix are to accomplish the following:

• Use natural strengths as enablers to their best advantage: maximize Quadrant 1.

• More fully develop and use nurtured strengths: hone Quadrant 2.

- Make irrelevant or deflect natural weaknesses that are derailers and disadvantageous to leadership: deflect Quadrant 3.

- Minimize or improve nurtured weaknesses: minimize or change Quadrant 4.

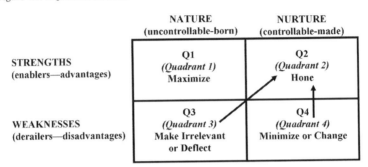

Figure 4.2: EQ MEASUREMENT AND IMPROVEMENT MATRIX

EQ is one of the most malleable of quotients, but it is one of the least changed quotients: understand why.

Genetic propensities or heritable traits are not totally duplicated. If they were perfectly duplicated, identical twins would always be thinking, acting, and feeling exactly the same. Research tests indicate the similarities approach 75%. According to standardized tests, tendencies are often incorrectly classified as natural because they are relatively stable over time. When calculating your own $LQ^{©}$, we would like for you to classify as natural things that you have little or no desire to change. For example, a couple of our friends smoke. Even though we both dislike smoking, we feel the person is better off if they admit it is dangerous and simply say, "I don't *want* to quit." We are not enamored of people who say they don't think it's bad for them, because that's not a good application of IQ. You will have a more accurate total $LQ^{©}$ if you admit that some tendencies are natural if you are not going to change them. Strong scientific evidence suggests that the propensity to become addicted to cigarette smoking is largely inherited. Maybe many tendencies should be considered natural tendencies for $LQ^{©}$ evaluation.

EQ is crystallized and rooted in biological evolution but not unchangeable because we are creatures of free choice and thought. We cannot always avoid emotions, but we can change our reaction to them. Of course, many of these traits do not have standardized tests, but we are taking liberties in these classifications since we are defining our Leadership Quotient as comprising items that have been shown to mold better leaders.

Personality is one area that many feel is inherited to a certain degree, but it is definitely an overriding influence on EQ regardless of its nature or nurture determinant. Personality has been shown to vary in about five major areas, which are often called "The Big Five Personality Traits":

1. Introvert versus extrovert. In *The Leadership Quotient*, we prefer to use internal locus of control versus external locus of control. We're not suggesting that a perfect correlation exists between introvert and internal, nor extrovert and external. However, we are aggregating them together out of convenience and because of normal observations.

2. Curious versus incurious. Curious people pay attention, while incurious people are inwardly focused and ignore their environment.

3. Disagreeable versus agreeable. Disagreeable people are contrarians and agreeable people are "yes-men."

4. Conscientious versus nonconscientious. This trait refers to those who care about what happens versus those who don't.

5. Stable versus instable. This trait is a measure of beta, or how much the person changes in response to his environment.

We have taken some liberty here and molded these five dimensions to our *LQ*©. For a more psychological treatment, look at any academic book on personality. These areas are related to emotions and should be considered as you review the EQ traits as we have classified them below. First, think about how you fit within the five personality dimensions mentioned above. Then see how these traits determine your selections on the EQ evaluative scale that is explained in the next section.

Normal Natural EQ Strengths—Quadrant 1 of the EQ 2X2 Matrix

Great leaders work through emotions by handling themselves and others. The truly gifted ones know how to use the heart and the head to motivate, guide, inspire, persuade, and create a synergistic attitude about organizational accomplishment (Goleman, Boyatzis, and McKee, 2002). They do this first by having emotional self-awareness that is based on an accurate self-assessment. They are confident but don't take themselves too seriously. These great leaders seem to exude a **commanding presence** and style because they are always aware of their attributes that demand respect. In the area of emotions related to your self-confidence, we like to remind people to first seek to "know thyself" before worrying about knowing others, and the only way to realistically know your own emotional self-confidence is through self-analysis and seeking feedback from others on a continual basis.

A commanding presence starts with self-assessment and awareness especially as it relates to emotional well-being. Again, we must see this not as cockiness but as reality of one's skill and self awareness of EQ. In his autobiography, General Chuck Yeager tells about a dogfight with German fighter planes in WWII. "There were sixteen of us and over two hundred of them…" and Yeager heard a fellow pilot call, "Hey, I've got six of them cornered at two o'clock. Come on up and have some fun" (Yeager and Janos, 1985, pp. 66 and 68). That pilot had either real control of his emotions, or he was crazy. Different jobs take different levels of control and being a fighter pilot in WWII definitely took a huge EQ. Yeager himself survived, in part because he understood the dangers and was able to recognize and stay within his physical limitations. On the other end of the spectrum is a person who is very cocky, and when you get to know her, you understand that it's just bluster. She is just trying to hide her insecurities beneath a tough exterior.

Normally, this commanding presence is initiated through first impressions. People who exhibit a commanding presence almost always make a great first impression, and people who make a poor first impression seldom have a commanding presence. We have met people who say that Michael Jordan simply dominates when he walks into a room, as does Colin Powell or Bill Clinton. You can never make a good second "first impression." Even if you are not a commanding-presence person, try to make the best first impression you can muster.

Closely akin to understanding if your presence is based on emotional self-awareness is the ability to control your emotions. **This awareness and control** is partly learned and partly inborn. Many feel that the ability to control and exhibit the appropriate level of emotion is mostly inherited. We are not so sure about this. However, we believe testing would show this to be relatively stable for most people. For those mature enough to read this book, it is very close to a trait that is imbedded so deeply it will be difficult to change. A lot of people do report this as a trait they do not control, so in the *LQ*© we refer to it as a natural strength. Both Bill Clinton and Ronald Reagan have exhibited this trait, though in differing ways.

We are combining a) emotional control and awareness, and b) self- and social awareness, because we feel that very few people are good in one area if they are not good in the other. People who are unaware of themselves are not normally in control of their emotions. Though the opposite might be true a little more often: People with self-awareness sometimes are not in control. Likewise with social versus individual awareness, people must be individually aware before they can be socially aware, though the opposite is not as true. We feel that combining a) awareness and control, and b) self- and social awareness, is more in reality than separating the two groups. If you feel you have one of a) or b) and not the other, then separate them for yourself.

Sensing others' emotions requires a lot of effort. First, commit to paying a lot of attention to others. Look and listen closely for emotional cues in what people say and do. We've often said to others, "I didn't know you were upset or bothered." The normal response was, "Yes, I know you didn't notice." They were simply telling us, "I noticed you didn't notice." Perhaps if they can see, we should be able to detect their discomfort in the first place! Intuition is felt by some to be the mind turning in on itself to reveal to us something we already know but are not aware we know. This is beyond the usual and rational in many cases, but intuition comes from experience and attention, and attempting to be intuitive. This is a people skill that we will explain in the People Quotient chapter.

High-EQ leaders continually scan what's going on in their environment and seek more information by asking questions. They use some level of abstracting and multivariate thinking to pull together what is really going on with people and their emotions. Regardless of your religious beliefs, Jesus as a figure in history reportedly exhibited this in an exceptional manner. As a favorite Bible verse implies, you will find only if you seek, you won't be given if you don't ask, and the door will remain locked to you until you knock. This is good advice for improving your EQ, no matter what your religion.

Leaders with high EQs know whom to ask and how to ask. They can read a situation and often know it's better to ask later or ask someone else, "What just happened with Dave?" Good advice is found in the old Jim Croce song: "You don't tug on Superman's cape; you don't spit into the wind; you don't pull the mask off the old Lone Ranger; and you don't mess around with Jim" (taken from Bill's jukebox). High EQs know how to apply that advice in leading people.

In Gardner's books on EQ, he writes a lot about empathy, caring, compassion, and other emotion-sensing results. We say there are a lot of appropriate sensing results, but the correctly exhibited EQ results seldom occur if one does not notice the emotions of others in the first place!

A final trait that we are listing as a natural strength is **entrepreneurial innovativeness**. This is a trait that many leaders have trouble with. But we have found there is an emotional side to being innovative in a unique and risky way. Some people are better equipped emotionally to step outside their norms and look at things differently and change their actions to meet their newly gained awareness. These people can adjust, adapt, or point others in new directions. They have the emotional strength to handle risk. Their emotions will allow them to break the daily grind and start doing things in a new way. Leadership authors have struggled to label this tendency. We refer to it as entrepreneurial spirit that is complemented by a sense of innovativeness.

David Kahn, the owner of about 50 Blockbuster stores and numerous other businesses, tells how he developed a business in his last couple of years of college that sold for hundreds of thousands of dollars. David exhibits this emotional attachment to entrepreneurial innovativeness. David seeks a way to improve and turn into a profit every product and service that he experiences. He is constantly telling others about new ideas they can use to get ahead.

Normal Natural EQ Weaknesses—Quadrant 3 of the EQ 2X2 Matrix

One of the most common problems with emotions is losing control when things don't go as we expect. Most of us do this, but to varying degrees. On the promotional schedule board in the operations room of a pro baseball team, one of the employees has written, "Days when Dick lost it!" Apparently, Dick has a temper. He also takes it pretty well, or the employee would not have written the note.

We have witnessed many who could not handle unexpected difficulty. Those people would lose their cool over a change in their schedule even when it was little or no real problem at all. On the other hand, we see those with great control. In fact, some seem to get calmer when things are bad. Dave does a lot of public speaking and one of his favorite speech-ending quotes is, "'If you can keep your head when all about you are losing theirs…' you probably don't realize how dire the situation is!" Then he goes on to recite Rudyard Kipling's "If." The joke works, because the leader in Kipling's poem understands the difficulty of the situation but is able to deal with the emotions that accompany it. To have a successful EQ, the leader needs to be able to keep his head when others about him are losing theirs.

John Madden tells a great story to indicate the kind of cool some people have and conversely others don't have. Madden considered his quarterback, Kenny Stabler, a great leader with high EQ. Stabler was one of the most successful college and pro quarterbacks of all time. This is the story according to Madden: Oakland and Baltimore were just about to start the second overtime in a sudden death divisional playoff game in 1977. Stabler walked over to Madden between periods. Madden was ranting and waving his arms as usual and suggesting plays left and right. Madden noticed Stabler was staring into the screaming crowd. Madden screamed, "What are you doing?" Stabler calmly said, "You know what, John?" Madden responded anxiously, "What, what!" Stabler replied, "All these people are really getting their money's worth today." Madden continued to rant. Stabler went back into the game and threw a winning touchdown pass. Madden said of Stabler, "The hotter it got, the cooler he got" (Madden, 1984, pp. 119-120).

The first natural weakness in EQ is the inability to keep your head when others are losing theirs, that is, exhibiting uncontrollable and destructive emotional excitability that leads to **emotional irrationality**. These leaders with low EQ have the opposite effect a leader is supposed to have because they cause some of the otherwise unconcerned to panic!

Trust is an enormously powerful thing and lack of it is even more powerful. In most ways, trust is a hygiene factor that we all expect to be there. As we drive down the highway, we trust hundreds of other speeding idiots to do what is right and stay on their side of the road. Those "nuts" are in control of thousands of pounds of steel that cannot stop for hundreds of feet. Fortunately, most of the time they do what you'd want them to and not too many get killed, although there are some 43,000 a year killed in vehicular accidents in the U.S. That is nearly as many Americans as were killed in all of the Vietnam conflict.

Dave and Bill traveled between Dallas and Birmingham in the course of writing this book. We both agree that the most dangerous part of the trip was driving to the airport. The plane is one of the safest places to be. Our lack of fear of flying is either because we're overeducated nerds who understand statistics too well, or we both have high EQs.

The point here is that we expect people to be trustworthy. A real problem arises when people are not trustworthy. Lack of trust destroys a leader. Most leaders are relatively trustworthy when they are being watched, but there are many examples of leaders who were not trustworthy when they had the opportunity to cheat and profit millions of dollars. This weakness of being **untrustworthy when not being watched** is often reported as an inherited weakness. We're not so sure it's a natural trait, but perhaps a gene will be found that indicates a propensity for this untrustworthiness. Many researchers and writers are beginning to think that there are genes that lead to many criminal activities (at least genes that lead to propensities to act criminally).

Another weakness we find is someone who emotionally can't adapt to change. This is different from keeping your head when problems arise. This is a basic aversion to change. Preservation of the species mandates that all of us have some fear of change. If you don't believe it, try putting your watch on the other arm, or put your wallet in the other pocket, or carry your purse on the other shoulder, or simply get another alarm clock. When something changes your morning ritual, does it upset your day?

Disruptive emotional reactions to life's insignificant changes show a certain level of "genetic" propensity for handling change well or not handling it well. People who can't handle a new toothpaste might not be able to adapt well to a new Enterprise Resource Planning system (ERP). **Inability to adapt emotionally** to change is a huge factor explaining why about 50% of the ERP implementations fail (Cortada and Hargraves, 1999; and Jacobs and Whybark, 2000). We suspect it is one of the primary factors that determine why many can't lead others into change. If the leader can't emotionally handle the change, how would one expect the followers to adapt? Emotions of the leader are powerful and rub off on the followers.

Many times, reluctance to change is exhibited as moodiness, which is a constantly changing response to a leader's environment. Moodiness that is inappropriate to the situation or the emotions of others is a poor trait to exhibit. We have told many MBA students that they must learn to control the outward display of their moods. We all have moods, but high EQ leaders know when to show them and when not to.

Emotional laziness is one of the most commonly reported EQ negative traits. Many people have trouble getting fired up about anything. And most say, "I can't get into it unless it is something I love." Well, that's not enough in the world of organizational leaders. High-EQ leaders must be able to generate enthusiasm for many things and lead the charge with the sheer force of their desire and enthusiasm. Unfortunately, "There is no lifeguard in the gene pool." Or some of us simply get all the cast-off genes as did poor Danny DeVito's character in the movie, *Twins*. So many times we have seen people who have low EQs because they are emotionally lazy. They try to get their followers to go forward, and it does not work because the followers are looking for emotional strength from the leader. But the leader is just too emotionally lazy to generate any feelings and effort at all. Think about failed political candidates: Often the problem was not their ideas, it was the lack of emotional strength they applied in selling them to the populace.

Dave serves on the board of trustees of a small Christian college. The board was in the closing phase of a particularly discouraging two-day meeting. The last agenda item was an address from the president of the institution. He was as discouraged and emotionally drained as the 30 board members. Yet as he stood to speak, you could see his energy increasing. He stood tall, purposely put his shoulders back and held his head high and delivered the most energizing speech in the college's recent history. High-EQ leaders exhibit energy when the followers need it most.

Some people exhibit emotional laziness because they are reclusive. Regardless of the excuse for it, emotional laziness is not a good feature or trait to exhibit.

Normal Nurtured EQ Strengths—Quadrant 2 of the EQ 2X2 Matrix

One of the most often reported strengths in EQ is **emotional maturity**. This is a fairly complex and difficult-to-measure trait, though we would bet that most of us know when someone has it and when they don't. It is in part the ability to adjust your internal emotions when new and different situations arise. It is knowing your preferences and limitations but being able to adjust beyond those limitations. There is no algorithm for emotional maturity. People simply seem to exhibit it to a greater or lesser degree; many seem to exhibit no emotional maturity.

If you are moving forward at a rapid pace in your leadership quest and have reached a high level, you've probably got emotional maturity. If you're stumbling in your leadership advancement, maybe you don't have it. Emotional maturity is most often a matter of time and exposure. But beyond time and exposure is the ability to recognize where you are in emotional maturity and make efforts to improve. Some leaders with low EQ seem to like being emotionally immature. Among our MBA students and consulting clients, we're aware of many low EQs who seem to think it's cute to continue to talk like a baby or giggle like a teenager or talk like a cool dude. That behavior is out if you want to be a real leader! It works for influencing toddlers or teenagers but not for adults. Baby-talking adults will stay in baby positions. Teenage actions will keep one at teenage jobs. We know staff members at both of our universities who try to identify with college-age students by including the word "like" in every sentence. It may increase their identification, but it's *not* going to increase their leadership. Think about it: Do you want to be led by someone who is at the same level as you, or would you prefer someone who exhibits more leadership skills? Even if the "common language" helps lead teenagers, it will prevent you from leading adults. Use your emotional EQ to change how you address followers. To have high EQ, adjust your language to a leadership level.

A 23-year-old preacher had to preach the funeral for a young friend who was tragically killed. Controlling his emotions would be difficult, but he wanted to because he had attended a wedding where the minister cried and it just destroyed the service. High-EQ leaders must control their emotions, even in their early 20s.

Managing your impulses and normal reactions through reframing means knowing when and how to challenge tactfully, using your sense of humor, and being enthusiastic about being challenged.

Some people challenge everyone on everything, and others never challenge anyone. We can see clearly that you must have a balanced approach and challenge when necessary and appropriate or your effectiveness will be nil. Reframe how you see your challenges to others. See your challenges as a chance for all of those involved to grow and a chance for you to advance your leadership cause. Forget using your challenges as a chance to prove you are right.

When and how to use your sense of humor is a great EQ trait. Dave and Bill both use humor often. But on the other hand, we have been in situations where it simply was not appropriate. Many instances have occurred of late where humor turned out to be politically incorrect and it has cost many their leadership positions. Using humor shows an approachability and ability to take life's problems in stride. Conversely, it can show a lack of awareness. Ronald Reagan had a great sense of humor and did not mind making fun of himself. Make sure you can take the humor directed toward you before you give it to others. Bill recalls when he asked his students why they did not laugh at his jokes, and one replied, "If you would say something funny, we'd laugh!" Now that was gutsy, but funny. Remember that self-regulation calls for some degree of selflessness. Be a courageous leader in the area of self-control.

Lastly, in this area of managing your emotional impulses be sure you know how to handle challenges. We never want yes-men or -women working for us, and the best way to assure we don't have them is to demand challenges from those who work for us. A famous person once said, "I don't want yes-men working for me, even if it costs them their jobs." Do you think that leader got challenged? Make everyone comfortable with appropriately challenging you. This does not mean you have to be a wimp, but it does mean you have to listen and often just accept the outcome.

Another area where we see people excel emotionally is through their **emotional attachment to success: valuating**. To be a positive, this cannot be an attachment that overrides everything, but it must be a strong attachment. People who are successful are emotional about their drive and desire to do the things necessary to be successful. They plan and work for success. They watch and listen for things they can do to improve themselves as leaders and as people whom others will want to follow. Taken to extremes this is a very bad trait, but when mediated with a healthy dose of reality and humility it can be a great complement to leadership. Yes, you must be emotionally attached to something if you are going to reach the highest levels in that "thing." You must temper this with the other good traits and not esteem success over ethics, values, the worth of others, or your own well-being. Your emotional attachment to success must be strong but tempered with higher callings and purposes. Your EQ for success should be directed toward a greater cause than pure power of success, or it will likely be a detriment rather than a positive influence.

We wonder at what level many of the corporate cheats were attached to success at any cost. They should have time to think about this as they are spending time in prison. Do you think those scandalous leaders had a *healthy* emotional attachment to success?

Experience in the area of **influencing others' emotions with cultural astuteness** is most often something you get just *after* you need it most. Americans are stereotyped as rich, independent, brash, loud know-it-alls. And yes, many of these stereotypes are true in part because we do have a lot to be proud of as Americans. Our educational, military, and economic might are unprecedented in world history. Even the poorest among those in the U.S. would be affluent in the majority of the 200 other countries in the world. America generates over 40% of the world's domestic product with less than 5% of its population. America spends more on its military than the rest of the world combined, but that spending represents only about 5% of our gross domestic product. Most individual states have a greater domestic product than all but a handful of the other countries in the world. Our society is educated, motivated, and full of opportunities. The problem is not that we should not be proud, but how we express this pride. Confidence and pride are great; cockiness and bragging are not. We must learn to be humble and try to be sensitive to the cultures and feelings of others. After all, we won life's lottery just by being born in America.

This does not mean that we have to totally understand other cultures or be a part of them. It simply means that we must seek to understand where other cultures are coming from and not try to impose our cultural standards on others. In many countries, the place of females is different than in America where equality should be the norm. We feel that the inequality in the rest of the world is wrong and we should hold to our values, but when we visit those cultures we don't need to try to impose our norms on them. Working quietly for a cause works much better than head-on confrontation in situations like this.

The relationship between bosses and subordinates in many cultures is very different from that seen in America. The difference among children, parents, and grandparents in many cultures is different than in America. The difference in client relationships is also very different in various cultures. Even within the U.S., we have great differences in use of body language versus verbal communications, between use of slang and proper English, between the role of fathers, between the respect of elders, on volume of music, and many more things. We generally know what is the correct standard, but the huge mistake is to assume that all standards are like ours. Yes, Dave and Bill are two fairly big and affluent, highly educated, older (ugh) white guys, and we are often stereotyped as believing that those whose standards aren't like ours must be wrong! Sad to say, but that is the way many think. We must reverse that thinking and realize what we are and what our cultural norms are, but appreciate that there are differences that are not wrong, just different. The level of appreciation, appropriate judgment, and action represents true culturally astute EQ. Without a bit of this, you won't go far in the leadership-development world.

Normal Nurtured EQ Weaknesses—Quadrant 4 of the EQ 2X2 Matrix

Conflict and change avoidance are reported weaknesses that many feel they have developed in their EQ. So many people just don't like conflict, mostly because so many simply don't know how to handle it. Bill knows that he lets things go and then goes overboard on conflict. He also knows that the best way is to address things up front and not let them get out of hand. But since he does not like confronting people, he waits until it's too late and then blows up. Consider this story. Bill is hurrying home one 100-plus-degree August day in Dallas, and his car breaks down about 20 miles from home. He takes off his coat and shirt and starts jogging to the nearest phone. About four miles later he stops at the phone and calls his house. The line is busy and there is no call-waiting and there are no cell phones. He hangs around, drinks a Big Gulp of Coke, and tries several more times. Yep, it's busy for over 15 minutes. So he jogs and walks to the next phone, another five or so miles, and yep, the phone is busy again. By the way, the phone eats about half of his dimes (see, a long time ago!).

Needless to say, he eventually walks and runs the entire 20 miles and is about dead when he gets home. His wife jumps all over him because he has missed his daughter's softball game and annual hotdog cookout. "Why didn't you call?" Well, Bill had meant to get on to his daughter and wife about always being on the phone, but he never had. Do you suppose he overreacted to this conflict now? Suffice it to say he did, and his ex-wife could attest to that. EQ lesson: Address conflict before it gets out of hand. In this area as well as many others, "the end depends upon the beginning" (quote from the movie, *The Emperor's Club*).

In addition to inability to properly and quickly address conflict at the right level at the right time, we see many leaders reporting change avoidance as a nurtured weakness in EQ. We are grouping it with conflict avoidance because both are simply the delaying of emotions and proper action. We say that you have to change with change. That sounds so simple that it may appear trite, but it is not. Humans by nature are creatures of habit and don't want to change when things are OK and sometimes even when things are bad. Many times, prisoners cannot handle freedom, and they do something to get put back in jail. No wonder we avoid change at our place of work. It is normally just easier to keep doing the same thing. We think it is a cheesy saying, but we must embrace change or not progress in every area of life. You will not become a leader, nor will you maintain leadership status, if you don't embrace change.

Lack of awareness of cultural issues is such a detriment in EQ that it is becoming one area in which successful leaders with this problem must change or get left behind. Think about Fidel Castro. He simply does not have a clue. Castro is egotistical and selfish to the nth degree. Castro will go to his grave causing irreparable harm to hundreds of thousands of people. Just think what Cuba could be today with a free market and free society. It is such a shame. We'd like for him to know that he will die not just as an utter failure but as a pure unadulterated disaster.

Bill's niece's husband, Ivan, escaped from Cuba in the early 90s. He thinks America is great, and he is amazed at how he can make money on so many things: cars, houses, labor, restaurants, and so on. Ivan has gained a great cultural awareness, and he understands that Castro is among the many postcard examples of lack of cultural awareness. Without world cultural awareness no one will remain a leader of enterprises in the future. EQ requires one to be aware of cultural issues in the area within which he must operate. And yes, it is different in rural Mississippi and London. And yes, it is different from the heartlands of the Dakotas and Dallas. Bill and Dave have lived and worked in those places and they know the differences.

You may not **like to persuade others**, but the art of persuasion is much needed in management. It's not enough to have ideas if you want to be a leader; you've got to convince others that you have ideas and that it's to their advantage to help you get those ideas implemented. It seems that a lot of people think they are weak at persuading others, mainly because they don't like to try to convince others that their ideas might be right. A simple story might do well here. A number of years back, Dave was teaching an undergraduate strategy class, and one young girl had really been put through the wringer for not being ready on the previous case. Dave suspected that Sara would be ready this time, so he called on her. "Sara, what would you do if you were president of Rocky Mountain Helicopters?" Sara had a great answer and recommended about five things and even said why she recommended the changes. Dave said, "You're wrong." His hope was she'd get a chance to shine. Sara lifted both hands in a sign of defeat and said, "I'm sorry I was wrong." This was not what Dave wanted, but it did turn out to be a teaching moment in which he could explain that we need to be in a position to persuade others of the value of our ideas and suggestions. The lack of desire or ability to persuade others lowers a leader's Emotional Quotient.

Many people are **blinded by emotional attachment** and cannot see the positives or negatives of others. This blindness can be hate or love, disliking or liking; but the effect can be devastating. The validity of a leader's emotional attachment to followers is key. However, it can start one way and go another, and that is OK if a leader is quick to pick up on the need to change the strength and form of attachment to key followers. Many of the leadership problems in the first Clinton administration were caused by Clinton having too many friends in the administration. There is nothing wrong with having confidants in key positions, but there is something wrong with not recognizing when that confidence is no longer warranted.

We often see the situation where a leader decides that a subordinate is no longer useful, then later the situation changes and the leader can't or won't use that person's input even though it's now very appropriate. The key here is to constantly assess others as well as yourself and realize that emotional attachments must be founded in situational and individual real accomplishments. Everyone must prove themselves over and over. We need to develop rapport with those around us that allows us to be truthful with them and tell them when their actions or support must change.

President George W. Bush is still proving his EQ, but we like what we see so far. Many of his closest advisors have differing opinions, yet he uses them and they are effective. Powell didn't agree with Cheney, Rice, or Rumsfeld on Iraq, but he changed and went along with his boss. This shows great EQ for Powell and Bush. Likewise, Rice and Bush disagree on affirmative action and college admissions, and Bush allows Rice to continue to disagree. Again, this shows high EQ on the part of Rice and Bush. She presented her side very clearly but not hurtfully or hatefully. Bush allows these disagreements. We wonder why more people don't give Bush credit for his EQ. EQ is more important than IQ, because when a leader expresses his IQ, there is only one person functioning. When he uses his EQ, multiple people are on the case. Know when to back friends and when not to. Know when to use input from detractors and when not to: exhibit the correct level of EQ.

Using the EQ Matrix

Evaluate yourself in each of the four quadrants, giving yourself a +1 for each of the strengths and a -1 for each of the weaknesses you have. If you can think of strengths or weaknesses that are more appropriate to you than those we have mentioned, score them +1 to -1, but be careful about just making up some traits. Divide some of the traits if you feel it's required. For example, you may be very emotionally aware, which is a positive, but emotionally out of control, which is a negative. Try to be realistic about a replacement trait; it's preferable to use those we have developed from our research with other leaders, which is supported by outside literature.

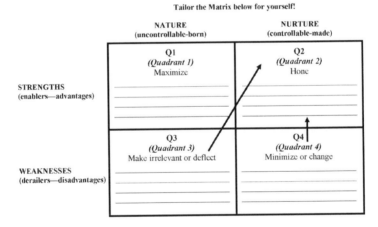

Figure 4.3: YOUR EQ MEASUREMENT AND IMPROVEMENT MATRICES

Evaluate yourself against the reported traits in this Matrix.

	NATURE (uncontrollable-born)	NURTURE (controllable-made)
STRENGTHS (enablers—advantages)	**Q1** _____ commanding presence _____ emotional awareness/control _____ sensing others' emotions _____ entrepreneurial innovativeness _____ (self-IDed trait)	**Q2** _____ emotional maturity _____ manage emotions via reframing _____ emotionally valuating success _____ cultural astuteness _____ (self-IDed trait)
WEAKNESSES (derailers—disadvantages)	**Q3** _____ disruptive irrationality _____ untrustworthiness _____ un-adaptable to change _____ emotional laziness _____ (self-IDed trait)	**Q4** _____ conflict/change avoidance _____ cultural unawareness _____ emotionally-avoid-persuasion _____ blind emotional attachment _____ (self-IDed trait)

Tailor the Matrix below for yourself!

	NATURE (uncontrollable-born)	NURTURE (controllable-made)
STRENGTHS (enablers—advantages)	**Q1** *(Quadrant 1)* Maximize	**Q2** *(Quadrant 2)* Hone
WEAKNESSES (derailers—disadvantages)	**Q3** *(Quadrant 3)* Make irrelevant or deflect	**Q4** *(Quadrant 4)* Minimize or change

Evaluating Your EQ Personal Profile: Strengths and Weaknesses

Doing Something About Your EQ!

Building a high EQ is a result of identifying what you know is under your control and what is not. The basic skills of identifying and ultimately using newfound skills for EQ development will serve you well, but only if you put in much sustained effort. You must practice improving your EQ by outwardly expressing your emotions, not just saying you have a handle on your EQ. Dwelling on the negatives insures you'll stay where you are.

We have observed four things when people evaluate their strengths and weaknesses in EQ.

1. Others don't always agree with our self-assessment as to what our strengths and weakness are.

2. Others normally think that a lot more of your traits are on the controllable side than you do.

3. Many have a negative trait that they potentially could control, but they feel they can't practically control it or at least won't control it.

4. Most people are more emotional than they appear to others.

So, you've identified everything. What now? First, check your evaluations with some trusted people. This is especially important in EQ. Next, come up with a strategy to address how you can work to improve those things identified as "under your control" in order to offset negative effects of factors over which you are relatively sure you have no control. Remember, in each of the four quadrants are three views.

1. First is the real or totally objective view. We simply don't believe humans can have this view; only God can.

2. Second, we see the perceived-as-each-individual-sees-it view. In this area, you need to rectify any discrepancies between how you perceive yourself and how others perceive you. If there is a continual disconnect between what you perceive and what others see, more often than not you should change your perception or at least work as if the perception of others is more representative of reality. Your goal is to get your perceptions as close to reality as humanly possible but with the realization that if the majority of those involved perceive something as true, you have to treat it as truth in order to change it.

3. Third, we see that regardless of perceptions, everything will eventually play out and the ultimate truth will be enacted as it comes into play in given circumstances.

Let's keep on with this topic for awhile. Again, the key is to make perceptions as near reality as possible but with an understanding that perceptions are in fact reality for the perceiver!

A couple of stories here show how some people just are not emotionally equipped yet don't seem to realize it. Jeff was a great computer programmer, yet he could not interact with anyone. You could ask him a yes or no question, and you could not determine his response. He said something like "Yea-oneunk" and shook his head at a diagonal. Ben was another programmer who could not speak to anyone. He walked by people looking down and toward the wall; he would not make eye contact. We later found out that both Ben and Jeff really loved their jobs and thought they fit in nicely and that they liked most everyone. Who could tell?

As We Said in the Introduction, "It's Time to Get Started; If Not Now, When?"

We know the reader should have gained some knowledge in this chapter. Some of the knowledge was based on science, some on logic, some on experience, and some on supposition; but regardless, we know that the important thing is what you do with the knowledge. It's not the EQ knowledge, it's your application of the EQ knowledge that will determine your long-term improvement as a leader.

Before we go on to the next chapter, we want to remind you that effective leadership requires a balanced fit among the many environments, behaviors, contexts, processes, contents, and needs. Figure 4.4 shows the interaction of 1) the leader, 2) the followers, and 3) the environments, which all need to fit. Put your EQ values in the triangle and see if your EQ forms enough of a foundation to help you progress as a leader. Regardless of the level of your current EQ, continue to work to improve it.

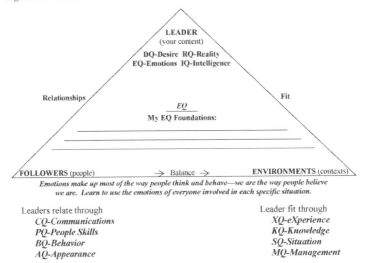

Figure 4.4: YOUR LEADERSHIP LEVERAGE TRIANGLE

EQ Conclusions

"Circumstances make men just as much as men make circumstances" (attributed to Marx in Pinker, 2002, p. 155).

Emotional Quotient is one of the more malleable of the Leadership Quotients. Intelligence Quotient, discussed in our next chapter, is by stark contrast generally considered to be one of the most fixed. In the area of EQ, we feel that the reader should commit to understanding and modifying his EQ. "Why?" you might ask. You should improve your EQ because it can be done, and EQ is a great determinant of leadership success. Lastly, nothing will serve a leader better than EQ improvement. An improved EQ will make all of your relationships better and indeed improve the quality of your life and leadership.

In addition to EQ being a very controllable factor, it is also one where the lines between what's natural and what's nurtured are very blurred. This is the opposite compared to the next section where we discuss IQ. The Intelligence Quotient has been shown to be mostly natural when it is measured in the traditional sense. To bring home this blurring or blending of nature and nurture for EQ, please consider the following about humankind:

> Man is not fully conditioned and determined but rather determines himself whether he gives in to conditions or stands up to them. In other words, man is ultimately self-determining. Man does not simply exist but always decides what his existence will be, what he will become in the next moment.
>
> By the same token, every human being has the freedom to change at any instant. Therefore, we can predict his future only within the large framework of statistical survey referring to a whole group; the individual personality, however, remains essentially unpredictable. The basis for any predictions would be represented by biological, psychological or sociological conditions. Yet one of the main features of human existence is the capacity to rise above such conditions, to grow beyond them. Man is capable of changing the world for the better if possible and of changing himself for the better if necessary.
>
> What he becomes—within the limits of endowment and environment—he has made out of himself. In the concentration camps, for example, in this living laboratory and on this testing ground, we watched and witnessed some of our comrades behave like swine while others behaved like saints. Man has both potentialities within himself; which one is actualized depends on decisions but not on conditions. (Frankl, 1992, pp. 133 and 135)

Your goal is to understand these complexities and make them meaningful and applicable to you and your situation now and as it will be in the future. Most people die regretting not mistakes but never trying. Listed below are some principles that we feel are very pertinent to your EQ improvement quest:

- EQ management is **attention, focus, desire, and locus of control**.

- **We choose because** of what **we value**, what is important to us, and it's a **mistake to think others value** as we do.

- We **don't describe** the world we see, we see the world we describe.

- **Beyond talent lie** discipline, desire, preparation, love, luck—but most of all, endurance.

- **Understand the difference in important and un**important versus **urgent and not** urgent.

- **Replace "try" with "do," and "should" with "could"**: language reveals you.

- Unfortunately, most people **don't improve, they keep playing** to strengths and never do things that are uncomfortable.

- Put yourself in a position to be **confronted in a meaningful way**.

- Don't think **self-esteem** comes from others.

- Realize that success is not a matter **of luck**.

- Reality emerges **as you reinterpret** "your" worlds.

Both Dave and Bill have been through many small trials and tribulations: most were self-made! But one thing we realize is that most of the worries we faced were more worries than realities. Looking back on the several worst days of our lives, we see that they generally played out to be basically nothing. Once a senior college student came by to see Bill at about 3:00 p.m. and was lamenting that she had missed the 1:00 p.m. class (she'd never missed before and the semester was about over). She said, "This has been the worst day of my life! My car would not start as I was going downtown to meet my mother for her birthday lunch. So I borrowed my roommate's car. We parked in a parking garage and I locked the keys in the car and we had to call a locksmith and pay him $30 for about one minute of work to open the car." All Bill could think was, "What an easy life you've had!" After telling this story to a class, Bill received a thank-you e-mail. It was from a young girl with the same story, except that as she hurried out of the parking lot she ran over a lady. After months of anguish the lady completely recovered, and the young girl's insurance covered all expenses and a settlement. This young girl said, "Now, four years later, I see this was not that bad after all. Thanks for talking about life with us and not just strategy. I think I'll be able to handle the next worst day of my life a little better than I did the first one." She improved her EQ four years after the worst day of her life just by listening and empathizing.

One area we are staying away from somewhat is group EQ. That's because we see group EQ as simply a collection of individual EQs. Many times we have been reminded that the consequence or by-product of a group is hiding the poor performers. It is true that leaders with low EQs don't want to improve the performance of poor performers, so they throw them in a group and let the team adjust. Managers need to ask their team members what this does to teamwork in their company. Group EQ has the same effect. You should give a group member time to learn either the job or EQ, but you must decide when to cut your losses and get rid of poor performers or group members with EQs that predict failure in your organization.

Druskat and Wolff (2001) wrote a good article on building a group's EQ, but we simply don't agree with the conclusions of the article. The authors sound to us like professors looking for a topic, not business experts with a proven solution. Druskat and Wolff said, "Inevitably, a team member will indulge in behavior that crosses the line, and the team must feel comfortable calling foul" (p. 84). This is just another example of a group that has one or more members with a poor EQ. The one who causes the problem has exhibited a negative EQ, but so have the group members who do not confront the offender. This case points to the need to insure that individuals learn about their EQ, or at some point, you cut your losses and get rid of them. Time and time again we see that people are simply too cowardly to confront poor performers and instead use training as a crutch. We know that people respond better to demands and strict guidelines of behavior than they do when the leader says, "They just need some training." So we won't waste much more time on group EQ. We just assure you that if you take care of individual EQ problems, you'll have no group EQ problems!

We will close this chapter with a few quotes from the *Field Leadership Manual 2000* (The Southwestern Company). Bill Cosby said, "I don't know the key to success, but the key to failure is trying to please everybody." Thomas J. Watson said, "Nothing so conclusively proves a man's ability to lead others as what he does from day to day to lead himself." Bobby Knight said, "The will to succeed is important, but what's more important is the will to prepare."

On to the IQ chapter to see if we can do anything at all about the intelligence fate has given us.

5

IQ, The Intelligence Quotient

Having a high IQ can become a disincentive to action. People with high IQs and analytical abilities often can see more and more layers to a problem, and as a result, they become paralyzed because they can't see their way through to a solution. When action is needed, they may be unable to take it. Psychologists have studied relationships between IQ and leadership. They have found that during times of relative calm, when there is no great premium on quick action, people with higher IQs are more effective as leaders than are those with lower IQs. But in times of stress, the relationship actually reverses itself. High IQ becomes an impediment to action, and the higher-IQ individual becomes a less effective leader than the lower-IQ one. Thus, the ability to think through alternative courses of action is important, but it is equally important to know when to wait and when to act. (Sternberg, 1996, p. 259)

The chapter on the Emotional Quotient used the ideas of Daniel Goleman to make a contribution to *The Leadership Quotient*. In this chapter on the Intelligence Quotient, we have a couple of authors to thank in particular. First, there is Howard Gardner and his seminal work on IQ, principally through his 1983 book, *Frames of Mind*. Next, we have Robert Sternberg and his work on successful intelligence. In this chapter, we are setting the stage for the traditional definition of IQ as it is approached with physiological testing and research using the ideas of Gardner and others; and we will contrast that with Sternberg's *Successful Intelligence*. Then we will describe the relationship of IQ to the Leadership Quotient.

While we don't want to limit the historical importance of IQ, we are convinced that you don't need to understand the concept any more in depth than we present it in this chapter. The Leadership Quotient relies on certain types of IQ, but not the type measured by traditional IQ tests. Sternberg writes, "IQ tests: Measuring IQ not Intelligence" (1988, title of Chapter 2). That's why it is *not* very important for you as an $LQ^{\copyright}$ leader to have a deep understanding about your tested IQ, but it is important for you to understand how your testable IQ can help or hurt your Leadership Quotient.

106

We need to address the question, "Is intelligence one thing or many? Clearly, it is many" (Sternberg, 1988, p. 72). In yet another work Sternberg says, "None of the currently available explicit theories seem to do justice to the full scope of intelligence, broadly defined. Perhaps no one theory ever could, whether that theory is explicit or implicit.…Although many of us *act* as though intelligence is what intelligence tests measure, few of us *believe* it" (Sternberg, 1985, pp. 39 and 43). We encourage you also to take specific note of the warning that begins this chapter: a high IQ does not always correlate with an effective *LQ*©.

For *LQ*© purposes, we like to remember the following definitions and comments:

> Intelligence is the mental capability of emitting contextually appropriate behavior in these regions in the experiential continuum that involve response to novelty or automatization of information processing as a function of metacomponents, performance components and knowledge acquisition components.…Even the most highly regarded of the currently available measures of intelligence, such as the Wechsler and Stanford-Binet intelligence tests, fail to do justice to their creators' conceptions of the nature of intelligence. (Sternberg, pp. 128 and 336)

The Relationship of IQ to *LQ*©

> *"[An intellectual is] a man who takes more words than necessary to tell more than he knows.…One who can think without moving his lips" (respectively, Dwight D. Eisenhower and Anonymous in Dillon-Malone, 2000, p. 162).*

As with the other quotients presented to this point, the individual and interactive effects of IQ often get applied in an unbalanced, inappropriate, or just plain wrong way that does not fit the people or environment involved. We want to state clearly that all things must fit the situation and people at hand, and they must be viewed regarding your wisdom to improve and contribute. The understanding of intelligence and the wisdom to apply what it can provide is the very essence of overall *LQ*©. You must realize that your tangible qualities related to IQ in and of themselves will NOT drive your success as a leader regardless of how high your tested IQ might be.

Intelligence is the best known of the quotients and is commonly thought of as "mental capacity." However, intelligence is a difficult concept. Most psychologists now agree that intelligence is a highly complex amalgam of a wide range of different sets of knowledge, skills, and abilities which are at best extremely hard to measure and define. Though IQ tests are designed to measure reasoning power, they are not totally indicative of true intelligence. Many feel that IQ tests measure how well someone can adapt to the form of assessment and that is in itself indicative of *true* intelligence. IQ as we know it does seem to predict how well someone can perform in the American educational system, but not how successful he will be in the many other facets of life. You probably know someone who earned all A's but failed at "life." Perhaps this explains the colloquial absent-minded professors we all know? In one study, IQs for professors and researchers were reported as 134, 128 for physicians and surgeons, 119 for accountants, and 85 for factory packers and sorters (Howard, 1991; we like this study because we are professors!). As we will see later, these scores may have more to do with the test than with those being tested! Or it may simply prove, as we've thought for some time, that IQ is an excellent measure of how well one will do in America's educational system and on college admissions tests. We have written this book for that very reason: There is a difference between IQ and $LQ^{©}$. Recall the "Asian intelligence myth" that provides a good example of the impact of IQ and how hard it is to judge. When using grades as a measure of performance, Asian students in American universities *perform* at a level that indicates their IQs are about 20 points higher. *Actually*, they are only a couple of points higher (Pinker, 2002).

Extending further, we see in Howard Gardner's pioneering book, *Frames of Mind* (1983), his notion of many types of intelligence. Gardner noted seven basic types of intelligence: verbal, mathematical-logical, spatial, kinesthetic, musical, interpersonal, and intrapersonal. Gardner's work seems to explain why traditional IQ tests are poor at predicting success in many of life's endeavors, such as leadership.

IQ is certainly a factor in leadership, but by no means is it the only factor or the most important. A high IQ can possibly help an interested person learn more about a situation and the people involved in that situation, thus allowing the high-IQ person to become more effective or successful. Or it could be that because of IQ someone just coasts along. We've seen both, but more of the latter.

Though IQ is important, it does not take as much intelligence as you might think to have a high Leadership Quotient. History has shown that people like Ronald Reagan and John Kennedy were great leaders who certainly were intelligent, but by no means were they mental giants. Yet many other very capable leaders were held back because it was assumed their IQs were *too* high. We suppose that some prospective leaders are so smart they simple don't see the need to build their other quotients. It's very normal to rely too heavily on your strengths and not try to improve your weaknesses. The Measurement and Improvement Matrices in each Leadership Quotient are designed to overcome that natural tendency. In our Ph.D. quest (this is where we met in 1990), we saw the smartest person never complete the program. As we all have witnessed: in many endeavors, brains are not enough.

The leadership literature is replete with theories espousing IQ, EQ, or a combination of both as predictors of successful leadership. Most have found, as Drucker said: "There seems to be little correlation between a man's effectiveness and intelligence…Brilliant men are often strikingly ineffectual; they fail to realize that the brilliant insight is not by itself achievement" (cited in Henninger, 2002, p. A16). Likewise, none of the major leadership theories—behavioral, trait, situational, contextual, or contingent approaches—fully answer our need to understand leadership as definable, teachable, and improvable.

The Leadership Quotient is a comprehensive view that includes the traditional theories we just mentioned, packaged in terms of the 12 definable, measurable, and improvable quotients. It is our belief that we must extend our understanding of IQ and how it is a building block for success in most professions. As with EQ, and the nature versus nurture debate, *LQ©* is blessed with a great book that gets us closer to the understanding of the true makeup of leadership and leaders. That book is Robert J. Sternberg's (1996) *Successful Intelligence: How Practical and Creative Intelligence Determine Success in Life.* Sternberg starts with a comprehensive description of the traditional methods of measuring intelligence: IQ testing. He then discusses how traditional intelligence measures were developed and what they really mean. Sternberg then discards the total importance of traditional IQ and replaces it with "successful intelligence," which he says is the kind of intelligence that matters in reaching life's important goals.

> We must never lose sight of the fact that what really matters most in the world is not inert intelligence but successful intelligence: that balanced combination of analytical, creative, and practical thinking skills. Successful intelligence is not an accident; it can be nurtured and developed in our schools by providing students, even at a very early age, with curricula that will challenge their creative and practical intelligence, not only their analytical skills. It is my contention that successful intelligence should be taught, because it is the kind of intelligence that will be the most valuable and rewarding in the real world after school—both in our work and in our personal lives. Our ultimate goal in understanding and increasing our intelligence should be the full realization in our lives of the intellectual potential we all have. (p. 269)
>
> Those who can recall facts, who may even be able to reason with those facts, don't necessarily know how to use them to make a difference, either to themselves or to anyone else. (p. 11)
>
> Conventional tests of intelligence are viewed as measures of only a small part of intelligence, not as measures of most or all of it. They focus on inert academic intelligence and not active successful intelligence....Successful intelligence, as I view it, involves analytical, creative, and practical aspects....Intelligence cannot possibly be measured in any large degree solely by the use of multiple-choice tests. Successful intelligence cannot be measured by such tests at all....Intelligence is primarily an issue not of amount but balance, of knowing when and how to use analytic, creative, and practical abilities....Schools tend to reward abilities that later in life are not very important....Intelligence is partially heritable and partially environmental, but it is extremely difficult to separate the two sources of variation because they interact in many different ways....An important element of intelligence is flexibility....Successfully intelligent people figure out their strengths and their weaknesses, and then find ways to capitalize on their strengths—make the most of what they do well—and to correct for or remedy their weaknesses—find ways around what they don't do well, or make themselves good enough to get by. (pp. 47-49)

Sternberg goes on to discuss such standardized tests as the SAT, MCAT, LSAT, GMAT, etc. He says those tests are measuring the same thing that is measured by traditional IQ testing: analytical abilities. "They should be referred to as measuring *academic intelligence.* Furthermore, the schooling on which they are based is Western schooling, which many children in the world do not receive" (p. 68). In all of these tests, he says we seem to place more weight on the predictive measure than on whether a person can actually do a thing or not: like preferring the weather forecast over the weather. In fact, the tests

> may predict people's grades in college with pseudoquantitative precision (p. 35)....And the perhaps sad fact is that most college admissions officers find high-SAT types to be just the kind of students the professors want: good at memorizing material, competent in academic skills, and savvy in test taking. (p. 37)
>
> [Sternberg asks,] "Why do we pay more attention to predictors than to performance?" (p. 140)... [He says further that everyone has intellectual strengths that can be developed, but that not everyone has developed them equally.] Yet people have enormous capacity to develop and manifest successful intelligence; how strange that so often we don't let them (p. 45)....By thinking to learn, they learn to think. (p. 151)

Sternberg writes an interesting analogy about why doctors, lawyers, and professors score high on IQ tests. He says it would be like requiring that they all be over 6' tall to get into their respective schools and then after they graduate measuring their height! Yes, they would all be over 6'. Likewise, when you require an IQ measure to get into the school, no wonder the IQ measures of graduates are high.

There is a reasonable apologetic for the use of standardized tests as a screen for college admissions. Most admissions personnel will admit that standardized tests are a forced choice. While they may predict success poorly, they are better than anything else that has been proposed. Colleges and universities use the standardized tests because they help the institutions toward a better use of their very limited resources: professors, classrooms, and dorm space. It's wise to accept only students who have increased chances of success.

These variations of IQ tests used for admissions to the professional schools might even be eliminated in favor of direct brainwave testing of intelligence in the near future. Zimmer (2003, p. E11) reported: "If neuroimaging grows simultaneously more powerful and less expensive, it stands to become a bigger part of our lives. Neuroscientists are now pinpointing brain regions that are most active in those who score high on intelligence tests. Will we judge the prospects of children someday with a brain scan instead of the SAT?" That's a distinct possibility. However, Sternberg simply said that our measuring methods and especially our teaching methods are simply wrongheaded.

> I have now been a psychologist for twenty-one years, and one thing of which I am certain is that I have never—not even once—had to do in the profession what I needed to do to get an A in the introductory course, as well as in some of the other courses. In particular, I've never had to memorize a book or a lecture (p. 125)....Telling students what to do is often unrealistic with respect to what will be required for later success (p. 130)....Academic tasks are given to you on a silver platter....Academic problems are often of little or even no intrinsic interest....Academic problems are

disembedded from people's ordinary experience….Academic problems often have just one "correct" answer. (pp. 229-230)

Through years of management experience and management teaching, we have never encountered—or heard an MBA student tell of encountering—a management problem that was presented as a multiple-choice question! In the classroom, we are much more inclined to give general directions and let the students figure out what is expected. Bill is known at his university for the general way in which he writes the senior project requirements. The instructions read, "Do a project." This often leads to multiple questions about form, format, length, media, topic, and outcome assessment. In one particular class meeting, a long question-and-answer session was finally ended when a student in the front row turned to his classmates and stated loudly, "It's like he wants us to figure it out for ourselves." Amen. Dave and Bill agree with Sternberg: "Thus, from our point of view, what students learn in courses is truly only a minor part of the college or any other educational experience" (Sternberg, 1996, p. 243).

Sternberg went on to identify the following six steps in problem-solving that need to be well understood for development of successful intellect: 1) recognition of the problem; 2) definition of the problem; 3) formulation of a strategy for solving the problem; 4) proper representation of information—avoiding our preconceived notions; mental sets, frames, models, fixation; 5) allocation of resources; and 6) monitoring and evaluation. Sternberg writes that the most important step is defining the problem, because if you solve the wrong problem, you have done only harm and no good for your real problem. Therefore, when a teacher just asks questions, he is not providing students with the most important part of problem solving: formulating the question.

On the topic of statistics and why the standardized tests are still the norm for admissions into almost all colleges and universities, Sternberg said: "I believe that academics and others love statistics because they cover up how poorly things are going at the level of individual cases. When statistical measures account for 10 or even 25 percent of the variation in a group, the level of individual prediction is quite poor" (1996, p. 228). We have to figure out a way to measure the 75% versus the 25% we are currently measuring. Hopefully, the changes to the SAT, that is, the requiring of essays, will help some in this area. But we have our strong doubts that the essay testing can be effectively graded. Three reviewers cannot grade over a million essays. The ability to look through bad grammar into the intelligence of the writer is a difficult judgmental task. The reviewers should be looking for experience and potential, not merely past academic success or good writing skills.

As experienced college professors, we admit our limitations in this endeavor. Even after a semester or two of personal interaction with students, it is still very difficult for us to judge intelligence from a written paper. This is a complex issue, but it's certainly an area we must address if we desire to help our readers more clearly understand their Leadership Quotient.

Ultimately, Sternberg lists the common characteristics and attributes that are found among successfully intelligent people (the list is an exact quote of his, but after each of the components he gives long explanations, which are not included here; this material is found in Chapter 8 of his 1996 book).

Successful intelligent people:

1. motivate themselves....By letting students lead me, I have entered areas that I never would have explored had I insisted on their doing exactly what I, not they, wanted.

2. learn to control their impulses.

3. know when to persevere.

4. know how to make the most of their abilities.

5. translate thought into action.

6. have a product orientation....They want results....If we demand that students merely "consume" information and feed it back on tests, once again we are depriving them of the kind of learning experience that will be of greatest benefit in the real world, and that is not how to use their intelligence.

7. complete tasks and follow through.

8. are initiators.

9. are not afraid to risk failure [or]...make mistakes, but not the same mistake twice.

10. don't procrastinate....We found that fewer senior executives had a variety of strategies for fighting procrastination. More senior and more successful executives did not have them for the simple reason that they had no need for such strategies.

11. accept fair blame.

12. reject self-pity.

13. are independent.

14. seek to surmount personal difficulties.

15. focus and concentrate to achieve their goals.

16. spread themselves neither too thin nor too thick.

17. have the ability to delay gratification.

18. have the ability to see the forest and the trees.

19. have a reasonable level of self-confidence and a belief in their ability to accomplish their goals.

20. balance analytical, creative, and practical thinking.

Following are some of the definitions of intelligence Sternberg includes: 1) the capacity to learn from experience and adapt to your environment; 2) metacognition—that is, understanding and control of your own thinking processes; 3) knowing when to use abilities; 4) beyond adaptation including an understanding of when to get out versus adapt; 5) beyond following trends to setting trends. But Sternberg ends by simply saying: "Successfully intelligent people buy low and sell high. They defy the crowd and, eventually, come to lead it" (1996, p. 189). "Thus, the true measure of your intelligence is not in a test score; it is in your willingness to develop your own talents" (1996, p. 150). The Measurement and Improvement Matrices that accompany each Leadership Quotient are an indication that we agree with Sternberg. Our ongoing crusade is to improve the leadership and life success of our readers. So when we write about the *LQ*©, we give you the opportunity to measure and improve it.

Perhaps it would be useful here to list the subtest or indexes of items tested for on a normal IQ test. This is not a primer on testing—there are plenty of those. Our intent is to make the reader relatively aware of what items are covered on IQ tests. Gregory, in his 1999 text, *Foundations of Intellectual Assessment,* has a very interesting table on "Mean Gains in WAIS-II Subtests, IQs and Index Scores" (p. 129). The table shows in summary form the Subtest/Scale/Index as follows:

• Vocabulary

• Similarities

• Arithmetic

• Digit Span

• Information

• Comprehension

• Letter-Number

- Picture Completion

- Digit Symbol-Coding

- Block Design

- Matrix Reasoning

- Picture Arrangement

- Symbol Search

- Object Assembly

- Verbal IQ

- Performance IQ

- Full Scale IQ

- Verbal Comprehension Index

- Perceptual Organization Index

- Working Memory Index

- Processing Speed Index

Though these sub-measures may not be totally meaningful, the pattern that is being measured with the Wechsler Adult Intelligence Scale is very clear. This test is a standard for measuring intelligence in the "normal" way. It has its efficacy as well as its limitations, many of which have been noted earlier in this chapter.

Guilford, in his seminal 1967 work, *The Nature of Human Intelligence,* gives 120 measures of intellect presented in a three-dimensional figure. The 5 operational dimensions are evaluation, convergent production, divergent production, memory, and cognition. The six product-factor dimensions are units, classes, relations, systems, transformations, and implications. The four content dimensions are figural, symbolic, semantic, and behavioral factors. This gives 120 measures: 5 X 6 X 4 as represented in Guilford's cube.

The purpose of this IQ chapter is not to gain an understanding of traditional methods of measurement, nor is it to explain the factors of intelligence from a testing definitional view. The purpose is for you to gain an understanding of your practical IQ as a means of measuring and improving your own personal Leadership Quotient.

History is replete with examples of leaders who have improved their own Leadership Quotients by identifying their shortcomings and working to improve them, albeit without the specific formula stated in this book. Abraham Lincoln, Thomas Edison, Woodrow Wilson, and Teddy Roosevelt—who was never without a book—are exemplars of both formally educated and uneducated leaders who worked to improve their IQs.

From a natural view, intelligence certainly developed early in the evolution of man. Mankind's physical shortcomings surely favored natural selection of the more intelligent humans who could figure out how to avoid danger, get the best mate or avoid a bad mate, and use all the skills they had to maximum advantage for all matters of livelihood.

Why Is IQ Next?

> *"Successfully intelligent people are flexible in adapting to the roles they need to fulfill. They recognize that they will have to change the way they work to fit the task and situation at hand, and then they analyze what these changes will have to be and make them (p. 153)....All of us know people who succeed in school but fail in their careers, or vice versa. They are a constant reminder that there must be more to success than school smarts....Making It in the Real World" (Sternberg, 1996, p. 220).*

You will note that IQ is below DQ, RQ, and EQ in our Leadership Triangle. That's because we consider IQ less important than the previous quotients. IQ is a factor that can help leaders, but as we have discussed, it can also be a hindrance. It is preferable that you think not of your specific IQ but of your overall successful intelligence, which we define as IQ that leads to $LQ^{©}$. That's because we believe our definition of IQ is more directly related to becoming a more effective leader. Also, successful intellect is more controllable than traditional IQ. A significant amount of IQ in its traditional sense is required to be a successful leader, but it is not that much above average. With large amounts of DQ and EQ, a leader can overcome many of the limitations of IQ as it is traditionally measured. Yes, it will be harder to get into institutions of higher learning without a high IQ, but it's not impossible. If you will think about the best leaders you know, we are confident that many of them did not get into the greatest universities or make the best grades, but they do exhibit a leadership intellect that is often vastly superior to that of many doctors, lawyers, and professors. We feel that the biggest drawback to an average IQ, as measured by traditional testing, is a person knowing he has an average IQ and allowing it to limit him. The second biggest drawback is the testing that is required to enter institutions of higher learning in the U.S.

If you want to be a leader and you feel your traditional IQ is low, work to improve your $LQ^{©}$ IQ (successful intelligence) and you'll improve both your traditional IQ and your $LQ^{©}$ IQ.

Description of the Intelligence Quotient and its Dimensions

As we begin the description of the IQ and its dimensions, we ask you to recall the generic version of *LQ*© as it applies to IQ. Remember that we have labeled them as follows:

Quadrant 1—the natural strengths
Quadrant 2—the nurtured strengths
Quadrant 3—the natural weaknesses
Quadrant 4—the nurtured weaknesses

You may want to refer to Figure 5.2 as we describe the dimensions of the Intelligence Quotient. Following are your goals throughout your *LQ*© journey:

1. Use your natural strengths as enablers to your best advantage: maximize Quadrant 1.

2. More fully develop and use your nurtured strengths: hone Quadrant 2.

3. Make irrelevant or deflect your natural weaknesses that are derailers and disadvantageous to you: deflect Quadrant 3.

4. Minimize or improve nurtured weaknesses: minimize or change Quadrant 4.

You will recall from previous chapters our admonition that genetic propensities or heritable traits are not totally duplicated. These inherited traits are probabilistic and impressionable through environmental influences. Again, if that were not the case we would see identical twins always thinking, acting, and feeling exactly the same. We are classifying things as natural when they are relatively stable over time as could be determined by some standardized tests. In fact, we would like for you to classify as natural things that you are not likely to change because of the difficulty or just because you don't want to change them. For example, a couple of our friends don't want to exercise. That's fine, but when they say they don't because they do not believe it's *good* for them, we want to choke them—and then there would be no need for them to breathe better! Their argument seems irrational, but we don't see it changing, so we would encourage them to put those traits under inherited because of their unchangeable nature. Do the same with IQ traits; just admit them and call them natural if you are not going to change them.

IQ is crystallized and rooted in biological evolution but not unchangeable because we are creatures of free choice and thought. We cannot always avoid our naturally inherited IQ, but we can change our feeling toward it and see it as much more malleable, and work to improve it. An example will make the point more clearly. One of our students is considered "so smart it's scary" by professors and fellow students, and in fact, he knows quite a lot about everything. When Dave was discussing his future with him, the student told Dave his IQ was about 125. This is indeed 25 points above average, but it is not off the charts. In further discussions, the student revealed that he has read some 50-100 pages a day beyond his course requirements for the last seven or eight years. Can you see how this college senior seems 10 times smarter than his fellow students? He does read about 10 times what most other students do. So he is brilliant when he talks to anyone, though his intellect would not be considered brilliant. Contrast this with another person we know who has an IQ of 129 but had read only three books by the time he was 35 years of age. How much smarter do you think the first person *appears* than the second? A lot.

Keep Figures 5.1 and 5.2 in mind as you review the following normally identified IQ-related traits and seek to understand where you might stand on those traits.

Figure 5.1: THE LEADERSHIP LEVERAGE TRIANGLE

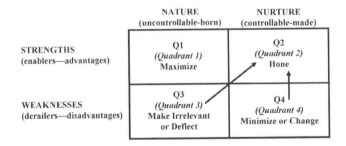

LEADER
(content)
Do you know your IQ?

Relationships   Fit

Understand and improve your EQ, RQ, and DQ
foundations through Successful Intelligence

FOLLOWERS (people)   → Balance →   ENVIRONMENTS (contexts)

LQ© IQ can be greatly improved. **Figure out why and how and then continually do it!**

Leaders relate through   Leader fit through
  CQ-Communications   *XQ-eXperience*
  PQ-People Skills   *KQ-Knowledge*
  BQ-Behavior   *SQ-Situation*
  AQ-Appearance   *MQ-Management*

Forget what you've heard about IQ or what your IQ of old is and learn what your *LQ©* IQ is so
that you can make it better or negate your old IQ if it's too high.

Figure 5.2: IQ MEASUREMENT AND IMPROVEMENT MATRIX

	NATURE (uncontrollable-born)	NURTURE (controllable-made)
STRENGTHS (enablers—advantages)	Q1 *(Quadrant 1)* Maximize	Q2 *(Quadrant 2)* Hone
WEAKNESSES (derailers—disadvantages)	Q3 *(Quadrant 3)* Make Irrelevant or Deflect	Q4 *(Quadrant 4)* Minimize or Change

Normal Natural IQ Strengths—Quadrant 1 of the IQ 2X2 Matrix

"Adults possess and exhibit many kinds of gifts, creativity, scholarship, leadership, physical, and so on, but not all are gifted in every respect" (source unknown).

The very obvious nature of this statement might elicit a response like, "No joke, Sherlock!" Related to the role of heredity in human traits, we should remember, "Even though individual studies may be faulted for particular reasons, we feel that in their totality they present a convincing story.…People accepting a role for heredity in human psychological traits are often suspected of being conservative politically, yet it should be remembered that heredity not only makes children similar to their parents, but also at times makes them dissimilar" (Vandenberg and Vogler, 1985, p. 3). "Most accounts in the psychological literature assume that intelligence is an innate capacity or learning potential" (Humphreys, 1985, p. 201), and this is what this first trait is all about. We will call it **memory, and it is the basis for most scholastically exhibited talents**.

Indeed, most professors have this kind of intelligence. Memory is the basis from which one could bi- and tri-forcate. That is how people bring together two or more things to generate a new thing or idea, and how they split things apart into understandable units. Without a good memory one cannot remember several things that could possibly be combined in a new and different way or for new and different purposes. There is no need to quibble about this point: There are many kinds of intelligence. Earlier in this chapter, we cited Guilford's list of 120 kinds of intelligence!

"Observations in the wild suggests that a single nutcracker hides some 30,000 seeds, more than half of which it is able to find over the next six months" (Mackintosh, 1994, p. 30). A good memory in and of itself is not enough. You must be able to apply it. Bill's dad, A. L. Service, could quote every poem you ever heard in your life. He had an unbelievable ability to read a poem once or twice and quote it. While he might miss a word or two now and then, it was uncanny how accurately he could quote a poem. He said it was because "I just know what the poet would say next." He loved poetry and would have loved to be a college literature professor. However, A. L. lacked one thing: the self-discipline to take a course from a professor he didn't like or complete a course which he was not excited about. A. L. finally gave up in his early 50s and never received a college degree. In fact, he graduated from high school only because he quoted "The Prisoner of Chillon." Can you imagine having a professor who could quote all of the poems you studied in college? A. L. could, but he never used those talents in an academic setting. That story provides evidence that just a high IQ in a limited area is of no use unless it is applied correctly. That's what we want you to gain as a result of reading *The Leadership Quotient*: the ability to apply your talents so they fit the people you encounter in the environments in which you find yourself.

Again, we will sidestep the temptation to argue about many other types of intellect than IQ. We will present some of them in the other chapters of this book, but we would say that people use their intellects *not* to create anything new, but to simply rearrange what is already there. God creates; humans discover. So what we call intelligence is merely the ability to discover and explain in a way that sounds impressive to others.

Michelangelo did not create the statue of David, he simply "found it" in a massive piece of rock. From the dictionary comes *War and Peace*, and from nature come quantum physics and the theory of relativity. In fact, just some 40 words make up 40% of the total of Shakespeare's collected works (Wills, 2003). Thus, a memory is required even though:

It is because what he said was not already known that we regard Einstein—and Newton, Faraday, Darwin, and other great innovators—as exceptionally intelligent. This is not the "intelligence" of existing knowledge. It is the "intelligence" of discovering or creating new knowledge. So, we find two very different kinds of intelligence: intelligence of stored knowledge and intelligence of processing, for problem solving. I suggest we may usefully call these potential intelligence and kinetic intelligence. Although distinct as concepts, they are found together intermixed, for some knowledge is needed for solving problems and some initiative is needed to apply knowledge appropriately. (Gregory, 1994, pp. 13-14)

Another area where intellect seems to surface as a natural ability is **rational adaptability, where we see those who are practical yet creative**. Chester Nimitz was appointed commander of the U.S. Navy in the Pacific after the Japanese attack on Pearl Harbor. His planning, strategy, and tactics were considered brilliant, as was his use of staff and resources. The bold tactics used in the Battle of Midway have gone down in naval history as a prototype, and indeed Nimitz was responsible for turning the tide of the war in the Pacific toward the U.S.'s favor. Nimitz exhibited a practical and creative adaptability that could be seen as a model of a God-given type of intellect. Many people might adapt, yet few can be creative in a practical way that manages risk. The adage that fortune favors the bold is indeed true. There is a type of brilliance that follows those who knowingly take calculated audacious steps to reach success. Nimitz without a doubt exhibited a rare kind of intellect where creativity and practicality come together at the most appropriate of times, maybe even changing the course of history.

Many computer geeks had more expertise than Bill Gates. But while his cohorts were playing games among a chorus of "gee-whiz" comments, it was Gates who put the elements together to create value via computer use. Do you have that type of intelligence? It's the kind that allows you to see how something used in one industry can be applied to another. It's the ability to take existing products and services and bundle them in new ways that provide value for consumers.

You have probably heard a person's intellect described as **quick or bright; often this person is considered a forecaster who can envision what's ahead**. Former Federal Reserve Board Chairman Alan Greenspan exhibited that type of talent by discovering a nearly flawless formula for interest rate adjustments that kept the economy growing while avoiding inflation and deflation. Comedian Robin Williams thinks so fast, you wonder if he has Attention Deficit Disorder. How can he process information so quickly to produce jokes instantaneously? Surely he has a superior intellect of this type. Then we see athletes, like football quarterback Joe Montana and basketball star Kevin Garnett, who adapt immediately to the defense that's constantly changing. Visionaries of the past, such as Churchill, must have been quite intelligent. The jury is still out on President George W. Bush and his move into Iraq. History may be able to tell us if he slowed terrorism or sped it up. We only hope and pray that peace will come to the Middle East and many lives on the Arab and Israeli sides will be made more worth living; if so, George W. Bush will be counted as a visionary.

This bright type of "uniquely exhibited" intelligence seems to be a natural trait in many, though it could be argued as nurtured. Our research with multiple people who have completed the Leadership Quotient questions encourages us to categorize this type of intelligence as natural. This quick-thinking intelligence has two parts: first, the ability to envision a future that's different than the present; and second, the intuition to act on it at precisely the correct time. Reagan knew *when* to call on Mikhail Gorbachev to "tear down this wall," ending the Cold War.

A lot of geniuses throughout history have exhibited superior **analytical, multivariant, and inductive thinking** that seems to be natural. Since we are talking about IQ—which is a psychological construct—we should mention Sigmund Freud's observations about genius. In *A General Introduction to Psychoanalysis*, Freud maintained that a genius is a person who "longs to attain honor, power, riches, and the love of women, but he lacks the means of achieving these gratifications. So,…he turns away from reality and transfers all his interest and his libido to the creation of wishes in the life of fantasy, from which the way might readily lead to neurosis" (Freud in Wolman, 1985, p. 859). Freud himself was perhaps the least multivariant thinker: for him, all problems stem from a lack of sexual fulfillment, and humans are driven by a single desire. We have dedicated an entire chapter to desire, called "The Desire Quotient," where we discussed how wanting to obtain a goal makes a large contribution to reaching it.

Wolman strongly disagrees with Freud and says, "Creative work is a combination of great abilities combined with superb self-discipline, and mental disorder reduces and may destroy any creative effort" (p. 859). Wolman continues on this subject: "Maslow (1970) studied the lives of several prominent people, such as Einstein, Beethoven, Lincoln, and others. On the basis of this study, he prepared a list of 15 traits of individuals who reached a high level of self-actualization.

1. The individuals who found self-actualization live very close to reality and judge life in a realistic and accurate manner.

2. Self-actualized individuals accept themselves for whatever they are and, at the same time, they are ready to accept others.

3. Self-actualized individuals display a great deal of spontaneous behavior; although they avoid anti-social or unusual actions, they show a great deal of originality and spontaneity in their thinking and overt behavior.

4. These people are usually devoted to solving a general problem. Their life is perceived as a mission rather than a satisfaction of their own personal needs.

5. Once in a while they have to move away from people in order to contemplate in solitude the problems they are coping with and to develop a more detached viewpoint.

6. They are not conformists. They develop their own ideas, rather independent of the *Zeitgeist* and cultural influences of their times.

7. The people who found self-actualization appreciate life; although they are not naïve optimists, they love life and they admire its beauty.

8. Some of them can reach beyond observable facts and have a deep feeling of ecstasy going beyond usual human experiences.

9. All of them are very much involved with social problems and display sympathy and compassion for humanity.

10. They develop close personal relations with a small number of friends.

11. Their approach to other people is thoroughly democratic, and they show respect for all other individuals regardless of race, creed, age and so on.

12. They would never choose inappropriate means to reach their goals. They enjoy just as much the road to achievement as they do their final goal.

13. Most of them have a good sense of humor.

14. They are creative and have aesthetic inclinations; they are interested in poetry, science, music and inventions.

15. Throughout their lives they retain intellectual independence and an independent outlook on life" (Wolman, 1985, p. 860).

Although not totally applicable to this chapter on IQ, these 15 so-called traits help us understand this natural trait of analytical, multivariant, and inductive thinking. It could be argued that Freud used non-multivariant thinking in his statement, while Maslow's 15 traits of exceptional people do exhibit a large amount of analysis and induction. Mackintosh reminds us of the complexity of intelligence: "A further source of temptation here is that we have a single word, 'intelligence,' for what we are talking about, as though there were a single thing or unitary trait for that word to refer to" (1994, p. 8).

Normal Natural IQ Weaknesses—Quadrant 3 of the IQ 2X2 Matrix

In this quadrant, we have compiled an amalgam of traits that don't seem to relate very closely. Our only defense is the one used by the X-ray technician, "I don't write 'em, I just read 'em." That's what we've done with many of these leadership traits: reporting what others have told us as they complete the Leadership Quotient.

We start with a **poor memory, which sometimes results in a poor vocabulary**. Many other things can be the cause of a poor vocabulary, and poor memory does not always result in poor vocabulary. But these two traits are reported together quite often in *LQ*© completion. In fact, very often the two are somewhat related.

Older people often suffer from a poor memory even though they are quite intelligent and can solve problems at a high level, given some time. Both of us have "senior moments" even though we are very active with young people and are required to keep mentally sharp so we can debate strategic management cases with experienced MBA students—whose intellect is often greater than our own! This makes the point quite well: You don't have to be the *smartest* person in the room to *lead* the people in the room.

This mental stimulation is often lacking in older people and seems to explain why they cannot remember things as quickly as they could earlier in life. Loss of practice dulls the ability to recall facts and problem-solving acumen. It has become widely accepted that continued interaction and use of memory is a good way to keep it. A recent article in the *Wall Street Journal*, "Lobes of Steel: Giving Your Memory a Workout," suggested very strongly that training may tone your brain just as the gym tones your muscles. The article cites many university courses on memory-training. "More recent studies have bolstered this notion that memory, like a flabby midsection, can be toned even late in life….If you want to exercise your brain, there are plenty of ways to do that…from reading to traveling to staying socially active" (Wysocki, 2003, pp. D1 and D8). Of course we know that exercise, diet, and physical and mental health play a large part in retaining what "natural" memory all of us seem to have in our earlier lives. Disregarding this somewhat normal decline of memory, it still seems that some people are blessed with a good memory; therefore, some must have a poor memory or we would have no way to say someone has a good memory!

Dave played the saxophone in high school, then didn't touch the instrument for 22 years. He found his nephew's sax sitting around unused, so he took it home and started tinkering with it. Suddenly, he was playing! It's frightening what's in your brain. Even more frightening: Experts agree that you never really forget anything, you just have trouble recalling it. High Intelligence Quotient leaders have the ability to recall the right facts at the right time to gain the followership of others.

Many examples indicate that a poor vocabulary lowers a person's Leadership Quotient. Harvey was born and raised in New York City, and worked his way through college driving a New York City cab. He talked fast and aggressively, as the stereotypical New Yorker does. Harvey incorrectly assumed that southerners thought slowly because they talked slowly. He soon realized that they were often brighter than he. He also realized that though he used good English, as did many of the southerners he could not understand, they were just not using the same brand of the English language he was. Learn the distinction between accents and word usage versus just poor grammar.

When Bill spent a semester in London, his wife recalls the look he got from English workmen as he asked them, "Do y'all want me to carry you upstairs and show you the problem?" Also, a young Russian Jewish immigrant could not understand being carried around the building, or what credit meant. Often poor grammar is obvious and often it's simply in the ears of the listener. Our point in this section is that IQ contributes to a heightened Leadership Quotient when the leader is able to use language in a way that helps followers identify with the leader and thus follow her.

We recall a couple of pro football players who played for the Houston Oilers years ago. Hoyle Granger was a Cajun who simply did not sound intelligent. Ode Burrell was very intelligent, but when he said, "thnk em guys tat block ferme," on national television, it gave the impression that all Mississippi State graduates were dumb. In fact, it was dialect and vocabulary, not IQ. Recall the story about the pro football player who said, after a devastating loss, "This is just football with blocking and tackling, it ain't rocket surgery." Now *he* was dumb. If you want to have a high Leadership Quotient, don't confuse low intellect with other problems. Often in business negotiations it's better to be smarter than you appear, as opposed to appearing smarter than you are.

A low ability to apply IQ is one we have all seen. Parents like to think this about their children. After coaxing a bright but unmotivated student through a senior-level strategic management class, Dave commented to the student's mother, "We know he inherited the brains, we just wonder what he's done with them!"

Some basic statistical analysis helps. Do you know where "all the women are strong, all the men are good-looking, and all the children are above average"? It's Garrison Keillor's mythical hometown, Lake Wobegon, Minnesota. Each weekly segment of his radio variety show, *A Prairie Home Companion,* ends with a story he's made up about the people and happenings in Lake Wobegon. He ends each story with, "And that's the news from Lake Wobegon, where all the women are strong, all the men are good-looking, and all the children are above average." Hold it: How many are REALLY above average? Half! That means half are below average.

Dave loves to ask seminar attendees to score their driving ability on a 100-point scale. After writing their scores on the flipchart, he explains that in reality half of the people in the room are below the 50 mark. Professors like Bill and Dave are the ones to blame: In school grading, anything below 60 is failing, so no one wants to score less than that. The problem is, that throws out 60% of the scale and forces us to crowd everyone into the top 40%. It's inaccurate and loses efficacy, because you lose the ability to compare abilities across a 100-point scale.

However, we don't want to think of ourselves, our students, our loved ones, or our workmates as "below average" when, statistically, half of them are at or below average IQ. We want to believe they are intellectually more capable than the average person. Seldom do we want to feel that indeed they are doing all they are capable of doing. Be realistic in this area and identify clearly if it's a matter of applying or having IQ.

We estimate that only about 10% of the students in our classrooms use a high percentage of their IQs. However, it could be that is simply all they are capable of doing. First, maybe they are simply average or below average. Second, maybe they have some form of illness, either mental or physical, and are doing all they are really capable of doing because of some limitation other than basic IQ. In our experience, we have seen many who suffer from some form of depression and struggle to advance to the fullest of their capabilities. It is a mistake to assume that all people are equally capable in terms of IQ capacity. In fact, just picking up this book indicates that you are probably using more of your intellect than many others. Many can't even make themselves read anything they perceive as any form of a self-help book.

Adam was a very intelligent student who never seemed prepared. When Bill asked him about it, Adam admitted that he had scored very high on an IQ test yet could not get motivated. Adam had wrecked a relationship with a beautiful and brilliant young woman and had almost flunked out of college several times. After getting to know Adam, Bill became convinced that Adam was doing the best he could because he faced issues Bill could not even begin to understand. We have high hopes for Adam and feel that he will find himself and be a great contributor and succeed to the level of his innate intelligence. But it may take him years, through which he will experience some difficult times. Adam is not using the fullest potential of his intellect, but he is possibly doing the best he can at present.

If your Leadership Quotient indicates you are not functioning at the highest level of your capability, we encourage you to analyze the reasons. We doubt that you can handle it yourself if you have tried for any length of time and still have not improved your performance.

Dave and Bill feel that we use a much higher percentage of our intellect than most people because of the nature of our jobs as professors. Yet we readily admit that we are like many people who operate under the level of performance that God has designed for us. And in fact, both of us are not so sure we want to use all of our intellect. We like the balance of our lives where we "waste" a lot of time enjoying life with frivolous hobbies and being with our loved ones!

Lack of preparedness and often nervousness are other traits that we find on many Leadership Quotient analyses. These two ideas may not intuitively relate, but we retreat to the same defense stated earlier—"We don't write 'em, we just read 'em."

Lack of preparation might be thought of as a nurtured weakness instead of a natural weakness. However, we think that more often some personality trait leads people to be prepared, just like some appear driven never to be prepared. Nervousness is also known to be partially a nurtured trait, but it does seem to become ingrained early in life and does not change, though people do learn ways to cope with it.

As co-authors, we have the same fear of failure that everyone else struggles with. We have purposely not put much effort into projects, so that if they failed, we could blame it on effort and protect the image of superior ability. We didn't want people to say, "We knew they were not capable." We prefer the criticism, "He didn't try very hard." This happened to Bill the night he decided he was really going to have to commit to the pursuit of his Ph.D. He was taking a few post-MBA courses at the age of 45 to test the idea of studying full time for a Ph.D. At a public event, his good friend, Terry Crain, introduced Bill by stating, "This is Bill Service; he just left the corporate world to get his Ph.D." Bill recalls waking up in a cold sweat that night thinking, "I'm now committed to a Ph.D. and what if I don't succeed?" Well, it *did* cross Bill's mind several times that he *was working on* a Ph.D., but Terry had *committed him*, even though she may not know it until she reads this book. Bill should probably thank Terry, because she aroused in him the realization that he had some Intelligence Quotient that was not being applied and that studying for the Ph.D. would cure that problem.

We encourage you to perform the same analysis. Be truthful with yourself and determine if there is a real reason you are not preparing or if it is simply laziness or habit. Writing about your IQ will move you toward an improved use of it as you prepare to build a higher Leadership Quotient.

Admiral Stockdale was Ross Perot's running mate in the 1992 presidential campaign. He is a brilliant man with an impressive IQ. As a Vietnam prisoner of war, he had been an inspiration to those around him, especially John McCain. His "Stockdale principle" resulted in the survival of many prisoners and is reported elsewhere in this book. Yet when Admiral Stockdale appeared onstage for a debate with the other much less intelligent and far from as savvy opponent, he simply could not speak convincingly. His "yes" and "no" were not what the audience was looking for and he seemed dim in spite of his great intellect and life accomplishments. He had a high IQ but could not apply it to deliver a high $LQ^{©}$. This book is designed to help you avoid the problem exemplified by Admiral Stockdale.

Another natural weakness that is often reported in this quadrant is a **poor impression of intellect**. We have all met people like this. Upon first meeting a person, he may be very quiet. You assume he does not have a lot of intellect. You're often wrong. In our Western way of thinking, we assume the person who talks most is the most intelligent. Asians often assume the opposite. A saying of Confucius relates, "You learn only while listening, never while speaking." Thus, often the highest IQ is owned by the person who speaks the least, not the most.

At first, we probably think a person who does not converse much might be dull, but so often we are wrong about people on our first meeting. Too often we don't know people for quite a long time and our assessments, especially of intellect, should wait for more proof. Don't confuse shyness with low IQ.

When intellectual presidents are mentioned, Abraham Lincoln should always be among them. Indeed, he and Richard Nixon were among the most brilliant of our presidents, yet few seem to know it. The misconceptions about Lincoln were caused by his simplicity in speech and his lack of formal education. The misconceptions about Nixon were because of Watergate. You can't make a second first impression. That's why so many people who have completed the Leadership Quotient are concerned about first impression. We have met many people who are initially assumed dull, who later proved us wrong. Just remember to give everyone an equal chance and make sure the first IQ impression you make is in line with your intellect. Whether this is natural or nurtured makes little difference. But remember: "[A] heritability of 30% to 40% means that 60% to 70% of the variation in general cognitive ability is due to non-genetic influences over which we may have some degree of control" (Vandenberg and Vogler, 1985, p. 50).

Normal Nurtured IQ Strengths—Quadrant 2 of the IQ 2X2 Matrix

> *"[T]here is little question that unraveling the complexity of environmental influences on IQ will pose a continuing challenge to behavioral science researchers in future years" (Bouchard and Segal, 1985, p. 454).*

We try to teach our students, seminar attendees, and consulting clients to **generalize** from one situation to another. We all need to be **thoughtful and reflective, and be able to use abstracting and reframing** so that we will not have to deal with the same problems over and over.

One of Dave's favorite keynote speech stories makes the point. The bush pilot shook his head in disgust as he landed his plane on a pristine mountain lake in the backwoods of Alaska to retrieve hunters he had left a week earlier. "I told you last week," he explained, "this Otter-style plane will carry the pilot, two hunters with gear, and one elk. I see you've killed two elk, and we can't take both of them home." The hunters pleaded their case: "We hunted at this same camp last year and loaded up two elk on an Otter just like yours." They used their Intelligence Quotient to call on all kinds of data about lift and the power of engines and elevation and the weight of every piece of equipment. The pilot finally agreed. "Your data seems right…let's load up and go home." So they loaded the pilot, the two hunters with their gear, and two elk into the plane. The Otter's huge single engine roared to life and the plane heavily lifted from the water. It struggled over the treetops and banked, heading for a pass in the mountains. They almost made it, but crashed just short of clearing the pass. But the plane crash-landed smoothly into heavy underbrush, so no one was killed. However, the side of the mountain was a mess of plane parts, hunters' gear, and dead elk. As the hunters emerged out of the underbrush, one said to the other, "Where in the world are we?" The other responded, "I think we're about the same place we crashed last year!"

It is our hope that, by increasing your Leadership Quotient, you won't end up "about the same place you crashed last time." Indeed, we face the same problems over and over in our lives. The inability to see the relationship of those events lowers our $LQ^{\copyright}$. Those with high Intelligence Quotients are able to see the similarities.

The Harvard Case Method is a popular business education technique because it exposes students to real-life business situations. The method is effective because students do more than answer questions; they determine what the questions *are*. For this case method to work, individuals must learn to generalize from one situation to another. This generalization requires a lot of thoughtful reflection.

We tell students to turn their radios down on their way home and think about what they have learned. It would do us all well to do this. Next time you dialogue with anyone, just think about what it means and what you might learn from it. We feel that we all must learn to learn from everyone in every situation. If you will do this reflection with the goal of seeing if you can reframe the situation to some problem or opportunity you are facing, you'll often find the most innovative and unexpected of solutions. Successfully intelligent people have a habit of reflecting, generalizing, and reframing, and abstracting what they have heard, seen, and done to improve how they address the current issues they face.

Curt Mueller was the founder and president of Mueller Sports Medicine, which at the time was attempting to be the largest sports medicine company in the U.S. Dave was accompanying Curt on an important sales call in central Texas. Curt and Dave were good friends and enjoyed conversing about sports and many other subjects. As they neared the office of the important buyer, Curt suggested, "Let's turn off the radio and stop talking while we think about this sales call." Curt was using his considerable Intelligence Quotient to improve his Leadership Quotient. He was thinking about his business, the distributor's business, the buyer's likes and dislikes, and the goal of the sales call. He was scripting out in his mind how he wanted to lead the buyer to place a large order for Mueller products. It worked. And it will work for you, if you apply your IQ to your $LQ^{\copyright}$.

It's a gross understatement to say that Microsoft founder Bill Gates is very successful. Gates is known for hiring people who are the best at what they do, although many of them are not computer specialists. He does this because he knows that his software must satisfy more than computer geeks. The creativity and Intelligence Quotient of his staff help Microsoft reach a wide audience of software users.

Vice President Dick Cheney is frighteningly smart when it comes to a scenario analysis. Cheney surely thinks about what has happened in the past and puts some level of abstracting to the new situation he faces. However, in at least one situation it appears Cheney's past experience and abstracting actually proved a disadvantage: some would say disaster. His experience had shown that intelligence reports are typically underestimates when it comes to matters such as Iraq having weapons of mass destruction. This "normal" trend caused those getting the estimates to think things were probably worse than reported simply because that is the norm for intel reports of this nature. Those of us who must wait for each individual lesson on a platter are destined for a lot of pain and suffering and likely not that much success. The ability to see the relationship of new problems to old problems increases your Intelligence Quotient and your ability to solve problems while increasing your Leadership Quotient. Yes, action beats inaction—but not always!

Another nurtured strength is found in **education for success: being effective, not just efficient**. Many people are educated but few take real advantage of their education. We are not talking just about formal education but also about self- and continuous education. One of the strongest determinants of success is the ability to scan the available information and make judgments about what is coming next and where to put your money and efforts. Most successful people have a vast network of information gathering, which allows them to see many things others do not. It is mostly because they make an attempt to pay attention to many variables at the same time. The entire discipline of business education springs from economic inequality. We challenge our students with this statement: "You want to get rich? Stand up, walk out of the classroom, and go fill a gap between supply and demand." Scanning many variables to find—and then satisfy—inequalities of supply and demand is very difficult to do. That's because many competitors are trying to do the same thing. Those with higher Intelligence Quotients will have subsequently higher Leadership Quotients to fill the gap between supply and demand.

If you think back to the 2003 Iraqi war, you can see that the decision to go to war was made with a lot of interpretation of information. We know that Secretary of State Condoleezza Rice had a lot to do with the decision. Even if you don't agree with the decision, you probably agree that Rice held among the highest Intelligence Quotients for this particular decision, thus she should have been involved in it. We also should be aware that she is highly educated and extremely bright. All of this should allow us to see that a lot of education, intellect, and care went into a very important and possibly history-changing decision. Condoleezza Rice exemplifies the education for success and effectiveness that goes along with that. She has been successful in part because of her education and her ability to process large volumes of information.

> When asked how history will treat the decision to invade Iraq, President Bush has responded, "I don't know." It may take years to see, but we do see that America did take action and try something because little else has worked for the past 30 years in the Middle East. The effectiveness of Rice's advice will be judged by history, but we at least know she is highly educated and intelligent and was well informed. Remember: "Intelligence cannot be well understood without reference to the internal representation of knowledge….External, contextual factors as well as internal, cognitive factors enter into the structure of intelligence, since what may be intelligent in one context may be superseded or become unintelligent in another" (Butterworth, 1994, p. 50). "No entity can learn without generating for itself the need to know" (Schank and Birnbaum, 1994, p. 84).

Wise and witty are nurtured traits that we have seen time and again, but in all of history, no one seemed better noted for this than Benjamin Franklin. His advice, in part from *Poor Richard's Almanack*, has stood the test of hundreds of years and will probably survive hundreds more. Former Education Secretary and morals author Bill Bennett has made himself into something of a current-day Ben Franklin by *not* heeding Franklin's advice, "Search others for their Virtues, thy self for thy Vices (p. 158)….The greatest monarch on the proudest throne is obliged to sit upon his own arse (p. 372)….A man wrapped up in himself makes a very small bundle (p. 415)….The secret of success is constancy to purpose (p. 471). [And finally,] thirteen virtues necessary for true success [include the following]:

- Temperance

- Silence

- Order

- Resolution

- Frugality

- Industry

- Sincerity

- Justice

- Moderation

- Cleanliness

- Tranquility

- Chastity

- Humility (Bruun and Getzen, 1996, p. 473)

Need we say more? Ben Franklin said enough; *wise* makes a strong contribution to your Intelligence Quotient, which contributes to your Leadership Quotient.

The last nurtured strength we have found in our research is **seeking, willingness, and curiosity that is exemplified with a true thirst for knowledge**. Leaders don't have much success if they don't first seek something. And then we have to be willing to accept what we learn or get or become. We see the thirst for knowledge in so many young children as they ask what and why and generally seem to just irritate us with their endless curiosity. Unfortunately, many elements of the typical school system and many parents stifle that seemingly bottomless desire to learn. So many adults seem to exemplify the attitude, "Why would I want to know that?" Many still are stuck in the old school and need to understand how they are going to *use* knowledge before they allow it to enter their brain. When someone says, "I'll never use that information, so I'm not going to bother with it," they have doomed themselves to mediocrity. All we have to do is tell students we are about to talk about something that won't be on a test and their eyes literally glaze over as they lean back and put up their own invisible shield. God forbid they should learn something that's *not* going to be on a test!! Those who are the most creative among us accept many non-useful things that later become of use as they figure new and better ways to do things. High Intelligence Quotient leaders learn from many sources.

Stephen Hawking's *Brief History of Time* is a tough read, yet it gives us insights from the most brilliant of minds. Hawking has continued to live years beyond any estimates of his life expectancy, mostly because he desires to learn more and understand more. What if more of us were like Hawking in using our intellectual capabilities? If we were, we could surely solve the world's challenges.

In closing this section, we want to remind you again that we aren't wholly worried about what's nature and what's nurture. Our purpose is to help you improve your own Leadership Quotient. There is little question that we are still wrestling with the complexity of the interaction of environmental and natural inherited influences on human intelligence. We will still be contemplating it 50 years from now. It is just too complex to solve simply because it is changing, be it ever so slowly, through evolutionary and daily influences on humankind's continued development.

Normal Nurtured IQ Weaknesses—Quadrant 4 of the IQ 2X2 Matrix

> *Apparently, intelligence and other mental functions are not totally separate entities independent from environmental influences. As previously mentioned, even the best seed will not turn into a plant if it was placed in arid soil. Innate abilities, big and small, may never come to fruition in a destructive environment. The earlier in life the hammer hits, the greater the damage. In some instances the blow can be devastating and the destruction irreversible to both intelligence and mental health. (Wolman, 1985, p. 868)*

One of the more obvious nurtured weaknesses that drag down the Intelligence Quotient is the **lack of reading or studying**. Very often this is exhibited by a person who does poorly on **standardized tests**. When George W. Bush was first mentioned as a presidential candidate, he knew very little about world leaders and geopolitical events, in part because he had not been running for president all of his life as many other presidents had been. However, he seemed to be a relatively quick study. He was able to overcome the denigrating comments about his alleged low Intelligence Quotient and was quite successful in televised debates with his opponent, Al Gore.

Once he became president, Bush surrounded himself with brilliant and successful people, not just friends. A quip on the Republican side of the contest goes like this:

- When George Bush walks into a room he knows he is *not* the smartest person there.

- When Bill Clinton walks into a room he knows he *is* the smartest person.

- When Al Gore walks into a room he *thinks* he is the smartest person in the room.

Bill and Dave are much like President Bush when we walk into a classroom of MBAs. The Leadership Quotient is *lower* with a high IQ leader like Clinton who acts like he knows he is smarter than others, but the *LQ©* is *higher* with a lower IQ leader like Bush who seeks advice and diverse opinions from his followers.

These analogies should make you aware that a high Leadership Quotient is obtained by leveraging more than what you have and more than you can reasonably learn. Leadership is about using the diversity and intellect of many others to accomplish more than one person can accomplish alone. None of us is as smart as all of us. Start with reading and studying, but seek the contribution of others and remember to thank them for their input.

Many people don't test well on the standardized tests that are the basis for most advanced educational programs in the U.S. The one thing we can say for sure is that we are missing a lot of capable people by using those tests as the chief criteria for admission to our advanced educational programs. We must realize that those tests are good predictors of who can be successful in passing tests in a given field, but poor predictors of who can be successful in the given profession. Also, a high score on a GMAT means you can probably pass the MBA program at most schools, but a low score is not nearly as predictive of failure.

Bill improved his GMAT from the 70th percentile to the 93rd percentile from age 28 to age 45. He attributes the improvement to massive amounts of reading. He read only a few books before the age of 35; this included textbooks, which he seldom bought in his undergraduate or MBA pursuits. He now reads his first-35-years equivalent or more every week. In this testing regard, think about the following: "Since intelligence changes over the life span (although an individual's ability relative to others may remain relatively invariant), then it follows that the indices used to infer ability necessarily must change" (Brody, 1985, p. 355).

If you want to improve your score on standardized tests, read more. Some people may need help with test anxiety, but that is rare. If you feel you do need anxiety-control help, contact a university and find out if the institution knows of a reputable person who can help you.

When we get to this next nurtured trait, **boredom, lack of interest, lack of focus or attention, and poor concentration**, we think first of Bill Clinton. He is without a doubt a brilliant man with many great attributes, and he was a successful two-time president of the most powerful nation in the world, but his Leadership Quotient faltered when he lost sight of what he was and what he was doing. His lack of focus led to the disastrous Monica Lewinsky debacle and eventual impeachment. Without this scandal, Clinton's legacy would be much brighter. If there is a bright side for the Clinton family, it's Bill's $10 million and Hillary's $8 million advance for their books that were a result of the scandal. So it paid off for Clinton in monetary terms. This trade-off is probably OK with Bill and Hillary now, but we doubt it will be on their deathbeds.

In a recent title basketball game where Samford University could have gone to the NCAA playoffs for the third time, Samford wormed its way to its first lead of the game with about two minutes to play. After the next turnover, when in-bounding the ball, the Samford player temporarily lost his focus and the ball was stolen for a slam dunk. Then on the next play a similar thing happened. Just because one person failed to concentrate for about two seconds, the season was ended. This kind of lack of focus can result in damage that in some organizational settings can't be repaired. High Intelligence Quotient leaders are able to focus and keep their attention on the situation at hand. Often, lack of leadership focus is not determined until it's too late. So take everything seriously in the beginning, as well as once you realize it's important.

Exhibiting **common sense and showing you are not clueless must start with the ability to learn from experience: too many people don't learn from experience**. Common sense is a learned trait that starts with an understanding of just how much we have to learn and how successful people are always looking for lessons in everyday events. We see so often the difference in students who have paid attention to and learned from their parents and those who have not. "Intelligence can be studied in three ways:

1. The adaptation of an organism to its environment;

2. The complexity of the system of mental structures required by such an adaptation; and

3. The individual know-how, that is, the ability of an individual to learn and use those complex structures in an appropriate way, according to the circumstances" (Arom, 1994, p. 138).

This brings to mind the 2000 presidential election, in which Al Gore tried to remake himself many times. Adaptation is a necessity in any battle, but it can be a hindrance when people see it as a shallow attempt to become something you are not. Al Gore had so much going for him that one must wonder, "What was he thinking?" Common sense would tell us that people like to see you adapt, but they don't like to think you have no firm foundation upon which your personality, intellect, and principles are based. Learn to learn and concentrate all the time.

Difficulties with **mathematics** are very common. So many leaders say, "I don't do math!" But you do! Even when you are comparing long-distance rates of 9 cents a minute to 1 cent a minute, you're NOT doing math. We seem to think it's math if we are multiplying 2 X 3! We have to wonder why so many leaders are able to use the excuse, "I'm no good at math." It's not acceptable to say, "I'm not good at reading!" It seems that the primary reason for not doing math is laziness. So many people are not willing to understand Math 101 before they go on to Math 102. Math is a subject that needs to be 100% mastered before progressing. When you make a 70% on the first math course and then a 70% on the next course, you then know 49% of what you need to know for Math 103: that's simple math. In Japan, you must master one math course before you progress to the next, and so it should be in the U.S. Think of this analogy: If you get the directions to a location 70% correct a few times in a row, can you ever find your way? The answer is no. But we allow our students to do this in math courses. It is possible in history courses to know a lot about what happened between 1800-1865 without knowing what went on before 1800. But even in history courses you need to know something about preceding events before you can describe *why* something happened. Perhaps we need to stigmatize lack of knowledge in math.

Just ask a normal college student to give you the square mileage of Louisiana. He will invariably say he doesn't know, and when pushed, will say something like 1,500. That would mean he thinks Louisiana is 15 by 100 miles! Try a question such as this and see how poor people are at estimating simple terms. When asked, one college senior said the population of the U.S. was 1,000,000 and another said no, it's more like a 1,000,000,000. When chastised about their replies, one said, "We don't have time to read; we're college students." So, we guess they'll have more time later?

A local newscaster was talking about Hurricane Andrew and its devastating financial impact on the economy of several states. She said Hurricane Andrew did over a million dollars in damage. This person did not stop to think how small the impact of one million dollars would have been. She was a real-life example of the humorous evil villain in the first *Austin Powers* movie, who held the world at ransom for "One Million Dollars," because he had been asleep for thirty years and had not kept up with inflation. It's funny in a scripted movie. It's not funny when you're trying to apply your Intelligence Quotient to increase your Leadership Quotient.

Is this the type of math we want our children to hear and think about? We all need to be able to estimate and understand when some numerical estimate is reasonable or not. We are not saying one needs to know the square mileage of any state or the population of the world's countries, but we need to be reasonable in our estimates. Bill was struck by an answer he got from several park rangers near Lake Superior a few years ago. When he asked how large Lake Superior was, he got the same answer from three separate rangers: "It's over 500 feet deep." What does that tell you about what those rangers were taught? Most importantly, it tells you they are not being taught to think at all.

Using the IQ Matrix:

Evaluate yourself in each of the four quadrants as you have done in the prior chapters.

Figure 5.3: YOUR IQ MEASUREMENT AND IMPROVEMENT MATRICES

Evaluate yourself against the reported traits in this Matrix.

	NATURE (uncontrollable-born)	NURTURE (controllable-made)
STRENGTHS (enablers—advantages)	**Q1** ___ memory/scholastic abilities ___ rationally creative ___ quick and bright ___ analytical/multi-variant/ inductive ___ (self-IDed trait)	**Q2** ___ thoughtful and reflective ___ education for success ___ wise and witty ___ true thirst for knowledge ___ (self-IDed trait)
WEAKNESSES (derailers—disadvantages)	**Q3** ___ poor memory and/or vocabu- lary ___ inability to use IQ ___ unprepared and/or nervous ___ gives poor impression of intel- lect ___ (self-IDed trait)	**Q4** ___ poor study/scholastic abilities ___ unfocused and inattentive ___ doesn't learn from experience ___ poor mathematical abilities ___ (self-IDed trait)

Tailor the Matrix below for yourself!

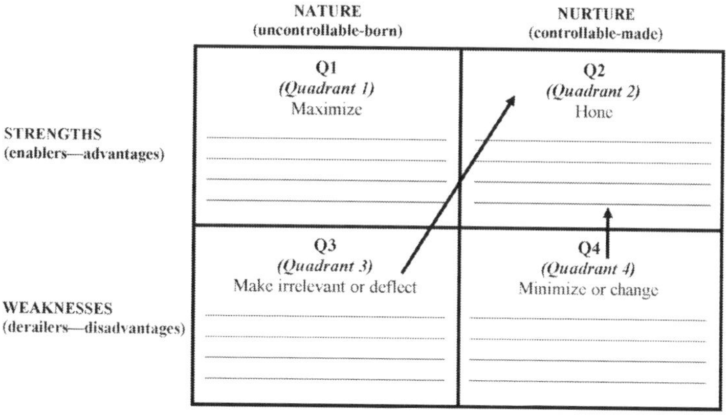

	NATURE (uncontrollable-born)	NURTURE (controllable-made)
STRENGTHS (enablers—advantages)	**Q1** *(Quadrant 1)* Maximize	**Q2** *(Quadrant 2)* Hone
WEAKNESSES (derailers—disadvantages)	**Q3** *(Quadrant 3)* Make irrelevant or deflect	**Q4** *(Quadrant 4)* Minimize or change

Evaluating Your IQ Personal Profile: Strengths and Weaknesses

Doing Something About Your IQ!

The Measurement and Improvement Matrices force you to identify what is under your control and what is not. As in previous analyses, include as unchangeable what you're not willing to change. The basic skills of identifying, limiting distractions, studying, learning, relearning, and ultimately using newfound skills for IQ development will serve you well only if you put in much sustained effort.

Practice improving your IQ by study and reading. Try learning some poetry or working crossword puzzles. Sitting still and expecting your Intelligence Quotient to come out of the TV will definitely lower your Leadership Quotient. Notice how sharp people of all ages are when they stay involved and are up to date on world affairs.

We have observed the following things when people evaluate their strengths and weaknesses in IQ:

1.   Others don't always agree with your self-assessment of your IQ.

2.   Others normally think that a lot more of your IQ characteristics are on the controllable side than you do.

3.   Many people have a negative trait that they potentially could control, but they feel they can't practically control it or at least won't control it.

4.   Most people have an intellect that plays out very differently than they often think it should.

5.   So many people think they are too intelligent to do menial work and therefore never accomplish anything.

6.   Many others don't realize the power of normal IQ when it's coupled with desire and focus.

Now you've identified the elements of your Intelligence Quotient related to your Leadership Quotient, as we are defining it here, not as you scored on some IQ test. What's next? We are sure those who have scored high on an IQ test want to believe in the test just as those who score low will try to deny it. But move on! Always check your evaluations with trusted people.

We are much more concerned with successful IQ than with traditionally measured IQ. Now come up with a strategy of how you are going to address your IQ. How are you going to work to improve your successful intelligence as it relates to your $LQ^©$? How are you going to improve your negatives and enhance your positives? But don't fall in love with what you perceive to be your high IQ. Leaders who do this end up with a high Intelligence Quotient but a low Leadership Quotient.

As We Said in the Introduction, "It's Time to Get Started; If Not Now, When?"

"No one approach to studying intelligence is apt to be 'complete.'…A continuing challenge for the future will be the integration of results from various paradigms of research so that our understanding of intelligence will be transparadigmatic rather than specific to the research approach that it happens to use" (Sternberg, 1985, p. 110).

We know the reader should have gained some knowledge in this chapter. Some of the knowledge is based on science, some on logic, some on experience, and some on supposition; but regardless, we know that the important thing is what you do with the knowledge. It's not the IQ knowledge, it's your application of the IQ knowledge that will determine your Leadership Quotient.

Before we go on to the next chapter, remember: Effective leadership requires a balanced fit among the many environments, behaviors, contexts, processes, contents, and needs. Figure 5.4 shows the interaction of 1) the leader, 2) the followers, and 3) the environments, which all need to fit. Put your IQ values in the triangle and see if your IQ is enough to help you progress as a leader. Regardless of the level of your current IQ, continue to work to improve your successful intellect.

Figure 5.4: YOUR LEADERSHIP LEVERAGE TRIANGLE

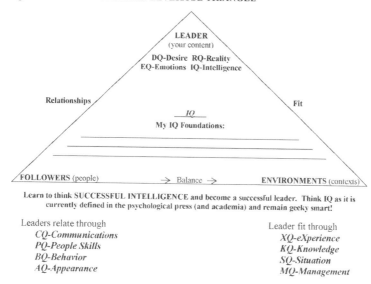

Impress by how good a leader you are, not how smart you think you are, even when you're right about your intellect.

IQ Conclusions

"What is intelligence? Intelligence is hard to define and descriptions are generally beset with paradoxes. Thus intelligence is attributed to those who have to think because they do not know a lot, and to those who know a lot and so do not have to think" (Gregory, 1994, p. 13).

IQ, as we have expressed it as part of *LQ©*, is among the most changeable of all quotients. However, it is normally measured as one of the least malleable of the Leadership Quotients. If you want to improve your Leadership Quotient, forget the normal IQ and begin to use the definition you found in the Measurement and Improvement Matrices.

Durban, in the fourth edition of his book on leadership (2004), says that about 40,000 books and articles have been written about leadership yet there is still no one clear definition of leadership. He simply sees it as influence and impact. He does suggest—as we have—that leadership in a current situation is more often a partnership than a dictatorship. This implies to all who aspire to be modern leaders that the old models of command and control may become things of the past, and we must realize that more often now than ever before, our followers have the right to say no unless the relationship is mutually beneficial. Perhaps this says that the traditional high IQ is not as important as an IQ that allows one to read others and not use others but benefit them in a way they see fit. Maybe the golden rule should now be, "Do onto others as they would have you do unto them." This requires an IQ that is focused on others, not on yourself.

Regardless, your goal must be to understand the complexities of real successful IQ and how that relates to your old-style measurable IQ; then make IQ meaningful and applicable to you and your situation now and as it will be in the future. Most people die regretting not mistakes but never trying. Listed below are some principles that we feel are very pertinent to your IQ improvement quest (Service and Arnott mixed with Sternberg [primarily Chapter 8, 1996]; Guilford [1967 and 1986]):

- Desire, attention, and focus are foundational to successful IQ for $LQ^©$.

- The ability to reflect and generalize is a critical element in continually improving IQ as it is useful in $LQ^©$.

- Successfully intelligent people learn how to motivate themselves before they worry about motivating others.

- Ability to remain flexible and accept criticism is a requirement of $LQ^©$ IQ.

- People with a high $LQ^©$ let others lead them in many ways, especially about what it takes to motivate others.

- Memory is important, but not necessarily a detailed memory; you must just be able to realize that something you know can be of use and where you can find out more if necessary.

- Ability to pull seemingly unrelated things together as well as to break down complex things into more manageable parts is of great help; this requires attention and practice.

- Innovativeness requires first and foremost an inquisitive, seeking attitude.

- Successful intelligence is the product of understanding the perspective of others better than they do.

- High-success IQ requires the motivation to acquire and store information of all types for potential future use.

- Ability to see relationships between things and potential transformations is essential to exhibited successful intelligence.

- Intelligence that pays off is tempered with self-reality and self-control.

- Knowing when to continue and when to cut your losses is key to renewed success.

- In successfully intelligent people, the desire to succeed overcomes the fear of failure; successes and failures really fear the same things.

- Successfully intelligent people have a clear bias for action.

- Making the most of good traits and the least of bad traits is true intellect.

- Action must be the result of thoughts and plans if you are to be successful.

- Procrastination is not the norm for successful people.

- Playing the blame game is out for successful IQ people.

- Self-pity is never a part of the independently minded, successfully intelligent person.

- Focus and attention are hallmarks of high IQ related to $LQ^{©}$.

- Success requires a certain level of delayed gratification.

- Knowing how much to take on and how much to let go is another hallmark of successful IQ.

- Be a learner, not learned.

- Think and think about thinking about thinking, and so on.

- Systems thinking—seeing the big picture and the details—is a requirement of IQ for $LQ^{©}$.

- Appropriate self-confidence is IQ.

- Thinking logically, emotionally, practically, creatively, and innovatively, and all types of thinking, are required in order to be a continual success.

We could add to this list Steven Covey's (1990) seven habits of highly successful people:

1.   Proactivity

2.   Beginning with an end in mind

3.   Putting first things first

4.   Thinking win-win

5.   Seeking first to understand before being understood

6.   Synergize

7.   Continuing self-renewal

A relatively substantial amount of progress has been made on studying the neurological basis for human intellect. Yet we must recognize how research evolves and that we are still a long way from understanding the neurological (or any other) basis of intelligence. Following is a wonderful example of the mental effort that has gone on in the literature related to intelligence testing:

> It is still valid to assert that intelligence is unitary, incompletely malleable, relatively invariant over the life span, substantially related to socially relevant intellectual achievements, related to the capacity to acquire knowledge in diverse settings, subject to the influences of motivational and temperamental processes that influence both scores on tests and the tendency to actualize one's intellectual ability, and subject to cultural influences that change the relationships between the test and the construct. (Brody, 1985, p. 384)

In the area of IQ we wonder, "Why can't researchers keep it simple?" It seems that most research articles on IQ are designed to make a normal person feel stupid. If this chapter makes you feel anything but encouraged about the ability to improve your IQ, you've missed the main point. You are in control of your own IQ as much as you are of your own EQ.

As a final note, we are staying away from group IQ because that is another topic for another book. We are talking about a person's own IQ; therefore, group IQ components have no part in $LQ^{©}$.

Conclusion

If you are lacking in one area, don't look for excuses but think instead about what Penrose said:

> I feel certain that there is no fundamental difference between mathematical and other kinds of thinking. It is true that many people find it difficult to cope with the abstract type of thinking that is

needed for mathematics, whilst finding comparatively little difficulty with the equally convoluted judgments that are involved in day-to-day relationships with other human beings. Some kinds of thinking come easily to certain people, whereas other kinds come more easily to others. But I do not think that there is any essential difference—or that there is more difference between mathematical thinking and, say, planning a holiday, than there is between the latter activity and understanding a music-hall joke. Human mathematical intelligence is just one particular form of human intelligence and understanding. It is more extreme than most of these other forms in the abstract, impersonal, and universal nature of the concepts that are involved, and in the rigor of its criteria for establishing truth. But mathematical thinking is in no way removed from other qualities that are important ingredients in our general ability for intelligent comprehension, such as intuition, common-sense judgment, and the appreciation of beauty. (1994, p. 107)

Remember these self-evident truths:

• You can't stop people from thinking—but you can start them thinking.

• Today's preparation determines tomorrow's achievement.

• The only difference between stumbling blocks and steppingstones is the way we use them.

• A mistake is proof that someone was at least trying to accomplish something.

• Two ways to make things better in the minds of the consumers: 1) hype, 2) make real improvements.

• Ideas are funny things. They don't work unless you do.

As Abraham Lincoln reportedly once said: "A capacity and taste for reading gives access to whatever has already been discovered by others…" or as Plato said, "Learning is a matter of remembering what is important," for "there are precious few Einsteins among us. Most brilliance arises from ordinary people working together in extraordinary ways" (source of these quotes is unknown). Dave and Bill both know that life has much more to teach them, and we are getting less intolerant of its lessons each day. Are you?

We have finished section one of *LQ*$^{©}$, which relates to traits that are primarily associated individually with the leader. The next section is about traits that must be viewed from a follower perspective. Though the traits in the next section are those of the leader, they are of little consequence unless they are viewed from the perspective of the follower. Regardless of the viewpoint, improvements often require what an army drill sergeant once said: "Sometimes the only way to make the Coke machine work is to give it a good kick." Yes—be enthusiastic, curious, ready, willing, devoted, and honest; but most importantly, kick it into high gear and just do it!

PART II
Follower Quotients

Understand what you feel is nonnegotiable, but do not have a personal doctrine so narrow that no one else's beliefs can get through. Communicate not to impress, but to share your meaning and to contribute to the general good. Go beyond words, programs, and formulas to build real relationships that are the beginnings, not the ends. The truth of how one communicates beyond the superficial is often very painful to all parties involved in sharing for authentic significance: understand and share the truth through real communication.

The theme throughout *The Leadership Quotient* is the need to learn to improve your leadership style with your followers in your specific environment. As a leader, it must be your goal to learn how **to fit in yet stand out** and make a difference through others. The road to personal leadership improvement starts with desire and self-awareness, goes on to continuous commitment to development, and ends with practice: application. The quotients in this section are presented from the perspective of the followers. While *The Leadership Quotient* is a book about improving your leadership, this section contains quotients that are intended to give you a better perspective of your leadership effectiveness from the follower's viewpoint. Look at Figure 6.1 and note the bottom left corner of the leadership triangle, where you will find the four "follower" quotients. Without followers there would be no leaders. Although the communication, people, behavior, and appearance aspects of leadership are traits or characteristics *exhibited* by the leader, they are of no use unless they are *exercised* in ways that appeal to followers.

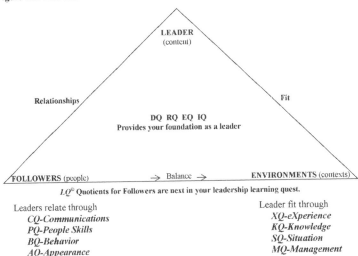

Figure 6.1: THE LEADERSHIP LEVERAGE TRIANGLE

In this follower section, you must shift your thinking. It's not how you think you communicated, but how *they* think you communicated; it's not how you think you treat and read people, it's if *they* think you are a people person; it's not how you look or behave, it's how *they* see you and your behavior. Think *"them"* versus "me."

As in previous chapters, we are again tapping into a variety of sources by combining research, exemplars, how-to's, popular press reports, experience, case reports, case research, and logic to help you build your own personal Leadership Quotient that will improve your effectiveness with followers in your specific environment. The first section of the book concentrated on the leader. This section will by nature be different because it looks at the followers affected by the leader's decisions and actions. The human interactions involved in leadership are so complex that reducing them to a handful of testable propositions or hypotheses simply cannot reflect the level of intricacy that exists with the leader-followers-environments interactions. Therefore, we developed the more inclusive $LQ^{\copyright}$ formula. As we've mentioned previously, "You kill something when you dissect it for analysis." Through *The Leadership Quotient* formula, you bring leadership *alive* in yourself instead of killing it through just studying it in others.

This section includes **Chapter 6: CQ—Communications Quotient, Chapter 7: PQ—People Quotient, Chapter 8: BQ—Behavioral Quotient, and Chapter 9: AQ—Appearance Quotient.** These four Follower Quotients help the leader discover how she is perceived by her followers and how her style fits their need to be led. As you read this follower section carefully, think about ***bal-***

ance, fit, appropriateness, and ***authenticity.*** Trying to be perceived as something you are not is a sure ticket to failure as a leader. Followers want authentic leaders above all.

6

CQ, The Communications Quotient

As you read this chapter, keep in mind that the theme is to improve your leadership communication by moving *from directing to connecting*. Ask any leader what she considers the most important leadership task. Communication is included as some part of the answer. Communicating with followers through many different forms and media separates successful from failed leaders. Communication is the backbone of leadership and the most important of the follower perceptions about a leader. Leaders don't communicate because they *think* they do, they communicate because the receiver understands the message the sender intended. Outcomes other than a "common understanding" are not communications. The word "communications" has as its root "comm," which means "to make the same." Other words that grow from this same root are "communal," "community," "communism," and "commune." All of these words mean to make something the same. When leaders communicate, the leader and the followers have the same understanding.

Unfortunately, it is becoming more difficult to communicate, not easier. It would seem that, with all of the current technologies, this statement does not make sense. However, the more sophisticated society gets, the more sophisticated leadership communications must become. One of the largest communication tools, television, is an interesting exception to the rule: The more complex the world gets, the more simple TV's message has become. Information technologies like e-mail have made it faster and easier to get a message out to vast numbers of people, but have increased the danger that the message will be misunderstood.

Every leader's goal must be to "really" communicate by beginning to move **from directing to connecting** in every single action she takes. A real communicator in today's world is a facilitator, not a dictator. The leader must be content to let others determine meaning, without specifically spelling out the details of the message. Many leaders feel they must *convince* others of what they know, when in reality it is much more important to allow others to *realize* what *they* know in this age of empowerment. A modern leader will move from the two-year-old mentality of "it's mine" to the mature view of "you own it" when leadership through empowerment and the self-sufficiency of all followers is the goal.

In a recent work of fiction, we found a real truth related to this issue. "In my sour moments, it strikes me that both sides seem much more interested in winning the argument than in alleviating…suffering" (Carter, 2002, p. 154). How often does this happen? The desire to win an argument overrides all logic and fairness! We often know we are misrepresenting facts to win an argument. In both the Democratic and the Republican 2004 National Presidential Conventions, many misrepresentations were made of the opponent's words or actions. On both sides, one can see clear misrepresentations that were surely purposefully proffered. We all know what Kerry meant when he said, "In a more sensitive way," and we all know what Bush meant when he said, "We can't win it." Either both parties (Democratic and Republican) are stupid or they misrepresented what was said. There are no other explanations to this type of rhetoric. You must answer this type of multiple-choice question even of your political party with only one of two responses: stupid or liar.

Recall how often you have seen the manner in which something is said, primarily in a politically incorrect manner, voiding a great argument for a truly greater cause. We all react to a message as if it is **all** the sender knows. When we talk about the need for minorities to get a better education, we are reminded of non-minorities that are uneducated; when we speak of 9/11, we are reminded of the plight of the Palestinians; when we speak of the need for responsibility, we are reminded of those who can't take responsibility; when we talk of governmental waste, we get reminded of the good government does; and so on. It is as if by saying one thing, we have proven we cannot possibly know another. This is simply not the case. We as educators know that there is more to every situation, but addressing one segment does not mean we don't know about others. This tactic of deflection is seen when the receiver has no logical objection to what one says but has a moral objection to what is being said. Remember this *deflection-from-a-truth tactic* and don't let your distracters get away with it!

> Competent hearers (who are usually also competent speakers) realize that speakers use communication to pursue their own ends, which may correspond in some respects to the ends of their audience, and differ in others. Communication is a special way of fulfilling an informative intention. An informative intention can be fulfilled in many ways. One way is to provide evidence, genuine or spurious, of the information one wants some to accept as true. (Sperber, 1994, p. 194)

Organizational Management and Leadership Starts Strictly as Communications

As stressed throughout $LQ^{©}$, the overriding purpose of management is to gain a sense of shared commitment on the part of the members of an organization and then lead the organization's members to the realization of that shared vision. These lofty purposes cannot effectively be met without a commitment to effective communications. You are probably reading this book to prepare yourself for expanded managerial and leadership responsibilities. Specifically, most of today's formal students and self-learners of management are seeking at some point a general manager's (GM) role. The intent of this book is to help you prepare yourself for an expanded leadership role. The 12 quotients will prepare you to operate in environments that are now unfamiliar to you. More discussion of those environmental issues are covered in the third section of the book.

Often individuals fail at higher levels because they choose to pay attention to issues that are not critical to their unit's success. We often tell our seminar attendees: "This seminar on Leadership Quotients will make the most efficient and effective use of the most limited resource there is: you!" Indeed, the most valuable asset today is the attention of top-level individuals. Managers naturally defer to their strengths and tend to address issues they know best, not those that are the most important to the organization's success.

Bill and Dave walked out of a New Orleans restaurant to see a fellow patron looking for his keys near a streetlight. The man was obviously perplexed, and we offered to help. After a few minutes of looking, Bill said, "I don't see them, are you sure you dropped them here?" "No," replied the inebriated gentleman. "I dropped them in the bar, but it's dark in there, the light's better out here." (Stories don't have to be true to make an impact.)

If you will honestly analyze your leadership strengths and weaknesses in each of the 12 quotients, you will shine light into leadership areas where you feel lost. Be brave; face and conquer your weaknesses. You can do it!

Don't put yourself in a functional ghetto where you deal only with issues within your own specific area of functional expertise. If you do, you will often address the wrong problems. Most executives have favorite solutions that they apply regardless of the problem. Many consultants suffer from this favorite solution syndrome. They have a tool they like to use, and they apply it to every problem. Give a child a tool and you will prove the axiom true—"To a boy with a hammer, everything looks like a nail." He will hammer everything within reach with the same tool. You're an adult. By the time you've analyzed all 12 Leadership Quotients, you will be a leader with a box full of tools to select from—so hammer away! But remember: Selection and proper identification of problems must always precede the solution phase, for if we solve the wrong issues, we have done nothing but ignore the real problems. Any current or future organization may have functions in-house or outsourced in whole or in part, but the general manager must be able to lead those under his charge, even those functions that are outsourced to others. This requires a solid CQ.

Attention, selection, and distinctive solutions are becoming key success factors for any member of an organization's top management team. None of these things work for a leader unless she can effectively communicate. Communicating with the many varied and unique specialists who make up the modern organization is a difficult job. Being able to communicate effectively with those who speak different functional languages like Human Resources, Research and Development, Information Systems, Legal, Accounting, Finance, Auditing, and Total Quality Management can be a complex nightmare.

A close examination of successful identification and definition of problems that leads to effective decision-making is enabled by selecting the right technology to use in communication. Particular attention must be given to the effective organization and management of the many varied functions, stressing decision-making and general executive competence, both of which are possible only because of communication. Regardless of where the leader starts, he must always end by analyzing the strategic interaction of all organizational departments affected by the communication. That greater purpose must override departmental or individual desires. The Communications Quotient seeks to help you understand how your specific communications style fits your followers in the current environment in which you work. The items you analyze in the Measurement and Improvement Quadrants will improve your organizational effectiveness and efficiency.

As a future general manager, you must address the following:

1. What **drives managers to select** specific problems, technologies, or other opportunities to improve work—human relations, knowledge, and other operational work?

2. How can leaders insure that their methods of problem and opportunity selection and solution development **meet the need for increased responsiveness** to customers—more speed, improved geographic reach, leverage of intellect, development of more and better leaders (you and others), and faster organizational learning?

3. How can selected problems and opportunities along with the selection of their "solutions" be **effectively and efficiently communicated** among the organizational members who can make those intentions happen?

Implementation of communications solutions that meet these overriding needs changes the nature of most tasks, the management and leadership needs, and the relationship of department and tasks to other activities within the organization. The more advanced the technology or solution, the more spectacular organizational change it generates and the more need there is for effective and efficient communications. How can a leader communicate these far-reaching changes? Success is in no small part determined by selecting the right issues to address, addressing them in an organizationally global and strategic manner, and—most importantly—communicating them to the people who can make them happen.

Competition forces all providers of products and services to make obsolete their own organization's products and services as well as forcing us as individuals to refurbish our own personal knowledge, skills, and abilities. If you don't make them obsolete, your competition will, organizationally or personally. The world's best organizational leaders keep no secrets. They compete within the open information framework that has some effect on all leaders. Keeping secrets is no longer an option, because when we do this, we most often keep secrets from people within our own organization, which leads to performance failure. People cannot reach goals they cannot see. Making others aware of what's needed for personal and organizational progress is effective communication.

Communication and Technology: A Contradiction of Sorts?

In today's technology-based world, communication is a word that has many meanings! At the most basic level, communication is a description of how people transfer ideas and information to other people. There are obviously many means of doing this. The communications media ranges from hand signals to the Star Trek-like feel of telepresence (a term used to describe video and audio linked with faxing or digital data links to make it possible for people to feel they are in the same room together even when they are continents apart); but regardless of the mode of dissemination, communication is the only way meaning is shared. Often in the current world of organizations, technology defines how meanings are transferred from one to the masses. This includes documents, video conferencing, voice, and directing and leading instructions, as well as all combinations and permutations of data and information. In our personal and professional lives, communication is a necessity. Business requires communication to manufacture, sell, and service its products. Communication theory describes the need for a message initiator, a message receiver, and a means to confirm that the message's meaning was understood. The key to effective communication is *mutual* comprehension.

Think about the cost of an ineffective communications systems. In a company of 72,000 employees spread over the world (one of Bill's former employers), what happens when the voice-mail system is just a bit off, the e-mail system is hard to use, and the cell technology is slightly out of date? What if the local paging system is old, or glitches occur in the video conferencing facilities? Add to that a local radio contact that is out of date and a server that is too small. If there is not enough power to the server, or the wide-area networks are not too effective, or the local area network is out of sorts, the leader has communications problems of a technical nature. When a computer or modem is slow, or a phone line is less than par, even a few hundredths of a second lost in each of hundreds of thousands of communications each day can cost your organization a bottom-line profit.

An example exists between Dave and Bill. The e-mail systems at our universities are not that good. We both have lost time each day because of slow e-mail systems. In fact, we both are sure we could produce another research article each year simply if our e-mail worked better and had more modern functionalities. (We're also sure that if the e-mail systems were fixed, we would find another excuse to blame it on.) One simple example: Most e-mail attachments must be saved and then opened in a word-processing application in order for us to use them. In a normal day, we might have to go in and out of e-mail 10 times just to read and respond to our e-mail (this particular problem was recently fixed at Bill's university!).

Human communication can be divided into two forms: verbal and nonverbal. Body language is a form of nonverbal communication. Almost 90% of interactive human speech communication uses nonverbal communication skills. We wonder what President George W. Bush meant when, in a recent interview on *Meet the Press*, he shook his head indicating "no" as he said "yes" (February 2004). Dave wondered, as he watched Diane Sawyer on ABC's morning show with the sound muted, if Diane was an actress or a journalist. Likewise, Bill recalls that he could tell exactly what Diane thought as she ***asked*** Mel Gibson questions about his *Passion* movie. Diane's actions and questions were definitely calculated more to give information than to get information: not very professional from someone who claims to be a pro! Both written and oral communications are effective, but the high Communications Quotient leader knows when to choose the correct type. Remember: What you don't say often speaks so loudly you really don't need to talk. Many mediums of technology can be linked for extending verbal and nonverbal communications.

Historically, humans have used technology to leverage their ability to communicate over distances that exceed speaking ability. In ancient times, humans realized successful hunting required a plan, which had to be flexible to match the field conditions. Man realized early in his existence that language played a role in his success. First, shouted commands, then relays of messengers, and later drums and amplification horns were used to signal movement and extend the range of one's voice for the purpose of command and control.

As man's sophistication grew, so did the reliance on communication technology. Several other examples include mirrors, flags, and light—or flash-based systems used to signal movements of armies and ships. Printing allowed for the compilation of policies, procedures, and maps to be used as means of communication. Improved technology brought into broad use the telegraph, telephone, fax, two-way radio, megaphones, television, computers, e-mail, the Internet, and—of late—telepresence.

Technology and communications are intertwined by the need to tell others what we do and how and why we do it. Another application of communications technology is enhancing the leader's public relations and corporate image. As competition in many markets becomes more accepted, we will be forced to increase our use of communications technology to operate more efficiently and effectively. Effective use of the Communications Quotient can significantly extend the leader's sphere of control.

The elements of effective corporate communication technology are easily understood when described in the following manner.

1. Language selected must be clear, concise, and understandable.

2. All communications should have proof of mutual meaning comprehension.

3. The media or means selected for delivery of the message have to be affordable and easily used.

4. All communications media should be interconnected.

5. There should be a record of all communication transactions, if not what was communicated, at least that there was communication (corporate fraud that has been perpetrated recently points to the need for such verification).

6. There should be a means to **evaluate the effectiveness** of corporate communications.

Since the beginning of time, there has been a need to develop communications resources. As our society and technologies have become more complex, we have become more reliant on others to advise us about our technology requirements. It is important to know what can be accomplished within your organization to meet communication requirements. Only you are the real expert in several of these decisions. You can hire someone, but they know only what they are told.

Regardless of how you do it, communication requires the understanding of several formulas that complement the basic CQ equation. First, understand that the foundation for successful leadership is communication, for only communication allows one to lead others:

COMMUNICATIONS EFFECTIVENESS = a function of the accurate alignment of sender's meaning and the receiver's understanding

DATA = Raw facts
INFORMATION = Data + Meaning
COMMUNICATIONS = Information + Mutual understanding
LEADERSHIP WISDOM = Communications + Proper use of shared meaning

Much of your effectiveness as a leader is measured by your ability to speak and write with clarity and conviction. However, your job as an organizational leader goes beyond personal communications to developing an organization that effectively interacts at all levels to foster an innovative, timely, quality-conscious, customer-focused organization. The myriad of choices within this framework can lead us to chase down numerous "rabbit trails" that do not contribute to our purpose of building your Communications Quotient. Statistics is an example. Regression, analysis of variance, factor analysis, discriminate analysis, meta-analysis, and many other statistical tools can be used to communicate an overall message. Our purpose with statistics would be to allow the data to reveal to us its meaning, not to torture it until it confesses to the meaning we desire. A decision is a choice made under varying degrees of uncertainty, and statistics can help reduce the uncertainty, making for a better decision, but only if we *allow* the data to communicate its real meaning to us: a deeper understanding of CQ.

Some other forms of management science, such as gaming theory, simulation, expert systems, decision support systems, artificial intelligence, PERT, CPM, brainstorming, and other related tools and methodologies should be considered for their communication value. The value of decision sciences tools is making meaning out of data. Some of these techniques can be quite valuable in improving a leader's Communications Quotient by increasing leadership meaning. If statistics or methodologies do not communicate clearly the "real meaning," avoid their use.

Communicating Effectively—Getting your Ideas Across—Technology or Not

In one-on-one or group settings, the following should always be the goals of communication:

- Completeness

- Conciseness

- Consideration

- Concreteness

- Clarity

- Courtesy

- Correctness

To accomplish these lofty and necessary purposes for a presentation, the leader should begin by analyzing the topic's purpose as it particularly relates to the audience for which it is intended. A good piece of advice is to let the receivers define your forms (the context), not your purpose (the content). Correctly identify if your objective is to sell, convince, generate enthusiasm, clear the air, negotiate, problem-solve, get support for a proposition, or simply to state a view. Then clearly identify the key people in your audience and what they need; their cultural specifics and hot buttons really are not necessarily just what you want them to be. From these identified items, prepare an outline of your message. Start with an introduction, support for your idea, and build up to a conclusion, which is based on proper research and logic. Always start by formulating in your mind the basic question you want to answer with your speech and then research it before you fully determine the answer you would like your audience to conclude from your words and actions.

Always practice listener-centered communication if you want it to be successful. When delivering presentations, follow these guidelines:

- Fire the speech writer: do it yourself

- Be prepared

- Be brief

- Be bright

- Be interesting

- Be gone: be seated

Enthusiasm and optimism are contagious, and good Communications Quotient leaders use them effectively by communicating their feelings. Harry Truman may have entered the White House the worst presidential speaker, but he left one of the best. His advice:

- Tell them what you are going to tell them.

- Tell them.

- Tell them what you told them.

Voice Power (Grant-Williams, 2002) proclaims that everyone has a voice that can be dressed up for success just as we have learned how to clothe ourselves for success. Breathing correctly, using your posture, molding your delivery, and writing speeches and rehearsing how you speak are all things we need to learn if we are to dress up our personal communications voice. All leaders continue to use their voice throughout their careers, yet few have worked to train themselves to maximize their effectiveness in speaking. One's voice can be a good or bad attention getter. Your voice can demand respect or simply get attention. Insure you know what yours does for you! Then to foster open and smooth communications, follow these steps:

- Build trust—strong relations

- Commit to sharing ideas

- Interact openly and directly

- Encourage expression of contradictory views

- Keep your boss informed

- Practice what you preach

- Use staff meetings and bulletin boards to inform, not for CYA (people see when someone is trying to cover versus inform or help)

- Do not shoot the messenger

- Return e-v-mail, mail, calls, visits, etc.

- Be a scribe

- Be as open as possible

- No surprises—internal and external scanning

For listening "actively" to oneself and others, whether one-on-one or as part of an audience, follow these guidelines:

- Hear—first seek to understand—look interested

- Interpret—it may just be a presenting complaint, so you need to paraphrase what you heard back to the sender

- Understand—from their perspective, not yours

- Don't interrupt—if you do, do so only to clarify your understanding

- Respond—do **NOT** focus on what you will say

  - focus on what someone else is saying

  - summarize what they have said

If you have trouble listening, try a trick we often use. Repeat to yourself mentally what you just heard. You'll pay attention if you do that. Speaking and listening both can be improved if you will treat communication as a problem to be solved and follow the following sequence:

- Define the problem, not the presenting complaint

- Discover and identify alternatives

- Evaluate alternatives

- Select—satisfice

- Implement

- Evaluate and revise

• "When the situation changes, I change my mind. What do you do?"

Building Flexible Organizational Communication Systems

OK, enough of that rabbit trail! Let's get back to when we are thinking about our entire organization and its needs, and say that we must start by determining what the communications requirements are if we wish to improve our Communications Quotient. Use a language that describes your performance desires. Define your terms in proper English, or the language of those you want to reach. Don't use jargon, marketing terms, or engineering formulas unless they are appropriate to the audience. For a plan to be workable, it must be understood at all levels. Ask these basic questions so you can understand your communications requirements:

1. What are your basic requirements?

2. How much of your existing communications meets your present requirements?

3. How much of your existing infrastructure can meet your new requirements?

4. Why consider communication technology changes?

5. How can you integrate or interconnect your organizational communication requirements?

6. When is the appropriate time to implement such changes?

7. Where can you find the help to accomplish this kind of survey?

The remaining question to be asked is, "Who can do it?" The basic development of communication requirements should be a corporate decision based upon a performance standard. Only your organization can develop such an evaluative and measurement document. What is a communications-based performance standard? It should result in a written inventory that lists all corporate communication activities as they presently exist. It should identify present deficiencies and suggest the changes necessary to improve the present situation.

The choice of appropriate technology is increasingly important to producing your highest Communications Quotient. We are going more in depth on this technological communications issue than we have in previous chapters, but this is a hot topic that we don't want you to miss.

Communications and Communications Technology: The Start of a Path for Understanding the Past, Improving the Present, and Creating a Future

This section takes us more into a pure communications subject, and it will feel as though we've left the Leadership Quotient for a few pages. Stay with us: This is important for your quest to understand communications. Communications technology is too complex to be addressed simply. Leaders have lots of communications face to face in the old fashioned way, but they are having an increasing number of interactions via new technologies made possible by computers and cellular technology and the like. Many parts of an organization are automatically linked via some form of electronic data interchange (EDI). A number of organizational processes are now accomplished computer-to-computer without human intervention. With this in mind, we need to address this question: What are some communications technology facts that might help increase your Communications Quotient in today's fast-changing and highly connected world? First we see technologies represented in two categories of delivery systems:

1. Wire—telephones, telegraph, computers, faxes, e-mail, and cable television are the best examples of wired systems for the most part, though there are wireless systems. The wired systems require that both the sender and the receiver be connected by hard wire from one location to the other.

2. Wireless—two-way radio, radio paging, data communications, and network television are basic examples of wireless delivery systems. Yet today, any of these examples can be designed and constructed to operate in either the wired or the wireless world. All communications technologies are some mediums/media designed to support communications from one location to another or to multiple locations, and can carry data, audio and even video.

Automated linking of an organization and its partners' systems is not simple, as anyone who has started an EDI (Electronic Data Interchange) or integrated enterprise-wide planning and communicating system (Enterprise Resource Planning System—ERP) can attest. Many of these huge ERPs are never implemented even after spending millions of dollars because the complexity becomes too great. A number of companies have gone out of business trying to implement these massive systems. Yet all organizations need some level of information for a decision-making process that allows leaders who are not communication experts to chart their organization's course with communications technologies that can accomplish the following:

• Improve overall organizational and individual efficiencies;

• Enhance accounting, financial, security, and record keeping to increase operations and administrative control while keeping costs down;

• Expand the utilization of all resources, human and otherwise;

• Improve measurement, compensation for results, and morale;

- Avoid lawsuits and limit liability as well as allow fraud audits if necessary (this might have helped us avoid many of the frauds we have seen of late; organizational controls are needed to help all of us stay honest);

- Project work: planning, estimating, scheduling, control, measurements, and adjustments;

- Standardize development, training, and secession contingency planning; often can be delivered or accomplished through the Web;

- Control inventories of parts, people, locations, knowledge, skills, abilities, etc.;

- Forecast upgrades and needed new features or facilities;

- Enhance utilization of Computer Aided Design and all forms of Computer Aided whatever;

- Track orders, purchases, and sales of products and services;

- Integrate all constituency relations;

- Manage: plan, organize, direct, control, reward, staff, strategize;

- Increase corporate image and public relation;

- Leverage everyone and everything; and

- Use a building-block approach to technology to be in position to take advantage of new communications technology advancements without having to junk everything.

You must first address this communications issue and understand how dependent you and your organization have become on so many various ways of communicating. To more fully realize any of these goals and objectives, it is important to take a large number of factors into consideration. Communications technology decisions involve consideration of the following:

- Determine what goal and objectives you want to accomplish with and through your information technology and systems used for communications.

- Inventory and list all of the communications technology your organization is presently using and what it is being used to accomplish.

- Determine what tasks are accomplished and how communications technology helps you accomplish them.

- Look closely at the kinds of technology interaction that are required to accomplish your essential task: interactions are the tricky part; individual elements in and of themselves are most often relatively simple.

- Understand who performs which tasks and the difficulties they experience and then define how their task might be made easier or more efficient or effective.

- Identify the communications technology interfaces that are presently a problem or an impossibility.

- Determine the technology changes, hardware or software, that can improve your personnel efficiency or effectiveness.

- Find out the internal intelligence capabilities or expertise that exists in your communications technology systems or people.

- Determine the level of communications technology integration.

- Determine the true requirements for communications technology capacity, speed, and backup.

- Assess what your organization's competitors are doing and what the vendors are providing.

- Assess the people factors of all communications technology: many people become wedded to their existing technology.

- Implement technological solutions that achieve communication goals and objectives, but allow the recovery of capital equipment costs in a reasonable amount of time.

- Achieve improved efficiency while maintaining and improving organizational public image, improving employee morale, and insuring longevity.

- Planning and implementing a more integrated communications technology must employ a building-block approach using widespread standards.

- Measure the cost-benefit of any communications technology upgrade over the projected life of the upgrade.

- Plan for the next upgrade by building in potential links with each upgrade.

Understandably, most organizations have allowed communications to happen over time, becoming so dependent on their "happen sense" net and cell technology that they cannot take the time to "fix" anything. Most leaders suffer from a low Communications Quotient because they are not fully utilizing all their resources. When organizational structure or technology changes—as they surely will—the leader is not in position to keep up with his environment.

In setting goals and objectives that measure the existing organizational performance, many other issues become apparent. Most organizations discover that their communications and technology systems are stand-alone systems that are being used together: they are not really integrated. Telephone systems are integrated with other systems yet they were not designed this way initially. Wireless communication systems are often stand-alone operations. In fact, all of the two-way, paging, tracking, e-mailing, computer, voice mail, and video could possibly be used together, but they most often are not integrated. Recognizing that all these separate communications operations are really vertical, stand-alone systems obviously indicates the need for evaluating and upgrading your communications technology. Your organizational goal should be the development of an **efficient and effective integrated communications system,** not just a comprehensive or convenient one.

While the solution is easily expressed with those six words, it is not easily implemented. That's because most of the existing communications technologies were implemented piecemeal without an overall evaluation and design. Leaders with a high Communications Quotient continually reevaluate organizational goals and objectives and assess how they relate to existing organizational communications technology. The internal and external forces for change are enormous and include many governmental as well as private entities. Many organizations could create an internal communications technology group comprised of those who do the job daily, led by an internal communications technology coordinator. Solicitation of ideas and methods from vendors, industry groups, and service personnel needs to be someone's job. With a group or person responsible, you can then start to determine what you really need.

In developing a communications strategy, it is important to recognize that decisions must be made because of competitive advantage or cost benefit. These cannot be determined without identifying corporate goals and objectives and determining exactly what communications, technological or otherwise, could improve the present situation. The key point is that without a viable corporate communications strategy that develops an integrated system approach to communication, achieving your highest Communications Quotient is not possible. A realistic strategy assists in prioritizing goals (in your language) and identifies how to best integrate all corporate communications systems and technology. The essence of a successful communications system is to integrate all aspects into a user-friendly system that allows for continuous growth. This is more preferable than a series of blocks of individual pieces of equipment that may be linked in subsystems. Unfortunately, some organizations find that to improve their telephones or data systems, they have to start from scratch. Flexibility and your corporate expertise, existing standards, and expectations improve your chances of getting what you need. How can you best avoid normal problems as you develop a viable communications system? Here are general rules or guidelines that experience has proven workable:

1. Create a communications group, team, or committee that has real worker representation and have one communications technology officer with influence running the group.

2. Seek and obtain the employees' descriptions of their communications problems, limitations, and needs; seek their help in defining what's needed for effectiveness and efficiency.

3. Compare and contrast what communications systems and technology others have inside and outside your industry; also understand what is available that is not currently being used.

4. Create a database of communications ideas.

5. Have review and test procedures in place prior to any purchases or commitments.

6. Develop a detailed written description of what services integrate with which existing systems; include how they integrate and how they should integrate.

7. Craft corporate-wide communication policies and procedures.

8. Consider the cost differences among owning, outsourcing, leasing, and renting services.

9. Understand the cost benefit trade-offs of each decision. Evaluate lowering or increasing costs and the facilities or services you'll get.

We are not attempting to tell you what specific communications technology could improve your Communications Quotient; we are just trying to get you to establish some general guidelines and directions. Most communications decisions a leader makes are affected by many factors:

- Business climate

- Industry advances

- Technology advances

- National association positions

- Governmental policies and regulations

- Federal Communications Commission's rules

- Future business decisions

All of these factors will influence communications strategy development. A successful communications technology strategy can outline the development of an integrated system that lasts for years. However, it will last only if flexibility is *built in,* not *built onto.* The hardware and software are available for the effective Communications Quotient leader to find and implement.

Yes, planning and implementing communications technology strategy is a complex activity for a number of reasons, but there is little doubt that it is worth it. There are differing opinions on what is the most productive and cost-efficient means to assess and validate your evolving strategy. Outsourcing the activities is often a good idea, but that is for an expert to decide. We feel that each and every leader should evaluate the real cost of her current communications systems so she can understand the cost/benefit relationship. The leader should never abdicate the responsibility of managing the communications systems. In fact, we feel it is harder to manage most things when they are outsourced or handed over to outsiders than it is when they are handled in-house.

Look at the formal and informal ways of communicating, and if you see much dissimilarity, you have a real problem. People must often use a different informal system because something is wrong with the formal system. Make sure the formal and the informal communications patterns and systems are relatively the same. If there is inconsistency between the two systems, the formal system should be changed. We hope this section has been general enough to cover many environments, yet specific enough that you can find some application. In other words, have we communicated with you? Now we turn to the specifics as they relate to our *LQ*©'s CQ. (Parts of this section were based on the work of Service, Whitman, Ammons, and Harper, 2000.)

Description of the Communications Quotient and its Dimensions

Look closely at Figure 6.2. This is the generic version of *LQ*© as it applies to CQ. Note we have labeled Quadrants 1, 2, 3, and 4. Refer to this figure as we explain the elements that comprise each quadrant. In each of the four quadrants, we discuss individuals who typify the trait and how it manifests itself in their observable behavior. These issues are discussed so that you can identify a "comparison other" to help you in identifying your own personal Communications Quotient as it related to your Leadership Quotient. We want you to apply these concepts and examples to your leadership style with your followers in your specific organizational environment because you learn better when you make specific and personal application of the ideas.

To identify a leader for comparative purposes, think of someone you know who exhibits an effective Communications Quotient that you would like to emulate. It might be you want to identify a leader you do NOT want to emulate or become more like. The leaders we discuss here are examples we have observed and can explain as universal examples. Think of your own "icon of Communications Quotient" as you read through the following descriptions. Your example may be a well-known public figure who is currently in a position of leadership, or perhaps a historical person. He or she could be a personal leader such as a boss, brother, mother, coworker, or friend. The main thing is to understand a trait someone else exhibits and how that relates to a trait you can control in order for you to develop a plan of action to improve your own Leadership Quotient.

The Greeks and Romans created myths so they could have a perfect example of the traits they admired. Comparing themselves to perfection provided for improvement of their lives. We want you to so the same thing. Dave does it in seminars. He asks small groups to identify a character from a TV series who exemplifies great leadership. If there are four small groups, at least one of them will nominate Andy Griffith. Dave has an example of *The Andy Griffith Show* cued up on the video and shows a five-minute segment as soon as a group mentions his name. "How did Dave know someone would mention Andy Griffith?" you might ask. Well, as a friend would say, "This is not Dave's first rodeo." He has conducted hundreds of seminars for years, so he is pretty confident someone will mention Andy Griffith. The seminar group continues to explain why Andy Griffith is such a great communicator, leader, and manager. At some point, a seminar attendee mentions that he seems perfect only because there is a script written for him. That's exactly the point. He's the 20th-century version of the Greek god: he's perfect. Comparing our leadership to his perfect leadership, we become better leaders. We will never lead like Andy Griffith, but we can improve our leadership, IF we continue to compare ourselves to perfection.

OK, back to the identification of strengths and weaknesses. Remember: Do not stagnate on the strictness of what is really under someone's control and what is not. We list things as natural or "no control" when they are things someone is not likely to change for whatever reason and things that have become ingrained early in someone's life. We identify things as natural when they appear to be things people have gained early on, perhaps they were born with, and things that they will not or cannot change.

Figure 6.2: CQ MEASUREMENT AND IMPROVEMENT MATRIX

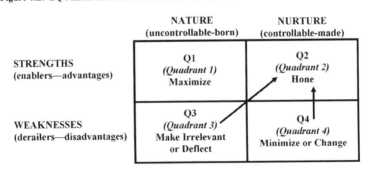

Remember: It's not how great *you* did telling people, it's how great *they* did understanding what you said that counts.

Normal Natural CQ Strengths—Quadrant 1 of the CQ 2X2 Matrix

Speaking is often the first trait that is noticed about a leader's communication ability. "She is just a natural speaker" is a typical observation. Those people are easy to listen to and convincing as public speakers as well as in personal situations. We often think of people as dignified in their speech or public speaking when they present their thoughts with clarity and conviction. Even those who have been trained to be effective speakers usually start with quite a lot of natural ability. The speaking talent is exhibited early on and indeed that talent is often what gets them on the path of choosing some form of speaking as a major contributor to their leadership style.

In this area, think about Matt Lauer of the *Today* show and how he seems to be so easy and effective in his speaking. His words and the way he uses them are pleasant and easy to listen to. You feel as though he is speaking only to you, not a national audience. On the other hand, try listening to Susan Estridge. It's almost impossible. How could she be on TV?

In history, we know of the Gettysburg Address and how Abraham Lincoln made such a lasting impact with a few well-chosen words. Lincoln was preceded on the podium by the governor of Pennsylvania, who spoke for over two hours. Lincoln felt inadequate with only the three-minute speech he had written on the train ride from Washington to Gettysburg. In the speech he even admits, "The world will little note nor long remember what we say here today…" Dave often recites the entire Gettysburg Address during speeches. When he does, he always pauses at that point to add, "It's 140 years later and we're still reciting the speech." If Abraham Lincoln is your icon of Communications Quotient, remember that he thought his words were not very meaningful, but they were. The same could happen to you. Choose your words carefully; speak with force and persuasion. You will make an impact.

Former President Bill Clinton is one of the most effective public communicators of our time. Very persuasive and realistic, he can convince an audience that he really means what he says and cares about each audience member personally. Barack Obama at the 2004 Democratic National Convention actually outshone Clinton in a speech. Remember that name! Obama made most of those watching speechless. On the other hand, President George W. Bush is not a natural orator like Bill Clinton. He makes "OK" public speeches, but it's obvious that it is not easy for him. He has to practice and receive coaching, and he still mangles a syllable now and then (by his own admission). If you're a natural born speaker, Bill Clinton might be your icon; if not, choose George W. Bush, who has made himself into an effective communicator.

One speech that stands out is Martin Luther King Jr.'s "I Have a Dream" speech. MLK's speech very well could have changed the course of history for the better. Consider what could have been the result if it had been Louis Farrakhan who led the way for civil rights for African Americans instead of MLK.

A second natural trait we have all observed is **listening**. An inclusive listener shows he is focused on what someone else has to say, not on what the listener himself wants to say. When someone is a good listener, you can see it and feel it. She is paying attention to you and clarifying what you mean, not what she wants to make of what you mean. To really understand and solve problems and make decisions, nothing is more important than listening. If the listener does not understand a problem or issue, he cannot solve it. This is the case very often where we solve problems we want to solve rather than the real issue. You might recall the story of looking for keys under the streetlight.

While in Europe, Bill was impressed by how, on the Tube or a train, you could sit right next to someone who was talking on the phone and not hear a word of his or her conversation. In America, you can normally hear a conversation several aisles over in the store or even in the car next to you at a stoplight. Bill said to a close friend in London, "You guys can hear a lot better than Americans for some reason." The reply was, "No, we cannot; we just pay more attention." The Briton made a good observation about our very noisy, communications-cluttered society. In our culture packed with messages, we have to be screamed at to get our attention. As Wayne's granddad said: "Wayne, if you'd just shut up and listen, you'd learn what I know as well as what you already know."

Popular icons such as Dr. Phil, Oprah Winfrey, Larry King, and Barbara Walters all appear to be great interviewers because they are great listeners. We have the feeling that our pastors are great listeners, as are many psychiatrists; but who really knows? A key here seems to be the ability to *appear* to be listening and really trying to understand. It seems that people are listening when their part of the conversation is accompanied by questions that indicate they really want to understand and not just be understood. Those interviewers on TV who simply want their opinion to be heard are really not that effective.

We generally see the logic behind some of what Bill O'Reilly and Rush Limbaugh have to say, but do we really need to hear what either of those guys thinks? I daresay anyone who has listened to either of those two for even a few hours can guess what Bill's or Rush's opinion will be with a 90%+ accuracy. Do we learn much from an entertainer? Maybe some, but not a lot of varied opinions, in part because they are good speakers and not good listeners. O'Reilly should occasionally practice what he preaches in the spin zone of spin zones not aptly called the "no spin zone."

When someone prefaces his communication to you by stating, "This is the honest truth," he is committing the liar's paradox. The person is either lying or not lying. Saying he is not lying does not change his status. Wouldn't a liar lie about lying? Ask yourself why someone must tell you she is honest, or a Christian for that matter; or is she not "spinning" the facts? It is, in all probability because you cannot figure it out from his actions or words, so he has to tell you, "I don't spin things!" Spin, honesty, enthusiasm, humor, and spirituality are among many things that must be obvious without a label or they are simply not as advertised. One local newspaper had a section on the front page, "Jokes," and yes, the title was needed! If you have to tell your followers you are their leader, you're not. Leaders who have a high Communications Quotient don't have to advertise their communications expertise or their leadership expertise.

A third trait that leaders cite in communication that they feel is natural or ingrained is that of being **outgoing, expressive, enthusiastic, and passionate**. We have all met someone who has had a profound effect on our lives. Perhaps it is a minister, boss, or professor, but it invariably is someone who is so passionate and enthusiastic that she makes us think about life and where we might be headed. He communicates not just with choice of words but with an outgoing expressiveness that makes us feel that he passionately believes what he is telling us.

Passion and enthusiasm for a topic are often more important than the technical correctness of the solution. The best salespeople are not always the people with the best products. Dave was a salesman with the Pripps beverage company of Sweden, who tried to replace Gatorade as the sports drink of choice in the U.S. In every measurable category, Pripps Plus was better than Gatorade. Because Pripps failed to communicate that message, the product failed. More specifically, the *product* didn't fail; the *message* about the product failed. The message of your leadership will fail also if you don't have an effective Communications Quotient.

The most convincing speaker is not always the one with the best logic, nor is the best professor the one who has the best material; but they are always the people who make you feel they really are passionate about their point of view, product, or your learning. Many people need to practice enthusiasm in their speaking and expression. It is very hard to get excited about a topic that the presenter is not excited about. When we give students the right to pick a topic or person to talk about, we really grade them down if they are not enthusiastic. If you cannot get enthusiastic about something you choose, how can you ever be enthusiastic about your Leadership Quotient?

Dave enjoys a seminar exercise where he selects a manager to "sell" buttermilk to his fellow seminar attendees. Dave pretends that an order has just come down from top management that everyone in the unit must drink buttermilk. He actually pours a cup for each attendee and sits back to watch the selected manager overcome the many forms of resistance to change that happen in all organizational change attempts. Often the "volunteer" didn't volunteer at all and doesn't like buttermilk herself. She will complain to Dave, "It's hard to sell something you don't believe in!" Yes, it is. That's why you will be a much more effective leader if you're leading a cause you care about and can show some emotion about.

The final trait that many feel is natural is a **genuine, humble honesty or expressed humility**. The recent *American Idol* winner, Ruben, was chosen in no small part because of his appearance of humility, honesty, and just being a nice guy. Jimmy Carter is respected not for what he did as president, but because of his actions since his presidency. Carter's work with humanitarian issues and Habitat for Humanity exemplifies what Americans want in the area of humility of otherwise famous people. Maybe what we see as humility and genuineness is faked, but we really want to see it in those whom we admire when they have held positions of power and influence. Perhaps this will be a problem for Hillary Clinton in her upcoming quest for higher political office. Maybe sad but true: Many followers still want more humility and genuineness from women than men.

Another exemplar in this area is Barbara Bush. Americans love Barbara because she seems to be a real mother and grandmother who will stand up for her kids and husband because they are simply that: her child or husband. Contrast Mother Teresa and Princess Diana. But remember: We really only know their public images, not the real person within. But we can use their public image to make assertions about their Communications Quotient because the CQ contributes to the Leadership Quotient only as followers perceive it.

Faking this area is dangerous, because once you are considered one who fakes humbleness and genuineness, you've blown it and you can't recover. Marsha often comes to a class and tells our students a story about a lady who came dressed very provocatively for an interview with a man. Marsha went out to greet the lady, and the candidate said, "I thought you were Marshal; if I had known you were a woman I would have dressed differently!" Marsha says, "That told me all I needed to know about her. I stood there with her for about two minutes and said, 'Thanks for your résumé. I'll call if I need anything else from you.'" Realize that often your actions tell people all they need to know about your genuineness and honesty. Often the leader's Communications Quotient tells the followers all they need to know about the leader.

Normal Natural CQ Weaknesses—Quadrant 3 of the CQ 2X2 Matrix

Many of the subjects in our Leadership Quotient study group report a natural weakness in the area of communications when the leader exhibits a **judgmental tone**, lacking empathy or understanding; lacking openness or directness. *Tonight Show* host Jay Leno talked about President Bush's statement of "pointing to the speck in a neighbor's eye while you have a log in your own." Leno says, "What was that all about, does anyone know what he meant?" Yes, Jay, we do, but it seems not many of us do. We all come short in so many ways that we must stop to ask, "How can we be so judgmental of others?" That's why we've written *The Leadership Quotient*: so you can "clean up your own act" so your leadership style matches your followers' needs in your specific environment.

Bill Clinton was a leader who could show empathy and "feel your pain." Many others, notably Ross Perot, left us feeling, "He doesn't have a clue." To have empathy that shows is a great trait, and not to appear to have it is often a deathblow, especially to a political future. Unsuccessful presidential candidate Bob Dole was a very capable leader in the political environment, but his followers (voters) didn't attach to him emotionally.

In this section, we're tempted to cite examples of public figures who seem judgmental. However, to do so would be to fall into our own trap, because then *we* would be judging. Former Minnesota Governor Jesse Ventura made one of his typical, outlandish comments about Christians being weak. His press secretary cleared up the governor's position for the media: "The Governor just can't stand intolerance!" If the governor really were tolerant, he would have to be tolerant of others' intolerance, so he would be intolerant. It's simple logic; don't get confused. Everyone is intolerant. Leaders with high Communications Quotients have the ability to help the followers improve their life (job performance, etc.) without judging them or telling them what to do.

We never said leadership is easy. After the publication of Dave's book, *Corporate Cults,* he participated in a debate with the human resources director from SAS. The company is always in the top ten "Best Places to Work" ranking in *FORTUNE* magazine. Dave didn't know the HR director was in the hall of fame of the organization hosting the debate, so Dave didn't do well. Dave came across as judgmental. One of the questions asked Dave to compare *Corporate Cults* and *Built to Last*, which seem to have somewhat opposite messages. Dave responded, "Read *Built to Last* to learn how to build organizations that last. Read *Corporate Cults* to learn how to build individuals that last." Dave's opponent pounced, "That sounds judgmental. Can you really tell people how to live their lives?" Dave was already behind in the debate and couldn't give the answer he really wanted to. What he wanted to tell the audience was that all books give instruction. Would you buy a book that didn't?

The Leadership Quotient tells you what to do. Hopefully, this book tells you what to do for your personal improvement in the leadership arena. We're laying out a formula, but you're the one who fills in the blanks and makes the judgments, not us. That's what leaders with an effective Communications Quotient are able to do: allow followers to see their errors and improve them without judging them.

Being open and direct is what most people want. Many interpersonal frameworks suggest you start with a compliment when you want to correct someone. That's OK with us, but the important thing is to get to the truth. Tell followers what they need to know, good *and* bad. Establish that you are open and direct and that you're not trying to manipulate them for your gain, you're trying to improve their contribution to the organization for their gain.

A second natural trait (a lot of this is acquired, but it is surely mostly acquired early in life and most often very hard to modify) is **clarity of speech often noted by accent, pitch, level, slang, or dialect**. We remind young students as they go for their first real job interviews that they need to sound and appear more mature, not less. Most of them need to reduce their use of the word "like" by about 50% or more. Filler words are also extremely distracting and need to be eliminated from a leader's speech. We are struck by the number of FOX reporters who continuously say "uhhh" and "ummm." Professional communicators should have corrected those distracting habits years ago.

Listen closely to some of the TV personalities such as James Carville and Susan Estridge, and you'll possibly get ill. We can hardly look at Susan Estridge as she makes her weird facial expressions. Or think about Carville as he said, "Drag a hunnerd doller bill thew a traller pork," it's almost more than one can stand. Try not looking at a talk show and just listening, and you'll notice the droning on of the incessant talking and it will drive you crazy.

Some people talk too high or too low. Dave has a friend who almost whispers when she speaks. When he asked about it, she responded, "I find if I talk low, people listen more carefully." Dave retorted, "I find if I say things that are interesting, people listen more carefully." There are many speaking errors; the key is to think about yours. What is it about your communication style that limits your Communications Quotient and thus your entire Leadership Quotient?

A third trait that many of our respondents categorized as a natural negative is **mannerisms**. The next time he is on TV, just watch William F. Buckley talk. Or recall what Simon said about *American Idol* runner-up, Clay: "I have to close my eyes to listen to you. Where did you come up with those facial expressions?" Clay listened and probably earned the runner-up position because he changed some of those extreme expressions.

Actor Jim Carrey uses his face to express a lot, but it seems that most of it is "dumb and dumber," which is acceptable for a comedian, but not an organizational leader! Get someone you really trust to watch you and tell you of any mannerisms that take away from your effectiveness. One executive management candidate had to be told not to stare at women's breasts. It was truly innocent, and he just did not like eye contact. Another example is when someone in an interview will not look you in the eye or stares you down: balance is the key.

Bill thinks Dave is successful partly because he just looks like a nice guy (and he really is). But his wife tells him not to frown when he watches TV. Apparently, when he concentrates, he looks surly. Frowning at the TV does not hurt his Communications Quotient, frowning at his students and clients will. Bill on the other hand looks a little sterner, but he, too, smiles when it is appropriate and looks mean when it's necessary. Bill's students saw him alone on the street corner about 1:00 a.m. in London and they said, "Wow, you looked mean." Bill responded, "But no one has ever bothered me; I guess it works!"

The last natural negative trait we have identified is **poor timing, and sometimes it almost appears on purpose**. Recall former Senate Majority Leader Trent Lott's statement about the late Senator Strom Thurmond and how it cost Lott his Speakership. Recall Jimmy the Greek's last statement on TV about black athletes being naturally better athletes, and you'll get the drift. Even Andy Rooney, whose purpose is to report the lighter side of life, has to be somewhat careful of politically incorrect statements. We feel that this has gotten out of hand, but we're not the followers. The message of this chapter is to form your Communications Quotient so it matches your followers.

We recall a former front-runner for governor of Texas who made a gaffe and told a joke around a campfire on a rainy night and it literally cost him the governorship. In fact, so many elections have been decided on a single saying. Here are some examples:

"He acquitted Willie Horton."

"He was born with a silver spoon in his mouth."

"Clayton Williams didn't pay any income tax last year; did you?"

"It's the economy, stupid."

"Read my lips."

"I did not have sex with that woman."

Normal Nurtured CQ Strengths—Quadrant 2 of the CQ 2X2 Matrix

This is an easy section, for we all know people who have nurtured their communications abilities and communicate an air of leadership that touches others as they pass by in daily life. Remember the saying: "What you do speaks so loudly I can't hear what you say." Make sure that your words are not overridden by your actions. It may take a thousand words to describe a picture, but there are probably not enough words to undo what someone sees us do!

The first trait we see exemplified and nurtured here is an ability to fit in socially. Yes, **social skills exemplified by one's understanding of** appropriateness, balance, and fit are an important part of your Communications Quotient. Confidence is what gives a leader the executive appearance. Samford University's president, Dr. Thomas Corts, looks and acts presidential even when he strides down the aisle to talk to the faculty in preschool workshops. This, however, is not all good because it does often result in an air about someone that stifles open and free sharing of ideas and information. Empowerment, not a picture of power, is the most appropriate form of social skills in today's complex world.

Dr. Terry Crane is a college friend of Bill's wife and was listed as one of the most powerful women in the Bay Area when she worked for Apple. She has continued to work in the Bay Area at a high-tech firm and lately as an executive for AOL. Terry is the epitome of social skills. She could talk to a doorknob, and we are confident it would answer back. She can discuss almost any topic with anyone, but she does not compromise. She is comfortable entertaining 5,000 at one of the most significant parties in Dallas, speaking at a college graduation, or working the crowd at an upscale ball; or she can talk one-on-one to the plumber.

Dr. Bill Hull, a minister and noted Biblical scholar, is another exemplar who can, in five minutes, act like anyone is his best friend, maybe because they are! He once introduced 15 people as a new committee and seemed to know more about each of us than we did. Bill could recall telling Dr. Hull all the information about his wife and children, but he did not know how Dr. Hull could recall it all.

Sadly, during the week we were writing this chapter, we had to pause to celebrate the life of Bob Hope as it came to an end. Bob Hope was an icon of understanding of what it took to get others to feel and see humor in any and every situation. He knew how to localize everything for the troops, making fun of their commanders and situation and himself, even as enemy fire was near his show. Old films of him visiting troops in the hospitals showed how focused he was on each individual and how he touched them, both with his own hands and heart.

The second trait we include in this quadrant is **writing and, consequently, reading** as a nurtured communications skill. We can all understand the need to write, especially today when e-mail is such a prevalent form of communication. The contribution of reading to the Communications Quotient is less clear. Reading is important because it is an important form of listening and the foundation for every writer. If you truly want to listen to what others have to say for learning, you must read so you will have a basis for understanding. TV and radio or personal conversations are just a small part of listening and communicating.

Alan Keyes attempted to run for president and was often on the talk shows during the 2000 elections. He epitomized the appropriate grammar and vocabulary of an exemplar we would love to have represented the U.S. However, he received little attention, in part because he was honest with his responses instead of being politically correct. How sad it is that Americans will not elect an honest-speaking person because we want those who can worm their way around what the definition of "is" is!

Commentator George F. Will's TV appearances and columns always show his education and precision, so he has an effective Communications Quotient. But so did those of columnist Lewis Grizzard, who wrote *Elvis Is Dead and I Don't Feel So Good Myself* and *If Love Were Oil, I'd Be About a Quart Low*. Grizzard's down-home manner has endeared him to millions. George F. Will spoke in Birmingham, Alabama, just before the 9/11 tragedy, where he predicted terrorism would hit the U.S. and then Americans would not be so indifferent to it as we had been for decades. Will and Grizzard exemplify people who can write and express themselves in a manner appropriate for their audience, gaining respect because of clarity and connection.

A third trait is one that many fear: public speaking, which we include under the title, **Making a Presentation**. Dave tells his management students, "The two greatest fears are death and public speaking, and we're going to cure one of them" (meaning you're going to make a presentation or die trying). He is unapologetic about it. Management is a discipline that requires you to make presentations. Leadership is too. This book is not about leading yourself; it's about leading others. How can you lead them if you don't communicate with them?

The ability to give a clear and concise presentation to help others learn, to motivate, or just to inform, is one of the foundations to success as an upper-level leader. We have discussed in the introduction to this section how to put together a good presentation, and we feel that everyone needs to practice this most critical of skills. However, we do know that sincerely being able to articulate your thoughts and persuade others is an invaluable skill that everyone can improve.

Colin Powell and Franklin Roosevelt are exemplars we all recognize as great speakers. Also, Martin Luther King Jr. and John F. Kennedy were great communicators. In a more close-to-home example, Bill recalls when he joined Chilton Corporation and was asked to update 200 contract clients on Chilton's new automated processing system. He worked for weeks preparing the speech, and just days before, his assistant told him that speeches at Chilton "make or break people." Then on Monday morning when he was to speak about 2:00 p.m. that day, Van Smith, the president of Chilton, called and said he was having lunch with Bill before his presentation. At the lunch, Bill told Van of everything he had planned to say: "You can't say that; they think we've been working on the system for years." Bill was hired to start the effort and knew the truth. It was a terrible speech and Bill to this day has difficulty with the embarrassment he felt covering up the truth—actually lying! We feel that the key to good presentations is sincerity, and when you learn to fake that, you've got it made. Or do you?

In making presentations, remember first and foremost: It is about the audience and not you. Secondly, you need to watch nonverbal communications as well as verbal. Lastly, use visual aids effectively and sparingly. We know too many people who turn over their speeches to PowerPoint, which can be a real mistake.

The last trait that is clearly a nurtured strength is **thinking and responding on your feet**. We have all seen facilitators who can balance formality and informality and just cannot be rattled. These people seem always prepared because they are. Think about what Henry Kissinger, one of the greatest negotiators of all time, said: "To win in negotiations, know more about the other person's side than they do." That is right: not more about your side, but more about their side. Most of us think we persuade from what we know, when in reality it is most often by first understanding where the other person is coming from.

JFK was a master at this and his debating skills won him the presidency. He could think, respond, and really connect with his audience. His appearance of poise and confidence overshadowed Nixon's knowledge, intellect, and experience. Another example would be Peter Jennings in his town hall meetings. He could connect with people, respond, and keep people on track. Learn to do this if you want to be a good leader: think preparation, preparation, preparation.

Normal Nurtured CQ Weaknesses—Quadrant 4 of the CQ 2X2 Matrix

Nonverbal communications such as **posture, expression, and movements** are most often more important than what is being said. How often have you watched someone talk and just could not hear them because of some facial expressions or other visual distraction? Nonverbal cues are much more important than we think they are. An entire chapter will address the Appearance Quotient, so we will not dedicate much space to it in this chapter. But we want to discuss the effect of nonverbal communications. These nonverbal behaviors are more often negative, for when they are positive they really are just neutral factors that do little "extra" good.

Joe Lieberman, Phil Gramm, and Steve Forbes are talented and intellectual individuals who will never be president because of their nonverbal communications. Someone needs to give Lieberman lessons on how to talk without whining because he always seems to be complaining about something even when he's not! Both Gramm and Forbes need lessons on eliminating "geekyness." Those things may not be real or important in the scheme of things, but they communicate weaknesses that we don't want in a leader of the free world.

A second trait that many seem to perfect is a style that **stifles communication**. "We live so much of our lives in chaos. Human history can be viewed as an endless search for greater order: everything from language to religion to law to science tries to impose a framework on chaotic existence" (Carter, 2002, p. 229). If we could encourage those who communicate with us, we would be able to understand the world as others see it and not as we see it. It seems the desire of many to be heard is so strong that it overcomes all else. These low Communications Quotient people seem to broadcast, "I'm smarter than you, so just shut up and listen." Nothing could be worse for a modern leader than for those around her to feel as though they can't speak and that anything they have to say is not important. Again, one has to wonder why someone has to feel as though they can't speak. Is it because they really know it all, or is it because they "can't handle the truth"? Makes you wonder why people don't want to hear what others have to say. This is probably alright for entertainers like Bill O'Reilly and Rush Limbaugh, but certainly not for a human resource director, CEO, or managers at levels where there is so much to know that they can't know everything.

We admire the interviewing skills of Tim Russert, who quietly pursues with facts and questions, not opinions. Compare "I'd like to know what you think" questions to "you listen to what I have to say" statements. Also ineffective are questioners who just want to make the interviewee feel warm and fuzzy. Which type of interviewer do we learn the most from over time? Remember these examples as you interview and talk to others. Listen to what they have to say; don't make them listen to what you have to say! Limbaugh and O'Reilly are just entertainers, and we must not forget that. You're not. You're the leader of people who expect you to communicate in a style that matches their will to listen in the environment in which you work. If you make all three fit—leader, followers, environments—you will have an effective Leadership Quotient.

Here we are reminded of most academic interviews where the professors interviewing for a new dean hardly give the candidate any time to talk. Bill came into a prearranged one-hour phone interview for a dean's job and observed that the interviewers talked about 50 minutes with 10 left over for the candidate. He quickly developed a questionnaire for all of the other nine phone interviews and directed only questions, not answers, to the interviewee. Informing the candidate can take place after you see if there is any mutual interest and a real fit.

Mike was an HR director who could simply outtalk or overtalk anyone. He would develop an opinion almost before anyone said anything and verbally beat you to death with it. One that really backfired on him was when his organization was bought out, and he was convinced he would be cheated out of his rightful executive security plan money. He quit and lost hundreds of thousands of dollars. He was so convinced he was right that he would not listen to the opinions of others. In addition to losing a lot of dough, he had a very hard time finding another job, in part because his skepticism showed. All of those who stayed after Mike received very generous payouts, and Mike left it all because he stifled everyone he talked to.

Ron was the vice president of a large information systems department, and he would not have people tell him anything negative in public. He liked to play junior psychologist with personal problems, but he stifled input on his or the organization's real actions. He said he didn't want yes-people when in fact that's all he wanted. He tried to make you think his ideas were yours but it did not work. Don't be a Mike or a Ron—sorry, guys, but you know it's true!

The next cultivated communications problem we see is **poor use of technology for communications**.

> I stare at the instrument, thinking—not for the first time—what a nasty, intrusive, uncivil thing the telephone really is, demanding, irritating, interrupting, invading the mind's space. I wonder why Alexander Graham Bell is such a hero. His invention destroyed the private realm. The device has no conscience. It rings when we are sleeping, showering, praying, arguing, reading, making love. Or when we just want desperately to be left alone. (2002 fictional work by Carter, p. 16)

A very wise lady led a thinkers' group called the Algonquin Round Table in New York. When the phone would ring, she would often shout out, "What fresh hell is this?" Yes, communications technology can add or detract from our Communications Quotient. Technology cannot replace other forms of communications, but properly used it can enhance the ability to communicate. When we (Dave and Bill) are on business all over the world, we use e-mail to communicate just as our students do as they travel the world. An acquaintance recently began using e-mail at 92 years of age just because he could communicate with his great-grandkids the way they were used to, not the way he preferred.

Ed is one of the best professors anyone has ever heard, and he loves to help students find themselves through new adventures. But his refusal to use e-mail or even have an answering machine makes him less effective than he could be. (Sorry, Ed, but you know it's true—he has just gotten both—alright, Ed!) Also, it seems a little odd that he wants others to stretch themselves but is reluctant to do so himself in this one area. No one should depend fully on technology for communications, but likewise no one should avoid it altogether. To really communicate to a variety of people, you have to figure out their preferred way and communicate in that manner with them. It's simple: You don't have to understand the technology to use it, just like cars, DVD players, dishwashers, etc.

The final trait we see in this area is **poor writing skills**. With the spread of e-mail and the continued importance of written proof, one can ill afford to be a poor writer. Here we do not mean the ability to impress with words, but the ability to put into writing what one wants others to understand. For leaders, being clear and concise beats being flowery every time.

As a college freshman, Bill barely passed freshman composition with a D. He did not write at all until he was well into his 30s, and then he often had help. One reason for this is that Bill read very little, perhaps three books by the time he was 30. He completed an MBA and didn't even buy his books: "I wasn't going to read them so why buy them?" Well, that gradually changed as he moved up into the higher managerial ranks. He became an avid reader and a relatively good writer. But still he must have a good editor! He really had to do this as he pursued his Ph.D. at the age of 45, where in his first semester he typed 580 pages of proofed output. What a way to learn to type!

We simply cannot see how one can get to higher levels of leadership in today's world without the ability to write concisely, clearly, and convincingly. Maybe it was possible years ago, but not now. E-mail and the written word are a must for progression if not actual leadership.

Now that we have finished describing the most common natural and nurtured CQ traits, it is time to look at the whole and assess yourself.

Using the CQ Matrix

As you can see from the previous sections, we gave many examples of communications traits that could help or hinder a person's quest for extended leadership responsibilities. A key here is to first understand clearly each of the traits and then honestly evaluate yourself in each of the four quadrants. Remember to use some additional help from those who know you best. Seek real feedback and use the principles noted in this section and you'll likely get it. Always use others when you are evaluating the way you look and come across in communications.

In evaluating yourself, put a +1 for each of the strengths and a -1 for each of the weaknesses you have determined are your communications traits and behaviors. If you can think of more appropriate strengths or weaknesses you have, list those and score them +1 to -1, but be careful about just making up some traits. Try to be realistic about a replacement trait; it's preferable to use those we have developed from our testing of the CQ or through the extant literature.

Figure 6.3: YOUR CQ MEASUREMENT AND IMPROVEMENT MATRICES

Evaluate yourself against the reported traits in this Matrix.

	NATURE (uncontrollable-born)	NURTURE (controllable-made)
STRENGTHS (enablers—advantages)	**Q1** ____ clarity and conviction in speaking ____ inclusiveness in listening ____ expressive-passion-enthusiasm ____ genuine-humble-honest ____ (self-IDed trait)	**Q2** ____ appropriate social skills ____ good writing and reading skills ____ good presentation skills ____ responding well on your feet ____ (self-IDed trait)
WEAKNESSES (derailers—disadvantages)	**Q3** ____ judgmental tone ____ poor clarity of speech ____ distracting mannerisms ____ poor timing ____ (self-IDed trait)	**Q4** ____ bad nonverbal expression ____ stifle others ____ poor use of technology for communication ____ poor writing skills ____ (self-IDed trait)

Tailor the Matrix below for yourself!

	NATURE (uncontrollable-born)	NURTURE (controllable-made)
STRENGTHS (enablers—advantages)	**Q1** *(Quadrant 1)* Maximize	**Q2** *(Quadrant 2)* Hone
WEAKNESSES (derailers—disadvantages)	**Q3** *(Quadrant 3)* Make irrelevant or deflect	**Q4** *(Quadrant 4)* Minimize or change

Evaluating Your CQ Personal Profile: Strengths and Weaknesses

Doing Something About Your CQ!

Identifying which CQ characteristics you feel are under your control and which ones are not requires a lot of introspection and self-honesty. Many people feel basically that everything is under their control and others feel they control very little. Again, just be realistic, and if you are not likely to change a trait, count it as not under your control. Be honest with yourself. Obtaining the skill of identifying, limiting distractions, studying, learning, relearning, and ultimately using newfound strengths for CQ development will serve you well. Practice improvement in your CQ by expressing outwardly your emotions about doing, getting, or being versus just saying you have the Communications Quotient down pat. Remember: If you dwell on the negatives you'll stay where you are.

We have observed that others often don't agree with our self-assessment as to what our communications strengths and weaknesses are. Also, others often think that a lot more of our traits are on the controllable side than we do. Maybe this is because we have traits that we are not going to change, simply because we don't want to or feel it is just too hard for the expected payback. Yes, most things of value require trade-offs and often trade-offs we are not willing to make. No matter, just be direct and open with yourself.

So, you've identified your Communications Quotient. Now what? Again, and especially in the area of communications, check your evaluations with some trusted people. Then come up with a realistic strategy to address how you can work to improve those things identified as under your control. That will help you offset negative effects of factors over which you are relatively sure you have no control. This will improve your CQ.

Remember: The key is to make perceptions as near reality as possible, but with an understanding that perceptions are in fact communication for the perceiver. In the 2003 Iraqi war, Americans were very convinced that we were liberating a people from untold hardships and cruelty. Yet hundreds of millions around the world felt America had imperialistic designs on the riches of Iraq. How do you change either perception? Press reports are always given by humans with human limitations to knowing Truth.

As We Said in the Introduction, "It's Time to Get Started; If Not Now, When?"

Put your CQ values in the triangle and see if your CQ is enough of a foundation to help you proceed to the next level of improving your $LQ^©$.

Figure 6.4: YOUR LEADERSHIP LEVERAGE TRIANGLE

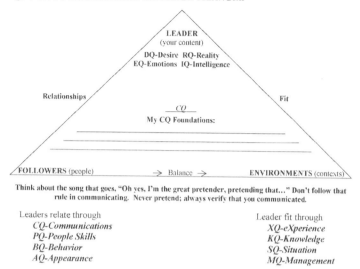

Think about the song that goes, "Oh yes, I'm the great pretender, pretending that..." Don't follow that rule in communicating. Never pretend; always verify that you communicated.

Leaders relate through
CQ-Communications
PQ-People Skills
BQ-Behavior
AQ-Appearance

Leader fit through
XQ-eXperience
KQ-Knowledge
SQ-Situation
MQ-Management

CQ Conclusions

Many current press stories will go down as classic lessons in communications. The stunning yet controversial success of Martha Stewart could be a study in communication. It seems that by failing to communicate her caring—if indeed there was any—Martha set herself up to be someone many wanted to see fall and fall hard (Byron, 2002). If people don't feel you care or have any empathy at all, they will look for reasons to see you fail; but on the other hand, if you communicate a caring and empathetic attitude people will overlook a lot.

We will go into specific types of communications such as performance appraising and coaching when we look at management. Also, we will look more closely at teams, conflicts, training, meetings, problem-solving, establishing cultures, openness, and trust within organizations more closely in other chapters, particularly the MQ chapter. However, all of the rules, descriptions, positives, and negatives identified in this chapter will help you in moving others to use more of their full potential just as they will help you reach more of yours.

Stating everything about an organization from mission, related goals, objectives, and final evaluative reward criteria as well as customer-centered messages in a way that is clear, simple, straightforward, and understandable to those receiving the message is the key.

Remember: As we said, it may take a thousand words to describe a picture, but it will take millions of words to negate what someone saw you do.

Time and again we find that employers are looking for communications skills, interpersonal skills, dependability, and initiative: Don't expect to go far in leadership if you don't have these traits to a reasonable degree. Learn how to influence through your communication, how to listen and understand, and how to negotiate and resolve conflict. "A man convinced against his will keeps the same opinion still" (Trompenaars and Hampden-Turner, 2002, p. 438).

Remember: I tell you, you forget. I show you, you might remember. I involve you in developing the meaning, and you understand. If you find the answer on your own, you've got wisdom.

Don't talk too much or too little, don't challenge too much or too little, don't over- or under-use humor or empathy, know when to take charge of the communications and when to let it ride; but whatever you do, have people say this of your commutations style: "His most outstanding leadership quality was that you knew where he stood" (Reagan as described by newsman Sam Donaldson, in Strock, 1998, p. 39). Nevertheless, don't try to be everything to everyone; and remember: We have one primary cultural orientation, and to think we have more is to err. "A man wrote me and said: 'You can go to live in France, but you cannot become a Frenchman. You can go to live in Germany or Turkey or Japan, but you cannot become a German, a Turk, or Japanese. But anyone, from any corner of the Earth, can come to live in America and become an American'" (Ronald Reagan as written in Strock, 1998, p. 28).

7

PQ, The People Quotient

Atlas chuckled. "Well, I only hope this little incident teaches you a lesson. You're a sweetheart, I know, and I'm [an SOB]. In this world the sweethearts have the friends, Norman, and the [SOBs] give the orders. The thing is, you're giving orders now, mister. You're trying to run a hotel, and you've got to become a little bit of [an SOB]. You'll never be a real one, that's a matter of talent, but you've got to work at it anyway." (Wouk, 1965, p. 323)

As you read this chapter, think about **connecting and reflecting on the perceptions of others** and moving from **fixation to adaptation**. These concepts sound easy, but they are not. How to touch the needs and desires of *others* is the very essence of a successful People Quotient for improved leadership effectiveness.

"High achievement requires a great degree of self-knowledge, as much as it does business acumen" (Hymowtz, 2003, p. B1). The self-knowledge you need in the PQ area relates to your ability to read and understand others. In the context of doing so, it is critical to be sincere about who you are because followers are extremely perceptive. Yes, most everyone is perceptive, but few use their perceptive abilities to their advantage. Most people, in fact, do not use their perceptive abilities to any advantage. They use them to push their agendas or confirm their suspicions before they seek to understand the usefulness of someone else's views.

Leaders with high People Quotients are able to escape the trap of being tough or singly focused on their own perspective, and are able to concentrate *not* on, "How can I use someone?" but instead, "How can we work together?" Just because you do not believe like me does not necessarily mean either of us is right or wrong. In all probability, we both are, and knowing the degree to which each person is right is the beginning of PQ wisdom.

In the end, it is not important to always know what to say or what to do, but it is important to care enough to exhibit the sincere desire to help: people don't care how much you know until they know how much you care. We understand as teachers that a willingness to be taught is the best way to teach. In fact, not knowing what to do, or not knowing the answer, is the beginning of wisdom. Admitting you are a fellow "seeker of knowledge" is often a strength when you want to connect with followers. Always knowing the answer beforehand is most often an "off-putting" characteristic. To truly establish a meaningful relationship, one needs to start at *another* person's point of need, instead of one's *own* point of need.

Bill and Dave have both been teaching for about 12 years. We have made a progression from asking, "What am I going to do with this class?" to, "What is this class going to do with me?" While we certainly have a syllabus and some concrete material to teach, experience has taught us that the best learning takes place when you ask questions that are not in the textbook. Consider the question we've just asked in terms of your group. Are you asking, "What am I going to do with this group?" or, "What is this group going to do with me?" You will have a much higher People Quotient if you ask the latter question.

The truth is that relating is more about reading and adapting than knowing, for we are all essentially alike. There is a very narrow margin of normality in humanity. Most people think and react along a narrow range that fits closely to a self-preservation, self-serving model. Leaders with the highest People Quotients have adopted the Golden Rule with one slight change: "Treat others as *they* would have you treat *them*," though that will not be too far from, "Treat others as you would have them treat you." Understanding and using the subtle differences makes a leader more real to others, more of a people person, not a self-serving person. This PQ skill, others over self, is *the* invaluable people skill.

OK, So What?

We can all point to living examples of "people" people. That is what we are talking about here. PQ is about the ability to relate *with* people and it includes the following:

- Relationships

- Relationship building and destroying

- Social skills

- Use of poise and demeanor

- Teaming

- Facilitating others

- Networking

• Reading others

As with the other quotients, all of these People Quotient concepts must be exercised in a way that produces a fit between the leader, followers, and environments, as shown in Figure 7.1. The emphasis on ability to relate to people from their perspective has changed quite a lot in the last 20 to 40 years. In the even more distant past there often was a need for followers to be dependent on a leader because followers were mostly ignorant and were given no real information, so there was a great deal of dependence. In current times, we see movement towards leader-follower relations that are mutually acceptable and benefiting as the only valid leader-follower relationships. Information and power are more equally distributed than they have ever been before, and this is resulting in a new model for effective leader-follower relationships. This model includes having the savvy to network within and outside organizations (Kilmann, Kilmann, and Associates, 1991).

People want a leader for direction, inspiration, validation, and relationships. Every enterprise is trying to develop leaders to help it in shaping an organization capable of meeting future needs that are, at best, unclear. When organizational change is required, things become confusing and stressful, and everyone looks for leadership—but not for leadership as defined by authority. They want a leader who leads by example, a leader who has earned his reputation and title, not a leader who has merely been appointed. Leadership is ***the*** reason organizational change succeeds or fails. "Around the world, the headlines state people have lost faith in their institutions and the individuals who lead them. But, is it leaders we have lost faith in, or ourselves? One hallmark of an optimistic people is a belief that one individual can make a difference. Yet somehow, we are not as convinced as we once were, that we can each become whatever we hope to be" (Kouzes and Posner, 1993, p. xxv). Leaders of the future must realize that people have specific needs:

• Direction—goals, objectives, measurements, rewards

• Knowledge—skills, development, training, information

• Resources—a place, tools, materials, money

• Support—approval, recognition, feedback, coaching, encouragement

All these elements (Byham, 1988) result in building relationships with people in an organization. People want desperately to belong, and leaders with high People Quotients are those who are able to tap into and satisfy that very basic need.

As a leader, you have to come up with a plan to meet followers' needs as *they* see them; you cannot just wish things would get better. This requires the ability to read people: PQ—a skill that can be learned.

We have seen again and again that leadership is a fusion of work and human relations. Leaders are not leading objects; they are leading human beings with dreams and desires. Your PQ skill will determine how well you speak to the hopes and dreams of others. Leaders need to help others realize their potential. It is such a heartbreaker that so many people die never realizing their dreams. Just think of the lost leadership potential.

If you want to be a leader, first realize people want leaders who want to serve. Then realize that they want a leader who will inspire them, validate them, give them solid direction, and most importantly someone with whom they feel they have a relationship. In the end, most followers simply want a leader who sees them as another person.

Dave is on the faculty at Dallas Baptist University. Keeping the same university president for 15 years is quite unusual. So, to celebrate the 15th year of DBU President, Dr. Gary Cook, faculty and staff were invited to write letters of appreciation for his leadership. Not one of the letters thanked him for leading the university. They all thanked him for personal kindnesses he had shown to them individually. *Leaders don't lead organizations; they lead people.*

Although Bill's university has good leadership, it is a leadership based too largely on dependency, and could be much better. His university sometimes exhibits the value of processes over people, although that is not what its Christian mission would espouse. Too often students and faculty are not the direction setters or main focus of concern; those things are the privy of top levels of hierarchy. Is this as it should be in a Christian university? When you set your standard higher and advertise yourself or your organization as being on higher moral ground, you have set a higher standard by which you are asking to be evaluated. It is obvious to so many that our low percentage of alumni donors is caused by favoring processes designed for administrators rather than students or faculty. Many seem unaware of this, perhaps because they never really ask! Yes, we do surveys asking some standardized questions, but we seldom go to faculty and students and ask for face-to-face feedback. This overall weakness will be developed in the MQ chapter, for so many organizational leaders lead with their own personal perspectives of truth versus the perspectives of their followers. Bill and many of his cohorts have personally been aware of many incidences where formal leaders did not have the PQ to pick up the phone and call someone. Many of our leaders let people find out via e-mail or interoffice mail of a decision that affected them personally. Bill and Dave both love their universities and really don't like to put them down, but we can always see room for improvements, and we use our simple examples here more for effect than real criticism: nothing is perfect!

Realize first that people can have influence over and leverage the power of others. Second, leadership is about the heart and the mind. Third, leadership is about human influence. Fourth, all humans perform actions that take care of what is important to them, to serve their unique values. Lastly, understand that it is a mistake to think others value what you do as you do. Thus, we suggest the following change to the Golden Rule: "…as *they* would have you do unto *them*." People are motivated in the way an organization desires them to be only when *they* really believe the relationship between effort and performance and organizational rewards is as the leaders proclaim. High-PQ leaders avoid ambiguous directions, they limit the search for solutions, and they learn from failures. Seek to understand others and you will have a high PQ.

People change what they do because *they see a truth* that influences their feelings (Kotter and Cohen, 2002). The ultimate test of all leadership is whether it gets people to commit their energy into improving things. Individual commitment alone can cause desired collective mobilization. "There are more than enough problems to go around, so take your share of the responsibility for fixing things. Push for an organizational culture of personal accountability" (Pritchett, 1993, p. 33). Start with your own accountability. Hold yourself accountable before you hold others accountable.

Remember the hard and the soft sides of leadership, which could be summarized along these indices:

1. heart and head

2. tangibles and intangibles

3. content and context

This idea could also apply to the analogy of music and art where there are those who are nearly perfect yet are not as successful as those with a unique style. In other words, being technically perfect does not guarantee success: you have to appeal to others. So it is with leadership, especially the relating-to-people aspect. This is the point we've been making via the Leadership Quotient triangle: Your leadership does not have to be *perfect;* it has to *fit* your followers and your environment. Hesselbein (2002a and b) says leadership is more a matter of how to be than how to do. Reading and relating to others' wants and feelings is an art that distinctively appeals to individuals and is developed by living a life for and with others.

"Attitudes are more important than facts" (Karl Menninger). "Nothing has any meaning in life except the meaning we give it" (Anthony Robbins). "Experience is not what happens to a [person]; it is what a [person] does with what happens to [him]" (Aldous Huxley). These quotes should hone your thinking and increase your understanding of the People Quotient.

The Theme of PQ

Leadership comes *only* from the relationships people form when they are doing things together. Therefore, you will become a leader only by virtue of your participation. When you participate without understanding the other people in the organization, you have a very low PQ. Organizations with low-PQ leaders will not survive. All organizations have *social capital*, which is the network of connections among people. These connections make an organization more than a collection of individuals out to achieve their own private purposes or successes. The collective organization must exhibit PQ so that members of the organization get the message, "It has to be more about the followers than the leaders." It is not altogether about being nice and liking and accepting one another, but it is about the necessity for collaboration involving many people. It is about demonstrating in practice what is of value to the group. Today's success and tomorrow's continuation of success are dependent upon enduring and effective leader-follower relationships, which must be reciprocal and voluntary.

"The leader has to set the tone for the quality of relationships" (Hesselbein and Cohen, 1999, p. 20). "What counts most in creating a successful team is not how compatible its players are, but how they deal with incompatibility" (*Sports Illustrated* advertisement, 2002). Many organizational problems result from a concentration on technical competence without serious regard for relationships, context, and process. To increase your People Quotient, you must develop a strategy for investing in and exploiting your and your organization's intellectual assets, especially as they relate to PQ: people understanding and respecting people. You can ultimately only improve the efficiency of knowledge workers through developing lasting relationships.

Both of us teach in MBA programs. Nationwide, employers of MBA graduates have complained for years that MBA programs turn out technical specialists who can't relate to people. There are only two things to concentrate on in an organization: tasks and the people who do them. Traditional MBA programs have concentrated too heavily on the task side at the expense of the people side because it is most often the only thing intellectual ineffectual professors can teach. Many attempts have been made to prop up technically-based MBA programs with people-oriented activities. The Wharton School tried sending their geeks (excuse us, MBA candidates) to a Philadelphia Phillies baseball game in an attempt to teach teaming skills.

Dallas Baptist University President, Dr. Gary Cook, returned to campus from an investigative visit to Regent University in 1994 and asked, "Instead of propping up the MBA, why don't we create a totally separate degree that concentrates on the people side?" "Oh, you mean give the customers what they *want*?" was our embarrassed reply. It was embarrassing because in the College of Business we teach customer service, but we don't always practice it very well. The Master of Arts in Organizational Management was created to meet the needs of students seeking a degree on the people side of organizations. Ten years later, it is nearly half the size of the traditional MBA program and is growing at a faster rate. It produces graduates who have lower task skills but higher people skills and thus a higher People Quotient.

Successful leaders see relationships in many multifaceted ways but none more important than in light of the people involved. Our advice is to first define something as the best it can possibly be, then add in the people for a reality check. We hate to say it again, but it is most often necessary to go outside of the normal boxes, frames, and models, and direct thinking toward developing truly innovative organizational members who have high PQs. You do not understand others without work and attention. A real "people person" knows that one cannot laugh if one is not willing to cry, and that we all must live life versus answer it to be truly fulfilled.

An understanding of self, others, and the basic principles of leadership is required as a starting point to building enduring relationships and a high People Quotient. However, beyond understanding of self and others, you must have the willingness and desire to actively incorporate these elements into your own life:

- realize

- admit

- take action

- measure

- improve

Realistically evaluating your PQ and establishing a plan for improvement must be one of your primary goals. Understanding all the principles presented here will help you in the journey to realizing how successful your leadership can become by increasing your PQ.

In *Good to Great* (2001), Jim Collins wrote that we need to start with the people. He used the phrase, "Get the right people on the bus," then allow them to figure out how to solve problems. He suggested that leaders don't solve problems, they find the right person to solve the problem. Franklin Roosevelt summed up his leadership style similarly. "I'm a train switchman," said FDR. "People come to me on one track and I switch them out on another track." He assumed—correctly, we believe—that a big part of leadership is getting the correct person-job fit. Get the people and then you can do almost anything. Understanding and relating to people is the only way to attract, hire, and retain the *right* people!

Dave was asked by a seminar attendee recently, "I graduated from an MBA program a few years ago. What are the new ideas in strategy since I've graduated?" Without hesitation, Dave answered, "Intellectual assets." The person worked in the drug industry, so Dave used this example: "What's Zantac cost, $2 a pill?" What part of that $2 goes to the actual product that's in the pill, maybe 8 cents? That leaves $1.92 for intellectual assets:

- Research and development

- Advertising

- Distribution

- Patent security

- Legal fees

- Insurance

- Packaging

- Service

- Manufacturing

All of these elements, everything outside the 8 cents for product, are categorized as intellectual assets. Intellectual assets are housed in the heads of *people*. Do the same analysis for the last set of tires you bought. If you paid $80 a tire, you can estimate the rubber that was cut off a plant in Malaysia is worth about 50 cents. Do the same intellectual assets analysis and you'll come to the same conclusion: People who own the intellectual assets are very important in producing value for the end consumer.

Always start by selecting the right person in the first place and then get him off to a great start. Establish the fact that you are a coach who will be sure that team members are rewarded for their commitment. Help people grow, advance, and see that their work is important. Do this by insuring that their contributions are recognized and rewarded. Do not tolerate abusive managers or toxic work environments. Do see people as fellow human beings and take time to listen, but mostly live the example you want them to exhibit in their work. Be positive, but also be straightforward about things people do wrong or of poor quality.

This advice will result in gaining and retaining the right people for it will build relationships between the organization (its managers and leaders) and the "right" people. These skills and behaviors are the essence of PQ, and a successful "coach" will surely exhibit a high PQ.

Pull others into meaningfully effective relationships through:

- Connecting with mutual understanding;

- Reflecting with and about them and your relationships; and

- Generalizing about their fit, yet understanding how they stand out (Branham, 2001).

These are three steps that lead to a high PQ. Good leaders don't push their way into relationships. As with many other quotients, PQ requires attention—but attention of a different kind: attention to what others value and want versus what you value and want for them. Once you identify some characteristics and other variables about someone that might be useful in developing a relationship with them, you must reflect back on similar people situations and learn to generalize to your new situation. That means you need to understand what will work with the new person and situation by understanding what worked in the past. In many areas we can afford to use tried-and-true methods and apply them to most problems. Indeed, this is why we developed formulas in math, science, and finance. However, we cannot develop single-use strict formulas in dealing with people. We can develop guidelines but not formulas. Recognize the difference and adjust your guidelines for useful individual formulas.

Bill O'Reilly's bestseller, *Who's Looking Out for You?* (2003), has some significant points to remember related to PQ. O'Reilly says that discovering whom you can rely on is the key to a happy and successful life and that cultivating and nurturing good friends is not easy. He says it starts with seeing people as who they are, not what we want them to be. O'Reilly agrees with the old adage, "We are whom we associate with." These are solid foundational points to a PQ that is genuine and supportive of one's leadership journey.

Yes, you can become better at reading others and applying what you know to building effective and lasting relationships, but only with considerable effort. Generally, people either develop these skills early on, or they never develop them. We don't mean to imply that it cannot be done, just that it is difficult. Below are other PQ skills that are of significance in today's info-interactive society if you want to be a better leader in all *LQ*© aspects.

Other Keys to PQ

For a good foundation, the best literary place to start is by reading classics such as the Bible, Simon's *Model of Men* (1957), and Sloan's *My Years at General Motors* (1963); Kennedy's (1987) study of the rise and fall of great powers; Lindblom's (1959) science of "muddling through;" Gleick's chaos theory (1987); JFK's *Profiles in Courage* (1956); Shapero's (1985) book on managing professional people; Reagan's (1990) description of his American life; Stalk and Hout's (1990) book on competing against time; and Schwarzkopf's (1992) proclamation that it does not take a hero. These and many others all have one very common theme. That theme is exemplified in another often-forgotten classic work, Stowe's *Uncle Tom's Cabin*. Stowe's work is often forgotten because it is not altogether politically correct even though it is in words and meaning very representative of the times and is considered by many as "the most popular, influential and controversial book written by an American" (Stowe, 1995, back cover). The theme of *relationships* as a key to accomplishment, theories, working, and living is exemplified in all of these works and many others. Why is there such a concentration on relationships in literary works? Because without relationships—formed by a high PQ—we could not reach meaningful goals.

Principles of Success Start and End with Relationships

Following are 10 principles of success that we have shared with classes and friends for years. Review these principles with the PQ in mind:

1. **Build and treasure relationships** for without them success is not worth it. Start and end with a relationship with a higher being. Follow this closely with relationships with friends and family; and, finally, extend it to all those you wish to influence. Remember that character, integrity, and ethics show. Always include fair and equal treatment to all. Remember the mirror test: without integrity we are nothing.

2. **Visualize the end you have in mind** for if you don't know where you are going you'll never arrive. Think big, but start small. Take Ben Franklin's advice to prepare well: "By failing to prepare we prepare to fail." This principle is truer with relationships than almost anything else, for if you do not want to develop a relationship, you will be successful at that.

3. **Set goals that are step-by-step ways to reach your vision.** Remember to focus. Set initial short-term goals that build to your ultimate goal, but never forget to work to help others out from their perspective before you seek to help yourself and serve your perspective.

4. **Be proactive and try.** Fear is an illusion that can freeze anyone out of action. Successful people and failures fear the same things, but the desire to succeed overcomes the fear for those who are successful. No one can achieve by being passive. It is better not to be good enough than not to try. The greatest of inventors had hundreds of failures. Thomas Edison said, "I know 5,000 ways not to build a light bulb." The first step in establishing a relationship is to try!

5. **Success is hard work; there are no shortcuts.** Put in the work and results will follow. Do not do things halfheartedly. Do not let others pull you down. Establishing relationships is quite often hard, so practice loving and caring.

6. **Teamwork wins the war even though an individual may win a battle.** Relationships that are successful reflect a selfless process: a win-win attitude. Talent or luck may win one or two times, but teamwork (an ultimate in multi-relationships) wins out over time.

7. **Learn, refine, and practice the fundamentals.** Plenty of people have ability, but few can apply it. Watch out for settling for instant gratification not supported by fundamentals! In *The 7 Habits of Highly Effective People,* Steven Covey (1990—worth mentioning many times) gives the following habits successful people exhibit: a) Proactivity, b) Beginning with an end in mind, c) Putting first things first, d) Thinking win-win—and I will establish a lasting relationship, e) Seeking first to understand, f) Synergizing, and g) Continuing self-renewal. See the link with relationship-building?

8. **Participate—set the example—I will be a good leader and a good follower!** Learn awareness: awareness of self, others, and the world around you. Back up your talk by example, not just

words. A picture of you in action will take thousands of words to describe and million of words to change the meaning of what people see you do. You must earn the title of leader or follower. Relationships are built on your actions more than your words. Servant leadership should be a goal.

9. **Learn to listen.** First, seek to understand before you seek to be understood. Develop an external focus and become an information junky. Leverage what you know in order to form a more perfect relationship.

10. **Reinvent yourself and commit to continuous learning—your personal relationship with learning.** Peter Drucker said, "Knowledge has become the key economic resource and the dominant, if not the only, source of comparative advantage." Knowledge of self and others is the basis for truly effective relationships. Your relationship with yourself can be strengthened only through continuous personal growth.

About Organizations and Relationships

Willingham (1997) points out that in the 1990s companies downsized, right-sized, and reengineered, firing their employees by the thousands. Management poured money into computers and information technologies. As a result, productivity has risen 1 percent since 1982 and employee morale is at a record low! Why? Because people are illogical creatures primarily driven by emotion. So how do we improve organizations? We improve people and how they deal with other people; that is, we improve relationships—not structure, policy, or procedures! Willingham says to start with what motivates behavior: understand progression of needs. Can you see that people desire relationships, not just a way to make a living?

To make the relationship shift, start focusing on enhancing employees' self-image for everyone has intellectual, emotional, and creativity centers. Grow a sense of self- and organizational alignment that spreads to others by:

- a shared purpose and vision

- meaningful job roles

- authentic mentors

- positive coaching and counseling that rewards results

- job security

- value for all constituents

- love and caring

Remember: People produce only as much as they think they can—or are led to believe they can—by those they consider their leaders. Learn to recognize behavioral styles (talker, doer, plodder, and controller) by observing employees' behaviors and blending your style with theirs. Hone your ability to lead effectively with:

- vision

- charisma—high-energy self-esteem

- character

- responsibility

- planning

- social skills

- achievement drive

- emotional stability

- tolerance for ambiguity

- decisiveness

- delegation

- positive outlook

- whatever it takes as long as it is moral, legal, ethical, and respectful

Be a leader who builds people by balancing doing and leading. People should think things out and not just accept conventional terms and the conventional way of doing things: get people to act this way! See possibilities in others even when they do not. Your beliefs can become self-fulfilling prophecies. Spend 80% of your time listening. EVERYONE needs a push sometimes. Practice discovery learning: Do not tell people the answer, let them learn it. Finally, understand and use synergy and empowerment with defined important goals and specific steps to reach those goals. Make the pledge to build effective relationships for yourself and your organization.

Relationships in the Technology-Information Age

In today's technological age, so many believe that communications technology will make or break organizations. Consequently, many seem to want to turn relationship-building over to technology such as cell phones, e-mail, and voice mail. Because of our flexible work hours, Dave and Bill both have answered the phone when the caller was taken aback by reaching us directly. "Oh, I thought I would just get your answering machine and leave a message" is the common response. So many people today avoid real interactions and do all their communicating via the Internet. This is a surefire way never to establish meaningful relationships. If you want to trust and be trusted, look the other person in the eye. A relationship is not:

- Technology
- Information
- Productivity
- Innovation
- TQM
- Teams
- Globalization
- Speed
- Connectivity
- Compatibility
- Customers
- Products
- Services
- Hardware
- Software
- Policies

- Procedures

A relationship consists of two humans who form a bond of mutual respect and trust. Technology and end-use are NOT the foundations of relationships—individuals' perceived and expressed values are. Hardware and software cannot feel, love, hate, question, respond, or react like irrational, emotion-driven humans. Things do not want or need relationships, but people desire relationships at their very core. If you learn to develop relationships because you really care for others, you will be a success; however, you might define success. If, on the other hand, you form no relationships, success will not matter and you will end up with no purpose or reason for living. So use technology as a tool, but do not rely on it for relationship building.

Human Resources (HR) Practices, Systems and Procedures, and PQ

Another area that deserves special attention when talking about PQ, or the relationship-based leading component, is the human resources function. In many modern-day organizations the human resources function has an undesired consequence. The HR function takes away relationships instead of building them. For all of the talk of strategic partnering that started some 15 years ago, little has changed. HR is espoused in the literature as a strategic partner, yet it remains a policing function in many organizations. The important question remains, "How can HR do its overall tasks and still help with relationship-building within an organization?" How can HR improve the PQ of an organization versus decrease it? That is in part the intent of this section and indeed an overriding purpose of this chapter on the People Quotient.

We have reviewed the literature, trying to determine how organizations can acquire, develop, and reward human resources to gain a sustainable competitive advantage while avoiding legal and ethical problems in a people-friendly, PQ-building way. We have *not* found a lot of practical material to help us. You can find theoretical pieces or academic exercises, but not much solid logical advice that is of use for an individual who wants to increase her People Quotient.

First, the primary HR objective should be to have and utilize the right people at the right time with the right skills and abilities motivated and committed to accomplishing desired organizational purposes. The basic HR objective implies the following:

- planning

- forecasting

- training

- development

- succession planning

- staff reduction readiness

- interviewing (entrance and exit)

- rewards and benefits

- policy development

In addition, for HR to be a success, these objectives and tasks are to be accomplished with equality and constancy. These purposes are very sterile in many cases and simply do not show emotion or caring. In addition, emotion can cause many problems, for without it, policies and procedures become only legal documents. As Henri Fayol showed about 100 years ago, a bureaucracy is very effective in accomplishing rule-based leadership without discrimination, but it has many limitations we cannot live with in this age of innovation and change.

Difficult HR issues arise in an environment where sustaining competitive advantage demands a shift from stability and control to innovation, change, and speed. In part, these issues are because of the restrictive application of many laws and the differing environments and cultures in which organizations exist.

We feel that there should be 10 basic premises for the HR model that builds the People Quotient:

1. **Value people** first and last and everywhere in between. Resolve the age-old conflict of "do unto others as **they** would have you do unto them" and "do unto others as you would have them do unto you." Reach an agreement with the employee on the resolution to this conflict given the organization's overriding purposes.

2. HR management and systems must **fit** your organization's resources, purposes, objectives, strategies, and people. Without some flexibility, you don't need people to make decisions.

3. **Insure that employees know** rules, policies, and expectations as well as organizational and personal objectives. Additionally, everyone must know the consequent rewards and punishments associated with all established guidelines. Apply guidelines and expectations in a consistent and predictable manner, yet realize that without exceptions you are not acting as a human. Be willing to go against policy when it is an absolute necessity. Be careful, but act on your own when necessary to be a leader!

4. **Provide a way for employees to question** or appeal management decisions. This implies that you should seek the approval of those who can hear an appeal before you take a critical action, i.e., firing or demotion. When investigating any charge, include impartial parties to gather information in a fair and systematic fashion.

5. **Always look at the body of research** in a topical area before trying any new system, rule, policy, pay or benefit system, etc. We think we know and often we do not. Remember who defines the product and its uses: the user, not the seller!

6. Put a **progressive disciplinary procedure** in place: train people about it and follow it.

7. When there are unique mitigating circumstances, remember to **be consistent** and realize that any exception becomes a rule and every rule has a life and meaning of its own. Make sure that any rule, expectation, and policy is logical and makes sense.

8. Always **follow the letter and spirit of the law**, and seek legal advice when in doubt.

9. In all matters involving employees, think **commitment to continuous, honest, two-way communications**. For what is done is often less important than how it is done. For example, in the legal system in America the means are more important than the ends.

10. Have an HR function to **insure that the hiring, training, and rewarding**:

    a. provide the best people in the most effective and efficient way,

    b. insure fair and equitable treatment,

    c. support organizational missions and values,

    d. support individual unit objectives,

    e. build a real strategic partnering mentality, not a policing mentality.

If you and your organization follow the intent of these rules, not just the letter of the rules, you will build a truly functional and effective HR. Efficiency comes second in a real relationship-supporting HR function designed and used to build the right People Quotient skills and behaviors.

Sustainable Leadership Starts with the Ability to Relate to People

Again, we are using a variety of approaches combining sound research, exemplars, how to's, popular press reports, experience, case reports, case research, and logic to produce a People Quotient that you can adapt and use repeatedly in situation after situation. The human interactions of people and relationship skills that are involved in effective leadership are so complex that reducing them to a handful of testable propositions or hypotheses cannot reflect the level of intricacy that exists with the leader-followers-environments interactions. That is why we developed the more inclusive $LQ^{©}$ formula and its very critical PQ component. Be careful not to kill every living complex human interaction, such as leadership, by dissecting it to search what makes it tick. People and relationships are far too complex to survive dissection. To be an effective leader, you must bring people-centered leadership *alive* through your actions and not kill it through studying it to death.

Remember some of our key words: ***balance, fit, appropriateness,*** and ***authenticity***. However, most importantly, remember that trying to be perceived as something you are not is a sure ticket to failure as a leader. Followers want, above all, authentic leaders. As stressed throughout *LQ©*, the overriding purpose of leadership is to gain a sense of shared commitment on the part of the members of an organization and then lead them to the realization of that shared vision. This lofty purpose cannot effectively be met without a commitment to establishing relationships person to person. Your purpose in reading this book should be to improve your ability to relate to others. This requires a combination of the ability to read and to ultimately empathize with and react to others from their perspective, not yours. *Relating is more about reading and adapting than about knowing.*

Description of the People Quotient and its Dimensions

In Hart (1989), the 100 most influential persons in history are ranked and the criterion used is the number of people they have affected. We see such humility and good as Jesus Christ (listed as number 3) and Buddha (4), contrasted with such evil as Adolf Hitler (35) and Genghis Khan (21). But also listed are Isaac Newton (2) and Aristotle (14). This shows that all types and behaviors can have influence if, ultimately, relationships are the desire.

Look closely at Figure 7.2. This is the generic version of *LQ©* as it applies to PQ. Note again the normal labeling of Quadrants 1, 2, 3, and 4, and refer to this figure as we explain what elements we have found in each of these quadrants. You need to have this 2X2 firmly ingrained in your working memory as you continue the *LQ©* journey to improved leadership. Remember that, in each of the four quadrants, we will once again discuss individuals who typify the trait and how it manifests itself in their observable behavior. However, our exemplars are presented primarily so you can identify a "comparison other" to help you in relating your own personal leadership traits, gifts, failings, or behaviors to those you have observed in others. We encourage you to do that because you learn better when you formulate your own examples. Relating is tough enough on its own, but it's impossible without lots of attention and focus. Observe PQ in others and relate that to what you need to do to build a great PQ for yourself. To identify a leader for comparative purposes, think of someone you know who exhibits leadership qualities you would like to have, then compare their qualities to yours.

It's also OK to identify a leader you do NOT want to emulate or become more like; or you might want to identify a leader whose exhibited People Quotient traits or behaviors are positive exemplars for you. Dave and Bill both have found they seem to learn the most from leaders they *do not* like. Perhaps that is because we pay more attention to things that hurt us than we do to things that support us. The leaders we discuss here are people we have observed and can use as universal examples. Think of your own personal examples as you read our descriptions. Public figures who are current or historical persons are helpful for many people, but others would rather think about personal leaders such as a "boss, brother, mother, coworker, friend," etc. The main thing is to attempt to understand a trait that is exemplified by someone else. Then decide whether you can or cannot control it, so you can develop a plan of action to improve or to make irrelevant where necessary.

As we have reminded you previously, don't get hung up on the strictness of what is under someone's control and what is not. Indeed, most things are under your control, but we list things as natural or "no control" when it seems we are unlikely to change them for whatever reason. We are identifying these early-acquired or not-likely-to-change items as natural because they seem to fit better in this category.

Figure 7.1: THE LEADERSHIP LEVERAGE TRIANGLE

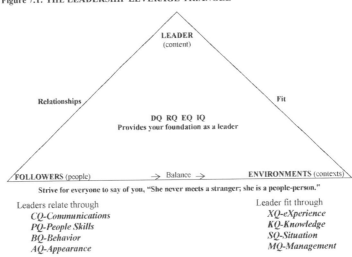

Figure 7.2: PQ MEASUREMENT AND IMPROVEMENT MATRIX

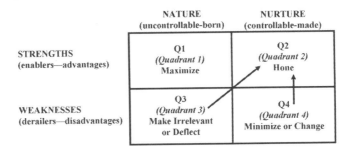

People who can read people are the luckiest people in the world!

Normal Natural PQ Strengths—Quadrant 1 of the PQ 2X2 Matrix

The first natural strength we find in this quadrant is **extroversion**. It's very common to hear some remark, "She is so outgoing and such an extrovert." That statement is very clear to everyone who hears it. Most of Bill's friends, upon meeting Dave, said something like, "He never meets a stranger." We all know what people are saying when they make those comments and we know people like this. Dr. Phil of TV fame is a great example of extroversion, though we cannot be sure if it is the TV image or the real Phil. We suspect it's for real: he seems to enjoy being with people.

Several people who completed the *LQ*© mentioned heavyweight boxer Mike Tyson in this area and we see why. Tyson seems to want to have everything fame can bring, but to be left alone. If you personally want to be a leader, do you suppose the Dr. Phil model or the Mike Tyson model would serve you better? It seems a dumb question, but many do not act as if they have found the right answer to this apparently obvious question. Perhaps the real answer to being an extrovert is a good personality that is inclusive in nature and truly wants to be out there learning from and dealing with others. Perhaps if you do not have a healthy dose of this trait you might rethink your potential as a leader.

It seems to us that this trait is either inherited or developed early in life. The point is, there is little change in extroversion throughout most of a person's life. Most people would agree that the tendency to be more extroverted is relatively stable and remains fairly constant throughout one's life.

For a real-life example, think about your high school reunion. The extroverts were leading the event, taking center stage, and managing things, just as they did 25 years ago. The introverts are still quiet and reserved. They have not changed very much, and it's likely you haven't either.

In our opinion, it would take only a little more extroversion for most people to be successful leaders. You do not have to be the life of the party to be a leader, but you do have to have some extroversion.

Dave attended a megachurch (more than 5,000 members) for ten years. Lake Pointe Church was founded by senior pastor Steve Stroope in a renovated bait house on the shores of Lake Ray Hubbard on the east side of Dallas. Thirty years later the church occupies a 5,000-seat arena-style worship center and two satellite locations. Dave has always been convinced that Steve Stroope is a natural introvert, but he knows how to "put on" the extrovert when it's required by his organization.

You may remember the extroversion-introversion index as the first element on the Myers-Briggs Type Indicator (MBTI). The MBTI is a well-known personality categorizing tool. It measures only where you get your energy; it does not say you can't operate in either environment. The MBTI makes the same assumption we start with in *The Leadership Quotient*. We assume you have natural tendencies that are either strengths or weaknesses but that you also have some nurtured strengths and weaknesses that are under your control. You are not condemned to a life of extroversion or introversion.

By analyzing your $LQ^©$, you can change and adapt it to fit the followers and environment that are necessary for you.

The tendencies to be introverted or extroverted are considered by most scientists as being highly heritable. We also have observed the nurtured part. We have observed many times how parents play to these tendencies of their children early on and in fact reinforce the tendencies and make people more introverted or extroverted. Start paying attention to how parents, family, and friends cater to a young child's tendency by reinforcing the child's need to be left alone or his need for high levels of interaction. We wonder how much these tendencies could be reversed if the child were nurtured differently.

The second trait that many report as a natural strength in the area of PQ is represented by the word **charismatic**. Some leaders are born with an air about them that attracts others to them. We see this early in elementary school where kids just flock to certain people. It continues through life, and it seems some people just attract others with their enthusiasm and energy. Sometimes we see the reason for the charisma. Michael Jordan certainly has the talent and the smile to win people over. Bill Clinton has that charm. Hitler captivated people with his enthusiasm. Billy Graham's charisma is based in sincerity. So little is known about his public image that it's hard to know what attracts people to Osama Bin Laden, but he certainly has the charisma to capture the hearts and minds of so many. Looking back through history, you find that charisma is a trait that many famous people exemplified. Often it could be seen by their physical imposition, but just as often they were not physically impressive at all.

George was a young student who came to talk to Dave. He said, "I'm just a little geeky kid and I don't have any luck with girls." Dave said simply, "George, you'll be fine. You are at a different level than most of the other students. In a few years all the women will be beating a path to you." George was about 5' 6" and small and dressed with a tie and a sports coat every day—as a 21-year-old junior in college! He was already an officer in his father's securities firm, handled some quite large accounts, and was very impressive in his knowledge of investments and the world in general. George has traveled the world from the Arctic to Antarctica, caddied for the top pro golfers, hobnobbed with Charles Schwab, and more. He's going to be fine. He even got to play golf with Phil Mickelson after Mickelson won the Masters. Being a world traveler with millions of dollars and dressing like a Wall Street executive makes one charismatic to educated mature 30- and 40-year-old women, but not to most 19- and 20-year-old girls. In terms of the Leadership Quotient Triangle, George *had* the leadership, but it didn't fit the followers in the environment he wanted to fit into.

Charisma is largely a matter of perception. One can do things to improve the level of one's perceived charisma. So if you do not have much of it, do not despair—the PQ Measurement and Improvement Matrices will provide some steps for you to improve your appeal to your followers.

Humility is most often reported as a natural trait in the People Quotient. The book, *Authentic Leadership: Rediscovering the Secrets to Creating Lasting Value* (George, 2003a), stands out to us as an exemplar of one area that is closely related to the type of humility we are talking about here. In his book, Bill George, former chairman and CEO of Medtronic, calls for responsible, ethical, and genuine leadership. He says that, after years of studying and practicing leadership, he has come to believe that leadership begins and ends with authenticity. George's authentic leadership is about a person being who he was created to be and not about adopting the styles and traits of others. He writes about five elements of leadership:

- Understanding one's passion for purpose

- Exhibiting core values in one's behavior

- Leading with the heart through compassion

- Establishing relationships—one's connectedness

- Demonstrating consistent self-discipline

These are the dimensions he feels represent the definition of true "authentic leadership." Finding a fit between an organization's values and your values, and leading a balanced life are keys to building an authentic organization where missions motivate and create real value for all constituents. Practicing stewardship to all the people you serve shows your values and that you are an authentic leader. Passion will result in superior results and innovation. "[B]e true to your values, build your relationships, practice self-discipline, and lead with your heart" (George, 2003a, p. 200). His ideas fit nicely into the Leadership Quotient Triangle, which agrees with George's directive to find a fit between your true self, your followers, and the organization, which we call environment.

George says, "Authentic leaders are dedicated to developing themselves because they know that becoming a leader takes a lifetime of personal growth....Leaders are all very different people. Any prospective leader who buys into the necessity of attempting to emulate all the characteristics of a leader is doomed to fail. I know because I tried it early in my career. It simply doesn't work" (George, 2003a, p. 12).

He writes about a discussion he had with leadership guru John Kotter, who challenged him, saying, "Bill, you're not thinking nearly big enough."

Near the end of the book, George exhibits the humility we are talking about when he says, "One of the great myths of the past decade is that CEOs are primarily responsible for the success of corporations" (p. 91). This statement says he is humble in the way we feel one should be in order to be a great leader. In *Good to Great*, Jim Collins found that leaders who changed their companies from good to great are people whose names you would not recognize. That's because they had the humility to put the organization first and themselves second. That's sometimes called servant leadership, when you put your followers first by trying to help them improve.

The last natural trait we see is being **compassionate**. In this area, there is no better example than that of Jesus Christ. Regardless of your belief, you can see in the New Testament a description of a truly compassionate being, Jesus, who exemplified what it would be like to be the perfect role model for love, sensitivity, and intuition about the feelings of others.

In the modern-day media world, the name of Oprah Winfrey is often reported to us by people completing the *LQ*© assessment. She is considered compassionate because of her trips to Africa and the way she connects with guests on her show. She seems to understand that she is fortunate and needs to be generous and compassionate to help the world be a better place.

Christians know for sure that they can never be a Jesus Christ or perhaps even an Oprah. However, they know that they can strive to be more like the compassionate model Jesus represented. Earlier in this chapter we asked you to think about an icon of perfection. Jesus Christ is that icon for Christians. The compassion for enemies and for those who do not care for us, as exhibited by Jesus, goes against every innate human characteristic for survival and perhaps that, in and of itself, is what makes Him so amazing. Seeing humans show compassion for those who would do them the ultimate harm is a heart-changing experience. "Sometimes you have to watch somebody love something before you can love it yourself. It is as if they are showing you the way" (Miller, 2003, p. ix).

Indeed, Christianity is an open religion, not a closed one such as it would seem to be from many reports we see in the media. Those who do not understand Christianity as open need to revisit the ultimate source on Christianity and not depend on the version portrayed in popular media sources. Even if we seem to have gained little compassion for others from nature, surely we are in control of how much we exhibit in the future. We can't be perfect, like Christians believe Christ was. But we can use His life as an icon to improve ours.

In each of these areas—extroversion, charisma, humility, and compassion—we see a common theme. Loving and caring for others, indeed, as we do for ourselves is against nature in most cases, but entirely possible, as has been shown throughout all of recorded history.

Normal Natural PQ Weaknesses—Quadrant 3 of the PQ 2X2 Matrix

As with the natural strengths we just discussed, this area is a little tricky. We might just as well classify most of these as nurtured. However, we are not, because these are traits that appear early and permeate most of the leader's life. Just as we see people remain extroverts, charismatic, humble, and compassionate all of their lives, so we see other people who remain self-serving introverts who are uncomfortable with human interaction most of their lives. Therefore, we are classifying these traits as natural for indeed they do appear early in one's life and seem to stay there until the day one dies.

The first natural weakness we found in our leadership study group was **self-serving**. In fact, many reported this as being **slick.** Some seem to think slick is a good thing, but the manner in which our leaders exemplify it, we don't agree. When slickness is conjoined with a self-serving bias, followers really dislike it and will not tolerate it in a modern leader. When there was a largely uneducated population, some seemed enamored by a slick operator, but those days are in the past.

Without being too judgmental, see if the following examples of opposite public images point up the comparison we're trying to describe:

Slick	*Real*
Bill Clinton	Jimmy Carter
Princess Diana	Mother Teresa
Jim Bakker	Billy Graham
Jerry Falwell	Martin Luther King Jr.
Pete Rose	Michael Jordan
Jerry Springer	Oprah Winfrey
Rush Limbaugh	Dr. Phil McGraw

There are, of course, many others. Don't get hung up on one of the specific comparisons you don't agree with. These names were given to us by the people who beta-tested *The Leadership Quotient* for us. The important thing is to think about where you are along the index between these two extremes. Some seem to have a trait that results in a selfishness that causes them to be perceived by others as untrustworthy.

The second trait we see reported in this area is being an **introvert**. Again, we all know people who don't want to interact with others, people who will barely speak to you even when you corner them. They would much rather play a video game or watch a movie by themselves than have to interact with anyone. Since this is not an either/or measure, all of us are along the continuum somewhere, so we get this way occasionally. Probably very few readers of this book would be introverts of this extreme nature.

Bill worked with many computer programmers who would rather be given written instructions and even written reviews and simply not have to talk to anyone. A hippie-turned-programmer, Don, even suggested automating the evaluation-and-review process so no human interaction would be necessary. Perhaps via the work-at-home trends, some of these introverts have found their niche. Strict introverts seldom become leaders, but they usually don't want to be. If you have some of this tendency, perhaps you should think about your leadership potential a little bit more realistically.

A third trait that is reported very often in the PQ area is that of being **uncomfortable with dissent**, change, interaction, or the emotions exhibited by others. We have all seen people who are very effective until someone disagrees with them or asks them to change something about the way they deal with others.

Bob was a great project manager who could plan and implement almost anything. However, when asked to change something, he went bananas and could not deal with it. It seemed he had to think of all of the possible contingencies in advance and build in the alternatives. He seemed to believe that careful planning—without alteration—was the only means to success. As you might guess, Bob did not remain a project manager long. High People Quotient leaders have learned how to embrace the unexpected while leading others. We cannot expect to have everything go just as we planned it. Just plan how you are going to schedule things the next time your child or grandchild visits, then see how close you remain to the plan during the visit.

Bill hates to admit it, but he does not like dissent. He seems to think that if someone disagrees with him, they have not thought about the issue enough because Bill feels he has seen every possible alternative and could not possibly be wrong. Surely, the other guy had failed to see all the alternatives and was just waiting for Bill to enlighten him. Well, Bill, you think of *most* perspectives and alternatives, but not *all* of them, so be prepared for some dissent.

The last natural weakness reported in the area of PQ is that of being **offensive**. We all know people who are offensive to those around them. Sometimes, it is easy to see or even smell what makes them so. Often they exhibit a "holier than thou" attitude or condescend to those around them. Some exhibit this offensive eminence and we really cannot put our fingers on why. Dave knows one guy who is just so smart that he projects something about his dislike for the average intellect. We are aware of a lady who seems to think she's God's gift to the world or something. It is easy to see why an immature child might exhibit this atmosphere, but not an adult. Educated adults know how little they know and realize they can never be sure how much smarter or better-looking they are than someone else. Indeed, at parties, people like to talk to medical doctors and even Ph.D.s, in part because they are surprised to find out how normal these people really are.

There is no reason for one to be offensive to another because we had little to do with our intellect or looks. Just as a brilliant student told Dave, "Yeah, I'm smart but I had nothing to do with it. Just like you had nothing to do with your big feet." (Dave wears a size 15 shoe; Bill only wears a size 13—too bad.)

This concludes the section on natural PQ weaknesses. We will summarize it by making one more high-versus-low People Quotient comparison: Why did the populace like Ronald Reagan more than they liked Al Gore?

Normal Nurtured PQ Strengths—Quadrant 2 of the PQ 2X2 Matrix

On to the nurtured strengths which start with the most often reported trait of **relating-connecting-personable**. We're reminded of the connection made by the late Dave Thomas of Wendy's hamburgers fame. Thomas starred in TV commercials for his company because he could relate and make a connection: he was personable. Perhaps there was something about his "common appearance" that made the viewer want to eat a Wendy's hamburger. There's more on that topic in the Appearance

Quotient chapter. This returns us once again to the idea of fit: Thomas's style fit his followers (customers) in the fast-food environment. He knew how to fit in and be "one of the guys." There may be times when we cannot be one of the guys, but leaders always need to connect and have others relate to them. Teenagers especially will not listen to those to whom they don't relate—but we are all more like this than we care to admit. You will be amazed at the things our teenagers tell us they've learned from a peer, when we've been trying to teach them the same thing for years!

Ray Romano plays the part of a character to whom the audience really relates. Even the title of the program indicates that "Everybody Loves Raymond." He is loved because his character connects with the audience. In leadership terms, there is a fit. Oprah connects with her audience. This is a social skill that few exhibit to the level of Dr. Phil or Oprah, but it is one that almost everyone identifies with and appreciates. We can learn a great deal about relating from these public examples. You can also learn a great deal from personal examples who are closer to your own life.

First Lady Laura Bush exemplified this to the ultimate degree when she was asked by CBS interviewer Tim Russert what she said to the families of those who had lost loved ones in the Iraq war. She said, "I just listen to them. They just want to tell me about the person they lost." That is genuine relating, and you do not have to say anything. We can learn a lot from that example of knowing when to talk and when to listen. People often do not want to hear what we have to say, but they want us to hear what they have to say. God gave us two ears and one mouth. Perhaps we're supposed to listen twice as much as we speak.

The second trait reported as a nurtured strength is **trustworthiness**. In the current climate of corporate cheating and public spectacles, we need to revert to an old value of trust. Recently, a TV personality was discussing the current climate of distrust for the media and how all of the media that we trusted were people of the past: Walter Cronkite, Michael Jordan, Arnold Palmer, and so on. Contrast those trusted names with Kobe Bryant, O.J. Simpson, and Pete Rose. On the business side, consider Ken Lay (recently deceased) of Enron and Bernie Ebbers (25 years—ugh!) of MCI, just to name a couple. What images do you get? We would bet it is not trustworthiness.

The old adage, "One rotten apple spoils the whole barrel," is true in human behavior and leadership as well. It takes only one member of a group or profession to cast dispersion on the entire group. The legal profession is a good example. Indeed there are many trustworthy lawyers, but many people do not think so. In a recent book, a young lawyer asked the senior partner how to become trustworthy. The senior partner said, "Try being worthy of trust." Too simple for many, but basically that is all there is to it.

We know that leading is teaching, and in teaching we are influencing, directing, guiding, helping, and nurturing because we believe in human possibilities. We must learn to help others reach excellence in everything they attempt. We want good plumbing as well as good medical treatment. To get this requires the faith that humans have when they lead and believe in their followers just as followers must believe in their leaders. Yes, one must believe in one's followers in order to be a trustworthy leader. A real leader must believe that others are worthy of excellence or she cannot trust. If you cannot trust, how can you be trustworthy?

Another reported nurtured PQ trait or skill is the **ability to read others**. This is an intuitive skill that enables the leader to predict how people are likely to react to events. We feel that this skill is more a matter of desire and attention than anything else. In fact, in a discussion in a class, it became evident that women are better at reading others than men are. It also became apparent that a large part of this has evolved in humans. In the not so distant past, the fate of women was more at the hands of men than most care to admit. Women had to be able to tell quickly foe from friend and with whom to align. Men on the other hand were much more capable of defending themselves, so other skills related to physical attributes became much more important. Therefore, women have evolved into the sex that can read people better. Perhaps it is also related to the sensitivity they have for their children and their needs. Many mothers seem to know why their child is crying—a skill not many men have.

Beyond the evolved part of intuition is the need to know about diverse kinds of people. "To know the right questions to ask you need some basic knowledge. By reading voraciously, Churchill knew the history of warfare and weapons through the ages, as well as the latest fantasies from science-fiction writers such as H. G. Wells" (Sandys and Littman, 2003, p. 159). Yes, studying people and situations of all types, fictional and otherwise, enables one to read people better. The heightened ability to read people is more a matter of desire and focus than many of the other factors we describe in *The Leadership Quotient.*

The ability to match people to jobs is an essential skill since human capital is the most important part of an organization. Judging who will be best in a certain slot or position is NOT what we are calling a PQ skill or trait. The trait of judging the ability of people to fill certain positions is a Management Quotient and will be discussed at length in a later chapter: MQ. The PQ part of this is being able to read how individuals will be motivated, honest, or a number of other human characteristics that indeed go into selection. The subject arises in this chapter because there is a great deal of People Quotient in first determining the type of person who is being considered for any specific position.

The last trait or skill that is reported as nurtured and a requirement for PQ is **networking**. Four rules of networking know-how will help you continually build your network if you go to new places, meet new people, follow up, and stay in touch:

1. Always listen more than you talk.

2. Always do something for another person before you ask them to do something for you.

3. Follow up and then follow-up some more.

4. Find innovative ways to stay in touch.

"It all comes down to who knows you—not who you know" (Henricks, 2003, p. 53). Networking has always been important for career success, but doing it the old-fashioned traveling way can take too much time for the benefit. The Internet makes networking more natural and efficient. We can stay in touch with friends and colleagues worldwide without disrupting anyone's schedule, and it takes little effort.

Victor and Skip are two of Bill's very-fast-moving former students who returned to campus to speak to his senior strategy classes. Victor and Skip are both consummate networkers. However, it seemed from their presentations that they approached networking differently. Networking is a natural outgrowth of what Victor does, but for Skip, networking is a purposeful effort to use every situation to network. Although some of their basic approaches are different, both Victor and Skip are successful at networking for the same reason: they are not users. They network with the genuine desire to help and be involved. Their networking helps others as much as it helps them. We close this section with another servant leader message: The key is to focus on others, not ourselves, in order to have a more effective PQ.

Normal Nurtured PQ Weaknesses—Quadrant 4 of the PQ 2X2 Matrix

The most common weakness we have seen reported here is **pretentiousness**. When someone pretends to like others or truly care about them, it comes across as a negative. Most of us would rather someone just say, "I don't care," than have them carry on with a false sense of concern. Once the fake is "outed," followers have no time for him. Nothing he does is worthwhile from that point on.

Think about the relationship between FDR and Churchill and how they managed to bring order out of chaos in times much like ours. It has been written of that situation, "We have learned the simple truth, the only way to have a friend is to be one." You cannot pretend to be a person's friend or to care about them for long. You will be found out. Act at the level of feelings you really have and understand that though one might be smarter than another, no one is better in every way than everyone else.

One of our co-workers was such a creep. He almost always kissed any boss' butt and really had a brown nose. He would not even look at a janitor. Another guy, on the other hand, was so rebellious he did the opposite. He would not give the boss any respect. Both of these approaches are wrong. Everyone is a human and deserves to be respected for that and their potential. If you are pretentious, stop it today!

A second area of concern of PQ is the **fear of deep relationships**. One of our students commented, "You really do care. I just could not believe it. I thought you treated me that way because you had to." Perhaps she had experienced false concern in which someone pretended to care about her but really didn't. Many people truly care and want to have a relationship that benefits both parties. In addition, many people are afraid that if they seek a relationship and fail, the hurt will be so great; therefore, they just don't seek a relationship. So often the person who fails and the person who succeeds fear the exact same thing. The only difference is that, for the victor, the desire to succeed overcomes the fear of failure. This is often true in relationships. Many do not attempt to have a meaningful relationship because they think they will fail. Try, and you'll succeed; or if you don't succeed you won't lose anything that can't be replaced. Thank God, people have an infinite capacity to love and respect others. As Louis Armstrong said: "I got a simple rule about everybody. If you don't treat me right—shame on you!" (Gardner and Reese, 1975, p. 19). Live and relate the way Armstrong suggests. If you have a great fear of relationships, write it in this quadrant and work on overcoming it.

A third trait that seems to be nurtured is a failure to really be **listening** when others are trying to tell you something. People talk to be heard, not to be talked to.

"One generalization that is supported both by research and experience is that effective two-way communication is essential to proper functioning of the leader-follower relationship.…Leaders, to be effective, must pick up the signals coming to them from constituents. In addition, the rule is if the messages from below say you are doing a flawless job; send back for more candid assessment.…The huge, complex organizations we have fashioned and the sophisticated control systems devised to manage that complexity reduce the amount of face-to-face communications between leaders and led. In addition, we pay a heavy price for the reduction.…Nothing can substitute for a live leader (not necessarily the top leader) listening attentively and responding informally.…Wise leaders are continuously finding ways to say to their constituents, 'I hear you'" (Gardner, 2003, p. 147). This means I hear not only what you say but also what you mean by what you say and your actions. Can you do that? Most of us cannot even hear someone plainly when they say a simple yes or no.

We recall one 50-year-old guy who said, "My mother wants me to move back in with her." We said, "No, she does not," and he said, "Yes, she does. She said so." Do you really think any healthy 75-year-old mother wants her son to move back in with her? Do not just listen to words, but pay attention to life's facts.

Mark Twain described meeting a prominent 19th-century industry baron who told him: "Before I die, I mean to make a pilgrimage to the Holy Land. I will climb to the top of Mount Sinai and read the Ten Commandments aloud." In response, Twain remarked, "Why don't you stay at home and *keep* them" (Ragsdale, 2003, p. C1). Twain listened a couple of levels deeper than what that person actually said. Could you do this?

The last reported PQ trait is **exclusivity or being withdrawn**. So many people cannot relate to others because they feel the other person is not good enough for them or does not fit into their club. We withdraw too often from others and prejudge how we could benefit from having a relationship with them. Why not think next time, "Maybe they can benefit from a relationship with me," or, "They are human and I am going to treat them that way regardless of how they fit my needs." So many have to feel that it is to their advantage to relate to another or they will not do it. That is a poor way to exhibit PQ. One person wrote as his chief PQ strength, "I watch people and ask them about themselves." Now, he exhibits a non-exclusivity that is the opposite of this weakness.

Now that we have finished describing the most common natural and nurtured PQ traits or skills as they have been reported to us, it is time to look at the entire matrix and assess yourself.

Using the PQ Matrix

> *Steve Reinemund, PepsiCo's Chairman and CEO, does not "invite inspirational speakers to give quick-fix recipes for self-improvement....[He simply] hopes that, in the end, the leadership program will help managers decide which specific strengths and talents they wish to build up, or whether they want to attempt to acquire new skills. Either choice is fine [he says, as long as the participants follow through.] The company has to give people the opportunity to grow, but they have to take responsibility for their own development and do it for themselves, not for me." (Hymowtz, 2003, B1)*

Nothing could be truer than Mr. Reinemund's statements when you are discussing the improvement of PQ. No one can do that for you; it is all you and what you make of it. You need to be realistic and ready for change if you want to improve in the PQ area.

As you can see from the previous sections, we gave many examples of people skills and traits that could help or hinder a person's quest for extended leadership responsibilities. A key here is to first understand clearly each of the traits and then honestly evaluate yourself in each of the four quadrants. Remember to ask for some additional help from those who know you best. Seek real feedback and use the principles noted in this section and you'll likely get help. Unfortunately, even your closest accountability partner will not tell you the entire truth, because you are too fragile to give or accept 100% honesty even with yourself, let alone with others.

In evaluating yourself as you've done before, remember to be realistic about a replacement trait.

Figure 7.3: YOUR PQ MEASUREMENT AND IMPROVEMENT MATRICES

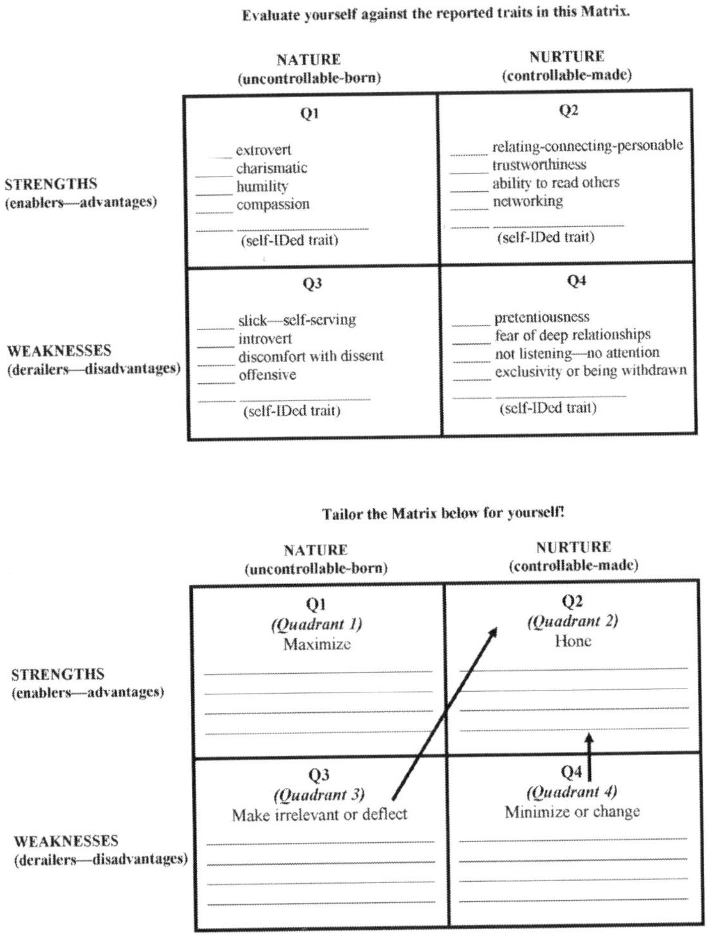

Evaluate yourself against the reported traits in this Matrix.

	NATURE (uncontrollable-born)	NURTURE (controllable-made)
STRENGTHS (enablers—advantages)	**Q1** ___ extrovert ___ charismatic ___ humility ___ compassion ___ (self-IDed trait)	**Q2** ___ relating-connecting-personable ___ trustworthiness ___ ability to read others ___ networking ___ (self-IDed trait)
WEAKNESSES (derailers—disadvantages)	**Q3** ___ slick—self-serving ___ introvert ___ discomfort with dissent ___ offensive ___ (self-IDed trait)	**Q4** ___ pretentiousness ___ fear of deep relationships ___ not listening—no attention ___ exclusivity or being withdrawn ___ (self-IDed trait)

Tailor the Matrix below for yourself!

	NATURE (uncontrollable-born)	NURTURE (controllable-made)
STRENGTHS (enablers—advantages)	**Q1** *(Quadrant 1)* Maximize	**Q2** *(Quadrant 2)* Hone
WEAKNESSES (derailers—disadvantages)	**Q3** *(Quadrant 3)* Make irrelevant or deflect	**Q4** *(Quadrant 4)* Minimize or change

Evaluating Your PQ Personal Profile: Strengths and Weaknesses Doing Something About Your PQ!

As We Said in the Introduction, "It's Time to Get Started; If Not Now, When?"

Remember: Effective leadership requires a balanced fit among the many environments, behaviors, contexts, processes, contents, and needs. Figure 7.4 shows the interaction of 1) the leader, 2) the followers, and 3) the environments, which all need to fit. We are repeating this message many times because we cannot say this too often. You will achieve fit when the triangulation of these three elements becomes second nature to you. Put your PQ values in the triangle and see if your PQ is enough of a foundation to help you proceed to the next level of improving your overall *LQ*©.

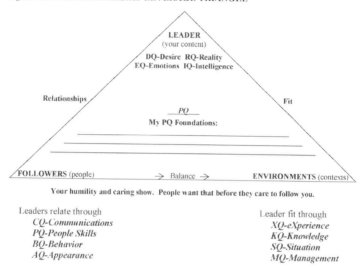

Figure 7.4: YOUR LEADERSHIP LEVERAGE TRIANGLE

LEADER
(your content)
DQ-Desire RQ-Reality
EQ-Emotions IQ-Intelligence

Relationships

Fit

PQ
My PQ Foundations:

FOLLOWERS (people)   → Balance →   **ENVIRONMENTS** (contexts)

Your humility and caring show. People want that before they care to follow you.

Leaders relate through
CQ-Communications
PQ-People Skills
BQ-Behavior
AQ-Appearance

Leader fit through
XQ-eXperience
KQ-Knowledge
SQ-Situation
MQ-Management

PQ Conclusions

As Keene (2000) said, our world is the result of interactions with many people within many environments, and the quality of those relationships will determine the effectiveness of the creativity that naturally takes place—these interactions are very much a part of the process that creates our environments. The role of leadership is to be a torchbearer, constantly scanning the environment looking for useful information to teach people so they become productive self-managed co-creators. It requires the power of trust and stewardship.

The art of leadership is seen as the ability to release the potential of individuals, and this unleashing is leveraged best by leaders with higher PQs. You need to dedicate a part of any leadership improvement effort to understanding your PQ and improving it. How much effort depends on your strengths and weaknesses in the PQ area as it relates to your other *LQ*© components.

A recent book from the Arbinger Institute, *Leadership and Self-Deception: Getting out of the Box* (2000), challenges each of us to ask ourselves when we meet someone, "Am I more interested in them, or in what they think of me?" It further challenges us to remember that, "We're all people…seeing others as people, we have a very basic sense about others—namely, that like me, they too have hopes, needs, cares, and fears" (p. 64).

The premise of this book is that we overemphasize our own virtue and end up inflating the value of our activities to justify our acts of self-betrayal. Self-betrayal is defined as someone doing something that is contrary to what they feel they should do. Think about this. How many times have you failed to do something you knew in your heart you should do because the other person was so irresponsible or ungrateful? Were *they* the cause of *you* not acting, or was it your own selfish action and self-betrayal? This is a form of PQ: PQ about self as it relates to others. Perhaps the first step toward being honest about others is being honest about yourself.

Theodore Roosevelt said, "The most important single ingredient in the formula of success is knowing how to get along with people" (Warner 1988, p. 22). In addition, Jean de la Bruyere said: "The best way to get on in the world is to make people believe it's to their advantage to help you" (Warner, 1988, p. 34). Both of these statements point to the importance of understanding PQ from the perspective of others, not just your perspective. In every $LQ^{©}$ quotient, it is important to understand the perspectives of others. But in PQ, the perspectives of others outweigh your own personal perspective. If we are trying to relate to others and influence them, we must learn to treat others as they would have us treat them.

Remember: Change for yourself or others related to PQ does not happen because of a change of mind; it happens because of a change of heart. For this reason, your PQ is going to be very hard to change. Regardless, as with the other quotients, the more realistically you identify your personal PQ components, the more likely you are to improve your PQ and your subsequent leadership potential. We did not say it would be easy, but we know it is worth it if your desire is to improve as a leader and as a human being.

In the next chapter, we will look at another follower quotient, the Behavior Quotient (BQ). There are indeed many examples that we are being slapped in the face with: Michael and Janet Jackson, Kobe Bryant, Scott Peterson, and many others remind us daily of the need to behave as if our mothers were always watching.

8

BQ, The Behavior Quotient

Your actions are speaking so loudly I can't hear what you're saying!

Leadership is all about behavior. Leaders behave differently than non-leaders. In this chapter, we will help you discover how you should behave with your followers in your environment.

The Leadership Quotient experience asks that you look deep inside your inner self to see what is really there. So many times we lie to ourselves about who we are and try to become someone we're not. In a previous chapter, we referred to that as "faking it." We do not consistently face the real person we are because we are scared of what we might discover. However, if we do not ask some tough questions of ourselves we will never find the answers of who we truly are. Inner reflection is very hard to do, unlike reflecting on the behaviors and actions of others. It surely seems that often we are quick to judge others but slow to judge ourselves. Some judge themselves much harder than others do, but they are the exception to the rule. We normally get satisfied with being stuck no matter how much we might wish to unstick ourselves; we most often wish something would change instead of working at changing it. This *LQ*© experience requires that you unstick yourself and look inward, and that is why this quotient might seem a contradiction. It is talking about your behavior as others see and perceive it, not as you see and perceive it. They know only what they see of you. Can you think inwardly enough to discover what others think of your Behavior Quotient?

In London, Bill had a theatre teacher named Rona who would insist that we look at every actor and ask, "Did she add to the intent of the playwright and director as she interpreted the play?" That is, "Did the way the actor performed benefit the moods, feelings, understandings, or emotions the playwright and director wished to be created and felt by the audience?" This was the question. Rona would say: "Dearie, I don't care if you liked her or the play. What I want to know is, did she add to the intent of the play?" Often Rona reminded us that a supporting cast member would bring the focus away from the leading actor or even some thing we were to notice in the play. She would say that the actor was overacting and not adding to, but taking away from, the overall intent of the play.

Let's apply Rona's lesson to our Behavior Quotient. In our daily actions, we must not interfere with others who are making leadership happen. When the limelight is on us, it might be bad for leadership. Would it not be appropriate to ask how your behavior relates to your acting as a leader or follower?

Business leaders now "perform" in a goldfish bowl —everyone is watching, thanks to Enron, WorldCom, and the like. We all should realize that business organizations are the most influential institutions in society and have replaced the political, religious, and home arenas as the entities that most direct our lives.

If you really want to succeed, act like it! Ambition is worse when you don't admit you have it; but if you do have it, exhibit it. Reframe and reshape your behavior to be an $LQ^{©}$ plus, not a minus. For authentic leader behavior, be decisive, be focused, add a personal touch, and read and study this section with an eye toward appropriate behavior modification.

We both like plays, movies, novels, and just about any kind of live performance. In part, we feel that these events are like highlighters of some part of life. Often the part of life seems insignificant at first, but as the performance unfolds we see that indeed the insignificant often becomes significant in the eyes of others.

We are reminded of a great play, *Dangerous Corner,* which had a nice run in London's West End theatre district. This play has a first and a second act that are identical until one point. In Act One, something happens that causes the music not to play, and people talk rather than dance. That talking leads to all kinds of discoveries, which really affect all the participants. In the second act, the music continues to play and none of the gruesome secrets are revealed. Think about the dangerous or opportunistic corners we all have come to at many points in our own lives. So it is with all our actions, that is, the few actions that most see us doing—our behavior—which might become a dangerous or lucky corner in the paths of our lives. Those few instances become a highlighter of who the person observing us thinks we are. Our behaviors are the highlighted actions that define us to others. They become our Behavior Quotient and we are judged by them, right or wrong, so always behave with care (didn't our mothers always tell us that?).

There is more to each person than you will ever know. John Maxwell, in his (2002) *Leadership 101: What Every Leader Needs To Know*, wrote, "Did you know that each of us influences at least ten thousand people during our lifetime? So the question is not *whether* you will influence someone, but *how* you will use your influence" (p. ix). Overall leadership ability, both natural and nurtured abilities, is a lid on how effective your influence can be. Leadership is so closely aligned with influence that the words are almost interchangeable. Leadership is a lifetime of growth and is a collection of skills, "nearly all of which can be learned and improved" (p. 13). "It's unfortunate because as long as a person doesn't know what he doesn't know, he doesn't grow" (p. 14).

Your external behavior is an exhibit of how others judge you as a leader. As we have said before: If it indeed takes 1,000 words to describe a picture, how many words must it take to convince someone who saw your behavior that it is not the correct indication of the person you are? The film and book, *Big Fish*, is an example, albeit fiction, of how there is always more to a person than we might believe, and unfortunately, we usually do not know it until the person's funeral.

We need help in accepting each other. We are all being judged by others continuously, and fortunately or unfortunately, people must judge by what they see of us. We feel that we should judge others by the standard by which we would like to be judged, but regrettably it is not what *you* think of your behavior but what *others* think. While appearances can be deceiving, appearances are all others see of you or me. That's why we've dedicated the entire next chapter to the Appearance Quotient. The study of the history of any individual is not limited by time, and we often change our minds as we get to know others in life or even after they've passed away, as we remember who they really were. However, in today's hyperactive world of work, we do not have the luxury of unlimited time. We hire, fire, decide, and move on with speed and assurance. Accepting others as they are, versus as we might wish them to be, must become a fact each of us understands. Behavior and actions are our movies to the world about each of us, and they reflect accurately to others who and what we are. If you want to be a leader, you have to be able to assess your BQ and adjust it to the followers in your specific environment.

When we finally sat down to write the Behavior Quotient chapter after weeks of study, we pondered the difference between the Behavior Quotient, the Appearance Quotient, the Communications Quotient, and many others. While we are departmentalizing those into separate chapters, we realize there is a lot of relationship between them. We concluded that BQ is the outward manifestations as others perceive them about the content of our other Leadership Quotients. Your BQ is judged by people, inside and outside your organization, who watch you. It is similar to organizational culture and climate. An organization's culture is made up of the actions, stories, rites of passage, ways of thinking and doing, etc., and climate is simply how it feels when you are in the organization. BQ is how you feel to be around. Behavior is like so many things that are more "caught" than "taught." You might want to remember the icons we mentioned in a previous chapter: From whom can you "catch" the kind of behavior that will improve your Behavior Quotient?

When Bill was first married and had young children, he was broke, as many young couples are, and he had to work on his own cars. He was so broke that he could not afford to own very many tools. That made it difficult to do some things, such as putting on shocks or a new muffler and tailpipe, with only a pair of vise-grips and a screwdriver. One day, as he was working on his car, his three-year-old daughter, Suzanne, was copying his behavior while "working" on her tricycle. She would beat her trike with the pliers and utter, "Shit, shit, shit." Where did she get this behavior?

Yes, people watch you; and quite often, they mimic what they see you do. As a leader, this is true with your followers, much like it was between Bill and little Suzanne. Your behavior can be seen as a lever by which you pull similar behavior out of your followers. Is it the behavior you desire? We all must accept the responsibility for making the most of ourselves regardless of what we see others do, but in the end, we are a composite of all we see and do. We most often know others are clever, reliable, or even trustworthy because of what we have observed them do—we have no better metric for measuring their behavior. We have comparison others—or icons, as we called them in a previous chapter—for all of our actions. Likewise, we are comparison others for followers when we are the leader.

As you read the remainder of this chapter, think about the fact that **my behavior highlights who I am to others and I may not get a second chance**. As you think about that, try to move from **behaving as I please, to behaving as if others are always judging me by what I do**. A simple story will do nicely to illustrate this point. Aunt Adia was an 80-year-old woman about 4' 10" who rented one of her rooms to a gentleman who was an alcoholic. One night, when he came in drunk, he was met by Aunt Adia and she said, "Shame on you, Mr. Jones." He responded, "I know I'm a sorry case; won't you please pray for me?" She quickly grabbed his hand and began: "Our dear heavenly Father, please help this poor ole drunk man…" To which Mr. Jones quickly replied; "Don't tell him I'm drunk; tell him I'm sick." Do you suppose He knows? Do you suppose mere people know when they hear us say one thing but see us act totally opposite? The concepts outlined in this chapter are intended to help you come to a more complete understanding of your Behavior Quotient as it contributes to your overall Leadership Quotient.

The Theme of BQ

It simply cannot be said too often: Leadership comes from the relationships people form when they are doing things together. Consequently, when you participate you must understand how your behavior will shape your image and substance as a leader. Just as an organization's culture is felt by the organization's climate, your leadership will be felt by the way you act. BQ—don't leave home without it!

Other Keys to BQ

Handy (1998) said: "However much we may deny it, the way other people see us does influence the way we see ourselves (p. 88).…I come from a long line of preachers, and preaching comes more easily to me than practicing (p. 103).…So much of the content of what I had learned was irrelevant, while the process of learning had cultivated a set of attitudes and behaviors which were directly opposed to what seemed to be needed in real life." Handy goes on to list seven qualities needed for success in life:

• Confidence

• Curiosity

- Intentionality

- Self-control

- Relatedness

- Communication

- Cooperation

Handy continues, "I am free, goes that message, to break free from my past and to recreate myself....The best is always yet to come if we can rise from our past....We can override that system, just as we can override the programming of nature....Where better to start than where we are?" (p. 254). Where better to start than to realize that your behavior, as it is witnessed and judged by others, is indeed you as a leader? Handy provides support and encouragement for our basic assumption: Understanding and improving your Behavior Quotient can improve your leadership.

Each semester Bill invites his graduating seniors to his home for a party. He does it for two specific reasons: first, to allow them one more chance to interact with each other, which is a metaphorical "door closing"; and second, to enable Bill to change his relationship with them. This metaphorical "door opening" is the commencement of a new relationship. The relationship is no longer professor-student, it is now adult-adult. He feels that as they enter their next phase, he would like them to see him more as a friend and mentor and less as a professor. His quirky "Bill-Rock Café" helps in a lot of ways because that's how students begin to see him as a person rather than as a professor. At one party, as Jeff was leaving, he said "Wow, I'd love to drive that Mustang." Bill threw him the keys to his coveted 1965 Mustang convertible. As Jeff pulled off, many students said, "Why did you do that? He'll probably never be back." Jeff was intelligent, but just not very responsible, and Bill had spent much of the semester really haranguing him. Bill decided it was time to show trust in Jeff. The coveted Mustang lurched and screeched as Jeff struggled with the manual transmission and manual steering. Bill had his doubts, but Jeff made it back with the Mustang—and himself—in one piece. Jeff began to act more mature after that experience.

Bill had exercised the "Pygmalion Effect" (you generally get what you expect) on Jeff. The idea is named for the mythical Greek sculptor who carved a rapturous woman in stone. Because of his overwhelming desire, the goddess Aphrodite made the statue come to life. Bill had so much desire for Jeff to be responsible that he gave him responsibility. Jeff responded as Bill wanted him to.

Bill's Behavior Quotient was copied by Jeff. Sometimes we get the behavior we expect from followers, so expect the best even if it means being disappointed sometimes. It would be so sad to never be disappointed by anyone, for if you never were let down by another then you would in no way ever trust another human.

In BQ, We Can Often Learn the Most from the Poor Behavior of Others

When people act normally we usually don't notice. We expect people to act normally and not to bring attention to themselves, but when they act abnormally it's predictable that everyone will notice. Good behavior is simply a hygiene factor that will normally not garner you very much appreciation because people expect it. However, when you are being considered for promotion, it's predictable that someone will produce a file of your bad behavior. How often have you heard a coworker say, "I just cannot understand why they promoted Dave and not me?" Overhearing this, we'll bet you've sometimes thought, "I know why. It's because John asked a goofy question of the big boss!" You want to ask, "Didn't you see John as he totally missed the fact that he should have gotten our guest something to drink, or when he slammed the door in the face of that customer?" He was not being mean; he just wasn't paying attention, and his behavior showed it.

People want to see that you are paying attention and picking up on things you need to be aware of. Little things mean a lot in big situations, and people figure you'll do the same as you have in the past. The best predictor of future actions is past actions. Your followers are looking at your behaviors as indications of the kind of person you are. They formulate their opinions on what they see, and often the person observed making a mistake never gets another chance. We're not saying it's fair; that's just the way it is. We can learn a lot from the poor behavior of others.

Bill George, the former CEO of Medtronic, took notice of the poor behavior of fellow CEOs: "The business world has run off the rails, mistaking wealth for success and image for leadership" (2003a, p. 96). In another article, George (2003b) wrote about "why it's hard to do what's right." Though neither Dave nor Bill is particularly enchanted with process, we can agree with Hope and Fraser (2003) who write, "Behavior change often follows process change. Therefore, organizations need processes that lead people to act legally and ethically."

Some Literature That Might Help!

Benton's (2003) *Executive Charisma* gives us the six steps to mastering the art of leadership and urges us to add substance to our style. Benton discusses charisma, self-confidence, poise, energy, and other skills that are important to a leader. In summary, he emphasizes the need for a leader to use his actions to encourage others to get useful things done. Benton stresses taking initiative and expecting others to accept you because you indicate through your Behavior Quotient that followers are significant to you. Integrity, confidence, and communications—verbal and nonverbal—all add the substance that you must have in order to lead. Following are Benton's six steps:

- Initiate first.

- Expect and give acceptance to maintain and gain esteem.

- Ask favors and questions.

- Stand tall and straight, and smile.

- Be human, using humor and hands-on approaches.

- Slow down, shut up; but most importantly, listen.

Your Behavior Quotient will be much improved if you can follow Benton's advice.

For too many people, winning always remains a mystery. For many others, they neither win nor lose, they simply mind-numbingly play the game. We are seeking to help you make yourself a leader who has made winning a way of life. Make your normal style of behavior under stress a winning style where your strengths are heightened and your weaknesses are put aside. Pay attention to your behavioral game. You can bet others are doing so.

We want each of us to adjust our behavior to improve our overall Leadership Quotient, but we should not sell our souls to accomplish our leadership goals. Only you can know if you are selling your soul or adjusting your behavior with honorable intent—that is not for anyone else to judge. You must learn to determine how your actions are perceived by your perspective followers who make you a leader—that's just about everyone.

For this purpose, there is no process that is perfect, but 360-degree feedback evaluative systems can be helpful in identifying weaknesses and helping improve performance with the development of new skills and competencies through awareness. To understand how others perceive you is the key, regardless of how you think you are, even when you are right! This system proves that everyone's input is important and provides a direct link between relationship management and performance (Tornow, London, and CCL Associates, 1998).

In the final analysis, no system works unless you work to make it work. Tools are tools and are only as useful as the craftsman using them. Start using any tool with the intent to improve dedicated relationships. Continually share knowledge interorganizationally with dedicated suppliers and all those you interact with, inside and outside your organization. End by creating high levels of trust throughout the extended enterprise with face-to-face sharing of problems and successes, analysis and evaluations, intended to move leadership throughout your organization (Childress, 2001). If your organization does not have a good 360-degree evaluative format, you should develop one to use for yourself. We've continually suggested in each Measurement and Improvement Matrix that you find a trusted colleague who will tell you the difficult truth about your leadership strengths and weaknesses. Thus, the Leadership Quotient acts as an evaluation system that focuses on how others perceive your performance and behavior.

Principles of Success Start and End by How Other People Judge Your Behavior

Others have no way to judge or evaluate you, other than the way you behave. Ask Al Gore, Jim Bakker, Martha, Madonna, or many others whose low Behavior Quotients have caused their fall from grace. They continually ask the public not to judge them by their few mistakes but by their many accomplishments. That request is sensible and one we should honor. But do we? No, we don't. We judge others by the behavior we wish to remember them by, not the behavior they wish us to judge them by. Each of us needs to remember this as we implement our Behavioral Quotient, because today's behavior may be the action that others remember us by!

Behavior in the Technology-Information Age

Our behavior is often exhibited via e-mail, video conferencing, or voice mail. That can be frightening. That could be significant. When you write someone an e-mail or respond to their e-mail (or snail mail), just remember that what you write will be in writing for all to see for all time.

In the aftermath of the Enron scandal, all the stored e-mails became part of a public record. Ouch! Think about e-mails you've sent today over your company's e-mail system. Would you like them to appear in the *Wall Street Journal* someday? That's exactly what happened to an e-mail exchange between an Enron employee and his "one-night stand" date in another city. Multiple court cases have maintained that the company owns every keystroke you make on your company-owned computer. Be careful. Electronic communication is very efficient, but it can last forever. Be careful that your Behavior Quotient doesn't come back to haunt you years from now.

Look at the Behavior Quotient as it appears in the *LQ*© triangle in Figure 8.1. This shows how perceptions are linked through the leader's and followers' behaviors as they relate in the leader-follower relationships. You will see that leader traits or actions are meaningless unless they are viewed through the eyes of the followers. Next, look at the 2X2 matrix that follows in Figure 8.2. We will develop the normal strengths and weaknesses that have been reported on the *LQ*© instrument and develop a profile of a good BQ using this input. These reported strengths and weaknesses will give you a comparison methodology by which you can determine if your BQ is a launching pad or a barrier to your leadership future.

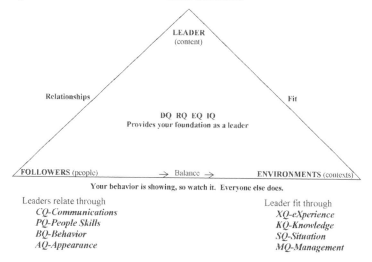

Figure 8.1: THE LEADERSHIP LEVERAGE TRIANGLE

LEADER
(content)

Relationships

Fit

DQ RQ EQ IQ
Provides your foundation as a leader

FOLLOWERS (people) → Balance → ENVIRONMENTS (contexts)

Your behavior is showing, so watch it. Everyone else does.

Leaders relate through
   CQ-Communications
   PQ-People Skills
   BQ-Behavior
   AQ-Appearance

Leader fit through
   XQ-eXperience
   KQ-Knowledge
   SQ-Situation
   MQ-Management

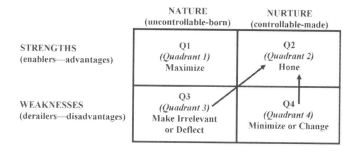

Figure 8.2: BQ MEASUREMENT AND IMPROVEMENT MATRIX

	NATURE (uncontrollable-born)	NURTURE (controllable-made)
STRENGTHS (enablers—advantages)	Q1 *(Quadrant 1)* Maximize	Q2 *(Quadrant 2)* Hone
WEAKNESSES (derailers—disadvantages)	Q3 *(Quadrant 3)* Make Irrelevant or Deflect	Q4 *(Quadrant 4)* Minimize or Change

We are to others as we behave, not as we say we behave.

Normal Natural BQ Strengths—Quadrant 1 of the BQ 2X2 Matrix

The most common natural strength that was reported by our test group of leaders was labeled **authentic-inspiring-trustworthy-moral**. This trait needs little explaining and most would agree it is a trait that forms early in life and indeed changes little throughout life. Part of the problem we currently have with corporate cheats is the belief that a college course on ethics will help. A survey we did with 100 college freshmen, 100 working MBAs (average age of 35), and 100 managers and executives (average age of 52) found one commonality. All groups agreed that these values are obtained before a person reaches college age and that they are gained primarily at home. Not one of the three groups felt that college education or work education would do much good. All the groups believed that two things would help: 1) courses on penalties, and 2) more control of compensation and stock options.

Our ethics-related, 25-question survey showed that all groups were very familiar with the most recent corporate scandals, and it showed that most people at all levels think that values are largely dependent on their leader's ethical behavior. Importantly, it showed that the 300 respondents thought that college ethics courses, corporate ethical policies, and new laws and rules would be much less effective than stricter penalties for corporate cheaters (Tevendale, Service, and Boockholdt, 2003).

In testing the Behavior Quotient with our beta group, the terms **courageous** and **brave** were repeated constantly. In this category, we found many mentions of names like **Nelson Mandela, John McCain, Jessica Lynch,** and **Admiral Stockdale** as solid exemplars who have exhibited this trait. Jim Collins wrote about the "Stockdale principle" in his book *Good to Great*. He wrote that it is a tremendous trait for an organization's leaders to exhibit. We feel it is indeed a principle we all should follow: Face the brutal reality of the moment, but have faith that all will come out in the end. This principle served many who were brutalized prisoners of war during Vietnam. The most notable of those was Arizona Senator John McCain, who was one of the most tortured of prisoners.

As we were discussing this, an MBA student said we should remove Jessica Lynch's name because we have since heard otherwise. Most in the class initially agreed, but we convinced them otherwise. She is mentioned here because of the brave way she just told the truth rather than taking credit for all the media said she did when she was captured by the Iraqi army. We think it is much harder to behave like a hero as others praise you and just tell the truth than it is to accept the praise and keep quiet. Jessica probably would be brave in many situations, or at least her behavior indicates to us she would.

Some part of courage and bravery is inherited, and a part is formed early in life, although there are many examples of people who led non-courageous lives, then stepped up to the plate and gave their lives in times of distress. Perhaps we all have this within us, just waiting for the proper moment to surface.

The third trait in this quadrant is **grace**. We cannot help but think of Jackie Onassis and her actions just after JFK was shot. She exemplified grace when she pulled the Secret Service agent into the speeding car and then held her husband's battered and bloody head. Finally, we see the picture of her in her bloodstained dress witnessing the swearing-in of LBJ on the plane en route to Washington. Certainly, Jackie O exhibited grace many times in her life.

Many leaders have shown grace and inspired others by their actions because followers have admired their ability to rise above and keep their heads when all others about them were losing theirs.

This is partly a natural trait and partly one that people are trained for very early in life: witness the training of royalty throughout history. Great Britain's now-deceased "Queen Mum" certainly had it, as does her daughter, Queen Elizabeth.

The final natural BQ trait is **being personable**. This trait is a focused dependability that makes the leader very responsive to others. Personable leaders seem to exude the attitude, "I'm your friend." Many actors and public figures have this at the mediagenic level, although it does not always translate to their personal lives. Princess Diana had this as far as we know, but we cannot be sure what it would have been like to work for or with her. We all have personal examples of people who are so personable that everyone thinks they are their best friend. In fact, we have seen many who appear this way because they *are* everyone's best friend, and they are not faking it. Some people just love people, and it shows. What about you? This natural BQ skill is certainly a plus for aspiring leaders. Your leadership ability will be reduced if you don't have an adequate level of *personableness*.

Normal Natural BQ Weaknesses—Quadrant 3 of the BQ 2X2 Matrix

Much like the natural strengths we just discussed, this area is tricky because of the highly intertwined nature of heritable and environmental influences. But we feel that there are certainly many weaknesses that could be classified as natural, because of their early onset and the strong influence of genetics on their initial development.

The first trait we see as a natural weakness is **lack of credibility**. It seems that the positive side of this trait can be within someone yet not surface until a great time of stress or need. Witness former New York City Mayor Rudy Giuliani or Enron whistleblower Sherron Watkins. Their credibility showed when it counted. Mother Teresa seemed to have it all the time. Perhaps Louis Farrakhan and Richard Scrushy could learn something from these exemplars about real credibility! Farrakhan and Scrushy appear to have this natural weakness. We have learned from many exemplars about lack of credibility. Unfortunately, the negative side of credibility that is exhibited seems to far outweigh the positive examples. Consider the credibility area of your Behavioral Quotient: Do you set the right credibility example?

The next natural weakness is a BQ trait we have seen too much of lately. It is **deceitful-cheater**. Too many corporate scandals have been coming to light of late, though most started years ago. We don't want to waste our words in this book re-reporting the scandals. John Ashcroft's often-maligned Justice Department is reported to be a puppet of the most corporate-friendly administration in our lifetime. Yet the Department has indicted more than 600 executives and obtained more than 200 convictions of executives for accounting irregularities that occurred mostly in the 1990s (Pulliam, Latour, and Brown, 2003, pp. A1 & A12). Some of the suspected executives probably have some degree of innocence, but there just cannot have been that many dumb, uninformed top executives. The jury did not buy WorldCom's Bernie Ebbers' plea of stupidity. Some of them just logically have to be guilty. For example, in the Pulliam article just referenced, we see Scott Sullivan admitting guilt after spending about $14 million on his own defense, even while his lawyers are proclaiming his innocence. Perhaps we do not need to hear from anyone's lawyer since we could write his or her script of complete and utter rhetoric. We can only hope that punishment is dealt out in proportion to the crime. While the deceitful cheaters lived in the lap of luxury, thousands of people lost tremendous amounts of hard-earned money that they were expecting to use in their retirement years or to better educate their kids.

We think Donald Trump is honest and basically a good person. But if we look back to the early 1990s, he was worth a *negative* $900 million and still lived the life of a king. We don't begrudge him that since he was taking great risk, which turned into success via ethical hard work. However, today we see so many living the life of kings on the backs of those who cannot afford decent places to live. Those modern-day reverse Robin Hoods steal from the poor so they themselves can live kingly lives. We ask, "Should they be allowed to reap the rewards of their purposeful deceitfulness?" Don't become a deceitful cheater.

This next natural weakness is one that every human has to some extent. Fortunately, with the proper training—mostly religious in nature—many people can overcome these tendencies and become decent human beings. This trait is exemplified by a **selfish, cowardly, hypocritical** demonstration of a low Behavior Quotient. Our human nature to some extent encourages selfish behavior, but many are exemplary in this area, both positively and negatively. It takes a lot of natural and nurtured willpower to overcome the tendency to look out for number one. Though it sounds strange, there are times when one has to be unselfish enough to be selfish or cowardly. Think about this, but don't end up being hypocritical about your own actions: admit when you are being unduly cowardly or selfish. We don't want to give examples in this area, but you should stop and think about people who exhibit these traits. Think about what Napoleon Bonaparte said: "A cowardly act! What do I care about this? You may be sure that I should never fear to commit one if it were to my advantage" (Gardner and Reese, 1975, p. 19).

The final natural weakness that we found in our research was defined as **disrespectful-aggravating or self-centered**. There are so many examples of this low Behavior Quotient that we don't know where to start. In addition, even when we are not sure if they are disrespectful or self-centered, we are definitely sure they are ignorant about what they say and how they say it. Former Chicago Bulls basketball star Dennis Rodman's off-court antics provide a good (bad) example. Radio shock jock Howard Stern is disrespectful, aggravating, and self-centered. People are disrespectful when they say things or do things that take advantage of the fears and ignorance of others. Many of us need to remember a central teaching of the Bible when we start to exhibit our natural self-centeredness: There is a God and we are not He!

Normal Nurtured BQ Strengths—Quadrant 2 of the BQ 2X2 Matrix

We start this more pleasant section of nurtured strengths with something that was reported in a recent book, *The Influentials,* by Keller and Berry (2003). They define **an Influential** as a person who brings important things to our attention. The authors claim that 1 in 10 Americans tells the other 9 how to vote, where to eat, what to buy, and so on. The authors explain who the Influentials are, along with their personalities. Basically, they are the optimistic activists who are constantly engaged in clear-headed attempts to think outside the orthodox box and confidently use their vision for change. They go to many events and belong to many organizations. They are voracious readers who trust their instincts, and they use multiple sources of information to learn, decide, and then act. They are pre-pared to be where the information is and to converse about it as they set a high pace. While doing so, they are at peace with themselves. They do not just *dream* about the future; they *build* it through their work and volunteerism, connecting at any and all levels. They accomplish through studying, reflect-ing, and connecting, but ultimately through action. Do you have this much-needed BQ trait? This trait seems to have some components that could be considered skills that are capable of being taught and learned.

The second trait we see reported as being a nurtured strength is called **trustworthiness**, and it goes in a different direction than the natural trait already discussed. It is a trustworthiness related to lead-ership that is exemplified when a leader **participates** and sets the example. It is a BQ leadership trait when you say to others through example, "I will be a good leader and a good follower."

Trustworthiness is a nurtured behavior that must be exhibited if you want to be a leader who is not blind. It needs some boundaries, requires constant learning, is not always easy, needs people, and must be earned by your behavior as judged by others.

We are often struck by the Christian concept of being nonjudgmental. We feel this Christian-influenced teaching is about motives and religious implications, not actions. In every respect, we should judge actions (what people do), but we should not judge beliefs (who people are). Bill and Dave judge students every day: We grade their papers, correct their bad logic, and dismiss their poor examples. We're admittedly tough on what they do, but we try to accept who they are in terms of race, ethnicity, gender, and belief systems. If one says she is a Christian, we are to leave that judgment to God. Denial is not truth; you get truth by accepting the truth as you see it about others and your-self, but with humility. High Behavior Quotient leaders do not condemn people they do not under-stand. As divided as the Christian church is, so is the rest of the world. So trustworthiness from a nurtured perspective does touch the very foundations of our religious and moral codes that we have acquired throughout our lives.

To be a trustworthy leader requires that you set the example and participate by being a good fol-lower and a good leader. We must learn awareness in order to truly be trustworthy as leaders: aware-ness of self, others, and the world around us. Back up your talk by example, not just words. Relationships of leadership trust are built on your actions more than on your words.

A third nurtured principle is **being savvy and flexible**. Though you may not always agree with them, Colin Powell and Donald Rumsfeld are true examples of this. Savvy requires years of work and effort. You don't become realistically savvy overnight, but you develop savvy by paying attention and reflecting on lessons learned and earned. It's sad to admit, but most of us learn lessons the hard way. If we had just listened, they would have been handed to us on a silver platter. One of our students sent an e-mail that said, "I know you already knew it, but you were right about everything. I now know it; keep pushing, maybe some others will get it while it has few consequences."

Savvy without flexibility is often unusable or very harmful. People or situations dictate many changes in the way we use our knowledge and skills. Often, using some method we know to be right is of value and maybe even the most ethical thing to do overall. Knowing when a coalition or consensus is more important than the technical correctness of a decision takes truly flexible savvy. Many know the right way, the technically best way, but that is often not as important as many other considerations. Each of us must realize what is right and worthy of fighting for; yet equally importantly, we must know what does not really make a lot of difference. Accountants call it "materiality." That means, "Is it significant enough to spend time chasing after?" The ability to recognize materiality will increase your Behavior Quotient because you will know what's worth "behaving" for.

The last trait can be defined in one word: **respect**. R-E-S-P-E-C-T, like the Aretha Franklin song. Followers want to "find out what it means to me!" This trait is earned by a steadfastness that is exhibited through a strong diligence that manifests itself in accepting actions of dependability and dedicated inspirational actions such as generosity and love. Michael Jordan, the Pope, Mother Teresa, Bill Gates, and Ray Kroc have our respect. They got it the old-fashioned way: they earned it. This trait is greater than the traits that others bestow upon you because of how others interpret the motives behind what you do. Everyone wants to *be* respected, but too few want to *earn* respect. Respect is another BQ trait that you can't leave home without!

Normal Nurtured BQ Weaknesses—Quadrant 4 of the BQ 2X2 Matrix

We start this self-made area of ugliness with a trait we see all too often in our heroes and media types: **pretentiousness**. The opinionated pronouncements of many are not backed up with any solid actions, only empty words. Witness the holier-than-thou words of many actors who rant and rave for higher taxes even as they live the lives of princes or princesses. It's not against the law to overpay your taxes. If you want higher taxes, you can have them by taxing yourself higher. But these people become pretentious when they go to a powerful governmental body to force others to do so. Or they trample the idea of free-enterprise capitalism as they squander the rewards of the system they claim to loathe.

Most of these pretentious people are simply empty-headed do-gooders. The problem is that they want to do good with *your* money, not *theirs*. We recall Rosie O'Donnell as she put her money where her mouth was and gave to the 9/11 fund. Do these rich celebrities not know what fools they make of themselves when they tell working-class people what *they* should be doing, yet themselves have millions they could put to good use? Look at the *good* exemplars in this area who are not pretentious and you won't see them having birthday parties that could build houses for scores of homeless or could send many street kids to four years of college.

The second trait is **temper** coupled with **cowardice**. What better example do we have than Saddam Hussein? His temper caused him to sacrifice the lives of thousands of his countrymen, yet he was such a coward that he emerged from a hole in the ground without a fight. Bill and Dave have dedicated their lives to teaching so our students can realize and take action when others try to use them to do things they would never do otherwise. History is replete with people who exemplify the willingness to do anything through others yet are so cowardly they do not do anything themselves. We think of the professional wrestler bad guys who will beg for mercy and then blindside the good guy with a chair. We know this is make-believe, but it's simply amazing how many leaders exhibit this trait in just as ridiculous a manner when they are faced with the slightest provocation.

The third nurtured bad trait is **greed**. Greed coupled with deceitfulness is an awful trait for a leader, yet we see it so often. Servant leadership is behaving in a way that develops followers at the expense of the leader. Greed is the opposite: it's the leader behaving in a way that profits the leader at the expense of the follower. There are multiple examples in the media every day, from religious leaders to media types, to business leaders. If you've heard the adage, "When you point one finger at someone else, there are four pointing back at you," then you'll know where we're going next with this greed idea. Many of us more common people suffer from greed just as badly as the big names do. The only difference is that our performance is not held up by the media for public scrutiny.

We cannot understand the example of Michael Milken, who could have legitimately earned millions, yet cheated investors so he could make even more. He is so smart; yet it seems $200+ million legally was not enough, so his greed pushed him to want to make over $500 million (and those are essentially individual yearly earnings figures).

The final behavioral trait is one that it seems many of us work to develop and then exhibit at the worst of times: that is **crudeness**. Mike Price was the short-term head coach of the University of Alabama's lauded football program. His public behavior indicates he could teach a class on crudeness. The "Dean of the College of Crudeness" would have to be radio shock jock Howard Stern.

It seems at times that Americans want their heroes to go to the limit, yet we punish those who go a bit too far. Janet Jackson's Super Bowl halftime act of crudeness provides an example for leaders *not* to follow. We feel that each of us is partly responsible for this over-the-top behavior. We allow it to creep into society, then act surprised when it reaches the forbidden level. We continue to watch movies and professional sports even as they spiral to the nadir of societal performance. Michael is an undergraduate student who recently wrote a paper in which he admonished the professional baseball owners who allow players to enhance themselves through extensive drug use yet will not allow metal bats or corked bats or doctored balls when the effect would be the same. What kind of example are they setting when they spend their Behavioral Quotient energies on protecting equipment instead of humans? Michael calculated the dollar value professional baseball owners receive through allowing drug usage via increased home run production. He concluded it's all about greed.

Early in his business career, Dave was riding in one of those large old Checker Cabs across the Triborough Bridge from Manhattan on the way to LaGuardia airport in New York City. Suddenly a gust of wind blew the hood open. Dave expected the cabbie to stop, but the cabbie did the opposite. He sped up! After about ten seconds of blind driving, the hood broke from its hinges and went flying over the cab, landing in the roadway behind, where other vehicles had to swerve around it. The cabbie laughed like it was an everyday occurrence, and kept driving to the airport. Sadly, some leaders are like that cabbie, leaving trash for followers to swerve around or clean up. Trash can take the form of incomplete projects, delayed goal completion, emotionally injured employees, bankrupt suppliers, and all forms of ethical violations and legal litigation. That's indicative of a very low Behavior Quotient.

Using the BQ Matrix

> *Most people claim they intend a certain thing, they have a vision, a mission, or at least a purpose, but we ask, "Can you determine that purpose by the way they act?" If not, is their stated purpose real? Even if it is real, who knows it is real? A superior being knows, and the one behaving knows, that her actions are not indicative of who she really is. To others, we are the person our behavior indicates we are.*

Again, the key is to first understand clearly each of the traits and then honestly evaluate yourself and the perception others have of you related to the concepts represented in each of the four quadrants. Use some additional help in this section because behavior as others perceive it is what we are talking about here, not behavior as you expect or want others to perceive it. Seek real feedback by pushing for honest answers and not being defensive when you get them. Then use the principles noted in this section and you'll improve the BQ component of your *LQ*©.

As you have done with the previous quotients, evaluate yourself. Behavioral traits are best if they are as others have identified them, not as you have identified them.

Figure 8.3: YOUR BQ MEASUREMENT AND IMPROVEMENT MATRICES

Evaluate yourself against the reported traits in this Matrix.

	NATURE (uncontrollable-born)	**NURTURE** (controllable-made)
STRENGTHS (enablers—advantages)	**Q1** ___ authentic-inspiring-moral ___ courageous and brave ___ grace ___ personable _____ (self-IDed trait)	**Q2** ___ influential ___ trustworthiness ___ savvy-flexibility ___ respect _____ (self-IDed trait)
WEAKNESSES (derailers—disadvantages)	**Q3** ___ lack of credibility ___ deceitful-cheater ___ selfish-cowardly ___ disrespectful or self-centered _____ (self-IDed trait)	**Q4** ___ pretentiousness ___ temper + cowardice ___ greed ___ crudeness _____ (self-IDed trait)

Tailor the Matrix below for yourself!

	NATURE (uncontrollable-born)	**NURTURE** (controllable-made)
STRENGTHS (enablers—advantages)	**Q1** *(Quadrant 1)* Maximize	**Q2** *(Quadrant 2)* Hone
WEAKNESSES (derailers—disadvantages)	**Q3** *(Quadrant 3)* Make irrelevant or deflect	**Q4** *(Quadrant 4)* Minimize or change

Evaluating Your BQ Personal Profile: Strengths and Weaknesses Doing Something About Your BQ!

As We Said in the Introduction: "It's Time to Get Started; if not Now, When?"

Put your BQ values in Figure 8.4 and see if your BQ is enough of a foundation to help you proceed to the next level of improving your overall *LQ*©.

Figure 8.4: YOUR LEADERSHIP LEVERAGE TRIANGLE

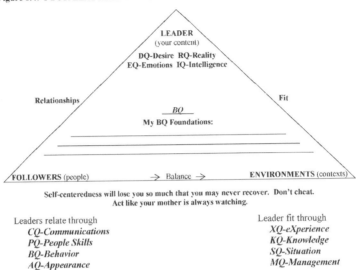

LEADER
(your content)
DQ-Desire RQ-Reality
EQ-Emotions IQ-Intelligence

Relationships   Fit

_BQ_
My BQ Foundations:

FOLLOWERS (people)   → Balance →   ENVIRONMENTS (contexts)

Self-centeredness will lose you so much that you may never recover. Don't cheat.
Act like your mother is always watching.

Leaders relate through
CQ-Communications
PQ-People Skills
BQ-Behavior
AQ-Appearance

Leader fit through
XQ-eXperience
KQ-Knowledge
SQ-Situation
MQ-Management

BQ Conclusions

Do not spend a lot of the time determining what *you* think are important Behavioral Quotients. To paraphrase a well-known colloquialism, "It truly is about *them*, stupid." We will all have lapses in our BQ, but hopefully they will be small enough for us to recover from. Most lapses of behavior have been minor for Dave and Bill to this point, though only time will truly tell! We must all realize that it is more important to manage our *Behavioral Quotient* than it is to manage our *subordinates,* because in no small part, they are the same thing. When a NASCAR competitor gets bumped from behind and his car spins out of control, the announcer will often say, "He just changed from a driver to a passenger." We must move from being BQ passengers to BQ drivers; responsibility is your toughest taskmaster. All things are difficult before they are easy, and the will to improve your BQ is more important than the will to succeed.

A quick reminder may be in order here. During the growth of the dot-com bubble, many experts thought the Internet would change the fundamentals of doing business. To some extent they were right; to some extent they were wrong. Online economic exchanges (often called EDIs—Electronic Data Interchanges—among other tags) are a fact. But they have not dominated the economy; most economic exchanges still occur the old-fashioned, face-to-face way (Pandya, et al., 2003). Of importance is the understanding that EDIs are relationships, even though they are electronic, and we cannot forget that our electronic behavior in this wired world makes up a great part of our BQ.

A lot of information and research about motivation and coaching is directed toward modifying behavior and coaching for leadership effectiveness. These topics will be covered in the MQ chapter and are not included in this chapter. That's because we are coaching you in hopes of improving your BQ. MQ is another matter about management, and of course this entire book is about developing your Leadership Quotient.

We loved what a couple of students wrote on their self-evaluations related to completing their own *LQ*© experience. "While I do lack a great deal of business experience, I feel my greatest deficiency is the lack of attention to what I have learned in the experiences I have had" (Lauren, one of Bill's undergraduates in 2003). "One of my weaknesses is a desire to talk about my strengths rather than my weaknesses" (David, another of Bill's undergraduates in 2005).

In the next chapter, we will look at the final follower quotient, the Appearance Quotient (AQ). There are indeed many examples that we are being slapped in the face with. Many others remind us daily of the need to appear as if our mothers were always watching—for we are to others as we appear! Few things related to people are purely logical. Most require a leap of faith to understand their meaning. So is the case with appearance.

9

AQ, The Appearance Quotient

Both Dave and Bill are tall, dark, and handsome, or so our wives and mothers have told us. We know mothers never lie, or so they told us! Talking about appearance and how it affects our chances of success is difficult if we are not young, tall, and slender, for even small children will quickly say that good-looking people are smart and nice and that the more appearance-challenged among us (ugly, some would say) are both dumb and mean. How did that get started? How did men ever convince women that we age better than they do? Look around and you'll see these stereotypes debunked but very much in use when we make decisions about hiring, marriage, friends, and leadership. What to do about appearance and its relationship to leadership is the very essence of AQ.

In some ways, this is a chapter we have dreaded. It seems that too much has been written about appearance, how you impress others, and appearing to be a leader. From popular media to politics to business, we are inundated with messages about the external. We wish the internal made a greater impact, but we must submit to society's demands and write a chapter about appearance. We're frankly concerned that not much can be added to the existing literature about appearance. However, it's important to analyze the Appearance Quotient and make any changes that will enable you to fit better with your followers in your current environment. Too much has been made of this issue, and we know we will write a lot that has been said a hundred times before, but we also know we have some good points that will contribute to improving your Appearance Quotient.

Something called the ego maintenance mechanism tries to tell us that we're right and others are wrong. When extended to the Appearance Quotient, we tend to think that the way *we* look is right and that *others* look wrong to us. Dave is a former member of Tall Texans, a social club for tall people. Men must be at least 6' 2" to join, and women must be at least 5' 10". Dave learned a lot about the comforts of this minor form of discrimination. "Gosh, it's nice to stand up straight and look people in the eye when you have a conversation," Dave observed. But there is great danger in discriminating against people because of their natural traits. While the discrimination practiced by the Tall Texans is not mean-spirited, it provides a great example of how we like people who are like us and tend to avoid those who are different.

Perhaps the value of looks started with the Christian reformation movements where the worth of individuals started to increase because of the freedom from patriarchal church control. Freed to determine largely on their own what is right, people started determining values and ethics for themselves; thus, their perceived individual value increased. Martin Luther is considered the father of the Reformation. Without him, much of the civilized world would still be under the control of a hierarchical church-state.

Next, official research seemed to begin with the classics and social research of people like Binet, Taylor, E. L. Thorndike, even Fayol and Max Weber with their thinking beyond the church and military models. We next saw a move to more normative views with Follett and Freud's psychotherapy and eventually data collection, training, and sensitivity T-groups with Bennis and Wechsler among many others. Then came Maslow and Skinner and retraining and behavioral groups, and industrial sociology with E. Mayo and R. Likert and D. McGregor trying to make more sense of organizational functioning.

This led to contingency models of leadership, which form the basis for the Leadership Quotient triangle of leader, followers, and environments. These models were forwarded by Vroom, House, and Fielder. This has led us to the use of political institutions and nonviolence in previously confrontational areas where influence through power developed.

This is where we are today in organizations, and we're sorry to report that many times the power of image rules over substance. We think that we are currently at the point where influence is through leaders who can share power, empower others, and even be nearly servant leaders, as their normal operating procedure. This is where appearance becomes an important issue in a different way than it was with the old survival-of-the-fittest charisma model. Today, appearance has become so important that leaders are attempting to be perceived as being something they're really not, through appearance. These scripted actions are aimed at making us believe people are the models we desire to follow.

Ask yourself, "**What would I change about my appearance**, if I could?" Bill says he would be a full 6' 2" instead of 6' 1.625", but who's measuring? Dave says he would be 6' 4" instead of 6' 5" so he could fit into airplane seats more comfortably. Both are generally satisfied otherwise. Pretty particular, aren't we? We will not bore you with the many equally shallow comments we received from our group of *LQ*© beta testers.

Our body-mass index is something we can change to a large extent. Our physical conditioning is almost totally within our control. For our general looks to fit within the range of normal for a leader in America is easy, because the range is very broad and mostly under our control. Most of us would be advised to forget about those little problems and work on our health or happiness and forget about minor details like feeling too tall or too short.

We see in so many areas three types of people: 1) those who wonder what happened to them, 2) those who watch what happens to them, and 3) those who make things happen for them. We want you to join the ranks of the third group and make the appearance thing happen for you to the best of your ability. Go ahead and get some books on etiquette, protocol, and civility so you'll know what is expected of you as a leader. Then you will at least know when you're breaking a rule, which you might do often to emphatically make a leadership point clear to your followers.

The images we see on TV and the movies are not reality. Look at movies and TV shows and ask yourself, "How many times have *I* met a doctor, lawyer, or cable repairperson who looks that good?" Not often, we'd bet. We were amazed that with the large number of ugly people in Hollywood, they cast a beautiful woman, Charlize Theron, to play the part of an ugly hag in the movie, *Monster.* In a recent *People* magazine interview, Drew Barrymore said, "If I'm lucky and good to myself, I can feel beautiful on the inside—and I can tell that shows on the outside" (Keeps and Sheff-Cahan, 2004). Yes, how we feel is almost as important as how we actually look.

Appearance can greatly be enhanced just by following these common sense guidelines:

- Hold yourself erect and use good posture.

- Maintain eye contact.

- Dress appropriately.

- Enter into discussions with poise and confidence.

- Have a pleasant voice.

- Understand what *good* small talk is.

- Focus on others.

- Avoid meaningless small talk.

Bill forgets the last one often. He tells bad jokes or makes down-to-earth comments in an attempt to belie the Ph.D. and come down to a more common level. Unfortunately, he often makes an impact, but not the one he intended.

Have you responded to the opportunities that your looks have given you? If indeed you have received the scum of the gene pool in this matter, don't despair. Everyone has weaknesses they will try to neutralize and strengths they will polish. Stay tuned: The Appearance Quotient Recognition and Measurement Matrices are coming in a few pages.

Recall all of the less-than-attractive people who have become great leaders, and improve in some other areas to offset this deterrent. We think education is a great way to offset deficiencies in looks.

Think about the professors you had in college. We're guessing few of them were "easy on the eyes." Maybe they sought a profession where looks were not important. Few care what a professor, doctor, or computer or research scientist looks like. So if you happen to be tough to look at, consider your options. Bill and his wife, Jan, recall one relatively plain-looking girl whom they both interviewed early in their careers. They both were talking about how striking she was, yet how plain she was underneath the makeup, glitzy clothing, and adept mannerisms. She was a good project manager because or in spite of looks (we're not sure which).

Start Thinking Differently About Appearance

This section is for the appearance-challenged among us. Unfortunately, some of us are truly not up to par when it comes to looks. Statistically, there has to be a certain number of the better-looking and the not-so-hot-looking. If perchance you are one of the unfortunate, we'd suggest a simple switch in thinking. Instead of thinking about appearance traits, start thinking about appearance skills and behaviors. Skills are generally classified into technical, interpersonal, and conceptual categories, and all of these can apply to appearance. Understand the technicalities of standing erect, posture, etiquette, and decorum, and mix these with the interpersonal skills necessary to show people you care about them enough to adjust behavior. When you do, you will find that others begin to perceive you as "better-looking."

Dave has had only one mentor in his professional life. He was hired right out of college to work for the Association of Tennis Professionals by then-executive director Bob Briner. By his own admission, Bob was not great to look at. He was overweight his entire adult life. But he was attractive. He had such a quick wit and great insight into human behavior that people were attracted to him. You can have a bad appearance and still be attractive. That's what the Appearance Quotient is all about.

"The issue of self-awareness, through various means, is becoming key in many organizations....The first step to leadership effectiveness is being aware of one's strengths, weaknesses, and personality characteristics" (Nahavandi, 2003, p. 80). In this area Richard Bolles' book, *What Color is Your Parachute?*, makes a contribution to your explanation. In the annual editions of this book, Bolles gives great guidelines to understanding yourself, the world, your mission, and how you might fit in and begin to stand out as a success in the world of organizations. Hints about appearance and behavior abound in these classic works of practical direction.

Acceptance of a Subscription to Life, which is to be Present in All of Life: Confront Versus Face

A few startling figures are important here. We make up our minds about another person in about five seconds. It takes five seconds to initiate a process, 21 days to start a pattern, and 100 days to start a habit. Eye contact is most effective when made during 60% of the time people spend together. Handshakes are best when they are two medium pumps with a fairly firm grip and a dry hand. The ways you enter a room and a conversation are more important than what you really say. Success in most leadership roles is 15% technical skills and 85% people skills.

Author Kurt Vonnegut gives very few public speeches. It was while sitting onstage ready to deliver one of those speeches that he learned a great lesson about public speaking. He was speaking at a college graduation. While the preliminaries were going on, the vice president of the university leaned over to Vonnegut and said, "I read your speech." "Oh," replied Vonnegut. "Did you like it?" "No," responded the vice president. "But go ahead and deliver it anyway. No one will remember what you say. They will only remember if you dressed appropriately and if they liked you." Appearance matters.

An ounce of image is indeed worth a pound of performance. Civility is not noticeable but being uncivil is! We do notice persons nonverbally before we notice them verbally. We like people who talk about us better than we like people who talk about themselves. Dave wrote 22 pieces of advice to his son, Lance, as a high school graduation gift. One of them reads, "The more you let people talk about themselves, the more interesting *you* will become."

We admire people because of how they dress. We admire them when they stay in good physical shape. Dave's wife, Cynde, delivers to him about twice a week weary complaints about a woman who shuffles and walks like it's her last step. This week, Cynde was asked by a person who had just met the shuffler if she indeed had mental problems. She doesn't. She just has a very low Appearance Quotient.

We often don't see what people look like because of how they sound. We prefer our news to be read by a good-looking person. You might recall a landmark legal case in Kansas City, where a female news anchor claimed she was fired because she was not good-looking enough. We value looks over intellect or sincerity. We prefer people to *look* nice over actually *being* nice. Obese, white-collar women are paid 30% less than slimmer colleagues are, yet men pay little penalty for being overweight" ("Obese," 2004, p. A1). Often we can overdo our daily acting, for as the famous actor Spencer Tracy said, "With acting, more is less" (per Bert Reynolds on a Biography Channel special, March 7, 2004).

Dave was leading a series of seminars for a federal government agency when he got into a very interesting discussion with one of the most insightful, intelligent people he had ever met. The woman was generally good-looking but was about 50 pounds overweight. "Oh, it's quite clear by casual observation," she said. "I've worked in government service for over 30 years, and people who work in the private sector, where there is competition, are much better-looking than government employees." Her point was that competitive, for-profit companies prefer better-looking people. Government, where there is no competition for the services they provide, can settle for the also-rans who don't have the looks to make it in the competitive environment.

Why not replace these superficialities with a couple of thoughts? First, try to encourage everyone with a smile and simply let them know they matter. Second, remember that we really don't get anything big until some time has passed. Divorces, deaths, illnesses, moves, losing a job, and many less impactful things may affect us personally more than we could ever think. Being pretentious, standoffish, or trying one-upsmanship is a ticket for disaster related to Appearance Quotient.

Honesty Facing Others

One of the hardest things to do is to tell someone about their appearance. Maybe we should not do it unless it is something they can do something about. Even when it is, your comments won't have any benefit unless they've asked for them. Bill has a student named Adrian who wants to start and establish his own company. Bill thought Adrian's dreadlocks, earring, and tattoo wouldn't help—but should Bill tell him? He didn't, but Adrian was smart enough to figure it out himself. When he arrived for the next class, Adrian had cut his hair, removed the earring, and covered the tattoo. His chances of succeeding just increased.

Dr. Phil McGraw (who is not that good-looking) recently said, "If you want better, give better....Everyone loves to be admired and respected (p. 181)....I strongly believe that the difference between winners and losers is that winners do things losers don't want to do....I've never yet seen a real, big-time successful person who was a lone wolf" (Bosch, 2004, p. 182). These principles certainly apply to appearance. Give more, respect others, work at difficult things, involve yourself with others, and you will improve your appearance. Can you understand why? Think about how often people get better-looking as you begin to know and love them for who they are. Why do we need heroes? Why do we need movie stars? Why do we need slogans and especially bumper stickers?

Leaders are figureheads who have to look the part or people will not take them seriously. But can't almost anyone *look* like a leader? If you will determine what it will take for you to look like a leader using what you have, your Appearance Quotient will shoot through the roof!

Here are a few words our Leadership Quotient beta testers used to describe the Appearance Quotient:

- Humility
- Enthusiasm
- Self-confidence
- Warmth
- Sense of humor
- Extroversion
- Stability

- Honesty

- Tenacity

- Work ethic

These actions make everyone's Appearance Quotient increase, and they have little to do with beauty.

Don't Fear Losing Because of Looks; Don't Run Away from Success

When you finally get a chance to succeed, don't run away from it, but approach it with confidence, worrying little about your God-given appearance. Dave worked for the Penn Tennis Company for a few years. The president, Dave Grant, was not that good-looking, but he was really smart and exuded such great energy that he had a very high Appearance Quotient. He was a great leader and was very highly respected in the tennis industry and in the broader sporting-goods business.

Life is not a Donald Trump *Apprentice* episode. Even "The Donald" is not as he appears in his show. Trump recently said, "This is the high point of my career. But I never viewed myself as having much of a low point" (Naughton and Peyser, 2004, p. 49). This comes from a man who, in the past, had a net worth of hundreds of millions of dollars—*negative* hundreds of millions of dollars! Talk about esteem and not fearing failure! Realize that even Christy Brinkley has had to have an airbrush for her looks. In reality, our appearance is as much about what we think we look like as what we actually look like. Bill and Dave jokingly disagree on a philosophical issue. Bill always suggests facing reality. Dave likes to deny it. He has never missed a day of work for sickness. Oh, he's been sick, but he denies it. "What's so great about reality?" Dave asks. Reality is divorce and bankruptcy and poor health. A little dose of reality-denying is good for you. If you think you don't look great, deny it! Being fearful about your appearance makes it a negative.

Numb to the Reality of the World—News has Become Entertainment

We are sure that the world has been "media-ated" into believing people are all nice-looking, yet these looks exist only in our imaginations. Human appearance is never as it seems. Recall Dave's discussion with seminar participants about the perfectionist leadership of Andy Griffith's TV character. There's a script; it's not real. The character's looks aren't real either; there's makeup.

We are directed to believe that people generally look different than they really do, causing many psychological problems when we try to look perfect as perfect is depicted on TV. Pay attention when the up lights are away from Barbara Walters, Carol Simpson, or almost any other TV personality. It seems there is no one on TV or in the movies who has not had some form of corrective surgery to make them look better—with the possible exception of Andy Rooney. In fact, Rooney said not too long ago that he was going to sue over his looks. He showed a picture of how he looked when he started doing TV and one of how he looks now, and we'd have to agree that TV (or something…maybe age) has made him look older. Perhaps he should sue CBS. In addition, we assume that many people have dyed hair, wigs, or some other form of help to look better. That's OK, but it's not reality. The world of reality is that most people don't look like those examples we see on TV and in the movies. Have you ever seen a real prostitute on the news? Did they look anything like Julia Roberts? No, they look like the *Monster* prostitute. Our newspersons and especially movie actors and actresses have numbed us to what the normal person actually looks and sounds like.

Even in drawings, women models are drawn out of proportion. Women are "six heads high." That means the body is six times the height of the head. In drawings, they want the model to look like she has longer legs, so they often draw her seven heads high. The normal female is not 5' 10" tall weighing 110 pounds. The normal male is not an Arnold; and even Arnold is not as he appears in the movies—ever seen a candid shot of him or Madonna? Dave was boarding a plane in San Diego recently. He had to look close to be sure the woman he saw in the airport was not Julia Roberts, because she looked a lot like Julia Roberts might look without makeup. We hope you get the point. Dave wasn't even sure what Julia Roberts would look like without makeup! It wasn't her. So readjust your form of what you should look like and don't let normal looks be considered anything bad as they are in so many forms of media.

Don't be Afraid of Someone Else's Fears—Life's not Always Easy, but It's Worth It if You Respond to the Opportunities You are Given

Most often, it is better to discuss a question without settling it than to settle it without discussing it. In addition, leaders are useless if their followers are incompetent or uninterested. Remember: In the end we never see things as they are truly are, but we see things as *we* are. You've probably heard the adage, "I'll believe it when I see it." Perhaps the converse is more true—"You'll see it when you believe it." We like to think of the song by the award-winning country group, Alabama:

> Give me one more shot,
> I'll give it all I got.
> Give me one day,
> Let me open my eyes to a new sunrise, I pray.
> Give me one more chance; I'll learn to dance the dance.

Take each new day and work on your appearance as much as you can, but realize you have 11 other quotients to work on also, so move on. Each of us has some unique appearance traits that will work for us. Our goal as leaders is to work to locate and use those potentialities. After doing this, we should help others do the same so we can be truly Leadership Quotient builders.

Now On to the AQ Traits that have been Reported to Us

"The lesson of disenchantment begins with the discovery that in order to change—really to change, and not just to switch positions—you must realize that some significant part of your old reality was in your head, not out there" (Bridges, 1980, p. 100).

Understanding what is reality about your appearance and its effect on your Leadership Quotient is difficult. But the most difficult part is changing what's in your head, not what's on your face. Not-so-great looks did not hurt the Leadership Quotients of Mahatma Gandhi, Eleanor Roosevelt, Winston Churchill, Adolf Hitler, or Mother Teresa.

Dr. Phil McGraw has many popular self-help books that are intended to help people change their lives. His book (1999) and workbook on life strategies (2000) are exemplars on how to address what you want to change, as is his recent book on weight loss. His most telling statement is on the first page of *The Life Strategies Workbook:* "Books don't change people. People change people" (2000, p. xi). He goes on to say, "Take a good long look at yourself. What do you see in the choices and outcomes...that you value or treasure about yourself?" (p. 21). He tells his readers to begin with their personal lives and to define what they want to do on autopilot and establish that as a habit.

Dr. Phil further reminds us that there is no reality, but only perceptions. It is all about you and your desire to change. He encourages the reader to stop blaming others for diet, exercise, or smoking problems. Bill recalls how his sister-in-law tried to blame her failure to quit smoking on the fact that everyone harped at her about smoking. What's worse is that Nancy was a psychologist who helped kids with behavioral problems. Wow—what did she think about the blame game? For you own good, realistically define your actual self and ideal self and make strategies to get the two more closely aligned (McGraw, 1999 and 2000).

Dave's award-winning book, *Corporate Cults* (2000), does an excellent job of showing how some corporate cultures are so strong that they even dictate appearance to lure individuals into an all-consuming path toward corporatism, taking away a lot of an individual's identity. Many people seem to want a pattern for their lives, including how they dress and appear.

A final note is called for before we begin the descriptions of the appearance traits. We are going to exclude those extremes such as disabilities and super-abilities, i.e., those of Michael Jordan, Miss Universe, et al., because most of us don't fit into those categories. For the disabled or disadvantaged in the appearance area, the only advice we offer is to think of your abilities, not disabilities. We have heard that advice and have seen it work with many people in the past.

Normal Natural AQ Strengths—Quadrant 1 of the AQ 2X2 Matrix

The first natural trait we found is being **attractive**. Being good-looking is a natural characteristic that really helps a leader. Some leaders emerge in organizations largely because of how they look. How you look in person is, in some cases, becoming less important than how you look on TV. Upper-level executives are increasingly exposed to the camera, and they must look good on the box. Donald Trump, JFK, and Bill Clinton are among the leaders who succeeded in part because of their medi-agenic looks. In JFK's case, it was because of the difficulties of the comparison other and how he appeared on TV. Nixon's sweating on the upper lip was famous. The experts define good looks in the form of symmetry, smoothness, and no overly unruly features. Some people are given the gift of beauty at birth and others have used plastic surgery and many other techniques to improve their attractiveness.

One of our beta group said, "I'm not especially tall," as he described his natural Appearance Quotient. Yes, a **good height-to-weight ratio** makes a large contribution to the Appearance Quotient. Anyone who is striking because of their physique is at a decided advantage. People notice them and want them to be the out-front person for their organization. One of our more attractive students, Julie, said her dad put her out front at the desk for their business with the instructions, "Just sit there and look good." As Julie recalled the story, she did what her dad said and it worked.

As we have said, overweight women are at the biggest disadvantage. They really have to have other Leadership Quotients to accommodate for this. A huge IQ and desire can overcome some of this, but it is not easy for a woman. Unfairly, men do not suffer as much for being overweight. But they do suffer from being under-tall. Men over six feet tall do better than those under six feet. Maybe it all starts early in life when youngsters look for the big guy to lead or when the slender woman is more acceptable. These characteristics have been "selected in" during the long-term evolution of the human race, and it seems that being selected out for special treatment makes us feel better and we do indeed become better.

The next trait is hard to explain, but you know it when you see it. We all know people who look **nice**. Looking nice is a decided advantage in America today for anyone aspiring to become a leader. Eventually looks and actions have to match, but often you can get away for a long time by just looking nice. We think here about the difference between the nice looks of Laura Bush and the not-so-nice looks of Dennis Rodman. Dave still lives in Texas, so he likes to use the example of country music legend Willie Nelson. Nelson's bad looks—torn jeans, scruffy beard, and extra-long hair—are part of his trademark as a kinky, off-center entertainer. If you want to be an entertainer, you should emulate Willie Nelson. If you want to be a leader, don't.

The final trait that many report as natural related to AQ is **confidence in appearance**. Our work in describing this trait was done for us by a Viagra TV ad that featured a good-looking, confident man who was asked by people all day, "What's changed about you?" "Did you get a haircut?" one asked. "Shave your beard?" another queried. "Lost weight?" guessed another. The advertisement ends with the confident man laughing into his cell phone in the parking lot as he leaves after receiving questions all day. The assumption is clear: Viagra improved his sex life, which improved his confidence, which improved his Appearance Quotient.

We have all known people who look "not that great," but their confidence increases their Appearance Quotient, so they win the prize. The prize may be the best-looking or most popular guy or girl, or a key leadership role. Look through your old high-school yearbooks where they selected the most handsome and the most beautiful and you'll see that there must have been something beyond looks in the selections. In Bill's yearbook, they should have said the guy with the best-looking car!! Confidence about appearance is gained at birth, or certainly early in life, and seldom changes throughout life.

Normal Natural AQ Weaknesses—Quadrant 3 of the AQ 2X2 Matrix

The first natural weakness we see reported is **unattractive**, often reported as **ugly**. I know we're continually calling on this excuse, but here it is again: "We don't write 'em; we just read 'em." Good, bad, and now ugly—our purpose is to help you improve your Leadership Quotient, and we're not going to let a few tough or embarrassing topics get in our way.

There is little we can say about this. We have heard anecdotal evidence that ugly people are nicer than attractive people. Logic tells us there may be something to that. After all, the forces of evolution dictate that elements of a species will defer away from its weaknesses and to its strengths for survival. It is probably very tough for people to realize this and understand how to deal with it.

We don't have much to say here except, "We're sorry!" This entire section of natural weaknesses is going to be short, because there is very little advice to give.

A **bad height-to-weight ratio** that is bad enough to report as a natural weakness is also quite often something a person can't control. For some people, doing the best with what they have is not enough. We have a young college student, Jon Michael, who is 42" tall and weighs about 70 pounds. He is so talented as a musician and his family is so loving that he is simply an "awesome person" according to his 6' 2" studly brother, Jason. Jon Michael is our hero as well. His size could be a disadvantage for him, but we will guarantee you it won't hurt him. If you feel disadvantaged in this area, try to be a Jon Michael and you'll be fine.

When someone has a **mean** trait, their Leadership Quotient is in real trouble. Some people do seem to have this from early life and there is not much hope for these types. Fortunately, many of them end up in jail and not reading a leadership book trying to improve themselves. If you feel you were born with a mean spirit, get professional help.

Some people don't really look that bad but they are **unconfident with their appearance**. This can be in part natural, but it also might be the way the person was treated early in life. In either case, professional help is probably the only answer. Mannerisms, grooming, poise, and alertness can help in this area, but if it is truly a natural trait, it is very tough to cure. Admitting a problem and working to overcome it are difficult when it is appearance-related and is formed early in life from a long-standing lack of confidence.

Normal Nurtured AQ Strengths—Quadrant 2 of the AQ 2X2 Matrix

One of the simplest ways to improve your appearance is to improve your **posture**. This goes beyond walking tall and straight, to include a natural easiness that says, "I belong and I'm fine." We all know there are certain sets of clothes that make us feel this way. Everyone can improve in this area by dressing and presenting themselves in a way that allows them to walk, sit, and act tall.

Bill recalls a poor, stray dog that ran around his neighborhood in Lancaster, Texas, that held her head down and kept her tail between her legs and looked un-proud because of posture. We already had three dogs we had adopted so we could not handle another one. After adoption by a neighbor, the dog's entire posture changed. She held her head and tail erect when walking as if to say, "Look at me. I'm special. Look who loves me now!" Parents and leaders of other areas of life, is there a lesson here?

A second nurtured trait often reported is called **decorum**, which we interpret as indicative of literary and dramatic propriety through good taste in appearance-related items and issues. People who use the right words and actions are way ahead in the leadership race. Understand proper decorum and develop it, for it is one trait that is easy to develop and use.

Recently, Bill stopped his car to let a lawn maintenance worker cross the street at his university. Bill noted how quickly and confidently the young Mexican man strode across the street. He commented to a fellow professor about how often he saw this young man and how quickly he worked and how confidently he held himself. We'd bet this young man will be running a crew soon, and we'd not be surprised if he ran his own company very soon. You can just tell when someone has the decorum of a leader about them.

Dave's brother, Gail, was doing behavioral research at Randolph Air Force Base in San Antonio. Gail and a couple of friends got the idea that they should be able to devise a test that would predict success and failure in flight school. If they could, the air force would save an incredible amount of resources by reducing the "wash-out" rate among pilots. The individual pilots who would eventually fail would be saved a lot of lost career time and the embarrassment of failure at flight school. The greatest predictor of failure seemed to be an inability to operate the flight stick that directs the plane. It takes a lot of hand-eye coordination and some people just don't have it, nor will they ever get it.

Gail has since retired as a full colonel after 30 years in the air force, but at the time, he was a commissioned officer. Gail really had the stereotypical air force Appearance Quotient: thin, good posture, athletic, brisk and efficient in movement. He could have been the guy on the air force recruiting poster. His research buddy was the opposite: a civilian who smoked a pipe, wore a scraggly beard, and favored an old sports coat with patches on the elbows. When Gail and his buddy went before the general to present the program that would save the air force millions of dollars each year, they were summarily dismissed. The researcher's Appearance Quotient did not fit the followers or the environment, so he couldn't lead.

But the data was there; it was still a very valid test. So Gail made two changes before presenting the idea again. One: he waited until the general was reassigned so he could present the idea to someone else. Two: he brought the researcher along, but made him the follower, not the leader in the presentation. The result: the general was astounded. "Why haven't we been using this screening mechanism in the past?" he demanded. Some 20 years later, they still use it.

The question is not, "Why haven't we been using the screening mechanism?" The question for *you* is, "Why haven't you adjusted your Appearance Quotient to more concisely fit the followers and the environment in which you lead?"

We are aware of a lady who is just a great person, and we really care about her. Unfortunately, her daddy left her a considerable amount of money, but he really should have sent her to charm school. The understanding of **appearance knowledge and skills** is invaluable for a leader. Here we are talking about knowing what it takes to have that put-together look that was carefully described in the 1980s book, *Dress for Success*. The book was about more than dressing; it had a lot of content about what we're calling the Appearance Quotient.

Confidence, understanding, empathy, loving, disapproving, and many other emotions can be communicated by the way you appear. It's beyond clothing, beyond etiquette, beyond posture, and includes all the appearance-related issues you can think of. If you can improve this AQ skill, it will pay tremendous benefits. A national organization of professionals teaches etiquette, dress, manners, and protocol that can help the more appearance-skills disadvantaged among us. We suggest you find and use them.

This last nurtured strength goes beyond the prior knowledge and skills and includes the ability to put those skills to work. Wisdom comes when one can use what one knows. It shows here with a heightened level of vitality, being distinguished, and having classical looks that result in dignity that is appropriate. It is a **polished appearance** that goes beyond just clean and neat and includes so much of the etiquette and manners we need to exemplify if we want to become top executives or leaders.

Dallas Baptist University, where Dave teaches, was one of the last holdouts that finally abandoned formal dress and allowed professors to teach in casual clothes. Dave is a pretty informal kind of guy but he didn't really mind wearing a tie, because that indicated a polished appearance. Now, the university matches its policies to its environment by having a dress code that changes depending on what stakeholder group is on campus. Formal Dress Days are indicated in the calendar for Board of Trustee meetings, graduation, and special symposia.

Normal Nurtured AQ Weaknesses—Quadrant 4 of the AQ 2X2 Matrix

The first nurtured weakness we see many people reporting for their own $LQ^{©}$ assessment is that of **poor posture**. It seems there is so much of this today, and frankly we don't understand why. More people than ever have good diets and can eat at a level that will allow good health and physical development. Many people are now working out, and it would seem that most would have good posture simply because they can.

So many people exhibit **poor decorum** that it makes us wonder, "What were they thinking!" The simple answer is, "Most often they weren't thinking, and it showed." It seems that for every person we know with appropriate decorum, we know ten with none or with extremely poor judgment about how to appear to others. Never forget: You are to others as you appear to them, not as you really are.

Thomas, an exceptional undergraduate, was addressing a young lady who said she did not want to appear more somber for a job interview than she really was. Thomas told her that she should consider changing the *range* of her behavior, not her total behavior. He said that she was exhibiting a very narrow range of behavior that would limit the range of opportunities she would be afforded. If she would open her behavior a little wider, Thomas said, she would be considered for more jobs and each of those additional opportunities might be the best prospect she could ever expect to get.

It is probably one thing to look bad and know it, and another to not know it! Often our off-color jokes or fun clothing are inappropriate, but to have **poor appearance knowledge and skills** is either stupidity or laziness. Both of them will significantly lower your Appearance Quotient. There is no good excuse for this type of failure. There are just too many options for learning how to dress for leadership success. Act as you want to be and you will become as you desire; act otherwise and you'll become that as well.

The final nurtured negative trait we see in the AQ is an **unpolished appearance**. We see that often and know it when we see it. Just a few examples are: dirty fingernails, women with worn shoe heels, men with crummy belts or watches, a frumpy dress or pants, granny shoes, hip shoes on a 58-year-old professor, a half-shaven look, tattoos, and dreadlocks. An unpolished appearance will give you an unpolished position.

Using the AQ Matrix

The first step to improvement is to understand clearly each of the traits and then honestly evaluate yourself using the concepts in each of the four quadrants. Use some additional help in this section, because appearance is about what others see of you. It is hard to really look at our own appearance without bias. Seek honest feedback, pushing for real answers and not being defensive when you actually get it. Then use the principles noted in this section and you'll improve your AQ component of your $LQ^{©}$.

As you have been doing in previous matrices, evaluate yourself, but don't trust yourself or your significant other here!

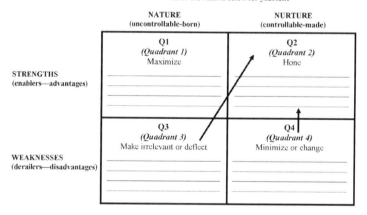

Figure 9.1: YOUR AQ MEASUREMENT AND IMPROVEMENT MATRICES

Evaluate yourself against the reported traits in this Matrix.

	NATURE (uncontrollable-born)	**NURTURE** (controllable-made)
STRENGTHS (enablers—advantages)	**Q1** ___ attractive ___ good height-to-weight ratio ___ nice appearance ___ confident about appearance ___ (self-IDed trait)	**Q2** ___ good posture ___ good decorum ___ good appearance knowledge ___ polished appearance ___ (self-IDed trait)
WEAKNESSES (derailers—disadvantages)	**Q3** ___ unattractive ___ bad height-to-weight ratio ___ mean appearance ___ unconfident about appearance ___ (self-IDed trait)	**Q4** ___ poor posture ___ poor decorum ___ poor appearance knowledge ___ unpolished appearance ___ (self-IDed trait)

Tailor the Matrix below for yourself!

	NATURE (uncontrollable-born)	**NURTURE** (controllable-made)
STRENGTHS (enablers—advantages)	**Q1** *(Quadrant 1)* Maximize	**Q2** *(Quadrant 2)* Hone
WEAKNESSES (derailers—disadvantages)	**Q3** *(Quadrant 3)* Make irrelevant or deflect	**Q4** *(Quadrant 4)* Minimize or change

Evaluating Your AQ Personal Profile: Strengths and Weaknesses

Doing Something About Your AQ! Get an Extreme Makeover?? Maybe Not!

Put your AQ values in Figure 9.2 and see if your AQ is enough of a foundation to help you proceed to the next level of improving your overall $LQ^{©}$.

Figure 9.2: YOUR LEADERSHIP LEVERAGE TRIANGLE

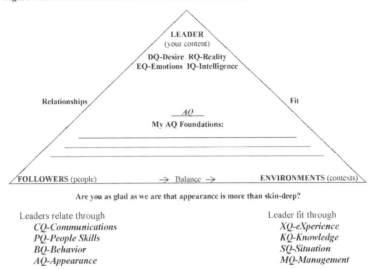

Leaders relate through
    CQ-Communications
    PQ-People Skills
    BQ-Behavior
    AQ-Appearance

Leader fit through
    XQ-eXperience
    KQ-Knowledge
    SQ-Situation
    MQ-Management

Closing AQ Comments

"**Make an Impressive Appearance.** By creating a polished appearance, a person can make slight gains in projecting a charismatic image.…In attempting to enhance your charisma through appearance, it is necessary to analyze your work environment to assess what type of appearance is impressive (Dubrin, 2004: p. 78).…Self-confidence is projected by such small items as the following:

- Neatly pressed and sparkling-clean clothing,

- Freshly polished shoes,

- Impeccable fingernails,

- Clean jewelry in mint condition,

- Well-maintained hair,

- Good-looking teeth with a white or antique-white color" (p. 374).

And we like to add that "more is less" when you talk about such things as jewelry, makeup, and all forms of accessories, for that matter. Never have over five things that distract from your message. The five include all accessories or personal enhancements such as wigs, flashy hairdos, nails, jewelry, big hair, makeup, unique ties or scarves, and so on, to include anything beyond the basics of clothing and self. Too much will take the attention away from you toward the accessories.

Appearances can always be deceiving. Bill recalls when he first met the 23 students he and his wife were going to live with for four months in the same relatively small six-floor house in London. Amanda seemed disinterested, Melissa seemed shy, Katherine seemed standoffish, and the three guys made almost no impression at all. Bill and Jan ended up being very wrong. It all started as they loaded the bus at London's Gatwick Airport. The three guys pitched right in to help load the luggage. At the other end of the bus ride, the guys ran the suitcases up the stairs with record speed. Even little Katherine's suitcase, which weighed 90 pounds (she only weighed 85), got up 99 steps in just minutes.

As the semester progressed, the group found that Thomas was a great piano player. Phil saw no wrong with anyone. Amanda—at 19 years of age—produced an 8-page typewritten itinerary and led 12 fellow students all over Europe, using her German and French as they went. The observations could go on and on. The 23 students had talents and traits that were not obvious by their Appearance Quotient. Julia was a natural beauty inside and out who could cook anything. Indeed, Bill learned another lesson about appearance at the age of 56: Expect the best and be disappointed occasionally; avoid being cynical 100% of the time to avoid the 2 or 3% who will let you down. Bill was never let down by any of his 23 students, though *he* let *them* down a couple of times early on.

With the next chapter, we launch into the final section of the book, **Part III**: **Environment Quotients**. Section III quotients have been grouped under "Environments" as a term used for situation, context, or even culture—organizational and otherwise. In this section we will explain XQ, the ***eXperience*** Quotient; KQ, the ***Knowledge*** Quotient; SQ, the ***Situation*** Quotient; and finally MQ, the ***Management*** Quotient. We group these quotients under "Environments" because they must first and foremost fit the environments within which leadership takes place.

In our next chapter, we look at the eXperience Quotient. Though we see that in general any experience is good, to be of the most use it needs to fit the environments: situations, contexts, cultures, etc. That is, it should be experience in a given industry or even sub-industry; or it needs to be in Japan not England, Alabama not New York, and so on. Of course there are commonalities, but there are also exceptions, as we shall note.

PART III
The Final Angle: The Environmental Quotients

"The past should be a springboard, not a hammock."—Ivern Ball
"Things ain't what they used to be; probably never was."—Will Rogers
(Reader's Digest, *"Quotable Quotes,"* 1997, p. 34.)

As we enter the final section of $LQ^©$, we want to remind you that it requires a lot of focus and courage to look at something you've seen multiple times and see it as if you've never seen it before. This is what you must do if you are to improve your experiences, knowledge, situations, and management quotients.

In the Leadership Quotient Triangle, the final angle depicts the environments or contexts where leadership takes place. This angle requires understanding about the situation and how to fit your leadership traits to the context in which you lead. The context of each new situation is unique, though many share a strong resemblance with situations you have seen in the past. The key is not to assume that new situations are exact matches of the past but to look anew, as we said in the introductory paragraph, and see the current situation for what it really has become. The better you become at identifying patterns from past experiences while understanding the nuances of new situations, the better your leadership will fit your environment. Using your experiences to improve your leadership is what this environmental section is all about.

In Chapter 10, the **XQ, eXperience Quotient**, is presented as the most critical of environmental quotients. XQ comes with time and different exposures, but only when the recipient of the exposure pays attention and focuses over time is the XQ developed in a way that helps the overall $LQ^{©}$ improve. The eXperience Quotient includes past accomplishments learned and earned, mistakes, seizing the moment, discernment, maturity, insights, generalizations, and shows how the leader can learn through reflection. A person with a high XQ can mobilize commitment, can foster consensus, has *good* hunches, can spread revitalization—institutionalize it, can monitor and adjust strategies and plans, and has assumptions that build mental models on how she views the world. XQ includes intuition, sound judgment, decisiveness, learning and showing by example, understandability, adaptability, and people and organizational savvy. With a solid XQ, the leader is better able to enact a situation to fit her own leadership strengths and better utilize the contributions of the followers at hand. "Find one or two people who have leadership styles you really admire. Follow them, observe them, listen to them and imitate the things that you like" (Motley, 1995, pages unnumbered).

Chapter 11, the **KQ, Knowledge Quotient**, is presented as the leader's ability to learn, pay attention, recognize, imagine, and keep up to date on workplace technologies. It also includes adaptability, innovativeness, and the ability to evolve. Knowledge—KQ—when combined with XQ goes beyond information to include the wisdom to apply what the leader knows to the correct situation at the right time. Indeed, it is possible to redefine or enact an environment that is more suitable for your success when you possess more knowledge than your competitors.

After clearly identifying an area of concern, acquiring useful knowledge is the next step to an answer that will solve a problem. This requires looking, listening, asking, and seeking as much as is practical given the time and money constraints as weighed against the payoff of the new knowledge. Once the information-building phase is completed, the leader has a solid foundation for developing useful knowledge.

Ignorance is no excuse. You simply have to do your homework in today's world where so much information of great value is available. The search for new knowledge must come to an end at some point and it must be applied. Our KQ chapter is about getting and molding the foundational knowledge necessary to proceed to wisdom and actual applied usage of the knowledge. Extending and extrapolating the available information or knowledge about your topic to your specific situation gets you closer to what you need for the most useful answer. Always ask yourself what assumptions you are using as you approach any new situation. The final step is to formulate knowledge and information acquired into workable solutions or concepts worthy of putting to use or testing to see if you have a practical solution.

Ask yourself, "Why can a rookie get new knowledge faster than an expert?" In today's over-wired world it's easy to get *too much* information yet not know how to interpret or extrapolate the information into application. Even a little wrong information can often be more dangerous than the assurance of knowing you don't know. After reviewing the KQ chapter, you'll know a little more of what you don't know.

In Chapter 12, the **SQ, Situational Quotient**, is the ability to interpret environmental cues. This quotient includes timing, instinct, political savvy, curiosity, flexibility, ability to simplify complexity, fitability, imagination, and circumstances. This includes a form of Strategic Intelligence that will be presented as a subset of the SQ. We also lean heavily on the Situational Leadership model developed by Hersey (1985) and Blanchard, which asserts that an effective manager varies structure and support based on follower needs and the situation at hand. SQ includes knowing when and where the time is to tell, sell, work for consensus, empower, or delegate.

Chapter 13, **MQ, Management Quotient**, is the final quotient chapter and includes a discussion of general administrative skills that could be categorized under systems and procedures, planning, organizing, controlling, and staffing. Other subcategories of the management quotient include teaming, process, ability to motivate, evaluating and managing personnel, information and knowledge management, quality, technological savvy, and strategic thinking. The chapter includes discussions on the effect of technical and functional expertise on the Leadership Quotient, as well as industry and organizational understanding. MQ is the knowledge of time-honored principles useful for getting groups to accomplish shared objectives in an efficient and effective manner. This chapter is similar to many overall management primers, but with a highly practical slant. Since this is a leadership book, we are purposely minimizing our coverage of management. The discipline of management has become a teachable and programmable skill that can be accomplished largely through standardized processes, information systems, and technology.

Don't trash the past, but don't assume your old ways will continue to help you fit the new world that is emerging. On to Chapter 10, where we will learn how to improve your XQ as it contributes to your overall Leadership Quotient.

10

XQ, The eXperience Quotient

Wouldn't you rather follow someone with experience? So far, we have found that having only one high quotient is not sufficient for leadership success. That changes with the XQ. The XQ stands out in its distinctiveness as the only quotient that can predict leadership success on its own. However, there is one rather large caveat. There is a proverb that applies here: "Experience is not what happens to a man, but what he does with what happens to him." This is true, since few would-be leaders really use their experience to develop their XQ. If we do develop a real XQ from understanding and purpose, then we can develop leadership wisdom. We define leadership wisdom as the understanding, adaptability, balancing, and fitability that comes as one grows and matures as a successful leader. You might not have the ability to recognize it in yourself. The purpose of this chapter is to help you acknowledge the abilities you have gained through experience as a means to improving your eXperience Quotient. Most people reading this book will have some level of XQ, but few have taken the effort to analyze and apply it. We want your Leadership Quotient to be supported by a healthy level of XQ. This chapter will show you how to recognize XQ, improve XQ, and apply XQ.

You will recall that in the Intelligence Quotient chapter we contrasted the traditional IQ of psychological testing with the successful IQ of leadership. We perform a similar analysis in this chapter: We contrast experience from XQ as it is used to develop an overall $LQ^{©}$. We are going to avoid any substantive references and use simply experience as the XQ basis, since that is what experience is. We want to look at not *just* who said it, or research evidence, but more practically we want to know whether the experience was learned or earned, and how it will improve your XQ and contribute to your overall $LQ^{©}$.

The XQ improves performance, but there are many ways in which experience can do the opposite—it can erect a barrier to learning. Experience can do that when the leader mistakenly thinks he knows everything and can't possibly learn something new, especially from a younger, less experienced practitioner in the field. That attitude prevents the leader from improving his position.

There are no humans from whom you cannot learn. If you think there are people in the "I can't learn from them" category, it's only because you *refuse* to learn from them. Start your XQ quest with the realization that we all have a lot to learn about leadership and ourselves and we will never know it all, but we must know enough to be successful.

Bill learned a lesson while teaching through a translator in Kiev. Bill was made aware that even the best of translators cannot keep up with a fast talker, since Russian words tend to be longer than their English counterparts. It was Bill's first experience lecturing through a translator and he was given a false sense of security by the translator, who assured him, "Don't worry about the way you talk; we understand 'Texan' and can keep up." Consequently, Bill talked like a Texan rocket for two hours, wondering why he got so little reaction from the audience.

After getting some advice from some English-speaking audience members, he cut his speaking speed in half the next day and the attention of his audience improved dramatically. Likewise, Harvey, our Jewish former New York cabbie, thought he did a great job as he presented Dun and Bradstreet's products to a group of Mississippians until he heard the Mississippians say as they left, "What'ta hail did that joooker jus' say!" Likewise, Carl thought that the group from Alabama really loved the Boeing Systems he had tried to sell them, since they were so friendly and nice; yet they bought absolutely nothing from his company. The opposite thing happened to him in New York: He got the cold shoulder from the prospective customers, but they bought the entire package he was selling.

Experience: Don't leave home without it! It is important for you to understand the validity of your current XQ if you are to develop a better one. It is not always what you know that will hurt you, but it is what you know that is *not true* that will hurt you. Learn to separate good experiences from bad experiences as you make them a part of your XQ toolbox for improved leadership performance.

When we write about our students, you will get the wrong impression if you picture a classroom of 18-year-olds. Bill and Dave teach in MBA programs, so quite often our students have very high XQs. They are accomplished business people, pastors, community leaders, doctors, and lawyers. Dave was teaching a graduate leadership class at DBU and one of the most experienced students was a lawyer named Gerald who had been on the Texas State Bar's Committee for Taxation. He owned and managed a real estate investment trust and had received an award as the REIT executive of the year. He had co-owned the Texas Rangers baseball team with George Bush. Throughout the semester, as the class worked their way through the learning and application of just about every leadership theory ever published, Gerald continued to apply them to what he thought was the greatest predictor of leadership he had ever seen: experience. "Wouldn't you rather follow someone who has experience?" he continually asked throughout the semester. Good theory. We like it. That's why we've written this chapter on the eXperience Quotient.

Is XQ one thing or many? Is it absolute or dependent? Is it natural or nurtured? Can it be improved or is it relatively stable over the life of a mature adult? Let's seek answers to those questions together.

Clearly, XQ can be good or bad, but one thing is true: We all have experience. XQ is like leadership: it is a set of skills that can be improved with analysis and effort. First, determine if you have ten years of experience or if you have one year of experience ten times. Most of us experience the same things over and over and really do not have that many new experiences unless we put ourselves into new positions often. If you will think about new, sometimes uncomfortable, positions as you read this book, your XQ will increase.

On to Our LQ©'s XQ

> *Thinking you know the rules of the game is often more dangerous than knowing you don't know. Ignorance is most destructive when you are unaware of it. To assume that others are like us or think like us and to assume that we understand a circumstance when indeed we do not is the start of leadership failure. Be aware of your own ignorance of new environments and let more experienced people help you. Though formal education is enduring, it can be a detriment when it keeps you from attempting to reread your new situation. Realize education can be like love and lust. Love is enduring and so is real wisdom through knowledge; lust is a fleeting thing and so is education until it becomes real knowledge one can use: real love represents the XQ you need.*

XQ can be presented in another three-dimensional figure (see Figure 10.1) with a content dimension, a context dimension, and a process dimension. We do not want to confuse you with another triangle, but it seems appropriate to use one again in this case. In Figure 10.1 we see that any one of the three angles can be critical to development of true *LQ©* XQ. As always, we see application, fit, and balance as the keys. In the university, most students learn content and are tested on content. Instructors do this out of a self-serving bias, so they can claim, "Look what I taught them." Of course, the student remembers little if any of the multiple-choice junk she learns and can apply very little of it in a few short weeks. Perhaps we would be better off helping students learn one principle they can use and apply than 1,000 we can test on?

We must also learn much about process as we do things together. And we learn about context as we are exposed to differing environments and cultures. The key is to be able to learn two sides of the triangle and figure out the other to develop a useful XQ, for seldom are we going to get exposed to all three angles at once. Remember Figure 10.1 and think about its message as you continue your study of this chapter.

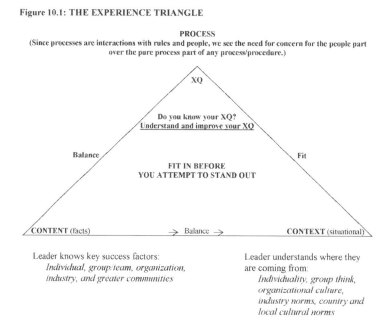

Figure 10.1: THE EXPERIENCE TRIANGLE

PROCESS
(Since processes are interactions with rules and people, we see the need for concern for the people part over the pure process part of any process/procedure.)

XQ

Do you know your XQ?
Understand and improve your XQ

Balance   Fit

FIT IN BEFORE
YOU ATTEMPT TO STAND OUT

CONTENT (facts)   → Balance →   CONTEXT (situational)

Leader knows key success factors: Leader understands where they
Individual, group/team, organization,   are coming from:
industry, and greater communities   *Individuality, group think,*
                                                              organizational culture,
                                                              industry norms, country and
                                                              local cultural norms

Learning and Leading with Questions in the Beginning = Leadership Wisdom!!

The understanding of experience and the wisdom to apply what experience can provide is the fundamental nature of overall $LQ^{©}$. You must realize that your tangible qualities related to XQ show as you work in an organization, and others know it even when you don't. Your experience and what you have made of it is obvious to your followers.

The key is to learn to build effective and efficient experience that can be used to improve and build you into a better manager and leader. Learning from the ordinary daily events of life as well as the idiosyncratic things that happen to you and others is in itself a learnable and teachable skill. Certainly "it" is an improvable skill for which we all have some innate abilities. We can all think back on our lives and realize how much easier it would have been if we had learned from the experience of others. Defining, understanding, and ultimately practicing the following XQ precepts is the start of an improved $LQ^{©}$ XQ experience.

XQ as Knowledge, Skills, Abilities, Actions, Appropriateness, Balance, Organizational Savvy, and Understanding How to Fit In Yet Stand Out

"Fortunate, indeed, is the man who takes exactly the right measure of himself and holds a just balance between what he can acquire and what he can use."—Peter Latham
"What we must decide is what we value rather than how valuable we are."—Edgar Z. Friedenberg
"We judge ourselves by what we feel capable of doing, while others judge us by what we have already done."—Henry Wadsworth Longfellow
(Reader's Digest, *"Quotable Quotes,"* 1997, pp. 14 and 16.)

Ultimately, a fairly common group of factors is found among successfully experienced people that goes beyond the normal leadership characteristics and traits. Success through experience is about substance that goes beyond teachings espoused in the typical leadership literature into the arena of actionable, relevant, and substantial precepts one can use to enhance realized leadership: XQ. Successful XQ is about these areas:

Knowledge—an interesting concept, because each of us really knows so much, some of which we can use and some of which we cannot use; or some of which we chose to use and some of which we chose not to use. Knowledge must *not* be minimized in its significance. You will see in the KQ chapter that intellectualizing something is the first step to being able to use it. Know:

1. The actual **potential** of self and others as well as real limitations.

2. Being **right does not always make you a winner**; when might makes right it costs.

3. Personal **difficulties normally exist** just in one's mind.

4. **Meaningful concepts and facts** about the arts, history, poetry, modern-day cultural norms, science, music, and inventions.

5. Playing the **blame game** is **out**.

6. **Stumbling blocks and steppingstones** often appear as the same things.

7. Today's **preparation** is the determinant of tomorrow's **achievement**.

Skills—practices that you have learned to use effectively; they can always be honed.

1. Establishing **meaningful relationships** because you care and it shows.

2. **Defining** and **solving problems**.

3. Building relationships between **things and people, and potential transformations**.

4. **Tempering experiences with self-reality and self-control**.

5. Making the **most of good traits** and the **least of bad traits** is true intellect.

6.   **Seeking—inquisitive** approach.

Abilities—apparent traits you put into use to gain skills and knowledge.

1.   **Motivating self and others**.

2.   Understanding you **can't be anything** you want to be: everyone is somewhat limited.

3.   Staying physically, spiritually, and intellectually **enthusiastically involved**.

4.   Pulling seemingly unrelated things **together**.

5.   **Breaking down the complex** into manageable parts requires attention and practice.

6.   Thinking logically, emotionally, practically, creatively, innovatively **as required**.

7.   Realizing **a mistake is proof** that you are at least trying to accomplish something.

8.   Perceiving that **ideas don't work unless you do**.

Actions—your behavior in most situations.

1.   **Starting with a smile** and concern.

2.   **Exhibiting honesty** and authenticity in all you do.

3.   **Influencing with a positive** and direct approach.

4.   Leading with action, **a clear bias for action**: translate thoughts into action.

5.   Working with self-actualized individuals and accepting them for whatever they are.

6.   Believing and living a **democratic approach**.

7.   Remaining **flexible** and **accepting criticism**.

8.   Developing plans from **solid thoughts**.

Appropriateness—almost nothing always works or fails.

1.   **Leading with questions** before you lead with answers.

2.   Practicing the **MAX MIN** principle with every Leadership Quotient.

3.   Desiring above all results, but **ethical results**.

4.   Being **involved** with social problems—display sympathy and compassion for humanity.

5.   Choosing **fitting means** to reach goals.

6.   Letting **others lead you**, especially about what it takes to motivate them.

7.   Practicing **self-pity must become a thing of the past**.

Balance—almost everything can be over—or under-done.

1. Allocating **yourself and your time**—your attention is your most valuable worldly asset.

2. **Using heart and mind** of self and others.

3. Developing **personal relationships** with many others.

4. **Enjoying the journey** as much as the final goal.

5. Having and using a good **sense of humor**.

6. Being **supportive and requiring responsibility** from self and others.

7. **Taking and giving** praise, responsibility, freedom, help, love, criticism, rewards, punishments, and many other psychological and physiological assessments and judgments.

8. **Taking on and letting go**.

Learning—it must never stop.

1. **Systems thinking**: seeing the big picture and how its parts fit together.

2. **To unlearn** and always work on both learning and unlearning.

3. **About a myriad of things from quarks to cosmos,** i.e., Vocabulary, Math, Decrement, Comprehension, Psychology, Sociology, Management, Pattern Recognition, IQs and EQs, Matrix Reasoning, Symbol Search, Objectivity, Subjectivity, Speed, Memory, Nature, Nurture, and especially *LQ*©!

4. **Caring, Adding Value, and Fun**.

5. About **your impulses** and how to control them.

6. You **can help others** do things you can't necessarily do, and vice versa.

7. **Something you know can be of use** and where to find out more if necessary.

8. To **store information** of all types for potential future use.

9. To **retrieve** needed information.

10. To be a **learner, not learned**.

11. **Thinking and thinking** about thinking about thinking.

12. **You can't stop people from thinking**—but you can start them!

Emotions—you have them, so use them.

1. **Starting, keeping going**, finishing, following through, getting feedback, and adjusting.

2. **Fearing the risk of failure less** than the inaction: go ahead, make mistakes, but not the same mistake over and over. We learn best by trial and error.

3. Procrastinating normally **leads to losing**.

4. **Accepting fair blame—don't** get into the blame game.

5. **Being reasonable** about self-confidence: watch over- or under-confidence in self and others.

6. **Balancing feelings**, facts, realities, and dreams: give everything a final reality check.

7. Seeing **life as a mission**.

8. Knowing when to be a **conformist** and when to be a **nonconformist**.

9. Being **less naïve** but **more optimistic**.

10. **Loving life** and living it.

11. **Having the desire**, attention, and focus foundations necessary for success.

Organizational Savvy—even if you don't work in an organization, you live in and with them.

1. **People want direction**, yet they can remain dependent—let them figure it out.

2. Focus and concentrate **your attention** where it will do the most good for the most people.

3. Understanding the **perspectives of others** better than they do.

4. Beginning with an **end** in mind.

5. Putting **first things first**.

6. Understanding and using **synergy**.

7. **Delaying gratification**.

8. Knowing how to **get others** to become and remain **innovative**.

9. Having the ability to **develop a vision** and get **others to share** it.

10. Understanding **risk/reward** and what **others value** versus what you value.

11. Understanding your organization's **distinctive competencies**.

Fitting in—whether you like it or not, it's a must.

1. Seeking first to understand **before seeking to be understood**.

2. Knowing **when to stay in the game and when to get out**; when to change jobs and when to stay; when to keep a product, line, or business, and when to divest it.

3. Thinking **win-win**.

4. Seeking self-actualization and **living very close to reality**.

5. **Delaying gratification** versus pushing for the quick solution.

Standing out—eventually you will have to do this to succeed at any level.

1. Preferring **action over inaction**: No decision is a decision and quite often the worst decision you can make.

2. Loving people and **their accomplishments**/self-actualization.

3. Becoming and **remaining innovative**.

4. Having and understanding yours and others' **distinctive competencies** and how they might work together.

5. Formulating **rules of your own** for leadership experience.

6. Having the **strong desire** to do and learn what it takes to lead.

7. Displaying quite a bit of **spontaneous behavior**.

8. Wanting to succeed **overcomes the fear of failure**.

9. **Learning before you teach**.

10. Reaching **beyond observable facts**.

11. Honing the **ability to reflect and generalize**.

12. Realizing **there is no leadership without risk**.

Learning to apply all of these pieces of wisdom would result in a super leader but perhaps one who is too perfect. Experience says that a person can be too good for a position and thus not get the position because there would be a lack of fit. There is a lot to experience, but that's why experience takes so long to develop and hone. Most often we don't get it until after we need it, but we can at least get it for the next time if we simply reflect on our learning experiences with the goal of being more prepared the next time. We will summarize this section by concluding that *as long as you don't know what you don't know, you won't grow!*

Description of the Experience Quotient and its Dimensions

In XQ—as we have done before—we are classifying traits as natural when they are relatively stable over time as could be determined by some standardized tests. We would still like for you to classify your own eXperience traits as natural when you are not likely to change them because of the difficulty or just because you don't want to change. Do this with XQ traits; just admit them and call them natural if you are not going to change them: "can't = won't" in this case!

Keep in mind the Measurement and Improvement Matrices as you review the following normally identified XQ-related traits, and seek to understand how they relate to your leadership environment. And remember: Learning to use the experience of others shows great maturity.

Normal Natural XQ Strengths—Quadrant 1 of the XQ 2X2 Matrix

The first natural strength we found among high XQs is **age**, which often gets intermingled with **maturity**. Though the two measures are certainly related, there is not a direct and perfect relationship. We are concerned about people who seek maturity too early. When our 22-year-old graduates are anxious to get married and play house we wonder about the wisdom of that decision, given a life expectancy that is approaching 90 years. One student who has had a lifetime dream of playing in the NBA is giving the European league a few years and says very maturely, "I just want to delay my maturity; so what if I'm 35 when I settle down?" We would tell him that when he is 60 he won't say, "I wish I had started at the bank five years sooner." He would worry about NOT giving the NBA a 10-year shot. We'd bet that when he is 90 he would regret not trying but would never regret trying and failing. He has a zero probability of success if he does not try and an infinitely greater probability of success if he tries.

We encourage our new college grads to experience life before being bound by it. "Ride your bike across Europe, be a ski instructor, or float the Nile," we tell them. Even better, go on a mission trip or spend a year with the Peace Corps. You will learn a lot more about leadership hiking the Appalachian Trail than you will being a first-level "gofer" in a large conglomerate. Those are encouragements to experience life. What we mean by "being bound by it" is taking on the responsibilities of a spouse, child, mortgage, and the "golden handcuffs" that grow the longer you're in a specific industry.

President George W. Bush has worked hard to get experienced people in his inner circle, like Colin Powell, Donald Rumsfeld, and Alan Greenspan. Howard Baker's successful negotiating of the forgiveness of Iraqi debt is another good example of using XQ. Ben Franklin was the wise old X factor who used age and maturity in the successful founding of the United States.

Although it's hard to get a high XQ early in life, it is certainly possible to improve it by recognizing what you have and using it to your advantage. You probably have more experience than you realize. Gaining experience from those around you can prove to be a great advantage in building your XQ. The major monotheistic religions of the world—Islam, Christianity, and Judaism—are all based on the concept of gaining experience from others along your own personal journey to God. These learning-from-others lessons should be transferred and used in leadership.

The second natural trait that was reported to us is **internal locus of control and extroversion**. Experience comes more readily to people who are courageous and are "out there doing it" while knowing in their own minds that they are in control. Many people show extroversion but feel they are at the very whim of the gods (external locus of control) and basically have no control. Former General Electric CEO Jack Welch and New York real estate developer Donald Trump are good examples of both internal locus of control (they think they are in control) and extroversion (they like being with people to accomplish goals). These icons of business success don't wait or worry about someone else making or breaking them; they'll do that themselves! While it's clear that all success is some combination of luck and timing, there is also a great deal of preparation and experience rightly and richly gained and used.

The third trait is **curiosity plus intuition or insight**. Few successful people become experienced without curiosity and fewer yet are good just because of curiosity. The combination of curiosity with insight or intuition is what produces success. Warren Buffett is curious, but he also has insight and a fair amount of intuition. Intuition and insight of course are part preparation and part "natural" or at least something developed early in life. Women are better at intuition and insight in part because throughout their development they used intuition more effectively than men. Good evidence suggests that women and men are born with the same level of intuition, but women build greater faith and use it more readily. Your curiosity is partly inherited; the rest is developed early in life. But it's never too late to hone and make better use of what you have.

The final normal natural strength we see being reported in the area of experience is **attention span/focus or at least a ratio** of time spent on something and the depth of attention per given amount of exposure. Surely, great basketball players like Michael Jordan have incredible focus that is increased by the pressure of the clock winding down near the end of a game. Golf great Tiger Woods has an impressive record of wins that can be somewhat attributed to focus. When we watched him go into a slump during the 2004 season, we had to wonder if a pending marriage and other responsibilities were shortening his attention span and diverting his focus. There is no offense intended; a slump for Tiger is better than the best of most.

Dave enjoys inviting sports psychologist Don Beck to speak to his classes. During a question and answer session, Dave gave Dr. Beck this case: "Please compare and contrast two college basketball players from the mid-1970s. One is a 6-foot 5-inch skinny white kid with no natural talent playing at a college in southern Illinois. The other is a 6-foot 7-inch skinny white kid with no natural talent playing just across the state border in southern Indiana. Why did Dave Arnott become a college professor and Larry Bird become an NBA All-Star?" Without hesitation, Dr. Beck answered, "Focus. Larry Bird concentrated on basketball, while you were going to class, participating in other extracurriculars, taking vacations, and enjoying the other parts of your life. Larry Bird succeeded because he was able to focus only on basketball." Good answer. You're welcome to disagree about our level of comparative natural gifts and many other details of the story, but don't miss the *point* of the story: Larry Bird continued to shoot 100 free throws at the end of every practice, even when he was one of the best players in the world. Focus and a long attention span is critical to gaining a high eXperience Quotient.

Normal Natural XQ Weaknesses—Quadrant 3 of the XQ 2X2 Matrix

As a corollary, if we see age as a natural strength, then indeed, it would seem plausible that it can be a natural weakness; and yes, **age and corresponding maturity** are natural weaknesses. Take Bill's three-year-old doll of a great-niece as she asks, "What is that?" about a "statute." When told, she said,

"I didn't know about Frosty the Snowman; my mother never told me about him." When another's grandchild says, "I like 'vertables,'" it's because she loved being in her grandmother's Mustang convertible. When a small child backs away from a cute puppy, it's because of an experience. Young children have no natural fear of something small and cute, though they have a well-developed fear of something large and ugly.

Our young students suffer from lack of experience more than age, although there is a skill of learning to get more out of any experience. We are amazed at the difference we see between students who watch and learn from their parents and those who don't. The stereotypical teenager rejects his parents' teaching, then agrees with their values somewhere in his mid-20s.

In the second natural XQ weakness, we see **external locus of control and introversion**. We see a vast amount of judgmentalism in this area. If there is one sin we are judgmental about it is judgmentalism: think about this one—who's being judgmental again?

When we stay within ourselves we can't possibly get as much experience. And even worse, because we feel we have no real control, we can't even learn from others. Introverts who feel they have no control have little chance of becoming leaders.

The third natural weakness is classified as **lack of curiosity**. This would seem a controllable trait, but it appears the propensity for curiosity is developed early and has a large amount of heritability within it. You see small children who are overly curious and others who appear to exhibit no curiosity. You have probably made the following observation about a child: "She is so naturally curious!" Exhibited curiosity is not very typical in adult leaders, probably because curiosity admits unknowing, which takes a great deal of humility.

A healthy dose of adult curiosity is required for a high eXperience Quotient. However, it has to be an applied curiosity, not curiosity about ethereal or theoretical matters, but curiosity about practical matters. McDonald's had success with a small test of vending machines that dispense video rentals, so they are broadening the test to all stores in the Denver area. This makes us curious because it does not fit our standard strategic efficient-use-of-resources model. But instead of predicting failure for the project, we're curious about what the McDonald's of the future will be like if this is a trend.

If you have a curiosity gap, you might consider filling it via a mentor or coworker. Find someone more curious than you and try to "draft" off their curiosity. Some people will always ask, "Why?" and others will never think to ask the question. If you don't have curiosity, use others who are natural *whyers* to improve your own XQ.

The final area of weakness that appears to be relatively stable and established early in life is a deficit of **attention and focus**. Some people just naturally have a short attention span. When it reaches the extreme, it's diagnosed as Attention Deficit Disorder. These are people whose active minds jump from topic to topic because they can't concentrate for a long period of time on anything. They focus on multiple things at the same time, but are unable to remain focused on a particular task.

We see two movements in organizations that actually encourage a short attention span. The first is the "doing more with less" dogma that takes over after a downsizing or restructuring. The workers are left with fewer people and more jobs to do. They have to multitask just to get their many tasks completed. In general, these decisions are good for the organization in the short term but bad for the leadership development of employees in the long term. It encourages short attention spans and causes employees to solve symptoms instead of problems because they are not allowed to focus on underlying causes.

The second encouragement is information technology. See if your experience is the same as ours: Do your IT people talk really fast and use a lot of abbreviations and acronyms? Our observation is that the entire industry grooms and rewards short attention spans among people who are encouraged *not* to focus on one thing at a time.

What to do about it? Here are a couple of suggestions. First, set a time limit and commit to stay focused on a particular project for a certain number of minutes. Start small, maybe five minutes. When distractions occur, ignore them. Close your door, or display your Do Not Disturb sign if you don't have a door. Don't answer the phone—that's what voice mail is for. Don't click on your e-mail when a new one arrives. Focus. If you get a great idea, or remember something that's important, scribble a note, but don't launch into another project. You think Bill and Dave haven't battled this problem while writing a book?

Here's a method Dave learned from Bill. Dave was getting divorced, going broke, and trying his best to flunk out of the Ph.D. program at the University of Texas at Arlington. He couldn't concentrate, so Bill offered to tutor him in statistics. Dave would come by Bill's house in the middle of the afternoon, and Bill would "preach" statistics at Dave for hours without stopping. The lesson to learn is this: find a friend who will help you concentrate. There's another lesson. When Dave's mind would wander and he would ask Bill a non-statistics question, Bill would grab a notebook and throw it on the floor in the doorway. "Now, when we leave the room, we'll remember to do what you just mentioned. Now back to stepwise regression," and Bill would preach on.

Dave has a technique for staying focused that he learned from leading seminars. It's just a more refined version of Bill's notebook on the floor. When a seminar attendee brings up a subject that is out in left field, Dave responds, "That's a good question, but it does not relate to what we're talking about now. Let's put it on the parking lot and we'll take it up later." He goes to a flipchart that is labeled Parking Lot and writes the idea on it. He uses a similar technique when writing a long document like this book, or when grading multiple papers. He keeps a notebook open beside his work. When ideas try to distract his attention, he scribbles down a key word that will remind him of the ideas later and stays on task with the writing or grading. On the parking lot right now as Dave is writing this are the following scribbled notes: "Gerald experience Bush," "Ignorant ex p. Rate," and "Butt to the chair." Stay tuned to see what those notes are about!

Leaders with short attention spans can be successful, but only when they structure their organization to have others follow them around and finish what they start. These types of people make up one great category of quick incremental innovationists who can be successful if they find the right people to support them. They usually have great personalities and are fun to be around if you are able to adapt when you see them mentally move on in mid-sentence. If you feel that you lack attention and focus, get people around you to pick up the pieces of incomplete projects you leave behind.

When Dave first started writing books, he sought out a writer who had a great eXperience Quotient. Among the many questions Dave asked her was one about scheduling time to accomplish writing projects. She had authored six books and had contracts for three more. At the time, she had two small children and was the wife of a busy executive. Dave asked, "How do you get the writing done?" "I glue my butt to the chair," was her earthy response. (And she has a lot to glue.) Dave took her advice. Most of his writing gets done during summer visits to his mountain retreat in Angel Fire, New Mexico. He will commit: "I will not have lunch until I've written 1,000 words." Then after lunch: "I will ride the ski lift to the top of the mountain only after I've written 1,000 words." Other rewards are dinner and going to bed.

Normal Nurtured XQ Strengths—Quadrant 2 of the XQ 2X2 Matrix

In this area, we see many examples of **varied exposure and objectivity** and how they have been put to good use. Surely, many world leaders have this; surely many, many people in today's travel-happy world have it. Then we must ask, "Why don't we see it put to better use?" To do so seems simple. Yes, many have much exposure, but few can view anything objectively. We see this with all of our major newscasters. They have exposure, but they see things through their rose-colored glasses. Remember, we don't see the world we describe; we describe the world we see. To improve your eXperience Quotient, be sure to get exposure, but find a way to incorporate it into your worldview or you'll miss the major implications.

One example here would be the difference in the Islamic East's and the Christian West's views of women. The Islamist thinks Western-heritage Christians exploit women; we think we give them freedom. We think Islamists persecute women; they think they protect and revere them. Without the proper objectivity we will never get to a solution because we see the situation through different lenses.

During a Christian Leadership Ministries conference, Dave learned a good objectivity lesson. The speaker was a biochemist whose access to the Chernobyl nuclear facility produced great research on the effects of radiation. "I go into my lab to answer one question," the scientist explained. "Because I follow the rules of science, I have written my hypothesis so it narrowly tests a specific theorem. However, while answering the question, I produce three more." At this point he was holding up one finger of his left hand and three on his right. He glanced from one finger to three, from three to one. "I'm getting ignorant at an exponential rate!" he exclaimed.

The scientist was right; and what he said concurs with another piece of advice, which Dave gave his son, Lance, upon Lance's high school graduation: "Education does not increase your intelligence; it just reveals your ignorance." That is true for Bill and Dave. Upon graduating from college, we thought we were pretty smart. When we got our master's degrees, we started to pull back the veil on what we didn't know. By the time we had earned Ph.D.s the view of the enormity of what we didn't know just overwhelmed us. We teach just to try to overcome our angst over our incredible ignorance. Thus, a high eXperience Quotient is not knowing everything; it's knowing what you know and what you don't know and acting on that information.

A second natural strength is a **love of learning**. We apologize for writing so much about our doctoral degrees, but that's where we met, so much of our relationship is based on that. "Ph.D." stands for "Philosophy Doctorate." "Philos" means love, and Sophia was the goddess of knowledge. So a person with a Ph.D. "loves knowledge." We should love it in all its forms; but like many other organizations, the Ph.D. "society" has adopted a certain type of learning, called "positive proof," which dominates the environment. There are many types of learning, and we endorse all of them.

Many people develop a love of learning early in life, but we also see people develop it later in life. For example, Bill has of late become interested in learning about psychological testing and theology, whereas in college he just wanted to know what was going to be on the test. Bill did not learn to love learning until he was in his mid-40s. We can all learn to love learning and work to learn from our mistakes. We see Franklin Graham as learning from his mistakes, and Thomas Edison and Ben Franklin as historic examples of people who loved to learn. James Michener loved to learn. His colossal books always started with literally years of study. He would move to an area and would work over the library and locals for information upon which to base his books. We love *Chesapeake, Centennial, Space, Texas*, and more. It seems John Jakes has done this as well. If you have never read his Bicentennial Kent Family Chronicles series, you've missed the development of America from the eyes of one who loves learning and teaching through fiction.

The third strength that people develop and use for leadership development is **attention to many things/diversity**. This may seem like a contradiction to our earlier section on focus. But it's quite clear that high-Leadership Quotient leaders are able to focus on both the short term and long term at the same time. They are able to see the forest *and* the trees. One study indicated that CEOs played the piano at a higher rate than the average public. Two inferences could be drawn from that study: 1) They saw the value of persistence, and 2) They saw how many small things (individual notes) can be synergistically aggregated to produce something beautiful.

Today's organizational environment is changing so fast that the leader cannot pay attention to just one area and continue to succeed. Many leaders did not foresee the rise of the computer, the PC, telecom, the car, airplanes, worldwide competition, empowerment, democracy, even Nazism or Communism, nylon, glass, word processing, air-conditioning (and the list could go on). Unless you learn to look at more and more varied things from different angles, you will miss much.

Looking at failed glue in a new light resulted in Post-it Notes. Looking at a three-year-old's question—"Why can't I see the pictures now?"—resulted in the instant camera. Looking at a chemical that dropped on a shoe resulted in Scotchgard. Looking at air travel as a replacement for bus and auto travel resulted in Southwest Airlines. A scientist who accidentally left an oven on overnight produced the super-hard tiles that protect the space shuttle when it returns to earth. Many bi- and trifurcations have resulted in untold new products and services. This attention to many diverse things with differing and new interpretations has become a must for an innovative leader of the future. Good XQ leaders learn to interpret the world as it is becoming, not as it has been. That reinterpretation requires attention to many diverse things and people.

The fourth and last reported nurtured XQ strength at first seemed a little strange to us. It is the **love of people**. Leaders who love to deal with people are better leaders. Perhaps they understand the need for relationships in order to accomplish goals. Perhaps they realize that few things of consequence have ever been done except by a group of committed people. Witness Christianity and the small number of disciples who have moved from a group of 12 to billions over the last 2,000 years. Leadership requires people, and what better way to lead than to love the people you are leading?

Think about what Napoleon said as he asked a general about Jesus. Napoleon asked, "Can you tell me who Jesus Christ was?" When Count Montholon declined to respond, Napoleon said: "Well, then, I will tell you. Alexander, Caesar, Charlemagne, and I myself have founded great empires; but upon what did these creations of our genius depend? Upon force. Jesus alone founded His empire upon love, and to this very day millions will die for Him….I think I understand something of human nature; and I tell you, all these were men, and I am a man: none else is like Him; Jesus Christ was more than man" (Zacharias, 2000, p. 149). Yes, still, after 2,000 years, Jesus moves people to do almost anything out of the power of love. Learn to influence when you are absent and you'll become a truly great leader.

Normal Nurtured XQ Weaknesses—Quadrant 4 of the XQ 2X2 Matrix

In the area of normally reported nurtured XQ weaknesses, the first and most often reported nurtured weakness we see is **limited exposure**. We can't be exposed to everything, but we can seek others with exposure and learn from them. So many of us can't think of walking in another's shoes because we won't try to think of this. Go out and visit places and people you are not comfortable with and you'll see how limited you really are: we have! Actually it is really tougher and more uncomfortable to have limited exposure than to be overexposed. So many presidential candidates—Ross Perot, Al Gore, Howard Dean, George Bush, John Kerry, and others—are not like us and have never been exposed to the common man and his plight.

Bill's wife, Jan, was working with a group of employees being laid off from a meat-packing plant when a young girl said to her, "How can I get a job like yours?" Jan asked the young girl about her experience and educational background. The young girl said, "When I was 15, my papa got burned up and I had to quit school and go to work here." Another older gentlemen was embarrassed for Jan to know he was 55 and could not read or write. He pretended his eyes were bad and that he had lost his glasses. We could cite a thousand things like this that have happened to us or others we are intimate with, but the point is: There are many things that we have never been exposed to. No matter how high your XQ gets, you will always have "blind spots."

Americans are the elite of the world. We are among the most educated and privileged by birth. Witness the results of the 2004 Olympic Games for one recent example. Americans represent 5% of the world's population, and those of us with at least a college degree represent 25% of Americans. Most of the people reading this book are in the elite 1% of the world's materially blessed people. By education level, Dave and Bill are 1 in 1,000, so we must try to think as others do. It takes effort to think as others do about leading or being led. Perhaps we all, as representatives of how the world thinks, are underexposed when we think of it as amount of firsthand exposure that may help us be better leaders in the world today. One of the best and quickest ways to get more exposure is through the experiences of others.

The second nurtured weakness we see in the area of XQ is almost hard to believe. It is a **disdain for learning**. We frankly know few who have this in a very general sense, but we know almost no one who does not have this weakness to some degree. Most of us don't want to learn in some area or another. In the area of religion, we see almost no one willing to learn about other religions. But if you think about it, and if religion is important to you, you need to learn about all major religions. For example, if you are a Christian, you believe that most of the Jewish faith is correct. Likewise, Islamic people must believe that a lot of the Christian Bible is correct. However, do these groups know this? Is this a form of disdain for learning, at least in one area? Just studying how the current Christian Bible came about would be very enlightening.

If you are interested, Nicolson's (2003) *God's Secretaries* is a fascinating though difficult book on the 50 people who translated and developed the King James Version of the Bible. The King James Version was developed between 1604 and 1611, using several earlier translations and the original Greek, Hebrew, and Aramaic texts. The key focus of Nicolson's book is the almost "virtual anonymity" of the backgrounds and personalities of the 50 translators. The book presents in old English the 15 rules that guided the translators: ugh.

We all suffer from a learning stubbornness in so many ways. As parents, we don't want to learn much about our kids' form of music or the type of movies they like or the books they read. We as leaders often care little about the new and different things our followers are learning unless those things are things we want them to learn. The conflicts we see in the world are most often the results of both sides having a disdain of learning what the other side believes. Think about the areas of learning for which you have disdain. Are your learning disdains healthy for a growing leader?

We already know what we know, but that is where we pay most attention in an argument or debate. We simply restate and focus on what we know, yet we already know our own point of view and attention. Recall the wisdom of Confucius from a previous chapter: "You learn only while listening." Why don't we seek to understand other points of view? We already know what we know just as surely as we don't know what we don't know! Many of us exhibit a nurtured weakness of **paying attention to what we already know**. Since we already have this weakness, why don't we all try next time to forget talking about our views, and listen carefully to the other person's view?

The last nurtured weakness we see reported is a **distrust of people**. We have found that starting from a point of trust results in a few disappointments, but frankly not many. Ask yourself, "Is it better to never trust anyone because you will be let down occasionally, or trust as a matter of habit and be let down occasionally?" It's a simple risk/return relationship, but so many people have retreated to the "protecting risk" end of the ratio and are getting almost no return!

Expectation theory often works too well. It makes us want our distrust of people to pan out so we can be right in our prediction! We think it would be better to trust and hope for the best, knowing that in some instances the fallen nature of humans will take over and you will be disappointed. Frankly, most people won't let you down if you show you trust them, and many will let you down when they know you don't trust them anyway. The best type of leadership control to have is for people to feel they don't *want* to let you down. More followers feel like they have a responsibility to their leader when the leader is depending on them than when the leader starts with the distrusting point of view.

Distrust of people is a developed weakness to which the media contributes in no small way. While we certainly defend the media's role in society as a challenger and questioner, we get frustrated about news that includes only the bad and evil things done, not acts of kindness and good that occur thousands of times more often than the reported bad things. Simply ask yourself on a daily basis, "Did I do more *bad* stuff than *good* stuff today?" The vast majority of people do infinitely more good things than bad. Believe that, and you'll have stronger and more dependable followers who will do good when you are watching *and* when you're not watching.

Using the XQ Matrix

Now that we have detailed what has been reported most often on our $LQ^©$ instrument, we need to begin the self-evaluation of our own XQ. Before we do, we'd like to report that Colin Powell is the most-often reported exemplar in the area of XQ. Frankly, we can see why. He is a person who seems to exemplify the best of experience. In Bob Woodward's 2004 *Plan of Attack,* Powell's power of experience, trust, values, party line, and taking responsibility while being a team player seem to exemplify all that can be good about experience. Likewise, even for his critics, Donald Rumsfeld is shown in a powerful light as having experience that has been put to good use. We really liked the way Rumsfeld led with questions when others supplied answers. He simply asks for the assumptions upon which the answers were based. This is a good way to question others about their ideas.

Now evaluate yourself in each of the four quadrants shown in Figure 10.2.

Figure 10.2: YOUR XQ MEASUREMENT AND IMPROVEMENT MATRICES

Evaluate yourself against the reported traits in this Matrix.

	NATURE (uncontrollable-born)	NURTURE (controllable-made)
STRENGTHS (enablers—advantages)	**Q1** _____ good age-to-maturity ratio _____ internal control locus + extro-version _____ curiosity + intuition-insight _____ good attention-to-focus ratio _____ (self-IDed trait)	**Q2** _____ varied exposures + objectivity _____ love of learning _____ attention—many diverse things _____ love of people _____ (self-IDed trait)
WEAKNESSES (derailers—disadvantages)	**Q3** _____ poor age-to-maturity ratio _____ external locus of control + introversion _____ lack of curiosity _____ poor attention-to-focus ratio _____ (self-IDed trait)	**Q4** _____ limited exposure _____ disdain for learning _____ attention to what I know _____ distrust of people _____ (self-IDed trait)

Tailor the Matrix below for yourself!

	NATURE (uncontrollable-born)	NURTURE (controllable-made)
STRENGTHS (enablers—advantages)	**Q1** *(Quadrant 1)* Maximize	**Q2** *(Quadrant 2)* Hone
WEAKNESSES (derailers—disadvantages)	**Q3** *(Quadrant 3)* Make irrelevant or deflect	**Q4** *(Quadrant 4)* Minimize or change

Evaluating Your XQ Personal Profile: Strengths and Weaknesses

Doing Something About Your XQ!

Instead of going over the normal routine to finish this chapter, we are going to do something very different. Just as we were trying to think of an approach to finishing this chapter, Bill received an e-mail from a student who was just graduating. The student wrote that he had found an assignment that summarized much of what he had learned during his college years, though he did not recognize it when he first completed the report. Here is that report as it was originally presented, though we have taken the liberty of bolding and italicizing key parts.

1/12/02 Leadership/Business Interview with Thomas Winstead

Denvill Thomas Winstead is the founder and president of Oral Arts Dental Laboratories Incorporated. Oral Arts was established in 1969 and was incorporated in December of 1970. Oral Arts' headquarters is in Huntsville, Alabama. In addition to Huntsville, Oral Arts has operations in Mobile, Alabama, and Maryville, Tennessee. In 2001, Oral Arts grossed 8 million dollars with approximately 140 employees. The following is an informal interview with Mr. Winstead regarding his business history and life perspective.

Q: What is greater than God, more evil than the devil, poor people have it, and rich people want it?

DTW: We're gonna get started off on this note, huh? Poor people have it and rich people want it? And it's greater than God? I'm thinking about it.

A: The answer is nothing.

Q: During your past work experiences, were you ever bothered by working under a boss and being subject to his rule?

DTW: Nope, that never did bother me; I've worked for others as well as myself. I started working around age 11 or 12. I had a paper route to start with. I sold the *Grit* newspaper. That was the first encounter I had with trying to set up my own business. I ordered the newspapers through the mail and I really enjoyed that job. It was actually my own business. I had a pretty good size route. I sold the newspapers for 10 cents apiece while riding my bike. Nope, it never did bother me to work for others.

Q: It is my understanding that you never exceeded an 8th-grade education. What personal attributes do you think you have that enabled you to be so successful with such little formal training?

DTW: I believe that common sense has a lot to do with it. Common sense is the real motivator and drive that allows you to figure life out, figure mechanics out, really anything without the formal education. If you don't have education and don't have common sense, it's going to be really hard to do much in life. If you've got both common sense and education, you can really exceed and excel. I think for me common sense had the greatest mark; that's God given. ***I've always had the will to learn from other people***, and I've always tried to associate myself with educated people, and I learned from them by my desire to succeed, by asking questions, and listening closely. I got my education through my association with educated people, respectable people, continued education programs, and through reading a lot. I've come to realize that not finishing school was a mistake, but I realized it too late, after I was providing a living for myself and my mother. I couldn't see any way to go back to school. So I continued to work. I realize that all the time. People who succeeded without education did it through more hard work and struggle than someone who was well educated. In my lifetime, it has made things very, very difficult. Lack of education has made things much harder, but by no means have I ever felt that it was too much of a battle and that I should give u p. I'm glad you asked that question. I sometimes don't tell young people that I didn't finish high school, and the reason I don't tell them is because I don't want them to think that they could quit and go out and start their own business and succeed. I would never want to contribute to a person thinking in a negative way like that. When I was raised up, how you were educated depended a lot on the family you were raised in, the time in which you were raised, and the area where you were raised. In my area, finishing high school was like finishing college: dropping out wasn't a big deal. In the country, families left it up to their kids whether to quit school or even encouraged them to quit in order to work. It was pretty much up to me whether or not I continued school. It was easier back then to succeed; however, the success depended on the type of business. I could never start a high-tech business because the education would prevent me from doing that. I think the important thing, whatever the type of business you get into, is that you've got to give 100% and do a good job, which in some ways is more important than working for the million dollars. ***If you work hard and treat people fairly and with respect, you can be more successful than just working for the dollar.***

Q: Has your lack of formal education ever bothered you?

DTW: It bothers me in writing letters and in doing math. No one around me realizes how much it really bothers me; I don't think that I display any sort of concern about my lack of education, but in my mind and in private, it bothers me a lot. It bothers me a great deal, because the things I get others to do for me, I could do myself. I'd do it myself, and in my opinion, do it a lot better and faster.

Q: When did you first realize that you wanted to create your own business?

DTW: Well, that was during 1968 in Vietnam. I was responsible for a dental clinic, and during that time, I realized that I could handle and accept that kind of responsibility. By being in charge of the enlisted personnel at the dental clinic I realized that I could have success, so when I got home from Vietnam I started Oral Arts. ***The experience in Vietnam built the basis towards my feelings of success and self-confidence.*** After I got back I was approached by a person in town who knew how hard I worked and encouraged me to start my own business. He co-signed the note with me at the bank to borrow the money I needed. That was the motivating factor for me starting the business. He believed in me based on his knowledge of my work habits.

Q: What was your motivation for starting your own business and how has that motivation changed?

DTW: That was the motivation for starting the business. That may sound strange, but when I got back from Vietnam I had no obligations to anyone. I had decisions to make, whether to start working for someone else or to start my own business. The night I got back I received two phone calls. One was an invitation to be a 50% owner in a business. I was against that idea because I really had no respect for that person and I did not want to be associated with him. The other call was from a dentist who said he would support the co-signing of $13,000 to start the laboratory business. He felt like I would do a good job and be very successful. In appreciation, I gave him a 25%, two-year discount on all his lab work. I paid the loan off in one year and continued giving him the discount for three years. I was so appreciative of him and didn't feel that two years was enough. That's just the way I believe. *I believe in fully paying back all my debts.*

Q: Successful people are said to exhibit certain beliefs and qualities. Can you identify any that you feel have been critical in your success as a person?

DTW: *I feel that one of my qualities is the ability to read people's actions and sense what a person really feels, not just what they are saying. In business I feel that is a very important ability to have.* There's no secret to moving to the top without the work. I feel like I've always had the quality about me that I've never minded working. One of my qualities and strong points is that *I don't feel better than anyone* else. Sometimes, and I don't say this critically, but sometimes that can be one of the downfalls of being highly educated. If a person is well-educated and has money, all of the sudden they feel better than anyone else. They try to hide that, but if they feel that in their mind, then they put out an aura about them that people can read and this can cause them to fail. I don't feel that way at all, I just humanly don't feel better than anyone else. I feel that's a very good quality in anybody. Another quality that I know I have is *the ability to ask an opinion and take that opinion and use it and not just listen for what I want to hear but listen to the real truth*. That's another great quality to be able to do that. I'm not stuck on myself or any particular way of doing things. I have my feelings about what is the best way to do things but, I don't have a problem changing my mind if I'm getting good advice. Another quality I have *is the habit of giving credit to people for their performance or ideas*. That, to me, is so wonderful to be able to do that. To be able to say that "he/she showed me that, or he/she told me how to do that."

Q: Would you consider yourself to be in a leadership position? Do you think people are born natural leaders or is that a learned skill?

DTW: I absolutely feel that I'm in a leadership position. I feel that education should give you the basics and overall knowledge as to what you need to do to be successful. That's my opinion because I never went to college. I feel that you're not born to be a natural leader; you acquire some basic skills that allow you to grow into being a leader, and you get that from your desire to better yourself, or in my case, the desire to have a job, and a future, and a job in the future. I think it's good to have to worry about your future to some degree. *By the age of fifteen I was already worrying about my future and what I would be doing in the future.* It was constantly in my mind as to what I would be doing in the future because of my lack of education. Would I live under a bridge? Would I have a job? Because I had no daddy, what would happen to me if something happened to my mother? I worked hard to please, and to have a job. My track record was that I learned more about my job than any person that had ever worked in that job; that's what I was told, that no one had ever asked as many questions as I did. That was giving me the knowledge and ability to get along with people. I learned to read people; I learned to see who was willing to give me information, skills, and knowledge. I began to learn what was on their minds rather than what was on their lips. I would go to the ones who had the willingness to help me along. That has helped me a lot in the leadership role. I think in some ways that there's no way that anyone can walk out into the world and be a leader.

Q: Tell me about some of the stumbling blocks you have faced in trying to manage people.

DTW: Getting a team together and getting them to work together as a team, getting them to care about their quality and their desire to do good work and even to be at work, have all been stumbling blocks for me. Creating incentives for them. Expecting too much, that was a big stumbling block for me, my expectations of others. For years I felt that everyone should work as hard as me. As a leader, that is not a good thing and can cause a lot of problems and headaches. *As a leader you've got to realize that you got there, and there was a reason that you're there and that you're going to be a little different from others.* As a leader you will be different; your difference is your willingness to work the long hours and do whatever is necessary; that's what got you there. Once you get there you need to forget it. You can't expect other people to do it. If they were doing that, they wouldn't be there with you to start with. Now, it's so much easier that I've learned all that.

Q: The coach can't, in himself, motivate a person to do something; the person has to motivate himself.

DTW: I know what you're saying and I can answer it really easily. You gotta realize that, number one, the people who work for you aren't going to work as hard as you and they're not as educated in the field as you are. *You have to educate them so that they can perform. You have to give them the latitude to learn. You've got to give them the tools to learn and the means of educating them and you have to praise them along the way.* That was another stumbling block that I had. I was too hard on my employees, which caused me a lot of grief; caused me *a lot* of grief. I expected a lot out of people who just walked in the door. I expected them to get in and work as hard as me, and that just isn't the way it is. I didn't realize that they needed more education at first. That caused me a lot of problems. If you praise them, and pat them on the back, and stroke them about the little things they do, that gives them the desire to do more and more. That's how you bring them up to other levels. You create a good working environment by giving them the means to do the job. That helps as well. The way you present yourself is very important in bringing people u p. It's how you conduct yourself around them, and your mannerisms around them. That was also a big stumbling block for me for years. That was a problem, but at the time, I really didn't know it. Flying off the handle and throwing things around or not being patient was a problem. You have to be patient. The only way that you're going to bring the employees up to a level of being productive is that you've got to be patient and control your anger and not display your anger. That's another stumbling block I had: getting angry and flying off the handle and allowing employees to see me angry. If you go into business, you would be much better off if you never allowed anyone to see you angry. You've got to be in control, and when you're angry, you're not in control of yourself or the situation and the people around you see that and it really hurts their feelings. One little instance can cause problems for weeks or even months. It takes a long time for people to forget that. That can be a major stumbling block.

Q: What about now that you're not working hands-on with the employees—how do you manage the company?

DTW: You have to educate the managers with all the experiences you've had. You have to teach them, and I've done that. Over the last 10 years I've had regular weekly meetings. *I realized 10 years ago the mistakes that I was making and made a commitment that I was going to change the management at the operation. I worked hard at having the meetings and coaching the managers to treat their people with respect and teaching the managers to take the responsibilities of the managing and don't let that filter down to the employees because they have their responsibilities to produce the work.* They don't need to hear a manager talk about business being off or quality being down. Some people are perfectly satisfied working eight hours a day and going home to their family and leaving business behind them. They don't care anything about the business aspect. It's not fair to them to hear anything about the business problems, so I coached the managers to lay off the management subjects around the hourly workers. I also encourage everyone not to bad-mouth others. You're always going to have it, but a leader's philosophy and goals will always filter down to the employees. It has filtered down that I don't want any profanity used during meetings. If they hear me using profanity, then they're going to use it. It's like raising a child: your child in many ways will reflect how you raised them in what you did and your reactions. It's the same way in business. If you are constantly displaying what you are coaching them into doing and the mannerisms that you use when you're around, they will eventually filter down. Getting people to perform is going to come from the managers, and I do that by telling them they're doing a good job and by coaching them and asking them questions to keep them accountable. ***I let the managers manage; I get out of their way.*** That's very important as a leader. If you're going to be a good leader and have a lot of people working under you, you've got to step back and give them freedom to manage. They will make mistakes, but you've got to be very careful when a manager makes a mistake. You have to understand that everybody makes mistakes. You've got to pat them on the back and say "Hey, don't worry about it; I know you're beating yourself up more than I ever could, so just don't do that; we're going to overcome this." You have to realize that they hate it a lot worse than you do, and you move on. That's not to say that no matter what they do or how many mistakes they make that you're just going to let it go. There are times when you've got to discipline and or even let someone go. It makes all of them respect you for doing it.

Q: What kind of changes do you think I will make by having a formal education in business?

DTW: In every aspect of the business your education will be beneficial. Education will give you the means to read and understand a financial statement so you can make adjustments that will affect the profit or loss. It will give you the resources to set goals and incentives for the employees. Your education will give you a certain amount of respect from the employees and business associations. Marketing will play a very important role in the success of the business; marketing will come from your education, and it will give you ideas. ***If your business is successful, marketing will play a major role in that success. I think the education will give the employees a sense of security; it will give them confidence in you to lead them and provide them with good advice. The education will give you confidence as well; you need to feel good about yourself. If you don't know how to handle a problem, an education will give you the knowledge to find what you need to solve the problem.*** With your background in business you'll project your ideas in a more understandable method. You will have the ability to write up an action plan or proposal in short order and that will be very beneficial. You will be able to take a financial report and do projections of what the business will do in a given time frame and implement action plans based on the results you want to achieve. I think your education will motivate you into achieving great success. You will have all these abilities; as a leader, these things are important and you will have them. You will be able to communicate to others both speedily and professionally. Because of your qualifications, you will recruit people who are more educated and this will help you reach a higher degree of business success. Your young age, demeanor, and education will rejuvenate the existing employees and attract the best in our field. The young people get excited that you're coming and know that a new and innovative attitude is coming. The older employees aren't bothered by it either. Another thing I think you'll do (which is very important) is that you'll bring spiritual leadership to the business, and I really believe this is going to be important. People will trust you more. This gives you the right attitude to deal with problems.

Your spiritual feelings will allow you to consult your employees who are having family problems and you will do things differently than a non-spiritual person. If you're a caring person, it will come out in the way you deal with people.

The following is a summarization of Thomas's business success by Pam Winstead, Thomas's wife.

Thomas has numerous strengths that have benefited him in developing and operating Oral Arts. *One of the most important has been his desire to embrace new technology and his ability to weed out innovations that will be accepted within the dental community.* If a product had value, then Oral Arts was among the first to make it available.

Another attribute is that he is a lifelong learner. He constantly strives to increase his knowledge of business-related topics as well as dental laboratory information. He reads, reads, and reads.

Thomas has a natural ability for marketing! He has a tremendous knowledge of the topics and products that dentists will be interested in. He has designed our printed ads for the professional journals we advertise in and gives our marketing director ideas for acquiring new business. Additionally, Thomas has *taught himself public speaking*, which was very difficult due to the difference in his education and that of the dentists. But he never allowed this difference to discourage him. He has addressed dentists as guest speaker at Case Western University and University of Texas as well as University of Alabama Dental School in Birmingham. He has given hundreds of seminars on dentistry throughout the United States, including Alaska and Hawaii.

And finally, Thomas never gives up on anything—in the past 23 years I've never known him to give u p. When something doesn't go well he just continues to make changes until finally a problem is solved or a technique is perfected.

As you can see, I'm very proud of what Thomas has been able to accomplish!

That's All, Folks

Dave and Bill don't think they can add anything of significance to this closing, so we are just going on to Chapter 11: The Situational Quotient. Just close with looking at Figure 10.3 and really thinking about your true XQ as it is and as you will make it become.

> *"The last thing one knows is what to put first."*—*Blaise Pascal*
> (Reader's Digest, *"Quotable Quotes," 1997, p. 21.*)

Figure 10.3: YOUR LEADERSHIP LEVERAGE TRIANGLE

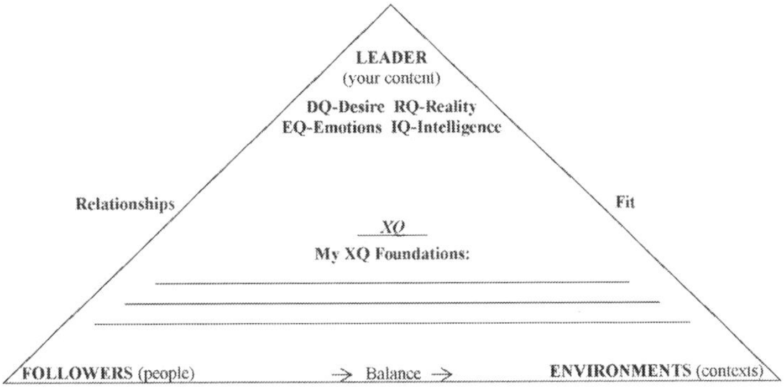

Experience is hard to get if you are too dumb to learn from others. It hurts to wait until we learn everything from our own personal experience.

Leaders relate through
    CQ-Communications
    PQ-People Skills
    BQ-Behavior
    AQ-Appearance

Leader fit through
    XQ-eXperience
    KQ-Knowledge
    SQ-Situation
    MQ-Management

11

KQ, The Knowledge Quotient

"Leaders have always needed to grow constantly as intellects, repositories of information, and guides of behavior, basing this growth on their collected wisdom. Curiosity and the desire for information seem to be self-regenerating phenomena. That is, the more we know, the more we want to know. The effective leader will always find ways to receive and process increasing amounts of information."—Warren Wilhelm

"Ask, and it will be given to you; seek, and you will find; knock, and the door will be opened to you."—Jesus

In the prior chapter, **XQ, eXperience Quotient,** was presented as the most critical of environmental quotients for it is through experience that we learn to deal with, work in, and indeed mold the environments within which we lead. This chapter will focus on another important environmental quotient, the KQ, Knowledge Quotient. In KQ, we see how one normally goes about acquiring needed useful knowledge.

A simple model of this is shown in Figure 11.1, Acquiring Useful Knowledge. As you can see, the first step after identifying a clear problem or area of concern is to seek information or knowledge about the problem or situation at hand. That is, to sincerely look, listen, ask, and seek. This has to be done in a way that weighs the time needed for the search against the potential payoff of expected new information. If time or money is not a factor, much work should be done to see what theory and research exist before attempting to look at the practical and more applied work. This is especially true if the task or situation is an important one. "Important" could mean many things, including "costly," "bet your company," or establishment of a new direction. A leader should know when something is important and when it is not. When you can't determine how important something is initially, treat it as important in the beginning and you'll never be sorry. The opposite is not always true!

Once the information-gathering phase has been completed, you will have a much better basis for developing useful knowledge. Ignorance is no excuse for the modern, educated leader. Leaders must do their homework. There is too much information of great value that can prevent blind leadership. "It turns out that as you learn about a subject/skill, one of the things you learn is how much there is to know, and consequently, you begin to appreciate how much you don't know....Recalling Darwin's conclusion that 'Ignorance more frequently begets confidence than does knowledge,' we need to be wary of those with the biggest egos, the ones who believe they are the best" (Dauten, 2004, p. 2L).

The search for knowledge must at some point come to an end, and one must know when it's time to stop gathering information and start taking action. However, when to get to work is not the main theme of this chapter. This chapter is about getting and molding the foundational knowledge necessary to proceed to wisdom and actual applied usage: within that definition of knowledge, we find the foundation for experience. Thus, the second step in our useful knowledge model is to extend and extrapolate the available information or knowledge about your topic to your specific situation. Perfect information is seldom available. If it were available, leadership would not be necessary. It's making judgments about the available information that makes leadership valuable. The closer the information is to perfect, however, the easier it will be to find an actionable leadership plan.

Two groups took different means of finding information in an innovation exercise. One group was assigned to find out what the normal blood pressure for humans was. They left the classroom and went to the Nursing School to get brochures on the topic. The other group was assigned to find the speed of light. Their response was that they didn't know, and didn't know how to find the information. Their excuse was, "We didn't know we could leave the classroom." Don't place restrictions on yourself. Unless told otherwise, use what others have learned as a basis for what you need to know. Continually challenge the assumptions you are using as you approach a situation. Often you will find that your assumptions are restrictions that are not necessary but have been placed there by you, not by the rules of your *game*.

The third step in our model is to formulate the knowledge and information acquired into workable solutions or concepts worthy of actionable leadership. As the model shows, you should limit the number of concepts to something that is usable for the purposes and constraints at hand. Then you can run experiments so you will know how to adjust your thinking in order to produce new or better knowledge.

Often the novice is better at getting new knowledge than the expert who often is inhibited by what they know. Time and again we see situations where people did not look further because they simply knew that heavier-than-air machines would never fly, there was no need to have a computer in one's home, and so on. Knowing can be a detriment; often we need to just go ask a kid! We remember when we were kids, hundreds of years ago back when Moby Dick was a minnow, the *Book of Knowledge* encyclopedia had a kid-friendly way of explaining everything. Today's youth have the equivalent of many Books of Knowledge available to them through the Internet. However, early in its development the Internet changed from an information source to an entertainment source. There is so much information available that we hear the joke, "I found it on the Internet, so it *has* to be true!" This provides many examples where it's better not to know than to know the wrong thing.

Several items in the current press have struck us of late. One is the constant reminder that the Library of Alexandria was pillaged and burned many times and much of the ancient wisdom was lost. Where might we be if we had the thinking of all the "greats" of history? Another is the current wisdom that is embedded in individuals who are alive and working today. The April 26, 2004, special issue of *Time* listed "The TIME 100: The lives and ideas of the world's most influential people." Beyond the arts, entertainers, and heroes, the list of leaders, scientists, and thinkers is breathtaking. There are predictions that humans are close to a frame-breaking theory that will link quantum physics and the theory of relativity to explain the very foundations of the universe and all of life. We are beginning to understand human genetics and "Adventures in Cloning" to a point where we could grow our own replacement organs. We are in the beginning stages of solving world poverty and understanding the differences that cause us to be divided across so many lines of religion and culture. The ideas represented by the best and smartest among us is humbling. However, this information should be encouraging. If we will use these brilliant thinkers and their knowledge as building blocks, we are much closer to solving the major human problems. If more of us built our KQ properly, using the knowledge foundations of the past and current thinkers as building blocks and steppingstones, not limits and stumbling blocks, where might we end up?

Knowledge begins and ends with doubt, or it is destructive. Knowledge in and of itself overlooks human emotions, though knowledge does not negate these more important human concepts: humans provide the limits, not the knowledge. Can you see the pitfalls of knowing it all? Indeed, we would say that this is the pitfall of infallible knowledge. We do not have infallible knowledge in any area. Another part of the difficulty of knowing is "knowing" how to share that knowledge with your followers.

Figure 11.1: ACQUIRING USEFUL KNOWLEDGE

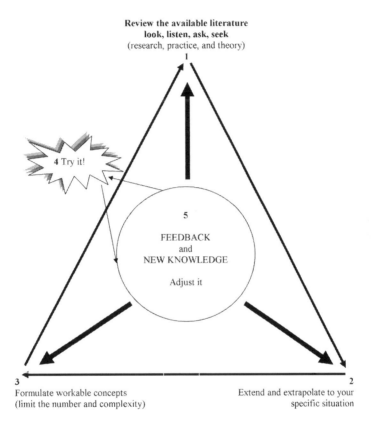

Review the available literature
look, listen, ask, seek
(research, practice, and theory)
1

4 Try it!

5

FEEDBACK
and
NEW KNOWLEDGE

Adjust it

3
Formulate workable concepts
(limit the number and complexity)

2
Extend and extrapolate to your
specific situation

KQ, the Knowledge Quotient, is the leader's ability to learn, pay attention, recognize, imagine, and keep up to date on workplace technologies. It also includes adaptability, innovativeness, and the ability to evolve. Knowledge goes beyond information, but stops at the point where wisdom is required, in order to apply what one knows to the correct situation at the right time. We discuss these "rubber meets the road" aspects of leadership in the XQ and MQ, among many other *LQ*© chapters. Churchill, in his 1948-1954 volumes on *The Second World War*, tells us indirectly why a leader or manager must be decisive yet seek more knowledge as well:

> To wait till everything was ready was probably to wait till all was too late (VI, p. 203)....In the problems which the Almighty sets his humble servants things hardly ever happen the same way twice over, or if they seem to do so, there is some variant which stultifies undue generalization. The

human mind, except when guided by extraordinary genius, cannot surmount the established conclusions amid which it has been reared (VI, p. 374).

We have written in previous chapters how restrictions to thinking get in our way when we wish to learn something new. These "frames," or "paradigms" as they are sometimes called, prevent us from seeing things in a new light. We filter everything through our experiences and predispositions, mostly because it's easier for us to do so. Recall from previous chapters how our worldview models and frames are muddled by the following *common traps*:

1. **Anchoring** to past events

2. Preference for **status quo**

3. **Sunk cost**

4. **Deciding without knowing the "why"**

5. **Preference for confirming evidence**

6. **Framing questions** to our liking

7. **Models** used to define everything

8. **Poor forecasting and estimating**

9. **Over- or under-confidence**

10. **Preference for an approach that's on the safe side**

Yes, the leadership research process is a continuous expansion of knowledge that involves the generation, acceptance or refutation, and application of ideas and theories. Perhaps more importantly, even when we act scientifically and try to understand, we cannot see things as they are because we are limited by the rules of science that constrain our thinking. Science itself provides a structured view of life. Only through acquiring knowledge by anticipation, research, making learning a habit, and continually seeking to improve and innovate will you become a more successful and effective leader. Remember that the academic, current-press, and instructive literature are filled with examples of organizations that did not learn the lessons provided in the knowledge that was there waiting to help them meet the future. If you will use the outcome of the KQ Measurement and Improvement Matrices, you can avoid the fate of many who would not learn because of these predispositions.

In the study of leadership directed toward improvement, it is not solving problems that counts, but being open to new ideas. The "Hawthorne Effect" demonstrated the irony about ideas: *they* don't work unless *we* do. Our goal is not to win the debate on how to become better leaders. Our goal is to help you develop the best questions and to help you realize more of your potential. Leading anything is based on the idea of leveraging what you know. High-Leadership-Quotient individuals need to leverage themselves and their followers through existing knowledge. There is no need to reinvent the wheel or a customer-service training program. There are no magic formulas or prescriptions. Only diligence, credibility, desire, and a lot of hard work can start the path to a better KQ. It is like playing golf, tennis, or any other sport: Knowledge of the fundamentals will put you way ahead of other competitors. *LQ*$^©$ as a whole can provide the fundamentals via the Measurement and Improvement Matrices contained in each chapter. Leadership is like golf: "It's not a game you win, it's a game you play." You will play better as you improve your KQ and, subsequently, your *LQ*$^©$.

So what really works? What do we really know? We think we collectively know a lot about leadership and leaders, yet little about *developing* leaders. *LQ*$^©$ is designed to remedy this, but it requires a great deal of sincere effort on the part of you, the leader. Start by tailoring to your understanding the simplest of concepts: the definition of leadership and its principle rules as outlined in this book. These principles in their entirety are a great foundation and provide *the best principles known at this time.* These principles are the foundational knowledge you need to begin to be successful in your leadership-improvement quest.

LQ$^©$ is the knowledge foundation for leadership, and it truly provides the knowledge that can become the first building block of a better leader if one understands and uses what is here for the taking. This is so true of much of the information available to us. We simply cannot or do not take what is there and use it. We feel this inability exists basically because we are restricted by our own self-imposed models, frames, constraints, and—yes—pure laziness. Most of us are so lazy we NEVER just stop and think, concentrating on using what we have or what we can get as foundational knowledge before we give up or complain about our circumstance.

Lessons Learned and Considerations

> *"As we look back at history, it should be evident that the builders are fundamentally different from the maintainers and changers....[Leaders need] extraordinary levels of perception and insight into the realities of the world and into themselves."*—Edgar Schein
> *"A capacity and taste for reading gives access to whatever has already been discovered by others."*—Abraham Lincoln

We should be reminded that nature has solved many complex problems randomly, but we should also realize it took thousands, indeed millions, of years to do so. Also we must realize that when man attempts to intervene it seems never to work, for if randomness is to work, it must be random, not somewhat random! So use a better approach and learn as much as you can to reduce the number of times you need to try. Never stop being enthusiastic, curious, ready, willing, devoted, and honest, but also know what those things really mean.

Knowledge—On Management and Change

"Let me first say, that as you pointed out, the book talks about irreversible changes, but changes that most executives have not really seen and reacted to. That's true of businesses and nonprofits. It is just as true of government agencies and churches. The ones most in need of change and mired in the past are the universities" (Drucker—about his 1995 book *Managing in a Time of Great Change*). Dave and Bill like to remind themselves of the fact that the universities, of which we are indeed a part, are the most mired in the past, especially when compared to the world of global organizations they teach about. Consider your view of reality in respect to the environments within which you operate, and ask, "How mired in the past is my organization?" Ask if there is new knowledge that could help you or others advance and improve as leaders. If you think not, then stop reading and go do something fun—you just don't get it!

Leaders of the future must have so much knowledge that is cross-disciplinary and cross-fertilized, and they must be cosmopolitan deep thinkers, managers, and learners who are comfortable operating across many boundaries as facilitators and integrators who can look beyond the obvious disciplines, functions, and cultural norms that we traditionally follow, especially in academia. These futuristic leaders must get extraordinary things done with power beyond the normal expertise taught in business schools or found in leadership books of the past. They must enhance employee capabilities and clarify values and norms to get the most from existing and new knowledge, for in true learning organizations the leaders are the best and most diligent of learners. They must continuously reassess the quality of all levels of leadership and the entire workforce and relationships at all levels. High-KQ leaders realize that there is a balancing act on how much time to expend on results and on relationships. Leaders are not arrogant or humble, they are realistic and work to increase their knowledge of emotional as well as content, context, and process factors related to their followers and situations.

Leveraging the enormous amounts of talent and creativity that lie dormant is the function of leadership learning and knowledge building: true KQ. As a knowledge-building leader, you are a bridge to the future where new knowledge meets the current needs as you direct others into learning and applying. Realize that no leader can know it all. The world is changing much too rapidly for that. Successful KQ leaders depend on others for information and have the confidence to make some mistakes so they can learn what to adjust and where to go next. Involve everyone in this quest for knowledge. These are the real KQ skills.

Tools for Building KQ

The effective KQ leader uses many knowledge tools. The first tool should be our daily newspapers. The *Wall Street Journal* is far more than a business paper; it is one of the best newspapers in the world—and it is a great source for keeping abreast. The next source for information is the Internet and its unbelievable amount of information, both good and poor. Third, we need to understand and be able to use some management science tools and methods such as ANOVA, Regression, Cluster Analysis, Structural Equations, Factor Analysis, Data Enveloping Analysis, and so on (ugh); and some other tools such as gaming theory, simulations, IS-MIS-DSS-ES-AI, and all matter of other computer and information systems; traditional tools of PERT and CPM, brainstorming, and other related techniques; and prototyping, modeling, and many other methodologies. We mainly need to know about the purposes of all these tools. Then we need to know how we can find out more about them, their use, and how to get them interpreted into useful knowledge.

The fourth tool for your toolbox needs to reside in your head. We call that tool "strategic action and thinking." It will be described more fully in the next chapter. The following sequence will help you obtain new knowledge more efficiently.

1. Always picture the desired future in your mind.

2. Focus on your desired vision of the future versus the most likely future.

3. Learn as much as you can about the situation.

4. Concentrate on the big picture and all of its parts.

5. Look for breakthrough ideas, but don't exclude the simple and mundane.

6. Be willing to think outside the box, but know what's in the box first.

7. Be alert to new patterns as well as past cycles.

8. View change as an opportunity.

9. Be willing to confront tradition, but have basic values that you hold dear.

10. Beware of pooling ignorance.

11. Give your ideas a reality check.

12. Go for it, measure it, adjust it, but just do it; always have a backup plan.

Overall, having an effective Leadership Quotient means taking action. No decision *is* a decision and quite often the worst decision. We observe that those with effective $LQ^©$s make decisions and:

1. See their task as maintaining operating conditions permitting the decision-making processes or systems in their organization to work effectively while keeping informed about operating decisions at all levels.

2. Understand the need to focus time and energy on a few issues (3-7).

3. Realize that they must work through others.

4. Have and value a sense of timing.

5. Don't like to be precise, and avoid a policy straitjacket.

6. Value trust and keep few secrets.

7. Have the need to be skilled as conceptualizers.

8. Are determined to exploit change.

9. Function effectively in an environment of continual change as a requirement.

10. Prefer people over process.

11. Muddle with a purpose.

12. Go for it, do it, measure it, adjust it, do a new "it."

This is the knowledge needed for a foundational and successful KQ.

The final set of KQ tools is: 1) becoming and remaining innovative, and 2) understanding and using technology for competitive advantage. We realize that there is a lot of industry, organizational, individual, or other knowledge you will need to succeed, but we also realize that we can't tell what the specific needs are for the many different types and levels of leaders who are reading this book. Therefore, we are going to go into detail only on points of universal knowledge that have come to the forefront of leadership learning necessities: areas where our current educational system is lacking in properly preparing us for leadership success. These ideas are so important that they deserve a section of their own.

Becoming and Remaining Innovative

There are two organizational imperatives for Leadership Quotient success: 1) understand how to become and remain innovative as an organization, and 2) understand why someone would do business with you or your organization. *Becoming and remaining innovative* is primarily a function of stressing the necessity for innovation and being innovative yourself. How can one accomplish this throughout a long and varied career when one is being pulled toward staying the same and just following rules and procedures? You can start by paying particular attention to the following driving forces:

1. Accelerating rate of technological development

2. Fast worldwide commerce

3. International media and travel

4. New values and ambitions of employees

5. Needing the ideas and support of all employees

6. Understanding the consequences of a strong culture:

    a. Local knowledge

    b. Cost of a strong culture

    c. When strong the wrong way, it's hard to change

7. Understanding the geopolitical nature of the current times

8. The changing nature of demographics

9. The quality and speed imperative for services and products

10. Democratization of the world's countries

11. Returning to religiosity and cultural roots

12. Shifting powers, trends, demographics, technologies, and new developments of all types

   Innovation is not primarily about technology, information, productivity, TQM, teams, globalization, speed, connectivity, compatibility, the customer, the products, the services, hardware, or software. It is about institutions and their management for all of the things above, but principally to realize a shared commitment on the part of the institution's members to satisfy needs others define through: 1) continuous improvements, 2) ever-changing functionality, and 3) systematic innovation. To these ends, knowledge available outside an organization matters more than inside information, and yet leaders often act as though technology and end-use are the foundations of management. In reality, it is customers' perceived and expressed values that must be our KQ foundations. Remember: We already know what we know, so focus on what you don't know that you should!

The wrong questions and the wrong theories matter little in hard science: things will still work as they do. However, in leading people, the underlying questions and theories are all that really matter because it is those suppositions that direct the power and course of leadership influence. Hardware and software can't feel, love, hate, question, respond, and react like irrational, emotion-driven humans! You have to have employees who express human emotions and understand those emotions as they are expressed by customers and potential customers. For in the end, innovation is people and their desire to improve or benefit from improvements or new alternatives they offer others.

There are many needs, opportunities, problems, solutions, and undefined innovative uses for technological or other innovative tools. Effective KQ leaders of the future have to be attuned to knowledge applications in many areas, and not fear technology or innovation but be able to apply it! Many leaders are surprised to find that most innovations are NOT technology-based.

Topflight organizational leaders are shifting emphasis from *management* of stability and control to *leadership* directed toward speed, empowerment, flexibility, and continuous improvement, all directed at organizational innovation. Innovation is using change opportunities and learning how to identify potential change. Any organization will falter and stumble if it is not innovative. Failure to innovate results in organizational decline, and the only truly sustainable competitive advantage comes through constant improvements. That's because innovations are quickly imitated.

Farren and Kaye tell us that leaders are bridges connecting people to the future. Yet, "No current trends lead inevitably to this envisioned future—it demands a leap of faith and an ungodly amount of hard work." Warren Bennis said that to be a truly innovative leader one must be curious and daring; and that study, travel, people, work, play, reflection, and mistakes are all sources of knowledge and understanding. Studying theories, innovative successes and failures, and relating this information to your collective experiences is the beginning of an innovative KQ foundation. Truly successful innovative KQ leaders see relationships in a number of different ways: as linear, sequential and serial, discrete, singular and independent, parallel and simultaneous, connected, murky, multiple, and interdependent. Effective KQ leaders continually seek to go outside of their normal "boxes, frames, and models" and direct their thinking toward developing true innovativeness within organizational members, starting with themselves.

Key KQ-*LQ*© Learning Objectives

To understand how to become more innovative as a person and develop a more innovative organization is one of the more difficult of the KQ foundational knowledges. Hundreds of books and thousands of articles have tried to do this over the past 25 years. In fact, Bill referenced hundreds of those in his dissertation. Not to worry—we won't mention them all, but we will spend considerable space giving you a practitioner-oriented version. First, understand that *innovativeness* indicates getting ideas to market, where they can create value for consumers.

What the bona fide *LQ*©-KQ leader needs to follow is a rapid innovation strategy for himself and his organization. Organizational innovativeness is critical to the profitability, adaptability, and survival of organizations. This proposes a new perspective of organizational theory (OT) based on speed, flexibility, and commitment that is emerging to replace the old OT perspective based on stability and control. We like to call this new strategic type Innovation Through Rapid Incrementalism, and it is becoming the only viable, sustainable, competitive advantage strategic type.

The cumulative effect of successive incremental improvements of established products and processes is larger than technological breakthroughs. The most important reason that competitive advantage is sustainable amounts to "constant improvements and upgrading" (Porter, 1990). In practice it requires learning KQ skills that are based on the new realities of flexibility, speed, experimentation, change, and innovation, which all must be supported by new management practices and research approaches. Drucker (1991) said corporations can become competitive only by being market-driven and by organizing their whole business around innovation. "The strategy itself is the innovation" (Drucker, 1985, p. 243).

Move from the Leader Being Innovative to Leading Innovative Organizations

Managers most often lose sight of the need to lead everyone to act like owners and share commitments. KQ leaders celebrate trying instead of fearing failure; they play to win; they are diligent and focused in pursuit of new things and new ways. They are able to look to others for help and take advantage of fate when it presents itself. To save space and make reading this chapter easier, we have listed KQ learning facts and objectives in Appendix 11.1. This appendix gives you a good idea of what your learning objectives must become if you are to develop an effective KQ. In some ways, we feel more explanation is needed for the reader to fully comprehend the depth and breadth of the knowledge and understanding necessary to stay innovative and new, but we will hold that for a later book where we can list the principles of innovation and more fully explain them.

To give you a little more specific taste, we will look at a part of understanding and being innovative. That is the area of technology. Technology is a very big part of innovation, yet KQ leaders are aware that most organizational innovations are not technology-based, as we have said. However, more and more of the blockbuster breakthroughs *are* based on technology. We don't want our readers to miss either the technology or the simple and mundane innovations, because all of them are useful.

Understanding, Obtaining, and Using Technology

An overall formulaic expression of this would be:

TECHNOLOGICAL SUCCESS = a function of:
(location + industry + organization + individual): Considering needs and perspectives.

A more complete formula would be:

EFFECTIVE TECHNOLOGY UTILIZATION MANAGEMENT = function of:
((national and global—governmental influences-pressures + markets + industry + cultures) + (industry—phase of maturity + level of technology + acceptance + ASK [abilities, skills, knowledge] requirements) + (organizational—structure + management-acceptance-focus-arrangements + production process type + culture + socialization + internal labor market structures + human resources practices + strategic choice variables + level of technology + phase of maturity of organization, people, products and services, markets, cultures, society, strategy) + (individual [end user]—social comparison-acceptance-focus + training + participation + ASK + technological sophistication + perceptions + attitudes + cultures)) ***all considering fit and balance among and between internal and external people and "things."***

These overall formulas must be understood in light of many different variables, according to what the leader wants to accomplish, and are actually made up of many even more complex relationships that could also be represented in formulas. This relatively complex relationship is mediated (that is, enabled) by necessity, commitment, and communications; and moderated (that is, strengthened or weakened) by an understanding and rationality of the players—real, perceived, or enacted. The problem becomes the density and richness of this information. The more prepared and knowledgeable the leader who is attempting to make this formula work, the more likely it will become a reality. The point is there is a great deal of complexity in almost any formulaic representation of organizational functions, and a leader must use extensive care when developing and applying one.

The key for a technological KQ that is lasting comes through developing a useful yet personal formula and then determining how to manipulate the identified variables. This exercise and the understanding that comes with it becomes the foundational route to success in accomplishment of managing and leading for technological application through technological KQ.

Looking more closely at the formula above, we see that indeed the pressures of location are intense and must be understood from every level if an organization is to be truly global. The cultural aspects alone can boggle one's mind when one must do business in Christian, Islamic, Buddhist, and other cultures.

The industry and its stage of development is another guiding force for technology. To really understand one's own industry is very difficult, because understanding the present is not important: A good KQ leader understands where the industry is going.

The next category of KQ variables is the very rich group of elements that make up the organization. The Management Quotient chapter (MQ), which follows, will present this in more detail. The key is alignment, both internal and external, and insuring that the formal and the informal structural situations are nearly the same. A disconnect with the way things are supposed to work and the way they really work indicates a big problem for your organization.

Finally, we see the individual leader's part of technology success. It is obvious that without innovative leaders an organization stands little chance of being able to use the latest and greatest of the available technologies. Remember that the pioneers get the arrows, but they get the glory as well…if they live!

When we hear the word "technology" we often think of Information Systems (IS) and Information Technology (IT): computers and telecom. Though IS/IT are the most common forms of technology now being exploited for competitive gain, they are *not* the preponderance of technologies. Many areas of robotics, genetics, telecom, plant and other automations, document capturing, medicine, and transportation are technologies outside of IS/IT. A great technology is a 2-wheel hand truck—unload a moving van without one and you'll totally agree! We present KQ specifics with somewhat of a focus on IS/IT because we see so many leaders having difficulties in these areas and it is Bill's area of expertise. The IS/IT knowledge reviewed here is meant to represent the depth of knowledge needed in so many other technology areas. We will intersperse other technological terms so that you can equate the IS/IT principles to other areas of technological need.

Staying Up with IS, IT, and Technologies in Your Field

After our discussion about how to remain innovative, we need to review the specifics of staying abreast of IS/IT and other technologies. Much of this was covered in the CQ chapter, albeit in a different fashion for a different purpose. But we will still present some overriding principles that can help you review and refocus your IS/IT understanding. These same types of knowledge are needed for many others areas of technology, depending upon the specifics of your industry. Chief among the concerns in any industry is determining which technology to use and which to avoid. These inclusion-exclusion decision skills are the essence of technology management, and they are difficult at best. The IS/IT area represents an area of universal concern from both a selection point of view and a management/leadership point of view. Few organizations are NOT dependent on IS/IT, and you must have enough knowledge to manage IS functions regardless of whether you do your IS/IT in-house or via outsourcing. Contrary to popular misconceptions, it is much harder to manage outsourced activities than those maintained in-house.

Most MBAs and even undergrads have a managerial finance and a managerial accounting course, but fewer have a managerial IS/IT course. This is a much-needed area of expertise, as our MBA candidates continuously tell us. We are giving you a flavor of the IS/IT functional knowledge you might need, though there is more to this discipline that we don't have space to mention in this chapter. You should always start any technological decision by defining the "what" of your needs before you consider the "how" of your decision. Too many people get hung up with how something will be done before they really define what the needs of the organization are. In all technologies, the "techies" start thinking about *how* before they understand *what*. Technology is all about leverage used to solve real problems and address real opportunities, and must start by addressing what you want to accomplish. These same goals must be the purpose of any technology. Having a certain technology, IS or otherwise, just to have the latest and the greatest is a disaster in the making. It is **not** about the latest and greatest, but it must be about using IS/IT and other technologies to accomplish these objectives:

1. Speed up, improve quality, lower cost, and/or expand scope.

2. Improve reliability and accuracy, make more complete, and/or provide linkage/interfaces.

3. Improve decision-making by reducing uncertainty.

4. Report or suggest, facilitate experimentation and "what-ifing?"

5. Differentiate by improving or expanding service and/or expanding customer base.

6. Address and keep up with current and future customer concerns.

7. Reduce manpower or other resource usage through increased productivity.

8. Meet a quality or functionality need you cannot meet otherwise.

9. Meet reporting or governmental requirements using by-products of normal business.

10. Improve effectiveness and efficiency.

11. Leverage human capital such as IQ and human strength.

12. Make people, processes, contexts, sales, marketing, support functions, products, and services more competitive through increasing their value, scope, functionality, or uniqueness.

The real $LQ^{©}$ question is this: How can we manage or lead our IS/IT functions, or other technology-based functions such as R & D, robotics, and plant automation, to better meet our potential? Or, personally: How can we use IS/IT or technology to improve our $LQ^{©}$? It all starts with better use of existing tools, and then proceeds to innovation of processes, methods, and self, before it goes to invention and totally new applications. Most everyone can use IS/IT at a high level. To get any competitive advantage or innovative edge from this technology is very difficult, to say the least. Every technology you choose—IS or otherwise—should have at least seven considerations:

1. The business goal—what is to be accomplished with the IS or technology.

2. The work practices or processes enabled/forced by the IS or technology.

3. What it looks like and does—data, text, pictures, sounds, motions, tasks.

4. Physical and knowledge components—the hardware and software.

5. The level of technology needed to support the correct IS or tech component.

6. People interfaces and interactions.

7. Human or machine competitive impacts as well as employee impacts.

Note that in actuality there is a circular relationship between technology and business needs: they drive each other. There is a tremendous value residing in information and forms of organizations and management that are directed at innovativeness. Business IS problems generally revolve around merging of the old and the new technologies. One example is using IT to address sustainable competitive advantage at any of the five points of Porter's five forces model: 1) power of buyers, 2) power of suppliers, 3) threat of new entrants, 4) possibility of substitutes, or 5) competition within your industry. Or we might see in a global sense that, internationally, IT—and the resulting IS—are forces for social, political, and economic change. This could also be said of most new technologies. People are disconnected or thrown out of work because they adapted technology for technology's sake, intending it to replace or leverage human activities, mental or physical. We have become so fascinated by gee-whiz technologies that there is very little that we might predict about technology that would seem farfetched.

Given these very broad conclusions, how can a leader's KQ of IS/IT help? Remember: We could be asking these questions of all types of technology, but we are using IS/IT as an example because it is Bill's unique area of expertise. First, you must avoid the common pitfall in using IS, that is, the common approach to just automating the old instead of rethinking the new way of doing business given the potentiality of IS/IT as it currently exists. The best way to avoid the common pitfall is to exercise an extremely disciplined approach to making forecasts, judgments, considering the extremes or preferences too heavily, or letting emotions rule. We do this by listening to and looking at a lot of other possibilities that are outside our preconceived notions and that take into account the "common traps" shown earlier in this chapter. One of IS's greatest potentials is in helping organizational leaders make more rational decisions by pointing out biases and alternatives outside of one's norms. You can build testing and disciplines into your Decision Support Systems (DSS) that can uncover errors in thinking before they become errors in decision and execution, or you can make them simply reporting systems. The design and basic approaches to using the systems are where the KQ leader excels or takes a step back into the past.

The focus of the topic of discussion here is a complex set of hi-low-no-technology tools, methods, procedures, models, and methodologies that can be tailored to meet clearly defined needs. And, as such, the best way to learn about the "tools" and their capabilities is to apply them. You are being asked this about IS/IT here, but you can ask the same questions about your technology. Simply put, KQ leaders must learn the capabilities of and their expectations for technology before using the technology. We can't go into a lot of detail about the required knowledge here, for that would require at least another book or two, but we can do the next best thing, which is to think through the application of some fairly well known tools. The following descriptions of organizational IQ contain elements that can help and have helped organizations fully utilize their information or knowledge through the proper application of IS/IT.

Organizational IQ and You: Building Your IS/IT KQ Foundation

Effective KQ leaders are prepared to manage the Information Systems (IS) and Information Technology (IT) part of the organization just as they manage other functions, such as accounting, finance, and marketing. Unfortunately, colleges and universities do not provide solid training in the IS/IT and technology management areas as they do in others. Therefore, we are providing a summary of what you need to know about IS/IT. A solid IS/IT and technology management KQ must include the ability to examine successful origination, development, implementation, and diffusion of information systems enabled by emerging technologies and decide on other emerging technological uses. Most non-IS/IT technologies require interfaces with existing IS to be of use. Concepts and techniques of strategic management of information systems and technology for competitive advantage must be explored by reviewing the interaction of IS, IT, and other technologies with other strategic variables related to the support of the overall organizational purposes. Leaders of the future must understand how to manage all technologies—especially IS and IT—toward improved organizational effectiveness and efficiency.

Of late, many authors have written a myriad of useful books and articles that could be used in developing a better IS/IT KQ. For a representative sample of this category of literature, see among others Albrecht (2003); Barner (2000); Barney (1991); Becker, Huselid, and Ulrich (2001); Cohen and Prusak (2001); Collins (2001); Flanagan and Safdie (1999); Gaynor (2002); Goldsmith, et al. (2003); Greenleaf (1991); Hackney (1997); Hruby (1999); Inmon (1998); Jick and Peiperl (2003); and Pinker (2002). There are a handful of books on general technology management, but they are mostly texts; and frankly, we could not recommend them, so we won't mention them. These cited authors look at topics such as teaming, developing innovative mindsets, evaluation and comparisons, leadership, and change. Their usefulness relates primarily to the attention needed for the human interface element involved in learning, managing, and leading the IS function. One must understand that the human element is the difficult part of managing technology. The focus must not be the technical aspect of IS and IT as you approach developing a solid managerial IS background. It is the interactive human element that really matters.

Future leaders of IS/IT and other technology functions must grasp: 1) what drives managers to adopt new information and other technologies to improve knowledge work and leverage human physical capabilities, and 2) how IT and other technologies can meet the need for increased responsiveness to customers, more speed, improved geographic reach, more functionality, more efficient use of labor, more safety, better quality, closer tolerances, leverage of intellect, and faster-learning individuals and organizations. Implementation of information systems and other technologies to meet these pressing needs often changes the entire nature of the task, the management of the assignments, and the relationship of the task to other activities within the organization. Indeed, the more capable the technology in terms of embedded knowledge or expertise, the more dramatic organizational change it generates.

Today the IS/IT trend is for the development and use of more expert systems (ES) that can replace the human expert in many areas. ES are designed by questioning an expert and programming her normal sequence of approaching and solving a problem. For a simple example, think of troubleshooting a car that won't start. A first question would be, "Does the engine make noise or turn over?" A second question would be, "Do any of the lights work?" and so on, with questions leading to a proper diagnosis of the problem. You would program what the expert does and allow the ES to lead you through the expert's normal analysis and efforts. You can think about an ES for many things a doctor does.

Another trend for IS/IT is to develop artificial intelligence—or AI—into IS. This implies more than rules; it implies a system that actually learns from what happens as it makes decisions. We could take our simple example of an ES for a car that won't start and let the system ask what works and what does not, and it could use the answers to build more rules as it records the results of its recommendations: thus it could become AI.

We just mention the ES and AI applications of IS/IT, for they are indeed replacing the need for humans who perform routine or programmable functions no matter how difficult or complex the functions may appear. Most management functions could be replaced with ES and AI because they are rule-based, but true leadership functions require judgment, so they could not be replaced.

The IS/IT Management Imperative—Equate to Other Technologies As Well

Former Federal Reserve Board Chairman Alan Greenspan recently said, "Information technology has begun to alter, fundamentally, the manner in which we do business and create economic value" (Melloan, 1999, p. A27). In the information age, the organizations that survive will be those that succeed in using computer-based information systems to provide sustainable competitive advantage. "Competitive advantage" refers to the ability of an organization to provide products or services that are distinctive and more desirable than those provided by the competition. Competitive advantage answers the question of why someone would choose to do business with your organization.

Greenspan further stated that these technologies did not "just happen, they were incubated," and that how they occurred could provide important lessons for organizations. We are presenting some leadership, managerial, strategic, and design guidelines that must be understood to enable the use of powerful new technologies in providing better information systems. These are the foundation of leading with IS/IT KQ. Understanding the leadership implications of IS/IT KQ requires new approaches for those who hope to exploit these new technologies. With that said, our overall question becomes, "How can you learn to manage those far-reaching changes?" We will first discuss how IS and IT can be better utilized in organizations, and then how IS needs to be designed to help high-$LQ^{©}$ leaders of the future understand how to manage IS/IT toward those ends.

They're Everywhere!

Computers, automation, software, and IT—the enablers of IS—are everywhere. Think about your typical day: software is in alarm clocks, coffee makers, microwaves, TVs, electric razors, and your car. You used all of these this morning, right? Before you got into your car the seat was automatically put back to "your" position when you used your remote to open the car (you and your wife are certainly not the same size nor do you like your seats adjusted the same, nor do you listen to the same radio station). The car's windshield wipers sense rain and click on for a minute. The car warns you it's time for an oil change and your brake pads are about to wear through. When you screech to a halt at the freeway entrance the computerized antilock brakes make sure the car stops straight even though the streets are slick. The traffic lights at the freeway entrance are computerized, you autodial someone on your cell phone, and you ask your car radio to seek another station even as you think to get directions to your first appointment on your in-car electronic map. Your computerized badge hanging on your rearview mirror gets you into your parking lot just as the one on your windshield paid your toll road fee automatically as you sped through the tollbooth. Then you get out your entry badge to get into your office, check your voice mail, and check your e-mail. "Beep-beep"—your personal organizer tells you it's time for that video conferencing session.

The restaurant where you eat lunch uses a computer to record what you ordered and to cook your meal. A quick check of your vibrating phone and you decide you don't want to talk to that guy at lunch. That afternoon, your broker calls you with a great buy that has just been brought to his attention by his computer's autotrack system. Your travel agent calls about some deal that is being offered for those in your group who are going to Italy this summer. On the way home, a stop at Wal-Mart is necessary to get the 15 things you want and to get some money from your debit card.

You arrive at home and the darned entry alarm has to be reprogrammed, as do the sprinkler system and the answering machine: there must have been a storm! Then as you sit down to a nice microwave meal, the phone system that autodials you gets alerted that you are eating and calls you! You wonder quickly why the "National Do Not Call Registry" did not block that crummy call. You finish eating while yelling at the telemarketer. As you say, "Take my name off the list," you think about getting one of those autobleepers for killing junk calls. But you are nice to the lady from the Disabled Veterans on the next call. She at least calls from home where you can see her name and return phone number. Now you can catch *The Oprah Winfrey Show,* which you missed (it was automatically TIVO'ed for you), and then you can call up a film, since you don't want to go to the video store. During the movie, you order those shirts you saw in a Land's End catalog. When they answer your call, they refer to you by name and know your size. You answer a few e-mails, schedule a few meetings, and update your Palm Pilot. The next day Land's End sends you another catalog that might interest you, since they see you are ordering shirts for your trip to Italy this summer.

At last you are ready for bed. You use your electric computer-controlled toothbrush, then your electric blanket, then the adjustable bed (you and your wife don't like the same firmness in a bed). Finally, you kiss your wife good night. She is real—no computer there—"Honey," she says, "put the TV on automatic snooze; I like for it to go off after I'm asleep." You dream about being on a deserted island without electricity—hey, heard about those wind-up radios?

Do you get the point? The real question is, "Does all of this stuff work like we think it should?" "Not quite," is most likely the answer. Why not? In part it is because most people who write software are less social than most of the rest of us because writing computer software is hard work. Programming requires the breaking down of activities into the tiniest of steps, and then stringing those steps into sequences that fit together. So the people who develop the software we use every minute of every day really don't think like we do, and they are generally not led very well. Our question quickly becomes, "Can we better lead the staff that designs and programs our IS so the products and services we use will more closely meet the needs of the average person?" The answer is yes, but first we must understand why and understand the contribution made by our Knowledge Quotient.

The Need for New Approaches to IS—Equate to Implementation of Other Technologies

An organization's IS are much more determinate of the products and services of our organizations than we really want to believe. And they actually drive how we accomplish our work. In addition to needing IS that are more people-friendly and allow more innovativeness, the need to improve competencies is being driven by a combination of interacting factors. They include instantaneously available global information, accelerating technological innovation, worldwide deregulation and privatization, and the opening of markets and competition (Linkow, 1999). Continuing on these themes, Cortada and Hargraves (1999) describe how IBM and other firms are moving into the "networked age." In the chapter, "How the Rules of the Game Are Changing," these authors list the 21 themes that are now defining the game of commerce and that, therefore, should help us mold our IS to accommodate commerce in the future. These themes illustrate the need for IS to capture, retain, and manage information from multiple sources while handling change and new avenues of interconnectivity. IS of today are powerful enough to aid in gaining a sustainable competitive advantage. Organizations now have the opportunity to gather operational and external data and manipulate it in ways that can transform the data into the basis for solid decisions. But to do this requires the transformation of data into information and the evaluation of that information using the judgment of a decision-maker. IS have the capability to take data, the raw material of living and doing business, and synthesize it in a fashion that develops useful knowledge for your KQ and your organization's IQ. Then this useful knowledge can be applied in decision-making.

Decisions are merely sets of choices under varying degrees of uncertainty, and knowledge is useful in decreasing uncertainty. But information and knowledge are not enough. To attain a sustainable competitive advantage, IS must retain the right *knowledge* until the right *time* and then communicate it to the right *people* who can use it. Indeed, it seems that few leaders understand these relationships well enough to develop truly useful information systems.

We simply are not gathering all the right data for true decision support systems, in part because it is impossible to map out all information that might be required in our rapidly changing world. Yet we must do this effectively because executive decisions are by nature ever-changing and non-repetitive, and we can see that this fact is even truer today than it has ever been before: things just get faster and more complex by the minute. Business intelligence applications are now possible using data-warehousing and online analytical processing. These are good technical solutions, but they are not solid foundations upon which to base decision support systems. In order to implement them for sustainable competitive advantage, IS need to capture the right information and provide design flexibility. We must resist the urge to get *prematurely physical* and select the systems before we decide truly what is needed to improve the lot of our organization, employees, suppliers, and customers while keeping our competition at bay.

A Leadership Perspective Needed for Real KQ

As Andrew Carnegie once said, "The only irreplaceable capital an organization possesses is the knowledge and ability of its people. The productivity of that capital depends on how effectively people share their competence with those who can use it" (Cortada and Hargraves, 1999, p. 82). Without the commitment to generating and sharing knowledge, no IS or other related technology will insure a competitive edge. Organizations can use a "garden variety" of decision, information, material, process, and telecommunications technologies to beat their competitors. Management of new technologies will transform how an organization does its business. That transformation can and will be difficult for an organization; an effective Knowledge Quotient among leadership then becomes the initial key to a successful IS/IT or other technology implementation.

Many managers fail because they don't properly execute management fundamentals—selecting, directing, evaluating, and rewarding. So regardless of the technology guidelines and direction we develop in a particular project, people and processes must be managed effectively. As Jim Collins said in his book, *Good To Great* (2001), getting the right people is the first step in improvement. We are identifying the criteria for effective IS/IT application, but we will precede that by stressing how to manage "human capital" to gain the full potential of IS or other technological applications.

One difficulty in structuring new IS applications in decision-making results from individual preferences and modes of operation. Everyone has developed frames of reference, contexts, histories, and educational experiences that can lead to bad (or at least skewed) decisions. These limit our ability to use information technology (IT) in innovative ways, as we have mentioned so often. To avoid the common pitfalls, the KQ leader must exercise an extremely disciplined approach to judgments. This point cannot be emphasized enough. Managers do this by listening objectively to others and considering possibilities that are outside preconceived notions. One of IS's greatest potentials lies in helping organizational leaders make more rational decisions by pointing out biases and alternatives outside of their norms. A good IS can help decision makers by presenting the current state as just another alternative.

Executives and managers are often overwhelmed by emerging technologies. The amount of available information is but one of the problems. The increased speed of technological change in the area of information is outpacing the ability of most organizations to research, evaluate, test, install, and use it for competitive advantage. Indeed, the speed of technological change means that we could all take 23.9 hours of our day just gaining new knowledge. We have to learn to focus our time and attention, and to use the time and attention of our followers, if we are to have a chance at staying abreast of the latest developments that might affect us and our organizations.

IS/IT or Other Technology Strategy for Competitive Advantage—Tough but Doable

A strategic competitive advantage can happen when a capable KQ leader applies technology to the strategic needs of the organization. The key is to insure that the technology being implemented provides functionality, quality, speed, cost advantages, or information needed by the organization to offer something of value that is rare, that cannot be easily imitated, and for which no real substitute exists (Barney, 1991). This indeed is a tough criteria that requires a lot of thought, knowledge, and hard work.

Identifying the issues that really matter in using technology for competitive advantage requires systematic innovation of our methods of learning. Information gathered from outside an organization is more important than information that comes from inside. Yet current IS capture mostly inside information. Likewise, any technology used must expand—not limit—an organization over time.

We see most leaders being more comfortable investing in physical capital than in human-knowledge capital. CEOs must be convinced that sound investments lie with people and a solid technology infrastructure, not just plant and equipment, and specifically IT hardware. Many think that by buying the latest, greatest, fastest, smallest, and most expensive piece of IT equipment they are in the networked age. Little do they know that *buying* is easy—*using* for success is very difficult! The following comments apply to all technology:

> The [technology] doesn't manage, the people do (p. 16)....You need to solve the management problems and get the relationships between functions sorted out before you can fire up the [technology]. (Jacobs and Whybark, 2000, p. 12)

Listed below are our guidelines for management principles to be followed to insure that strategic development is directed toward using technological tools for gaining and maintaining a competitive advantage, not just for the sake of being a leading-edge user:

1.   Understanding the overriding necessity of gaining a **shared commitment** to an organizational purpose that places the ultimate value on the human capital.

2.   Building **human resources systems and policies** that support the hiring, training, and rewarding of people who see the necessity for, and can add value to, the principles of speed, innovation, and recognition of the necessity to meet changing customer needs.

3.   Instituting the cornerstone of improvement— **measurement**.

4.   Understanding that **relationships and discipline** are keys to successful management. This applies to constituents—organizations, self, and all human resources.

5.   Perceiving that the new rules of commerce require a **flexible broadening** of awareness, perspectives, and alternatives.

6.   Knowing that the understanding of individual and organizational **frames and biases** is a way to expand alternatives and reach new horizons.

7.   Committing to **usefulness that is defined by customers,** not technology.

8. Insuring that "necessary" **function-centered automation** must always override technology-centered functionality.

9. Showing that **flexibility** is the key to survival.

10. Having management recognition and rewards that direct the organization toward continuous improvements, adding of new features that meet changing needs, and systematic innovation: **reward trying**, not just success!

11. Knowing that **capturing information outside** of an organization matters more than inside information.

See—we said it would not be easy! A technology will not contribute to a sustainable competitive advantage without recognizing in its design the human resources, customers, relationships, and ability to recognize change. The objective of all technology design is to provide leverage that supports these overriding leadership essentials. In other words, the technology should not be the end in itself; the end should simply be how the technology allows an organization to more effectively and efficiently meet the needs of some of its constituents.

Remember: We said that Knowledge Quotient leaders must recognize the need to shift emphasis from the management of stability and control to leadership directed toward speed, empowerment, flexibility, and continuous improvement. Furthermore, these improvements must be directed toward product, service, administration, process, and managerial and organizational innovation. The power of new technologies makes management especially critical for organizations to become and remain innovative—indeed, even for organizations to survive. Technology must be flexible enough to be adaptable to changes in the organization's management and its external environment. This is also true for other technologies such as plant automations or telecom automations.

Technological change, specifically using IT in IS, has led to success for some organizations. However, using high technology for IS does not guarantee success. Many important innovations relating to IS for competitive advantage are mundane, involving no breakthroughs. All information innovations have the potential of providing competitive advantages and should be viewed as critically as major technological information systems changes. How do we take advantage of the "hi-low-no-tech" IS promised potential? Effective KQ leaders start by formulating an IS strategy for competitive advantage.

Formulating a Technology Strategy

A strategy that allows organizations to achieve technology's potential is developed according to the following guidelines:

1. Identifying all information, processes, and interfaces used in an organization's value chain.

2. Identifying potentially relevant technologies in other industries and under scientific development.

3. Determining the likely path of change in key technologies.

4. Determining which potential technologies are most significant for competitive advantage and industry structure.

5. Looking at the key information and processes—that is, those that take the most time or cost the most—and select some for updating or replacement; don't forget you might have to totally revamp everything, but try to do it incrementally, not all at once.

6. Assessing a firm's relative capabilities in important technologies and the cost of making improvements.

7. Selecting a technology strategy that reinforces the firm's overall competitive strategy.

8. Reinforcing individual business unit technology strategies at the corporate level to support the overall corporate technology strategy.

9. Insuring that technology supports organizational strategies and fits organizational capabilities, resources, and needs.

10. Doing it, measuring it, adjusting, and going back to step one!

Managers who follow the above steps to formulate a technology strategy, however, must implement a consistent reward structure. All too often, poor KQ leaders say they want one thing, but they reward for another. Managers often say they want quality and profit, yet pay for production and sales. They preach the need for service, but measure work by number of customers handled or the length of the customer service phone call. They seek long-term profits, but manage and control by quarterly earnings. They talk about the need for innovation, but punish failure. Management's commitment to continuous innovation and change must be shown through its reward systems (Service and Boockholdt, 1998).

Regardless of the industry or the circumstances, getting the right people to identify the right problems is more important than determining the correct answers. Therefore, rewards must be geared toward identification and not necessarily toward solution. To help this process, an IS designed for strategic advantage must have the ability to capture, store, and retrieve volumes of information from customers and potential customers. This requires implementing the IS strategy.

Likewise, any technology, from the large-scale ERPs to walkie-talkie-type systems, requires a strategic plan, SMART (**S**pecific **M**easurable actions that are **A**ttainable, **R**elevant, and **T**ime-bounded) objectives, and proper rewards. Never forget the human interface element when implementing any new technology.

Implementing an IS or Other Technology Strategy

Bill Gates is usually considered an effective KQ leader. Gates (1999) says that how you gather, manage, and use information is the chief determinant of whether you win or lose. The information flow is the lifeblood of any business. The right information must reach the right people at the right time. He goes on to say that most organizations have the technology they need, but they don't always know how to use what they have. The only way to make money today is to solve customers' problems. An organization must build its technology infrastructure to add value to the business it is in.

Outlined in Appendix 11.2 is a development process that has been successful in creating systems or selecting other technologies for competitive advantage. It is a repetitive process: its steps are repeated when new information or technologies become available. It has been successful because it facilitates innovation and accommodates changes in the organization's environment.

Managers can use this process to develop effective IS for competitive advantage or as criteria for selecting other technologies. The most effective way to gain and sustain competitive advantage often involves speed—in designing, building, and delivering. The effective way must add value for key constituents. Most often we see exceptional performers rapidly adopting new technologies without necessarily changing niches.

Success Components of IS

The above discussion includes suggestions for identifying and developing IS for competitive advantage. These suggestions, however, lead to the following questions: "How do managers identify ways of deploying IS in their organizations to achieve competitive advantage?" and "How do managers know that their IS/IT adequately serve this purpose?"

We feel that an organization must work to determine the success factors of its chief technology applications, and we are providing an example of success components that apply to IS in particular—but they also apply to any other technology application usage. The IS success factors are shown in outline form in Appendix 11.3.

These factors are useful guidelines for developing IS aimed at a competitive advantage, and as we said, they can be applied to any technology you might wish to use. Look at these principles closely, for they can give you great guidelines for all management and leadership issues. We feel strongly that the effective KQ leader will start any IS/IT or technology re-evaluative process with the correct questions. Again, we are using IS primarily because that's what we know, but these questions can be adapted for any technology reevaluation. Remember: If the questions themselves are wrong, the answers are simply irrelevant. Experience and research have pointed to the questions shown in Appendix 11.4 as questions that must be addressed for a valid IS/IT or technology change to occur.

All technology employed must be about leverage used to solve real problems and address real opportunities. Success comes when major problems are solved (effectiveness), price performance is improved (efficiency), and the users are satisfied (competitive advantage).

Why and How Do Leaders of the Future Study IS/IT and Emerging Technologies?

How to Stay Abreast of the Latest and Greatest

Most leaders are overwhelmed by IS and IT and all types of emerging technologies. The increased speed of technological change and the increasing capabilities of IS and IT are outpacing the ability of organizational leaders to grasp them. Those leaders are having difficulty researching, evaluating, choosing, developing, testing, installing, and monitoring technology use for daily business needs, let alone for competitive advantage. The effective KQ leader will figure out a way to help aspiring managers better handle these technology capabilities and align them with other organizational functions that are much more comfortable to manage. That is KQ at its technological best.

Theory and Practice

How We Got Here and Where We Are Going

From the American university perspective and understanding that every country now competes globally, we need to recall that, at the end of WWII, America appeared to be unstoppable. The U.S. basically ruled the world technologically and economically. America was the stronghold of steel, automobiles, electronics, aviation, aerospace, computers, and communications. In the past 25 years, the U.S. has lost much of that leadership to—among others—Japan and Germany, and, of late, India and China. However, America still reigns supreme in the services industries. But logic and history predict that America's leadership will not last for long. When an entity becomes profitable and known, it is duplicated and leapfrogged. What if America's major competitors become more successful in the service arena? Be warned: Our intellectual jobs are being farmed out to India at an alarming rate. This is where the alignment of strategy and technology can potentially help the U.S. retain the leadership position in services and regain the top spot in manufacturing.

In order to realize these potentials, upper management can no longer think of computers, networks, and other technologies as "black boxes" and cell phones that can be managed only by techies for techies. All technologies, especially IS, must meet organizational needs; any organizational technological component must share a mutual understanding of its part in the organization's purpose. Tech projects must align with global missions and objectives, and it is necessary to understand the technology's specific part in attainment of those overall purposes. Specific ways to measure the results and related rewards must be put into place. Realistic and relevant cost-effective approaches to information needs must be properly addressed.

Knowledge Quotient leaders should study technical aspects, but this should not divert them from the major purpose. Keep asking yourself three critical questions as you review technology concepts and trends:

1. How will this help in leading any technology function?

2. How will this help in strategic alignment of technology and the overall organization?

3. How can technology be used to sustain strategic competitive advantage?

To be a leader with an effective Knowledge Quotient, you must have an overriding goal to understand enough to lead technology functions as well as you would lead another, more familiar, function. What is needed is a solid knowledge base of the technology you are managing, a conceptual way of thinking that allows you to figure out how to lead in unique situations where you encourage innovation in technology as well as you do in less complex areas. You don't have to be able to *do* it all, but you do have to *understand* it all at a conceptual level. We have supplied a small amount of what you might need to be able to develop that conceptual thinking in technological areas, especially IS/IT. Appendix 11.5 shows some interesting points to ponder in the IS/IT area. Develop some similar points for yourself in your area of technological concern.

Technology Conclusions

We encourage you to remember that technology success is **not just** functionality, information, productivity, innovation, TQM, teams, globalization, computers, IS/IT, speed, connectivity, compatibility, the customer, the products, the services, hardware, or software…it is the KQ of leadership within the institution. Moreover, its purpose must be to realize a shared commitment on the part of the institution's members to satisfy the needs of others with: 1) continuous improvements, 2) meeting changing needs, and 3) systematic innovation that allow the organization to develop a distinctive competency that further allows it to understand why someone would chose it over the competition.

We need technologies, computers, networks, and systems that do things, not challenge the users to figure out a way to do things. Often technologies are far too complex. The technology should be quiet, invisible, and unobtrusive. Our technology complexities and frustrations are largely due to the attempt to cram far too many functions into a single box that sits on the desktop. To develop better technologies, KQ leaders need to hire people with human-centered skills, who will find out what customers want and desire—avoid technology-centered and marketing-minded people as systems developers. This is the framework for KQ success. Everything else is window dressing. This is no different for managing technology: the rewards still drive the behavior. Ultimately, it will be up to the KQ leader to find out how his/her organization can stay up on technology and take advantage of technological innovations as they come at an ever-increasing pace.

We realize that we've written perhaps too much about innovation, technology, IS, and IT, but in our defense we are trying to demonstrate the depth of knowledge required in just one area in which the leaders of the future must lead and manage: technological application. Yet you need to appreciate that we have written so little of what you will need to know to be a successful, technologically astute leader. Leaders of the future have to have a large KQ related to technology.

Be truthful and realize that most people are lazy in many areas of knowledge acquisition. When areas are outside our expertise we have a hard time knowing what we need to know—develop some trusted advisors in key knowledge areas of your organization, profession, and industry. A general manager must know enough to manage accounting, finance, R&D, IS, technologies of all types, HR, legal, and so on. Some failed to get the correct level of accounting knowledge and are in jail to prove it!

It's now time to see what has been reported on our $LQ^{©}$ instruments as hallmarks of someone with a good KQ. In this section of KQ, we are going for brevity, since we have covered so much up to this point. Keep in mind our triangle and 2X2 matrix as you review the following normally identified KQ-related traits, and seek to understand where you might stand on those traits.

Normal Natural KQ Strengths—Quadrant 1 of the KQ 2X2 Matrix

The first trait that was reported to us as a natural strength is **driven-thirsty- seeker**. It seems we all know people who just can't ask or know enough. They always want more. It seems from what our parents say that this is natural, and Dave and Bill have a fair amount of it. One of our young students reads some 100 pages a day outside his schoolwork: that's a high KQ!

Many seem to gain new knowledge, but fewer seem to **recognize the important** things that constantly appear on the horizon. This second trait does seem to be natural, because some people are good at understanding what is important in the area of new knowledge. Alan Greenspan seems to exhibit this quotient very well.

The next natural trait that is reported very often points to being **innovative and technologically astute**. We feel OK about linking these together, since most people who are innovative also use technology well. The opposite, however, is not always true. Michael Dell is often reported in this area.

The final trait reported as a natural characteristic is **awareness and constant scanning**. Those who constantly look at their environment and are aware of everything seem to be ahead of the rest of us. These high-KQ people see the new products and services and often can't understand why we can't see them. Peter Lynch is arguably the best mutual fund investor of all time. He tried to tell us in his first book that we could be good at identifying what is going to be the next and latest and greatest company: boy, was he wrong! Since he apparently has this trait naturally, he assumed all of us would have it. It's a KQ trait that few have.

Normal Natural KQ Weaknesses—Quadrant 3 of the KQ 2X2 Matrix

If you really think about it, you will see that most people struggle to keep up with the latest developments. Thus, the first natural weakness we found among our respondents was **not evolving**. We know that most people are victims of conditioning: They like the status quo and don't want things to change. The "same old same old" is simply comfortable, safe, and easy. How many times have you heard, "I just wish things would quit changing; I like things the way they used to be in the good old days." If you think about it, overall the *good old days* have basically been *now*. The world is getting safer, freer, and more educated and affluent; but it is hard to see that with the doom-and-gloom trends in the overly dramatized and under-factual reporting that is called newscasting. Sadly, it seems that Ralph Nader comes to mind in this area!

The second natural weakness reported is **not being stimulated to desire new knowledge**. It seems that many leaders desire no stimulation that will get them to want new knowledge. Perhaps this is why we see so few people returning to the university for more education. Though of late a lot of adults are going back for more education, they remain a small percentage of those people who *could* go back. Most people remain where they first stop on the formal-education ladder. It would make sense that most end up where they start on the information-education ladder as well: that is indeed sad. Archie Bunker, of the *All in the Family* TV show, could be the poster boy for this trait.

The third natural weakness says that people **can't recognize new things**. Try showing something new to someone, and in general, you'll see that they have a hard time visualizing how and for what it might be used. Most can't figure out what to do with something new. Just think about the first time you saw a fax, cell phone, new features on a car, and so on. We'll bet many of you have a tough time figuring out how to use something until you are told what it is for!

Bill is an old-time programmer who wrote computer programs in Assembler Language (close to machine language), yet he can't figure out how to program his VCR. Yes, he exhibits some of these natural weaknesses: **technologically or innovatively challenged**. Many would not recognize an innovative possibility if it fell from the sky and hit them on the head. It seems the world is full of technologically and innovatively challenged people. Perhaps that is why we have few entrepreneurs and even fewer inventors. Young kids are not this way, so why should you be?

Normal Nurtured KQ Strengths—Quadrant 2 of the KQ 2X2 Matrix

One of the best strengths a KQ leader can develop relates to systems thinking. That is the ability to see the whole and the parts. It seems many are good at one or the other, but few are good at both. **Balancing micro- and macro-focus** is a unique nurtured trait that we discovered among the beta testers for *The Leadership Quotient*. Balancing looking at the big picture and the small picture is difficult, but good KQ leaders are able to do it. On the national scene, you might contrast the micromanaging presidency of Jimmy Carter (who kept the White House tennis reservation form in his desk) to the macroempowerment philosophy of Bush 41, who saw the work of the country being done by "a thousand points of light."

Some people have **persistence in pursuit** of knowledge of any kind. It seems that those special people among us won't quit asking and wondering and trying. Remember: Dave was frustrated at the "sniff-and-scurry" theme of Spencer Johnson's book, *Who Moved My Cheese?*, so he wrote a response titled *Who MADE My Cheese?* It's a book about the value of persistent production. Persistence is a good trait to improve and is relatively easy for most of us to do better. So just do it. Radio talk-show host Rush Limbaugh is good at this, though the way he exhibits it is not necessarily a good example you should follow! Stephen Hawking is great in his area of expertise.

Even when the KQ leader is not naturally innovative or techno-minded, she can learn from others in the organization and encourage others to be so. This group of people have nurtured their strengths and made sure that they at least **push and recognize innovation and technology** and how it could be better put to use. You don't have to be innovative to use innovations, and you don't have to be a technocrat to use technology!

The final nurtured strength we see belongs to those leaders who **grow with knowledge because they know it reduces uncertainty**. This is something we all can learn, and this will help us move away from the preferred status quo when it is indicated that is the right thing to do. All leadership ultimately calls for decision-making. The more knowledge one has before making a decision, the less the uncertainty that the solution will work.

Normal Nurtured KQ Weaknesses—Quadrant 4 of the KQ 2X2 Matrix

So many today are **closed- or narrow-minded**. But do you suppose that has gotten worse, or better, in the past few years? We would all think that it gets better with more information, but we have seen where a little information causes people to think they know when they don't.

Many people are **distressed over new things**. Yes, new things make our old things obsolete and often make the leader himself obsolete! The most likely part for many is not learning, but retreating and making their world narrower and narrower. At some point, the KQ leader needs to stop distressing and start using. Realize that recognizing distress over something new is the first step in recovery and application.

We get frustrated when our university students say, "I can learn about things I like." Well, so can most everyone, but the truly successful learn from anything and everything and everyone. If you exhibit an **illogical learning tied only to liking** attitude, change it now.

So many leaders have a low KQ because they **say no to technology or innovations**. When it affects us or makes us have to expend any effort, we get lazy and say that's not progress—well, maybe it is.

This concludes our very quick tour of the natural and nurtured weaknesses of the KQ leader. Now is the time to determine your own KQ.

Evaluating Your KQ Personal Profile: Strengths and Weaknesses

Using Your KQ Matrix

As you've done many times before, evaluate yourself in each of the four quadrants. After plotting and identifying your strengths and weaknesses on Figure 11.2, think about your real KQ as you review Figure 11.3 and the note pertaining to this KQ unique leadership triangle. You will increase the curiosity part of your KQ as you think about changing it to match the turbulent environment in which you lead others.

The Situational Quotient is Next!

We purposely spent a large portion of our KQ chapter on technology because we believe that tech knowledge will increasingly become a part of the competitive advantage of all organizations. The KQ leader who has the ability to direct his company to the right match of tech to his specific environment will be the long-term winner.

The next chapter is about the part of the organizational environment that we have termed "The Situational Quotient."

Figure 11.2: YOUR KQ MEASUREMENT AND IMPROVEMENT MATRICES

Evaluate yourself against the reported traits in this Matrix.

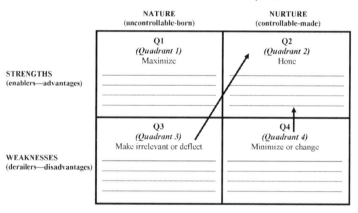

Tailor the Matrix below for yourself!

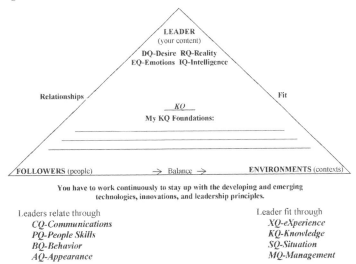

Figure 11.3: YOUR LEADERSHIP LEVERAGE TRIANGLE

In today's complex global-technological world, where time, size, speed, quality, and functionality are rapidly changing, we continuously have to learn to manage new and different areas. A certain level of understanding is required to manage or lead any function; therefore, KQ is not stagnant. It will keep you learning!

Appendix 11.1: Facts and Learning Objectives Critical to KQ

1. Believe that organizational innovativeness is critical to the profitability, adaptability, and survival of organizations. Know that the single largest reason for the decline of organizations is their failure to innovate.

2. Understand the new perspective of organizational theory (OT) based on speed, flexibility, and commitment, which is replacing the old OT perspective based on stability and control.

3. Realize that the cumulative effect of successive incremental improvements in and modifications of established products and processes outpaces efforts to achieve technological breakthroughs: go for hits, not home runs—and some home runs will come naturally! ALL innovations, big or small, technology-based or not, are important for inclusion in strategic planning and strategic processes.

4. Be able to develop new management practices and research approaches required for the new realities of flexibility, speed, experimentation, change, and innovation. Learn to manage the innovation process without stifling it.

5. Organize your organization around innovation. "The strategy itself is the innovation" (Drucker, 1985, p. 243). It is necessary to structure an organization and manage its people in a manner that fosters innovativeness.

6. Develop organizations for excellence with a large capacity for dealing with paradox. Your guiding theory must be dynamic so you can handle both stability and change, considering the tensions and conflict inherent in human systems. Excellent managers and leaders in outstanding organizations have a knack for dealing with paradox and ambiguities and many of our "management" theories are not designed to take this into account. In order to simplify, remain internally consistent, and be applicable to many situations that can be replicated, most theorists tend to eliminate contradictions. We need more malleable and dynamic theories to address change before stability. Stability and control are being replaced by innovation and change as the guiding principles of new management and leadership theory. This does cause conflicts for many, but we must address the dichotomous situations that exist in the real world of organizations not the contrived situations we find so often in our ivory towers of academia.

7. Understand and explain your frames and models, since people do not go in empty-headed but take with them various frameworks. Know how your rose-colored glasses distort your views.

8. Understand that an element common to faltering corporations and their leaders is that they could not or would not adjust to the new reality of collapsed time frames. They waited until later; then it was too late.

9. Realize that a common series of management processes is required to become and remain innovative. Among these are focus, consensus, forecasting needs, improving understanding, structuring awareness in a useful manner, being credible, understanding many viewpoints, understanding synergy, developing ever-broadening support, identifying opposition and indifference, building in structural flexibility, understanding the risk-reward relationship, experimenting as a way of life, and formalizing commitments from all business partners.

10. Understand Drucker's "Discipline of Innovation":

    A. Innovation is purposeful change focused toward economic or social potential.

    B. Entrepreneurship requires commitment to systemic practice of innovation.

    C. Sources are flash of genius, systematic search (within and outside organizations), unexpected occurrences, luck, incongruities, process needs, industry/market changes, demographics, change of perception, new knowledge.

    D. Principles:

    Purposeful analysis of sources of new opportunities, look, ask, and listen

    Preference for simple and focused

    Prefer work over genius—but don't exclude either

    Hire for talent, integrity, knowledge, diligence, persistence, and commitment

    Don't discount luck; use it if it appears, but don't count on it!

11. Understand managing innovation as an uncertainty-reduction process.

    A. Can be incremental, radical, evolutionary, revolutionary, enabling, and disruptive.

    B. Reduction of uncertainty—ends and means.

    C. Solutions and problems coexist for the choosing in all organizations.

    D. Key issues—observant people, valuing experience, linking different technologies and concepts, perseverance, group problem-solving and valuing individuality, potential opportunities that arise, recognizing what might destroy organizations and/or markets, communications, product champions, matching technology and markets; and messy processes such as bootlegging, skunk works, conscious purposeful search.

12. Facilitating innovation in large organizations requires an understanding of:

    A. Innovation = Conception + Invention + Exploitation.

    B. Size—more depersonalization—fewer lateral and vertical communications.

    C. Innovation players: ideators, inventors, technology gatekeepers, champions, sponsors, commercializers, and entrepreneurs and intrapreneurs.

    D. Relay-race and stovepipe models are out—overlapping is the way.

    E. Office of innovation and group review.

    F. Encouragement for idea generation and initial screening.

13. Develop an appreciation for visionary leadership and strategic management relating to:

    A. Transformational leadership: envisioning the desired future organizational state; articulating and communicating visions; and empowering followers.

    B. Leadership as an interactive phenomenon.

    C. Gestalts and metaphors for the process of innovation within organizations—for style, process, content, and context, e.g., timing, audience, players, music.

    D. Look at a variety of innovative leadership styles: creator, idealist, and so on.

    E. Look at Change masters as defined by Kanter (in Henry and Walker, 1991).

14. The three stages of a Change master's journey: formulate and sell a vision, find the power to advance the idea, and maintain momentum.

15. Know and practice the skills needed for innovation: kaleidoscope thinking, communications, persistence, coalition-building, working through teams, sharing the credit, and making the team the hero.

16. Understand the impact of innovation and creativity management on organizational culture and climate. Leaders—or managers, for that matter—cannot fear proven technology; they must use it much like we use automobiles, faxes, airplanes, or PCs: knowing the capabilities without having to understand the technology.

17. Know there is **no** one best way to organize projects for innovation; but above all, top management must really want and stimulate people to be innovative for innovativeness to have a chance of becoming an organization's guiding light. Determine how to make your organization "innovative by design."

18. Know how to choose a new product strategy:

    A. Sell to the broadest possible market.

    B. Use customers/users in design.

    C. Focus on commercially viable translation of ideas.

    D. Work on the integration between departments.

    E. Keep the sources of innovative ideas as wide and diffuse as possible.

    F. Create or allow as many different independent centers of initiative as possible.

19. Understand that, as a strategic weapon, time is the equal of money, "productivity, quality, and even innovation" (in Stalk and Hout's, *Competing Against Time*, 1990).

20. Realize the danger of bottled change, without avoiding it.

21. Determine what separates winners from losers in new products through knowing *The Discipline of Market Leaders* (Treacy and Wiersema, 1995):

    A. Market leaders don't try to be everything to everyone.

    B. They know different customers value different things.

    C. Choose a value discipline that stresses either:

        i. Operational excellence—price-dependability.

        ii. Distribution, information, equipment, the "best deal."

        iii. People who follow the rules.

    D. Product leading strategy featuring: performance-features-quality-performance-innovative people.

    E. Service or customer-intimate strategies featuring customer's partner, empowered-customer-intimate people.

22. Know how to evaluate what are true motives and reality versus what are excuses.

23. Know how to build and treasure relationships. It revolves around *them* before *you!*

24. Understand and practice visualizing.

25. Know how to set step-by-step goals necessary to reach a vision: use SMART objectives, as defined in this book, as a guide.

26. Always be proactive and try: go for it; then you can adapt and adjust.

27. Believe that there are no shortcuts: teamwork and hard work are foundations.

28. Recommit to self-renewal.

Know that you have to understand, accept, and live with the PAST; exist and succeed in the PRESENT; yet remain flexible and poised for the opportunities of the FUTURE.

Appendix 11.2: Development Process for Creating Successful Technologies

Think speed, design, effectiveness, efficiency, and customer value.

1. Select processes for design or redesign with promising payback, risk-reward ratios, or cost-benefit projections. But remember the intangibles may be more important than the tangibles—don't discard things that may be very hard to measure.

2. Identify enablers for new process design. These are people, equipment, processes, governmental or other incentives: many things are enablers.

3. Define business strategy and process vision. Know where you are; then define where you want to be, and the strategies will fall out.

4. Understand the structure and flow of current process. When you understand the flow of your organization's work, you can locate the areas that need the most help.

5. Measure the performance of the current process. Know where you are; then you can know if you have improved things.

6. Design the new process. Start with what you want to accomplish and be very careful to design in the needed flexibility and ease of production.

7. Prototype the new process. Test before committing. Figure out a way to lower the risk of your organization implementations—pilot testing, gradual implementation, or other evolutional approaches.

8. Implement the process and associated systems. Just do it!

9. Communicate ongoing results of the effort. Measure, report, adjust, refine, and continue to monitor.

10. Build commitment toward this type of solution by obtaining feedback from users and making adjustments. Listen to those most affected by the technology.

Appendix 11.3: Success Components for IS and Other Technologies (Service and Maddox, 1999)

AIMING—ROBUSTNESS THROUGH FUNDAMENTALS
1. Complete database
2. Continuous upgrading
3. Fast innovation/New products
4. Linkage to all necessary product, services, customers, suppliers, etc.

CAPTURING—MARKET AND CUSTOMER FOCUS
5. Service added
6. New pricing structures
7. Low-cost provision
8. Speed/Timing or being first
9. Keeping info from customers and non-customers
10. Anticipating future needs and maintaining maximum flexibility

BALANCING—PROVIDE MORE FUNCTIONAL LEVELS TO STRATEGY
11. Making IS and/or IT [all types of technology] support an organizational objective
12. Point to a distinctive competency
13. Know your business and apply IS/IT [all technology] to business needs
14. Redesign or incremental improvement

MEASURING—BEHAVIORAL/STRUCTURAL-INFRASTRUCTURE/FOCUS
15. Benchmarking
16. Assess risks
17. Assess infrastructure
18. Assess managerial impact
19. Assess organizational structures impact
20. Assess managerial focus

DESIGNING and INTEGRATING—DEVELOPMENT PROCESS
21. Quality and design
22. Lock-in and lock-out—for customers and value chain
23. Integrate products
24. Simple solutions
25. Define existing processes
26. Maintenance of special features
27. Testing ideas before committing

Appendix 11.4: Questions to Guide Technologies Application Change Decisions

1. How can we recognize opportunities for IS/IT or other technologies?

2. Should we rent, buy, or build this (ask about each one) new technology? How can we rent, buy, or build what we need?

3. What level of IT is required in our new IS? What level of any technology?

4. How can we transition from legacy systems to client server technology if that is where our organizations currently operate? Transformations from old technology to new technology are more difficult than starting with no technology.

5. What will the role of an Information Systems Division or technology group be versus the role of end users in the development?

6. Why are IS and other technologies so difficult to get in on time and on budget, and how can we avoid those pitfalls?

7. What can IS or the technology do for our distinctive competency?

8. How will we use IS or the technology for our basic business practices, innovativeness, and TQM?

9. How will EDI be used inter- or intra-organizationally?

10. How will we secure our systems and technologies?

11. How will we find and evaluate applications and integrating software or other technologies?

12. How will we apply CBA and other justification methods to IS/IT and technology?

13. What are our heightened expectations for IS/IT and other technologies, and how will we meet them?

14. For in-house development, when will we use SDLC, prototyping, and RAD (Rapid Applications Development)?

15. What parts will be done in-house versus outsourced or purchased?

16. How will backup and security be handled?

17. Do we understand the tech-terms and definitions that will be used in our organizations' new technologies?

18. What are the legal, ethical, social, personal, and personnel issues involved with the development?

19. Have we decided how we will do something before we decide what we will do? All techies immediately start thinking about how.

Appendix 11.5: Points to Ponder About IS and IT and Their Place in Organizations

1. IS center on information and doing justice to business needs by applying IT. The IS should reach beyond computers and networks to sustainable competitive advantage. Most CEOs think their organization's IS are not totally within their control! Many say that the PC bigots have simply taken over from the mainframe bigots. They see the main issues as a common language, a need to shift the levers of change from IT back to strategy, and the proper application of what's old with IS and IT before getting into what's new with IS and IT.

2. TQM and IS: The most effective way to gain and sustain competitive advantage is speed—in designing, building, delivering, etc. The second most effective way is by adding value. However, speed and value come from "the only difference-maker"—people.

3. Strong individual performers and leading organizations adopt new technology quickly, with or without changing niches.

4. Nine themes of the new IT industry: 1) computers are becoming commodities; 2) consolidation and restructuring are occurring; 3) account control is dead—proprietary is out; 4) revenues and profits are shifting to services; 5) the software industry is becoming a parts industry; 6) the playing field is leveling; 7) new distributional channels are moving to the fore; 8) power is shifting from vendor to customers; and 9) the future of technology is being shaped cooperatively.

5. Today's robotics is more about IS and IT than about mechanics. Most robots don't look anything like people; in fact, many are roving tables with PCs on them!

6. We must extend exchanging best practices through computer-aided systems—i.e., AI or ES, and link organizational units within and outside an organization to facilitate: 1) fast and efficient communication—EDI (electronic data interchange), 2) shared memory and systems, 3) solutions or at least solution methods, and 4) innovativeness in all that we do. Many organizations have an "anti-learning" culture where experimentation is discouraged and the sharing of solutions falls prey to competition among units. So few can learn from competitors simply because they won't!

7. The presupposition that there are distinct businesses or industries, indeed even sub-industries, is an old idea whose time has come and gone. In today's global world, companies do not respect traditional industry paradigms and virtual partitions, or even trademarks and confidentialities, for that matter.

8. Wal-Mart's biggest success is probably in their unparalleled involvement in the affairs of their suppliers. They don't ask; they tell!

9.   A Brookings Institution economist found that in 1982 hard assets accounted for an average of 62% of a firm's market value for U.S. manufacturing and mining companies. By 1992, this had gone down to 38% (Stewart, 1995a, p. 157). And today there are many tremendously successful enterprises that have almost no tangible assets.

10. Be reminded: The way to win against Bobby Fischer is, don't play him at chess.

11. U.S. consumers spend much more on PCs than on TVs and other related entertainment devices.

12. Information is the most expensive item in products and services: Look at any organization's budget and add up what is spent keeping up with taxes, accounting and control, reporting internally and externally, advertising (brochures, catalogues, communications internally and externally), IS, conventions (just informing, faxing, e-mailing, newsletters, networks internally and externally), overheads (PowerPoint, research, software, training, videotapes, and so on); and estimate the value of the time people spend finding, updating, maintaining, and using information: you will be floored at the cost.

13. Creating and spreading knowledge among the members of an organization is the basis of innovation. Information is the basic requirement for the creation and spread of knowledge. In today's complex, fast-paced business world, IS and IT offer the ability to capture information from internal and external sources, and the ability to categorize, maintain, and update the captured information; until, finally, information becomes useful knowledge.

14. The terms "mainframe" and "midsized processor" have been replaced with the term "server," and when you consider the percent of information yet to get digitized, you can see that mainframes are with us to stay. Schlender said that in 1996, and it is still true!

15. Louis Gerstner said, "I start every day with customers, but this is an *industry* that starts every day with technology…[because] the customers are changing the way they're thinking about information technology (source unknown)."

16. Wal-Mart's 675,000+ associates are encouraged to know about the business, its profitability, and its systems and technology, because as CEO David Glass asks: "How do you run a $100 billion corporation?" He indicates you do it with knowledgeable employees and his information on one store at a time (source unknown).

17. Instantaneously available global information, accelerating technological innovation, worldwide deregulation and privatization, and the opening of markets and competition are simply moving organizations into a networked age.

Cortada and Hargraves (1999) described the new themes leaders must understand in their chapter, "How The Rules of the Game Are Changing." The following multiple themes that are now defining the game of commerce should help us mold leaders who can accommodate commerce in the future (list directly taken from pp. 26-27).

1. Design, build, sell, and buy anywhere, anytime.

2. Time—and location-independent work and play.

3. Free or unlimited consumer choice.

4. Free for all—no or very low entry or exit barriers.

5. Globally optimized resources (predictive, sense and respond, customer-supplier linked).

6. Global knowledge accessibility.

7. Value networks (seamless, dynamic, focused competencies, disintermediation, and assembly of new value coalitions).

8. Increasing consumer power and move to presumptions (versus consumption), i.e., the consumer will order and schedule production and delivery of offering.

9. Electronic and physical channels will coexist for a while.

10. Consumers will use multiple channels—physical to digital—in all aspects of their lives.

11. Customer segmentation will occur in three tiers (all of which will be used simultaneously): first, by moment of value of event; second, by disposable income; and third, by technology astuteness of the user.

12. Firms will become more customer-intimate and will be more precise in targeting consumers.

13. Though individuals will have network access, the degree of exploitation of interconnectivity will be higher between business and business than between business and consumer in the near term.

14. Firms will shift to Customer Life Share capture rather than Individual Transaction profitability.

15. Owning the content is no guarantee of winning the future. Owning the context (or access of navigation point) will provide the most leverage.

16. Government intervention will occur on strategic issues, though it may not be successful.

17. While disintermediation will occur in many areas (direct enablement), re-intermediation will occur in others (where collaboration increases group power).

18. While business reach or brands may be more global, production and customer reach will be more through multi-local approaches.

19. Consumer preferences and adoption rates are ethnocentric despite ubiquitous channel access.

20. Different regions of the world may end up at different points.

21. Unusual global exchanges will form, e.g., risk securization and exchange.

12

SQ, The Situation Quotient

A true leader understands it is normally not the situation but one's reaction to the situation that makes one become the leader. Those with high SQs do not appear to be brilliant; they appear to be prepared. They understand what's going on and develop strategies to address the situation to make it come out to their advantage. They know that coming into a situation understanding the situation and its circumstances produced effective leadership time after time.

The Situational Quotient is the leader's ability to read a situation and strategize how to make their leadership fit the followers in the specific situation. When a person **shifts his thinking for leadership superiority toward versatility of thought and deed related to understanding the situation at hand**, then his true measure of SQ becomes apparent. SQ includes a great sense of timing and understanding of circumstances as well as measured reactions to the situation as it actually exists, not as we wish it to be. SQ is about using a realistic understanding of the situation to develop a strategy that works.

Viktor Frankl gets our nomination for the Situation Quotient Hall of Fame. *Man's Search for Meaning* is a classic book on surviving by understanding one's situation and accepting the cruel facts without becoming a part of them. Frankl exemplified intellect and spirituality as he accepted his merciless circumstance and chose to deal with it in a manner befitting a saint. Much good has come from the application of therapies developed by Frankl as he reflected on his tortuous experiences. During Frankl's three years of imprisonment in WWII concentration camps under appalling conditions, he started a search for the deeper meaning of human existence. By growing as a human being and finding meaning within the horror and suffering, Frankl exhibited an exceptionally high SQ.

We have reviewed hundreds of books and articles for *LQ*©, and we are amazed at the abundance of leadership material. While all of it has some level of application, much of it contains very simple themes. The simplicity of the message is revealed in many leadership books by their titles: *Fish!*

Sticks; The Go-Getter; Who Moved My Cheese?; Teaching the Elephant to Dance; Martha Inc.; Use What You've Got, and Other Business Lessons I Learned from My Mom; Mexicans and Americans; Poplorica; Monday Morning Leadership; 10 Minute Guide to Leadership; Who Says Elephants Can't Dance?; The Seven-Day Weekend; Celebration of Fools; When Giants Learn to Dance; The Hothouse Effect; The Productive Narcissist; Confessions of an S.O.B.; The Responsibility Virus; The 21 Most Powerful Minutes in a Leader's Day; Passion and Discipline: Don Quixote's Lessons for Leadership; Geeks and Geezers; A Survival Guide for Working With Humans; Leadership Secrets of Attila the Hun;…of Lewis and Clark, Dilbert, Tony Soprano, Machiavelli, Shakespeare, and so on.

We could go on, but you get the point. Perhaps the list of leadership titles reaches its nadir with the title, *The Leadership Secrets of Santa Claus.* Many of these books are reasonably good and contain some useful principles and even thoughtful ideas. But most of these books are simple and don't assume—as we do—that the reader knows the basic principles of management that fill most of the super-hero and the self-help leadership books on the market today. Admittedly, we have used some of these ideas in *The Leadership Quotient.*

Our objective is to move your thinking toward a Frankl model of realistic complexity of leadership: a model that you can figure out how to apply, not a simplistic view of leadership that any "dummy" could use. If there isn't a *Leadership for Dummies*, there should be (there is!!). Our concern about the list of leadership books we just compiled is that few are of sufficient depth to allow an intellectual person to better comprehend the richness of the fruitful interrelations possible between the leader, followers, and environments. Because of the varied factors in the complex world of organizational leadership success, it should be apparent that success is possible only through diligent work and study. Organizational leadership success is impossible through the quick fixes offered by leadership self-help books. We can't see how you as a leader could profit from reading how another great person led in her specific situation because you are not in that situation. Instead, you need an understanding of the reality of the complexity of the interactions of the leader, followers, and environments, which produces a better $LQ^{©}$.

When studying this SQ chapter about interpreting situations and developing strategies, keep the following SQ Commandments in mind:

1.   Start any planning session by asking, "**How are we serving the 'why'** of our organization's existence through the strategies we will develop and follow?" "If a company does not know why it exists, then it will never know if it is failing or succeeding" (Zacharias, 2000, p. 12).

2.   Think **testing before fully committing** whenever possible.

3.   Be a leader who **uses situations to develop leaders** rather than gather followers. Recognize the potential that everyone has to be a better leader.

4. Make **solutions expanding, not limiting**.

5. **Remember timing** when you address any situation and its strategic solution: there are good and bad times for everything.

6. Use situations to **apply the leadership principles** you have learned to grow as a leader and to grow other leaders.

7. Know, among others, the **Situational Leadership model theory** used by Blanchard that asserts that an effective manager varies structure and support based on those being managed and the situation at hand. This is the ability to realize when and where is the time to tell, sell, work for consensus, empower, or delegate. **Do not be hampered by theories**, but do not disregard them either!

8. **Use fortitude, perception, judgment, and ultimately wisdom** when defining a situation or addressing the strategy for any situation.

9. Use systems analysis and **problem-solving techniques** when identifying situations. Regardless of your chosen method: a) start by defining your issue accurately and completely, b) continue to fiddle with the issue to better define it, c) remain flexible to inside- and outside-the-box ideas, d) prepare relentlessly, e) involve everyone all the time, f) forge alliance, and g) challenge all ideas—ask what the underlying assumptions are. Also, note that the normal sequence followed by systems analysts is a good guide for everyone to follow in strategic problem-solving. Systems analysts start by clearly identifying and documenting problems and opportunities in light of the current systems, and then they develop new concepts to fill in or replace where appropriate. These problems, opportunities, and requirements then become the backbone of a new design for the required systems. Rapid Applications Development and test-and-go systems are replacing many of the old systems developed under the Systems Development Life Cycle approach. These new test-before-you-leap concepts point a strategist toward thinking, testing, measuring, adapting; and retesting, rethinking, readapting; and so on.

10. Know **what is developing with a situation**, not just what exists about a situation. "Figure out what awaits you on the other side of the hill.…Most people make the mistake of planning only on the basis of what they know. The trick is to lay what you do know against all there is to know, make the subtraction, and then try to find out as much as possible of the needed-to-know unknown" [recall the KQ chapter?] (Safire and Safire, 2000, p. 18).

11. Remember: **It is better to discuss a situation and not decide** than to decide without discussing (as we've said in many other quotients).

12. **Approach each new situation with the truth**, not what you hope to find. Start by clearly writing down what you hope to find and then see if you can *disprove* it.

13. Become a **strategic thinker**, not just a strategic planner.

14. **Visions can be powerful** when they are shared and understood.

15. Wake up and **observe**; don't just see.

16. Fully comprehend **fit, balance, and what is appropriate** as they relate to **leaders, followers, and situations** at hand.

17. **Strategy** does not deal with future decisions; it **deals with decisions for the future**.

18. Remember history and **the time it has taken to solve major issues**. It was 500 years between the Magna Carta and the Declaration of Independence, and it was 110 years from the American Civil War Reconstruction to the Civil Rights movement!

19. Given the freedom, people on average over time make wise choices.

20. To fully understand a situation, make it specific and simple: **put it in writing**.

Test your assumptions, test your theories, test all thoughts; **but in the end, you must act**. All strategies must **ultimately be doable** for you and your organization. Before we move on in SQ, we need to differentiate between our RQ chapter and what we are espousing for SQ.

SQ Versus RQ from Chapter 3

> *When you are looking, are you looking closely, or from afar: is it a relationship, or a mirage? Be reminded of the following chaos theory example: Imagine slowly pouring water from a glass. When it's viewed normally it looks very smooth, but when it's viewed from a much closer, microscopic view it looks messy and quite confusing with little molecules scrambling all over!*

We defined RQ in Chapter 3 as the varying interpretations of reality and the resulting implications and interactions. We saw that when perceptions of events are not defined very near to reality, imbalance and inappropriate actions that limit a leader's capacity to perform the leadership function normally follow. We said that leadership RQ requires two things: 1) more information, and 2) the wisdom to validly interpret and use the information. A valuable RQ lesson was to understand anew (or for the first time) something about yourself or your situation that others already (or have always) perceived.

Chapter 3 also contained the four dimensions of RQ:

1. your personal self-assessment and orientation

2. your ability to accurately understand how others perceive you

3. your ability to read your current situation

4. your ability to perceive the direction of larger environments

Successful people and leaders want to help others in their learning journeys.

SQ Versus RQ; The SQ in This Current Chapter

On the other hand, SQ is strictly about interpreting and handling the situation at hand as it develops, not about interpreting reality as it is or is likely to become. As such, it is more of an immediate skill than a visioning skill. We call it "envisioning," which denotes the immediacy of the vision. Because of this immediacy, it is even more influenced by the common weaknesses people have related to the filters (see other chapters if you've forgotten the filters) by which they interpret the world.

We admonish the real SQ leader to handle situations with care, understanding how your normal filters distort the situation and being sure your definition of the situation is clear before you develop a strategy to handle it. If you strategize for the wrong situation you might have a perfect strategy, but it would evolve to address the wrong situation. Therefore, we suggest that as you evaluate a situation you remember these simple, yet powerful, points:

• Don't try to be perfect in any situation. Do try to improve over prior similar situations: understand satisficing.

• Don't assume a current situation is exactly like a prior situation. Do identify the subtle as well as major differences.

• Don't fail to know what is inside the box, fail to go outside the box, or fail to see others' boxes.

• Don't fail to see what others see as outside or inside the boxes.

• Don't give up on yourself or others when you are discovering what's inside and outside the box for your situation.

• Don't deny you've been in the box when you have been.

• Don't just focus on what others are doing wrong. Do focus on what you and others can do right.

- Don't worry whether others are helping you in the situation. Do worry whether you are helping others.

- Don't fail to realize that no answer is also an answer: no interpretation of a situation is an interpretation.

- Don't fail to see that the reverse side of a situation also has a reverse side.

- Don't forget that God gives us the tools but does not use them for us.

- Don't forget that it takes an unusual mind and a lot of willpower to analyze the obvious and the status quo of a situation anew.

- Don't fail to seek information about others' failures and successes in similar situations. Do understand what is similar and what is dissimilar.

- Don't fail to reconcile the claims of differing stakeholders and be prepared to manage any problems you may stir up.

- Don't fail to stay on the issue and just fix something that is out of sync (idea taken from the Arbinger Institute, 2000, p. 166, with many modifications).

The first rule of properly defining a situation is to be careful to insure that you are not describing what you want versus what is really there. We will now look at a subset of SQ, strategizing, and see how we must understand strategy in order to become better leaders through enhanced $LQ^{©}$ SQ. After this section on strategy, we will look at modeling your response to the situation.

Strategy: Developing and Understanding Your Strategic Intelligence

Strategy is a journey from planning to implementing, evaluating, and adjusting—but always paying attention and focusing on the right things. We must progress from strategic planning to strategic thinking to, ultimately, strategic leadership. A primary intent of this $LQ^{©}$ SQ section is to help you reach more lofty heights as a strategy-maker. Developing strategy is a skill every would-be leader must hone.

Strategy starts with a vision that clearly provides a picture of what one desires to be at some time in the future. Then it naturally evolves to the development of specific actions necessary to reach the stated visions. These specific actions, moves, or allocations are strategy. From these strategies come goals, which must ultimately be translated into objectives with **S**pecific **M**easurable actions that are **A**ttainable, **R**elevant, and **T**ime-bounded. We call these **SMART** objectives.

The purposes of objectives meeting these SMART criteria are guidance, measurement, indications of adjustments or redirection, and motivation. Indeed, we have moved from strategic planning to strategic management to strategic thinking to strategic leadership. Strategic leadership is serious and hard work directed toward determining how to translate visions and missions into actions that individuals and organizations can actually take.

Think through the different levels of what we have in the past called strategy, and try to separate the ***doing*** from the ***formulating***. The *doing* consists of: 1) administrative preparing of components, 2) operational implementation issues, 3) functional and operational supporting actions, 4) organizational system support arrangements (HR, R&D, IS, Legal, etc.), 5) measuring, monitoring, motivating, and rewarding tools, and 6) related consensus and implementation issues. The *formulating* consists of: 7) the creative developmental issues. In some ways, we should think about issues 1-6 as the micro-strategic issues, and issue 7 as the macro-strategic issue. Here we are stressing the macro-strategic issue, for that indeed is the difficult issue. When it is done wrong, everything else is in vain, for we would implement the wrong things in a very efficient manner! If you get this *what* down correctly then the *how* follows rather predictably without too much difficulty, and the strategy becomes manageable.

The difficult part is deciding exactly what your strategies are to be. Anyone can say they have a vision of being number one in their industry. Likewise, most everyone can come up with measures that can specify what you mean by number one: market share leader and volume of sales are examples. Many people can develop specific SMART objectives with a little training and practice; many can develop monitoring systems, given some of the project management systems that are available. But precious few are creative enough to develop original strategies that can guide an organization toward meeting a specifically identified situation.

The difficult part of the process becomes what is in between the vision and your identified measures of situational success. What actions or moves will propel you or your organization into the desired position that you have envisioned? This generally requires some innovation and new approaches. Will it be through new products (R&D)? Will it be through the best quality (TQM)? Will it be through the best procurement (JIT)? Will it be by offering the most features (functionality), or the best service (best in the world)? Most likely, the advantage will come through a combination of most of the prior components. However, whatever the delivery mechanism, advantage will ultimately come through customer-perceived value, that is, value as the customer defines it. Then, accomplishing these "things" becomes the real strategic issue.

A Starting Point: Understanding Strategy in Today's World

Strategy normally starts with development of a vision to address an acknowledged situation and then progresses to formulation of specific strategic initiatives that can be implemented within the organization. To give the strategy a chance of success and to know when success is met, one must develop measures: feedback and monitoring mechanisms. Then actions must be taken to adapt, adjust, or change as the measures indicate—not looking for what you desire, but for what is actually happening.

Key success factors are attention, focus, fit, and balance. It's important to remember that strategy, in today's hyper-competitive world, must emerge as you reinterpret your ongoing actions that are designed to make your vision really happen. The desirable strategic cycle, as it has evolved, is represented in the following ten steps:

1. Understand the real situation or problem, not the presenting complaint or your perception of the situation. Understand the **strengths and weaknesses (SW)** of yourself, your top management team, and your business and industry; and its environments and the **opportunities and threats (OT)** that exist in these complex arenas (Porter, 1980, 1985, and 1990). Every situation is viewed in three ways:

    a. The real or objective truth—only God really knows this.

    b. The differing perceptions of all those involved.

    c. How the situation gets enacted or played out. The key is for your perception to be as close as possible to reality and to manage the others involved in order to get them to play out the situation as you perceive it or want it to be. When a person is in charge, she can use power to make sure the situation plays out as she desires. However, when she is no longer in charge, she must use influence, manipulation, management, and politics to direct others to think her way (Gerloff, 1985).

2. Define and then **continually reassess and redefine** as appropriate:

    a. **Why would someone do business** with your organization? Every organization must have something of value that causes customers to choose that organization over its competitors. Your situational strategy must not change this competitive advantage because it's the reason for the firm's existence.

    b. How can your organization **become and remain innovative**? This is the key to a sustainable competitive advantage—something that is of value, rare, hard to imitate, and makes substitutes unlikely (Barney, 1986, 1991, and 1995). The key is constant incremental reinvention of your organization's distinctive competency. Any strategy must insure that innovativeness is not destroyed.

3. **Notice things**—pay attention to the right trends and developments; never assume that any trends or developments do not affect your organization (Davenport and Beck, 2001).

4. Clarify and interpret what you see and project as the **direction of trends** of doing business that are developing in your industry and its greater environment (Cortada and Hargraves, 1999).

5. Formulate **new beliefs and understandings** of how your **organization fits** into its industry and its all environments—how they currently are and how they are becoming (Tichy and Devanna, 1986).

6. **Focus your desire and commitment.** Understand what you might do (is there a market for it?), what you can do (do you have the expertise or resources to do it?), what you want to do (is it within the organization's mission—desires?), and what you ought to do (is it right?). Do these things to establish a vision that is a mental image of possible and desirable future states that has foresight, breadth, uniqueness, consensus, accountability, and doability.

7. **Develop viable alternatives.** Always give status quo the same criteria as the other alternatives. Understand why you choose an alternative.

    a. Picture the future and focus on your vision of the future.

    b. Learn as much as you can about the situation.

    c. Concentrate on the big picture and all of its parts.

    d. Look for breakthrough ideas.

    e. Be willing to go outside the box or stay inside the box.

    f. Be alert for patterns and cycles.

    g. View change as an opportunity.

    h. Be willing to confront tradition but hold to your basic values.

    i. Beware of pooling of ignorance.

    j. Give your ideas a reality check.

8. **Decide and go for it.** Develop strategies to pursue the purpose and overall missions and visions dictated by the situation you are addressing. Strategies are moves and actions—"things" you are going to do to complete established objectives. Balance committing to a course of action with testing the waters and adjusting when you see it must be done.

9. Measure—**feedback. Establish SMART objectives** and use them, but do not fail to adapt if something indicates you should, e.g., when there is an economic downturn you cannot expect to continue as normal. Recall **S = Specific, M = Measurable, A = Attainable, R = Relevant and/or Realistic, and T = Time-bounded**.

10. **Adjust and continue #1-9** (not necessarily sequentially).

High-Situation Quotient leaders are good at strategy because strategy is the leader's interpretation of the situation he is in. As we have pointed out, strategic thinking is a never-ending, circular process and does not follow the normal study, plan, execute, evaluate, and adjust model. It should be more of a rapid incremental process of attention and experimentation. Strategies are the plans of actions and moves that describe resource allocation and other activities for dealing with the factors facing an organization as it attempts to improve its competitive position. **Like visions and missions, strategies change; but successful organizations develop strategies that focus on core competencies, developing synergy, encouraging and motivating organizational members, and creating value for all constituents.** Strategy is implemented through the systems and structures that are the basic architecture for how things get done in an organization. But first and foremost, strategy is about understanding the situation that encompasses the people. It is through people—leaders, followers, customers, other stakeholders, or the public at large—that goals get accomplished (DeKluyver and Pearce, 2003).

Learn to make your strategies focused and clear to everyone. This helps to build a performance-based culture where you can execute your strategies in a more efficient and effective way. Keep your talent by having flat organizations that are fast and involve everyone (Joyce, Nohria, and Roberson, 2003).

The Variables that can be Manipulated to Realize Strategies

Your strategic role as an organizational leader is to build organizational capacity for realizing a sustainable competitive advantage by addressing identified situations, e.g., meeting a competitor's low pricing, adding new functionality in response to competition or customer demands, establishing a new or sustainable segmentation, and so on. You do this only by building a learning organization that the Situational Quotient leader matches to the environment as both the organization and the environment change. Then the SQ leader uncovers new market opportunities, focuses existing resources, and accumulates new resources.

Often the question becomes, "How can you change an institution?" First, realize that organizations are arenas where coalitions vie for dominance, and often it takes a crisis to trigger action. Yes, organizational values and norms (culture) make it hard to transform organizations. Innovative ways to reinterpret existing knowledge, bend the frame of stodgy organizations, and develop solid strategies to accomplish the "new and different" are a must for long-run organizational survival. Organizational success in accomplishing strategies is a function of how one arranges, develops, changes, or uses the organization's policies, systems, and people, related to the following:

1. Culture and climate. Culture is the system of norms, beliefs, and values that shape how an organization behaves. It is among the most difficult aspects of an organization to change. Changing an organization's culture is as difficult as changing the personality of a full-grown person. The

climate is simply how the organization feels, that is, how the culture actually plays in reality (Arnott, 2000).

2. Environments. Adapt or enact new environmental directions or structures.

   a. Objective Environments:
      1. Demographics
      2. Political and legal
      3. Technological
      4. Economic
      5. Governmental or locational
      6. Ecological—physical environments

   b. Subjective cultural environmental views:
      1. Subsistence—methods
      2. Cultural—manmade and physiological
      3. Socio-social systems—interactions, roles, laws, current concerns
      4. Individual—psychology
      5. Inter-individual or socialization—sociology
      6. Projective—myths, fantasies, and religion

3. People. All constituents who have a stake in the organization and their level of involvement.

4. HR practices. The subsystems, policies, procedures, and guidelines that direct hiring, training, and rewarding.

5. Characteristics of the products and services. How closely they fit the organization's distinctive competency and the external environments.

6. Management to Leadership—allocation and attention. Management is needed to keep people in the known: for stability and control. Leadership is needed to move people into the unknown: for change and innovation.

7. Structure. This is the backbone of the organization and how departments and people are arranged.

8. Markets and marketing. Markets set the pace and the tone for your products. They determine what you can sell and the functionality that must be a part of an organization: the demand. Marketing can change things about one's markets. Marketing can create demand and new markets.

9. Systems. Beyond the automated IS, IT, and MIS, to include all organizationally related systems.

10. Policies, procedures, and rules. Remember that rules develop a life of their own and often become an end in themselves.

11. Technology use and level of sophistication.

12. Fit and balance before standing out.

   Though these situational variables are key, they are affected greatly by:

   a. felt necessity,

   b. exhibited commitment,

   c. realized communication, and

   d. ultimately desire of the organizational members as a whole.

   Indeed, we see 1 through 12 as independent variables that determine the dependent variable, organizational success; but those independent variables are mediated by the variables shown as "a" through "d." These relationships are then moderated by:

   a. organizational type, e.g., governmental, for-profit, charity, etc.;

   b. organizational size—could be market cap, assets, number of employees, sales, or locations;

   c. level of automation—for both production and doing business; and

   d. other industry norms, e.g., level of competition, number of players, distinctive competencies, etc. (based on works of Service and others, 1999, 2000, and working papers).

A formulaic expression of this would be as follows:

Organizations' Success in realizing strategies = F (Culture + Environment + Constituents + HR + Characteristics of Products + Management + Leadership + Structure + Markets + Marketing + Technology + Fit/balance/stand-out) as enabled by catalysts of necessity, commitment, communication, and desire; moderated by organizational type, size, and automation, as well as industry.

This overall formula must be understood in light of many different variables according to what one wants to accomplish, and is actually made up of many complex relationships that could also be represented by a formula.

Kaplan and Norton (2001), in *The Strategy-Focused Organization*, stress that in today's highly competitive business climate it has never been more important to implement solid strategies. They present the Balanced Scorecard as a method where an organization uses strategies to create value. The Balance is among 1) financial—growth and profitability; 2) customer—quality and experience; 3) internal business processes—line management and best practices; and 4) learning and growth—relationships and skills. The key is to set up objectives and measures for all of these perspectives to guide the organizational members as they work day to day. Regardless of specific systems or names for them, strategies need to be translated into operational terms, aligned with all organizational units and members, making strategy everyone's continuous job. Leadership must lead the charge for change, but must *not* develop strategies in a vacuum or keep the scorecard only at the top.

Textbooks are usually better for formal learning than the practical knowledge we are encouraging via *The Leadership Quotient*. But the following could be of use to those who are still confused about strategy. Pearce and Robinson's (2005) *Formulation, Implementation, and Control of Competitive Strategy* says that strategic management is the set of decisions and actions that result in the formulation and implementation of plans designed to achieve a company's objectives. Because it involves long-term, future-oriented, complex decision making and requires considerable resources, top-management participation is essential. That's what we're saying about the Situation Quotient: A leader makes decisions that result in actions to accomplish organizational goals.

Strategic management has become a three-tier process involving corporate-, business-, and functional-level planners, support personnel, and workers. At progressively lower levels, strategic activities become more specific, narrow, short-term, and much more action oriented, with lower risks but indeed less opportunity for dramatic impact (adapted from p. 19). We like a lot of what these authors have to say, but overall the text is just too academic and somewhat out of touch. In *The Leadership Quotient*, we stress that we are talking a level or two above this, because we are talking about reality for you, your followers, your environments, and your organizations.

Dess, Lumpkin, and Taylor's (2005) *Strategic Management: Creating Competitive Advantages* (2nd edition) is a good strategy *textbook*. These authors list four attributes of strategic management: 1) directed at overall organizational goals, 2) includes multiple stakeholders, 3) has short-term and long-term perspectives, and 4) recognizes trade-offs between effectiveness and efficiency. They also list the following three processes: 1) strategic analysis, 2) strategic formulation, and 3) strategic implementation. Further, they write about the interaction of corporate governance and stakeholder management as well as discuss environments of globalization, technology, and intellectual capital. A good strategic view can occur when the reader does as the authors suggest and looks closely at the consistency of their visions, missions, strategic objectives, and goals. The authors do a good job of relating an accurate academic view of strategy; however, the book is weak at the applied level.

We recommend two books for their concise packaging of strategic concepts. The first, *Essentials of Strategic Management* (J. D. Hunger and T. L. Wheelen, 2003, 3rd edition), is a great text to use if you are charged with developing a strategic plan. It provides a nice checklist on what you should include in your strategic plan. The second book, *Strategy: A View From The Top: An Executive Perspective* (C. A. de Kluyver and J. A. Pearce II, 2003), is an excellent book for an executive who is overseeing a strategic plan. You will not be disappointed by either of these books. Our experienced MBA students praise these books as the best they had in their MBA experience.

However, one recent book by Mintzberg, Ahlstrand, and Lampel (2005), entitled *Strategy Bites Back,* is head and shoulders above the rest in terms of reality. Though it is not a text, it does cover the essentials in a somewhat unorthodox way. Its tidbits of wisdom are no less true because they often appear somewhat trivial. It is an excellent humorous and spirited read that can appeal to the reader's emotions. It does give the reader a differing view of successful strategy and its many faces.

The Reality Quotient is a Step Toward an Improved Situation Quotient

A first step in understanding and improving your SQ is another intelligence called the Reality Quotient (RQ). **Reality Quotient,** as discussed in detail in the beginning of the chapter, is the measure of one's ability to judge and recognize reality. It includes seeing and understanding self, others, and situations in the present and as they are becoming. Correctly clarifying inclusiveness, consensus, objectives, forward-sightedness, and visions about what the world of your organization is becoming are all part of the leader's RQ. All of the great ideas in the world are of no value to the leader if he cannot make them "real." The more accurately a strategic leader can interpret the reality for his followers, the more influence he will exercise over the group. Everyone defines a reality, and the better you are at interpreting the reality for your followers, the more effective a strategic leader you will be. The key is to determine how much of the future is externally driven by chance, and how much the leader can effect by matching leadership style to the followers in the specific situational environment.

When your RQ results in a solid interpretation of reality, you can use your SQ to insure that you properly address the situations you have identified as critical. Here again, we see RQ as an important introductory understanding of the situational environment and followers as they are and are becoming (a futuristic task). Conversely, SQ is more of a "here and now" concept.

Clarify Your Reality and the Most-Needed Learning for Leadership or Management

To rise to leadership levels in an organization where real strategy is made and a high SQ is required, the leader must follow many prescripts that are hard to define and that require extraordinary judgment and wisdom for effective application. There are no magic bullets for organizational strategy and direction. Many times, we confuse knowing a few things—or even an inordinate number of things—with the wisdom and desire to apply them. SQ requires specificity of reality/future and situation/now.

Everything is changing before our eyes, yet we cannot always recognize where it is going. The past is not always a good indicator of future situations. To clarify the future requires judgment and good decision-making. Too often we focus on just a specific area, such as management, human resources, information systems, operations, globalization, quality, customer service, societal and ethical issues, finance and accounting, marketing, career management, life management, and leadership, when we need to look at all of these areas together.

You as a Strategist—Managerial and Leadership Purposes

The "organizational" leadership intent of learning about your RQ, SQ, and strategy is to help prepare you to lead the many functional areas and individuals from a general manager's (GM) perspective. This is where strategic thinking must go beyond an individual functional area to include issues in other unfamiliar areas that are of significance to an organization. Often, leaders fail at higher levels because they fail to define the situation, by paying attention to the wrong situational cues. Therefore, successful identification, definition, origination, alternative development, implementations, decisional and diffusion issues of problems and opportunities all become part of the leader's composite SQ. Particular attention should be given to the effective organization and management of the many varied functions, stressing decision-making and general executive competence. A real leader does this by exploring the concepts and techniques of leadership and management as she applies them to the many functional and strategic areas within her organization. The strategic effort should always include the strategic interaction of all organizational departments to gain support when important issues are addressed.

Too often, a person stays in a lower-level manager's position because of his SQ. He continues to handle each new situation at a low level and responds only from the perspective of his functional area. To succeed in moving to higher levels, think as if you are in the level you desire: improve your SQ to the level of your leadership aspirations, not your current position.

What Gifted Strategists Do

Any improvement in your knowledge or skill base results in an SQ increase. That's because strategy formulation is about realistic interpretation of the situation. People who are exceptional at strategy are able to think about things both more *closely* and more *distantly*. They are the people who can change their minds quickly when they get new information or see something is not working. They look, listen, and notice as they constantly scan the situation, looking for that golden nugget of information that is critical to success. They can take abstractions and envision what they would look like if they were bent, reshaped, or combined in new and differing ways. They are multitask thinkers and doers. They go outside their normal disciplines and patterns of thinking by reflecting on things and categorizing them in new and innovative ways. This litany of skills is a long and difficult one to compile, but high-SQ people can do it.

Lessons Learned and Considerations

The lessons we have witnessed, if not learned, on the journey to becoming better strategists are shown in Appendix 12.1. These lessons revolve around attention, focus, learning, accepting reality, and being clear about the *who, what, where, when, why, how, might, can, want,* and *ought* of strategy. Apply them if you can, but don't get discouraged by their number. Good leadership concepts that are complete come in big packages!

We have great faith in the strategic management of situations because strategy is something that can be learned, practiced, and improved. Your style is not *the* determining factor, though it is a factor. Achievement of strategic thinking and leadership is a matter of finding better ways to be of use and to use what you notice. The more time you devote to learning, and the less to maneuvering for power, the more successful you will become. Many are doomed by unknowns—attempt to define the unknowns and how you can handle them.

SQ as Molding Your Response to the Situation Contrasting with Blanchard's Situational Leadership Model

Ken Blanchard, of *One Minute Manager* fame, trains leaders using his Situational Leadership model. His approach and concepts are sound and very helpful to aspiring and growing leaders. In his model, Blanchard defines two basic dimensions of behavior to use when working with a follower: 1) **supportive**—from high to low, and 2) **directive**—from high to low. The levels of each of these two behaviors are used to determine when one needs to use leadership behavior that stresses: 1) delegating, 2) supporting, 3) coaching, or 4) directing. A delegation style of leadership should be the style of choice when you must give the assignment to a self-reliant achiever who is capable and committed. A supporting style should occur when you have a capable, cautious leader who is moderately competent and committed. A coaching style should occur when you have a disillusioned person with some competence but a low level of commitment. Finally, directing is the leadership method of choice when the delegatee is an enthusiastic beginner with low competence yet high commitment.

These four styles can also be used to determine the areas where those receiving assignment could be developed. For example, in coaching you would need to address why the delegatee was disillusioned and provide for some training for required competencies, and you would need to look at reward-system changes that could improve levels of commitment. We would expect that for those to whom we could delegate, we would be more of a colleague and a mentor; and on the other extreme, where we direct associates, we could see the need for clear goals, action plans, and very frequent feedback.

When you delegate, you should let the person go and consequently grow. This is a case where you empower and recognize the value of the employee through your actions: just let him do it. On the other extreme, when using directing, do not empower, but assist with problem and solution definitions, providing close supervision and rapid feedback. In a more moderate range when you must use a supporting behavior, you can help more in solving the problems and defining the how-to's as well as evaluating work as the work takes place. Coaching can include interactive problem and solution definitions interspersed with instructional lessons and interactive feedback.

Following are the objectives of Blanchard's Situational Leadership:

A. Understanding leadership as the art of influencing others.

B. Understanding the three skills needed to be an effective situational leader:

   1. Capability to diagnosis willingness and ability.

   2. Ability to be flexible in using leadership styles that vary from levels of autocracy to democracy.

   3. Partnering for performance.

C. Ability to apply diagnosis, flexibility in styles, and partnering for performance.

Now that we have a basic understanding of Blanchard's Situational Leadership styles and appropriate behaviors and development model, let's look at how that model differs from our Situation Quotient (writings of Blanchard and others, 1984, 1985a & b, 1991, 1999, 2003, as well as conference attendance).

Molding Your Response to the Situation Via *LQ*$^{©}$

We see good uses for Blanchard's Situational Leadership explanations and guides. However, our SQ extends this, and the leadership styles chosen by a superiorly trained *LQ*$^{©}$ leader will be much deeper and broader, considering various key factors along many dimensions of the leader, followers, and environments. They will allow you to fit in and stand out in any conceivable leadership situation. The 12 Quotients you learn within this book give you 96 desirable skills and traits. They also give you 96 undesirable skills and traits. All of these 192 skills and traits are ones you can change, fit, adapt, mix, and match, in an almost infinite number of ways, to insure a customized *LQ*$^{©}$ that will enable you to form the proper relationships with your situation and your followers.

That said, don't get too complex; and just remember to look at the Leadership Triangle and 2X2 Measurement and Improvement Matrices for each of the quotients. You are encouraged to simplify for your own special skills, abilities of your followers, and uniqueness of your environments. We say you must build yourself as a leader to the point where most of the considerations and adjustments come almost as second nature. We know that too many of the consultants and leadership writers of today avoid the necessarily complex issues and make leadership something simple so it can be easily taught and remembered. We are too sincere to tell you it's that easy. Furthermore, if you value being a world-class leader you must take the time to understand the more complex and complete picture that to date only $LQ^©$ can provide.

Donald Rumsfeld advocated what he called the "'toolbox approach' to problems, noting that if the only tool you have is a hammer, then every problem looks like a nail. Thus it was essential…never to approach problems with only a hammer because life is complex and not all problems are nails" (Woodward, 2004, p. 281). $LQ^©$ is a toolbox where we have endeavored to include all the known leadership tools made apparent and available.

Successful $LQ^©$ leaders and strategists want to help others in their strategic-learning journeys, and they do this by improving their own SQ and the SQ of their followers. When you can identify a situation correctly and develop a strategy for solving problems and changing paradigms, you will become a better leader. Just remember all situations involve you as the leader, your followers, and the varied contexts within which the situations take place. Our Leadership Triangle, as depicted in Appendix 14.1, provides the best composite of the interactions within our models.

We like to tell people that they need a strategy for every situation. Next time you are faced with a personal or organizational situation, clearly identify the situation and then develop a strategy for handling it. No situation is too small. Be a leader who correctly identifies situations and carefully constructs strategies for addressing problems. Be a strategic thinking, situation-interpreting leader with an effective Situation Quotient.

Description of the Situation Quotient and its Dimensions

As you read the next section, think about the 2X2 Matrix and Triangle, so that you might correctly identify situations and develop strategies to address skills that can be earned and learned for your leadership growth.

Normal Natural SQ Strengths—Quadrant 1 of the SQ 2X2 Matrix

We start this section with the normally reported trait of **comfortable with new circumstances**. Here we find SQ leaders who are receptive and understand that the situation is more what you make of it than it is the actual circumstances of the situation. Bob Hope, Jay Leno, and David Letterman are exemplars in this area, but in a roundabout way. Time after time they have shown us in a humorous way that we are faced with a new reality that we must become comfortable dealing with. We think all those in high public office should listen to what these exemplars have said in many situations and realize that understanding the comedian's point could make you comfortable with the new circumstance of your latest flaw if it were ever made public. You may have to think about this one, but it could be worth it. If you do NOT have this trait, the comedians might give you a clue of what to do.

The second natural trait we see reported is the ability to be a **simplifier**, and we would certainly say that Michael Dell is an exemplar in this area. Dell brought together the hard sell of hardware that changes quickly and the ease of use of the Internet to allow customers to get what they want and need in the most efficient manner possible. This simplification has really bound us to ordering just what we need; or, in the cynic's view, is it really what we are told we need? Regardless, Dell's system has simplified getting what you need and knowing what you get in the very dynamic arena of personal computers.

A third trait is that of timing where people seem to subtly **seize the moment**. The Google Guys adjusted their IPO to apparently seize a *good* moment to go public. Likewise, Sir Richard Branson seems to be an example of this trait. His new vision of capitalism, demonstrated and enhanced by his photogenic media personality, has made him an example for all who want to latch onto a new and different way to make it big in the world of business (Trompenaars and Hampden-Turner, 2002).

The final natural trait we see reported among our *LQ*© testers is the combination of skills that are **observant-aware yet realistic**. Hugo Levecke, Chairman of ABN AMRO Lease Holding, has been described as one who has always met the challenge of renewal in his 17 years of leadership (Trompenaars and Hampden-Turner, 2002). Likewise, we think of Linus Torvalds, of free software fame, as a person with this trait. We can foresee the day when Linux puts Microsoft out of the operating-system business (see *Time*'s April 26, 2004, Special Issue on "The TIME 100").

Quite a few people mentioned traits of "in the mix," "involved," and "jumping in." We see these traits as key parts of all the other traits we show above as natural strengths of SQ.

Normal Natural SQ Weaknesses—Quadrant 3 of the SQ 2X2 Matrix

A most frequently reported trait was that of **aloofness**—unawareness or inattentiveness.

Hare (2004) described JC Penney's leaders as unaware of their arrogance and self-serving attitudes, which led to indecision and bad decisions. Hare's work is relevant, and it can help leaders to learn about how situations evolve and what causes them to go bad when the leader has a low SQ.

This trait also exemplifies itself by those who appeared wrapped up in themselves and their views. Here we can think of no more contrasting example than former President Lyndon Johnson. As president, he had circumstances that worked to his and America's detriment, e.g., Vietnam, but others that worked to his advantage, i.e., the Civil Rights laws for which he was responsible for passing. Ronald Reagan seemed to be the opposite when he understood the circumstances related to Communism and the fact that the U.S. could spend the U.S.S.R. out of existence—we did, and the U.S.S.R. is no more. Reagan often seemed unaware of himself and his image, and focused on serving the betterment of the American people.

The second natural weakness we see is a **complexifier**. Bill recalls a great professor named Mel who loved metaphors. However, his metaphors were deep. We could understand them only after he explained them for a couple of hours; but aren't metaphors supposed to act somewhat as "hooks" we can easily latch onto?

A third weakness we see as natural is **not assimilating into reality**. First, one has to see it; but so many people, when confronted with situational reality, just don't absorb into it. We see Bernard Lewis, as he tries to understand the roots of Muslim rage, as one who has spent his life telling others about reality that most people will not assimilate into (see *Time*'s April 26, 2004, Special Issue on "The TIME 100").

The final natural weakness we see reported is that of **overreaction to new circumstances**. We see some low-SQ people with this trait who seem to have quietly seething personalities just looking for something to overreact to. Here we think about how the *American Idol* candidates often overreact to the valid criticisms of Simon Cowell. Simon is almost always accurate in his cutting wit, and says what almost everyone is thinking but is afraid to express. We see those who listen and follow Simon generally improving, and those who ignore his words losing out and wondering why.

Next, we turn to the nurtured strengths as they have been reported.

Normal Nurtured SQ Strengths—Quadrant 2 of the SQ 2X2 Matrix

In the areas of nurtured strengths, many leaders told us about **appropriate versatility**. This is where people learn how to be highly adaptable, flexible, fitable, and exhibit decisiveness that shows their sense of timing fits the new and unusual situation in which they find themselves. Here we can think of no better example than those represented in Tom Brokaw's (1999) *The Greatest Generation*. It certainly seems that the generation written about in his book was exceptional at versatility and figuring out new circumstances quickly. The young people who stormed the beaches at Normandy quickly became the best fighting men the world had ever seen, and their learning and experience live on today in the personnel of the American military. After winning WWII, that generation came back to America and started the U.S. on a productivity growth path that had been unprecedented in all of history.

A second trait we see defined as a nurtured strength is that of being **analytical and visionary**. We see this often as smart luck, but it certainly is more tactical and strategic than it is lucky. Tom Peters, in his 2003 book on re-imagining, says he is mad about leaders with egos that prevent them from seeing that we are on the verge of the largest and most profound wave of economic change in a thousand years. He says we keep clinging to the models of old and are not innovating and empowering at the rate that can save our organizations. He stresses speed, cunning, and surprise as the keys to winning in our hyper-competitive world of commerce. We see how this book's pronouncement could be combined with Kunstler's (2004) need for hothouse organizations. These are organizations that cultivate new ideas in such a way that they become bastions of the creative processes spawning genius to come up with new ways, knowledge, products, and services that are exceptional in their own time. Kunstler examines the ideas, perceptions, social interactions, values, and other factors that exist in creative organizations, and shows how to develop strategies for building those creative communities in your organization. Not only do we have to worry about our own SQ, but more important perhaps is insuring that our organizations collectively have SQ, wherever it might come from! To reach these goals, one must find leaders who are analytical and have the vision to tactically and strategically lead us to better times.

The third nurtured SQ strength we found was that of **consciously reading** the situation. We see here an awareness of the situation and people at hand. Many people reported pro quarterbacks in this area. More pointed to Peyton Manning than to any other quarterback. Manning does take his abilities to the max through his knowledge and capability of reading the situation and personnel at hand with accuracy and speed. This allows him to lead his team to strike at the right weakness very quickly and effectively. Manning gets the most out of what he has to work with, showing a real ability to adapt to the situation second by second: another aspect of SQ at its best.

The final nurtured SQ strength that was reported to us by our beta group was being a **steady, unflappable, street-smart facilitator**. Unflappability and boldness under pressure exemplify those with this trait. This trait is obvious in Secretary of Defense Donald Rumsfeld and British Prime Minister Tony Blair. Rumsfeld (Woodward, 2004, p. 43) said, "I to ask a lot of questions of people I work with and I tend to give very few orders." He does not seem to suffer from the doubting that gets so many people overwhelmed by problems when the situational scenarios they project produce hundreds of permutations about what to do. Acting will make you stronger and more committed—which is often as important as the chosen course of action. Tony Blair acted, saying, "…no choice is perfect, no cause ideal.…But on this decision hangs the fate of many things" (Woodward, 2004, p. 373).

Normal Nurtured SQ Weaknesses—Quadrant 4 of the SQ 2X2 Matrix

We now turn our attention to the normal nurtured weaknesses of SQ, a category that is headlined by **poor assumptions**. We think the real reason for most poor decisions is the weakness of the assumptions upon which the decisions are based. Yes, there are other reasons, but our assumptions do indeed direct us. At some time or another, all of us have used poor assumptions when making a decision. Here are a few casual assumptions you may have accepted just today:

• We assume that others act this way or that because of our inaccurate assumptions.

• We assume that the reason for the day's change in stock prices is how they were presented on the nightly news.

• We assume that the TV evangelist is preaching the Bible.

• We assume we know why Bill Clinton did what he did.

• We assume that President George W. Bush was wrong about Iraq.

- We assume that President George W. Bush was right about Iraq.

- We assume we know why our husband didn't like the exercycle we got him for Christmas.

- We assume we know why our wife did not like the book, *Slimmer Thighs After 40*, we got her for Christmas.

Check and recheck your assumptions and don't assume they stay correct for very long.

The second trait we see reported to us as a nurtured weakness is the **failure to grasp and understand life's historical lessons** both personally and in the larger worlds within which we work and live. Horowitz (2004) tells us of the dumbest moments in business history. One in particular that really stands out was when a plaque was prepared thanking James Earl Ray for keeping the Martin Luther King Jr. "Dream" alive. James Earl Jones was the real person to thank. Recall that James Earl Ray was King's assassin—what a situational error.

On a more organizational basis, we see Pandya, et al. (2003), who said that the dot-com bubble from the beginning had some people reading the situation as a revolutionary force in changing the world while others saw it as speculative mania—SQ would help us know the difference. There are definitely technological effects that one must see, effects of knowledge more widely dispersed, and alliance opportunities that have to be viewed differently. Communications and related ramifications are also new keys, and there are surely many other effects related to e-commerce, but perhaps the most important effects are the integrative effects on value chains and the elimination of middlemen. We don't want to tell you what we think the final dot-com answer is because the final answer has not been determined yet. Those who think they have this answer are surely wrong and lack the proper SQ. All of these add thoughts to how to have an SQ-intelligent organization.

A third area of nurtured weakness related to SQ is **judgmentalism**. As authors of a book about leadership, we admit that we have to be judgmental or we wouldn't write anything worth reading. Yes, we make the judgment that you will become a better leader by following our advice. Would you read the book if you assumed the opposite?! We humbly suggest, however, that this book is more self-help than "author-help." You're the one making yourself a better leader by following the advice, as it relates specifically to you and your situation, that you discover in each of our Measurement and Improvement Matrices.

The final nurtured weakness we see is that of being **inappropriate for the circumstance at hand**. We think of Ray Romano's character on *Everybody Loves Raymond* as his own TV dad said, "You dumb bastard." Time after time, Raymond showed that he did not have a clue. Yes, his TV wife was going to kill him, but he still just didn't get it. If you've going to be an effective SQ leader, you need to be able to handle the circumstance at hand in a politically correct manner.

As in previous chapters, we now advise you to evaluate yourself against the SQ as it should be for you, compared to your current SQ. This gap is in effect the area for which you must develop a strategic plan for improvement. So get after it and build a better SQ!

Using the SQ Matrix

As you have done in previous chapters, evaluate yourself in each of the four quadrants.

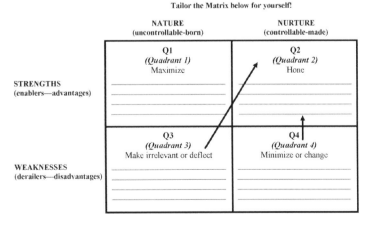

Figure 12.1: YOUR SQ MEASUREMENT AND IMPROVEMENT MATRICES

Evaluate yourself against the reported traits in this Matrix.

	NATURE (uncontrollable-born)	NURTURE (controllable-made)
STRENGTHS (enablers—advantages)	**Q1** ___ comfortable with new circumstances ___ situational simplifier ___ seizes the moment ___ observant-aware-realistic ___ (self-IDed trait)	**Q2** ___ appropriate versatility ___ analytical and visionary ___ consciously reading ___ steady, unflappable—street-smart ___ (self-IDed trait)
WEAKNESSES (derailers—disadvantages)	**Q3** ___ aloofness and/or unawareness ___ situational complexifier ___ won't assimilate into reality ___ over-reaction to new circumstances ___ (self-IDed trait)	**Q4** ___ poor assumptions ___ failure to grasp history ___ judgmentalism ___ inappropriate for circumstances ___ (self-IDed trait)

Tailor the Matrix below for yourself!

	NATURE (uncontrollable-born)	NURTURE (controllable-made)
STRENGTHS (enablers—advantages)	**Q1** *(Quadrant 1)* Maximize	**Q2** *(Quadrant 2)* Hone
WEAKNESSES (derailers—disadvantages)	**Q3** *(Quadrant 3)* Make irrelevant or deflect	**Q4** *(Quadrant 4)* Minimize or change

Evaluating Your SQ Personal Profile: Strengths and Weaknesses

Doing Something About Your SQ!

Develop a strategy for your own SQ improvement. You might use Dr. Phil's seven steps for creating a strategy for getting the life you want:

1. Express your goals clearly in terms of specifics about events and behaviors.

2. Make sure your goals can be measured.

3. Assign time frames to all goals.

4. Make sure your goals are about things that are truly under your control.

5. Develop a program and strategy that will get you to your goal.

6. Break down your goal into doable steps.

7. Create a sense of accountability for progress toward goal accomplishment (taken from McGraw, 2000).

Identify what you feel is under your control and what you feel is not. Basic skills of identifying, limiting distractions, studying, learning, relearning, and ultimately using newfound skills for SQ development will serve you well. Also, practice improvement in your SQ by expressing outwardly your emotions about doing, getting, or being versus just saying you have the Situational Quotient down pat. Remember: If you dwell on the negatives you'll stay where you are. When you are attempting to use the SQ knowledge, apply what Zacharias said: "Anytime Scripture is quoted for the express purpose of advancing one's selfish aims, light is turned into darkness" (p. 154). Know your motives for your own development.

In America, 1 in 10 people tells the other 9 how to vote, where to eat, what to buy, and so on. Basically, these optimistic activists are constantly engaged in clearheaded attempts to think outside the orthodox box and confidently use their vision for change, and we might be able to use what they have to say to adjust our own SQ. But beware, and seek a clear understanding of any pronouncements. You know this type of people—they go to and belong to everything; they are voracious readers who trust their instincts; and they use multiple sources of information to learn, decide, and then do. They are prepared to be where the information is and to converse about it as they set a high pace but are at peace with themselves. They do not just dream about the future; they build it through their work and volunteerism, connecting at any and all levels. They accomplish through studying, reflecting, and connecting, but ultimately through action (Keller and Berry, 2003). Instead of listening to them, why not become one yourself through your superior SQ?

A real SQ leader knows that all top leaders need to see themselves as developers of talent. Fred Hassan is the chairman and CEO of Schering-Plough. He says he has seen people who can speak three to four languages and still have a narrow view of the world, just as he has seen people who speak only English be very effective in different cultures. Jeffrey Immelt, chairman and CEO of General Electric, says that when he meets someone, he doesn't quiz them to see if they could do the job or if they exhibit smoothness. He looks instead for someone with great instincts for his markets, his business, and his subordinates—it is truly about people. He seems to see people as pretty much the same everywhere (Green, et al., 2003). These authors point to parts of an SQ. "In my own work I am constantly and happily surprised by how impossible it is to extinguish the human spirit" (Wheatley, 2001, p. 1). Don't be surprised at how much spirit people exhibit, but do use all of the spirit people want to give: SQ for *LQ*©.

SQ is about strategy and social change. It requires recognition of need, a process, content, and context. Our SQ framework guides the leader to make better decisions and reap the rewards of those decisions. It is not meant to limit options but to help pick the best ones, with room for diversions as appropriate. Do not focus on a particular thing, but do focus on people and leaders and ask, "Where is my SQ going to be in 5, 10, 15 years? What strategic milestones will help this come true?"

SQ is about meeting the challenges of our increasingly virtual world (Cohen and Prusak, 2001). Core competencies must revolve around "creativity, entrepreneurial zeal, and institutional dynamism" (Cortada and Hargraves, 1999, p. 27). "Whenever an individual or a business decides that success has been attained, progress stops" (Thomas Watson, Sr., cited in Miller, 1989, p. 83). Make change happen fast for your SQ.

Start by evaluating where you are and where you need to be, and identify the strategies to get you there. The next chapter is about the Management Quotient. In that chapter, we will explain that even though there is a great difference between leadership and management, a leader can have a high Management Quotient.

Figure 12.2: YOUR LEADERSHIP LEVERAGE TRIANGLE

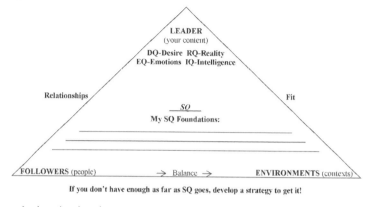

If you don't have enough as far as SQ goes, develop a strategy to get it!

Leaders relate through
 CQ-Communications
 PQ-People Skills
 BQ-Behavior
 AQ-Appearance

Leader fit through
 XQ-eXperience
 KQ-Knowledge
 SQ-Situation
 MQ-Management

Appendix 12.1: Lessons Learned While Becoming a Better Strategist

1. New structures, associated measures, and rewards are often necessary.

2. Status quo is often the easiest, but not often the best.

3. You will all see theft, fraud, and ethical lapses: how will you react to them?

4. Nothing breeds failure like success.

5. So many reward systems are circumvented or lead to the wrong results: change them often.

6. In many organizations there is no direct correlation between leadership development and opportunities.

7. Who you know has a greater impact than what you do.

8. What do you do when a company can't afford pay raises? Be innovative. Start by making sure people know how your organization is doing: use open-book management.

9. Don't let people develop their own compensation, but do use their input about what they do.

10. Improve someone's life!

11. Think building relationships versus making a sale.

12. Professionals carry their tools in their heads: they often aren't the best managers.

13. Poor management causes many problems. Don't be the problem as you progress!

14. Every success, every reward system, every leader, every manager, etc., has a catch: nothing stays perfect in this world.

15. Measure *it* and *it* will improve, but be sure what *it* is! And from whose perspective *it* is defined. It does depend on the definition of what *it* is.

16. You've got to figure out ways around competitor moves when the moves are price or image.

17. Corporate cultures are living things and you can feel them. Corporate culture is communicated mostly through actions and seldom through formal statements.

18. Show people what is in it for them.

19. Traditional methods don't work for unique services and unique customers: many are off-limits to professionals.

20. Look at the lost CBA—the cost of not doing. There is always a price to not doing something—understand it well.

21. Leaders have to continually assess which group they are trying to lead.

22. Seventy-five people can't make every decision—what's the limit on a number? And how will decisions be made with a large number of equals?

23. Management often exhibits a strong resistance to change. The higher the organizational level of the resister, the more effect the resistance has.

24. To be effective, leaders must have the will, means, knowledge, and wisdom to understand what they know and don't know.

25. You've got to figure out how to use low-paid people with poor attitudes and work ethics.

26. You have to figure out how to work with groups you don't control.

27. Be honest with yourself. Just because you wish it doesn't make it true.

28. Ninety percent of all the people I've ever known have tried to treat me fairly. Sometimes I would not let them! What about you?

29. Intimidation does not play well for long.

30. If you're liked by everyone you work with, you're probably doing something wrong.

31. How do you get people to value quality and service the same way you do?

32. The only power worth having is power that you can or will share.

33. Governments and unions offer significant challenges. How do you prepare for this?

34. Many management jobs are poorly designed. If a job is a continual people-killer, it's designed wrong or you're staffing it with the wrong kinds of people.

35. Cutting back is not a strategy; it's a reaction.

36. Relating to technology, innovation, and level of problems and opportunities, some live on the bleeding edge and others in the backwaters.

37. Innovation for one may be standard for another. An innovation is something new or different for you or your organization.

38. Comprehend strategic action and thinking.

39. Understand the difference in the strategic roles of management and leadership.

40. Always end with the analysis of the *might, can, want,* and *ought* components of strategy.

41. Continue to make structure follow strategy.

42. Recognize the strategic relevance of ten current themes in organizational strategy: globalization, radical change, leadership culture, innovation, ethics, beyond TQM, beyond reengineering, teaming, empowerment, and customer relations.

43. Know when a structured versus an unstructured decision process is warranted.

44. Know how the behavioral and cultural theories of organizations relate to strategy and strategic fit.

45. Understand the current competitive forces within industries, life cycles, and competitive advantages.

46. Accomplish with generic strategies in mind.

47. Develop and use distinctive organizational value chains for different organizations.

48. Realize that strategies are formulated but emerge as they are implemented and situational changes occur.

49. Always generate alternative scenarios.

50. Know how to use current IT-based search methods to generate information on organizations and industries.

51. Understand that strategic excellence can be developed in products, market class/user, technology, production, sales and marketing, management and human resources, distribution, natural resources, size or growth, and returns and profits.

52. Comprehend why sustainable competitive advantages must be valuable, rare, inimitable, and non-substitutable.

53. Understand the meaning of fit and balance as they relate to strategy, management, and leadership.

54. Understand your strengths and weaknesses as a leader or manager.

55. Understand what it takes to prepare for your career choice.

(This list was developed by Bill and Dave over 10 years of teaching MBA and other experienced professional students.)

13

MQ, The Management Quotient

"The more you learn, the less you know." The "less" we know about management is that there are only two things: Tasks and People. After reading thousands of books over our combined 100-plus years of life, if we had to read just one book on management it would be Drucker's classic, Management: Tasks, Responsibilities, Practices *(1973). A close second would be the Bible, particularly the New Testament.*

Management is getting things done through others, or, in our simplified version: Tasks and People. Its functions center on planning, organizing, directing, controlling, and—most importantly—staffing. Hundreds of management or supervisory primers more than adequately cover all of these five functions. All of these texts are prescripts and theories about how to handle and control people to accomplish a common purpose within organizations. These books provide tested theories and even some practical applications, but none of them are worth the paper they are printed on if you can't make applications from them.

Management is one of the easiest things you will ever do…after you have done it for about 20 years! The first two to five years it seems impossible; the next two to five it seems doable but tough; and finally management becomes easy because you've mastered it, and then you retire!

To be successful as a manager, take a job as a manager; and look, listen, and ask for help from those savvy managers to whom everyone turns when there is a problem. To be successful, observe and emulate those you admire. The basis of all education is to start with what people know and extend to what they don't know. Whose management style do you want to emulate so you can learn what you don't know? Who will become your perfect management icon?

Mentors can be great sources of advice and inspiration. Once you identify your icon for perfect management, your style will improve because you know what the target is. Then you start to understand:

- The requirements of your job

- The jobs of your subordinates

- The mission of your organization

- The responsibilities of your department or unit

- The personalities and desires of your subordinates

- Your superiors' wishes and their personalities and desires

- The wishes and desires of your customers

- The desires of the owners

- The industry and sub-industry you are in

- Your organization's internal structures

- The markets you operate in

- Your products and services

- The direction of technology and innovation in your industry

- Where your organization is today and where it is headed

- The political, technical, and regulatory trends of your environments

- The future of your products and services.

Oh, by the way—you need to really understand psychology and sociology, as well as be an expert on drug and alcohol abuse; and don't forget about the federal, state, and local laws you need to know. And your organization will have a lot of automated systems and rules, policies and SOPs that need to be second nature to you. Know these things, and then keep your moods steady; be strong but friendly; know when to be nice and when to be firm; know how to read people, how to dress, how to speak and behave; how to get the information you need and what information to ignore. Then figure out what is important and what is not, and you've got it made. Then get into an area that really fits your life's interest. Wait—one more thing: You need to be able to show employees that you care, or be able to just fake it.

You can either subscribe to this very difficult list of management success requirements, or subscribe to the "Bill and Dave simplified formula": Tasks and People. Remember: The purpose of *The Leadership Quotient* is to simplify leadership, not make it more complex. We have simplified leadership by reducing it to 12 quotients. We have simplified management by reducing it to Tasks and People.

We faced a dilemma in developing this MQ chapter because there is a lot of good management literature on the bookshelves. We wanted to give you something different. Just because we don't mention something does not mean we don't know it or that we consider it unimportant. As all authors do, we have selected the management topics that we think most relate to *The Leadership Quotient* framework.

We started this chapter talking about Drucker and his classic *Management* book. In the mid-1970s Bill was studying for a test that would give him a CDP (Certified Data Processor) certification. Several organizations were trying to establish this certification along the lines of the CPA. Initially, the developers wanted this to be a tough test; and, indeed, there were only a handful of people passing all five parts of the exam. Bill knew he was weak in the Practice and Theory of Management section. When he sought advice from experts, many of them directed him to the Drucker book. Bill bought and read the book. He passed his entire CDP test on the first try, and contributes his success on the management section largely to the information he found in the Drucker book. He went on to manage for the next 15 years, during which time he received an MBA and many promotions. He feels he was successful as a manager and executive and completed the MBA and Ph.D. partly because of what he learned from Drucker. This basic management book receives our highest recommendation.

When we reviewed Drucker's 811-page, 61-chapter book for our MQ chapter, we were amazed at how current it all seemed! From the discussions of how difficult it is to manage service institutions and their knowledge work and workers, to the need for social responsibility and ethics, to the need for innovation and even the challenges of the future, it seems Drucker had it figured out long ago. We fully understand that parts of the Drucker book could seem off-putting to some young students. An example is when Drucker says, "But does the man who spends $7,000 on a new Cadillac buy transportation, or does he buy primarily prestige?" (p. 83). Today's young people often miss the point, and think, *$7,000 would buy a new car? And a Cadillac is prestige? And women* don't *buy cars?* They often miss the timeless lessons of why we buy Infiniti versus Nissan, Lexus versus Toyota, Acura versus Honda, and so on. Dave's strategy students have led this very same discussion in their team presentations. Since he teaches at a Christian university, there is a responsibility to use the Christian worldview. Just this semester, a student team analyzed the auto industry and probed Drucker's question about the Christian purpose for the industry: transportation, or prestige?

Another story will help here as well. When Bill came to Samford University in 1993 and began his second career as a university professor at the age of 48, he was confronted by Dr. John Cousins as he was about to teach the introductory management course. John, who had been a Catholic priest before earning a Ph.D. from Harvard, said, "You can do anything you like, but I'll fight you like hell if you try to change the Drucker book as the primer for our introductory management course." (Yes, Cousins really cursed a lot!) Bill had no objections to keeping the book. However, a few years later, after John had left the university, Bill was pressured to switch to a more modern management text filled with asides, pictures, graphs, and all kinds of colored diversionary drawings. It seems students today can't read; they want pictures! We are frustrated with modern texts that are designed more to entertain than to educate our students. What are we teaching people? Drucker's 1973 book is 811 pages of nothing but words—not a single chart, picture, model, or aside!!

We appreciate what Drucker said, and we should constantly ask, "What is our business, and what should it be?" We embrace his continuous call for an organization to become and remain innovative. If you will recall, we have written much in $LQ^©$ about knowing why people do business with you and figuring out how to become and remain innovative. We got this from Drucker originally and have confirmed it over many years of application and study.

Before we go on to our own attempt to define MQ, we would like to repeat some of Drucker's concluding remarks (1973, pp. 807-808):

> In this century, society has become a society of organizations. Every major social task in this society is being performed in and through large, managed institutions. As a result, the great majority of people in developed countries work as employees. They work as members of managed institutions and within a managerial structure and organization.
>
> In this century, society has become a knowledge society. More and more of the members of developed society make their living by putting knowledge to work. More and more acquire their qualifications through long years of formal education. More and more of them are managers themselves or work as knowledge professionals with direct responsibility for performance and results.
>
> The two developments are interrelated. Because of the emergence of the society of organizations, one can now make a living through knowledge work. In addition, because of the availability of large numbers of people with substantial formal education, large institutions are possible and can be managed.
>
> Management is both the carrier and the result of these two developments. It is the organ through which the institutions of the society of organizations can be made to function and to perform their mission. And management itself is such a "knowledge." It is a discipline with its own subject matters, its own skills, and its own expertise. Above all, the managers of these institutions in a society of organizations form the leadership groups of the society.
>
> Unless this society of organizations destroys itself, managers as a leadership group and management as a discipline and challenge will remain with us. To repeat the *leitmotiv* of this book, we are moving from management boom to management performance. It is the task of *this* management generation to make the institutions of the society of organizations, beginning with the business enterprise, perform for society and economy; for the community; and for the individual alike.
>
> This requires, first, that managers know their discipline. It requires that they know management.
>
> We hear a great deal today about the manager of the future. But the important man is the manager of today. And the first requirement is that the manager know his craft, his tools, his task and

responsibility. The first requirement is that he be able to function....(To page 811—what is shown next).

What is needed to break out of the straitjacket of old slogans and old issues is management performance. This first requires performance as a technocrat. It requires performance that makes the manager's organization capable of supplying to society and economy the contribution for the sake of which it exists, such as economic goods and services and the capital fund for tomorrow. But it also requires performance beyond the immediate mission, beyond technocracy: performance in making work productive and the worker achieving and performance with respect to the quality of life. But above all, it has to be performance with respect to the role and function of the manager. If he is to remain—as he should—the manager of an autonomous institution, he must accept that he is a public man. He must accept the moral responsibility of organization, the responsibility of making individual strengths productive and achieving.

AMEN! We intend for the rest of this chapter to act as a guide to the tasks and people of management. We will discuss the tools of the trade of management in the most simplified terms we can. Our intention is to avoid the common book versions of today's management world that are by over-hyped, media-driven, over-informed yet under-knowledgeable do-gooders who author trite and meaningless metaphors as a means of relating *their* management advice. As managers, we must come to grips with the necessity of improving the world through the organizations where we live and work. To act responsibly and accordingly, we have to start with a good basic MQ.

Management—An Important Step Required for Those Wishing to Lead Today's Organizations

The path to organizational leadership goes through management. Leaders who cannot prove effective and efficient in managerial roles seldom get to handle leadership roles in business organizations. We suggest that non-business organizations, such as those in the realm of politics, produce worse leaders because they don't have the management requirement that we're writing about. Unfortunately, management is not a requirement in some environments, such as politics, religion, and education. Thus, we often find leaders who don't know how to manage. We are sure the management requirement makes better leaders who have a higher overall Leadership Quotient.

The Basics of Management Success

Unfortunately, most managers are not very good. Half are below average, and we have found that average is relatively poor. We tell students they will find that most managers are poor at the task. When we mention that, our experienced MBA students agree, and the normal undergraduate does not. However, when those undergraduates come back to our classes to present guest lectures years later, they always seem to remember this part and say, "When Dr. Arnott (or Dr. Service) tells you most managers are no good, they are right—they aren't!" It is fairly easy to excel at management, not because management is easy, but because it's done so poorly! It starts with the simple desire to be better and ends with the understanding that it is not about *you*, it is about *others!* Followers—or subordinates, as they are often called in management texts—are the keys to being successful as a manager. First, start treating and calling them partners, colleagues, cohorts, or some similar title. That helps you get away from the principle of "I'm the boss." If you really *are* the boss, you can always act like it when absolutely necessary. We like what our friend Uri (Director of the Kiev Business School's MBA program) said about almost everything we asked: "Not exactly." Keep this and Bill's favorite answer—"It depends"—in mind, as we offer our simplistic primer to management. In fact, all you need to know is how to: 1) balance everything and everyone, 2) fit yourself, everyone else, and every situation, 3) do what is appropriate, 4) know that the correct answer is not exactly correct, and 5) understand that it depends. Yes, once you know what it takes to balance, fit, be appropriate, be exact, and understand what it depends on, you have it made. Experience will tell you that it's not easy to do! But increasing your Management Quotient will certainly lead to a higher Leadership Quotient.

Just as we were completing *LQ©*, a very famous and, we feel, accurate management professor and researcher, Henry Mintzberg, came out with a book entitled *Managers Not MBAs: A Hard Look at the Soft Practice of Managing and Management Development* (2004), which added real credence to our pronouncements in *LQ©*. "The practice of management is characterized by its ambiguity....That leaves the managers mostly with the messy stuff—the intractable problems, the complicated connections. And that is what makes the practice of management so fundamentally 'soft' and why labels such as experience, intuition, judgment, and wisdom are so commonly used for it....[On the work experience for MBAs,] what is the use of a few years of experience, especially when it is not managerial (p. 13)?...To conclude, we need leaders with human skills, not professionals with academic credentials" (p. 18).

"They never tested their own assumptions (p. 26)....[T]he United States alone now produces upwards of a million people per decade who believe that they have the capacity to manage by virtue of having spent two years in an academic school of business. It is to this unexamined yet flourishing proportion that we now turn" (p. 29).

"As businesses work valiantly to bust down the walls between their 'silos,' business schools work valiantly to reinforce them. Business schools teach a great deal about managing change, notably that it has to get past existing categories. Yet because business schools themselves cannot, they remain more or less where the two foundation reports of 1959 put them" (p. 32).

"To conclude, the typical business school today is about specialization, not integration, concerned with the business functions, not the practice of managing (p. 36)....Synthesis is the very essence of management. Within their own contexts, managers have to put things together in the form of coherent visions, unified organizations, integrated systems, and so forth. That is what makes management so difficult, and so interesting. It's not that managers don't need analysis; rather, it's that they need it as an input to synthesis, and that is the hard part. Teaching analysis devoid of synthesis thus reduces management to a skeleton of itself. This is equivalent to considering the human body as a collection of bones: Nothing holds it together, no sinew or muscle, no flesh or blood, no spirit or soul....[on MBAs—Roger Martin of the University of Toronto in the *Financial Times,* September 11, 2000]. They were clever and knowledgeable, but had no overarching framework to apply to problems that ran across the academic disciplines they had studied" (p. 37).

Mintzberg says that managers (and we say leaders as well) need the following five mindsets: 1) reflection—managing self (knowing others is intelligence, but knowing yourself is wisdom), 2) analysis—managing organizations, 3) worldliness—managing context (managers need to get into other people's worlds), 4) collaboration—managing relationships, and 5) action—managing change (chart on page 278). Effective managers function at an interface between reflective thinking and practical doing. "To manage is to bring out the positive energy that exists naturally within people. Managing thus means engaging based on judgment, rooted in context....Leadership is a sacred trust earned from the respect of others" (p. 275; all prior quotes from Mintzberg, 2004). Sorry, MBAs, but it's essentially true!

We both have Ph.D.s and understand the value of education and academic research, but more importantly, we understand the limitations of education. People who have never lead or managed, but only taught, researched, or consulted, simply cannot know what they don't know about management and leadership. Bill says very directly, "During my entire MBA and Ph.D. I did not learn a tenth of what I learned during my 15-year journey in management." Yes, Henry—it takes a lifetime of commitment to be a good manager or leader!

The fog of management is about persuasion and bringing people together to accomplish overriding purposes. Before you can become a top leader in the world of organizations, you must be an excellent manager who can clear the fog and make clear the path to accomplishment. A manager can keep people on track and move them to action. You must move without the clarity of hindsight, but with the knowledge of past actions and resulting performance. The following is an outline of the topics we will write about in the next section. As with previous chapters, you will conduct a self-analysis at the end of the description, so start to think about your strengths and weaknesses relative to these management tasks.

Management From Start to Finish—Our Views About Management

Understanding management history—Good managers must pull in many resources and use knowledge from many areas and disciplines to foster the creativity required to keep an organization alive.

As we move through this section on management, we really don't want you to think we are dumbing down the material, and we really don't want you to think we are being cute for cute's sake: it's for learning and fun! We have studied management for years, and laugh at the simplicity of much of the academic research. When we were Ph.D. candidates together, one of our favorite professors used to say, "Sometimes good research is like busting through an open screen door!" (It's simple and obvious.) We are adding a humanistic-realistic approach to what others have said, as well as adding our own viewpoints to build MQ.

It took management to build the pyramids and the cathedrals of Europe; to win battles for Greece and Rome; and to erect Stonehenge. However, management as a discipline is only about 100 years old. It has not been around long because the modern organization is not old. One-hundred fifty years ago, organizational management was generally not needed in areas other than the government, military, or church, for we were a world of individual farmers and cottage industries.

The study of business as definable theories and disciplines began in the discipline of economic theory. Three basic assumptions guide economics theory:

1.   Markets are free.

2.   People's actions are rational.

3.   All market participants have perfect and equal information.

Everything we teach in our colleges of business is based on these simple precepts. Our management discipline has its roots here also. We would ask you to consider, "Are these assumptions always true?" We think you would agree that there are many exceptions to these basic rules of economics. Markets are not totally free anywhere in the world, humans never act absolutely rationally, and no one has complete and perfect information (insiders occasionally get it, but that's illegal and unequally dispersed). Based on these facts, one must rationally conclude that the theories of economics and consequently management are wrong because they are based on invalid assumptions. So, what should the management assumptions be?

The following three MQ assumptions will give us a good start: 1) Markets, even in the U.S., are highly regulated and are influenced by many factors related to the differing environmental views we have discussed in prior chapters. 2) People often act emotionally from their hearts, rather then using intellectual rationality from their heads. When they act rationally, it is usually in just their areas of expertise. 3) Information is always limited in some way. Even if it were perfect and equally dispersed, we would all understand or use it differently.

These assumptions are more nearly correct and point to the real management theories that are of value: 1) You are at the mercy of the markets, and they are driven by many influences. This means you must know all the environmental, physical, and psychological influences that can change the markets. 2) People often act out of emotion, not rational logic (logic is normally about 10% of most decisions). Therefore, you must spend more time thinking about *their* emotions than *your* logic if you want to manage for change. 3) People interpret information as they want, given the filters we've mentioned in previous chapters. You must be informed and able to inform others if you wish to influence.

We know that the contingency views discussed by many academicians are correct. That's the basis for the $LQ^©$ triangle that includes the points you need to bring together in order to triangulate management: leader, followers, and environments. Keep these three variables in mind as we review some of the aspects of management.

Management definitions and overview—*Ask of any management principle, "Does it make sense and fit the distinctiveness of my situation?"*

All management frameworks must fit the environment, mission, people, core competencies, and technologies in which they are implemented. If it does not make sense, it is not right for managing people. And as we've heard before, "If it does not fit, you must acquit" yourself of the theory!

"BASIC ASSUMPTIONS ABOUT REALITY are the PARADIGMS of social science, such as management. The scholars, writers, teachers, and practitioners in the field usually hold them subconsciously. Yet those assumptions largely determine what the discipline—scholars, writers, teachers, practitioners—assumes to be REALITY" (Drucker, 1999, p. 3). Management is about people integrated into common ventures for universal purposes in organizations that operate within complex environments. Thus, the manager must understand the environment in which he is operating.

Management decision-making: types and styles—*Make decisions for fast incremental innovation and development of people.*

Decisions are choices under varying degrees of uncertainty. To improve decisions we need to reduce our uncertainty. Start by using the real assumptions and the theories they imply when making a decision. Many decision-making frameworks can be arrayed across a continuum of two opposite types of decision-making, with the leader making all decisions on one end of the spectrum and the group making decisions on the other end. Organizations are like humans where you must take a holistic approach to understand the whole and all of its parts (Brache, 2002). The decisions that must be made within organizations must take a holistic-humanist approach.

"A decision is a judgment. It is a choice between alternatives. It is rarely a choice between right and wrong. It is at best a choice between 'almost right' and 'probably wrong'—but much more often a choice between two courses of action, neither of which is provably more right than the other" (Drucker, 1967, p. 143). Learn to satisfice and take the best decision given the resource, time, human, and personal limitations. Leaders with a high Management Quotient will always *make* a decision because no decision *is* a decision, and most often it's the worst decision.

The environments of management—*Learn to manage your environments to have a higher Management Quotient.*

Managers work in relatively complex organizations, and all organizations operate in competitive arenas under governmental and societal constraints. The media largely establish the environments we manage in because hype is the method of choice for organizations to sell their products. Quality and service are second to who *hypes* the products. If we could view our purchases externally, we would determine that we are a rather dim bunch of people for the simple reasoning we use when choosing the products and services we buy. Much of our persuasion in this area is gained by commercials we see on TV. The commercials we see in our printed press and on TV are windows on who we are as a people. The 90-second "in-depth" issue reports on the nightly news are also very telling. It takes more than 90 seconds to learn about a topic.

The Functions We Normally See in Management Texts

Human Resources for personal growth and selection—*The key to promotion lies not in what you have done in the past, but in what you are capable of at the next level.*

To increase your Management Quotient, become a bit of an expert on HR. A fact of organizational management is that you can and will be sued for anything. *The HR Answer Book,* by Smith and Mazin (2004), is a quick read that should be all you need for a few years, provided you keep your ear to the ground. Rulings come every day that can get you into hot water. Sexual harassment, ethics, values, leadership development; psychological disorders such as disabilities, illegal discharge, employment of illegals, and employee privacy are huge—watch developments in these areas.

Planning—*insures the possibility of survival for you and your organization.*

"By not daring to take the risk of making the new happen, management takes, by default, the greatest risk of being surprised by what will happen. This is a risk that even the largest and richest companies cannot afford to take. And it is a risk that not even the smallest need take" (Drucker, 1998, p. 52). If you do not plan obsolescence of yourself and your product, you or your organization will have a very limited life! As has been said repeatedly, by failing to plan you plan to fail. Planning is relatively simple and should take a strategic slant. See our SQ chapter for a more complete description of strategic planning, but start today and commit to spending time at the beginning and end of each day planning the next. Never fail to re-plan and to throw out plans that have become impossible because they were bad in the first place or the environment made them untenable. It seems few managers can properly balance the persistence of a "damn the torpedoes, full speed ahead" attitude with "analysis paralysis," but the expert Management Quotient leader can.

Organizing—*Reorganizations are often a cover for not knowing how to improve the organization. Organization is important, but if you have the right people, it's a lot easier!*

Effective Management Quotient leaders are able to work in a span of control from 1 to 400. You need to be sure everyone has a part and knows it. Responsibility and authority need to match. Balance spontaneity and organization. Reorganize self and others often. Stop what you are doing long enough to get organized. The MQ leader's job is to fit together the tasks and people in a way that accomplishes the organization's purpose. Insure a match between the formal structures and the informal structures. Do **not** worry as much about location in the structure as about influence of the person in the structure. Organize for ease of communications, innovation, controls, process, people, keeping people honest, taking advantage of opportunities, speed, steadiness, new directions, and so on. Use all capabilities to maximum potential benefit.

Directing—*Normally it's the manager and how she gets people to become codependent that causes the need for continued directing.*

    To be an effective Management Quotient leader, start thinking about self-direction from knowledge and experience coupled with the correct motivation. We don't want too many people in today's organizations who just sit and wait to be told. If you want to use the hands and the head of every worker for innovativeness, then you need to refrain from directing others as a matter of course. Directing people keeps them organizational "children" when they need to be organizational partner-citizens. In any case, where you have to direct someone repeatedly as to how to do their job, it's either you or them who needs changing. Good managers get people to think and self-direct.

Controlling—*Just enough controls to keep people honest.*

    We say basically the same thing for controlling as we said for directing. Your goal is to have self-controlled individuals and teams.

Staffing—*"Surround yourself with an inner core that complements your leadership"* (Maxwell, 2002, p. 80).

    To have a high Management Quotient, you need to create an organization that people love to be associated with. To get and keep the best people:

1. Be an organization that people really want to work for.

2. Select the right person in the first place.

3. Get off to a great start—the way people are oriented into an organization is the biggest determinant of their contribution.

4. Coach and reward to maintain commitment.

Good people leave because:

1. They see no link between pay and performance.

2. They do not perceive growth or advancement opportunities.

3.   They do not see their work as important; or their contributions are not recognized.

4.   They do not get to use their talents.

5.   They have unclear or unrealistic expectations.

6.   They will no longer tolerate abusive managers or toxic environments (Branham, 2001).

To retain talented workers, the effective Management Quotient leader will arrange the organization so that these six reasons become irrelevant in the organization. Discovering upon whom you can rely is the key to a happy and successful life in and outside organizations. "When all is said and done, your ability as a leader will not be judged by what you achieved personally or even by what your team accomplished during your tenure. You will be judged by how well your people and your organization did after you were gone" (Maxwell, 2002, p. 108).

In selecting people for your organization, often you have to put up with a weakness to get a great strength (Drucker, 1967). "No executive has ever suffered because his subordinates were strong and effective" (Drucker, from Maxwell, 2002, p. 95). Hiring is a solemn responsibility and the ticket to management failure or success.

The Real Tough Management Functions

The objective of this section is to give you useful information for the advancement of your MQ. Our intent is to give you a view that you may not have and spur you to think anew.

Motivation—*Good managers have no second-class subordinates. This attitude results in self-motivated employees!*

Motivation occurs best when you focus more on your subordinates than on yourself or your superiors. Let your passion show and let others see you accomplishing above and beyond. "Remember that optimism and strength of character are contagious" (Sandys and Littman, 2003, p. 263). If you are fulfilled in your job, your subordinates have a better chance of being fulfilled in theirs. Treat all with respect: "As you chart the course of your life, determine to be the one that walks hand in hand with others, valuing human life to the maximum, treating all with respect" (Paul Corts, cited in Williams, 2003). In a recent study, 86% of the workforce cited fulfillment and work/life balance as their top career priority (NASPI, 2004, p. 2I).

Teams—*The primary use of teams today is to hide poor performers and allow fearful managers to avoid doing the real job of management.*

One of the more difficult issues today is to make teams effective when you have very different groups within the same team. Often the groupings seem to view each other with suspicion and skepticism. Look at Karp, Fuller, and Sirias's 2002 book on *Bridging the Boomer-Xer Gap* for an excellent guide to creating authentic high-performing teams with differing types of people, baby boomers and Xers, or otherwise.

Experienced yet low-MQ managers avoid the hard choices required to fire poor performers, quite often in the name of diversity. Diversity is many things, but it is never an excuse for not performing or for causing others not to perform. When we discuss teams with an MBA class, this is what we always hear, so do not fool yourself—teams do **not** work that well in American organizations. Teams for teams' sake is not a good Management Quotient decision.

A couple of good books related to teams are *The GE Work-Out* (Ulrich, Kerr, and Ashkenas, 2002), and Butler's (1996) book that gives us 72 good ways to make smart decisions in meetings.

"Coming together is a beginning; Keeping together is progress; Working together is success" (Henry Ford). "Never doubt that a small group of thoughtful committed people can change the world; indeed it is the only thing that has" (Margaret Mead). But be prepared for the inevitable problems of personal conflict, confused goals, jumbled goals, and poor leadership that often appear in teams.

Teams are not machines. They are individuals with talents, prejudices, ambitions, and fears. They must be led, motivated, and nurtured to work. Too often we have a *mob*, not a *team*. A mob does not rely on interdependence. It has no real commitments or goals, and talents are not identified and used. A mob distrusts and a team trusts. Teams are open and honest. Mobs are not. Conflict is left unresolved in a mob. Mobs are lazy and just follow blindly, whereas teams work together to solve and address situations. On a real, self-directed work team, a mistake can be celebrated if it was a well-conceived plan that failed. Are you building a mob or a team?

"I want to know whether the leader believes in the followers" (Gardner, 2003, p. 90). Use teams for work that needs teams, not for individual work.

Creativity-innovation—*"The best way to get a good idea is to have a lot of ideas" (Pauling in Sandys and Littman, 2003, p. 160).*

"Is it possible to foster creativity? The question is not easily answered (p. 67)....In all relationships of influencing, directing, guiding, helping, nurturing, the whole tone of the relationship will be...the generative element...that runs beneath the surface" (Gardner, 2003, p. 89). "Wherever you see a successful business, someone once made a courageous decision" (Drucker, in Bruun and Getzen, 1996, p. 469). Be alert and see it, find it, do it; but stay ahead. The only way to create a new future is to visualize what it will look like and then work to make it happen.

Most of us do not even recognize innovations, so how can we put them into use? We must continually establish new systems and structures to create alignment for handling the increasing speed and volume of information. A manager must use everyone through deeper relationships to realize sustainable innovativeness (Harris, 2003a). "Leaders have no office hours. Work flows seamlessly into the rest of life" (Sandys and Littman, 2003, p. 118).

Organizations need innovators to say here is how we could make it work; and inhibitors who say here is why it won't work (Dauten, 2004). The good Management Quotient leader mixes and matches people in the organization for innovation. Elvis Presley's mix of country and rock is an example—he took two things that already existed and put them together.

God creates; humans discover. Innovation is discovering new combinations for things that already existed. Edison mixed elements in a way they had not been mixed before. Steve Jobs, Michael Dell, and Bill Gates, among many others, simply saw how existing ideas could be combined and brought to market for profit. In the end, all innovativeness requires quiet time to watch and think.

Communications—*"One generalization that is supported both by research and experience is that effective two-way communication is essential to proper functioning of the leader-follower relationship....Leaders, to be effective, must pick up the signals coming to them from constituents....Wise leaders are continuously finding ways to say to their constituents, 'I hear you'"* (Gardner, 2003, p. 147).

Without communication, we would have no management or leadership. Don't use technology to avoid face-to-face relationships. Real relationships are the basis for long-run management effectiveness, and they require personal, live interactions.

Managing Change—*Learn how to manage change or it will manage you.*

You are part of an organization, and your entire organization is part of a much larger system that you must understand to have an effective Management Quotient. When the system around you changes, you must change. The soul of a company is found in the hearts of its employees. You must address the heart of any change as well as the logical view if you are to create a future in which you can succeed. Change does not happen because people think differently; it occurs more because they have a change of heart (Kotter and Cohen, 2002).

Change is the mantra of our global, fast-paced world. To meet these new requirements be agile, learn to learn, manage risk, stick to the right things, avoid busy work and the wrong things, don't establish a culture of fear, and avoid developing a "management model of the week."

Dr. Phil McGraw's TV show gave us some good guidelines for handling change, albeit his guidelines were for weight control. We have modified his directions, and feel the following guidelines will help you master the fear of change.

1. Right thinking—understand the reasons for the change and shift your thinking from dreading change to embracing change.

2. Healthy feelings—your mental state on anything is important and when you dwell on the negatives of change you are not being healthy at all. A variation on the Serenity Prayer is a key here.

"God grant me the understanding to change that which I can and to accept that which I cannot change, and the wisdom to know the difference."

3. No-frills encouragement—figure out a way to encourage yourself to embrace and make the needed change; reward yourself for completed steps toward change.

4. Mastery over change—don't let it control you; you control it.

5. High response costs—set up a system that makes it hard *not* to change.

6. Intentional action—do things to remind yourself of your area of change.

7. Your center of support—let others know about your change and help you change.

As a manager you often are the last to see a needed change. Ineffective Management Quotient leaders simply can't or won't see the forest for the trees, or vice versa. "Experts are less likely to challenge convention than perceptive amateurs" (Sandys and Littman, 2003, pp. 34-35). A good manager realizes that large change is normally the last option. Try to accomplish large change in small incremental sections for your own well-being and for the sanity of your subordinates. Improve the parts, not the whole (Andrews and Johnson, 2002).

To get people to change, you must show them how it will hurt them *not* to change, and help them to change. Give no special dispensation to hardcore cases. Three current interconnected challenges from employees—bad attitudes, poor performance, and resistance to change—require new forms of change management. The only way to handle these challenges is to eliminate the payoff of negative actions by holding employees accountable (Chambers, 1998). Surveys show that employees with bad attitudes do not feel they have bad attitudes. Perception is reality for them. This calls on the best of the leader to help employees understand that their bad attitudes must change.

Managing conflict—*"Almost all our faults are more pardonable than the methods we think up to hide them" (Maxwell, 2002, p. 28).*

Start and end each bit of conflict with respect and humility, and never think you are better than anyone else. The key to conflict is listening, not talking. Discuss everything and then take action. Listening, focus, and visible recognition of feelings, as well as content-balanced inquiry, advocacy, and judgment, are necessary to keep talented people (Harkins, 1999). Recognize that conflict is inevitable and that you can minimize it only by creating fair policies, correct hiring, identifying the real sources of conflict, and putting into place a resolution system that fits your organization. Describe the conflict properly and have an open-door policy: intervene with care (Blackard and Gibson, 2002).

Conflict is neither good nor bad; it is what we make of it and how it's done. Subordinates are highly sensitive to signals sent out by their boss. It is very easy to turn high achievers into under-performers with constant rejection and criticism. The majority of bosses have to work to overcome aggression, impatience, and tendencies to micromanage. You can be tough without killing someone (O'Loughin, 2003).

Managing time—*We all have the same amount of time, and it's simply our choice how to use it.*
We hate time management. We all have time to live, love, exercise, work, play, and accomplish just about anything we want to. "Just about anything" is different from "everything." In a world that is limited by time and resources, good Management Quotient leaders know how to make choices that produce success, for themselves and for their organization. We have to allocate our time and attention understanding balance, fit, appropriateness, and most importantly the perceptions of others. Our lives become out of balance when we do not have enough time, but time is *all* we have! At the end of our time, all our time is taken away, and the only thing left of our time is what we have helped others make of themselves.

Managing unique functional areas or areas that think they are unique—*is easy!*
Bill was a manager of systems and programming groups for years. From those experiences he learned it is not hard to manage unique functional areas. It is simply a matter of understanding the basics about the functional area and then getting people you trust to handle it for you. The main problem we see in managing unique functional areas is not a lack of knowledge but an unwillingness to learn enough to manage those functions just like you do anything else, using visions, missions, SMART objectives, and rewards as appropriate.

Don't fear managing unique functions or highly educated or intelligent people—love it! Everyone is by definition a human and no different from you. A few points on IQ or a few more years of education do not *automatically* make one better able to direct others than you.

International management—*is more a matter of attitude than of experience.*
The chief reason for difficulties in global businesses is the lack of managers with appropriate skills to relate to people from different cultures and countries. The following 12 fundamental management-interpersonal skills will help you develop an international MQ:

1. Establishing credibility—not appearing boastful or arrogant.

2. Giving and receiving feedback—appropriate level of directness.

3. Obtaining information—don't equate subjective perceptions with facts.

4. Evaluating people—without offending.

5. Working on a global team—watch the tendency to defend national interest.

6. Training and development—trainers must train differently in many cultures.

7. Selling—speak their language. Learn to introduce yourself and to say thank you before you ever visit a country.

8. Negotiating—confidentiality differs from culture to culture.

9. Strategic planning—strategic mindsets are very different from culture to culture.

10. Transferring knowledge—smoothly is an important competitive differentiator.

11. Innovation—set up systems that encourage: different in differing cultures.

12. Managing change—requires tremendous momentum (Gundling, 2003).

The first step is to "know what you don't know"; then read, study, focus, ask, and accept, to learn and then use what you have learned nonjudgmentally.

Managing through empowerment and shared responsibilities—*Based on in-depth interviews of 60 of Europe's top business leaders, Childress (2001) stresses distributing leadership all down the line because concentrated power means no freedom (de Geus, 1997).*
Empowerment has to be a two-way street: they have to want, and you have to be willing to give. Make it a rule to get and keep the best people if you desire to share responsibilities. This is a requirement in today's overly complex world, where no one person can know it all.
Managing intelligent, confident professionals who love autonomy is difficult and requires:

1. clarifying your role and the roles of others,

2. building relationships one at a time,

3. having deep insights into people,

4. valuing differences in people,

5. showing interest in others' interests,

6. dealing differently with different people,

7. throwing down a challenge,

8. nurturing juniors,

9. asking and listening,

10. being there,

11. building trust, and

12. integrating new people (McKenna and Maister, 2002).

To develop managers who can be empowered and trusted to share responsibility, try being a coach versus being a manager/director. As you coach for empowerment, remember the nine things the best coaches do:

1. Take time to listen.

2. See employees as people.

3. Care personally about employees.

4. Set good examples.

5. Encourage.

6. Don't pull rank.

7. Keep people informed.

8. Praise people.

9. Be straightforward about things people do not do well (Branham, 2001).

Disperse leadership responsibilities across your organization until you have leaders at every level. This builds a sense of commitment by letting employees engage in activities that connect them by building a sense of trust in their organization and each other. Give all people the right to connect and demonstrate their value, which is often termed "social capital." Social capital can be shared and grown if it is accomplished through delegation and empowerment.

Honesty and ethics—*"Always do right. This will gratify some people and astonish the rest" (Mark Twain, from Gardner and Gardner, 1975, p. 114).*
"Thank you, Enron, Arthur Andersen, WorldCom and HealthSouth. You woke us up. The business world has run off the rails, mistaking wealth for success and image for leadership" (George, 2003b, p. 96). "In America, the bosses of big companies command only slightly more respect in pub-

lic-opinion polls than used car salesmen. Rebuilding that trust will be slow work....At the same time, leaders of large companies are increasingly in the public gaze. A company's boss is now expected to take personal responsibility for its fortunes as never before" ("Tough at the Top," 2003, p. 3).

The goal should be to ensure a spirit of transparency in all we do, developing a culture of accountability and participation of all people that is above reproach, and reflected in a corporation's reporting system (DiPiazza and Eccles, 2002).

Social responsibility—*We are a society of organizations, and as such, all organizational managers must respect the society within which we live and realize that if the society is not doing well, then neither will our organizations.*

Our possibilities as humans, acting in groups called organizations, are unlimited, but only if we take societal responsibilities seriously; for without a solid free and open society, little progress will be possible or meaningful. Indeed, social responsibility for the modern stockholder firm is on a continuum from *none* (other than making a profit), to *molding and shaping our world* to fit the highest of moral and ethical values. The problem with the latter extreme becomes who defines the highest of moral and ethical values. As we've said before, this is a danger we must face.

Staying ahead of the new realities—*"Able business leaders are alert to the political climate and to world economic trends" (Gardner, 2003, p. 138).*

Simple answers have not emerged from management research because we face complex problems with complicated answers based on many conditions and exceptions. The length and breadth of the world of organizations, and its various histories, starts and falters, conflicts, habits, regulations, rules, and randomness, has led us to a relatively difficult state. We have tried so many answers and found that many problems seem to be beyond the ability of mankind to solve. There are still profound mysteries in many of our aimless courses and our random achievements. Yet we must continue to strive, for the heartrending truth is we have no choice but to work in the reason-bewildering future. Effective Management Quotient leaders have to stay up with all matter of environmental information. Staying up with the latest and greatest is not easy, but it's absolutely necessary.

Not being a chicken!—*Management requires courage, and we have seen too many chicken managers.*

You will work with the shortsighted, the unethical, the dumb, the unqualified, the boring, the unmotivated, the destructive, the scatterbrained, the know-it-alls, the rude and crude, and all other types of people. Don't be one of those "types," and never be a chicken manager. Face your fears and run toward them, not away from them.

Picking information and issues—*Address the important and urgent.*

Read, learn, and struggle to make up for weaknesses in leading. Be a sponge for information, especially during a time of crisis, leading with questions designed to develop loyal partners. Seek and learn from every conceivable source, but be careful—much of what you read cannot be generalized to your specific leadership followers in your specific environment. Remember to address the urgent *and* important.

Honesty over political correctness—*America has the means to solve its most pressing issues, but we lack the will to openly discuss them. If we won't talk freely about the most pressing of issues, then we can in no way expect to ever solve them. Let's start a movement to throw out political correctness and replace it with honesty and openness.*

Political correctness has so clouded the truth. The hurt feelings that would emerge if we abandoned political correctness would be temporal. When people don't say what they really think, you don't have a starting point on changing them or understanding where they are coming from. Because people do not say, does not mean they do not think. We have cited many instances of otherwise effective Management Quotient leaders being destroyed because of a failure to be politically correct. Among the silliest is the use of the terms "him" or "her." We know men and women can be leaders or managers, and by using "him" we do not exclude women, or vice versa, as some would seem to think.

We want more managers to fix things, not just talk in a politically correct fashion. We all need to worry much more about what **is** than about the **way** something is said. In an attempt to be politically correct, people have gotten away from the real problem, and that is the real problem!

Effectiveness over efficiency—*Take effectiveness over efficiency every time.*

Being effective means doing the right things, as opposed to being efficient, which means doing things the right way. It is so easy to see that even if you do things the right way you've done nothing of good if it's the wrong thing you've done right. It's often said about computers that are programmed wrong, "They can make mistakes so much faster!"

Managing professionals who love autonomy requires a special understanding of effectiveness. Take on **effectiveness** issues **before** you worry about TQM, procedures, and **efficiency**!

People over process—*Take people over process every time and fire those who don't—especially business school professors and deans, as well as QC-TQM experts!*

"Any business that concentrates on its internal mechanisms more than on the customer is, ultimately, a bad business" (Handy, 1998, p. 10). We see many who act as if the process were an end unto itself. Management is about people first or it is about failure.

The realities of diversity*—Take diversity of thought over diversity of appearance every time.*

The meaning of diversity is a matter of where you live: black and white in the South, Hispanic in Texas and California, and "other" categories in other areas. We know diversity is more a matter of how one thinks than how one looks. It's how one *is,* not how one *ought to be* based on one's physical traits. Diversity in thinking produces successful organizations, not diversity in the physical measures that are often used—gender, race, and ethnicity. Reality is that diversity is much deeper than the physical measures of skin color, sex, or age. Management Quotient leaders who learn this lesson will be much more effective.

Managing systems, rewards, rules, and Standard Operating Procedure*—An excess of rules inescapably weakens all rules.*

"No matter what one's line of business, too much emphasis cannot be placed upon the necessity of perfecting from the outset a thorough organization and system" (Montgomery, 1911, VI, p. 175). But to avoid rules and systems becoming an end unto themselves, they must be killed occasionally. It's like burning down a forest and letting it regenerate and regrow. When we have tried to interfere with nature, we have messed up and caused more fires. Controlled burning of rules, systems, and SOP works just like it works for national forests. Reward systems get stale, and people figure out how to manipulate them to their advantage. Rewards should be established from a balanced perspective of what the receiver values and management needs to have accomplished. Contrary to popular belief, good managers must not fear reward systems that discourage unwanted behaviors. Both positive and negative rewards work. We have come to fear negative rewards, and that has caused us lots of problems. Though fear is not good, it's not all bad. Poor Management Quotient leaders have gone to the extreme, and no one fears any consequences. Make consequences for actions a way of life and continually reevaluate your rewards, rules, and systems.

Roles*—Your first role is the image of your organization that comes from your actions and words.*

When we think of the roles of a manager, we must first think of the public image of an organization and how that image is simply a mirror of the actions of the dominant coalition of managers and leaders. *Guerrilla Publicity,* by Levinson, Frishman, and Lublin (2002), tells you how to toot your own horn at a lower cost. The authors discuss how to make publicity work for you instead of advertising by creating a buzz about your organization and its products. It is about having a succinct message that everyone knows and promotes. Learn to do that with your organization, because you won't have an effective Management Quotient if your organization doesn't succeed.

The Civil Corporation, by Zadek (2001), shows us how corporations must take the lead in forming alliances and partnerships by understanding the need for corporations to accept the role of good citizenship on a wider scale and to be part of the solution, not the cause of the problems.

Learn the management and leadership roles of: 1) figurehead, 2) spokesperson, 3) negotiator, 4) coach, 5) motivator, 6) team builder-leader-member-player, 7) problem definer, 8) problem solver, 9) entrepreneur, 10) intrepreneur, 11) champion, 12) strategic planner, 13) doer, 14) delegator, 15) mentor, and 16) thinker. Once you understand these roles, you've become a real Management Quotient $LQ^©$ manager and you will know when, where, why, and how to use these roles for effectiveness and efficiency.

Strategic Development—*"Speed is a great asset in war and business" (Sandys and Littman, 2003, p. 253).*

We covered strategy in the SQ chapter, but we have one more book to recommend: *Strategy Maps,* by Kaplan and Norton (2004). We like the value-creating process they discuss where they see the need for companies to focus on differentiating a value proposition either in operations management, customer management, and innovation, or in meeting societal expectations. The authors discuss risk, innovation, and intangible assets, but they say that ultimately they are talking about all strategy revolving around some form of continuous innovation.

"Try as you might, you can seldom carry out a strategy exactly as planned. You must do your best with the hand you've been dealt (p. 241)....Long-term strategies are often complex and need to constantly evolve (p. 242)....Formulating a strategy is an intellectual process. Keeping it going is about willpower" (Sandys and Littman, 2003, p. 248).

Diversity of self—*The NAACP and its expressed distaste for diversity recently struck us silent. It is sad indeed that a group that should represent diversity at its best chastises all diversity of thought among the race it was formed to help!*

So many of us think race, age, and sex when we think of diversity, strictly because that is what the media tell us to think! Forget the political correctness of the topic and think about diversity of mindset. That's the important diversity to have in organizations. Learn the double-loop learning method for real diversity—maybe even the quadruple loop: listen, repeat, apply, give/get feedback, and redo—but learn to think diversely yourself; then you will know real diversity when you see it. Learn to empathize with your enemy and those you don't understand, and you'll see another side to your own views.

Speaking in public—presentations—*"Of all the talents bestowed upon men, none is so precious as the gift of oratory....*He who enjoys it wields a power more durable than a great king. He is an independent force in the world. Abandoned by his party, betrayed by his friends, stripped of his offices, whoever can command this power is still formidable" (Churchill, as cited in Sandys and Littman, 2003, p. 43).

Fundamentals and learning—*You must first exhibit the courage to speak and hear the truth before you can really learn anything: courage is built on candor, purpose, will, rigor, and risk.*

Make every experience interactive learning. Think about management fundamentals as you review the following principles of Gwartney and Stroup's (1993) *What Everyone Should Know About Economics and Prosperity*:

The Ten Key Elements of Economics (from page 2):

1. Incentives matter.

2. There is no such thing as a free lunch.

3. Voluntary exchange promotes economic progress.

4. Transaction costs are an obstacle to exchange; reducing this obstacle will help promote economic progress.

5. Increases in real income are dependent upon increases in real output.

6. The four sources of income growth are a) improvements in worker skills, b) capital formation, c) technological advancements, and d) better economic organization.

7. Income is compensation derived from the provision of services to others; people earn income by helping others.

8. Profits direct businesses toward activities that increase wealth.

9. The "Invisible Hand" Principle—market prices bring personal self-interest and the general welfare into harmony.

10. Ignoring secondary effects and long-term consequences is the most common source of error in economics (must trace not merely the immediate results but the results in the long run, not merely the primary consequences but the secondary consequences, and not merely the effects on some special groups but the effects on everyone [p. 27]).

Further contemplate our related principles: 1) private ownership—by owning the right to learn and the results of learning, people will learn; 2) freedom of exchange—know what is in it for you and understand the trade-offs; 3) competitive and efficient—a level of competition always helps people do hard things; and 4) free trade—freely trade your time for learning. A manager's job is more about helping others in their learning journeys than it is about one's personal learning experience. The managerial help for learning must be about encouraging and facilitating, for you cannot *make* people learn. Management is *not* a corrective device; it is a device to lift restraints, encourage, and often push.

You cannot have a learning organization if you fear new ideas and new courses of action—managers must get the useful information that is available to them. Good people are attracted to and stay with companies that embrace excellence and are committed to values, vision, creativity, trust, and respect—to learning. Culture is key to keeping people who learn.

Management education should result in more tolerance, not less. Many management research findings and theories are confusing and contradictory. If you want people to learn new and different things, be careful with criticism—speak to the other person's agenda and ask for clarification and, finally, fill in the picture. No one gets ahead by copying status quo. Few of us progress in life without an adaptive capacity and a youthful curiosity and zest for knowledge.

Managing yourself and moving on up—*"Your most important job is to be the marketer for the brand called You" (per Tom Peters, in Dauten, 2003, p. 1G).*

Make the image of you one that invokes others to think of your name as dependability, motivation, passion, and a lifelong learner who creates a higher level of relationship with their associates (Dauten, 2003).

"During college, most students learn how to find the best professors. Knowing how to do this makes their college years much easier. But good instructors also teach lessons that stay with you for life. Now as you commence your career in the real world, your task is to find one more great teacher. Your first boss can make all the difference in the world" (Falvey, 1999, p. 25). "Your first boss is important because of all of the unwritten rules you need to learn....The rules are different everywhere and you can't figure them out for yourself....Remember, you have just as much right to fire your boss as he or she has to fire you" (Falvey, 1999, p. 28). Don't stay wrong long when it comes to a boss.

"Networking has always been important to career success, but doing it the old-fashioned way—at association meetings, social events and on business trips—can be time-consuming and difficult. Today, the Internet makes networking far more efficient. It allows you to stay in touch with friends and colleagues worldwide, at any time of day, without disrupting your schedule or taking much time and effort" ("How Much Can the Internet Help Executive Job Hunters?" 1999, p. 13).

We close this section of MQ with a more complete description of managing yourself and your career, but we leave you now with this advice. Manage your image at all times; manage your substance at all times; and make each experience an opportunity to advance your connections or knowledge and you will become the *LQ*[©] manager of the future.

Religion's impact on management and leadership—who, what, when, how, and why—*We are aware that the road to religious tolerance, individual freedoms, and the governments that guarantee those blessings has been crooked, crowded, rough, and bumpy; but the tough road unquestionably has led us to* *freedom of choice for the opportunity of success and fulfillment. We simply cannot get hung up on the errors made during a historical journey and thereby deny the correctness of where we have arrived. Errors are made in reaching most worthwhile destinations, but those errors, no matter how bad, do not make the destination bad. Sometimes, the means are bad, not the ends. If you think we are saying the ends justify the means, you're in denial!*

We are saying "no" to political correctness and including a section on religion. It seems required because religion, more than any other factor in the world, has affected how we manage and lead others. Today, more than at any other time in our memories, religion plays a part in the world and its direction. In many ways it seems we are back to the days when the world was fighting for the dominant religion, i.e., the Crusades and Spanish attempts to Christianize the New World. We hope you don't take this section wrong, for we are not telling you how or what to believe; we are showing you some basics that can help you in understanding how religion has shaped us and most of the world. Judeo-Christian views have shaped American thinking on leadership study and teaching just as those views are the foundation for capitalism—which is the best system ever devised to generate the wealth necessary to solve problems we face today.

Leadership is the only answer for building a future that's worth living in, and management is a precursor to leadership. Yes, Bill and Dave are Christians and Americans with views shaped by those facts. Everyone on earth is a product of the nature and nurture that we wrote about in earlier chapters. Don't let people fool you and don't fool yourself—you are made by many things that have happened to you and your ancestors, purposeful and otherwise.

In *For the Glory of God: How Monotheism Led to Reformations, Science, Witch-Hunts, and the End of Slavery,* Stark (2003) defined his work as social science, not as philosophy or religion. He took great pains not to imply or deny the existence of God or to express his own personal religious views. He said that humans naturally seek explanations for the meaning of our existence. We believe as Stark said: People seek religion not just for things they desire but for meaning, dignity, hope, and inspiration. Stark starts by stating that in the advanced and less sophisticated societies "monotheism may well have been the single most significant innovation in history" (p. 1). He says that religion has been responsible for many of the good things that have happened in the world and that many people simply don't want to admit that fact. Stark further asserts that reforming impulses are an aspect of all religious organizations and that the Christian Protestant Reformation, started as early as the second century, was the foundation for democracy and individuality, and thus today's leadership.

More foundational understandings of Judaism, Christianity, and Islam should help us develop more useful leadership models, roles, and teachings. The frameworks of our understandings of organizations, management, leadership, and many other concepts related to our environments are truly religion-based. Denying this fact does not make it less so. The thoughts, theories, and theologies that resulted in more modern understandings of religions serve as a model for our study of such abstract yet observable concepts as organizational leadership. Understand the history of religions to understand the history of leadership. We all suffer greatly from cultural limitations, and our modern media and political correctness keep us in a limited-perspective mode. Move out of these problems through a greater understanding of your limits.

"So, then, let us finally be done with the claim that religion is all about ritual....It was not the 'wisdom of the East' that gave rise to science, nor did Zen meditation turn people's hearts against slavery. By the same token, science was not the work of Western secularists or even deists; it was entirely the work of devout believers in an active, conscious, creator God. And it was faith in the goodness of the same God and the mission of Jesus that lead other devout Christians to end slavery, first in medieval Europe and then again in the New World. In these ways, at least, Western civilization really was God-given" (p. 376).

Can you see Stark's points—that religion has provided our foundation for governments, social-cultural systems, prosperity, leadership, and understanding of the world in which we must live and lead? Do NOT blame religion; instead, blame our limited interpretation and use of religion. Stark clearly shows that religion led us out of the Dark Ages into the light, and out of slavery to freedom and opportunity. Do not let religion reverse that trend because we misinterpret it.

Listed below are some points that we all need to contemplate as we are thinking about religion and its impact on our world and our understanding of management and leadership:

- God and our definitions of God are not one and the same—humans do not have the words to describe all God is. The agenda for the realm of God is not the agenda of our idols of words: we characterize God by our analogies since they are all we have.

- Honor all questions in the search for truth—do not claim to have all answers.

- Explanations to or about ourselves are human inventions.

- Christian, Jewish, and Islamic education should be the search for truth rather than the indoctrination of a form of religion—whether it is comfortable or not.

- Christianity, Judaism, and Islam are not just to be believed, but to be lived.

- No religion, including Christianity, Judaism, and Islam, has ever come in as a totally new thing. As C. S Lewis said, "When I was an atheist, the whole Christian thing looked very probable to me; now that I am a Christian, Christianity often looks very improbable to me."

- Regardless of your religion, Jesus, Mohammed, and Moses (the Ten Commandments) were defining moments in the journey to the meaning of God.

- Not agreeing with someone's religion should not keep us from using their insights.

- As Christians, God is real to us and Jesus is our window to God. Islam has Mohammed and Judaism has Abraham and Moses.

- Many of us know a lot of the Bible/Koran/Torah, yet do not live an integrative Biblical/Koran/Torah and Talmud life.

- Islam and Christianity differ in many ways that can't be resolved. One simple example is that Islamic people think Christians exploit women; Christians think we give them freedom. Islam teaches revering women; Christianity, in one view, teaches that women should be subservient to men. Perspectives are very different and basically impossible to change when they relate to one's religion.

- I have no final answers; do you? There is a truth if there is a God (and we believe there is), but only God can know that truth that we are seeking. Perhaps that is why He made us—to search for the truth.

- All real searches for knowledge must begin and end with doubt.

- There is a God and we ain't Him.

Handy (1998), in *The Hungry Spirit*, ties religion and capitalism, and the freedoms they give us to succeed, together nicely. He makes suggestions for social entrepreneurship and adjustments to our corporations and their members. He says corporate members should become corporate citizens with rights and responsibilities. "Nobody can prove to anyone else's satisfaction that their beliefs are right (p. xv)....A truly open society accepts that there is no such thing as an absolute truth (p. xiv)....[I]f you believe that most people are capable and can be relied upon, they will often live up to your expectations. Optimists are always prey to disappointment, but life without hope is dismal (p. 6)....There are two great hungers and the greater hunger is 'Why?'...Money breeds creativity. Money also brings choice, and freedom of a sort (pp. 4-5)....Money is a necessary but not sufficient condition of happiness (p. 6)....Markets don't work where the human cost of failure is unacceptable (p. 8)....Any business that concentrates on its internal mechanisms more than on the customer is, ultimately, a bad business" (p. 10). These principles support our 12 Quotients for religion and capitalism and have provided the framework of opportunity for work and success.

"Capitalism, then, would revert to its proper role, as a philosophy designed to deliver the means but not necessarily the point of life....Capitalism helps the poor to escape from poverty (p. 50)....Creativity, choice and responsibility, morality and community are the fruits of capitalism (p. 53)....To be free to move when opportunity knocks. To be free to leave when it stops knocking" (p. 65). Are we fortunate or what?—Leaders know that we are.

Choice makes the need for leadership. Yes, you can break from a past to a new *LQ*© you.

As we said, Dave and Bill are both blessed to be Christians and Americans, and we proudly proclaim both titles. As such, we would like you to think of a few facts. Christians are about one-third of the world's population and control over two-thirds of its wealth. Americans are 5% of the world's population and control about 40% of the world's domestic product. America spends more than all of the other 200 countries combined that have a military on our military and we do it with about 6% of our GDP—thus we have a responsibility to help the world with our power (regardless of your persuasion of whether we are doing it correctly or not, it's a responsibility). Do these facts say we are right or wrong?

Christians are among the most generous people in the world, yet we give away only about 2% of our total incomes. Over 90% of Americans say they believe in God and about 60% say this is very important in their lives. As Americans, we are the most blessed people in all of history, both freedom-wise and monetarily. The American minimum wage for one hour of work is about three day's, income for over 2,000,000,000 people! We spent about $7,000,000,000 on Halloween in 2003, and that is more than the GDP of most countries in the world. With these simple facts we must ask, "Will Americans use the blessings we have to make the world a better place? Will those reading this book work to lead in such a way as to squander or spread wealth, well-being, and freedom? Thinking beyond Christianity and America, will all the religious peoples of our small planet use their religions for good or for ill?"

While this section might seem like rabbit-chasing, we deem it necessary, since we need to go ahead and admit facts about the most important foundations to the thinking of leaders and would-be leaders. Nothing is more important in the thinking and actions of the majority of people in the world than their very personal and real religions. We do not want to put anyone off, but we care about all elements that produce the Leadership Quotient, and religion is a major factor.

***So much for religion—on to our pronouncements about the future for MQ and* LQ**©—*Make a difference, or simply nothing will make any difference.*

Peter F. Drucker said that the average retirement age in the developed countries will have to go up to about 75 for healthy people (the majority at that age) before 2010; sounds good to Dave and Bill—what about to you? Economic growth will increasingly have to come from productivity in the developed countries. There will be no dominant single world economic power, though the world economy will be highly competitive and turbulent. Information needs of organizations will change rapidly. Knowledge will make resources mobile since knowledge workers carry their trade in their heads. The meaning of organization will change and there will continue to be more and varied ways to organize. The art and science of management will continue to evolve and be used more outside of business organizations. Drucker ends by saying he will make no predictions, for the items presented here have already happened (1998).

Use our predictions—rambling and unorthodox—as a "straw man," and then make your own: 1) the world will become freer and safer, 2) Americans will continue to have weight problems—in spite of the no-carb fad—because we are lazy (sadly, colon cancer will increase with the no-carb diet), 3) we will continue to have a worldwide energy crunch, 4) China will become much more dominant, 5) the last bastions of Communism are on their very last legs and will soon fail, 6) religion will be more important to more people worldwide, 7) Microsoft will not move much unless they buy some other firms, 8) new technologies and new biological discoveries will astound us, 9) leadership will prevail over management, 10) higher education in the U.S. will experience some profound changes—directed toward reality, not provability, 11) U.S. markets will continue to rebound, 12) travel will rebound, 13) there will be more terrorist attacks, but the numbers of people affected will be smaller, 14) interest rates will rise, 15) unemployment will mediate in the U.S. but not in western Europe, 16) Russia will experience some kind of crisis because they are not totally accepting capitalism, 17) in spite of the increased emphasis on ethics, lapses in ethics will still occur, 18) people will rush to buy our book, 19) entertainment will move from team sports, except for football (we have to have our violence), and lastly, 20) Rush Limbaugh will marry again after another round of drug rehab—please prove us wrong, Rush! Stop for a few minutes and think about the trends you can see for yourself and the worlds within which you must exist.

We see the need to realize that one must continually learn to learn. A continuous search for knowledge makes life worthwhile for the learner and the beneficiary of the knowledge. Trends toward freedom, free trade, cultural identity, education, information, self-reliance, reduction of government, affluence for all, and tolerance have some momentum; but sadly on the reverse side, we see decadence and decline, for the already successful and evil seem unstoppable. Effective Leadership Quotient leaders are able to stress the potential for good and at the same time stifle the potential for evil that so many great powers have suffered throughout history.

Self-managing and the management career—*managing up to move up.*

Most of you who really desire leadership within the corporate world will ascend to high levels within large, publicly-traded companies and must at some point learn how to manage a board of directors. We think that managing a board is akin to managing your boss, which is the most important task of management. So practice managing your boss and you'll be ready for managing a board. Managing subordinates is nothing compared to managing your boss—learn to do this to have a really high Management Quotient.

Staying ahead as a manager requires that you and your organization learn at all levels. Everyone within your span of control needs to scan the environment, suggest changes, come up with new programs and systems, and take advantage of environmental trends and shifts to become a topflight manager of the future in the present. Major shifts in your thinking must happen to match shifts when they occur:

1. in the thinking of the majority of others you must deal with;

2. within and because of technology;

3. because of regulatory and legal requirements;

4. in the customer values and preferences;

5. with new followers or situations;

6. with many other issues that change daily in our global, intensely competitive, environment.

In *Career Warfare*, D'Alessandro (2004) gives us ten rules for building a personal brand and keeping it. He says: 1) don't be too generic, 2) don't throw in the towel, 3) ask for opportunities and promotions, 4) make sure your assignments provide opportunity, 5) control the change you see coming, 6) gamble shrewdly, 7) develop your brain, 8) tinker with success, 9) don't lie or cheat, and 10) be conscious that every day you are building a reputation called "you." He tells us to act like we are expensive and worth it, use our bosses in building our brand, learn about all the correct management tools, act like it's always show time, pick enemies and battles carefully, and realize that the higher your position in an organization, the more of a target you become.

"Meaning is not something you stumble across, like the answer to a riddle or the prize in a treasure hunt. Meaning is something you build into your life. You build it out of your own past, out of your affections and loyalties, out of the experience of humankind as it is passed on to you, out of your own talent and understanding, out of the things you believe in, out of the things and people you love, out of the values for which you are willing to sacrifice something. The ingredients are there. You are the only one who can put them together into that unique pattern that will be your life. Let it be a life that has dignity and meaning for you. If it does, then the particular balance of success or failure—as the world measures success or failure—is of less account" (Gardner, 2003, p. 53).

When plotting and planning your management career, recall Drucker's words:

> Knowledge workers are likely to outlive their employing organization....The average life expectancy of a successful business is only thirty years—and in a period of great turbulence such as the one we are living in, it is unlikely to be even that long. Even organizations that normally are long-lived if not expected to live forever—schools and universities, hospitals, government agencies—will see rapid changes in the period of turbulence we have already entered. Even if they survive—and a great many surely will not, at least not in their present form—they will change their structure, the work they are doing, the knowledges they require and the kind of people they employ. Increasingly, therefore, workers, and especially knowledge workers, will outlive any one employer, and will have to be pre-

pared for more than one job, more than one assignment, more than one career. (Drucker, 1999, p. 163)

Words to remember for management excellence—*"Every time I encounter utterly first-class managers they turn out to have quite a lot of the leader in them"* (Gardner, 2003, p. 116).

Just because we did not mention a management topic does not mean we don't think it's important. It does mean that we felt you should already know it or that it's in too many places for us to take the time to repeat it. However, you should realize that we did spend a lot of time repeating simple concepts because all management principles in the end must be simple, and also because some things are so important that you must be reminded of them. There is so much to management and becoming a better manager, and so we are closing this descriptive section with some words to remember. If you don't get them, then reread the book! Management is:

> Truthfulness; Openness; Passion and Compassion; Discipline—Give and Have; Love; Respect—Self and Others; Selflessness; Conviction; Courage; Persuasiveness; Listening; Speaking; Responsibility; Empowerment; Imagination; Innovative; Inventive; Resilient; Caring; Fun; Accomplishment; Productive; Learner and Learned; Speed; Balance; Fit; Appropriate; It Depends; Not Exactly; Dreaming; Acting; Measuring; Testing; Reinventing; Desire; Achievement; Preparation; Deciding; Going for It; Staying in It; Leadership; Observing; Listening; Discussing; Reading; Thinking.

A little story of what can happen to you—*"Try not to become a man of success, but rather a man of value"* (Albert Einstein, quoted in The Book of American Value and Virtues, *eds. Bruun and Getzen, 1996, p. 526).*

"The faculty at the University of Heidelberg rejected the thesis, probably due as much to their deficiencies of imagination as to actual faults of Oberth's theories (p. 24)....Von Braun, who exploited good ideas wherever he found them, incorporated it in his plans for his space station (p. 75)....The overall Apollo program eventually required the direct involvement of about 20,000 industrial and university contractors and the participation of 400,000 people (p. 154)....When the Third Reich collapsed, von Braun unashamedly switched his allegiance to the victor. He became a leader in the United States space program and the prophet of space travel. Because of his tireless promotion, he was the man who sold the moon. Sadly, because of his complicity with the Nazi cause, he also sold his soul to reach that goal" (Piszkiewicz, 1998, p. 203). Be successful as a manager but understand the price of your success as you determine how to gain success: quick and dirty, or over a lifetime of committed learning.

Why MQ Is Next

People usually start as supervisors or team leaders, and they develop into higher-level managers if they do their jobs well. In all modern organizations, you must fit in as a manager before you can stand out as a leader. You must first be able to provide stability and control, before you are allowed to shake things up and be innovative for the future. You must first survive before you can make progress toward a better tomorrow for you, your organization, and the world as a whole. We are all a part of the world, and we only can survive if it does. The stability and civility of the world determine your quality of life. By understanding these facts, we learn to manage the FISO (Fit In—Stand Out) of leadership. The following paragraphs will go into detail about the varied components that make up the Management Quotient that enable you to become a good manager capable of being promoted.

Description of the Management Quotient and its Dimensions

What others have said makes up a real and effective manager—*The theme of MQ is, "It's not about you." "The purpose of your life is far greater than your own personal fulfillment, your peace of mind, or even your happiness. It's far greater than your family, your career, or even your wildest dreams and ambitions" (Warren,* The Purpose-Driven Life, *2002, p. 17—We like this title and the book lives up to the hype).*

As we reviewed the 800+ completed $LQ^{©}$ instruments, we avoided using the normal planning, organizing, directing, and controlling terms associated with management. In fact, those who used these terms were, in general, the younger and less experienced respondents. One of the amazing facts was that teams and teaming were mentioned only twice; and the word "powerful" was mentioned only once. Jack Welch and Donald Trump were the most often cited examples of managers. A few people mentioned as exemplars were very interesting, and we will use them in the Strengths and Weaknesses section below.

As we present what our $LQ^{©}$ surveys have revealed, remember the tasks of management, for one with real MQ must begin with a shift in thinking **from controlling to relationship-building** and **from directing to coaching**.

Normal Natural MQ Strengths—Quadrant 1 of the MQ 2X2 Matrix

The first reported trait we are calling **selflessness: always considering others over self**. Most $LQ^{©}$ instrument respondents alluded to this in some way. Many talked about unselfishness, really caring for others, or simply love, but most pointed to people who give credit to others first, or those who don't seem to care who gets the credit. Rick Warren, the author of *The Purpose-Driven Life* (2002), was mentioned several times, as was Sam Walton. Of course, we all know the stories of Sam going to his Wal-Mart stores in his old pickup truck with his sack lunch. Walton's attention to others is legendary.

Warren's book was mentioned a number of times because of our Bible Belt respondents, and in fact, several mentioned the Lead Like Jesus Leadership Conference that Rick hosted in Birmingham in late 2003. Bill, along with 25 students, was able to attend the conference, thanks to a really outstanding leader who is the retired president of Alabama Power. The conference was excellent, and though it had a strong religious slant, as the title would suggest, Warren and Ken Blanchard did an excellent job of giving the 300,000+ participants (most via video linkup) solid managerial values they could really use, regardless of religious beliefs.

We lumped a number of responses into the "others over self" category. Words like "serve," "service," and "ethical" occurred many times. In all of these cases, the words associated with these terms pointed to a certain level of selflessness. We know service belongs in this category, but perhaps ethics belongs somewhere else. For simplicity's sake, we categorized it here.

The second natural trait we see reported is **decisiveness**. General Patton and the movie characters of *True Grit* were mentioned often in this area. It seems that people do recognize that the ability to make a decision in light of imperfect information is a necessity for management or leadership greatness. As we have said, at some point you've just got to make a decision, even if it's wrong! A decision gives everyone involved a point of reference and a place to start adjusting, whereas no decision leaves everyone hanging and not knowing how to adapt or adjust. If you don't decide, you can bet your competition will.

The third reported trait we see as natural is the ability to **motivate**. A lot of people talked about Donald Trump in his hit TV show, *The Apprentice,* where "you're fired" were the dreaded words that seemed to motivate contestants. The legendary coach, Bear Bryant, was mentioned by several respondents and more especially by a couple who played for the Bear. Bear Bryant and the legendary Grambling coach, Eddie Robinson, who was also mentioned in this area, motivated with their mere presence. Most of us have to work at it, but then we suppose that Eddie and Bear had to work at it the first years of their amazing careers.

The final natural trait we see reported is **organized**. People talk about people who always have everything in order and because of this, execute or act to accomplish all tasks at hand. Often people included words like "logically organized" or "methodically organized." Many mentioned military leaders like Tommy Franks and Norman Schwarzkopf. We all know people who appear to have it all together because they can locate anything and everything; they know who, what, and when about everything they are involved in. The organization we are talking about usually results in people having a clear mind because all the known facts and figures are in their proper places: a place for everything and everything in its place.

Normal Natural MQ Weaknesses—Quadrant 3 of the MQ 2X2 Matrix

The first natural weakness we see reported is **self-serving**. This one seems to be easy to spot in political candidates, bosses, TV characters, and of course, our own managers. People don't work well for managers with a "you work for me" attitude. The self-centered approach of Alabama Supreme Court Judge Roy Moore, when he defied the very court he worked for, showed an unbelievable level of self-serving and self-centeredness he could not disguise.

Fidel Castro is the poster child for self-serving people. He has ruined the lives of millions with his "me at any cost" approach. Castro will be remembered by the world as a total and utter disaster mainly because of his self-serving weakness.

The second natural weakness we see reported is **indecisiveness**. It seems that most people are indecisive. Many today are so baffled by the number of choices available that they are made stagnant by the vastness of the alternatives: choosing just not to decide. Even though it may seem that many get into hot water for deciding for the wrong reasons or making the wrong choices, it has been the experience of almost all managers that non-deciders lose out quickly.

We mourn the recent passing of Ronald Reagan even as we celebrate his great life, and we must all admit that he was anything but indecisive. In fact, early on, he was called an out-of-control cowboy, and a warmonger, among many other things. His declaration of the Soviet Union as the Evil Empire caused a wave of criticism; but eventually, his unwavering and narrowly directed purpose of destroying Communism resulted in the freeing of hundreds of millions of people—Reagan was very decisive. Krauthammer's (2004) article title says about all we need to know: "He Could See for Miles: Reagan had a vision and the courage to endure all doubters" (p. 94). That's why Reagan was decisive—he was convinced of his convictions.

The third reported natural weakness that was reported to us is **unethical**. With the myriad of corporate scandals we have today, just pick your own poster child for this one. Sadly, you have plenty of choices.

The final reported natural weakness we see is **perfectionist**. We see many who say they are perfectionists, yet we can't see it. Most self-proclaimed perfectionists just like to tell you how you could do it better versus just doing it better themselves. Many past executives felt they knew it all and that no one could do it like them. This is often called the "savior complex." It's when the leader thinks he is the only person who can "save" an organization. Sometimes the threats to the organization are real, and sometimes they are created to give the savior a reason for leadership.

Perfectionists and saviors often are effective for a time, but then the organization outgrows their ability to know it all and they became history. It's one thing to want things to be perfect and help others reach that, and another just to complain because things are not perfect. Is Disney's leader, Michael Eisner, an example of this weakness, and possibly was our former President Jimmy Carter? You decide; but we are confident you know a lot of people who are perfectionists, and even more who claim to be.

Normal Nurtured MQ Strengths—Quadrant 2 of the MQ 2X2 Matrix

The first nurtured strength we see reported is a manager who really **empowers** others by giving away a part of her own power. Some are good at delegating and seem so good at trusting and picking people to trust. For empowerment to really work, it must be freely given and freely accepted, and it must result in a trusting attitude of mutual respect and understanding. LBJ did not do so well in delegation or empowerment related to the Vietnam War, but the elder Bush did a great job of empowerment with the first Gulf War.

One interesting example was given with the *I Love Lucy* show of old. Someone said, "Lucy could empower Ethel to do all her dirty work." We have seen this type of empowerment, and it works for the short run. Empower for the growth of others and you will have an effective MQ.

The second nurtured trait we see reported can result in someone being called a **systematizer**. This is someone who can develop a system or a unified set of procedures and policies that can work to relieve people of the burdens of managing in some respects. Henry Ford was mentioned here. Robert McNamara established rules and systems for the Defense Department in the 1960s—some were successful, and others were not. Curtis LeMay did this with the firebombing of Japanese cities near the end of the Second World War, and the system killed many more people than both of the atomic bombs used to end the war with Japan.

The third trait we see is that of **mentor**. Usually one that becomes a mentor has been mentored. Here we like to think of a young man in the George W. Bush White House, Dr. Eric Motley. Eric tells the story of how his aunt helped him move out of the "Turtles" reading group at school; how his granddad was willing to sell his car to get Eric into college; how a teacher told Samford University's president to "give this young man a scholarship"; and, finally, how the rector of the University of St. Andrews in Scotland, where Eric was working on a master's degree, said, "A young, brown man like you needs a proper Ph.D.," as he gave Eric a scholarship to complete his Ph.D. Eric says so many helped and mentored him that he simply could not fail to help others. Remember Dr. Eric Motley. Eric will make an impact in this world because of his mentors and protégés.

In the area of mentoring, we also want to mention coaching, for the two can be and often are used together. People coach their protégés as they show and tell them how to work through their own management dilemmas. Coaches see their management jobs in a different light than directors see theirs. A coach teaches versus directs. Chose your mentors and protégés carefully, and learn to be a **mentor-coach** manager, not a **director-boss** manager.

DuBrin's (2005) *Coaching and Mentoring Skills* is an excellent little book on these topics. DuBrin says of coaching and mentoring:

> You probably have some experience in coaching whether or not the activity was given a formal label. If you have helped someone else improve his or her performance on the job, on the athletic field, in the musical band, or on the dance floor, you have some coaching experience. In the workplace,

coaching is a method of helping workers grow and improve their job competence by providing suggestions and encouragement. An effective coach displays the following skills and characteristics: empathy, active listening, ability to size up people, diplomacy and tact, patience toward people, concern for the welfare of others, self-confidence, non-competitiveness with team members, and enthusiasm for people (p. ix)....Mentoring is also a method of helping others grow and develop, but it involves a greater range of helping activities and skills than coaching. In Homer's tale, *The Odyssey,* Mentor was a wise and trusted friend as well as a counselor and adviser. A **mentor** is generally defined as an individual with advanced experience and knowledge who is committed to giving support and career advice to a less experienced person. The less experienced person is the **protégé** from the French word for "protected" (p. x)....All mentors should be coaches and master the skills involved in effective coaching, but not all coaches need to be mentors. Any worker of any level can coach another team member. A mentor, however, is more experienced in some important aspect of the job and wiser than his or her protégé. (p. xi)

A final nurtured trait of the Management Quotient is the ability to **find and attract talent**. These people seem to have figured out how to judge who is good for what job, and then they can get them to take the job. We'd bet that Donald Trump is this way, as are many others. In the book, *Brotherhood of the Bomb* (Herken, 2002), Robert Oppenheimer is described as the manager at Los Alamos who recruited the people who enabled the U.S. to develop the first atomic bomb. Oppenheimer seemed to have many problems, but he could recognize and then get the right people to help him with the most difficult tasks.

Normal Nurtured MQ Weaknesses—Quadrant 4 of the MQ 2X2 Matrix

This section really could go on quite awhile. We all see so many poor if not downright pitiful managers. We often wonder why so many are poor at managing others; and then we realize how poor they are at managing their own personal lives: bankruptcies, divorce, lack of education, drug use, alcohol and tobacco addiction, obesity. When you realize that many people can't manage their personal lives, it's easier to realize why they can't manage others. We often wonder aloud to our students if their future employers care whether we teach them management principles or knitting or shooting free throws. The future employer just wants to know if the person can "get their act together and show up," which is proven by getting accepted to college, enrolling in the class, and showing up for class.

The first reported nurtured weakness we see is that of **laziness**. We remember when a man was a man and had to get up to turn the TV channel and open a can or bottle with an opener and even push in a clutch as he drove in the heat without power steering: wow, we were tough! Now, we basically don't have to lift a finger, and we don't. Too many of us aren't good managers because we are lazy and don't want to do the homework necessary to be good managers. Reread the first section of this chapter if you don't recall what all it takes to be a good manager. Contrary to the belief of most followers, it's harder to be the manager than a worker. Managers work longer hours and spend more of their free time preparing for the future then do non-managers. The biggest problem with being an executive is that you basically have to commit your life to it. Many refuse promotions into the ranks of management because of the loss of freedom the move entails. Many try management and go back to their old job when they see that "hey, I'm in charge now" causes them to have to really begin to work. Managers at any level can't check their heads and hearts at the door at 5:00 p.m. Most upper-level executives have no quitting time. Going to dinner with clients and applicants is not that much fun for very long, and neither is business travel. We'd rather stay at home and have some time of our own, so we consequently got out of management and went back to get Ph.D.s. We are too lazy for management—are you?

The second reported nurtured weakness we see is that of **micromanagement**. If you can't let go, but have to have your hands on everything, you will always have a low Management Quotient. At some point, a manager's job goes beyond what the individual can do and becomes what the manager can get others to do. It is indeed very difficult to know the level at which to hold on and the level at which to let go; just as it is difficult to know whom to trust with what, and whom not to trust. This indeed takes some trial and error. Though we seem to think people naturally know these "when to hold and when to let go" truths, nothing is further from the truth. Most will tell you they have been burned; and many can share with you the secrets they now use to appear to be natural managers who know when to control and when to let go. In actuality, they know that in part a subordinate is to be more trusted when the subordinate admits ignorance than when the subordinate says he is infallible.

A third nurtured managerial weakness is **greed**. Greed is not good. Greed is the root of most evil. We are confident you can think of many examples of people who got too greedy for their own good. It seems that there is really not a little greed, for the greedy just become more greedy—makes sense if you think about it!

The final nurtured weakness we see is an **unwillingness to confront**. To be a good manager you have to confront people with good and bad things. You have to be willing to say, "You are fired," and many other tough words. Poor Management Quotient leaders are unwilling to just say no. As simple as it sounds, human beings don't naturally like to confront others, and yet some of the most successful managers develop a skill that allows them to confront quickly and easily. Most managers (those who have short careers for the most part) are not willing to say what needs to be said. Jim McNerny, CEO of 3M, and Bob Nardelli of Home Depot seem to be leaders and managers who will confront and tell people what to do. We are not sure at this point if Jeff Immelt, Jack Welch's replacement, will be as good at confronting people at GE as Jack Welch was—but then hardly anyone is!

Using the MQ Matrix

For the last time, evaluate yourself in each of the four quadrants in Figure 13.1.

Figure 13.1: YOUR MQ MEASUREMENT AND IMPROVEMENT MATRICES

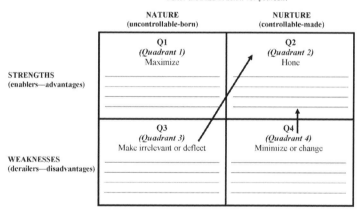

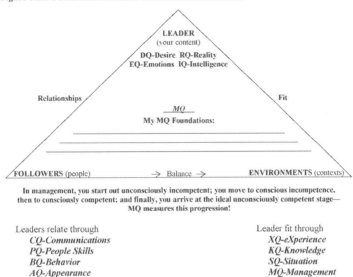

Figure 13.2: YOUR LEADERSHIP LEVERAGE TRIANGLE

In management, you start out unconsciously incompetent; you move to conscious incompetence, then to consciously competent; and finally, you arrive at the ideal unconsciously competent stage—MQ measures this progression!

Leaders relate through
 CQ-Communications
 PQ-People Skills
 BQ-Behavior
 AQ-Appearance

Leader fit through
 XQ-eXperience
 KQ-Knowledge
 SQ-Situation
 MQ-Management

Evaluating Your MQ Personal Profile: Strengths and Weaknesses

Doing Something About Your MQ!

Great managers know:

- it's not about self. it's about others;

- it's not about personal visions, it's about collective visions;

- it's not about personal fame, it's about organizational fame;

- it's not about money, it's about lasting rewards;

- it's not about self-development, it's about developing others; and

- management is hard work.

While we were writing this section, we saw former President Bill Clinton on a TV interview saying, "Only a fool does not look to explain his mistakes." Be self-critical, analytical-correcting, and ultimately self-assured, and you will improve your MQ to the level necessary to have a shot at becoming a real *LQ*$^©$ leader. Just get to work!

MQ Conclusions

> *What is in one's history affects how one acts and thinks.... "When making decisions, it's very important to me to be aware of all my feelings....I didn't change because of analysis, but analysis allowed me to change. It gave me the self-assurance to be self-determining rather than determined by circumstances. I was aware that life can be very fast-paced, and I had a hunger to do a lot in a short period of time....I ask myself, 'Am I interested, relaxed, tense or bored, and what is this candidate doing to make me feel one way or the other?'" (Daniel Vasella, Novartis's Chairman and CEO, quoted in Hymowtz, 2004, p. B1).*

Continued self-understanding is the key to MQ development over time.

Before we move on—We had available to us a multitude of subtopics to include in this chapter. We started to write about all of them; then we decided that you could read many of the books that are available on those topics. Though they are often too simple, these books do provide a starting point for improving your Management Quotient.

The final chapter of *LQ*$^©$ should help you pull the entire Leadership Quotient framework together.

14

The LQ©, Conclusion

"Those who travel are never the same when they return home from their journeys. Change cannot be escaped. Perspectives are stretched, and the truth about the world makes a little more sense....It's all about what you decide to make of it. Expect the world, because that is what you are getting."—Andrew Michel, from Samford University's "London Program News and Views," Winter 2004

The New Fad: The No-Fad Approach

We appreciate Andrew's refreshing view about the world. But we didn't include the part about why he traveled in the first place: he was burned out after two full years of college. That's not much compared to what many people go through, and what you will experience as you build your own Leadership Quotient that matches your leadership style with your followers in your environment. Still, wouldn't it be nice if all of us could experience what Andrew experienced? But then, we can, can't we?

It seems that a journey is first and foremost a matter of how one's mind is set and not so much about the experience one actually goes through. Your journey is to a more successful leadership style. It does not have to be in London, of which Samuel Johnson said, "…When a man is tired of London, he is tired of life." It does not have to result in climbing a mountain or jumping from a plane at the age of 80, as former President George Bush did. It comes from a journey within your mind, a journey of learning, a journey of growth.

We hope you have made *LQ©* a journey of learning and growth. We promised a somewhat irreverent, but genuine, approach to leadership, and we hope you think we have delivered. We have not hesitated to criticize long-standing leadership and management traditions or the spoutings of the popular media. The "how great I art" and silly "parables" currently selling like hotcakes exemplify all that is wrong with leadership development. They promise a quick fix, but seldom deliver any substance. We challenge you to use the effort you would waste on fads. Put it into *LQ©* and build a lasting foundation upon which to launch the new you as an effective and successful leader. $LQ^©$ will make you into a leader who can recognize and adapt your leadership style to fit the people and the environment.

We admonish you to finish strong and learn the lessons that provide a foundation for your life as a learning regenerative leader. That foundation must rest on sound principles of others before self and understanding that leadership is influence, beginning to end. It's simply your choice: pay the price of the fad over and over, or start doing it the $LQ^©$ way right now. The chief danger in following a fad is that it delays working on the really important foundational principles that in the long run are the only hope of success.

$LQ^©$ was conceived to help us all become better leaders. It is intended to help each of us fill the void of who we currently are, and even more importantly, who we can become as leaders. In the realities of all organizations there are problems, because organizations are collections of people, by people, and for people; and when people work together, there will be problems. When you start your journey toward organizational leadership, you need a road map. Formal academic education will make its contribution, but there is more "travel information" you need. Leadership is so much more than a position; it is a balanced process accomplished within differing contexts that encompasses various and diverse human followers. It is understandable when closely observed, and it has definite knowledges, skills, and abilities. Therefore, leadership influence is a set of learnable and teachable principles that are available to everyone who seeks them. Those are the basic assumptions behind the development of *The Leadership Quotient*.

$LQ^©$ is a road map that starts by making the overall path look easy with one simple triangle framework of leader, followers, and environments. Then those principles are extended to further identify the real potholes, shortcuts, and even new paths that must be recognized for one to truly succeed as a leader in a world of complex followers and convoluted situations. Each of us must learn to accept "what is" versus "what we wish to be." We also need help in gaining the wisdom and courage to know what can be changed within ourselves, within our followers, and about our environments, so we can become all we can be. This requires so much knowledge, understanding, and—ultimately—wisdom. Things are seldom as they originally seem, and even less often, things are as others tell us they are. Each of us who wants to become a better leader must develop frameworks that can guide us. We need paradigms for making sense of the world of leadership. That is what $LQ^©$ can do if you work with and through it.

We are not offering the normal quick fix; instead, we are offering the starting blocks for one wishing to become a future leader. The momentous issues we face in our overly complex and mostly open world cannot be solved with the same attitudes and thinking that produced the problems. "All the king's horses, and all the king's men, couldn't put Humpty together again." That's because the king made the rules, built the wall, and set all the paradigms under which the problem was created. Someone from outside the kingdom is needed to solve the problem. That's what we've humbly attempted to do with *The Leadership Quotient.* We want you to take a step back from the "kingdom" you work in and try to make yourself a better leader with your followers in your environment.

Most of the academic texts and articles give us the solutions that worked in the past. An improved *LQ$^©$* will move you toward the ability to develop new answers to future problems with an understanding of the irreducible complexities of complex problems. We must avoid making the same mistakes over and over again by using the old arguments and solutions. If it didn't work then, what makes you think it will work this time? Even those solutions that worked in the past must be justified anew, because even the solutions that worked before will not necessarily work again because situations and people change. Have a clear and precise reason for trying a solution that has succeeded in the past. Judgment and wisdom are the basic requirements for application of all principles and lessons. You don't develop that judgment or wisdom overnight from a book you read or something someone told you was the hidden secret to success. The secret is no secret; it's just old-fashioned work, as we have outlined in *The Leadership Quotient.* The lottery is a tax on people who are bad at math. Pop psychology theories of leadership are a leadership lottery for people who don't want to accept that leadership development is tough, personal work.

We have equated leadership fads to dieting fads, some of which work, but all of which have a cost. In dieting, some of the costs have been deadly; others have actually helped for a while, but most of them delayed the real change that was needed and produced a roller-coaster effect. Leadership development is much like weight control: At some point, you have to practice the basics of healthy eating and exercise. Then you continuously practice the fundamentals in your newly acquired and *balanced* lifestyle. In personal leadership development, you have to learn the basics of leadership style, followers, and environments to reach an understanding that it's about people and influence viewed with a *balanced* perspective. There are no magic bullets or pills, no single or even simple secret answers. There is only *balanced* hard work and discipline behind your becoming an effective leader who can *fit* the *leaders, followers,* and *environments* facing you so that you can indeed *stand out* as an effective leader who has honor and lasting respect.

It is amazing that people are still looking for quick fixes in health, management, and leadership. But perhaps we should not be surprised when humans seek a shortcut to happiness. It's like the choice of lifting weights or taking steroids to get more muscular. We make short- and long-term choices in leadership and many other areas of life. The drugs of leadership development are the fads that are sold every day that lead to the ethical scandals like Enron, WorldCom, HealthSouth, Tyco, and Adelphia. Sadly, popular culture encourages us to seek the quick fixes like the lottery and gambling to improve our lives. Even when they buy a book or see an article on an appropriate leadership topic that could provide a portion of the demanded fix, only a very small percentage of people actually read them for the good they can provide. So often we seek methods to change *others,* when it's *we* who need changing. Words and intentions are plentiful, but deeds are precious few: read and study to change yourself first. Don't waste your time on quick fixes or risk jail by cheating. Learn the basics and practice them. We have provided 12 basics of leadership success in this book.

This final chapter of *LQ*© will review the fundamentals of leadership, and we will summarize some of the things you need to know about all the quotients individually and as a whole. Though we have criticized fads, fads are not normally wrong. Fads just simply are not all there is to it. Often, as the term indicates, fads are very temporal and act as a "soup of the day" to help you get back on track. Fads are normally a small factor that can be of help when they are put into the context of the people and places where you need them. In fact, we have used basically all of the fads as support for the principles we have developed for this book. Fads can be of significance when they are used with a *balanced* understanding of how they fit in yet stand out. Used on their own, fads have a price, and most of the price is the neglect one gives to learning the basics as one practices the fad. But when used to supplement a solid program based on good principles, a fad can be a nice additional touch. We suggest it's better to work out your leadership desires with a lifetime workout program than with the 10-minutes-a-day approach. Depending on a fad is like depending on a snack for lunch, missing a night's sleep to catch up on some work, avoiding your boss because you don't want the bad news, or avoiding your spouse because you've messed up. These temporal solutions, which we call fads, are OK occasionally, but don't make a habit of them if you want to live a healthy, wealthy, and wise life.

We are reminded of James, a young man of 26 who lost a lot of weight over a couple of months. When we asked James how he did it, he said he started shooting pool every night for a couple of hours. What does that tell you? It tells you that James was in absolutely terrible physical shape and basically did nothing before he began his pool-shooting exercise routine. This example points out that if you're bad enough, anything will help, in exercise, management, or leadership.

For a Fad to be of Value, YOU Must Understand the Whole

"The belief that chance represents either insufficient knowledge or indifference is sometimes referred to as the subjective definition of randomness: according to this view randomness exists only in the minds of individuals, not in the objective world" (Bennett, 1998, p. 154). "From where we stand the rain seems random; if we would stand somewhere else, we could see the order in it" (Tony Hillerman, quoted in Bennett, 1998, p. 109).

We are struck by these words in so many ways. We think of them as we argue, and we contemplate the many wars throughout the world and current challenges we are faced with in our lives and times. Just think if everyone could see the perspective from afar or close up as would be the best for the correct view. We could solve so much because so often there is little difference in views, but there is no mutual understanding of differing views. In part the problem is that we don't listen, in part that we don't know; but mostly it's that we don't care to know. Leaders care enough to change, but they must change themselves first. We know that the current times in which we find ourselves require real leadership—leadership that can come only with study and dedication.

Four out of five corporate change efforts in America fail. That's an 80% failure rate for restructuring, reengineering, TQM, and teaming. Why? These failures are most often caused by management and leadership blunders—blunders caused normally by a belief in a "fad." The most successful leaders start with the primary objective desired and continually increase the number of individuals responsible ("involve 'em to sway 'em"). Then they ensure everyone knows how their performance is tied to the change objective. Make sure everyone understands the objective. Everyone should know how they will be rewarded if the change effort works. They should know what's in it for them if it works and how they will suffer if it fails. Then encourage creativity, innovation, and imagination when implementing the change. Concentrate your organizational design efforts on how people work, not on the structure. Structure is a facilitator, not a cause of change. Leaders must exhibit honesty and understand that it is important to stimulate and sustain behavior-driven change throughout an organization.

Themes of Quotient Chapters—You Simply Must Understand At Least This About Each Quotient

"Without ambition, one starts nothing. Without work one finishes nothing. The prize will not be sent. You have to win it."—Ralph Waldo Emerson

Chapter 1 introduced you to the *LQ©* and the **balanced triangulation** necessary to be a good leader, the need to **understand and mold** yourself as a leader, and the way to **read** followers and develop relationships as well as how to **fit** into differing environments. We repeatedly stressed the need to understand appropriateness, and the types and levels of relationships and fits that are required to become a more effective leader. We stressed that learning to be a better leader requires a lot of knowledge and understanding. We started the journey to real leadership understanding, not a "fad" or a "how great I art" view of leadership as you get so often in our too-busy world. The following seems to capsulate the topic of Chapter 1:

There are only two types of business books: the Obvious and the Envious. Most are compilations of cliché truths. Their success seems to rest on reassuring readers that they already know everything. Then there are the books that tell the stories of successful people or organizations, the best of which leave you wishing you could have been a part of them. Rarely is the issue in business writing whether or not a conclusion is true; more often it is just how often you've already heard the truth.

So it was a surprise to read *Career Warfare*, by the chairman of John Hancock Financial Services, David D'Alessandro, and find that there might be a new category to add: the Obvious, the Envious, and the Obnoxious. (Dauten, 2004, p. 1G)

In Chapter 2, we wrote about the quotients that are unique to you as a leader and how they can be molded and improved. We began by discussing the Desire Quotient, the first of the Leadership Quotients. We saw that you must ultimately **develop and use newfound skills related to Desire**. Development of your Desire Quotient was given as an intelligence that will serve you well, as will measuring and understanding your DQ. But to become even better at leading, we suggested practicing improvement in your DQ by expressing outwardly your emotions about doing, getting, or being, versus just saying you have the Desire. We're sorry it sounds like a cliché, but you must learn to "pump yourself up" about your own leadership development. We admonished you not to dwell on your DQ negatives. We began showing you what you can learn in the area of passion, commitment, and self-discipline that will allow you to make your strengths more important and your weaknesses irrelevant by building a solid and effective DQ.

In Chapter 3, we talked about your Reality Quotient. We saw that people who claim to have a natural RQ strength say they are realistic about themselves, others, and their situations. And we admonished you to develop for yourself a better RQ through realism about **yourself**, **others**, and **the situation**. One of the most critical qualities of a leader is the capacity to see the world and its people as they are becoming, not as you would like to see them become. That is a very good definition of RQ.

Next, we saw in Chapter 4 emotional intelligence as measured by the Emotional Quotient, which we defined as the sum total of **your ability to know and use your emotions and to read and use the emotions of others**. We saw that emotions can be good or faulty guides. But a good EQ is simply the wisdom to separate the defective from the appropriate emotion. Most failures we see in America today are not failures of intellect, but the results of emotional impairment. We saw IQ and luck contributing some 20% to success in life, and therefore, we determined that there were other more significant factors involved. EQ was consequently identified as a huge factor in leadership success.

In Chapter 5, we discussed the Intelligence Quotient and tried to shift your thinking from the IQ of old, which measured your ability to do well in American educational institutions, to a **successful IQ**, which is much broader and more important for a leader than the heretofore identified IQ. The educational system, current and past, was criticized severely for not working to recognize and develop a real successful IQ as opposed to an outdated, memory-based academic model. We ended by suggesting you should improve your $LQ^©$ IQ, and we discussed some of the ways to do it. To improve your IQ, start with DQ-RQ-EQ as foundational understandings that will lead to a real $LQ^©$ that can destine you for leadership greatness at the level you desire.

Starting Part II of $LQ^©$, we said that the theme throughout $LQ^©$ was the need to learn to identify, understand, change, and direct yourself, others, and your situations toward becoming more of what you can become as a leader. We challenged you as a leader to learn how to *fit in* yet *stand out* and make a difference through others. The road to personal leadership improvement starts with desire and self-awareness, goes on to continuous commitment to development, and ends with practice via application. The quotients in the second section were presented from the perspective of the followers. While *The Leadership Quotient* is a book about improving your leadership, this section contains quotients that are intended to give you a better perspective of your leadership effectiveness from the followers' viewpoint.

The first chapter of Part II, Chapter 6, the Communications Quotient, was the first on the follower quotients. In this chapter, we reminded you that, to improve your leadership communication, you needed to move ***from directing to connecting***. Communications was presented as the backbone of leadership and the most important of the followers' perceptions of a leader. We discussed in detail the Information Systems and Information Technology communications connections necessary for an organization to function well. We also provided a guide on how a leader develops a truly communicative organization. We challenged you to learn to communicate with others from their perspective, not yours.

Every leader's goal must be to "really" communicate by beginning to move from directing to connecting in every action they take. A real communicator in today's world is a facilitator, not a dictator. The leader must be content to let others determine meaning, without specifically spelling out the details of the message. Many leaders feel they must *convince* others of what they know, when in reality it is much more important to allow others to *realize* what they know in this age of empowerment. A modern leader will move from the two-year-old mentality of "it's mine" to the mature view of "you own it," when leadership through the empowerment and self-sufficiency of all followers is the goal. The truth related to this issue is that communication is the way to fulfill the intention to inform. We use communication to provide evidence and prove our evidence, to convince others that what we say is true. Remember that organizational management and leadership starts and ends strictly through communication.

In Chapter 7, we discussed the People Quotient and challenged you to shift your thinking a little. We stressed the need to think about **connecting through reflecting** on the perceptions of others and moving away **from fixation to adaptation**. We presented the People Quotient as the ability to escape the trap of being tough or singly focused on our own perspectives, and to move instead to the perspective of how can we work together. The new model of a leader is based on relationship-building, social skills, networking, and reading others. We all know people who are "people" people, and that is indeed what your PQ needs to reflect.

Chapter 8 discussed the Behavioral Quotient: BQ. In this chapter, we were reminded that often **our actions speak so loudly that no one can hear anything we say**. We know that leadership must be exhibited through our behavior and that in our fishbowl world everyone is looking to see what the leader does, not just what she says. To be a leader one has to act like a leader first and foremost. We were reminded that each of us influences at least ten thousand people during our lifetime and our behavior leads that influence. BQ says that your behavior highlights who you are to others.

Close behind behavior is appearance, and Chapter 9 was about the Appearance Quotient, AQ. This chapter is about how your appearance can have an effect on your leadership success. Appearance starts with what God gave us, but it goes into posture, etiquette, decorum, and the mix of interpersonal skills necessary to show people you care about them even before they see you act or hear what you have to say. **An appearance polished for leadership will start you off on the right foot as you begin your lifetime leadership development journey.**

In our third and last section of *LQ*$^{©}$, we looked at the final angle in our Leadership Quotient Triangle: the environments where leadership takes place. This angle required understanding about situations and **how to fit your own traits within the context of where you must lead**. The four quotients in this section were about gaining and using experience, knowledge, situational understanding, and management principles to improve your leadership.

In Chapter 10, we challenged you to answer whether you would rather follow someone with experience or not—XQ: The Experience Quotient. Then we showed you the **common group of factors that have been found to lead to success as people build experience**. We discussed the knowledge, skills, abilities, actions, and organizational savvy that allow you to truly fit in yet stand out. We showed you what successful XQ is about and how to improve yours, not just from your own experience, but from the experience of others.

In Chapter 11, we presented the KQ—Knowledge Quotient as the leader's **ability to learn, pay attention, recognize, imagine, and keep up to date** on workplace technologies. It included adaptability, innovativeness, and the ability to evolve. KQ goes beyond technology, to application of what one knows, to the correct situation at the right time. We looked again at the filters through which all our experiences and predispositions move, and advised you about the following common traps: anchoring; status quo; sunk cost; not knowing the why; confirming-evidence; framing; modeling; forecasting and estimating; over- and under-confidence; the safe side. We challenged you to develop the knowledge of these traps and the beginnings of the understandings necessary to apply leadership logic to what we learn as new knowledge, that is, improve your KQ.

Chapter 12 was about the Situational Quotient, SQ. We said that SQ determines a leader's ability to read a situation and strategize how to fit into it or make it fit your available followers within the environments in which they must operate. We asked that you **shift your thinking for leadership superiority toward versatility of thought and deed related to understanding and developing strategies to meet the situations at hand**. SQ was shown to include a great sense of timing and understanding of circumstances, as well as measured reactions to the situation as it actually exists, not as we wish it to be. SQ was also presented as strategic thinking and knowing more than the other guy about the reality of the situation one faces. SQ is about using a realistic situational understanding to develop a strategy that works. Those who correctly interpret the world as it is becoming will take more of the world's rewards than will those who misinterpret what the world is becoming.

In the final chapter on quotients, Chapter 13, MQ, we presented the Management Quotient. The MQ chapter was presented as **a guide to the task, responsibilities, and practices of management**. We discussed the tools of the trade of management as they exist in today's world of over-hyped, media-driven, over-informed yet under-knowledgeable do-gooders who try to lead for their own benefit without serving others. We showed how to come to grips with the necessities of acting to improve the organization for everyone if we wish to become managers who ultimately can lead other managers. We have to know we are responsible and act accordingly, and we have to start with a good basic MQ. We finally presented *management as an all-important step on the way to becoming a leader in today's organizations*.

The Appendices

We would like to briefly point you to Appendices A and B before concluding this chapter. Appendix A provides models of the overall lessons of *LQ©*, the lessons of each of the 12 quotients, and how *LQ©* fosters innovativeness. It also provides a clean-slate Matrix for each of the 12 quotients, plus forms for you to use in developing your personal leadership improvement plan for each of the quotients. We know you can figure out what to do in this area. Remember to express every planned task in terms of SMART objectives that are doable. So much improvement is possible, and the key is for you to admit that and just do it.

Lastly, Appendix B is a clean copy of the *LQ©* assessment instrument with a new and thoughtful slant for you to use after studying all of the leadership quotients.

Conclusions

> *"I think it is a great tragedy in life that people live and die and never find a dream around which they can feel resonance, a tragedy in part because a dream is available to people who seek it and a tragedy in part because of the lost and unrealized potential of individuals" (Clawson, 1999, p. 95).*

Thankfully, we always have a chance to start a new dream; and as, fortunately, we do not have to be right about everything, we define God and leadership with man's limits, and both are entirely beyond those confines. We have always had to search for theology, and we always will. All disciplines are used in theology: 1) history, 2) Scripture, and 3) experience, just as they should be used in all of leadership and leadership development. Yes, our system has problems, but it's as the old saying goes, "It's the best one we've ever seen." Only capitalism can provide the incubator for leadership that can make the world worth living in. Don't forget that "the danger never dreamt of, that is the danger" (A. Nicolson, 2003, p. 105). And we can't prepare for all the "never dreamt ofs"—yet we can prepare adaptable learning leaders who can effectively meet and solve those challenges of the unknown, if we will pay attention to the lessons of *LQ©*. *LQ©* provides a leadershipology. And yes, a lot of that theology has some Biblical views; yet we would say you don't need the religiosity to get the leadology—though it might not hurt!

We are reminded of the message of two great books, *Sarum* and *Pillars of the Earth,* both in part about the building of the great cathedrals in Europe. Both indicate that a stonemason must believe he is building a monument, not carving an individual stone. Likewise, you must think of building yourself as a leader beyond the individual stones of the principles we have given you. You must see the real complexity of the interaction of the whole, while practicing the individual simple principles.

We have offered so much that some will consider it daunting, to say the least. It's really not that tough. It's like building a house: the first bricks may seem so far from the finished house, just as the first day of biking across America seems so intimidating. They appear small as you get well into the journey, and at the end, the start seems, well, just insignificant. Start by hiring and associating with people who are smarter than you, people who will really challenge you. Then delegate more to them than you feel comfortable doing, and end up by always putting yourself on the spot—time after time! Finally, when you are perplexed, just remember: It's simply a matter of balance, fit, and relationships.

Until you can put in your own words the lesson of $LQ^{©}$, you don't have it. You should be a leader seeking faith in yourself as a leader through understanding of self, others, and the environments. A tall order, but one we are all capable of to some extent.

We really hope you will become a leader and learn to love being one. It is funny: Sometimes we don't learn to love something until we see someone who really loves it. Maybe that will happen to you and leadership. We love it and hope it shows, so maybe you'll grow to love it. We hope we have helped show you the way.

> *"Writing a book is an adventure. To begin with it is a toy and an amusement. Then it becomes a mistress, then it becomes a master, then it becomes a tyrant. The last phase is that just as you are about to be reconciled to your servitude, you kill the monster, and fling him about to the public"* (Winston Churchill, read and copied at Blenheim Palace, March 2001).

A person who is right all the time is a liar, dumb, or never tries much of significance: be none of these.

Here's our secret and our fad for leadership success:

    Our Secret: There is no secret.
    Our Fad: The no-fad fad.

Go get 'em!

Appendix 14.1—Workbook for Self-Improvement Models, Matrices, and Planning Documents

Appendix 14.2—*LQ*© Instrument

APPENDIX A

LQ© Models & Workbook for Self-Improvement

Contents

Notes on Using the Matrices and Self-Improvement Planning Documents

As you develop a strategy for your own overall *LQ$^{©}$* improvement, we would suggest following the ten steps below for creating a strategy for becoming all the leader you can become (a modified form of Dr. Phil McGraw's [2000] goals for getting what you want in life):

1. Clearly and honestly assess yourself for each of the 12 quotients.

2. Clearly express your goals in terms of specifics about events and behaviors. Be truthful and honest and don't establish goals you cannot or do not intend to accomplish.

3. Set doable goals that you can and will measure.

4. Define your objectives for each goal as SMART goals. S=Specific, M=Measurable, A=Attainable, R=Relevant and Realistic, T=Time Bounded.

5. Make sure your goals are about things that are truly under your control, or figure out how to get someone else to help you. This may require professional help—a coach or counselor.

6. Develop a program and strategy that will insure that you accomplish each objective.

7. Objectives must be doable steps.

8. Establish whom you are going to work with to support your development.

9. Network to learn specifics about your followers and your environments.

10. Create a sense of accountability for progress toward goal accomplishment: provide rewards and punishments as appropriate to help yourself complete your improvements.

Remember that you must always be careful about identifying what you feel is under your control and what you feel is not. The skills of identifying, limiting distractions, studying, learning, relearning, and ultimately using newfound skills for quotient development will serve you well in all areas of your life. Practice improvement in your Qs by expressing outwardly your emotions about doing, getting, or being versus just saying you have a quotient down pat. Remember: If you dwell on the negatives you'll stay where you are. When you are attempting to use your Qs knowledge, know your motives for your own development.

Study and understand Figure 14.1, *LQ$^{©}$*'s Lessons—Overview, before you complete the assessments.

Never forget what Mark Twain said—"We do not deal much in facts when we are contemplating ourselves." Never lie to yourself!

Figure 14.1: *LQ©*'s LESSONS—OVERVIEW
LQ© - THE LEADERSHIP QUOTIENT: THE LIFESTYLE FOR LEADERSHIP SUCCESS

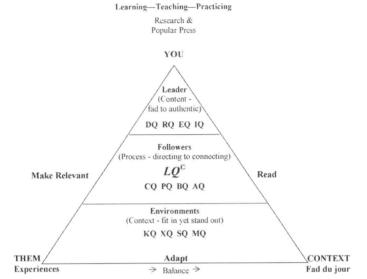

Learning—Teaching—Practicing

Research &
Popular Press

YOU

Leader
(Content -
fad to authentic)

DQ RQ EQ IQ

Followers
(Process - directing to connecting)

LQ©

CQ PQ BQ AQ

Make Relevant   **Read**

Environments
(Context - fit in yet stand out)

KQ XQ SQ MQ

THEM   **Adapt**   **CONTEXT**
Experiences   → Balance →   **Fad du jour**

FUNDAMENTALS FOR INNOVATIVE LEADERSHIP
Learn to understand the quotients and apply them to yourself, your followers, and your situations.

$LQ©$ = f(AQ-Apperance + BQ-Behavior + CQ-Communications + DQ-Desire +
EQ-Emotional + IQ-Intelligence + KQ-Knowledge + MQ-Management +
PQ-People + RQ-Reality + SQ-Situation + XQ-eXperience a no-fad zone)

To Be An Innovative Leader:
Categorize your strengths and weaknesses versus the ideal for all 12 Quotients.

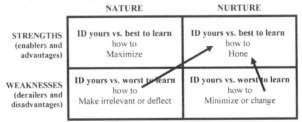

	NATURE	**NURTURE**
STRENGTHS (enablers and advantages)	**ID yours vs. best to learn** how to Maximize	**ID yours vs. best to learn** how to Hone
WEAKNESSES (derailers and disadvantages)	**ID yours vs. worst to learn** how to Make irrelevant or deflect	**ID yours vs. worst to learn** how to Minimize or change

Figure 14.2: DQ LEADERSHIP PRINCIPLE. Moving yourself and your organization from good to great.

You as a Leader
Look, listen, ask, seek, use your energy to become more intense
(research, practice, and theory).

Understand your capabilities and possibilities:
persistence, discipline, and internal locus of control.

Having a strong DQ encourages, inspires, and builds confidence in followers.
DQ properly channeled allows accomplishment of the seemingly impossible.

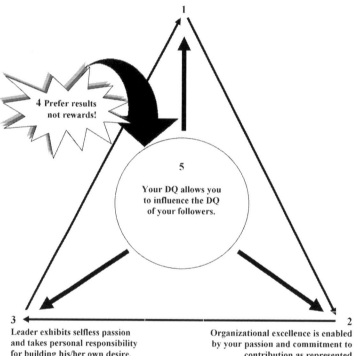

1

4 Prefer results not rewards!

5
Your DQ allows you to influence the DQ of your followers.

3

Leader exhibits selfless passion and takes personal responsibility for building his/her own desire.

2

Organizational excellence is enabled by your passion and commitment to contribution as represented by your DQ.

Figure 14.2A: DQ MEASUREMENT AND IMPROVEMENT MATRICES

Evaluate yourself against the reported traits in this Matrix.

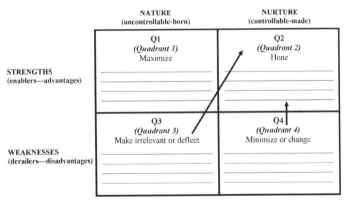

	NATURE (uncontrollable-born)	NURTURE (controllable-made)
STRENGTHS (enablers—advantages)	**Q1** _____ high-need type _____ persistent personality _____ appropriate tenacity _____ selfless passion _____ (self-IDed trait)	**Q2** _____ self-disciplined _____ I'm in control _____ passionate _____ commitment to contribution _____ (self-IDed trait)
WEAKNESSES (derailers—disadvantages)	**Q3** _____ no natural enthusiasm _____ no commitment, attention, or focus _____ misplaced urgency _____ selfish passion _____ (self-IDed trait)	**Q4** _____ lack of enthusiasm for right things _____ rewards over results _____ lack sense of urgency _____ don't know S&W of desire _____ (self-IDed trait)

Tailor the Matrix below for yourself!

	NATURE (uncontrollable-born)	NURTURE (controllable-made)
STRENGTHS (enablers—advantages)	**Q1** *(Quadrant 1)* Maximize	**Q2** *(Quadrant 2)* Hone
WEAKNESSES (derailers—disadvantages)	**Q3** *(Quadrant 3)* Make irrelevant or deflect	**Q4** *(Quadrant 4)* Minimize or change

FIGURE 14.2B: Desire Quotient (DQ)—My Improvement Plan and Commitment

1. I acknowledge the following shortcomings:

2. This is how I will improve on the shortcomings:

3. This is how I will measure my progress:

4. These are the people in my support group for the changes I will make:

Figure 14.3: RQ – To be a leader with a high RQ you must understand the realities of the current environments and followers, and use these to build a better understanding of the new realities of the future.

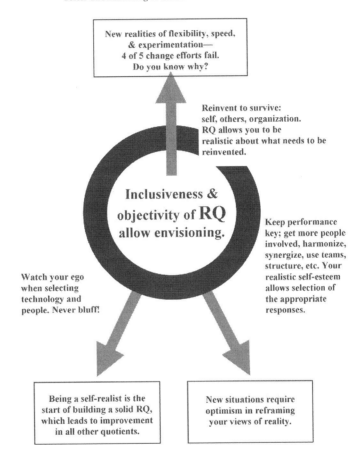

New realities of flexibility, speed, & experimentation— 4 of 5 change efforts fail. Do you know why?

Reinvent to survive: self, others, organization. RQ allows you to be realistic about what needs to be reinvented.

Inclusiveness & objectivity of RQ allow envisioning.

Keep performance key; get more people involved, harmonize, synergize, use teams, structure, etc. Your realistic self-esteem allows selection of the appropriate responses.

Watch your ego when selecting technology and people. Never bluff!

Being a self-realist is the start of building a solid RQ, which leads to improvement in all other quotients.

New situations require optimism in reframing your views of reality.

Figure 14.3A: RQ MEASUREMENT AND IMPROVEMENT MATRICES

Evaluate yourself against the reported traits in this Matrix.

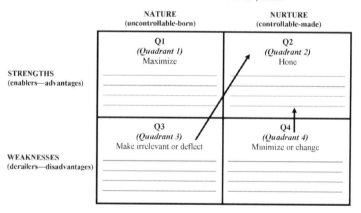

	NATURE (uncontrollable-born)	**NURTURE** (controllable-made)
STRENGTHS (enablers—advantages)	**Q1** ___ self-realist ___ realist about others ___ situation-realist ___ self-esteem _____ (self-IDed trait)	**Q2** ___ inclusive ___ better objectivity ___ envisioning ___ consensus—not yours _____ (self-IDed trait)
WEAKNESSES (derailers—disadvantages)	**Q3** ___ inflated ego ___ poor self-image ___ inability to interpret reality ___ self-image bluff _____ (self-IDed trait)	**Q4** ___ can't reframe views ___ unfounded pessimism ___ unfounded optimism ___ consensus for its sake _____ (self-IDed trait)

Tailor the Matrix below for yourself!

	NATURE (uncontrollable-born)	**NURTURE** (controllable-made)
STRENGTHS (enablers—advantages)	**Q1** *(Quadrant 1)* Maximize	**Q2** *(Quadrant 2)* Hone
WEAKNESSES (derailers—disadvantages)	**Q3** *(Quadrant 3)* Make irrelevant or deflect	**Q4** *(Quadrant 4)* Minimize or change

FIGURE 14:3B: Reality Quotient (RQ)—My Improvement Plan and Commitment

1. I acknowledge the following shortcomings:

2. This is how I will improve on the shortcomings:

3. This is how I will measure my progress:

4. These are the people in my support group for the changes I will make:

Figure 14.4: EQ—Requires you to understand and use the emotions of others and yourself.

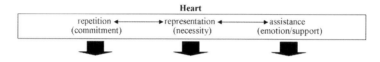

Actions for a New Heart and Mind High-EQ Leader

1. VALUATING—presence and awareness and control of emotions
2. SENSING EMOTIONS OF OTHERS—look, listen, and ask
3. ENTREPRENEURIAL INNOVATIVENESS—requires solid emotional control
4. EMOTIONAL MATURITY—not always age-related
5. MANAGING EMOTIONS—by reframing your views of emotional issues

EQ = MORE THAN YOUR EMOTIONS

6. EMOTIONALLY VALUATING SUCCESS—you do what you emotionally value
7. EMOTIONAL CULTURAL ASTUTENESS—requires stability and exposure
8. AVOID DISRUPTIVE IRRATIONALITY—handle change head-on
9. NEVER BE UNTRUSTWORTHY—awareness of trustworthiness in all cultures
10. EMOTIONAL LAZINESS IS A KILLER—don't avoid; confront appropriately

Figure 14.4A: EQ MEASUREMENT AND IMPROVEMENT MATRICES

Evaluate yourself against the reported traits in this Matrix.

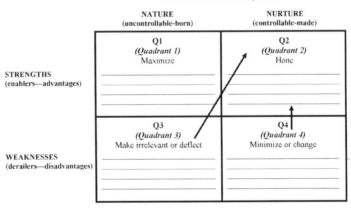

	NATURE (uncontrollable-born)	**NURTURE** (controllable-made)
STRENGTHS (enablers—advantages)	**Q1** _____ commanding presence _____ emotional awareness/control _____ sensing others' emotions _____ entrepreneurial innovativeness _____ (self-IDed trait)	**Q2** _____ emotional maturity _____ manage emotions via reframing _____ emotionally valuating success _____ cultural astuteness _____ (self-IDed trait)
WEAKNESSES (derailers—disadvantages)	**Q3** _____ disruptive irrationality _____ untrustworthiness _____ un-adaptable to change _____ emotional laziness _____ (self-IDed trait)	**Q4** _____ conflict/change avoidance _____ cultural unawareness _____ emotionally-avoid-persuasion _____ blind emotional attachment _____ (self-IDed trait)

Tailor the Matrix below for yourself!

	NATURE (uncontrollable-born)	**NURTURE** (controllable-made)
STRENGTHS (enablers—advantages)	**Q1** *(Quadrant 1)* Maximize	**Q2** *(Quadrant 2)* Hone
WEAKNESSES (derailers—disadvantages)	**Q3** *(Quadrant 3)* Make irrelevant or deflect	**Q4** *(Quadrant 4)* Minimize or change

FIGURE 14.4B: Emotional Quotient (EQ)—My Improvement Plan and Commitment

1. I acknowledge the following shortcomings:

2. This is how I will improve on the shortcomings:

3. This is how I will measure my progress:

4. These are the people in my support group for the changes I will make:

Figure 14.5: IQ—as we define it is successful intelligence and is very susceptible to improvement.

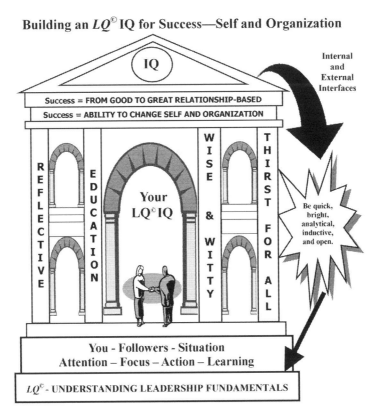

Figure 14.5A: IQ MEASUREMENT AND IMPROVEMENT MATRICES

Evaluate yourself against the reported traits in this Matrix.

	NATURE (uncontrollable-born)	NURTURE (controllable-made)
STRENGTHS (enablers—advantages)	**Q1** _____ memory/scholastic abilities _____ rationally creative _____ quick and bright _____ analytical/multi-variant/inductive _____ (self-IDed trait)	**Q2** _____ thoughtful and reflective _____ education for success _____ wise and witty _____ true thirst for knowledge _____ (self-IDed trait)
WEAKNESSES (derailers—disadvantages)	**Q3** _____ poor memory and/or vocabulary _____ inability to use IQ _____ unprepared and/or nervous _____ gives poor impression of intellect _____ (self-IDed trait)	**Q4** _____ poor study/scholastic abilities _____ unfocused and inattentive _____ doesn't learn from experience _____ poor mathematical abilities _____ (self-IDed trait)

Tailor the Matrix below for yourself!

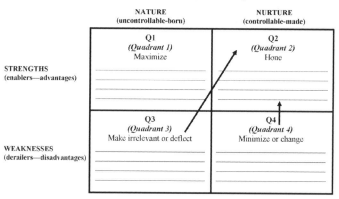

	NATURE (uncontrollable-born)	NURTURE (controllable-made)
STRENGTHS (enablers—advantages)	**Q1** *(Quadrant 1)* Maximize	**Q2** *(Quadrant 2)* Hone
WEAKNESSES (derailers—disadvantages)	**Q3** *(Quadrant 3)* Make irrelevant or deflect	**Q4** *(Quadrant 4)* Minimize or change

FIGURE 14.5B: Intelligence Quotient (IQ)—My Improvement Plan and Commitment

1. I acknowledge the following shortcomings:

2. This is how I will improve on the shortcomings:

3. This is how I will measure my progress:

4. These are the people in my support group for the changes I will make:

Figure 14.6: CQ—Practice two-way open communications.

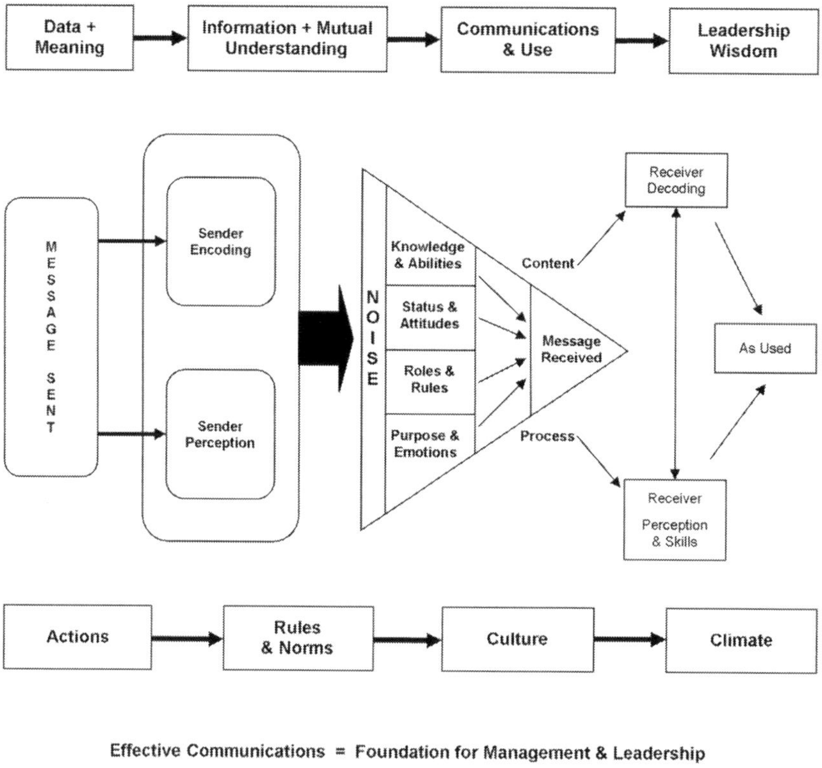

Effective Communications = Foundation for Management & Leadership

Communications: The Foundation of Successful Management

Communications accomplish the following:
- Enable one to lead others.
- Measure leaders by their ability to speak and write with clarity and conviction.
- Develop interaction at all levels to foster an innovative, timely, quality-conscious, customer-focused organization.
- Provide a method by which you can understand yourself and how you communicate before you ask others to improve their communication skills.

Figure 14.6A: CQ MEASUREMENT AND IMPROVEMENT MATRICES

Evaluate yourself against the reported traits in this Matrix.

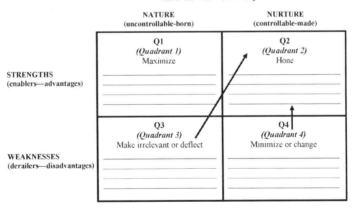

Tailor the Matrix below for yourself!

FIGURE 14.6B: Communication Quotient (CQ)—My Improvement Plan and Commitment

1. I acknowledge the following shortcomings:

2. This is how I will improve on the shortcomings:

3. This is how I will measure my progress:

4. These are the people in my support group for the changes I will make:

Figure 14.7: PQ—Relationships—learn to read people! PQ = PEOPLE PERSON

What	How
1. Build and treasure relationships. Requires appropriate charisma, humility, and compassion.	1. Start with a higher being, friends, and family, and add professional relationships. Character, integrity, and ethics show.
2. Visualize the end you have in mind. Learn to read others.	2. Think big, but start small. Ben Franklin said, "By failing to prepare we prepare to fail."
3. Set goals that are step-by-step ways to reach your vision of becoming a people person.	3. Focus. Set initial short-term goals that build to your ultimate goal.
4. Be proactive and try. Be an extrovert.	4. Successful people and failures fear the same things, but for the successful, the desire to succeed overcomes fear. Not good enough beats not trying.
5. Success is hard work—there are no shortcuts. Networking works.	5. Put in the work and results will follow. Don't do things halfheartedly. Don't let others pull you down.
6. Teamwork wins the war even though an individual may win a battle.	6. Selfless process—always think win-win. Talent or luck may win one or two times, but teamwork wins out over time.
7. Learn, refine, and practice all the LQ© fundamentals.	7. Covey's 7 habits of effective people: Proactivity Begin with the end in mind Put first things first Think win-win—establish a relationship Seek first to understand Synergize Continued self-renewal
8. Participate. Set the example: "I will be a good leader and a good follower. I will be both!" Be an extrovert about leadership.	8. Learn awareness of self, others, and the world. Back up talk by example. Earn the title of leader or follower. Servant leadership should be a goal.
9. Learn to listen. Start all networking by asking and listening to how you can help the other person.	9. Develop an external focus. Become an information junky. Leverage what you know.
10. Reinvent yourself and commit to continuous learning. Never stay content with how well you read others.	10. Drucker said, "Knowledge has become the key economic resource and the dominant, if not the only, source of comparative advantage."

Figure 14.7A: PQ MEASUREMENT AND IMPROVEMENT MATRICES

Evaluate yourself against the reported traits in this Matrix.

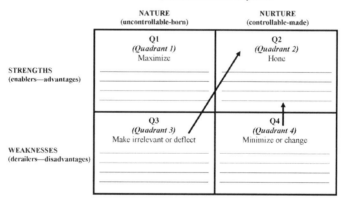

	NATURE (uncontrollable-born)	NURTURE (controllable-made)
STRENGTHS (enablers—advantages)	**Q1** _____ extrovert _____ charismatic _____ humility _____ compassion _____ (self-IDed trait)	**Q2** _____ relating-connecting-personable _____ trustworthiness _____ ability to read others _____ networking _____ (self-IDed trait)
WEAKNESSES (derailers—disadvantages)	**Q3** _____ slick—self-serving _____ introvert _____ discomfort with dissent _____ offensive _____ (self-IDed trait)	**Q4** _____ pretentiousness _____ fear of deep relationships _____ not listening—no attention _____ exclusivity or being withdrawn _____ (self-IDed trait)

Tailor the Matrix below for yourself!

	NATURE (uncontrollable-born)	NURTURE (controllable-made)
STRENGTHS (enablers—advantages)	**Q1** _(Quadrant 1)_ Maximize	**Q2** _(Quadrant 2)_ Hone
WEAKNESSES (derailers—disadvantages)	**Q3** _(Quadrant 3)_ Make irrelevant or deflect	**Q4** _(Quadrant 4)_ Minimize or change

FIGURE 14.7B: People Quotient (PQ)—My Improvement Plan and Commitment

1. I acknowledge the following shortcomings:

2. This is how I will improve on the shortcomings:

3. This is how I will measure my progress:

4. These are the people in my support group for the changes I will make:

Figure 14.8: BQ—Your behavior is you to everyone but you—shift from power to influence.

FOR A HIGH BQ
you must understand these new requirements.

FROM	TO
Deceitful (corporate cheats)	Authentic (inspiring morals)
Selfish coward (be neither!)	Courageous and brave (often this is not easy)
Poor credibility (it's easy to get and hard to lose)	Trustworthiness (it's hard to get)
Self-centered (natural)	Focus on others (nurture)
Disrespectful (everyone sees and remembers this)	Respectful (starts with self-respect)
Greed (never good regardless of the movie!)	Sharing (you'll have more this way)
Crude (you know when you are)	Classy (best to be too classy)
Lose temper (easy)	Control temper (hard)
Ungraceful (many exhibit)	Grace (few have true grace)
Stuck-up (habit)	Personable (new habit)
They influence you (easy way out)	You're an influential (you think before you influence)
You're responsible (they want it)	They're responsible (they need it)
Taking responsibility (let them)	Giving responsibility (hard for you)
It's the content (not really)	It's the process and the context (reality)
It's management (old way)	It's leadership (new way)
Guessing your answers (lazy way out)	Learning as working and proving it (harder)
Stifle (you know it all)	Empower (only way to develop)
Hold tight (you'll never move)	Letting go (life's great)
Behave like you want to be a leader (you'll never become one)	Behave as if you're a leader (you'll be one soon)

Figure 14.8A: BQ MEASUREMENT AND IMPROVEMENT MATRICES

Evaluate yourself against the reported traits in this Matrix.

	NATURE **(uncontrollable-born)**	**NURTURE** **(controllable-made)**
STRENGTHS **(enablers—advantages)**	**Q1** _____ authentic-inspiring-moral _____ courageous and brave _____ grace _____ personable _____ (self-IDed trait)	**Q2** _____ influential _____ trustworthiness _____ savvy-flexibility _____ respect _____ (self-IDed trait)
WEAKNESSES **(derailers—disadvantages)**	**Q3** _____ lack of credibility _____ deceitful-cheater _____ selfish-cowardly _____ disrespectful or self-centered _____ (self-IDed trait)	**Q4** _____ pretentiousness _____ temper + cowardice _____ greed _____ crudeness _____ (self-IDed trait)

Tailor the Matrix below for yourself!

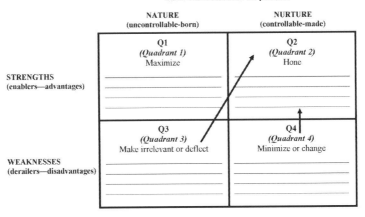

	NATURE **(uncontrollable-born)**	**NURTURE** **(controllable-made)**
STRENGTHS **(enablers—advantages)**	**Q1** *(Quadrant 1)* Maximize	**Q2** *(Quadrant 2)* Hone
WEAKNESSES **(derailers—disadvantages)**	**Q3** *(Quadrant 3)* Make irrelevant or deflect	**Q4** *(Quadrant 4)* Minimize or change

FIGURE 14.8B: Behavior Quotient (BQ)—My Improvement Plan and Commitment

1. I acknowledge the following shortcomings:

2. This is how I will improve on the shortcomings:

3. This is how I will measure my progress:

4. These are the people in my support group for the changes I will make:

Figure 14.9: AQ—Requires you to really assess what you have and do not have related to appearance—maximize your good points and don't worry about your bad.

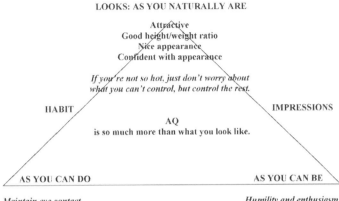

LOOKS: AS YOU NATURALLY ARE

Attractive
Good height/weight ratio
Nice appearance
Confident with appearance

If you're not so hot, just don't worry about
what you can't control, but control the rest.

HABIT   **IMPRESSIONS**

AQ
is so much more than what you look like.

AS YOU CAN DO   **AS YOU CAN BE**

Maintain eye contact	*Humility and enthusiasm*
Dress appropriately	*Self-confidence and warmth*
Enter discussions with poise and confidence	*Sense of humor and extroversion*
Have a pleasant voice	*Stability, honesty, and tenacity*
Focus on others' work ethics	*Effort and energy*
Avoid meaningless small talk	*Speak as you wish to become*

These actions increase AQ, yet they have nothing to do with beauty.

Always have the following:
- Neatly pressed and sparkling clean clothing
- Freshly polished shoes
- Impeccable fingernails
- Clean jewelry in mint condition
- Well-maintained hair
- More-with-less jewelry, makeup, and all forms of accessories

Figure 14.9A: AQ MEASUREMENT AND IMPROVEMENT MATRICES

Evaluate yourself against the reported traits in this Matrix.

	NATURE (uncontrollable-born)	NURTURE (controllable-made)
STRENGTHS (enablers—advantages)	**Q1** _____ attractive _____ good height-to-weight ratio _____ nice appearance _____ confident about appearance _____ (self-IDed trait)	**Q2** _____ good posture _____ good decorum _____ good appearance knowledge _____ polished appearance _____ (self-IDed trait)
WEAKNESSES (derailers—disadvantages)	**Q3** _____ unattractive _____ bad height-to-weight ratio _____ mean appearance _____ unconfident about appearance _____ (self-IDed trait)	**Q4** _____ poor posture _____ poor decorum _____ poor appearance knowledge _____ unpolished appearance _____ (self-IDed trait)

Tailor the Matrix below for yourself!

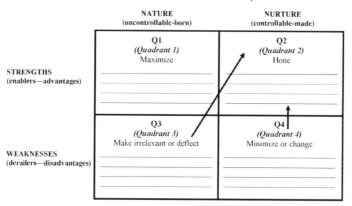

	NATURE (uncontrollable-born)	NURTURE (controllable-made)
STRENGTHS (enablers—advantages)	**Q1** _(Quadrant 1)_ Maximize	**Q2** _(Quadrant 2)_ Hone
WEAKNESSES (derailers—disadvantages)	**Q3** _(Quadrant 3)_ Make irrelevant or deflect	**Q4** _(Quadrant 4)_ Minimize or change

FIGURE 14.9B: Appearance Quotient (AQ)—My Improvement Plan and Commitment

1. I acknowledge the following shortcomings:

2. This is how I will improve on the shortcomings:

3. This is how I will measure my progress:

4. These are the people in my support group for the changes I will make:

Figure 14.10: XQ—The sum total of what you have done and learned from what others have done.

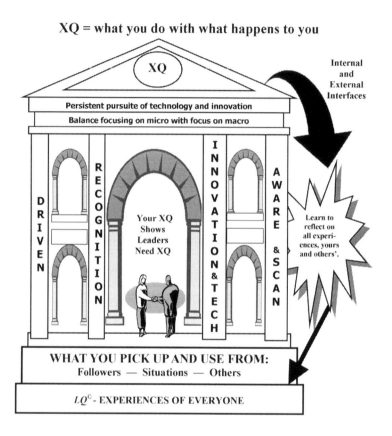

Figure 14.10A: XQ MEASUREMENT AND IMPROVEMENT MATRICES

Evaluate yourself against the reported traits in this Matrix.

	NATURE (uncontrollable-born)	**NURTURE** (controllable-made)
STRENGTHS (enablers—advantages)	**Q1** ____ good age-to-maturity ratio ____ internal control locus + extro-version ____ curiosity + intuition-insight ____ good attention-to-focus ratio ____ (self-IDed trait)	**Q2** ____ varied exposures + objectivity ____ love of learning ____ attention—many diverse things ____ love of people ____ (self-IDed trait)
WEAKNESSES (derailers—disadvantages)	**Q3** ____ poor age-to-maturity ratio ____ external locus of control + introversion ____ lack of curiosity ____ poor attention-to-focus ratio ____ (self-IDed trait)	**Q4** ____ limited exposure ____ disdain for learning ____ attention to what I know ____ distrust of people ____ (self-IDed trait)

Tailor the Matrix below for yourself!

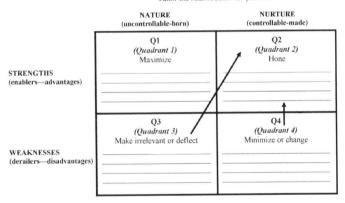

	NATURE (uncontrollable-born)	**NURTURE** (controllable-made)
STRENGTHS (enablers—advantages)	**Q1** *(Quadrant 1)* Maximize	**Q2** *(Quadrant 2)* Hone
WEAKNESSES (derailers—disadvantages)	**Q3** *(Quadrant 3)* Make irrelevant or deflect	**Q4** *(Quadrant 4)* Minimize or change

FIGURE 14.10B: eXperience Quotient (XQ)—My Improvement Plan and Commitment

1. I acknowledge the following shortcomings:

2. This is how I will improve on the shortcomings:

3. This is how I will measure my progress:

4. These are the people in my support group for the changes I will make:

Figure 14.11: KQ—This is all about acquiring and ultimately using new, useful knowledge.

ACQUIRING USEFUL KNOWLEDGE

- Review the available literature (fads, research, practice, and theory).
- Look, listen, ask, and seek with a thirst for knowledge. Balance micro and macro focus, pushing technology and innovation to reduce uncertainty.
- Constant scanning and awareness must become persistent in your behavior to develop a great KQ.

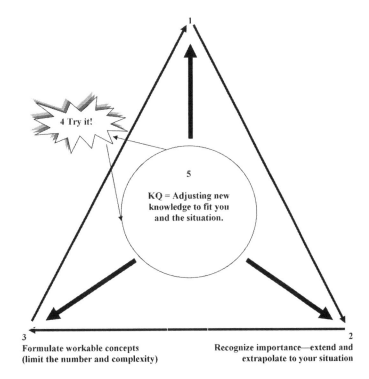

Figure 14.11A: KQ MEASUREMENT AND IMPROVEMENT MATRICES

Evaluate yourself against the reported traits in this Matrix.

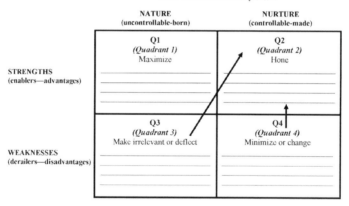

	NATURE (uncontrollable-born)	NURTURE (controllable-made)
STRENGTHS (enablers—advantages)	**Q1** ___ driven, thirsty—seeking knowledge ___ recognize the important ___ innovative and technology-astute ___ awareness and constant scanning _____ (self-IDed trait)	**Q2** ___ balance of micro and macro focus ___ persistence in pursuit ___ push/recognize innovation or technology ___ knowledge reduces uncertainty _____ (self-IDed trait)
WEAKNESSES (derailers—disadvantages)	**Q3** ___ not evolving—often too slow ___ no stimuli enough for desire ___ can't recognize new things ___ technology/innovatively challenged _____ (self-IDed trait)	**Q4** ___ narrow-minded ___ distress over new things ___ learning tied to liking ___ say no to technology or innovation _____ (self-IDed trait)

Tailor the Matrix below for yourself!

	NATURE (uncontrollable-born)	NURTURE (controllable-made)
STRENGTHS (enablers—advantages)	**Q1** *(Quadrant 1)* Maximize	**Q2** *(Quadrant 2)* Hone
WEAKNESSES (derailers—disadvantages)	**Q3** *(Quadrant 3)* Make irrelevant or deflect	**Q4** *(Quadrant 4)* Minimize or change

FIGURE 14.11B: Knowledge Quotient (KQ)—My Improvement Plan and Commitment

1. I acknowledge the following shortcomings:

2. This is how I will improve on the shortcomings:

3. This is how I will measure my progress:

4. These are the people in my support group for the changes I will make:

Figure 14.12: SQ—Correctly identifying situations and developing strategies to address them are skills you must earn and learn.

No situation is more critical than your current SQ situational understanding.

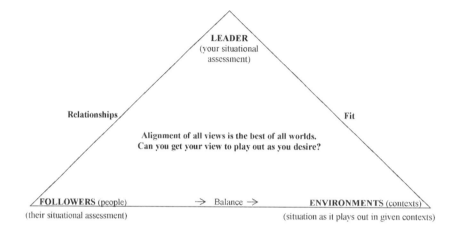

Any situation may be viewed in three ways:

1. The perceived view
2. The objective or real view
3. How things are enacted

We strive to have our view closer to reality and to make sure our view plays out in the end.

Figure 14.12A: SQ MEASUREMENT AND IMPROVEMENT MATRICES

Evaluate yourself against the reported traits in this Matrix.

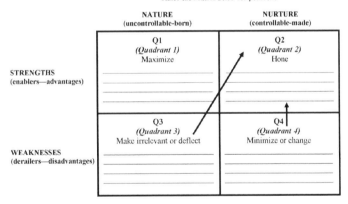

	NATURE (uncontrollable-born)	**NURTURE** (controllable-made)
STRENGTHS (enablers—advantages)	**Q1** ___ comfortable with new circum-stances ___ situational simplifier ___ seizes the moment ___ observant-aware-realistic _____ (self-IDed trait)	**Q2** ___ appropriate versatility ___ analytical and visionary ___ consciously reading ___ steady, unflappable—street-smart _____ (self-IDed trait)
WEAKNESSES (derailers—disadvantages)	**Q3** ___ aloofness and/or unawareness ___ situational complexifier ___ won't assimilate into reality ___ over-reaction to new circum-stances _____ (self-IDed trait)	**Q4** ___ poor assumptions ___ failure to grasp history ___ judgmentalism ___ inappropriate for circumstances _____ (self-IDed trait)

Tailor the Matrix below for yourself!

	NATURE (uncontrollable-born)	**NURTURE** (controllable-made)
STRENGTHS (enablers—advantages)	**Q1** *(Quadrant 1)* Maximize _____ _____ _____ _____	**Q2** *(Quadrant 2)* Hone _____ _____ _____ _____
WEAKNESSES (derailers—disadvantages)	**Q3** *(Quadrant 3)* Make irrelevant or deflect _____ _____ _____	**Q4** *(Quadrant 4)* Minimize or change _____ _____ _____

FIGURE 14.12B: Situation Quotient (SQ)—My Improvement Plan and Commitment

1. I acknowledge the following shortcomings:

2. This is how I will improve on the shortcomings:

3. This is how I will measure my progress:

4. These are the people in my support group for the changes I will make:

Figure 14.13: MQ—First, be a great manager, then shift from management to leadership through understanding the following dichotomies:

Management	Leadership
Information hub [I'll tell you what you need to know]	Gets problems solved [lets you have a say and asks]
Content [rules and processes]	Process and context [people]
Power [drives]	Empowerment [allows, then mentors and coaches]
Vertical integration [we do it all]	Alliances [can't always be #1]
Experts [stay narrow]	Teams [expanded knowledge]
Lifetime employment [never works anyway!]	De-jobbing [your job is what it takes]
Stability [stay the same]	Innovativeness/change [the way to survive]
Invention [not very likely]	Innovation [likely continues]
Caution [a really risky scheme]	Experimentation/speed [survival over time]
In-house [only if best in world]	Outsourcing [use the best]
I [win]	We [win-win]
Control [demands respect]	Trust [is respected]
Autocrat [administrates—authority]	Coach [leads—goodwill]
How [not enough time]	Why [makes the time]
Credit or blame [fear]	Shared responsibility [enthusiasm and fixes it]
Administrator [watches the bottom line]	Facilitator [watches the horizon]
Maintain [gets worse on its own]	Develop [use everyone and every thing]
Accept status quo [and don't improve]	Challenge [to always get better]
Surrender to context [it controls you]	Master context [you control it]
A good soldier [gets killed]	Own person [kills the enemy]

Figure 14.13A: MQ MEASUREMENT AND IMPROVEMENT MATRICES

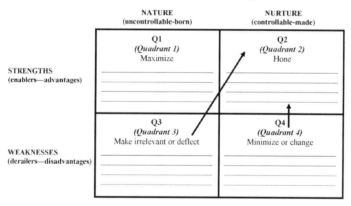

Evaluate yourself against the reported traits in this Matrix.

	NATURE (uncontrollable-born)	NURTURE (controllable-made)
STRENGTHS (enablers—advantages)	**Q1** _____ selflessness—others over self _____ decisiveness _____ motivated and motivator _____ organized _____ (self-IDed trait)	**Q2** _____ empower—delegate _____ systematizer _____ mentor _____ find and get talent _____ (self-IDed trait)
WEAKNESSES (derailers—disadvantages)	**Q3** _____ self-serving _____ indecisiveness _____ unethical _____ self-proclaimed perfectionist _____ (self-IDed trait)	**Q4** _____ laziness _____ micromanager _____ greed _____ unwillingness to confront _____ (self-IDed trait)

Tailor the Matrix below for yourself!

	NATURE (uncontrollable-born)	NURTURE (controllable-made)
STRENGTHS (enablers—advantages)	**Q1** _(Quadrant 1)_ Maximize	**Q2** _(Quadrant 2)_ Hone
WEAKNESSES (derailers—disadvantages)	**Q3** _(Quadrant 3)_ Make irrelevant or deflect	**Q4** _(Quadrant 4)_ Minimize or change

FIGURE 14.13B: Management Quotient (MQ)—My Improvement Plan and Commitment

1. I acknowledge the following shortcomings:

2. This is how I will improve on the shortcomings:

3. This is how I will measure my progress:

4. These are the people in my support group for the changes I will make:

Figure 14.14: *LQ^e* **principles for realizing innovation through a rapid incremental innovation strategy.**

One of the two organizational imperatives we have harped on is the need to become and remain innovative. This figure depicts how that can be accomplished with and through LQ^e.

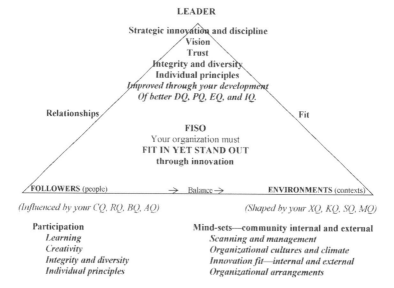

The strategy works only for those who:

- Adequately fund, and—yes—reward and encourage innovative experimentation.
- Stay in the game.
- Live with the PAST; succeed in the PRESENT; position for the FUTURE.

APPENDIX B

A New LQ© Instrument

"*I can be viewed by some to have a great leadership potential and by others as just an average employee who does what he is told and is a self-motivator at best. This perception on various levels is very different and makes me curious as to what positives or negatives they see in me. We all ought to pay close attention to what people say about us and how they perceive us. However, there are some people whose opinions I do not value, and I take what they say about me with a grain of salt. Conversely, others speak and I listen—no matter how good or bad the comment.*"—*Jamie, one of Bill's MBA students, Summer 2004*

Notes on Using the Following *LQ©* Self-Assessment Form

1. In each of the 12 quotient areas, you are trying to identify a "comparison other" to help you in identifying personal leadership traits, gifts, failings, or behaviors you have observed in others or yourself. To identify a leader for comparative purposes, think of someone you know, or know of, who exhibits leadership qualities you would like to have more or fewer of, and compare their qualities to yours. It might be that you want to identify a leader you do NOT want to emulate or become more like; or you might want to identify a leader whose exhibited traits or behaviors are exemplars for you.

2. For your public figures, use current or historically known persons.

3. For your personal leader, just identify who the person is, i.e., "boss, brother, mother, coworker, friend."

4. Think about the traits your identified leaders have and then assess how close you are to those leaders as a percentage. For example, a favorite leader for many in the area of DQ is Thomas Edison, and you might feel you have about 10% of the DQ of Edison. *Do NOT get hung up on percentages. The intent of the percentages is just to get you to think about yourself, i.e., traits and characteristics you have and do not have and what you might, can, want, or ought to do about them.*

5. When you are responding to questions about your own personal quotients, do not get hung up on the strictness of what is really under your control and what is not. Yes, most things are under your control to some degree, but list things as "no control" when they are things you are not likely to change for whatever reason.

6. Many people have a deeply entrenched delusion that they can know or do things with a near-perfect certainty—don't be one of those types!

7. Search for exemplars who are substance versus sound bites or media hype.

AQ: Appearance Quotient

Appropriate dress, mannerisms, physical appearance, poise, demeanor, etc.

1. Name a **well-known person** who exemplifies **AQ**: _____.

    How does **this leader** exemplify **AQ** (circle one)?   In a positive way   In a negative way

    Estimate the percentage to which your **AQ** is like that of **this leader**: _____%.

    List **AQ** words that define **this leader**: _____ _____ _____.

2. Name a **personal leader** who exemplifies **AQ**: _____.

    How does **your leader** exemplify **AQ** (circle one)?   In a positive way   In a negative way

    Estimate the percentage to which your **AQ** is like that of **your leader**: _____%.

    List **AQ** words that define **your leader**: _____ _____ _____.

ABOUT YOUR AQ:

3. List a **positive** which you control: _____.

4. List a **positive** over which you have **NO** control or are unlikely to change: _____

_____.

5. List a **negative** over which you have **NO** control or are unlikely to change: _____

_____.

6. List a **negative** which you control: _____.

BQ: Behavioral Quotient

Exhibited ethics, sense of necessity, courage, motivation, commitment, etc.

1. Name a **well-known person** who exemplifies **BQ**: _____.

    How does **this leader** exemplify **BQ** (circle one)?   In a positive way   In a negative way

    Estimate the percentage to which your **BQ** is like that of **this leader**: _____%.

    List **BQ** words that define **this leader**: _____ _____ _____.

2. Name a **personal leader** who exemplifies **BQ**: _____.

    How does **your leader** exemplify **BQ** (circle one)?   In a positive way   In a negative way

    Estimate the percentage to which your **BQ** is like that of **your leader**: _____%.

    List **BQ** words that define **your leader**: _____ _____ _____.

ABOUT YOUR BQ:

3. List a **positive** which you control: _____.

4. List a **positive** over which you have **NO** control or are unlikely to change: _____

_____.

5. List a **negative** over which you have **NO** control or are unlikely to change: _____

_____.

6. List a **negative** which you control: _____.

CQ: Communications Quotient

Verbal, written, body language, tone, dialect, appropriateness of words, etc.

1. Name a **well-known person** who exemplifies **CQ**: _____.

    How does **this leader** exemplify **CQ** (circle one)?   In a positive way   In a negative way

    Estimate the percentage to which your **CQ** is like that of **this leader**: _____%.

    List **CQ** words that define **this leader**: _____ _____ _____.

2. Name a **personal leader** who exemplifies **CQ**: _____.

    How does **your leader** exemplify **CQ** (circle one)?   In a positive way   In a negative way

    Estimate the percentage to which your **CQ** is like that of **your leader**: _____%.

    List **CQ** words that define **your leader**: _____ _____ _____.

ABOUT YOUR CQ:

3. List a **positive** which you control: _____.

4. List a **positive** over which you have **NO** control or are unlikely to change: _____

_____.

5. List a **negative** over which you have **NO** control or are unlikely to change: _____

_____.

6. List a **negative** which you control: _____.

DQ: Desire Quotient

Effort, drive, persistence, conveying a sense of urgency, etc.

1. Name a **well-known person** who exemplifies **DQ**: _____.

    How does **this leader** exemplify **DQ** (circle one)?   In a positive way   In a negative way

    Estimate the percentage to which your **DQ** is like that of **this leader**: _____%.

    List **DQ** words that define **this leader**: _____ _____ _____.

2. Name a **personal leader** who exemplifies **DQ**: _____.

    How does **your leader** exemplify **DQ** (circle one)?   In a positive way   In a negative way

    Estimate the percentage to which your **DQ** is like that of **your leader**: _____%.

    List **DQ** words that define **your leader**: _____ _____ _____.

ABOUT YOUR DQ:

3. List a **positive** which you control: _____.

4. List a **positive** over which you have **NO** control or are unlikely to change: _____

_____.

5. List a **negative** over which you have **NO** control or are unlikely to change: _____

_____.

6. List a **negative** which you control: _____.

EQ: Emotional Quotient

Self-awareness and management, social awareness, empathy, exhibited mood, etc.

1. Name a **well-known person** who exemplifies **EQ**: _____.

   How does **this leader** exemplify **EQ** (circle one)?   In a positive way   In a negative way

   Estimate the percentage to which your **EQ** is like that of **this leader**: _____%.

   List **EQ** words that define **this leader**: _____ _____ _____.

2. Name a **personal leader** who exemplifies **EQ**: _____.

   How does **your leader** exemplify **EQ** (circle one)?   In a positive way   In a negative way

   Estimate the percentage to which your **EQ** is like that of **your leader**: _____%.

   List **EQ** words that define **your leader**: _____ _____ _____.

ABOUT YOUR EQ:

3. List a **positive** which you control: _____.

4. List a **positive** over which you have **NO** control or are unlikely to change: _____

_____.

5. List a **negative** over which you have **NO** control or are unlikely to change: _____

_____.

6. List a **negative** which you control: _____.

IQ: Intelligence Quotient

Intellect—commonly thought of as "mental capacity."

1. Name a **well-known person** who exemplifies **IQ**: _____.

   How does **this leader** exemplify **IQ** (circle one)?   In a positive way   In a negative way

   Estimate the percentage to which your **IQ** is like that of **this leader**: _____%.

   List **IQ** words that define **this leader**: _____ _____ _____.

2. Name a **personal leader** who exemplifies **IQ**: _____.

   How does **your leader** exemplify **IQ** (circle one)?   In a positive way   In a negative way

   Estimate the percentage to which your **IQ** is like that of **your leader**: _____%.

   List **IQ** words that define **your leader**: _____ _____ _____.

ABOUT YOUR IQ:

3. List a **positive** which you control: _____.

4. List a **positive** over which you have **NO** control or are unlikely to change: _____

   _____.

5. List a **negative** over which you have **NO** control or are unlikely to change: _____

   _____.

6. List a **negative** which you control: _____.

KQ: Knowledge Quotient

Continuous expansion of base of useful information, keeping up, etc.

1. Name a **well-known person** who exemplifies **KQ**: _____.

   How does **this leader** exemplify **KQ** (circle one)?   In a positive way   In a negative way

   Estimate the percentage to which your **KQ** is like that of **this leader**: _____%.

   List **KQ** words that define **this leader**: _____ _____ _____.

2. Name a **personal leader** who exemplifies **KQ**: _____.

   How does **your leader** exemplify **KQ** (circle one)?   In a positive way   In a negative way

   Estimate the percentage to which your **KQ** is like that of **your leader**: _____%.

   List **KQ** words that define **your leader**: _____ _____ _____.

ABOUT YOUR KQ:

3. List a **positive** which you control: _____.

4. List a **positive** over which you have **NO** control or are unlikely to change: _____

_____.

5. List a **negative** over which you have **NO** control or are unlikely to change: _____

_____.

6. List a **negative** which you control: _____.

PQ: People Quotient

Ability to relate with *people; relationships, social skills, listening, etc.*

1. Name a **well-known person** who exemplifies **PQ**: _____.

How does **this leader** exemplify **PQ** (circle one)?   In a positive way   In a negative way

Estimate the percentage to which your **PQ** is like that of **this leader**: _____%.

List **PQ** words that define **this leader**: _____ _____ _____.

2. Name a **personal leader** who exemplifies **PQ**: _____.

How does **your leader** exemplify **PQ** (circle one)?   In a positive way   In a negative way

Estimate the percentage to which your **PQ** is like that of **your leader**: _____%.

List **PQ** words that define **your leader**: _____ _____ _____.

ABOUT YOUR PQ:

3. List a **positive** which you control: _____.

4. List a **positive** over which you have **NO** control or are unlikely to change: _____

_____.

5. List a **negative** over which you have **NO** control or are unlikely to change: _____

_____.

6. List a **negative** which you control: _____.

MQ: Management Quotient

Planning, organizing, controlling, directing, staffing, mentoring, etc.

1. Name a **well-known person** who exemplifies **MQ**: _____.

   How does **this leader** exemplify **MQ** (circle one)?   In a positive way   In a negative way

   Estimate the percentage to which your **MQ** is like that of **this leader**: _____%.

   List **MQ** words that define **this leader**: _____ _____ _____.

2. Name a **personal leader** who exemplifies **MQ**: _____.

   How does **your leader** exemplify **MQ** (circle one)?   In a positive way   In a negative way

   Estimate the percentage to which your **MQ** is like that of **your leader**: _____%.

   List **MQ** words that define **your leader**: _____ _____ _____.

ABOUT YOUR MQ:

3. List a **positive** which you control: _____.

4. List a **positive** over which you have **NO** control or are unlikely to change: _____

   _____.

5. List a **negative** over which you have **NO** control or are unlikely to change: _____

   _____.

6. List a **negative** which you control: _____.

RQ: Reality Quotient

Clarifying inclusiveness, consensuses, seeing current state as it really is becoming, etc.

1. Name a **well-known person** who exemplifies **RQ**: _____.

   How does **this leader** exemplify **RQ** (circle one)?   In a positive way   In a negative way

   Estimate the percentage to which your **RQ** is like that of **this leader**: _____%.

   List **RQ** words that define **this leader**: _____ _____ _____.

2. Name a **personal leader** who exemplifies **RQ**: _____.

   How does **your leader** exemplify **RQ** (circle one)?   In a positive way   In a negative way

   Estimate the percentage to which your **RQ** is like that of **your leader**: _____%.

   List **RQ** words that define **your leader**: _____ _____ _____.

ABOUT YOUR RQ:

3. List a **positive** which you control: _____.

4. List a **positive** over which you have **NO** control or are unlikely to change: _____

   _____.

5. List a **negative** over which you have **NO** control or are unlikely to change: _____

   _____.

6. List a **negative** which you control: _____.

SQ: Situational Quotient

Ability to read a situation and fit into it; timing, and circumstances.

1. Name a **well-known person** who exemplifies **SQ**: _____.

   How does **this leader** exemplify **SQ** (circle one)?   In a positive way   In a negative way

   Estimate the percentage to which your **SQ** is like that of **this leader**: _____%.

   List **SQ** words that define **this leader**: _____ _____ _____.

2. Name a **personal leader** who exemplifies **SQ**: _____.

   How does **your leader** exemplify **SQ** (circle one)?   In a positive way   In a negative way

   Estimate the percentage to which your **SQ** is like that of **your leader**: _____%.

   List **SQ** words that define **your leader**: _____ _____ _____.

ABOUT YOUR SQ:

3. List a **positive** which you control: _____.

4. List a **positive** over which you have **NO** control or are unlikely to change: _____

   _____.

5. List a **negative** over which you have **NO** control or are unlikely to change: _____

   _____.

6. List a **negative** which you control: _____.

XQ: eXperience Quotient

Past accomplishments learned and earned, mistakes, firsthand, etc.

1. Name a **well-known person** who exemplifies **XQ**: _____.

    How does **this leader** exemplify **XQ** (circle one)?   In a positive way   In a negative way

    Estimate the percentage to which your **XQ** is like that of **this leader**: _____%.

    List **XQ** words that define **this leader**: _____ _____ _____.

2. Name a **personal leader** who exemplifies **XQ**: _____.

    How does **your leader** exemplify **XQ** (circle one)?   In a positive way   In a negative way

    Estimate the percentage to which your **XQ** is like that of **your leader**: _____%.

    List **XQ** words that define **your leader**: _____ _____ _____.

ABOUT YOUR XQ:

3. List a **positive** which you control: _____.

4. List a **positive** over which you have **NO** control or are unlikely to change: _____

    _____.

5. List a **negative** over which you have **NO** control or are unlikely to change: _____

    _____.

6. List a **negative** which you control: _____.

Bibliography

Abernathy, W. J., & Utterback, J. M. (1988). Innovation over time and in historical context. In M. L. Tushman, & W. L. Moore (Eds.), *Readings in the management of innovation*, (2nd ed.) (pp. 25-36). New York: HarperCollins.

Aczel, A. D. (1999). God's *equation: Einstein, relativity, and the expanding universe*. New York: MJF.

Albrecht, K. (2003). *The power of minds at work*. New York: AMACOM.

Aldrich, H. E. (1979). *Organizations and environments*. Englewood Cliffs, NJ: Prentice-Hall.

Alter, J. (2003, November 3). Robert's rules for rummy. *Newsweek, 43*.

Andrews, D. H., & Johnson, K. R. (2002). *Revolutionizing IT*. Hoboken, NJ: John Wiley & Sons.

Arnold, H. J. (1982). Moderator variables: A clarification of conceptual, analytic, and psychometric issues. *Organizational behavior and human performance, 29*, 143-174.

Arnott, D. (2000). *Corporate cults: The insidious lure of the all-consuming organization*. New York: AMACOM.

Arom, S. (1994). Intelligence in traditional music. In J. Khalfa (Ed.), *What is intelligence?* (pp. 137-160). New York: Press Syndicate of the University of Cambridge:

Ashby, F. C., & Pell, A. R. (2001). *Embracing excellence*. Paramus, NJ: Prentice Hall.

Ashkenas, R., Ulrich, D., Jick, T., & Kerr, S. (1995). *The boundaryless organization*. San Francisco: Jossey-Bass.

Axelrod, A. (2003). *Nothing to fear*. London: Portfolio the Penguin Group.

Barber, B. (1996). *Jihad vs. McWorld.* New York: Ballantine.

Barner, R. W. (2000). *Team troubleshooter.* Palo Alto, CA: Davies-Black.

Barney, J. (1986). Organizational culture: Can it be a source of sustained competitive advantage? *Academy of Management Review, 11*(3), 656-665.

Barney, J. (1991). Firm resources and sustained competitive advantage. *Journal of Management, 17*(1), 99-120.

Barney, J. (1995). Looking inside for competitive advantage. *Academy of Management Executive, 9*(4), 49-61.

Baron, R. M., & Kenny, D. A. (1986). The moderator-mediator variable distinction in social psychological research: Conceptual, strategic, and statistical considerations. *Journal of Personality and Social Psychology, 51*(6), 1173-1182.

Bate, P., & Child, J. (1987). Paradigms and understanding in comparative organizational research. In J. Child, & P. Bate (Eds.), *Organization of Innovation East-West Perspective* (pp.19-49). New York: Walter de Gruyter.

Becker, B. E., Huselid, M. A. and Ulrich, D. (2001). The HR Scorecard. Watertown, MA: Harvard Business School.

Beer, M. (1980). *Organization change and development.* Santa Monica, CA: Goodyear.

Begley, S. (2004, April 18). Self-esteem builds on achievement not praise for slackers. The *Wall Street Journal*, B1.

Behe, M. (1998). Intelligent design theory as a tool for analyzing biochemical systems. In W. A. Dembski (Ed.), *Mere creation: Science, faith & intelligent design* (p.178). Downers Grove, IL: InterVarsity Press.

Belasco, J. A. (1990). *Teaching the elephant to dance.* New York: Crown.

Benioff, M., & Southwick, K. (2004). *Compassionate capitalism.* Franklin Lakes, NJ: The Career Press.

Bennett, D. J. (1998). *Randomness.* Cambridge, MA: Harvard University.

Bennis, W. G. (1989). *On becoming a leader.* Reading, MA: Addison-Wesley.

Bennis, W. G. 1997. *Managing people IS like herding cats.* South Provo, UT: Executive Excellence.

Bennis, W. G., Spreitzer, G. M., & Cummings, T. G. (2001). *The future of leadership.* San Francisco: Jossey-Bass.

Bennis, W. G., & Thomas, R. J. (2002, September). Crucibles of leadership. *Harvard Business Review, 80*(9), 39-46.

Bennis, W. G., & Thomas, R. J. (2002). *Geeks & geezers.* Boston: Harvard Business School.

Berger. L. A., & Berger, D. R. (2004). *The talent management handbook.* New York: McGraw-Hill.

Bernstein, P. L. (1998). *Against the gods: The remarkable story of risk.* New York: John Wiley & Sons.

Blackard, K., & Gibson, J. W. (2002). *Capitalizing on conflict.* Palo Alto, CA: Davies-Black.

Blake, R. R., & Mouton, J. S. (1984). *Solving costly organizational conflict.* San Francisco: Jossey-Bass.

Blanchard, K. H. (1991). *The one minute manager meets the monkey.* New York: Harper Trade.

Blanchard, K. H. (2003). *The one minute manager: The world's most popular management method.* New York: Random House Audio Publishing Group.

Blanchard, K. H., & Johnson, S. (1985). *The one minute manager.* New York: Penguin Group.

Blanchard, K. H., & Johnson, S. (1985). *Building one minute manager skills.* New York: Penguin Group.

Blanchard, K. H., & Lorber, R. (1984). *Strategies for putting the one minute manger to work.* Old Greenwich, CN: Listen & Learn.

Blanchard, K. H., & Zigarmi, P. (1999). *Leadership and the one-minute manager.* New York: Morrow/Avon.

Block, P. (1988). *The empowered manager.* San Francisco: Jossey-Bass.

Boa, K. D., & Bowman, Jr., R. M. (2002). *20 compelling evidences that god exists.* Tulsa, OK: RiverOak.

Bolles, R. N. (1981). *The three boxes of life and how to get out of them.* Berkeley, CA: Ten Speed Press.

Bolles, R. N. (1995). *The 1995 what color is your parachute?* (A new edition is published yearly. All editions provide the basic necessities.). Berkeley, CA: Ten Speed Press.

Boone, M. E. (1991). *Leadership and the computer.* Rocklin, CA: N. Dean Meyer and Associates.

Bosch, L. (2004, March). Dr. Phil: Your total life makeover. *Good Housekeeping,* 119,

Bossidy, L., & Charan, R. (2002). *Execution: the discipline of getting things done.* New York: Crown Business.

Bouchard, Jr., T. J., & Segal, N. L. (1985). Environment and IQ. In B. B. Wolman (Ed.), *Handbook of intelligence* (pp. 391-464). New York: John Wiley & Sons:

Bourgeois, III., L. J., McAllister, D. W., & Mitchell, T. R. (1978). The effects of different organizational environments upon decisions about organizational structure. *Academy of Management Journal, 21*(3), 508-514.

Boyacigiller, N. A., & Adler, N. J. (1991). The parochial dinosaur: Organizational science in a global context. *Academy of Management Review, 16*(2), 262-290.

Brache, A. P. (2002). *How organizations work.* New York: John Wiley & Sons.

Bradley, B. (1998). *Values of the game.* New York: Artisan.

Brandrowski, J. F. (1990). *Corporate imagination plus.* New York: McMillan.

Branham, L. (2001). *Keeping the people who keep you in business.* New York: AMACOM.

Bridges, W. (1980). *Transitions: making sense of life's changes.* Cambridge, MA: Perseus.

Brody, N. (1985). The validity of tests of intelligence. In B. B. Wolman (Ed.), *Handbook of Intelligence* (pp. 353-390). New York: John Wiley & Sons:

Brokaw, T. (1999). *The greatest generation.* New York: Random House.

Brooker, K. (2001, May 28). The chairman of the board looks back. *Fortune,* 62.

Bruun, E., & Getzen, R. (1996). *The book of American values and virtues.* New York: Black Dog & Leventhal.

Burgelman, R. A., & Sayles, L. R. (1986). *Inside corporate innovation: Strategy, structure and managerial skills.* New York: The Free Press.

Burns, T., & Stalker, G. M. (1961). *The management of innovation.* London: Travistock.

Burnside, R. M. (1991). Visioning: building pictures of the future. In J. Henry & D. Walker (Eds.), *Managing innovation* (pp.193-199). London: Sage.

Burrows, B., & Helyar, J. (1990). *Barbarians at the gate.* New York: Harper & Row.

Butler, A. S. (1996). *TeamThink.* New York: McGraw Hill.

Butterworth, G. (1994). Infant intelligence. In J. Khalfa (Ed.), *What is intelligence?* (pp. 49-71). New York: Press Syndicate of the University of Cambridge.

Byham, W. C. (1988). *Zapp!: The lighting power of EMPOWERMENT.* Pittsburgh, PA: Development Dimensions International.

Byron, C. (2002). *Martha inc.* New York: Wiley.

Campbell, G. M. (2002). *Bulletproof presentations.* Franklin Lakes, NJ: Career Press.

Carlzon, J. (1989). *Moments of truth: New strategies for today's customer-driven economy.* New York: Harper & Row.

Carnegie, D. (1985). *How to enjoy your life and your job.* New York: Simon & Schuster.

Carr, D. K., & Johansson, H. J. (1995). *Best practices in reengineering.* New York: McGraw-Hill.

Carter, S. L. (2002). *The emperor of ocean park.* New York: Vintage Books, Random House.

Carter, V. B. (1965). *Winston Churchill: an intimate portrait.* New York: Harcourt, Brace & World.

CEOs: The Vision Thing. (1993, January 28). The *Wall Street Journal,* A14.

Chambers, H. E. (1998). *The bad attitude survival guide.* Reading, MA: Addison-Wesley.

Cheyfitz, K. (2003). *Thinking inside the box.* New York: Free Press.

Child, J., & Bate, P. (Eds.). (1987). *Organization of innovation east-west perspective.* Berlin: Walter de Gruyter.

Childress, J. R. (2001). *A time for leadership.* Los Angles: Leadership Press.

Churchill, W. S. (1949). *The second world war (6 volumes).* London: Cassell & Co. LTD.

Clawson, J. G. (1999). *Level three leadership: Getting below the surface.* Upper Saddle River, NJ: Prentice-Hall.

Clegg, C., Unsworth, K., Epitropaki, O., & Parler. G. (2002). Implicating trust in the innovation process. *Journal of Organizational Psychology, 75,* 409-422.

Cohen, D. and Prusak, L. (2001). In Good Company: How Social Capital Makes Organization Work. Watertown, MA: Harvard Business School.

Cohen, M. D., March, J. G., & Olsen, J. P. (1972). A garbage can model of organizational choice. *Administrative Science Quarterly, 17*(1), pp. 1-25.

Collins, J. (2001). *Good to great: Why some companies make the leap…And others don't.* New York: HarperCollins.

Collins, J. (2003, July 21). The 10 greatest CEOs of all time. *Fortune,* 55-68.

Conner, D. R. (1998). *Leading at the edge of chaos: How to create the nimble organization.* New York: John Wiley & Sons.

Conner, J. (2000). Developing the global leaders of tomorrow. *Human Resource Management, Summer/Fall, 39*(2 & 3),147-157.

Corcoran, B., with Littlefield, B. (2003). *Use what you've got & other business lessons I learned from my mom.* New York: Portfolio.

Cortada, J. W. and Hargraves, T. S. (1999). *Into the networked age.* New York: Oxford University.

Cottrell, D. (2002). *Monday morning leadership: 8 mentoring sessions you can't afford to miss.* Dallas, TX: CornerStone Leadership Institute.

Cottrell, D., & Layton, M. C. (2004). *175 ways to get more done in less time!* Dallas, TX: CornerStone Leadership Institute.

Covey, S. (1990). *The habits of highly effective people.* New York: Simon and Schuster.

Covey, S. (1991). *Principle centered leadership.* New York: Summit Books.

Craig, M. (2000). *The 50 best (and worst) business deals.* Franklin Lakes, NJ: Career Press.

Crouch, N. (2004). *Mexicans & Americans.* London: Nicholas Brealy.

D'Alessandro, D. F. (2004). *Career warfare.* New York: McGraw-Hill.

Damanpour, F. (1991). Organizational innovation: A meta-analysis of effects of determinates and moderators. *The Academy of Management Journal, 34*(3), 555-590.

Dauphinais, G. W., & Price, C. (Eds.). (1998). *Straight from the CEO.* New York: Simon & Schuster.

Dauten, D. (2004, May 16). What you don't know. The *Birmingham News*, p. 1L.

Davenport, T. H., & Beck, J. C. (2001). *The attention economy: Understanding the new currency of business.* Watertown, MA: Harvard Business School.

de Geus, A. (1997). *The living company.* Boston: Harvard Business School.

Deal, T. E., & Kennedy, A. A. (1982). *Corporate cultures.* Reading, MA, Addison-Wesley.

DeKluyver, C. A., Pearce, II, J. A. (2003). *Strategy a view from the top: An executive perspective.* Upper Saddle River, NJ: Prentice Hall.

DeMarco, T. (2001). *Slack.* New York: Random House.

Despain, J. and Converse J. B. (2003)....*And dignity for all.* Upper Saddle River, NJ: Prentice Hall.

Diamond, J. (1999). *Guns, germs, and steel: The fates of human societies.* New York: W.W. Norton.

Dillon-Malone, A. (2000). *The cynic's dictionary.* Chicago, IL: Contemporary Books.

DiPiazza, Jr., S. A., & Eccles, R. G. (2002). *Public trust.* New York: PricewaterhouseCoopers.

Dolan, P., & Thom, E. (2003). *True to our roots.* Princeton, NJ: Bloomberg Press.

Dotlich, D. L., & Cairo, P. C. (2003). *Why CEOs fail.* San Francisco: Jossey-Bass.

Drucker, P. F. (1967). *The effective executive.* New York: Harper & Roe.

Drucker, P. F. (1973). *Management: Tasks, responsibilities, practices.* New York: Harper & Roe.

Drucker, P. F. (1980). *Managing in turbulent times.* New York: Harper & Row.

Drucker, P. F. (1985). *Innovation and entrepreneurship.* New York: Harper & Roe.

Drucker, P. F. (1986). *The practice of management.* New York: Harper & Row.

Drucker, P. F. (1988). The coming of the new organization. *Harvard Business Review, 66*(1), 45-53.

Drucker, P. F. (1989). *The new realities.* New York: Harper & Row.

Drucker, P. F. (1990, November 1). [Closed circuit TV presentation]. The University of Texas at Arlington.

Drucker, P. F. (1991, February 7). How to be competitive though big. The *Wall Street Journal*, p. A14.

Drucker, P. F. (1993, February 2). A turnaround primer. The *Wall Street Journal*, p. A10.

Drucker, P. F. (1995). *Managing in a time of great change.* New York: Truman Talley Books/Dutton.

Drucker, P. F. (1996). The shape of things to come. *Leader to Leader.* Premier Issue, pp. 12-18.

Drucker, P. F. (1998). *Peter Drucker on the profession of management.* Boston, MA: Harvard Business Review Book.

Drucker, P. F. (1999). *Management challenges for the 21st century.* New York: HarperBusiness.

Druskat, V. U., & Wolff, S. B. (2001, March). Building the emotional intelligence of groups. *Harvard Business Review,* 80-90.

DuBrin, A. J. (1996). *Reengineering survival guide.* Cincinnati, OH: Thomson Executive Press.

DuBrin, A. J. (1997). *10 minute guide to leadership.* New York: Macmillan Spectrum/Alpha Books.

DuBrin, A. J. (2004). *Leadership: Research findings, practice, and skills.* New York: Houghton Mifflin.

DuBrin, A. J. (2005). *Coaching and mentoring skills.* Upper Saddle River, NJ: Pearson Prentice Hall.

Dyer, J. H. (2000). *Collaborative advantage.* New York: Oxford University.

Easterby-Smith, M., Thorpe, R., & Lowe, A. (1991). *Management research.* London: Sage.

Eisenhardt, K. M. (1989a). Building theories from case study research. *Academy of Management Review, 14*(4), 532-550.

Eisenhardt, K. M. (1989b). Making fast strategic decisions in high-velocity environments. *Academy of Management Review, 32*(3), 543-576.

Eppler, M. (2003). *The Wright way.* New York: AMACOM.

Fayol, H. (1949). *General and industrial management* [C. Storrs, Trans.]. London: Pitman. (Original work published in 1916)

Field leadership manual 2000. (2000). Nashville, TN: The Southwestern Company.

Finkelstein, S. (2003). *Why smart executives fail.* New York: Portfolio.

Fisher, R., & Ury, W. (1983). *Getting to yes.* New York: Penguin Group.

Fombrum, C. J. (1992). *Turning points: Creating strategic change in corporations.* New York: McGraw-Hill.

Fong-Torres, B. (2003, March 30). I owe America my life: An interview with Carlos Santana. *Parade,* pp. 4-5.

Ford, H., with Crowther, S. (1922). *My life and work.* Garden City, NY: Doubleday.

Foster, R. N. (1986). *Innovation: the attackers advantage.* New York: Simon & Schuster.

Frankl, V. E. (1992). *Man's search for meaning.* Boston, MA: Beacon Press.

Franks, T. (2004). *American soldier.* New York: Harper Collins.

Fullan, M. (2001). *Leading in a culture of change.* San Francisco: Jossey-Bass.

Fuller, T. (1995, July-August). Does business need leaders? *Business Horizons,* pp. 1-4.

Fulmer, R. M. (1997). The evolving paradigm of leadership development. *Organizational Dynamics, 25,* 59-72.

Fulmer, R. M., Gibbs, P. A., & Goldsmith, M. (2000, Fall). Developing leaders: How winning companies keep on winning. *Sloan Management Review, 42*(1), 49-60.

Galbraith, J. (1973). *Designing complex organizations.* Reading, MA: Addison-Wesley.

Galbraith, J. R., Lawler, E. E. III, & Associates. (1993). *Organizing for the future.* San Francisco: Jossey-Bass.

Gardner, F. (Ed.). (2003). *Living, leading, and the American dream: John W. Gardner.* San Francisco: Jossey-Bass.

Gardner, H. (1993). *Frames of mind.* New York: Basic Books.

Gardner, J. W., & Reese, F. Gardner. (1975). *Quotations of wit & wisdom.* New York: W.W. Norton.

Garratt, B. (2003). *Thin on top.* Yarmouth, ME: Nicholas Brealey.

Gaynor, G. H. (2002). *Innovation by design.* New York: AMACOM.

George, B. (2003). *Authentic leadership: Rediscovering the secrets to creating lasting value.* San Francisco: Jossey-Bass.

George, B. (2003, September 29). Why it's hard to do what's right. *Fortune, 148*(6), 95-100.

Gerloff, E. A. (1985). *Organizational theory and design.* New York: McGraw-Hill.

Gerstner, L. V., Jr. (2002). *Who says elephants can't dance.* New York: HarperBusiness.

Gibson, C. B. (2001, June). Metaphors and meaning: An Intercultural Analysis Of Concepts Of Teamwork. *Administrative Science Quarterly.* Retrieved February 1, 2006, from www. findarticles

Giuliani, R. W. (2002). *Leadership.* New York: Miramax Books.

Glaser, B. J., & Strauss, L. J. (1967). *The discovery of grounded theory.* Chicago, IL: Adline.

Gleick, J. (1987). *Chaos: Making a new science.* New York: Viking Penguin.

Glover, C., & Smethurst, S. (2003). Creative license. *People Management, 9*(6), 30-34.

Goldenberg, J., Horowitz, R., Levav, A., & Mazursky, D. (2003, March). Finding your innovative sweet spot. *Harvard Business Review,* 129.

Goldsmith, M., Govindarajan, V., Kaye, B., & Vicere, A. A. (2003). *The many facets of leadership.* Upper Saddle River, NJ: Financial Times Prentice Hall.

Goleman, D. (1995). *Emotional intelligence.* New York: Bantam.

Goleman, D. (2000). *Working with emotional intelligence.* New York: Bantam.

Goleman, D., Boyatzis, R., & McKee, A. (2001, December). Primal leadership: The hidden driver of great performance. *Harvard Business Review*, 42-51.

Goleman, D., Boyatzis, R., & McKee, A. (2002). *Primal leadership: Realizing the power of emotional intelligence.* Boston: Harvard Business School.

Goold, M., & Quinn, J. J. (1990). The paradox of strategic controls. *Strategic Management Journal, 11,* 43-57.

Govindarajan, V., & Gupta, A. K. (2001). *The quest for global dominance.* New York: John Wiley & Sons.

Grant-Williams, R. (2002). *Voice power: Using your voice to captivate, persuade, and command attention.* New York: AMACOM.

Green, S., Hassan, F., Immelt, J., Marks, M., & Meiland, D. (2003). In search of global leaders. *Harvard Business Review, 81*(8). 38-45.

Greenleaf, R. F. (1987). *Teacher as servant: A parable.* Indianapolis, IN: The Robert K. Greenleaf Center.

Greenleaf, R. K. (1991). *The servant as leader.* Indianapolis, IN: The Robert K. Greenleaf Center.

Gregory, R. (1994). Seeing intelligence. In J. Khalfa (Ed.), *What is intelligence?* (pp.13-26). New York: Press Syndicate of the University of Cambridge.

Gregory, R. J. (1999). *Foundations of intellectual assessment.* Needham Heights, MA: Allyn & Bacon.

Grove, N. (1997). *National geographic atlas of world history.* Washington, DC: The Book Division National Geographic Society.

Guilford, J. P. (1967). *The nature of human intelligence.* New York: McGraw-Hill. .

Guilford, J. P. (1986). *Creative talents.* Buffalo, NY: Bearly Limited.

Gundling, E. (2003). *Working globesmart.* Palo Alto, CA: Davies-Black.

Gwartney, J. D., & Stroup, R. L. (1993). *What everyone should know about economics and prosperity.* Tallahassee, FL: The James Madison Institute.

Handy, C. (1998). *The hungry spirit.* New York: Broadway.

Harari, O. (2002). *The leadership secrets of Colin Powell.* New York: McGraw-Hill.

Harborne, P., & Johne, A. (2002). Many leaders make light work in banking innovation projects. *Journal of Financial Services Marketing, 6*(3), 267-280.

Hare, B. (2004). *Celebration of fools.* New York: AMACOM.

Hargrove, R. (1998). *Mastering the art of creative collaboration.* New York: McGraw-Hill.

Harkins, P. (1999). *Powerful conservation's.* New York: McGraw-Hill.

Harmon, R. L. (1996). *Reinventing the business.* New York: The Free Press.

Harper, B., & Harper, A. (1990). *Succeeding as a self-directed work team.* New York: MW Corporation.

Harris, J. (2002). *Blindsided.* Oxford: Capstone.

Harris, J. (2002). *Facilitating others: A Christian view of leadership.* Alabaster, AL: Smokey Road.

Hart, M. H. (1989). *The 100: A ranking of the most influential persons in history.* New York: Carol Publishing Group.

Hartley, R. F. (2000). *Management Mistakes And Successes* (6th Ed.). New York: John Wiley & Sons.

Henninger, D. (2002, December 13). There must be a real reason for Bush's success. The *Wall Street Journal*, p. A16.

Henricks, M. (2003, July). Grow your contacts. *Southwest Airlines Spirit*, 50-53.

Henry, J., & Walker, D. (Eds.). (1991). *Managing Innovation.* London: Sage.

Herken, G. (2002). *Brotherhood of the bomb.* New York: Henry Holt.

Hermalin, B. E. (1998, December). Toward an economic theory of leadership: Leading by example. The *American Economic Review*, 1188-1206.

Hersey, P. (1985). *The situational leader.* New York: Warner.

Hesselbein, F. (2002, Winter). A time for leaders. *Leader to Leader*, 4-6.

Hesselbein, F. (2002). *Hesselbein on leadership.* San Francisco: Jossey-Bass.

Hesselbein, F., & Cohen, P. M. (Eds.). (1999). Leader to leader: Enduring insights on leadership. The *Drucker Foundation's Award-Winning Journal.* San Francisco: Jossey-Bass.

Hesselbein, F., Goldsmith, M., & Beckhard, R. (Eds.). (1996). *The leader of the future.* The Drucker Foundation. San Francisco: Jossey-Bass.

Hesselbein, F., Goldsmith, M., & Beckhard, R. (Eds.). (2002). L*eading for innovation: And organizing for results.* The Peter F. Drucker Foundation. San Francisco: Jossey-Bass.

Heymowitz, C. (2003, September 9). Pepsico chief executive asks future leaders to train like athletes. *The Wall Street Journal,* p. B1.

Hickman, C. R., & Silva, M. A. (1984). <u>*Creating excellence: Managing corporate culture, strategy, and change in the new age.*</u> New York: NAL.

Himsel, D. (2004). *Leadership Sopranos style.* Chicago: Dearborn Trade Publication.

Hoover, G. (2001). *Hoover's vision.* New York: Texere.

Hope, J., & Fraser, R. (2003). *Beyond budgeting.* Watertown, MA: Harvard Business School.

Horowitz, A., & editors of *Business 2.0* (2004). *The dumbest moments in business history.* New York: Portfolio.

Horton, T. R. (1996, January). Selecting the best for the top. *American Management Association,* 20-23.

Howard, R. (1991). *All about intelligence.* Marrickville, MSW: Southwood Press Pty.

Huber, G. P. (1991). Organizational learning: An examination of the contributing processes and a review of the literatures. *Organization Science, 2,* 1.

Hubner, H. (1986). Innovation management—Art and science. In H. Hubner, (Ed.), *The art and science of innovation management* (pp. 427-441). *Proceedings of the Fourth International Conference on Product Innovation Management,* Innsbruck/Igls, Austria, August 26-28, 1985. Amsterdam: Elsevier Science.

Humphreys, L. G. (1985). General intelligence: An integration of factor, test, and simplex theory. In B. B. Wolman, (Ed.). *Handbook of intelligence* (pp. 201-224). New York: John Wiley & Sons:

Hunger, J. D., & Wheelen, T. L. (2003. *Essential of strategic management.* (3rd Ed.). Upper Saddle River, NJ: Prentice Hall.

Hunt, D. M., Magruder, S., & Bolon, D. S. (1993, March 2-6). Questionnaire format: A test of juxtaposed vs. separate scales. In K. A. Vaverek, M. A. Williams, & The Mescon Group, (Eds.). *Proceedings of Southwest Division of the Academy of Management* (pp. 371-373), New Orleans, LA.

Hymowtz, C. (2003, September 9). In the lead: Pepsico executive asks future leaders to train link athletes. The *Wall Street Journal*, p. B1.

Hymowtz, C. (2004, June 15). Once a psychoanalyst, Novartis's chief uses his skills to manage. The *Wall Street Journal*, p. B1.

Hynd, G. W., & Wills, W. G. (1985). Neurological foundations of intelligence. In B. B. Wolman, (Ed.). *Handbook of intelligence* (pp. 119-158). New York: John Wiley & Sons.

Iacocca, L. (1984). *Iacocca: an Autobiography.* New York: Bantam.

Imai, M. (1986). *Kaizen: The key to Japan's competitive success.* New York: Random House.

Jacobs, G., & Macfarlane, R. (1990). *The vital corporation.* Englewood Cliffs, NJ: Prentice-Hall.

Jackson, K. (2000). *Katye: The story of a cancer survivor.* Birmingham, AL: Katye Luvs Cats, LLC.

Jackson, P. Z., & McKergow, M. (2002). *The solutions focus: The simple way to change.* London: Nicholas Brealey.

Jacobs, F. R., & Whybark, D. C. (2000). *Why ERP?* New York: McGraw-Hill Higher Education.

Jarboe, J. (1989, April). A boy and his airline: No kid ever had more fun with his favorite toy than Herb Kelleher has in running Southwest Airlines. *Texas Monthly*, 98-110.

Jelinek, M. (1979). *Institutionalizing innovation: A study of organizational learning systems.* New York: Praeger.

Jelinek, M., & Schoonhoven, C. B. (1990). *Innovation marathon: Lessons from high technology firms.* Oxford: Basil Blackwell.

Jick, T. D., & Peiperl, M. A. (2003). *Managing Change.* (2nd Ed.). New York: McGraw-Hill.

Johnson, S. (1998). *Who moved my cheese?* New York: G. P. Putman's Sons.

Jung, D. I., & Avolio, B. J. (1999). Effects of leadership style and followers' cultural orientation on performance in group and individual task conditions. *Academy Of Management Journal, 42*(2), 208-218.

Kanji, G. K., & Moura e Sa, P. (2001). Measuring leadership excellence. *Total Quality Management, 12*(6),:701-718.

Kanter, R. M. (1983). *The change masters.* New York: Simon and Schuster.

Kanter, R. M. (1989). *When giants learn to dance.* New York: Simon and Schuster.

Kao, J. J. (1991). *The entrepreneurial organization.* Englewood Cliffs, NJ: Prentice Hall.

Kaplan, R. E. (1991). Creativity in the everyday business of managing. In D. A. Kolb, I. M. Rubin, & Osland, J. S. (Eds.).*The Organizational Behavior Reader* (pp. 270-278). Englewood Cliffs, NJ: Prentice-Hall.

Kaplan, R. S., & Norton, D. P. (2001). *The strategy-focused organization.* Watertown, MA: Harvard Business School.

Kaplan, R. S., & Norton, D. P. (2004). *Strategy maps.* Boston, MA: Harvard Business School.

Karp, H., Fuller, C., & Sirias, D. (2002). *Bridging the boomer-Xer gap.* Palo Alto, CA: Davies—Black.

Kash, D. E. (1989). *Perpetual innovation: The new world of competition.* New York: Basic.

Katz, D., & Kahn, R. L. (1978). *The social psychology of organizations.* New York: Wiley.

Keene, A. (2000). Complexity theory: The changing role of leadership. *Industrial and Commercial Training, 32*(1), 15-20.

Keeps, D., & Sheff-Cahan, V. (2004, February 23). Learning curves. *People,* 86-92.

Keller, E., & Berry, J. (2003) *The influentials.* New York: The Free Press.

Keller, R. T. (1986). Predictors of the performance of project groups in R & D. organizations. *Academy of Management Journal, 29*(4), 715-726.

Kennedy, J. F. (1964). *Profiles in courage* (Memorial Ed.). New York: Harper & Roe.

Kennedy, P. (1987). *The rise and fall of the great powers.* New York: Random House.

Kerlinger, F. N. (1986). *Foundations of behavioral research.* (3rd Ed.). Orlando, FL: Holt, Rinehart and Winston.

Khalfa, J. (Ed.). (1994). *What is intelligence?* New York: Press Syndicate of the University of Cambridge.

Kilmann, R. H., Kilmann, I., & Associates. (1991). *Making organizations competitive: Enhancing networks and relationships across traditional boundaries.* San Francisco: Jossey-Bass.

Kilmann, R. H., Saxton, M. J., Serpa, R., & Associates. (1985). *Gaining control of the corporate culture.* San Francisco: Jossey-Bass.

Kim, W. Chan, & Mauborgne, R. (2003, April). Tipping point leadership. *Harvard Business Review,* 60-69.

Klein, G. (2003). *Intuition at work.* New York: Doubleday.

Klein, J. (2004, May 17). The perils of a righteous president. *Time,* 25.

Klein, M., Napier, R. (2003). *The courage to act.* Palo Alto, CA: Davies-Black.

Kolb, D. A., Rubin, I. M., & Osland, J. S. (Eds.). (1991). *The organizational behavior reader.* Englewood Cliffs, NJ: Prentice-Hall.

Kotter, J., & Cohen, D. (2002). *The heart of change.* Boston: Harvard Business School.

Kotter, J. P. (1988). *The leadership factor.* New York: The Free Press.

Kouzes, J. M., & Posner, B. Z. (1987). *The leadership challenge: How to get extraordinary things done in organizations.* San Francisco: Jossey-Bass.

Kouzes, J. M., & Posner, B. Z. (1993). *Credibility: How leaders gain and lose it, why people demand it.* San Francisco: Jossey-Bass.

Krass, P. (Ed). (1998). *The book of leadership wisdom.* New York: John Wiley & Sons.

Krauthammer, C. (2004, June 14). He could see for miles: Reagan had a vision and the courage to endure all doubters. *Time,* 94.

Kriegel, R. J., & Patler, L. (1991*). If it ain't broke…BREAK IT.* New York: Warner Books.

Kuhn, T. S. (1970). *The Structure of Scientific Revolutions* (2nd Ed.). Chicago: University of Chicago.

Kunstler, B. (2004). *The hothouse effect.* New York: AMACOM.

Kyne, P. B., & Axelrod, A. (2003). *The go-getter.* New York: Times Books.

Lacey, R. (1986). *Ford: The men and the machine.* Boston: Little, Brown.

Landry, T. (1990). *Tom Landry: An autobiography.* New York: HarperCollins.

Laurie, D. L. (2002). *Venture catalyst.* Cambridge, MA: Perseus.

Law, F. (1969). *Modern great Americans.* Freeport: Books for Libraries Press.

Levering, R., & Moskowitz, M. (1993). *The 100 best companies to work for in America.* New York: Doubleday.

Levinson, J. C., Frishman, R., & Lublin, J. (2002). *Guerrilla publicity.* Avon, MA: Northan: Adams Media; Roundhouse.

Lewis, C. S. (1952). *Mere Christianity.* San Francisco: HarperCollins.

Lewis, C. S. (1996). *The problem of pain.* New York:: HarperCollins.

Lindblom, C. (1959, June). The science of "muddling through." *Public Administration Review*, pp. 79-88.

Linkow, P. (1999, July). What gifted strategic thinkers do. *Training & Development,* 34-37.

Lundin, S. C., Christensen, J., & Paul, H. (2003). *FISH! STICKS.* New York: Hyperion.

Maas, J. (1998). Winning' em over: A new model for managing in the age of persuasion/getting it done: how to lead when you're not in charge. *Sloan Management Review 40*(1),103-104.

MacArthur, B. (1999). *The penguin book of twentieth-century speeches.* London: Penguin Books.

Maccoby, M. (2003). *The productive narcissist: The promise and peril of visionary leadership.* New York: Broadway Books.

Mackay, J. (1995). *Robert Service vagabond of verse: A biography.* Edinburgh and London: Mainstream.

Mackintosh, N. (1994). Intelligence in evolution. In J. Khalfa, (Ed.). *What is intelligence?* (pp. 27-48). New York: Press Syndicate of the University of Cambridge,

Maier, N. R. F. (1991). Leadership principles for problem solving conferences. In D. A. Kolb, I. M. Rubin, & Osland, J. S. (Eds.). *The Organizational Behavior Reader* (pp.294-303). Englewood Cliffs, NJ: Prentice-Hall,.

Mangalindan, M. (2003, April 8). Larry Ellison's sober vision. The *Wall Street Journal*, p. B1.

Manz C. C., Bastien, D. T., Hostager, T. J., & Shapiro, G. L. (1989). Leadership and innovation: A longitudinal process view. In A. H. Van de Ven, H. Angle, & Poole, M. S., (Eds.). *Research on the management of innovation, volumes 1 and 2* (pp. 613-636). Cambridge, MA: Ballinger,

Manz, C. C., & Neck, C. P. (2004). *Mastering Self-Leadership* (3rd Ed.).Upper Saddle River, NJ: Pearson Prentice Hall.

Manzoni, J-F., & Barsoux, J. L. (2002). *The set-up-to-fail syndrome: How good managers cause great people to fail.* Boston: Harvard Business School.

Marquardt, M. J. (2004). *Optimizing the power of action learning.* Palo Alto, CA: Davies-Black.

Martin, R. (2002). *The responsibility virus.* New York: Basic Books.

Mauzy, J., & Harriman, R. (2003). *Creativity, Inc.* Boston: Harvard Business School.

Maxwell, J. C. (2000). *The 21 most powerful minutes in a leader's day.* Nashville, TN: Thomas Nelson.

Maxwell, J. C. (2002). *Leadership 101: What every leader needs to know.* Nashville, TN: Thomas Nelson.

Meeker, M.(1985). Toward a psychology of giftedness: A concept in search of measurement. In B. B. Wolman, (Ed.), *Handbook of Intelligence* (pp. 787-800). New York: John Wiley & Sons:

Messick, D. M., & Bazerman, M. H. (1996, Winter). Ethical leadership and the psychology of decision making. *Sloan Management Review, 9-22.*

McCain, J., & Salter, M. (1999). *Faith of my fathers.* New York: Random House.

McGrath, J. E., Martin, J., & Kulka, R. A. (1982). *Judgment calls in research.* Beverly Hills, CA: Sage Publications.

McGraw, P. C. (1999). *Life strategies: Doing what works doing what matters.* New York: Hyperion.

McGraw, P. C. (2000). *Life strategies workbook.* New York: Hyperion.

McKenna, P. J., & Maister, D. H. (2002). *First among equals.* New York: The Free Press.

Meacham, J. (2003, October 20). FDR, Churchill, and us. *Newsweek, 62-63.*

Mento, A. J., Steel, R. P., & Karren, R. J. (1987). A meta-analytic study of the effects of goal setting on task performance: 1966-1984. *Organizational Behavior and Human Decision Processes, 39,* 52-83.

Michels, A. J. (1992, December 28). Nothing comes to those who wait. *Fortune, 54.*

Miller, D. (2003). *Blue like jazz.* Nashville, TN: Thomas Nelson.

Miller, L. M. (1989). *Barbarian to bureaucrats: Corporate life cycle strategies.* New York: Clarkson N. Potter.

Miller, W. C. (1987). *The creative edge.* Reading, MA: Addison-Wesley.

Mintzberg, H., Raisinghani, D., & Theoret, A. (1976). The structure of "unstructured" decision processes. *Administrative Science Quarterly, 21*(2), 246-275.

Montgomery, R. H.(Ed., 3 volumes). (1911). *The American business manual: A complete guide to modern systems and practice.* Emeryville, CA: P.F. Collier & Son.

Motivating People. (2003, January). *Harvard Business Review.* 41-47.

Motley, E. L.(1995). *Lesson learned and observations made: A student's perspective on leadership.* Birmingham, AL: Privately printed by Hanna Steel Corporation.

Murray, A., & Lehner, U. C. (1990, June 25). What U. S. scientist discover, the Japanese convert into profit. The *Wall Street Journal,* p. A1.

Nadler, D. A. (1998). *Champions of change.* San Francisco: Jossey-Bass.

Nahavandi, A. (2003). *The art and science of leadership* (3rd Ed.). Upper Saddle River, NJ: Prentice Hall.

Naisbitt, J. (1982). *Mega trends.* New York: Warner Books.

Naisbitt, J., & Aburdene, P. (1985). *Re-inventing the corporation.* New York: Megatrends.

Naisbitt, J., & Aburdene, P. (1990). *Megatrends 2000.* New York: William Morrow.

NASPI. (2004, April 18). Five keys to satisfaction in any career. The *Birmingham News,* pp.1I & 2I.

Naughton, K., & Peyser, M. (2004, March 1). The world according to Trump. *Newsweek*, 48-57.

Neuharth, A. (1989). *Confessions of an S.O.B.* New York: Doubleday.

Nicolson, A. (2003). *God's secretaries.* New York: HarperCollins

Nickolson, N. (2003, January). How to motivate your problem people. *Motivating People,* 57-65.

Niebuhr, R. (1964). *The nature and destiny of man a Christian interpretation: Volume 1: Human nature.* New York: Charles Scribner's Sons.

Nohria, N., Joyce, W., & Roberson, B. (2003, July). What really works. *Harvard Business Review,* 42-52.

Norman, D. A. (1998). *The invisible computer.* Cambridge, MA: The MIT Press.

Nutt, P. C. (2002). *Why decisions fail.* San Francisco: Berrett-Koehler.

Oakley, E. and Krug, D. (1991). *Enlightened leadership.* New York: Fireside.

Obese white-color women get paid…(2004, March 4). The *Wall Street Journal*, p. A1.

Olesen, E. (1993). *12 steps to mastering the winds of change.* New York: Macmillan.

O'Loughin, J. (2003). *The real Warren Buffet.* London: Nicholas Brealey Publishing.

Ouchi, W. (1981). *Theory Z.* Reading, MA: Addison-Wesley.

Paine, L. S. (2002).*Value Shift.* New York: McGraw-Hill.

Pandya, M., Singh, H., Mittlestaedt, R.E., & Clemons, E. (2003). *Knowledge @ Wharton: On building corporate value.* Hoboken, NJ: John Wiley & Sons.

Parker, R. C. (1982). *The management of innovation.* New York: John Wiley & Sons.

Pascale, K., & Athos, A. (1981). *The art of Japanese management.* New York: Simon & Schuster.

Pearce, T. (1995). *Leading out loud.* San Francisco: Jossey-Bass.

Penrose, R. (1994). Mathematical intelligence. In J. Khalfa, (Ed.), *What is intelligence?* (pp. 107-136). New York: Press Syndicate of the University of Cambridge,

Perlow, L. A. (2003). *When you say yes but mean no.* New York: Crown Business.

Perlow, L., & Williams, S. (2003, May). Is silence killing your company? *Harvard Business Review,* 52-68.

Perot, R. (1992). *United we stand.* New York: Hyperion.

Peters, T. J. (1987a, Winter). Facing up to the need for a management revolution. *California Management Review,* 7-37.

Peters, T. J. (1987b). *Thriving On Chaos.* New York: Alfred A. Knopf.

Peters, T. J. (1992). *Liberation management.* New York: Excel.

Peters, T. J. (2003). *Re-imagine!* New York: Dorling Kindersley.

Peters, T. J., & Austin, N. (1985). *A passion for excellence.* Delran, New Jersey: Macmillian.

Peters, T. J., & Waterman, Jr. R. H. (1982). *In search of excellence.* New York: Warner.

Phillips, D. (1992). *Lincoln on leadership.* New York: Warner Books.

Pinker, S. (2002). *The blank slate: The modern denial of human nature.* New York: Viking.

Piszkiewicz, D. *(1998). Wernher Von Braun: The man that sold the moon.* Westport, CN: Praeger.

Porter, M. E. (1985). *Competitive advantage.* New York: Macmillan.

Porter, M. E. (1990). *The competitive advantage of nations.* New York: Macmillan.

Pritchett, L. (1995). *Stop paddling & start rocking the boat.* New York: HarperCollins.

Pritchett, P. (1993). *Culture shift.* Dallas: Pritchett & Associates.

Pritchett, P. (1994). *The employee handbook of: New work habits for a radically changing world.* Dallas: Pritchett & Associates.

Pritchett, P., & Pound, R. (1991). *Business as unusual.* Dallas, TX: Pritchett Publishing.

Pulliam, S., Latour, A., & Brown, K. (2003, March 3). Reaching the top: U.S. Indicts WorldCom chief Ebbers. The *Wall Street Journal,* pp. A1 & A12.

Quinn, J. B. (1980). *Strategies for change: logical incrementalism.* Homewood, IL: Richard D. Irwin.

Quinn, J. B. (1988a). Innovation and corporate strategy: Managed chaos. In M. L. Tushman, & W. L. Moore, (Eds.), Readings in the management of innovation (2nd ed.) (pp. 123-137). New York: HarperCollins.

Quinn, J. B. (1988b). Services technology and manufacturing: Cornerstones of the U. S. economy. In B. R. Guile, & J. B. Quinn, (Eds.), *Managing innovation: Cases from the services industries* (pp. 9-35). Washington, D. C.: National Academy Press,

Quinn, J. B. (1991). Managing innovation: Controlled chaos. In D. A. Kolb, I. M. Rubin, & J. S. Osland, (Eds.), *The Organizational Behavior Reader* (pp. 575-590). Englewood Cliffs, New Jersey: Prentice-Hall,

Quinn, J. B. (1992). *Intelligent enterprise: A knowledge and service based paradigm for industry.* New York: The Free Press.

Quinn, J. B. (1993, February 3). *Presentation to Doctoral Students and Faculty.* The University of Texas at Arlington.

Quinn, J. B., Doorley, T. L., & Paquette, P. C. (1990, Winter). Technology in services: Rethinking strategic focus. *Sloan Management Review,* 79-87.

Ragsdale, B. A. (2003, November 9). Groundless defense. The *Birmingham News,* p. C1.

Reagan, R. (1990). *An American life.* New York: Simon and Schuster.

Reich, R. (1993, July 6). Firms need prodding to improve workplaces. The *Wall Street Journal,* p. A1.

Reichheld, F. F. (2001). *Loyalty rules!* Watertown, MA: Harvard Business School.

Rhinesmith, S. (1996). A *manager's guide to globalization: Six skills for success in a changing world* (2nd ed.). New York: McGraw-Hill.

Robbins, H., & Finley, M. (1995). *WHY TEAMS DON'T WORK: What goes wrong and how to make it right.* Princeton, NJ: Peterson's/Pacesetter Books.

Robbins, S. P. (2002). *The truth about managing people.* New York: Financial Times/Prentice Hall.

Roming, D. A. (2001). *Side by side leadership.* Bard Press.

Ropo, A., & Hunt, J. G. (1991, December). A dynamic case study perspective for management and organizational research. An unpublished report from Professor J. G. Hunt Institute for Management and Leadership Research, College of Business Administration Texas Tech University, Lubbock, Texas.

Rosen, R. H. (1996). *Leading people.* New York: Viking Press.

Rummler, G. A., & Branche, A. P. (1990). *Improving performance.* San Francisco: Jossey-Bass.

Safire, W., & Safir, L. (2000). *Leadership.* New York: Galahad Books.

Salmon, W. A. 1999. *The new supervisor's survival manual.* New York: AMACOM.

Sandys, C., & Littman, J. (2003). *We shall not fail: The inspiring leadership of Winston Churchill.* London: Portfolio the Penguin Group.

Schank R., & Birnbaum, L. (1994). Enhancing intelligence. In J. Khalfa (Ed.), *What is intelligence?* (pp. 72-106). New York: Press Syndicate of the University of Cambridge.

Schwarzkopf, H. N. (1992). *It doesn't take a hero.* New York: Bantam Doubleday Dell Publishing Group.

Scott, G. G. (2004). *A survival guide for working with humans.* New York: AMACOM.

Scott, S. K. (2004). *Mentored by a millionaire.* New York: John Wiley & Sons.

Semler, R. (2004). *The seven-day weekend.* New York: Portfolio.

Senge. P. (1990). T*he fifth discipline.* New York: Doubleday/Currency.

Service, R. W. (1940). *Collect poems of Robert service.* New York: Dodd, Mead.

Service, R. W. (1945). *Ploughman of the moon, an adventure into memory.* New York: Dodd Mead.

Service, R. W. (1948). *Harper of heaven, a further adventure into memory.* London: Ernest Benn.

Service, R. W., & Boockholdt, J. L. (1999). Factors leading to innovation: a study of managers' perspectives. *Creativity Research Journal, 11*(4), 295-311.

Service, R. W., & Maddux, H. S. (1999). Building competitive advantage through is: The organizational information quotient. *Journal of Information Science, 25*(1), 51-65.

Service, R. W., Whitman, J., Ammons, D., & Harper, L. (2000). The material in this section was based in part on work for a jointly developed and never used communications training course.

Shapero, A. (1985). *Managing professional people.* New York: The Free Press.

Shinn, S. (2003, March/April). LUV, Colleen. *Based*, 18-23.

Shook, R. L. (1990). *Turnaround: The new Ford company.* New York: Prentice Hall.

Shostack, G. L. (1988). Limitation is the mother of innovation. *Journal of Business Strategy, 9*, pp. 51-52.

Simon, H. (1957). *Models of men.* New York: Wiley.

Skinner, K. K., Anderson, A., & Anderson, M. (Eds.). (2001). *Reagan: In his own hand.* New York: The Free Press.

Slater, R. (1999). *Jack Welch and the GE way.* New York: McGraw-Hill.

Sloan, A. P. (1963). *My years with general motors.* New York: Doubleday.

Smith, M. J., & Kiger, P. J. (2004). *Political.* New York: HarperCollins.

Smith, S. A., & Mazin, R. A. (2004). *The HR answer book.* New York: AMACOM.

Sperber, D. (1994). Understanding verbal understanding. In J. Khalfa, (Ed.). *What is intelligence?* (pp.179-198). New York: Press Syndicate of the University of Cambridge,

Sports Illustrated Advertisement. (2002, December 2). In *People* Magazine, 28.

Stalk, G. Jr., & Hout, T. M. (1990). *Competing against time.* New York: Macmillan.

Staubach, R., with Ludsa, F. (1980). <u>*Roger Staubach: Time enough to win.*</u> Waco, TX: Word.

Steckler, N., & Fondas, N. (1995, Winter). Building team leader effectiveness: A diagnostic tool. Organizational Dynamics, 20-33.

Steinbock, D. (2001). *The Nokia revolution.* New York: AMACOM.

Stern, J.M., & Shiely, J. S. (2001). *The EVA challenge.* New York: John Wiley & Sons.

Sternberg, R. J. (1985). Cognitive approaches to intelligence. In B.B. Wolman, (Ed.), *Handbook of intelligence* (pp. 59-118). New York: John Wiley & Sons.

Sternberg, R. J. (1985). *Beyond IQ: A triarchic theory of human intelligence.* New York: Cambridge University.

Sternberg, R. J. (1988). *The triarchic mind.* New York: Viking Penguin.

Sternberg, R. J. (1996). *Successful intelligence: How practical and creative intelligence determine success in life.* New York: Simon & Schuster.

Stewart, T.A. (1995a, October 2). Trying to grasp the intangibles, *Fortune,* 157-159.

Stewart, T.A. (1995b, July 10). What information costs, *Fortune,* 119-121.

Stewart, T. A. (2001). *The wealth of knowledge.* Doubleday: New York.

Stirr, T. (1997). *Miller bolt: A modern business parable.* New York: Addison-Wesley.

Stoltz, P. G. (2000). *Adversity quotient at work.* New York: HarperCollins.

Stone, F. M. (1997). *The manager's balancing act.* New York: AMACOM.

Stowe, H. B. (1995). *Uncle Tom's cabin.* Hertfordshire, England: Wordsworth Classics. (Original work published in 1852)

Straw, B. M. (2000, September). What bandwagons bring: Effects of popular management techniques on corporate performance, reputation, and CEO pay. *Administrative Science Quarterly.* Retrieved February 1, 2006, from www.findarticles.com

Strock, J. M. (1998). *Regan on leadership: Executive lessons from the great communicator.* Rocklin, CA: Strock Enterprises.

Sull, D. N. (2003, June). Managing by commitments. *Harvard Business Review*, 82-91.

Summitt, P., & Jenkins, S. (1998). *Reach for the summit: The definite dozen system for succeeding at whatever you do.* New York: Broadway Books.

Sun Tzu. (1963). *The art of war.* [S. B. Griffith, Trans.]. New York: Oxford University. (Original work created in 500 B. C.)

Taylor, S., & Gryskiewicz, S. (2003, January/February). The search for solutions: Choosing the right approach to generating ideas. *Leadership in Action 22*(6),14-18... The Center for Creative Leadership. Hoboken, NJ: Wiley Periodicals, Inc.

ten Have, S., ten Have, W., & Stevens, F. (2003). *Key management models.* New York: Portfolio.

Tevendale, B., Service, B., & Boockholdt, J. (2003). Have we become jaded to corporate scandals? *Birmingham Business Journal, 20*(23), p. 30.

Tichy, N. M. (2002). *The leadership engine.* New York: HarperCollins.

Tichy, N. M., & Devanna, M. A. (1986). *The Transformational Leader,* Canada and The United States: John Wiley and Sons.

Time Special Issue (2004, April 26). The *Time* 100: The lives and ideas of the world's most influential people. *Time,* entire issue.

Tracy, B. (2002). *Focal point.* New York: AMACOM.

Trompenaars, F., & Hampden-Turner, C. (2002). *21 leaders for the 21st century.* New York: McGraw-Hill.

Tornow, W. W., London, M., & CCL Associates (1998). *Maximizing the value of 360-degree feedback.* San Francisco: Jossey-Bass.

The leadership secrets of Santa Clause. (2003). The Walk the Talk Company, Dallas, TX : Performance Systems Corporation.

Tough at the top. (2003, October 25). *The Economist,*3-22.

Ulrich, D., Kerr, S., & Ashkenas, R. (2002). *The GE work-out.* New York: McGraw-Hill.

Useen, M. (1998, November). Corporate leadership in a globalizing equity market. *The Academy of Management Executives,* 43-59.

Van de Ven, A. H. (1989). Nothing is quite so practical as a good theory. *The Academy of Management Review, 14*(4), 486-489.

Van de Ven, A. H., Angle, H., & Poole, M. S. (Eds.). (1989). *Research on the management of innovation, volumes 1 and 11,* Cambridge, MA: Ballinger.

Vandenberg, S. G., & Vogler, G. P. (1985). Genetic determinates of intelligence. In B. B. Wolman, (Ed.), *Handbook of intelligence* (pp. 3-58). New York: John Wiley & Sons.

Vlamis, A. S. (1999). *Smart leadership.* New York: AMA Publications Division.

Von Bertalanffy, L. (1968). *General systems theory: Foundations, development, application.* New York: Braziller.

Vroman, H. W. 1995. *Innovation in professional education: Steps on a journey from teaching to learning.* San Francisco: Jossey-Bass.

Vroom, V. H., & Jago, A. G. (1988). *The new leadership: Managing participation in organizations.* Englewood Cliffs, NJ: Prentice Hall.

Walesa, L. (1991). *The struggle and the triumph: An autobiography.* New York: Arcade Publishing.

Warren, R. (2002). *The purpose driven life.* Grand Rapids, MI: Zondervan.

Watkins, M. (2002). *Breakthrough business negotiation.* San Francisco: John Wiley & Sons.

Watson, T. J., Jr., & Petre, P. (1990). *Father, son & co.: My life at IBM and beyond.* New York: Bantam Books.

Weick, K. E. (1969). *The social psychology of organizing.* Reading, MA: Addison-Wesley.

Welch, J. (2001) *Jack: Straight from The gut.* New York: Warner Books.

Westly, F., & Mintzberg, H. (1991). In J. Henry, & D. Walker, (Eds.). *Managing innovation.* London: Sage.

Wheatley, M. J. (2001, Spring). Innovation means relying on everyone's creativity. *Leader to Leader*. Retrieved February 1, 2006, from http://www.pfdf.org/

White, J. (1986). *Excellence in leadership.* Downers Grove, IL: InterVarsity Press.

Whitney, D. C., & Whitney, R. V. (1996). *The American presidents: Biographies of the chief executive from Washington through Clinton* (8th Ed.). Pleasantville, NY: The Reader's Digest Association.

Whyte, G. (1989). Groupthink reconsidered. *Academy of Management Review, 14*(1), 40-56.

Williams, R. L. (2003, December 14). Hard-driving nurse among 250 grads. The *Birmingham News,* p. 23A.

Williamson, D. (2002, March). Was Hitler a weak dictator? *History Review,* p. 9.

Willingham, R. (1997). *The people principle: A revolutionary redefinition of leadership.* New York: St. Martin's Press.

Wilson, E. O. (2000). *Sociobiology: the new synthesis* (25th Anniversary Ed.). Cambridge, MA: Harvard University.

Wolman, B. B. (Editor). (1985). *Handbook of intelligence.* New York: John Wiley & Sons.

Wolman, B. B. (1985). Intelligence and mental health. In B. B. Wolman, (Ed.). *Handbook of intelligence* (pp. 849-872). New York: John Wiley & Sons.

Woodward, B. (2004). *Plan of attack.* New York: Simon & Schuster.

Wouk, H. (1965 and 1999). *Don't stop the carnival.* New York: Little, Brown.

Wrapp, H. E. (1967, September/October). Good managers don't make policy decisions. *Harvard Business Review,* 91-99.

Wysocki, B., Jr. (2003, April 29). Lobes of steel: Giving your memory a workout. The *Wall Street Journal*, pp. D1 and D8.

Yasuda, Y. (1991). *40 years 20 million ideas: the Toyota suggestion system.* Cambridge, MA: ProductivityPress.

Yeager, C., & Janos, L. (1985). *Yeager: An autobiography.* New York: Bantam.

Yeager C., & Leerhsen, C. (1998). *Press on! Further adventures in the good life.* New York: Bantam.

Young, Y. (1992). *The discovery of Luther.* Cambridge: Cambridge University.

Zacharias, R. (2000). *Jesus among other gods.* Nashville, TN: Thomas Nelson.

Zadek, S. (2001). *The civil corporation: The new economy of corporate citizenship.* Sterling, VA: Earth-Scan.

Zaleznik, (1989). *The managerial mystique: Restoring leadership in business.* New York: Harpers & Row.

Zimmer, C. (2003, June 9). Peering into the brain. *Newsweek*, pp. E10-E11.

About the Authors

Bill Service, during his 22 years of successful non-academic experience, demonstrated his ability as a problem solver and executive before receiving his Ph.D. in 1993.

He is an Associate Professor at Samford University School of Business in Birmingham, Alabama.

As an award-winning professor, Bill publishes extensively in areas of strategy, leadership, innovation, management, and teaching. He facilitates MBAs, undergraduates, and others in improving themselves and their organizations.

Dave Arnott is a professor, author, speaker, consultant, and seminar leader who teaches strategic management at Dallas Baptist University in Dallas, Texas.

He's the author of *Corporate Cults* and *Who MADE My Cheese?* He has appeared on the CBS program, *48 Hours*, and has been quoted in *Fortune* magazine and many other publications.

Dave is also a motivational speaker and seminar leader on the topics of leadership, management, and strategy. Before entering academia, he had successful careers in sports promotion and the sporting goods industry. He's a retired marathoner, and he once rode his bicycle across the United States.

978-0-595-38741-0
0-595-38741-1

28315554R00273

Made in the USA
Lexington, KY
12 December 2013